Genocide in the Age of the Nation-State

Volume II
The Rise of the West and
the Coming of Genocide

Genocide in the Age of the Nation-State

Volume II:
The Rise of the West and the
Coming of Genocide

Mark Levene

I.B. TAURIS
LONDON · NEW YORK

Published in 2005 by I.B. Tauris & Co. Ltd
6 Salem Road, London W2 4BU
175 Fifth Avenue, New York NY 10010
www.ibtauris.com

In the United States of America and Canada
distributed by Palgrave Macmillan a division of St Martin's Press
175 Fifth Avenue, New York NY 10010

ISBN 1 84511 057 9
EAN 978 1 84511 057 4

A full CIP record for this book is available from the British Library
A full CIP record is available from the Library of Congress

Library of Congress Catalog Card Number: available

Typeset in Garamond by JCS Publishing Services
Printed and bound in Great Britain by
TJ International Ltd, Padstow, Cornwall

Contents

'And so you killed the snake.'
'That is not killing', said Mrs Jolley, propping the spade. 'That is ridding the world of something bad.'
'Who is to decide what is bad?' asked Miss Hare.

Patrick White, *Riders in the Chariot*

Introduction to Volume II,
The Rise of the West

In the first volume of *Genocide in the Age of the Nation-State* the aim was to offer some conceptual and broad historical frame of reference for the full study that would follow. *The Rise of the West* begins that larger process. As the title implies, the arrival of what we understand as the specific phenomenon of genocide is here treated as a sub-plot of a more general historical development whose origins lie in Europe.

The purpose, however, is not to proffer some identifiable moment when genocide began. On the contrary, implicit in this study is the view that there is no one single historical point of departure. The more one might seek to find some original crystallisation, perhaps in the wake of the dramatic events of 1789, or even 1492, the more one is equally drawn to events from earlier centuries still when an assault directed by the state, or its agents, against some organically-connected communal group or other, appears to take on an entirely exterminatory thrust. That our study has resonances even of the decline and fall of the Roman empire may not entirely surprise.

That said, there remains something of an enigma as to why our phenomenon emanated from this particular geographical source. The answer, as is posited here, is not a simple one. On one level, at stake is the very nature of Western state formation, empowerment and expansion, played out in both domestic but also increasingly colonial contexts. Warfare against other states and peoples figures very largely in this aspect of the narrative, and readers, thus, will find a number of references to War Types One, Two and Three, a full exposition of which can be found in the chapter entitled 'Definitional Conundrums' in Volume I: *The Meaning of Genocide*. The use of this typology is essentially heuristic and, on its own does not provide an explanation for genocide. Nevertheless, readers may wish to be reminded of the typology as follows:

- Type One: State war against other sovereign states.
- Type Two: State war against other sovereign states or nations who are perceived to be 'illegitimate'.
- Type Three: State war *within* the boundaries, or other territories, controlled by the sovereign state, against national or other groups who are perceived to be illegitimate.

Given the historical universality of armed conflict, however, these notions or aspects of warfare alone would not explain the emerging and more specific relationship between the West and genocide. Nor is the Western rise to a global hegemony – and with it the subordination or subjugation of other peoples – necessarily sufficient to an answer.

Rather, what is being suggested here is a correlation between that rise and a Western model of humanity, albeit as it metamorphosed from its essential Christian foundations to a more overtly and stridently secular one. Again, with regard to what we know about Western tendencies on the cusp of that shift, especially with regard to its own developing sense of enlightened progress, human rights, and hence tolerance, such a conclusion can only be viewed as paradoxical, if not downright contradictory. But then who said that the wefts and warps of historical development have to add up to a neat and tidy geometry? The road is often unexpected, frequently convoluted and usually ill-lit. Nowhere is this more so, perhaps, than in instances of genocide.

Perhaps this may explain why what is consciously intended as a historically synoptic four-volume survey of the subject is, even so, less concerned with detailing an exact chronological plot and more with developing a thematic approach and geared towards introducing the reader to broad patterns, processes and interconnections between what may often be quite unfamiliar instances of genocide. Three basic trajectories are offered with regard to the subject matter of this volume. Hence the three parts to *The Rise of the West*, themselves divided into two chapters apiece.

The first considers the initial great surge of Western expansion, conquest and settlement across the oceans to the Americas and antipodes, and its impact on native peoples in these regions, from the late fifteenth century and for the next 400 years. Paradoxically, the avant-garde initiators of this process were still, within this same period, attempting to complete the colonisation and/or market-driven reorganisation of continental, or island peripheries closer to home, necessitating some cross-reference herein between state policies towards, and treatment of, indigenous 'savages' and those on more distant frontiers.

If the taming of humanity to suit both Western economic imperatives and cultural sensibilities was arguably at its crudest in these frontier contexts, there was also a more markedly metropolitan milieu in which it was played out. Our second trajectory, thus, takes the destruction of the Vendée as its fulcrum, in order to work both backwards and forwards from its moment to consider the West's striving for people-homogeneity, on the one hand, and its marked, even phobic aversion to what was perceived as foreign or heterodox, on the other. It will be argued, however, that the uniformity derived from religious foundations in pre-modern Europe proved even more rigid, and indeed dangerous, in the emerging era of the nation-state. Nor were new ideological challengers to the 'nation's supremacy capable of genuinely breaking out of its binary, even Manichaean tendencies'. On the contrary, concepts of an improved, even utopian, social order based on race, or even class, only reinforced modernity's potential for lethally tidying up human material perceived as surplus to requirements and/or, more pointedly, as extraneous 'other'.

This full potential was not realised in metropolitan contexts until after the great 1914 watershed. However, there was a great deal of actual exterminatory violence in the new imperial domains which European nation-states awarded to themselves in the decades leading up to the First World War. While, again, at the outset of our third and final section, we will focus on the destruction of the Herero as arguably the best-known case of late-colonial genocide, our purpose, rather, will be to demonstrate how this was part and parcel of a much wider landscape of *fin-de-siècle* extreme violence perpetrated by European imperialists as they met increasingly tenacious native resistance. However, the wider, fundamentally destabilising impact of the Western world on those 'old' empires, which remained technically independent of, or simply adjacent to the West's hegemonic reach, is also an important aspect of this story. *The Rise of the West* thus concludes with cases of genocide, or at least massive exterminatory violence, perpetrated by four such empires against indigenous peoples in their own not fully consolidated frontier regions, but very much as a consequence of those hegemonic pressures, in the half century leading up to the general global cataclysm of 1914.

ONE
To the Frontiers

1. European Conquerors and Sundry 'Savages'

An increasing number of aborigines in the land – were it possible that the race should increase – would be a curse rather than a blessing ... their doom is to be exterminated; and the sooner that their doom be accomplished – so that there be no cruelty – the better will it be for civilisation.

Anthony Trollope, *Australia*, 1875[1]

The nobility of the Redskin is extinguished ... The Whites, by law of conquest, by justice of civilisation, are masters of the American continent, and the best safety of the frontier settlements will be secured by the total annihilation of the few remaining Indians. Why not annihilation? Their glory has fled, their manhood effaced, better that they should die than live the miserable wretches that they are.

L. Frank Baum, editorial, *Aberdeen Saturday Pioneer*, January 1891[2]

What is to be done with the black Australian and Papuan? Is fusion, extrusion or isolation to be fostered in this case. Is their extermination (assuming such to be contemplated) to be allowed to proceed without remonstrance from the Metropolis?

Sir Harry Johnston, 'The Empire and Anthropology', *The Nineteenth Century and After*, July 1908[3]

A leading novelist and social commentator (British); a newspaper editor who would later be best known as author of the celebrated children's novel *The Wizard of Oz* (American); a towering figure in the imperial advance and later colonial administration of Africa (British); Trollope, Baum and Johnston were something more than just average opinion formers in societies which, at the time of their writing were generally acknowledged as either global hegemons of the now or not too distant future. This makes their obvious vexation on the issue of the 'natives' all the more perplexing. After all, none of the three seems to evince any qualms over their country's rights not only to be ensconced in but to take titular right to lands inhabited by other peoples for thousands of years. The presence of white men of European background in the Americas or Oceania in historical terms may have been a very recent blip, but the implicit wisdom here is that it is normal, just and proper.

The vexation, thus, is not about this, it is about what to do with the 'natives'. The clear inference is that they represent an inertial drag on future agendas. Somehow the problem has to be made to go away. Maybe, as Trollope, seems to suggest, this can be done by a conjuring trick called 'doom', perhaps even without cruelty, though whether his concern here is for the Europeans or the natives remains opaque. Baum, a man altogether less worried about mincing his words, calls for their outright extermination. Johnston, perhaps as one might expect from a public political figure with an eye to both long-term ramifications and posterity, seems to be seeking some deferral on the matter, the inference being that the final decision ought to come from some higher authority of state. Significantly, all three writers posit the problem as if it were one which ought to be considered as of that moment, albeit with Baum implying that some action may have been undertaken previously. Nevertheless, in each instance, it is assumed that extermination is not a given, the already accepted bedrock of state policy, but rather an option which might be entertained, at some – preferably sooner rather than later – stage as a basis for resolution.

The very fact that these authors present the case for genocide as one of wish-fulfilment rather than empirically grounded reality, poses an interesting conundrum for us as latter-day observers of the avant-garde Western powers in their drive to expand, develop and ultimately consolidate their national and imperial frontiers. By the late 1870s, these processes, at least on the north American continent and in the antipodes had already reached culmination and practical completion. In other words, if genocide – as delineated in the first volume of this work – were the issue, it would mostly likely have occurred *before* rather than after this juncture.

New World Populations and their Demise: A Subject for Controversy

It is generally recognised that the encounter between an emerging 'West', as initially represented by a handful of European maritime states from c.1450 onwards and the peoples of those regions of the world which they directly conquered and intensively settled – what the great environmental historian Alfred Crosby dubs 'neo-Europes'[4] – was not simply disastrous for the latter in socio-economic, cultural and political terms but involved a massive demographic haemorrhage which wiped out or severely reduced long-standing native populations. But the question still remains, was it genocide?

The controversy surrounding this issue has tended to group around two key questions. Each, as we shall see, is at the very nub of repeated and often highly acrimonious debates between those who make claims that genocide took place – whatever the particular case – and those who seek to refute or deny it. As a result, the relevant evidence and data marshalled by either side is rarely value-free but is collated or selected to support an already-formulated agenda. The first question is about numbers. Were there many people in these regions before the arrival of Westerners, assuming intensive and successful land cultivation, or only a few, more sparsely distributed hunter-gatherers? Advocates that genocide did take place are generally keen to have the figures high, their adversaries to keep them low. Both, of course, would claim to make their extrapolations on the basis of objective scientific evidence, not subjective bias. Yet the disparity in their findings with regard to the main bone of contention, the population of the pre-Columbian Americas, is very striking.

Alfred L. Kroeber, for instance, generally recognised as the dean of American anthropology, published findings in 1939 that proposed that no more than 8.4 million people inhabited the hemisphere, making it a largely vacant wilderness. This was all the more the case in the northern part of the continent, which Kroeber, however, rather less than objectively, put down to 'insane, unending, continuously attritional warfare' and 'the absence of all effective political organisation, of the idea of the state'.[5] Nevertheless, Kroeber's figures of less than a million pre-Columbian natives in today's United States and Canada, prefigured in the work of his leading predecessor, James M. Mooney, have been largely taken up by the Smithsonian, the leading American research institute, as if they were canonical, their upper limit of 2 million still conveniently making of the catastrophe which befell this population in the centuries after 1492 a reality somehow more digestible than if the real figure had been 18.5 million. This is the possible number of pre-Columbian north Americans offered in an entirely alternative reading by Henry F. Dobyns, in 1983. Indeed, this anthropologist's many years of research led him to conclude that the Americas as whole sustained a potential 112 million pre-1492 inhabitants, a number considerably in excess of the contemporaneous European equivalent.[6] If many demographers such as Woodrow Borah and Sherburne F. Cook of the so-called 'Berkeley school' – which began producing findings at variance with that of the Kroeber version from the 1950s onwards – consider Dobyns' most recent figures a touch inflated, their own independent findings tend to operate on numbers above Dobyns' preliminary 1966 estimate of 12.5

million north of the Rio Grande, and on the basis of a hemispheric total some-thing 'upwards of 100 million'.[7]

If this is very much the new wisdom, if there were something in the region of 8 million inhabitants in Hispaniola and 25 million in central Mexico at the point of Columbian contact, then it makes the second question – how did they die? – all the more compelling and stark. For die they did. Hispaniola, the West Indian island of first Spanish settlement, had an estimated aboriginal population of 4–5 million in 1496, 100,000 – some of whom had been forc-ibly imported from other islands – in 1508, and only an estimated 20,000, ten years later. By 1535, these Arawak indigenes were to all intents and purposes extinct. The Mexican population went into similar freefall, losing some 18.75 million of its number in the period 1520–4 and descending downwards to a brink of around 1 million in 1605, an estimated 97 per cent loss from its pre-Columbian norm.[8]

Similar proportions of loss were repeated almost everywhere throughout the Americas and antipodes. Australia, for instance, also registers a 97 per cent loss, though given the smaller aborginal population of possibly three-quarters of a million at the time of first concerted British settlement at Botany Bay, in 1788, and a huge – if inhospitable – landmass into which to retreat, the speed of attrition to an all-time low of 60,000 by the 1920s was necessarily slower.[9] Island populations were even more vulnerable. Tasmania lost its entire pure-blooded indigenous population of perhaps 4,000 or 5,000 from the period of first settlement in the early 1800s through to 1876, the vast majority dying in the first thirty years.[10] More than a century earlier, Spanish landfall in the Pacific Marianas reduced a much larger indigenous Chamorro population of 60–70,000 to a mere 1,500 in a similar time-frame.[11]

There is, of course, a straightforward epidemiological explanation for these human disasters, which nobody disputes. The parlance is virgin-soil epidemics, in other words, death by contact with microbes brought by European popula-tions, for which the indigenous peoples had no inbuilt immunity. How else can one explain the extinction of three-quarters of the Mexican population in a four-year period? If it was smallpox here, it was typhus, measles, influenza, mumps, even the common cold elsewhere.[12] Nothing could destroy like nature itself. But this is not the point at issue. Rather, it is a case of whether epidemi-ology can or cannot be regarded outside its social and political context. If it can, then one can go along with Katz's assertion that 'microbes not militia',[13] or, put another way, pathogens not policy, are to blame, making human action, in the process, an irrelevance. Indeed, one might go beyond this to argue, as Katz does, that as the *conquistadores* and their successors had a mat-erial interest in the survival of native populations so that they could labour for them, the ensuing mass mortality was not simply 'unintended' and 'inadvertent' but entirely contrary to the incoming Europeans' design or purpose.

The problem with this line of reasoning is it fails to take sufficiently into account the circumstances of the incomers' arrival or their long-term aspirations. They came, after all, not to discover, or even simply to trade – as was the case, though on highly unequal terms, in Asia – but to possess in entirety the lands which previously had been enjoyed by the native populations and to alter radically, indeed irreversibly, their usage in ways which suited the incomers' own quite different economic and cultural requirements. However, as it was patently obvious that the natives would not be giving their most precious possession to the Europeans for free and as they, the Europeans, certainly had no intention of negotiating purchase on an equitable basis, they could come by it by one means only – violence. Given that the number of interlopers was originally small and the number of incumbents large, a lot of violence. Indeed, even where the demographic balance shifted in the incomers' favour, land possession still assumed physically subjugating or alternatively eliminating the natives. To suggest thus, argues an author like David Stannard, that 'microbial pestilence'[14] on its own killed the indigenous millions of the Americas fails to take into account the repeated abuse, rape and massacre, the scorched-earth destruction of agricultural crops and animals, the starvation, induced trauma and psychic numbing which, interdependently with microbes, sapped the indigenes' will to live.

Perhaps one could argue for elements of self-inflicted violence in this matrix. In the Spanish and Portuguese conquered territories, for instance, as native dispossession was succeeded by forced labour, or forced concubinage, women simply stopped having babies, in itself, says Stannard, a 'blueprint for extinction.'[15] But if this, like intentional miscarriage, infanticide and suicide was an act of ultimate despair, responsibility for it clearly rested with the conquerors. For Stannard, all these elements are evidence of a racially motivated will to genocide which, concomitant with disease, resulted in Native American collapse. Ward Churchill has gone even further in developing this connection, proposing that in many specific cases, the Europeans specifically and intentionally introduced smallpox or other microbes as an early form of bacteriological warfare.[16]

The evidence that these and other commentators marshall on the scope, scale and relentlessness of the European onslaught on the New World thus confirms overwhelmingly that mass unnatural death at least here was anything but a by-product of some unseen force of nature but actually integral to the European's agenda of conquest. If one were to go one stage further and agree with Tony Barta in his assessment of the impact of British colonisation on the Australian aborigines, that even without the intent, the very nature of their takeover inevitably had to lead to extermination, then one would be left with little option but to concur that it is colonisation itself which is 'genocidal *tout court*'.[17]

Two further questions thus pertain. Firstly, should we see in the Europeans who spread across the seas to the Americas and Oceania and there sought to impose their will by right of conquest, the authentic precursors as well as transmitters of the phenomenon of genocide in its modern variant? Secondly, and perhaps more contentiously, though necessarily a question at the core of this study, should we treat all the mass violence that they undoubtedly perpetrated there as evidence of genocidal intent – as Stannard and Churchill largely seem to do – or should we rather see these outcomes not as a single continuous sequence but rather as a series of perpetrator responses to a variety of not altogether similar circumstances, some of which, as a result, would fit into a pattern of genocide, others of which – while still resulting in mass murder or mass death – would not?

The answer to the first question rather depends on whether one sees European permanent conquest and settlement beyond the continent as a dramatic rupture with the past or simply as a continuation of a much older pattern of displacement of one group by another. The ubiquity of this dispossession and displacement in the human record is not to be doubted, what is virgin territory for one human population is ancestral home to another. In which case, one might argue, the whole of history – and indeed much of man's prehistory – may be genocidal.[18] Certainly, even if our assumption that the expansion of the West on a global scale, in terms of direct settlement, was a critical harbinger in the emergence of the modern world – and hence critical to our understanding of its genocidal corollary – we can hardly ignore the historical record of Western expansion on the continent or peripheries of Europe itself which preceded it. In other words, if the roots of *modern* genocide lie in 'Western' conquest and settlement, we still have the problem of locating its initial, possibly pre-Columbian moment.

The second question is not predicated on any dispute over the scope or scale of the *direct* post-Columbian mass killing which Stannard and Churchill adumbrate. A cursory reading of the atrocities committed by Cortes at Tenochtitlan in 1518, or Pizarro at Cajamarca in 1532, or, for that matter, in that same decade by the expedition of the German, Nicolaus Federmann, en route to the lands of the Muisca at the supposed fabled heart of the El Dorado – for which all the *conquistadores* were then frantically searching – would confirm that what they did in mass murder was quite equal to the accomplishment of any *Einsatzgruppen* unit operating in the Russian borderlands of 1941–2.[19] Which might make doubly strange any suggestion that this initial, largely Spanish conquest did *not* involve genocide. However, the issue at stake is not the anatomy of atrocity *per se* but what these repeated massacres were designed to achieve: not the wholesale extermination of the Mexica, Inca or Muisca but the wholesale destruction of their political structures and autonomous power so that, suitably subjugated, their populations could be put to enforced work, in effect enslaved, in order to enrich their new Castilian masters.

The knock-on effects of these onslaughts, not least in the thorough over-turning of a religiously sanctioned and informed purposefulness to native culture were, in addition to the direct killing, certainly as devastating as the effects of genocide on any society which has undergone it. And the ultimate point of the exercise – to find a short-cut to power both for the *conquistadores* personally and, more importantly, for the protean Spanish colonial state – had, in this sense a commonality with the purpose of genocide. Native American productivity, and indeed excess productivity, as forced out of them by unrelenting coercion, was to be harnessed almost entirely to goals set by the Spaniards, the value of that productivity accruing to them not as a surplus but practically in its totality, at minimal capital outlay to themselves.[20]

Here, in the hyper-exploitation of an emerging *encomienda* system, was a short-cut to power just as potent as the extermination of peoples who stood in the way of land acquisition, or had possessions of a material or other kind which the perpetrators coveted. But while the two procedures, hyper-exploitation and extermination are akin and may – as we will see – often be carried forward closely intertwined with one another, they are not necessarily one and the same. There are conditions in which extermination may also emerge *out of* hyper-exploitation, most obviously when native peoples revolt against their oppressors, leading to the latter's retributive over-kill. But while examples of such insurrections, followed by their bloody extirpation – are proof that the potential for genocide existed in the dominant Iberian-controlled parts of the New World – these were not a *major* facet of their experience.[21]

We are thus left with a paradox. While many peoples, particularly as a result of the initial encounter, were literally wiped out to the tune of millions, demanding the import of further millions of enslaved Africans to fulfil and perpetuate the hyper-exploitative project, this was not a policy or strategy geared towards killing the natives or their replacements outright but extracting as much labour out of them as possible, either *in situ*, or in specific locales such as the Bolivian silver-mines of Potosí, where, as a result, they continued to die of exhaustion, accident, abuse and sickness on a massive scale. By contrast, though mortality rates in statistical terms were significantly smaller (though so too were the actual numbers of native peoples involved) in the territories of North America and Australia mostly settled by Anglos, the incidence of something we could specifically describe as genocide was much higher. Why was this? Simply put, the Spanish and Portuguese sought mostly to *encapsulate* their surviving natives, forcing them against their will to do their bidding but ultimately acculturating and assimilating large numbers of them into an increasingly *mestizo* (and one might add demographically revitalised) society. By contrast the Anglo-Americans strove to *disgorge* themselves of their natives in order to dispense with farming of a traditional intensive kind – as largely practised by their Iberian counterparts – in favour of an agro-business increasingly geared towards the global market-place and in which the role of the natives as producers had no place whatsoever.

Yet if this is to propose that the difference between the nature of violence in Iberian as opposed to Anglo zones of occupation is more than simply a question of semantics but is grounded in divergent socio-economic imperatives – of crucial significance, of course, to the contours of their respective, subsequent developments – it still leaves open how the Anglo model necessarily produces genocide. Desiring to get rid of the natives, as either surplus to requirements, or in order to make way for settlers of 'one's own kind' may tell us half the story. But it still leaves perplexingly unanswered, as our introductory testimonies also imply, how it is that official British colonial or US native policy set themselves up not as the exterminators of their aboriginal populations but as their benign protectors. Does this simply underscore that these regimes were schizophrenic; publicly saying one thing but covertly (or not so covertly) doing quite another? It is absolutely clear, as will be demonstrated, that while the Anglo-Americans did not commit one single, all-embracing and ongoing genocide against all native Americans any more than the British did against their antipodean aborigines, they did commit repeated acts of this kind against scores of native peoples, either directly through their military or police arms or through the usually authorised or semi-authorised agency of settlers.

Somehow, then, that part of the explanation for an outcome of genocide grounded in the colonial agenda – the desire for land and with it vacant possession – needs to be married with some other active element if we are to overcome the apparent lack of a preconceived governmental motive geared towards extermination. On one level that element is provided by the natives themselves. Their refusal simply to vacate or even more conveniently 'fade away' provides an obvious dynamic to the conflict that gives to the ensuing denouement a strongly functional flavour: government wants land – natives resist – outcome genocide. But there is surely something more here. The very fact that the 'victims' do not passively let it happen but fight back, often actually rather successfully against overwhelmingly superior forces in technological, demographic – and epidemiological – terms, gives to them, in the minds of the 'perpetrators' a potency ripe for radical, even extreme projection. Perhaps not least because what the perpetrators so often perceive they are up against is that most potent archetype of all: the savage.

Savages

Ethnocentricity is common to all mankind. When Amerindian tribes refer to themselves in their own tongue as 'the people' but give often derogatory names to those around them they are doing no more nor less than human groups since time immemorial have done when confronted with 'outsiders'.[22] The fact that this condition is historically universal, all human groups living at the very least with the knowledge of others but with the vast majority inter-acting socially and economically both with their contiguous neighbours and often far beyond, lends to it a clear socio-biological imperative. If one's own group's norms and customs with regard to its economic foundations, occupa-tional including gender divisions, culinary and sexual practice, as well as rites of passage, are seen not simply as preferable to others but are grounded in belief systems which give to it a distinct, even special spiritual meaning, then not only does this provide important markers distinguishing 'us' from 'them' but – possibly except for man-made or natural catastrophes – might serve to preserve, enhance and vitalise group cohesion and integrity for generation upon generation.

These normal human assumptions founded in the legacy of a common hunter-gatherer past, however, become rapidly mired as soon as the issue at stake is no longer simply group culture but 'civilisation'. Here the distinction between normal as opposed to alien, correct and seemly conduct versus the grotesque and gauche, also more pronouncedly translate as that between superior and inferior, or serious worth compared with that of no intrinsic value whatsoever. Historically, the key point of reference for this discourse in the West is classical Greece, the peoples beyond the pale of the Hellenic-speaking and thinking world being referred to as 'barbarians'.[23] Yet it is equally visible in the worldview of ancient Assyria, particularly with regard to concepts of harmony and order at the imperial centre versus the chaos of the unsettled periphery, as it is evident, also in the self-image of imperial Japan and China, the latter, for instance, not only seeing the nomadic peoples beyond the Great Wall as uncouth but, from the early modern period, encroaching Europeans too.[24] Clearly, the civilised versus barbarian dichotomy is entirely in the eye of the beholder. By any objective criteria the densely settled, politically highly organised, heavily urbanised world of imperial Persia, was in its own terms at least as sophisticated as the Greek society which dubbed it barbarian, just as the urban town-planning and architectural splendour of the Aztec or Inca could equal, if not surpass, anything the invading Castilians had on offer.

If the civilised–barbarian rift thus has an inbuilt toxicity in its highly subjective thought processes, there remains a bottom line in the acceptance by the self-proclaimed former that the latter, though separate and living beyond the boundaries of order and good governance, are nevertheless people with whom one could justifiably and even equitably engage in social and material exchange. The same is not true, however, with regard to savages. The two terms, barbarian and savage, are, of course, often used interchangeably. But this in a sense obfuscates a critical distinction. Barbarians are human beings whose social, cultural and material level is deemed far below one's own. But they are still recognised as like oneself – human. With savages, this is not at all clear. The very term denotes something that comes out of the woods.[25] In the European middle ages, indeed, the notion of *homo ferus*, a wild man, referred to a creature who was neither fully man nor fully beast. Yet the idea was so accepted that it appears as late as in the eighteenth-century system of biological classification devised by Enlightenment botanist, Linnaeus.[26]

While thus being labelled a savage, or a barbarian, in each instance tells us more about the psyche of the describer than those so described; the image of the former is an altogether more potent one: that of an unclad 'creature' emerging from 'the realm of physical nature ... the habitat for man's instinctual drives – a panic landscape of procreation and fertility'.[27] What is so interesting about this is that it contains almost equally overwhelming measures of repulsion and attraction, on the one hand, a terror of primeval, sexual urges whose affront to Christian order and seemliness would demand immediate stifling, yet on the other, the fantasy of an unfettered freedom, perhaps even of a return to some prelapsarian Utopia. Such biblical points of reference were clearly in the heads of some Europeans who encountered aborigines. The Rev. Samuel Marsden, one of the first clerics in Australia, considered their condition a special punishment derived from the sins of their ancestors in the Garden of Eden,[28] presumably the same ancestors as his own. By contrast Captain Cook, on his *Endeavour* expedition, some thirty years earlier, painted the scene as if they were still there:

> They may appear to some to be the most wretched people on earth but in reality they are far happier than we Europeans: being wholly unacquainted not only with the superfluous but with the necessary conveniences so much sought after in Europe, they are happy in not knowing them. They live in a tranquillity which is not disturbed by the inequality of condition ... they have very little

need of clothing ... they seem to set no value upon anything we gave them, nor would they part with anything of their own.[29]

If this rendering was very much in vogue with the Rousseauesque discovery of 'the noble savage' living a free, innocent and untrammelled existence in an Arcadia refound, even then the image could be drastically turned on its head. An officer, Julien Crozet, who had been on a French expedition to the south Pacific in this same period as Cook, returned to Europe to insist:

> that among all created animals there is nothing more savage and dangerous than the natural and savage peoples themselves. I ... found nothing but vicious tendencies among these children of nature: and they are all the more dangerous in that they greatly surpass Europeans in physical strength.[30]

The problem with all these renditions, wildly oscillating as they are between the positive and the utterly negative, is that they do nothing to suggest that these subjects of critical observation might be, in essence, human beings like 'ourselves'. The bull *Sublimus Deus*, issued by Pope Paul III in 1537, may, after long deliberation, have confirmed the status of the native Americans as 'true men' in the eyes of the Catholic Church, albeit ones in urgent need of taming.[31] A century on, a dominant environmentalism in emerging Enlightenment thought certainly postulated that, as New World natives were clearly products of a paradisiacal environment, they had the human capability to attain levels of culture and sophistication which European settlers attributed to themselves.[32] If, thus, there was the barest, although grudging, acknowledgement that New World peoples were members of the same species and that contained within this reality was some 'minimal humanity',[33] it was either in the degeneracy of that condition or its exotic peculiarity that the subject primarily entered an emerging Western consciousness. Indeed, once nineteenth-century anthropology had taken hold of it, such notions were simply elevated to that of scientific wisdom; the 'savage' henceforth being classified as the autochthonous remnant or residue of the oldest, most primitive elements of humankind, his/her position on the lowest rung of the evolutionary ladder explaining in turn his or her thoroughly wayward, immature and irresponsible behaviour; like a child in his nonage.[34]

It followed that even if one admired their 'natural' attributes there could be no genuine basis for an equitable cultural or economic intercourse with such lesser peoples, let alone a compromise over the key issue: ownership of land. And this, of course, was at the very essence of the ensuing dynamic. The imperative to have, control and retain the land was for the incoming European not simply an abstraction associated with a good idea called 'progress', it was, by the time of the great eighteenth- and nineteenth-century surge of British settlement in the Americas and antipodes, an economic-cum-demographic *sine qua non*. Behind the explorers, missionaries and penal convicts were potentially millions of would-be British and other European settlers whose scope for self-improvement in their own homelands was itself foundering on the rock of market forces. There could be no question of 'the right of wandering hordes to engross vast regions – for ever to retain exclusive property to the soil ... which would feed millions where hundreds are scattered'.[35] So wrote Sir George Arthur, the British administrator of Tasmania in 1826, at a critical moment in the nascent colony's conflict with its aboriginal peoples. The sentiment amongst the incomers, however, was practically universal. Expropriation was the name of the game, the only issue for the Europeans was how to justify it.

The answer came from their own 'construction' of the savage. The natives had already forfeited their land rights by dint of who they were and how they behaved. One could not allow them to perpetuate their yearly rounds of inter-tribal warfare, which Europeans interpreted as a state of Hobbesian war 'of all against all'[36] – further proof, if needed, of their social decomposition and law-less anarchy (Europeans, of course, never went to war) – nor countenance their hold over a resource from which Providence demanded a fruitful agricultural productivity. Half a century before the Enlightenment philosopher, John Locke, had famously articulated how the Christian work-ethic, combined with the power of the market-place, would transform the land into a basis for won-drous wealth creation, the Puritan divine, John Cotton, had already succinctly stated the case for European supercession: 'In a vacant soyle, hee that taketh possession of it, and bestoweth culture and husbandry on it, his righte it is.'[37] The savage did not do anything with the land, had no sense of ownership or obligation to it, he just was what he was, an indolent 'strolling savage'[38] mov-ing apparently without rhyme or reason around a landscape to which he had no specific connection. These notions were, of course, a complete travesty of the truth: both Australian aborigines and their north American counterparts having not only a deep reverence for the land at large, but specific economic and spiritual ties to quite discrete territories in which they did not wander but 'commute',[39] and which they had shaped and adapted into an environment designed to maximise their return from it both in game and crop production.

The more perspicacious early European pioneers and settlers were actually quite aware of this sustainable management system and, indeed, of the degree to which certainly many of the north American natives were as dependent on agricultural and horticultural practices as were they themselves. How else could early English New England and Jamestown settlers have survived their first critical winters except through gifts and purchases of abundant native

corn?[40] In later years frontiersmen were regularly more than eager to participate in military campaigns into Indian country, simply because of the known
cornucopia of agricultural foodstuffs which they might plunder.[41] But if this
was common knowledge, why was it wilfully ignored for the most part? The
answer is damningly simple. It would have undercut the entire principle upon
which the British and Americans sought to make good native dispossession:
namely that the land was either empty or ill-used. The first element in this
sophistry had been cited by New England settlers in the 1620s, i.e. almost at
the very outset of British north American colonisation, in order to expropriate
unenclosed native land which they coveted. But the concept of *vacuum
domicilium*[42] actually made a greater running in Australia where, under the
nomenclature of *territorium nullius*, a legal decision in 1889 declared the whole
continent to have been an unoccupied 'waste' prior to the eighteenth-century
British 'discovery' of it.[43]

Here, then, was the perfect mechanism for getting a continent not simply
on the cheap – but for free. As aborigines had no property, they could not be
entitled to compensation for it. If this represented the most stunning short-cut
to development conceivable, there was a slight glitch in its unhindered application in the Americas, the right of discovery alone giving land title being
contradicted by case law which emanated from the period of original Spanish
conquests. Not all of the clerical establishment in Spain had accepted either
the *conquistadores* or Crown's untrammelled rights over the natives. In particular on matters of enslavement, either directly or indirectly through *encomendia*,
there was a fierce and protracted debate culminating in a famous open airing
of the two sides of the argument conducted before the Holy Roman Emperor,
Charles V, at Valladolid, in the summer of 1550. Though inconclusive, the
more humanitarian position represented by Bartolomé de Las Casas – himself
an early eyewitness to and commentator on *conquistador* atrocities – over his
hardline rival Sepúlveda, tended to carry through into subsequent Crown prescriptions governing future conquests.[44] If this, arguably, was too little, too
late, the vast majority of the damage to native American life and liberty
already having been done, the fact that the dispute, at least in part, turned on
the actual status of the natives – informing, for instance, Paul III's 1537 pronouncement on their humanity – did have a certain bearing. This was not
least because a leading ally of the Las Casas position was the leading Dominican jurist, Francisco de Vitoria, usually acknowledged as the principal founder
of the study of international law, and in many respects a prototype for Raphael
Lemkin, who sought to internationally outlaw genocide.

Vitoria held the natives to be *gentes*, sovereign nations who formed organised and independent polities. In the context of a *jus gentium*, a 'law of nations',

Vitoria proposed that what was legally binding on Europeans in their dealings with each other equally applied to these native polities.[45] These prescriptions were to inform Western legal doctrine significantly henceforth. In a famous case *Worcester vs. Georgia*, brought nearly 300 years later, before the US Supreme Court, Chief Justice John Marshall ruled that Indian nations are 'distinct, independent political communities ... their territories completely separated from that of other states'.[46] The very fact that a native American people, the Cherokee, had appealed to law in this way, against Georgia, a state of the Union which was trying to dispossess them of their remaining ancestral lands – many had already been evicted – in itself represented an important departure. That they won – an earlier ruling, though equivocal on their actual independent status, however, confirming their 'unquestionable ... right to the lands they occupy'[47] – should have been a signal victory. Yet not only in practice were the vast majority of the Cherokee, along with nearly all the remaining native peoples of the Eastern seaboard, evicted in the wake of the ruling, but their enforced deportation – under military jurisdiction to inhospitable and alien territory of what was then commonly referred to as the Great American Desert hundreds of miles away, with ensuing mortality rates on a gigantic scale[48] – was an authentic harbinger of the great wave of European, Caucasian and Middle Eastern deportations committed by agenda-driven regimes a century later.

The message from the Cherokee episode was a simple one. British or American colonisers would abide by their own legal rule-book when it suited them; where it did not, they would simply change it, or circumvent it. Two years before the Marshall ruling, in 1830, Congress had already passed an Indian Removal Act, which gave to the federal government the right to move the eastern natives westwards, if necessary by force. Thus, instead of sending federal troops to protect native land rights as upheld in the courts against the thousands of settlers pressing down with vindictive Georgia state encouragement upon them, President Jackson, chief architect of the removal policy, is reputed to have remarked: 'John Marshall has made his decision, now let him enforce it.'[49] Forty years later, in 1871, the US Congress decided, in effect, that it wanted the entire land within the compass of the trans-continental state to come under its jurisdiction. With the remaining unsubdued tribes clearly no longer strong enough to oppose it, Congress simply abrogated all the 'treaties' that it had made with the tribes, thereby terminating at a stroke the 'sovereign' facade by which they and their British predecessors had operated in the Americas for the previous 250 years. If they had consciences to salve on the matter – though there is no particular evidence that they did – fifty further years on, in the 1920s, the lawyers would come to their unequivocal assistance, arguing the renowned international legal experts, Oppenheim and Lawrence that, as tribal societies were not sufficiently developed to be 'sovereign' entities, they were *ipso facto* outside the family of nations. It thus followed that the territories 'tribals' inhabited could be legally claimed by a foreign power.[50]

If all this would suggest that when it came to the question of land, indigenous 'savages' would under no circumstances be allowed to stand in the way of European colonising agendas, there still, perhaps surprisingly, remains a problem – or more obviously a paradox – in seeing this as an inevitable prelude to genocide. For official British colonial or American policy towards the natives was founded on the principle that this terminus could be circumvented by 'civilising' the 'savage'. Bring him on, better him, elevate his condition, show him the benefits of ordered society and he would give up his barbaric customs, pagan superstitions, above all his 'strolling' habits and settle down to a life of sedentary, productive labour.[51] His 'problem' condition, in other words, would evaporate. Here, in 1835, is Governor Gawler, addressing a group of aborigines in Adelaide:

> Black men. We wish to make you happy. But you cannot be happy unless you imitate white men. Build huts, wear clothes and be useful ... you cannot be happy unless you love God ... Love white men ... learn to speak English. If any white man injure you go to the Protector and he will do you justice.[52]

At the beginning of the twentieth century such sentiments were to be a good deal more pithily encapsulated, this time in a north American context, in the dictum: 'Kill the Indian, save the man': a programme of forced assimilation or, more honestly put, ethnocide. The coiner of the term, Indian commissioner Frank Leupp knew what he was about.[53] By breaking up the communal structure of the now thoroughly subdued Plains Indians and with it the last vestiges of their customary, collective land holdings, he could free up the surplus for the benefit of still land-hungry homesteaders. Such a policy assumed the complete destruction of native culture, and with it the eventual disappearance of the natives themselves. Having said that, it did implicitly proffer a sort of deal to them. This read something like: 'assimilate to European customs, standards and dominant religion and we will not only promise not to kill you – as might befit savages – but we will look after you as our special "wards" even let you legally own a little land, or alternatively – in the Australian aborigine case where any issue of native sovereignty was forfeit from the start – find you some work'. The nature of the deal thus was entirely of 'a take it or leave it' variety and even in its basic premise offered neither full citizenship, genuine colour-blind tolerance nor the equality of opportunity with which to succeed on the white man's terms. All that could objectively be said in its favour was that it was somewhat better than the original Spanish principle that, as less than human, the 'savage's' only purpose in life was as a servant or slave, the Enlightenment counter-thesis propounding that it was indeed his very humanity which gave to the 'savage' the potentiality – 'the saving grace' – with which to receive and benefit from civilisation.[54]

Yet, if to the more multiculturally minded Westerner of the twenty-first century, this prescript may seem utterly misguided and perverse, one has to acknowledge that its thinking – to which American and British colonial native policy remained in principle steadfast – was designed *to avoid* extermination. Indeed, both polities believed that they had a specific and direct 'hands on' duty to this end. It is implicit in the instructions that Arthur Phillip, the first governor in Sydney, brought with him from London to conciliate the natives; 'live in kindness with them' and punish those who would 'wantonly destroy them',[55] just as it is, almost simultaneously, though in more systematic form, in the programme devised by Henry Knox, the man vested with responsibility for Indian affairs by President Washington, in the newly created United States.[56] In both instances the assumption was that the state would paternalistically hold the ring between native and settler, allowing for an orderly transfer of land to the latter – in the American case through its sale. This thereby also allowed time for the educators, missionaries and other on-the-ground transmitters of *la mission civilisatrice* to get to work to detribalise the natives and so make them ready for absorption and, indeed, biological assimilation – through miscegenation – into white society.

The fact that for 150 years prior to Phillip's remit towards the aborigines, the British government had been presiding over exterminatory campaigns against north American natives, or that Knox – himself a major landowner – in his capacity as secretary for war, was party to similar campaigns, does not seem to have deflected either them or their successors from believing that they were operating, not only as neutral arbiters in settler–native disputes, but with a benign interest in the welfare of the natives. Clearly there was something more than simply paradoxical going on here. On the one hand, British and American policies remained committed throughout to keeping both sets of indigenes *alive*, even if the logical consequence of this was their dispossession, degradation yet dependence upon the dominant society that had brought them to this miserable and utterly marginal condition in the first place. Yet on the other hand, successive governments of both states were wilfully, repeatedly and directly responsible for a series of onslaughts on specific tribes which amounted to partial or total genocide.

An insight into this gaping contradiction is again strikingly exemplified by the case of the Cherokee, one of the five so-called 'civilised' tribes of the American south. Having suffered repeated war, demographic collapse and enforced land surrender throughout the eighteenth century, a substantial proportion of them began to take the European prescript about their savage condition at face value and, in the early years of the republic, to reorientate their lifestyle, economy and culture accordingly in order 'to read, dress, talk, vote and worship like white Americans'.[57] They also happened to make this dramatic shift on residual native lands which were some of the most fertile in the trans-Appalachian region and at a moment of time when the whole southern economy was re-orientating itself dramatically towards a monocultural cotton production geared increasingly towards a British textile market. The Cherokees' cardinal sin, in other words, was to play according to the white man's rules far too successfully: to reorganise themselves as property-owning home-steaders; to defend these property rights adroitly in the American courts; while at the same time beginning to compete with whites in areas such as cotton production in the dominant market-place – even, in some instances, through adopting the white practice of black slave-labour for the purpose.[58]

Yet, instead of applauding the Cherokee for their acumen, entrepreneurship and good sense, white frontiersmen increasingly vented their passions against those who had 'no right to alter their condition to become husbandmen when 'the Georgian soil was destined to be tilled … by the white man … not the Indian'.[59] Here, then, was a basic conflict of interests that 'the civilising of the savage' discourse could neither have imagined nor could solve. The Cherokee had the land and with it its natural as well as mineral wealth – Appalachian gold having been recently discovered – while affirming their 'fixed and unalterable determination never to cede one foot more'[60] to those, like the state of Georgia, that both coveted yet claimed the Cherokee territory as rightfully theirs. In such circumstances what native peoples were supposed to do was to bow out gracefully by agreeing to what Benjamin Hawkins, then chief US agent to southern Indians, had recommended to the Cherokees' Creek neighbours; namely, sell the land for a good price (sic.), accept further annuity payments for the losses incurred, as well as gratefully receive further assistance in the adoption of civilised ways.[61] This was a very convenient way, of course, of absolving the European colonisers from any inference of negligence or lack of equity towards those who were being asked to politely disappear. The problem in the Cherokee case was that not only had a majority among them already fully adopted 'civilisation' but had shown a particular and acute grasp of its method and intricacies in 1827 by holding their own constitutional convention, consciously on the lines of the US model and in which they declared not only their sovereign and independent status but their intention to form a representative national government.[62]

Subtly and brilliantly, Cherokee 'savages' had broken the rules once again. They had emulated exactly the American process of state formation but in order to forge their own consciously and overtly modern national identity. Thereby they could also critically refute the colonial premise that sovereign territory could be ceded away from the Cherokee 'nation'. Not surprisingly, Georgia branded the constitution 'a presumptuous document' while broader, dark murmurings claimed the Cherokee convention was threatening the very conception of the United States.[63] In a critical sense, this was entirely true. The only 'peaceful' way the American state, in both its federal and separate state entities, could expand territorially was through the sale of tribal lands to the west, the process of which was also assumed – mistakenly – to be the necessary prequel to the detribalisation and hence obliteration of Indian communal life. The only alternative was to precipitate Indian tribes into armed resistance, paradoxically giving to the Americans, as to their British predecessors, the apparently sound *bona fides* with which to claim that they were fighting 'legitimate' Type One forms of warfare against sovereign nations and with that rights of territorial conquest, when the Indians were suitably defeated and crushed. The fact that the Anglo-Americans actually fought these wars as Type Three struggles against 'illegitimate' adversaries operating on territory they already considered as their own, underscored the double standards involved. It was as good a reason as any as to why the Cherokee refused in the 1820s to play the military card.

Doubly paradoxically, however, by successfully deflecting that possibility, the Cherokee exposed an even greater Anglo-American potential for extreme violence. The latter's colonial drive for land and power was founded upon the peculiar casuistry that it could be both unfettered yet legitimate. Native 'savages' were expected to play to these rules. The Cherokee exposed the flaw by borrowing the white man's mantle of juridical legitimacy to articulate their own alternative conception of sovereign power founded on communal solidarity. It was exactly the sort of strategic insight which was likely to have colonial adversaries fulminating with accusations of savage treachery. But it was hardly the Cherokee obstacle alone that tore away at the humanitarian veil. Wherever the colonial advance was met with Indian tenacity, resilience and refusal to submit to *force majeure*, the recourse to savage imagery was practically instantaneous. It could only be exacerbated where the natives continued to act *against* projective type. Militarily, where Indians did fight back, not only invariably did they not run away, or fall down like nine-pins as savages were supposed to do in the face of modern weaponry and disciplined soldiery, but they sometimes were so successful that, in spite of massive demographic losses through epidemics and starvation, they were able to stymie the colonial advance for years, if not decades.[64] A critical factor in this process was repeated, concerted efforts to create religiously inspired pan-tribal alliances, a strategy which at the time, and in traditional historiography, has often been discounted as beyond the wit or mental horizons of the Indian nations.[65] This is a rather surprising assertion when one considers that, in spite of all the expectations and hubris of Washington's nascent republic to make a great, concerted push to the Mississippi, it was actually forced to sue for peace along the Ohio River boundary, after the most humiliating defeat of its army, at the hands of the Shawnee-led pan-Indian forces, in November 1791.[66]

The spectre of a resourceful Indian unity driving military and settlers from forts and homesteads and unimaginably defeating the forward march of the colonial project was, thus, just a little too much to contemplate for the proponents of an emerging 'Manifest Destiny'. It would be much simpler to charge that Indians were the treacherous pawns of outside conspiracies, the French in the case of the great Pontiac-led wave of resistance to the last major British colonial advance in the 1760s, the British themselves in the case of the last great quasi-millenarian wave of pan-tribal resistance in the 1812 war.[67] Outside interference was, of course, less easy to conjure up in the equally determined if less chronicled Australian aboriginal resistance to the British.[68] Either way, frontier settlers at the immediate receiving end of indigenous fight-back were, clearly, particularly prone to rant and rave against the alleged vicious treachery, bloodlust and sado-erotic murderousness of their opponents. Settler lore in the antipodes, as in the Americas, was indeed notably fixated on orgies, not just of unmerciful murder perpetrated against innocent settler mothers and their children, but with an openly racist undercurrent provided by tales of 'white' women kidnapped, ravished and then butchered by black 'demonic, subhuman brutes'.[69] The charge, too, of cannibalism further conjured up the irredeemable inhumanity of the 'savage'.[70] In the Americas, additionally, it was supported by stories of scalping of victims both alive and dead, offering the supposedly most potent of all the mutilations in the arsenal of savage bestialities.[71]

All these lurid horror stories – much contested as they rightly are[72] – provided the essential rationalisation for a projective retribution. The self-confident narcissism of, for instance, early to mid-seventeenth-century Puritan New Englanders sitting as it did so uneasily with the actual insecurity and tentativeness of their hardly established settlement toeholds, was just the volatile mix necessary for explosions of an unforgiving violence. It was the General Court of Massachusetts, not their surrounding indigenous neighbours, who repeatedly offered bounties for the scalps of Indian men, women and children. In other words, a bounty hunters' impunity was legally sanctioned by the perceived savagery of 'the other'.[73] But then, whenever the Indians posed an obstacle to settler territorial advancement, the metaphors of projection were regularly trotted out in the Americas and antipodes as consistently as anything we know from a more familiarly genocide-prone twentieth century. A plague of vermins became the imagery of colonial fighters as they sought to stamp out the extraordinarily fierce native insurgency of the 1670s when the Wampanoags and some of their Indian neighbours mounted a last-ditch struggle to defend their dwindling homelands, in south-eastern New England, in the so-called 'King Philip's war'. It led to a popular ditty: 'A swarm of flies, they may arise a nation to annoy, / Yea rats and mice or swarms of lice, a Nation may destroy.'[74] Two hundred year later, when the Third Colorado Volunteer Cavalry Regiment rode unprovoked and unopposed into the sleeping Cheyenne encampment at Sand Creek, to commit one of the better reported – and hence more infamous – massacres of US history, their rallying cry was 'Nits make lice'.[75]

But, while it is easy enough to identify the religiously inspired fundamentalism of Puritan New Englanders or the sheer bloody-mindedness of tough-living American (or Australian) frontiersman as the culprit, we should be wary of assuming such unmitigated venom and murderous intent was their monopoly. Not only could it take hold at the highest levels of state, but in conditions of crisis it even had avowed supporters of the Rousseauesque vision of native gentility floundering intemperate. It is surely no accident that President Jefferson, better known as a native accommodationist, should weigh in with his own most vituperative denunciations, most particularly at the very juncture of the early 1800s when the state's whole future – predicated as it was on westward expansion – came up against the brick-wall of the most seriously concerted pan-Indian opposition in its history. The only US response, wrote Jefferson to his secretary of war in 1807, was war *à outrance* pursued until the resisting tribes were 'exterminated or ... driven beyond the Mississippi'. There could, he implied, be no accommodation in such circumstances, only a situation – and here he referred to the Powhatans and Pequots destroyed by the English at the outset of their north American settlement – where 'they will kill some of us or we shall destroy all of them'. Returning again to the theme in 1812 and 1813, when the fortunes of the Indian allies, already on the wane, were turning to abject defeat, Jefferson – while reiterating that they, the Americans, were 'obliged' to drive the 'backward' Indians 'with the beasts of the forest into the Stony Mountains 'or somewhere else 'beyond our reach' – also offered an alternative solution where they would be 'extirpate(d) from the earth'.[76]

What drove Jefferson to pronounce, in these last words, something that had an almost biblical resonance of holy war in it? Was it simply a utilitarianism of state which, with its preconceived timetable for the incorporation of the North-West Territory, was not going to let a unruly clutch of obdurately immovable tribes get in its way? Or was it actually impelled by a much deeper anxiety, that the Shawnee political-spiritual leadership of Tecumseh and his more avowedly prophetic brother Tenskawatawa, really did have some magic potency upon which might perpetually founder an American self-image as the moral and political force of an irreversible, enlightenment-based progress?[77] The resort to some Christian religious sanction as a counter-magic to that of the Indians was more implicit than explicit in Jefferson's exterminatory prediction. But not so in that of Massachusetts' divine, Cotton Mather's description of the early colonists' burning to death of hundreds of sleeping Pequot, mostly women and children, as 'the just judgement of God'.[78] Similarly, 200 years later, the former Methodist preacher Col. John Chivington would pronounce, prior to taking his cavalry into Sand Creek, that 'I have come to kill Indians and believe it right and honourable to use any means under God's heaven.'[79] The motif is surely more than a simple case of the Western godhead being repeatedly invoked to excuse perpetrator 'blood lust'. It is a motif, one might add, with neither Chivington nor Mather on the psychological or any other margins of 'Anglo' society, but rather articulating an elite unanimity of colonising purpose against a real and 'radical alternative'[80] as posed by the 'savage'.

But if that alternative clearly existed, not only in the realms of Euro-American imagination, but arguably in actual political territorial and cultural terms, its frightfulness for the Anglo-American conquerors lay in the very ontological condition of the opponent. From the mid-nineteenth century, the new 'scientific' wisdom sought to offer an overtly racist explanation to the supposed propensity of the 'savage' toward violence and treachery located in the inferior shape and form of the Indian's cranium.[81] But even a critical proponent of this sophistry, such as the leading southern surgeon, Josiah Nott, continued to intermix with the pseudo-science his own image of the savage skulking 'untamed through the forest', just as Francis Parkman, the celebrated early twentieth-century historian, would present his 'ideal' rendition – the Ottawa warrior Pontiac – as 'the Satan of this forest paradise'.[82] In every critical respect, this was the same terror-laden imagery that overtly Puritan settlers had deployed from the very outset of conquest. Moreover, one has to ask, if New England pioneers and Victorian scholars alike were so convinced of the intellectual and physical inferiority of the natives, why was the prevailing image of them, women and children included, as devils incarnate, or as equal to, if not the same as the most dangerous, cruel and supposedly frightening animals of the forest: the wolf, the lynx the cougar?[83] Could it yet again be that the 'savage' represented an aspect of themselves which, when apparently faced with its potent allure – like the ancient Hebrew *vis-à-vis* the Midianities – they could not handle, and which, instead they strove to exorcise through an extirpatory violence?

Speculative as this may be, it is clear that in American and antipodean contexts Anglos acted out their conflict with the native possessors of the land and natural resources they coveted as if it were primarily a contest between civilisation and savagery and in which the supposed 'moral gulf' between the two justified the Anglos' actions as logical, purposive and measured – however genocidal the outcome.[84] True, providing the natives gave way, and accepted the inevitability of conquest, the colonists' mailed fist remained gloved. As soon as it was seriously resisted, however, thereby frustrating their expansionist agendas, the full panoply of 'savage' imagery – deceit, treachery, conspiracy and bloodlust – would be almost instantly deployed as the basic ground rules with which to justify a massive and exterminatory overkill. Vocal liberal opinion, usually, though often crucially aroused at the metropolitan centres of the American and British states, represented an important inertial drag denying the full genocidal potential of this trajectory on many occasions. But it could never overwhelm it completely for two basic reasons. Firstly, the dissenters shared the same basic premise about native savagery; their quarrel with the protagonists of extirpation thus being about method – a matter of whether the 'savage' could be reformed into something other than what he/she was, or was not. None of these liberal 'do-gooders', however, were prepared to advocate abandoning trans-continental advance and consolidation in the aboriginal interest. And this, of course, is the second reason why the position of the 'dissenters' lacked cogency or a popular mandate, even though their argument was being enunciated in societies that increasingly prided themselves on their democratic voice. Everybody who was on the inside of white society as a settler, later immigrant or even, in the British case, as part of a domestic constituency, was in some respect a beneficiary of the colonial short-cut of dispossession, including those in the British Aborigines Protection Society, or the Quaker-informed American 'Friends of the Indian', who wished to 'preserve' the native.

Moreover, their preoccupation was hardly one widely shared. It was not only frontiersmen who, as on the occasion of the Denver opera house meeting *after* Sand Creek, shouted down the senator who timidly suggested it might be better to civilise the surviving Indians rather than kill them, with cries of 'Exterminate them! Exterminate them!'[85] Back on the eastern seaboard, the cause of scourging 'the red wastes where the barbarian peoples of the world hold sway'[86] – President Theodore Roosevelt's piquant turn-of-the-century declaration on the subject – was considered a perfectly proper, commonsensical and indeed vote-winning one, as an earlier president, Andrew Jackson, had already proven. But whereas when the 'savage' strove to defy this encroachment, his actions were always portrayed – and believed – as that of a wildman unable to control his irrational and murderous instincts, the white's man's retaliation was always, by contrast, that of rational and legitimate self-defence. And, of course, it was always that way round; civilisation in defence of peace and progress, savagery bursting in upon it; despite the obvious sophistry involved.

But if this underscores a truism, that without a generally held thought system to support and legitimise it there cannot be a sufficient basis for the involvement or at the very least acquiescence of a significant part of the dominant population in an act or acts of genocide, does this particular thought system begin with Anglo aggrandisement onto an American and antipodean stage? Or can we trace it back to earlier European origins? If modern genocide – at least in part – begins with 'the West's struggle against "savagery"', where exactly do we locate its wellsprings?

Eastern Frontiers

If the concept of 'barbarians' in the West was nothing new, nor were agendas of conquest which legitimised themselves by the claim of being civilising missions. The obvious model was Rome, whose advance implied both subjugation and/or enslavement of defeated peoples but also the possibility of being inducted as citizens into the realm of a law-based *pax Romana* for whoever among the remainder complied. The empire, of course, brooked no opposition, whether external, as famously from Carthage, or from the imperial peripheries as with Judea, Dacia, or the British confederates of the Iceni. But even displaced peoples from beyond the imperial frontiers, including clearly 'barbarian' and potentially very threatening Goths, Huns, Vandals and Suevi were given admittance on the premise that they could be assimilated to civic society and made to settle down. Widely seen as a fatal wrong-turning leading to the empire's demise,[87] the basic premise nevertheless survived Rome's fall to be incorporated into the Christianising message imbibed by the post-imperial Frankish kingdoms, Pope Gregory the Great's argument 'in favour of a kindly, rational and accommodating approach to the unbeliever',[88] providing the essential framework for an inclusivist if expansionist West. If this raised questions about the exact place of the Jewish monotheists in Christendom (just as, in parallel from the seventh century AD, it posed similar questions about the place of Christian as well as Jew, in an expanding Islamic imperium) the benefits of civilisation were proffered to the pagan outsider as the natural but enticing corollary to conversion.

But what if the 'pagan' refused the bribe? For centuries the Frankish frontier had been pushing steadily and almost relentlessly outwards from its core Romano-German heartlands to the north and east, subduing barbarian peoples through war, but ultimately also assimilating them into this newly emerging European political, economic and cultural system, primarily through the Christian conversion of their native aristocracies.[89] This civilising 'trickle-down' of a process, however, came up against something very much like a brick wall in the eastern Baltic. It did so at the very time – in the twelfth and thirteenth centuries – when Latin Christianity was becoming militant in its efforts to redeem Jerusalem from Muslim overlordship, the result of which was the crusades. The papal call to 'Holy War' over Jerusalem was also replicated in similar calls for the reconquest of Muslim Iberia, and a Northern crusade against the so-called Wends and other pagan peoples of the Baltic frontier. Whereas, however, the conquest of Jerusalem, or Andalucia, might be posited as legitimate recoveries of territories previously Christianised and long civilised – even the 'infidel' Saracen being grudgingly recognised, on the latter score, as such – the great expanses of Baltic forest and swamp were for the crusaders not unlike the seventeenth-century Americas encountered by the Anglos, that is, inhabited by utterly alien 'savages'.

In fact, one could take the comparison somewhat further. The Baltic might be imagined as an untamed wilderness. However, like north America, its resource base – not least the human one in slaves and the animal one in furs – made it an obvious asset in trading terms. Yet even more lucrative wealth-creation prospects beckoned for any duly mandated organisation hoping to channel settlement from the increasingly overpopulated western Europe into a new 'virgin site' developmental programme. Throughout this whole period 'Western' designs on the region thus jockeyed with those of other proto-Russian, Swedish and Polish agendas – not unlike the seventeenth- and eighteenth-century inter-state struggles for north America – but with the additional similar problem that the natives themselves represented the critical political factor in the equation, blocking the total territorial conquest of any one of these states. And not just as a political factor. The obdurate refusal of the Baltic peoples to be civilised via Christianity but instead to hold on successfully to their actually highly organised religious practices, festivities and sites – focused as they were in nature and things natural – also posed an obstacle to a European cultural advance predicated on its own allegedly God-given powers.

Indeed, the challenge was much more powerful than that, for it posed the perpetuation of a genuine 'pagan' *alternative* at a juncture when a significant proportion of recently converted Christians in many respects remained only nominally so. At the time of the first northern crusade in 1147, its great promoter, Bernard of Clairvaux, wrote a famous letter in which he stated: 'We expressly forbid that for any reason whatsoever they should make a truce with those peoples, whether for money or for tribute, until such times as, with God's help, either their religion (*ritus*) or their nation be destroyed'.[90] In other words, there could be no accommodation or arrangement with pagans, only total submission at the point of the sword. By degrees, the various Wendish tribes, the point of Bernard's immediate attention, were whittled down, subjugated and absorbed by the conquerors. But further to the east – deeper as it were into the Baltic forests and swamps – the Prus and Lithuanians proved more intractable.

These peoples were quite distinct from the the Slavic Wends, and certainly more aboriginal in the sense that their languages point to their being descendants of some of the very earliest Indo-European migrants onto the continent, some 3,000 years earlier.[91] Like the Indians of north America – or indeed the Wends – they could not be categorised as a commonality but as a diversity of quite distinct tribes melded together through cultural zones of linguistic identity and shared religious practice and custom. We know insufficient about these rites because of their swamping or direct obliteration by the forces of 'civilisation'. We do know that tree-worship was integral to all the Balts, that they had sacred groves and cults of the dead and – as with so many pagan peoples – human and especially horse sacrifices, which, within the framework of yearly cycles of festivities and rituals, were considered 'as the essential guarantees of the health, security, success and identity of the family, village and tribe'.[92] Pitted against this nature-centred riposte to the Christian godhead from the early thirteenth century was a handful of military-cum-religious orders whose origins lay in the defence of Christian enclaves and holy sites in Palestine. The one which ultimately matters in this narrative was the Order of the Teutonic Knights.

The Teutonic Knights have no exact parallel with any more modern entity, in spite of Himmler's predilection to see them as the authentic progenitors of the SS.[93] It is true that they adopted an efficient, systematic and almost robot-like diligence in their task of extirpating their adversaries and that, like both *conquistadores* and SS, they used this professional military expertise not only to justify their unfettered autonomy but also to make claims for specific territorial dominion – in this case the lands of the Prus. Moreover, while the SS – like the Knights – might claim that they had dedicated their lives to a particular purpose and this was carried forth with an equivalent degree of fanatical zealotry, the former were under no vow to live a life of dour austerity, unflinching self-chastisement or segregation from women as were the warrior-monks, nor were they required to understand this as the sum-total of their personal route to heavenly salvation. On this level, the order's intense military monasticism was peculiarly medieval, as was the literal Manichaeism in which the Knights conceived themselves as agents of good triumphing over evil. Yet, clearly, on this latter point the gap between the medieval and the modern rather dramatically narrows. Indeed, if crusader aspirations directed towards redemption in the after-life and even martyrdom to arrive there seem to run very much against the grain of the essentially very terrestrial motives for modern genocide, the mindset which demands unremitting, exterminatory war, as set out in the *Livonian Rhymed Chronicle* of 1290s, and whose anonymous author was probably a member of the Teutonic Order, sounds very much more modern than medieval.[94]

Of course, all medieval wars were almost by the very nature of the technology employed vicious and brutal. Nor could there have been, particularly for those who might have served apprenticeships on the frontiers of the Levantine crusader states, any illusions about mercy or quarter being given either in the face of battle, at the point of surrender, or for the women and children caught in the tide of advancing or retreating armies. Yet there is arguably something qualitatively different about the thirteenth-century struggle against the Prus which places it much more closely in the category of genocide. Certainly, the Wends or, for that matter, peoples such as the Saxons, caught up earlier on in the path of the Frankish Christian advance, suffered unremitting massacre until they submitted, while later on, the Lithuanians, in their own struggle with the Teutonic Order, avoided total destruction through their own political-military prowess, enabling them ultimately to convert on their own terms. By contrast, for the Prus – as a people – these options never seem to have arisen.

The explanation for the specificity, and with it exceptionality, of their destruction is partly circumstantial, partly a matter of the contradictory nature of their strength and weakness. The Prus stood as an obstacle to an unbending and militant church at a juncture when the threat of Mongol invasion from the east gave to its apocalyptic mindset a particular crisis-ridden edge. The fact that Prus religion helped give to their political resistance a dynamic vigour with which to ride out the initial crusader onslaughts of the

1230s, thus, would have had the Teutonic Knights redoubling their projection of them as savage devils. Yet, at the same time, the tribal nature of the Prus and their inability – unlike the Lithuanians – to forge a political unity, meant that their struggle, though fought over many decades, gave the long-term advantage – as with that between settlers and Indians on the eighteenth-century American eastern seaboard – to the materially, technologically and politically stronger party. This involved, of course, a genuine rather than imagined dynamic of conflict, the subordinated Yatwingians – the most significant of the Prus tribes – repeatedly rising up against the new political-cum-religious order in guerrilla-style insurgencies which in turn were met by retaliatory counter-insurgency and massacre often carried out by bands of converted Prus auxiliaries.[95] Genocide, in this sense, emanated from a War Type Two which, after nominal Teutonic Order conquest, turned into a unrelenting War Type Three.

But if a resultant 'creeping' genocide evolved out of an unbridgeable *Kulturkampf*, one can also see how, as this developed, it carried with it its own 'modernising' genocidal logic. The Teutonic Knights had been originally invited in to subjugate the Prus by a Polish Mazovian duke and then given a religious mandate for the task by Gregory IX in 1230. But, having begun, successive masters of the order could see that actively eliminating the Prus provided them with an opportunity to sidestep dependence on either pope, Holy Roman emperor or Polish prince. A region practically cleansed of its native inhabitants provided land for free which could be then developed on the order's own terms: a short-cut to power; and to state formation. There was no shortage of compliant German and other European settlers – in effect 'new' Prussians – to participate in this transformative, 'civilising' project. Under the order it is estimated that some 100 new towns and 1,000 new villages helped repopulate the region while, of course, providing enrichment for the order.[96] Surviving Prus were forced to accept Christianity as the price for their personal liberty, though clearly in other areas discriminated against on grounds of *ethnos*.[97] Swamped by the new settlers, in a country whose very physical contours had been radically altered, whose familiar place-names had all been consciously changed, whose sacred trees had all been ripped out and obliterated, the fate of these survivors, as that of the Prus language itself, was now one of a rapid ethnocide.

There is one thing more about this medieval episode that also makes it significant as a signpost to a genocidal modernity: its seeming inevitability. By the time of the destruction of the Prus, Latin Christendom's outward march from its Romano-German core had been going on for centuries. In this way it was already seen as preordained that civilisation should flow 'from the higher west to the lower east' as if it were a 'cultural gradient' (*Kulturgefalle*) 'replacing barbarism with sophistication'.[98] In these terms, the clearing away of pagan savages and their replacement by a new imported breed of orderly, settled Christian 'Prussians' was simply the last stage in a natural – and normal – process. Indeed, viewed from the vantage point of 1862, the very time when the colonial frontier was being brought to a speedy terminus in north America, there was, thought the nationalist and rabidly social Darwinian German historian Heinrich von Treitschke – foretelling Frank Baum's comments a little later – an imperative to get it over with quickly.

> In the unhappy clash between races, inspired by fierce mutual enmity, the blood-stained savagery of a quick war of annihilation is more humane, less revolting, than the specious clemency of sloth which keeps the vanquished in a state of brute beasts.[99]

According to this reading there could be no half-way house between civilisation and savagery, no accommodation for peoples who could not get up to speed themselves; only a clear developmental logic that demanded a zero-sum game. For Nazi acolytes of Treitschke's analysis, the path hewn by the Teutonic Knights was also the path of the future.

Islands and Enclaves

In fact, two centuries after the final extirpation of Prus insurrections, the ambitions of the Teutonic Order were rapidly collapsing in the face of repeated defeat at the hands of the Slavic Poles, proof if anybody needed it that there was nothing inevitable about Western or more specifically German advance. Yet, at this very juncture, a new colonial project was emerging on Europe's western maritime margins which would have profound ramifications both for the course of world history and for its genocidal offshoots.

The seaborne drive of a a handful of early modern European states south, and south-west, in search of the sources of African gold and Indian spices were, at their fifteenth-century outset, both highly tentative yet also high-risk efforts to accumulate wealth and power by means of the short-cut. Their immediate aim was to cut out the middle man, traditionally in European terms the Venetians, the opportunity being in part provided by the dislocation to Levantine trade brought about by the rapid advance of the Ottomans. Yet this agenda did not proceed by some blueprint – how could it, when no cartographer or seaman advising the Portuguese or Castilian crowns had any well-grounded empirical evidence as to exactly how it was to be accomplished?

The Portuguese Vasco da Gama thus, reached the desired Indian objective some years after the Genoan Columbus, on behalf of Castile, had first inadvertently arrived in the Americas. An important staging post in this unseen process, however, was the takeover and colonisation of the Atlantic islands of Madeira and the Canaries.

Uninhabited Madeira was settled by the Portuguese from the 1420s onwards. Its dense forests were rapidly cut down and replaced largely by a single, though highly labour-intensive cash crop, sugar cane, which was so explosively successful in European and Near Eastern markets that it provided a major incentive for the similar colonisation of the seven islands of the already better-known Canary archipelago. There were, however, two problems on this score. Firstly, in addition to the Portuguese, the Castilians and the French were also contenders for the islands, the result being that they became an early focus for European imperial rivalry. The second, more significant problem for all these would-be claimants was that they were already inhabited.

It is estimated that some 80,000 Guanches, as they were known, inhabited the Canaries at the time of European conquest.[100] They were the descendants of peoples who had crossed the sea from Africa, possibly beginning in the second millennium BC, but who, certainly from the early centuries of the Christian era, had been isolated from broader human contact or developments except for whatever ships may have ephemerally strayed across their path. The Guanches, therefore, were a unique branch of the human family, having retained a highly individual Neolithic culture which, had it survived, would have provided social anthropologist and palaeoethnographer alike with an endless source of research and delight. As it was, notes Crosby, with appropriate acerbity, the attention that the Guanches deserve was never received, for 'they were, with the possible exception of the Arawaks of the West Indies, the first people to be driven over the cliff of extinction by modern imperialism'.[101] One might quibble on this score that it was the native Prus who deserve this dubious distinction, though, of course, Crosby is not charging genocide for the Guanches, *only* extinction. But, then, there is a case to be made for the former, too.

The Europeans may not have set out to exterminate the islanders but, by the same token, they would not be deflected from their intention of controlling the islands. In response, the – by all accounts tall and extremely formidable – Guanches resisted, very successfully, and the ensuing, spiralling dynamic of conflict rapidly took on the familiar contours of an exterminatory war; not least because the contest, from the Europeans' standpoint, should have come quickly to a foregone conclusion. Countering the Guanches' weapons of wood and stone, the Castilians were, by the time of the expedition

authorised by Ferdinand and Isabella of Spain in 1478, deploying 'all the paraphernalia of European warfare',[102] including armoured horsemen and cannon.
Yet this was an extraordinary three-quarters of a century on from the first
Franco-Castilian campaign of 1402. Whatever the supposed technological discrepancy between European civilisation and Canarian savagery, with all the
other assumptions which went with it, it was self-evident on the ground that
God had not directly authorised the speedy victory of the former. The Castilians were forced instead to seek other explanations, most tellingly that behind
the Guanches was really a foreign power, Portugal.

As we have already noted, perpetrator justifications for the genocide of a
targeted group commonly focus on the latter's alleged role as surrogate for
some other malevolent human – if not cosmic – power which is intent on sabotaging their own legitimate agenda. It is true that for a brief period, at the
height of the Castilian campaign, the Guanches were in alliance with the Portuguese and were able to draw some military support from them. But by the
Treaty of Alcaçovas, in 1483, significantly the first in a long line of carve-ups
signalling the new era of European imperialism overseas, the Portuguese and
Castilians came to terms about who would have what in the west African
coastal and island trade.[103] The Castilians got the Canaries. The Guanches, of
course, were not consulted. Instead, they were forced back on their own native
tenacity to defy the Castilian will, ensuring that the latter's frustration would
become all the more overwhelming, and that their commitment to the physical destruction of the islanders all the more absolute.

In the end, in September 1496, Guanche resistance on their last unsubdued
mountain redoubts of Tenerife was brought to a dramatic end by the wholesale
death of the defenders through *modorra*, an unspecified virgin-soil disease. In
other words, one could argue – as with the Americas – for pathogenes not policy as the ultimate cause for the islanders' demographic collapse. By this
juncture too, many thousands of Guanches had been sold into slavery – many
for hard labour in Madeira – while others had survived liquidation by fighting
as proxies for the Spaniards. The fact that there were a few Guanches reported
by European travellers to the islands as late as the 1540s might similarly mitigate against a charge of genocide, just as during the course of the fighting, the
propensity of the defenders, like the Prus before them, to massacre their opponents whenever they were in a position to do so, would also seem to be at odds
with a common, if simplistic perception of victim passivity in the face of death.

If then, the direct physical onslaught on the Guanches did not on its own
lead to their complete extinction, and even if it is true to say it was compounded by other factors, the causal relationship between their demise and the
violent birth-pangs of the modern world are less easy to dismiss. The misfor-

tune of the Guanches – an island people whose ongoing health, security and survival was entirely dependent on their sustainable management of a fragile and limited eco-system – was to be in the immediate path of a protean tendency whose economic rationale was quite distinct: the need to make money. Not simply for its own sake, though that was significant enough, but in order to fuel the aims of one of an initial handful of Western states in their competitive power-play with each other. The destruction of the physical landscape which was home and sustenance to the original Canarians in order to make way for an entirely different one, geared to the production of sugar, wine and wheat was also, thereby, a first step in a transmission belt translating wealth into ships and guns and the means to conquer other 'virgin' lands with which to continue the process.

The Guanches could not be allowed to be party to any of this for the simple reason that this would have legitimised their land-holding rights and in so doing undermined the economic underpinnings of a wealth-creation programme precisely founded on their expropriation. This did not mean the Guanches, in principle, were entirely expendable. If they had simply surrendered, an absolutely minimal future of enforced labour or slavery could have been their lot – albeit at home, or far away – thereby aligning their position with the majority of both native Americans and imported Africans in the Spanish and Portuguese spheres of colonisation. Who can be surprised, however, that most chose resistance, or that after defeat those who lingered did not do so for long, succumbing rapidly to alcohol abuse or the sort of psychic numbing recognisable in the case of the La Palma warrior, Tanausu, who, exiled to Spain, is said to have died of despair and self-imposed starvation? It was an end which one contemporary observer noted was 'a thing very common and ordinary'.[104]

*

The Castilians had *not* set out to exterminate the Guanches. Yet the end result was this all the same. Moreover, the almost complete extinction, within a matter of years, of the Arawaks of the West Indies would seem to suggest an emerging pattern in the encounter between Western colonisers and aboriginal populations in which island or other environmental-niche dwellers were particularly vulnerable to such a fate. The case of the native Tasmanians, three centuries later, can only reinforce this assumption. Indeed, the complete eradication of the autochthonous element of this population in the seventy years after the first white settlement on the south Australian island, in 1803, has been repeatedly taken as a unique example of British-organised genocide.[105]

Yet, though its history is well-documented, its categorisation as the *exception* to the non-genocidal colonising norm is highly problematic, in part because this fails to engage with the broader incidence of British settler genocide – especially in the antipodes – in part because the Tasman example itself, on closer inspection, largely mitigates against the specific charge.

The British colonisation of Van Dieman's Land (later renamed Tasmania) began initially, as in so much of their empire-making, to keep out another potential contender – the French.[106] Once claimed, the island's future seemed to be closely tied up with its perceived role, like that of its mainland predecessor at Botany Bay, as a military-run penal colony for transported British convicts. Violence, thus, was intrinsic to the contours of the colony's early development with specific knock-on effects for the native–white encounter. Escaped convicts were certainly one element in this equation, paradoxically injecting a considerable lawlessness into what was intended to be a model, if utterly draconian, prison society. However, the convicts' compunction to kill the aborigines they encountered or to steal their women was hardly unique to them. Another element in the equation was the urgent need to feed a close-to-starving colony prior to its becoming self-sufficient: one can again note parallels here with the very first precarious years of the Anglo-American eastern seaboard settlements. Competition with the natives – in the Tasmanian case for kangaroo and wallaby, the native's primary food source – was followed by the gradual erosion of the animals' heavily forested eco-system as the Europeans shifted to agriculture and began moving up the Derwent River from the first primary settlement at Hobart. These basic ingredients inevitably led to increasingly direct and bloody confrontations with the natives.[107]

There were estimated to be between 3,000 and 4,000 Tasmanian aboriginals at the outset of British settlement. Like the Guanches they were not a unified totality but consisted of some nine distinct groupings operating in perhaps fifty autonomous bands.[108] Like the Guanches, too, they represented a quite unique stone-age culture, distinct from that of the Australian mainland, probably the result of their ancestors having crossed the then land-bridge from the continent some 30–40,000 years ago. When the land-bridge disappeared, as a result of the rising post-glacial sea levels that created Bass Strait around 8000 BC, the red-brown, palaeolithic Tasman hunter-gatherers were marooned on their island until the arrival of the Europeans.

Early observers, like Cook and the French naturalist Labillardière, were particularly taken with the natives' hardy yet gentle and cheerful character.[109] The recurrent tendency of white convicts-turned-bush-rangers plus whalers, sealers, soldiers and latterly settlers to poison, torture and enslave the natives, or simply go out on hunting parties with their lurcher dogs, to bag a score or two – as if they were kangaroos – however, clearly threw this natural native disposition heavily off balance as, spear against musket, they fought desperately back. But what turned this 'war of random encounter inexorably ... into one of extermination', was not convict or settler violence *per se* but a dramatic economic developmental shift geared towards the global market.[110] Just as the catalyst had been sugar in the Canaries, tobacco in Virginia, cotton in the Carolinas and Georgia, so here the vehicle determining extermination was sheep.

In the first years of European encroachment, this window of opportunity had not been apparent, profit mainly accruing not to the new settlers but to sealers of various nationalities who plied the island's coastal waters. By the 1820s they had so systematically massacred the until then huge populations of seal and sealion, that hardly any were left. As sealers' fortunes fell, however, that of the free settlers, attracted to Tasmania by its mild England-like climate and possibilities of making money from wool and woollen products, dramatically rose. Not only did the island prove first-rate stock-rearing country, but the surge in profits in the wake of a British 1822 reduction in duty from specifically Australian wool exports became the single most critical factor in the metamorphosis of vast tracts of dense jungle into clearly defined if extensive pastures. The sheer explosion of this on-the-hoof near-monoculture speaks for itself. Between 1816 and 1823 the ovine population quadrupled in size to 200,000, more than trebling again to 682,000 in 1830 and reaching 911,000 in 1836, by which time there were more than twenty sheep for every white person.[111] Concomitantly, the white population rose in this same period from 2,000 to 23,500.[112] This was particularly excellent news for the emerging 'planter' class with the capital to invest in, or even better speculate in, land. All the more so as the wool boom and the accompanying one in real estate was being to a considerable extent subsidised in the form of bonded (i.e. enslaved) labour allocated by the lieutenant governor to 'deserving' landowners. A convict-built north–south trunk road from 1824 similarly opened up large-scale commercial logging possibilities.[113]

If these developments then represented yet another familiar short-cut to economic 'take-off', for the surviving aborigines – by 1830 outnumbered by sheep by a factor of 1,000 to 1[114] – they represented literally a sentence of death. To survive, in other words not to starve to death, they had no choice but to protect their dwindling resource base, which meant, in effect, attacking fences, property, sheep and, where possible, the intruders themselves. The so-called 'Black War' of aboriginal guerrilla attack and settler retaliatory over-kill had been building up in tandem with the wool boom since the mid-1820s. By 1830 the aborigines, in settler perception, had become so bold and successful, however, that a committee of inquiry set up to consider the causes of 'black' hostility saw a systematic and coordinated plan of campaign in their actions which popular rumour put down to the existence of a white leader.[115] Even worse, in the view of Lieutenant Governor Arthur, they had 'lost the sense of the superiority of white men and the dread of the effect of fire-arms'.[116] No longer simply attacking the 'miscreants' who had abused them but 'a different and totally innocent class',[117] – Arthur's loaded assumption about the distinction between escaped convicts and respectable settlers – white fatalities in the war peaked at forty-three in 1830.[118] Objectively considered, this represented the last ditch and frantic effort of the aborigines to stave off disaster. The effect upon settler society, however, was to have it sliding into something close to panic.

With the savage again rearing its 'spearing … murdering' and 'treacherous' head, the call was up to make a clean breast of it and 'annihilate them at once'.[119] Perhaps not surprisingly some of the most vocal demands of this nature came from large landowners, notably Roderic O'Connor, who had accumulated for himself 65,000 of the choicest acres of the island, and who proposed that some of the more notorious aboriginal killers among the convicts be put to legitimate and gainful employment to finish the job.[120] If this certainly represented the more radical settler view, there remains something of a question mark over the role of Arthur, the head of the island administration.

Arthur is the critical player in this saga. In practice a one-man government with dictatorial powers at the best of times, there is nevertheless a view that this colonial administrator, with some years of experience in the Caribbean behind him, sought a peaceful resolution of the conflict. His veering towards more radical action, including a declaration of martial law in 1828, thus came from pressure from prominent settlers in Van Dieman's Land Executive Council demanding a *carte blanche* to attack the remaining aboriginal bands with impunity.[121] It is certainly true that this was not Arthur's own intention, or that of his Colonial Office masters in London, who, at this juncture strongly under the sway of anti-slavery campaigners, wanted a policy of sedentarising, and civilising the savages via Christianity and without violence.[122] The problem is that this supposedly enlightened, assimilationist intent was completely at odds with the settlement programme as developed and encouraged by Arthur himself. It was he, from his arrival in 1824, who had been the single most important factor facilitating and accelerating the linked processes of infrastuctural and economic expansion and it was he, too, who had signalled who would most particularly profit from these developments by appointing the venal O'Connor as land commissioner. In this role O'Connor had oversight for the opening up of 'unoccupied' lands brought into play by the building of the central spine road, which he was also to survey. Not only, thus, did Arthur provide the necessary conditions for a form of mini state-building predicated on sole white occupation of the vast majority of the island, but he also had a personal interest in its success, acquiring a large fortune through land investments which neatly dovetailed with major infrastructural projects, of which he, of course, as governor, had advance knowledge.[123]

When, thus, in the crisis year of 1830, having failed to keep the surviving aborigines out of the settled area by other means, Arthur instituted the infamous 'Black Line' to finally drive them into a geographical cul-de-sac where they might be captured, his apparent reluctance on the matter is somewhat contradicted by the physical *force majeure* which he deployed. In addition to 550 troops, practically every able-bodied man, convict and free settler alike, was called out. They were to participate in a human cordon stretching across most of the island, the aim of which was to flush out the remaining aboriginal bands very much in the manner of a pheasant drive. Robert Hughes reports that the beaters carried with them 1,000 muskets, 30,000 rounds of ammunition and 300 pairs of handcuffs. According to Arthur they were filled 'with the most zealous and cheerful alacrity'.[124] In fact, despite this overwhelming show of force, the whole episode proved a fiasco bordering on farce.[125] All but two aborigines escaped the dragnet. The majority were clearly still at large.

Having failed to subdue the native threat by straightforward coercion, Arthur opted – one might say reverted – to that of persuasion and conciliation. Engaging the services of a middle-aged Presbyterian missionary, George Robinson, for the purpose, the official Tasmanian policy now was to make contact with the aborigines so that they might recognise the futility of continued resistance and in order that they might voluntarily give themselves up in return for a promise of government protection and sustenance. To this task, Robinson proved remarkably tenacious and ultimately successful, bringing in over the following five years what proved to be the remaining 195 pure-blooded aborigines of the thousands who had once lived on the island.[126] In this sense, the full-scale genocide demanded by the settlers had been averted, Robinson's highly paternalistic kindness towards his charges even offering a model for the classic assimilationist creed that godless savages, after all, could be civilised, Christianised and, indeed, Victorianised.

A more jaundiced view, however, would be that this 'benign' method had exactly the same, single goal as that of people like O'Connor: namely restricting, bottling up and finally excluding the aborigines in entirety from the one key asset – *their land* – by which the conquerors of this remote and peripheral backwater sought to integrate themselves into a modern, metropolitan-dominated world. After all, the vast majority of aborigines had already died by the time Robinson had got to them, if not from direct, violent encounter with the whites, then from the diseases they had imported. Confined to the offshore and not very salubrious Flinders Island, the natives continued, despite Robinson's initial best efforts, to die in droves. Just as with the remaining Guanches, they died, if not directly from observable neglect, bad conditions and European illness, then from alcohol-assisted anomie, homesickness and the pointlessness of it all. Tellingly, there were few and ultimately no births on the island to make up for deaths. Nor would belated return to another tiny reservation on the Tasman mainland in 1840s, with even more rigorous budgetary restrictions on its management, be enough to stem the tide of extinction. After 1876, the only remaining Tasmans were the half-breed descendants of the sealers and their aboriginal concubines.[127]

At least such miscegenation proved that there was a perfectly sound biological alternative to the inevitability of native extinction propounded by the 'doomed race' theorists.[128] Nevertheless, as this antipodean near-genocidal trajectory reached its pitiful conclusion, another markedly similar tragedy was being compressed into a much shorter time-frame, in an environmental enclave a continent away. Again the perpetrators were Anglos, this time in the newly created Californian state of the American Union, the specific area the north-western mountainous Yolla Bolly country in Mendocino County, and the main victim target, the Indian Yuki tribe.

*

Over 100 tribes inhabited the California region on the arrival of the white man, indicating an exceedingly rich cultural diversity. Made up of different language groups and living in closely defined areas, each – mostly quite small – tribe fiercely defending the territorial integrity upon which its balance between population and food supply depended, the Yuki grouping nevertheless stands out as, in some respects, quite exceptional. Partly this was linguistic, the Yukian group representing a small, isolated – and indeed antiquated – speech family whose modern European equivalent would be Basque, this singularity being further reinforced by the anatomical distinctions between Yukians and the majority of their neighbours. Like the Tasmans, for instance, they were unusually short, which in the view of anthropologists make them closer to being authentically autochthonous Californians than any other native group. However, the very geographical isolation of the main core of the Yukis, in Round Valley, a high, heavily forested valley region in the coastal range, further accentuated this distinctiveness; unlike most other Indians, their economy was entirely one of hunting, fishing and gathering. Their dependence on game, salmon, nuts, acorns, berries, bulbs and grass seeds was absolute, the carefully harvested abundance of these resources sustained a significant population through the sever winters. It has been estimated that before Anglo contact, there were at least 3,000 Yuki and, if one were to include the neighbouring Wailaki and Lassik, around 11,000 indigenes in total in the Yolla Bolly country, each group, by all accounts, with its own extremely elaborate and ritualised religious life.[129]

Because of their northern isolation, the Yuki were fortunate to avoid the Spanish policy of kidnapping or herding all coastal California Indians they could find for enforced labour, mostly in Franciscan coastal missions, until a very belated Spanish expedition up beyond San Francisco in 1821. This was on the cusp of the country becoming part of a newly independent Mexico. If these raids represented a continuation of standard *conquistador* practice in the Americas, with the usual disastrous epidemiological results – Stannard estimates that death largely through disease had collapsed a formerly extraordinarily healthy native Cailfornian population by at least 75 per cent by 1845[130] – its lasting legacy for the Yuki was not so much in the actions of the Spanish themselves but in the American mimicry of the policy when the territory passed in 1848 to the United States at the end of the Mexican war. The new California state legislature almost immediately passed a law that allowed citizens to indenture Indians as servants for ten or fifteen years. As a result, when Anglo trappers began encroaching on Round Valley in the early 1850s, its natives – most particularly the young women – were looked upon as fair and legitimate game in their own right, or as a source of trade with the Mexicans further south. This, of course, was not identical with genocide. Even so, when, less than a decade later, in 1860, the question of what to do with the Round Valley Indians became a critical one for the Californian state, one, albeit minority, recommendation proposed the problem could be speedily expedited by compulsorily indenturing all of them.[131]

By this juncture, however, the crisis of encounter had moved rapidly from one of possible enslavement to one of incontestable extermination. All of California was being swamped by white incomers in the 1850s, in the wake of its gold rush. However, while this vast influx impacted disastrously on the Indians of Round Valley the immediate crisis was not an issue of numbers: there were still only nineteen white men there in the autumn of 1856.[132] Nor was it the discovery of gold. Rather, what entryists, like Serranus Clinton Hastings – a vastly powerful and rapacious entrepreneur intent on building up holdings in different parts of California – realised was that this extraordinarily beautiful and well-appointed enclave represented the perfect environment with which to feed the white incomers and thereby make a huge financial killing. The immediate issue thus became, as in Tasmania, one of land ownership and land use for the raising of stock: not in this case sheep but thousands of horses, cattle and hogs. As the first two, however, lived on grasses and seeds, the last on acorns and nuts, their numerical increase could only rapidly undermine the Indians' carefully managed food supply. Faced with starvation or simply being shot down by stockmen, the natives had litte choice but to turn to the state for protection and survival. This was given, at least in theory. The California legislature declared Round Valley an Indian reservation in 1856, the idea being that it would be developed as a communal farm with its own stock and with the Indians providing the labour themselves, under federal supervision and training.[133] If this then represented the classic contours of the benign state coming to the rescue of the defenceless Indian, shielding him from the ugly side of modernity and even providing soldiers to ensure his safety, one has to ask what went so terribly wrong. How did these 'liberal' good intentions end up in an unmitigated bloodbath?

Again, at first sight, the contradiction between the principle and the practice seems quite bewildering. The US government did not lack information as to the discrepancy, being fortunate in having an intelligent and energetic man on the spot, special treasury agent J. Ross Browne, who reported back explicitly on the massacres perpetrated by the settlers. In turn, a five-man commission, appointed by the California state legislature in 1860 to investigate the troubles, found – in its majority report – that it was the Indians exclusively who were on the receiving end of the violence and that the solution lay in the US Congress buying the nonetheless illegal settlers out and confirming the whole valley a native reservation. There were calls too, to both sack and bring to justice Thomas J. Henley, the utterly corrupt Indian superintendent of California, who was not only in cahoots with Hastings but had used his position to take over a substantial part of the valley as well as government stock intended for the reservation, for himself. On both fronts these calls were repeated time and time again. Yet, not only did Henley append his name, in 1859, to a nine-person Hastings-led 'settler' petition calling on California governor, John B. Weller, to take action on their behalf *against* the Indians (at a time when Henley was under criminal investigation), but Weller in return authorised the settlers to form a volunteer company, the Eel River Rangers, to undertake it themselves.[134]

The situation illustrates the way the 'Anglo' state always ultimately sided with the interests of capital, property and development, whatever the murderous ramifications. Indians, as Indians, of course, never counted as property owners. The US government explicitly stated as much in its 1859 secretary of interior's annual report, Indians having no 'right of exclusive occupancy in any specific lands'.[135] Thus, when Indians killed hogs or horses they were property-destroying and dangerous *criminals*, regardless of the obvious reason for their actions – starvation. By contrast, when venal Indian commissioners, like Henley, milked the system for all it was worth, or the government itself cut its allocation to the reservations on grounds of fiscal stringency, there might be voices of reprimand and dissent but nobody was going to go out with a gun and shoot the malefactors. Yet, when the Round Valley whites did exactly this on any flimsy pretext, the one truly remarkable thing in the Yuki's case is their restraint in response. When they finally did kill one particularly vicious settler and rapist of Indians, John Bland, whom even army officers described as a 'a lawless ruffian', the Eel River Rangers took this as yet another excuse to declare an Indian open season.[136] And with complete impunity. On an earlier occasion when it was not a white settler but a valuable grey stallion which was killed, H. L. Hall, the leading Indian tormentor in the valley and Hastings' and Henley's stockman employee, put together a small posse which proceeded to hunt down and slaughter 240 Yuki men, women and children.[137] This, however, was not exceptional. Indeed, it was very much the norm. Another early settler, Dryden Lacock, who had worked on the reservation, attests that from 1856 through to 1860, such posses went out two or three times a week, killing on average fifty or sixty Indians on each trip. This, notes researcher Virginia P. Miller, would, on the conservative estimate of two trips a week killing *only* fifty Indians, compute as 5,200 deaths a year.[138]

Nor was direct shooting or battering to death the only form of murder. Strychnine, a newly introduced poison much preferred by hunters for dispatching wolves – another trans-continental target for extermination – was commonly laid in the Yuki rancherias, just as previously Tasmanian aborigines had been enticed to their deaths with flour and sugar laced with poison.[139] All this certainly tells us a great deal about the mentality of the direct perpetrators. Walter S. Jarboe, another Hall-like figure, who was leader of the Eel River Rangers wrote to Governor Weller justifying his actions thus:

> ... the Ukas are without doubt the most degraded, filthy, miserable, thieving lot of any thing living that comes under the head and rank of human beings ... They are so inferior in intelect (sic.), so devoid of feeling that they stand by cooly and unmoved and see their companions shot down by scores without evincing the least symptoms of sorrow and boldly avow their determination to continue their hostilities and kill our Citizens and stock so long as they live ... They have had warning after warning but all to no avail ... It may be that nothing short of extermination will suffice to rid the Country of them to make them cease their thieving and murderous course.[140]

But if this would seem to put the onus for these repeated atrocities on a sadistic, blood-crazed thug, behind whom the absentee landowner Hastings was able to tweak his influence, as first chief justice in the California Supreme Court – very much in the same manner as Tasmania's leading magistrate O'Connor had brought similar pressure to bear on a reluctant Arthur – ultimate responsibility for the Yuki slaughter must still rest with Weller and, hence, the state. The California governor may have given the appearance of putting the brakes on an outright act of genocide by warning Jarboe not to conduct indiscriminate warfare against women and children. Yet the very fact that almost in the same breath he also gave him authority to operate against those 'who are known to have been engaged in killing the stock and destroying the property of our citizens',[141] – the very point of departure of the Hastings-initiated petition – could be equally interpreted as a green light to Jarboe to do more or less as he pleased. The inference is further reinforced by the subsequent granting of most of the $11,000 which Jarboe charged the state government for his services, and for the final letter which Weller wrote him congratulating the Rangers for doing 'all that was anticipated', adding 'his sincere thanks for the manner in which it (the campaign) was conducted'.[142]

The consequences of these actions speak for themselves. In 1864, all that remained of the estimated Round Valley Yuki population of 3,000, were eighty-five men and 215 women. This demographic collapse had, in other words, been the product of a mere nine years of settler–native encounter. The evidence, moreover, suggests that a very considerable proportion of this collapse was due to direct physical violence either as sponsored by the Californian state or to which it conveniently turned a blind eye. Indeed, there was one notable occasion when a posse of settlers took it upon themselves to walk onto the reservation to massacre starving Wailaki while its superintendents looked on. Eighty years later, in 1944, the native population of Round Valley consisted of ten full-blooded Indians buttressed by several dozen of mixed blood.[143]

How, then, should we evaluate these case histories in relation to the broader canvas of genocide and its avoidance? Were what happened to the Tasman aborigines or the Yukis particular and peculiar aberrations that had as much to do with the bad luck of their physical geography as anything to do with the wilful malice of the colonisers? Such a verdict would certainly be reassuring to most British-settler descended Americans and Australians who might not be able bring themselves to accept that some of their forebears committed repeated genocide. Unfortunately, neither Tasman nor Round Valley examples represent a deviation from the main thrust of Anglo conquest and settlement but only a microcosmic insight into its bitter but inexorable logic.

At the height of the Round Valley massacres in 1860, duly authorised volunteer regiments were also slaughtering the Wiyot Indians, not very far away on Humboldt Bay, while other Californian tribes, too, notably the Yahi, Yana and Tolowa were also in similar fashion being brought to the edge of extinction.[144] Not even enslaving Indians seemed to suffice anymore. A horrified regular army lieutenant, Charles Hubbard, caught up in a military sweep aimed at removing the last Indians from the upper Mattole river area, in 1863, reported that 'even squaws and children that have been domesticated for months and years', were 'without a moment's warning' being cold-bloodedly murdered by their owners 'and with as little compunction as they would rid themselves of a dog'.[145] Why keep wretched Indians when there was an increasingly plentiful supply of dirt-cheap labour in the form of Kanaks, Chinese and *mestizo* Mexicans? These peoples, too, might be perceived by Anglos as equally wretched and vile, but at least they seemed pliant and there was no particular onus on employers or the state to look after them.[146] Could it have been that California governors throughout the 1850s publicly and vocally mandated volunteer units to go and out and exterminate Indians because it was the most obvious, convenient and *cheapest* solution to the crisis of this new state's consolidation within the Union? Was it because this method, as Weller's successor, Governor Leland Stanford coyly put it, 'accomplished for less expense than the General Government now incurs under its miserable management of Indian affairs'?[147] By these efficacious means the land was cleansed of large numbers of natives – overall the Indian population of California declined from some 150,000 in 1845 to an estimated 35,000 in 1860.[148] And with the problem thereby resolved, the 'bleeding hearts' – like Hubbard, who called for 'perpetrators of these horrible crimes against humanity'[149] to be brought to justice – were effectively sidestepped.

Thus, if there always remained among the colonisers – often army officers, like Hubbard – those who genuinely adhered to the state's official assimilationist position, this voice of authentic Western liberalism was also paradoxically one, like that of the native itself, which was crying out in the wilderness. For a simple rule applied: whenever the logic of extermination was questioned, one reminded one's interlocutors of the obstacle one was up against: a great terrifying horde of treacherous, murderous and, of course, godless savages. Yet if the threat of the savage striking back and denying the land upon which one's unfettered drive to power was founded was the bottom line in the Anglo justification for resorting to genocide, it did not have to wait for its overseas imperial moment before it could fully crystallise. If the broad contours of the West's rise to genocide can be tentatively located in an earlier eastern frontier, in a critical sense a specifically Anglo trajectory emerges from a 'British' domestic-colonial context.

Savages on the Doorstep: Gaelic Irish and Scots

To speak of colonialism emanating from the British domestic scene may super-ficially seem like something of a contradiction in terms, particularly when one considers that the common usage of the term 'British' stems from an attempt to forge a hybrid but inclusive national unity, in the wake of the 1707 Act of Union between England and Scotland.[150] This union also comprised the Celtic Welsh (and Cornish) – just about – as well as the English and Lowland Scots, and arguably laid the foundations for the first modern nation-state. By any reckoning this was a remarkable achievement when one recalls the long centu-ries of violent conflict and animosity between these diverse peoples. What matters here, however, is not so much who was accepted within this national embrace, but rather who was left outside it; specifically two groups on the archipelagic periphery – the Gaelic Irish and Highland, also Gaelic-speaking, Scots.

Gaeldom may have always been geographically peripheral, given a prima-rily English dominance founded on more favourable environmental and climatic conditions, but even in spite of war and conquest, these areas had – right up to the early modern period – held their own as quite distinct political economies and cultures. The formation of a proto-capitalist society founded on an English core, however, threatened to change all this, not by absorbing the Gaelic peoples as partners in this new ostensible wealth-creation programme but rather by eliminating them from the equation altogether so that their ter-ritorial assets might be freely available to more 'productive' English and Lowland Scots. Again, we have to be wary of reading into this some precon-ceived teleologic, not least because Britain, as the forerunner nation-state, had no blueprint for its accomplishment. Nevertheless, it is clear that, from the sixteenth and seventeenth centuries onwards, the ancestral Gaelic homelands had become for their would-be colonisers, frontiers to be subdued, tamed and civilised, concomitant to there being an increasing tendency on the latter's part to look down upon the Gaelic peoples as not simply inferior beings but aboriginal savages.

Indeed, it is striking in the degree to which the slanderous invocations made against American and later, antipodean 'first peoples' simply replicated Anglo venom directed at what were nearly always referred to as the 'wild' Irish.[151] Many English commentators of the period seem to have taken it as a given that the Irish were the local Red Indians[152] and even when this Atlantic connection was not developed there was still the stock-in-trade more conventional wisdom to fall back on, that the they were actually the bastard descendants of the Scythians, 'the most barbaric people known to the ancient world'.[153] It followed that when, in 1655, Charles Fleetwood, the then Lord Deputy in Ireland, empowered to carry out the Commonwealth's mass ethnic cleansing of the country, pronounced in justification that 'the Irish are abominable, false, cunning and perfidious people', he was doing no more than stating what most literate Englishmen took to be an honest and true characterisation of the facts.[154] Indeed, soldiers and others associated with an Elizabethan punitive military expedition more than eighty years prior to Fleetwood were already variously describing the inhabitants they encountered as wild, barbarous, indolent, parasitic, treacherous, blasphemous, thieving, violent, murderous, incestuous and sexually licentious.[155]

Arguably, dark talk of Irish cannibalism, and of the roasting of their victims, injected into these English mental constructions a more obviously exotic element which more closely aligned the Irish stereotype to the allegedly godless, pagan devil-worshippers on the other side of the Atlantic.[156] There was a problem here, of course. Many of the Elizabethan adventurers in Ireland were part of a highly educated and talented 'Renaissance' elite who knew full well that the Irish were Christians (and had indeed been so sometime before the English). That they were Catholic Christians, as was the case with some of the Scottish Highland clans, would hardly have endeared them to English Protestants at a time of unrelenting, vicious and increasingly trans-European conflict across this religious divide. Even so, putting the Irish entirely outside the universe of Christian obligation required their 'mere' Catholicism to be subordinated to an imagery which confirmed their more lowly place in the human hierarchy. As another Elizabethan commentator put it, the Irish more 'than in any other part of the world that is know' were 'like beastes, voide of lawe and all good order'. It followed that no action against them could be 'too seveare'.[157]

All this conveniently served a very English purpose in Ireland: the forfeiture of Irish-held land in favour of English colonies. Or in the parlance of the time: plantations. Sixteenth- and seventeenth-century plantations, on whichever side of the Atlantic they were founded, were considered to be a product of enterprise deriving from an emerging English or Scottish national community, but which in turn were expected to 'raise commercially desirable commodities' for the benefit of the commonweal.[158] As in the Americas, so in Ireland it was the degeneracy of the people not the environment itself which denied this potential. Hence the fault could be logically righted only by handing over the governance of the country to those who would make it virtuous and ordered.[159] For English commentators the Irish habit of herding their cattle round the country like nomads – in fact the quite 'normal' and traditional pastoral practice of transhumance – living for much of the year out in the open in woods and bogs, not to say within the social framework of chieftain-led tribes and clans, were all evidence of a brutish backwardness. The issue of Ireland in all such discourses (and these, of course, closely paralleled or prefigured those over the future of the American continent) was not so much over what to do with the land – that was practically a given as technically the English Crown had claimed Ireland by right of conquest since Norman times – but what to do with *the people*.

Should there be an attempt to convert the Irish to the 'righteous' path of Protestantism, make them virtuous and civil like the English themselves, even integrate them into an English-led civil order through intermarriage, as some assimilationist advocates from the period of Elizabeth through to Cromwell proposed? Or was long-standing Irish lawlessness, obduracy and refusal to acculturate to 'superior' English norms, as their 'more 'hawkish' opponents argued, proof that this would be an utterly wasted effort? It is surely significant that neither 'hawks' nor 'doves' in this debate had any intention of meeting the Irish half way, anymore than later imperialists would have done with regard to Australian aborigines. The only issue at stake, with Rome very much another early imperial model to presumptuously emulate, was how exactly to proceed with the civilising project.[160]

A critical signpost to an emerging English hard line on the matter is the anonymous late Elizabethan tract *A View on the Present State of Ireland,* generally attributed to the humanist poet and crown official in Ireland, Edmund Spenser.[161] *A View* does not propose extermination *per se* but rather encapsulation, the English effectively taking over the country beyond the traditional Pale of Settlement around Dublin, through a radical and comprehensive, not to say scientifically organised, programme of reform. On the one hand, this would dismantle the old social organisation of the entire island of Ireland and on the other replace it with English-settled plantations in which the Irish populace would be absorbed into that of the incomers' custom and religion. The whole programme would be accomplished under the strict and authoritarian tutelage of military governance. Indeed, the tract is unapologetic in its prescription that violence, or the threat of violence, is the necessary method for the achievement of this reforming order.[162]

But even supposing this policy were adopted, what did one do if the Irish still refused to be reformed but actually took up arms against it? Then, logically, bar abandoning the colonising project altogether – about as remote a

possibility as conceivable – one's only recourse was to consider even more drastic remedies. *A View* does not flinch from these possibilities, though it avoids
the prospect of direct slaughter by positing that, in the face of the scorched-
earth policies that would be inflicted on the starving Irish resisters, they would
then turn on and devour one another. The reference to a convenient cannibalism is clearly an extension of the then current English myths about the Irish.
The concept of an intentionally created famine, however, is entirely factually
drawn from Elizabethan military campaigns launched against the uprisings in
Ulster and Munster in the last three decades of the sixteenth century.[163] If
famine, by inference, was Spenser's preferred if ultimate method of resolving
the Irish problem, other commentators with hands-on experience of the fighting were much less coy about enacting a direct extirpatory violence. 'How
godly a dede it is to overthrowe so wicked a race the world may judge: for my
part I thinke there cannot be a greater sacryfice to God', proudly wrote one of
the lieutenants of the first major Elizabethan expedition to Ulster to the
queen's chief minister, Burghley, in 1574, describing how they had harried
men, women and children into woods and plains with the onset of winter so
that they would freeze and starve to death.[164] What is significant, of course, is
that this onslaught on non-combatants was not some one-off, devised by a
commander in the field acting on his own volition, but rather part of an
emerging state-authorised policy of war without restraint, in clear contravention of the accepted rules of war. In this sense, not only did it represent an
innovation in terms of English military practice, but one that was to become
its standard operating procedure in the course of subsequent mid-seventeenth-
century Irish campaigning.

Can we thus trace the origins of the English experience as genocidal perpetrator in the Americas and antipodes to events in late sixteenth- and early
seventeenth-century Ireland? Indeed, are developments on both sides of the
Atlantic, at this same time, indicators of a common toxicity in an emerging
political economy of empire? The answer is both yes and no. On the one hand,
the same closely linked mix of territorial consolidation and commercial entrepreneurial interests as in the Americas, provided irresistible grounds for a
programme of state-sponsored expropriation of the Irish and Scottish Gaels.
One might go a cynical stage further, with regard particularly to the Scottish
Highlands, and say that, as with Tasmania, profit by way of the introduction
of a four-legged crop – Cheviot sheep – was utterly dependent on at least drastically reducing if not entirely eliminating its two-legged inhabitants. One
might even go a stage further still and posit that, given the demands of a rapidly growing British population and increasingly urban-based economy, the
imperative to sweep away political economies resistant to the trajectory of the

modernising core made genocidal sense. Thus, removed of their recalcitrant inhabitants the territorial and other assets of these regions might then be brought within the orbit of, and in turn properly integrated – tabula rasa-like – within, the totalising frame of the national economy.

The notion is appallingly neat but historically flawed. For one thing, the reduction of Britain's traditional peasant society was hardly exclusive to the Celtic fringe. On the contrary, its heartlands were the English shires, where profit-driven enclosure of the commons by wealthy landowners had been pre-ceding apace for centuries, leading directly or indirectly to the dispossession of the vast majority of English tenant farmers who had become surplus to requirements. If the mass eviction of much of the Scottish Gaeltacht through the Highland Clearances was indisputably more extreme, partly because it was compressed into a shorter time-frame, partly because it was often instigated by chieftains who had abandoned their own clan followers, it was nevertheless still part of the same general pattern.[165] It was a pattern which, though brutal and dehumanising, was no more genocidal in itself than the dispossessions which would occur throughout the world as relationships between land and people rapidly unravelled in the face of an emerging international market-place.[166] Moreover, and rather problematically, the majority of Gaelic dispos-sessions tended to occur some time after the danger of actual genocide had passed, rather than the other way round, as one might expect. The Highland Clearances began some forty years after the obvious crisis moment, the col-lapse of the Jacobite rebellion of 1745. Ireland, it is true, had seen attempts at limited dispossession through the various plantation schemes of the Eliza-bethan and early Stuart monarchs as well as more pointedly during the Cromwellian settlement. Even so, intensive Anglo-Scottish colonisation of one particular region, Ulster, did not properly get underway until the reign of Willam and Mary, again some forty years after Cromwell's extirpation of the Irish revolt.

The fact that we can identify in both these cases a moment of genocidal potentiality – if not necessarily its actuality – must also confirm that the behaviour of British state-builders towards Gaelic peasants was, in some fun-damental respect, quite different from their behaviour towards English ones. However, if the imperatives of dispossession *alone* cannot properly explain it, neither can 'Anglo' charges of Gaelic savagery as a single cause. After all, the savage – whether the Australian aborigine or, for that matter, the English indigent – could always, in principle, be tamed and thereby, again in principle, brought within one's universe of obligation. The danger from the Gaels, or more accurately the perceived danger, was that they might overturn and destroy that universe. In this sense, being placed where they were on the domestic periphery of the emerging British state provided them with a potency that the 'savages' of the Americas and antipodes could never fully realise. The fact, moreover, that this threat appeared to crystallise not only at very specific moments of broader national crisis but, in so doing, always throwing up in its wake deep-seated anxieties about French or Spanish intervention on 'British' soil,[167] provided ingredients for much more mainstream politically driven genocidal scenarios which, in the Americas and antipodes were not always, if at all, self-evident.

Yet, as in all genocidal scenarios, the discrepancy between the reality of the Gaelic threat and its perception by those who faced it is rather stark. True, the charge sheet against the Irish in the 1640s, and many of the Scottish clans a hundred years later, is a long and serious one. They had either instigated or participated in armed and violent rebellions against the crown, had welcomed foreign troops, or emissaries, onto 'British' soil providing them with a potential launching pad for more serious attacks on its heartlands and had themselves provided strike forces for this purpose. Moreover, both rebellions were tainted by association with the cause of the Stuart kings or later pretenders, which by degrees – particularly after the judicially sanctioned execution of Charles I in 1649, even more so after the successful 'Glorious Revolution' against his son, James II in 1688 – became synonymous with reactionary, Catholic and hence 'foreign' efforts to subvert an agenda of national consolidation, elite-monopolised wealth creation and imperial conquest. The fact that both parts of the Gaeltacht included core bastions of an opposing and outlawed Jacobitism and were, to greater or lesser degrees, involved through their own elites in the various abortive conspiracies, scares and insurrections which punctuated the transition to an ultimately Hanoverian 'Great Britain', did arguably make them a hostile and treacherous fifth column.

However, in an important sense this tells us much more about the xenophobic, vituperatively anti-Catholic and increasingly single-minded agenda of Europe's first authentic nation-state builders and, as such, of their refusal to brook any sort of accommodation with those whose primary aim was to safeguard and defend their own fragile political-cultural autonomy. The attempted Irish coup of 1641 was one such attempt to seize opportunity from a growing civil strife on the other side of the water, in order to reassert a modicum of Irish self-rule.[168] Certainly, it dramatically misfired, some thousands of Anglo-Scottish settlers paying for it with their lives. Certainly too, its instigators found themselves by default, rather than design, lined up on the side of the Crown against Parliament as the ensuing internecine wars in the three kingdoms of England, Ireland and Scotland began to unravel. This ensured that the outlook for the Irish would be grim should Parliament win, as indeed

it did. That the power behind Parliament, led by Oliver Cromwell, was actually the most radical and ideologically driven regime in English history, and a
military one to boot, however, turned grimness into catastrophe. Cromwell's
Commonwealth imbibed the whole Puritan account of the Irish coup in which
300,000 Protestants had supposedly been massacred – there were only
125,000 settlers *in toto* in Ireland. Apparently, this all was part of a carefully
constructed conspiracy engineered by Charles, that behind Charles was the
papacy, this explained why Ireland was crawling with Franciscan friars and
Jesuits, why the king's army in England was full of Irishmen, and, in short,
why the Irish were no more nor less than the forces of the devil incarnate.[169]

When thus, Lord Protector Cromwell personally led a Commonwealth
army across to Ireland in 1649, not simply to flush out the last vestiges of royalist resistance but to exact revenge for the 1641 massacres, he was acting out
a model perpetrator's 'never again' syndrome. 'Never again' would the Irish be
allowed to harm righteous Protestants but also 'never again' would they be
allowed to defy English order as beyond the Pale of Settlement they had effectively done for hundreds of years. Nor, ever again, would they be allowed to
offer Ireland as a geo-strategic toehold for England's enemies. Ironically,
Cromwell's personal role in what then transpired is largely overplayed, while
what happened after he left the country in November 1651 is seriously under-
estimated. True, Cromwell must take responsibility for the indiscriminate
retributive slaughters committed by his soldiery against the garrisons and
populace of Drogheda and Wexford, at the outset of his campaign.[170] Even so,
these atrocities fall into a familiar and standard pattern of early modern European siege warfare where failure to surrender a town provided the attackers
with the justification to offer no quarter when it was eventually taken. In spite
of the several thousands of combatants and non-combatants massacred at
these two places, these cannot add up, in themselves, to a specific charge of
genocide. However, can we look at the larger mortality rates from the wars
and come closer to the charge?

Considered overall, an Irish population collapse from 1.5 or possibly over 2
million inhabitants at the onset of the Irish wars in 1641, to no more than
850,000 eleven years later represents an absolutely devastating demographic
catastrophe.[171] Undoubtedly the largest proportion of this massive death toll
did not arise from direct massacre but from hunger and then bubonic plague,
especially from the key outbreak between 1649 and 1652. Even so, the relationship to the worst years of the fighting is all too apparent. Having said
that, a broader perspective again would remind us that these were not untypi-
cal results of early modern warfare. It was not just across the Atlantic in the
wars conducted against Indian 'savages' that 'scorched earth' was practised as

a standard means of denying an adversary his resource base and sapping his morale. Such practice was intended specifically to terrorise 'enemy' non-combatant populations in Europe too. The resultant population losses as hunger, exposure and disease set in are very telling. In the Seven Years War between 1756 and 1763, for instance, an estimated 70,000 Pomeranian civilians lost their lives, with as much as a quarter of the population of the New Mark of Brandenburg disappearing through death or flight.[172] In these terms, what happened to the Irish in the mid-seventeenth century might be viewed as certainly on the extreme end of an early modern warfare spectrum but not in itself entirely exceptional.

Yet, as Ian Gentles has pointed out, a great deal of the Irish killing came in *the aftermath* of the conventional war.[173] This was the period when Cromwell was back in England, but Irish guerrilla bands (the original 'Tories') continued to operate to deny to the generals and commissioners whom the Lord Protector had left in charge any semblance of a successful post-war pacification. It was a situation where these authorities, unable to defeat a largely unseen enemy, began to take more and more desperate measures against the Irish population as a whole, to the point where mere contemplation of exterminating the Irish population began to be translated into reality. Scorched-earth operations became something more. As the English standing army in Ireland swelled to 35,000 it systematically laid waste the corn and cattle upon which fighters and general populace alike depended, cut down the woods in which the Tories hid and also attempted to control the residence and movement of everyone across the country. In this process great swathes in the centre and south of Ireland where the insurgency remained strong were declared free-fire zones. Absolutely anyone found within these zones, said the official proclamations of early 1652, could be 'taken, slain and destroyed as enemies' along with their cattle and other goods.[174]

What happened in Ireland in the early 1650s, thus, is recognisably akin to the 'dirty' counter-insurgency wars of the twentieth century where an imperial or colonial power, or its proxies, seeks to win a struggle against an alternative political programme by treating not just the insurgents but their whole supporting population as equally guilty and thereby expendable. Irish soldiery fighting in the English Civil War had already been shown no mercy when captured. In Ireland, apprehended priests and friars, whatever their actions, were similarly strung up or shot. However, when the generals responsible for the counter-insurgency operations began to make absolutely no distinction between combatant and non-combatant, a significant Rubicon was crossed. But to consider their actions as impelled by an impassioned anti-Catholicism, or in the case of Sir Charles Coote – the most notoriously brutal of the commanders on the spot – as an example of a self-made 'new English' land-owner with a personal interest in recovering his estates lost in 1641, only tells us half the story.[175]

In England, in spite of the violent religious antagonisms engendered by the Thirty Years War on the continent, Cromwell was attempting to grant tolera-tion to Catholics and non-Catholics alike. His Irish policy thus stands in marked contrast: a conscious attempt to reduce a distinct ethnic population, not simply on grounds of their religious predisposition, but also for demon-strating their potential to challenge the mono-directional and monopolistic thrust of an Anglo-Protestant dominated British Isles. In this sense, too, the genocidal process that began to emerge after 1651 was neither simply a short-term military strategy nor impelled purely by the voracity of a handful of entrepreneur speculators, although some of them were in military uniform. It was part of an intentional long-term political policy. Granted, there were dra-conian yet non-lethal aspects to it, England's first Navigation Act of 1651, for instance, by denying the Irish the use of their own shipping, successfully destroyed with one blow the basis for an independent trading potential that had become evident in the years of unrest between 1641 and Cromwell.[176] Interestingly, such economic sabotage would, in Lemkin's original 1944 pre-scription as to the meaning of the term, count as an aspect of genocide where it could be shown to be part of an overall plan aimed at the disintegration of a national group's essential foundations.[177] But what arguably clinches the case for the prosecution is when these elements are put alongside the 1652 Act for the Settlement of Ireland.

The Act, and the parliamentary legislation which succeeded it the following year, is the nearest thing *on paper*, in the English and more broadly British-domestic record, to a programme of state-sanctioned and systematic ethnic cleansing of another people. The fact that it did not include 'total' genocide in its remit, or that it failed to put into practice the vast majority of its proposed expulsions, ultimately, however, says less about the lethal determination of its makers and more about the political, structural and financial weaknesses of the early modern English state. For instance, though the Act begins rather ominously by claiming that it was not its intention to extirpate the whole Irish nation, it then goes on to list five categories of people who, as participants or alleged supporters of the 1641 rebellion and its aftermath, would automati-cally be in forfeit of their lives. It has been suggested that as many as 100,000 people would have been liable under these headings. A further five categories – by implication an even larger body of 'passive' supporters of the rebellion – were to be spared their lives but not their property. Here the underlying Com-monwealth intention, as underscored by the succeeding legislation, becomes clearer still. The expropriated were to be required to move on pain of death to a designated area in the most westerly corner of Ireland and so make way for a new massive wave of Anglo-Scottish settlers who would supersede them. Certainly, at the time, it was generally assumed – as well as taken as read by the then Lord Deputy in Ireland, Lieutenant-General Ludlow – that the expulsion order applied to the entire Catholic element of the Irish population regardless of whether they had, or had not participated in the rebellion.[178]

Of course, one could argue that bottling up a native people on a Connacht reservation whose bounded contours – the river Shannon and the Atlantic Ocean – prevented their natural egress was one rather important step separate from genocide just as, in rather similar vein, were the 1830s deportations of the Cherokee and other Eastern seaboard peoples to reservations across the Mississippi, or for that matter the Nazis' 1939–40 grand projected removal of Polish Jewry to a reservation in the Lublin region. Yet all three examples evince the same basic rationale: namely the intention to eject a troublesome population whose place within the broader national or colonial frame had been definitively and permanently revoked, while using their expropriated land or other assets for the benefit of a national consolidation. That in the case of the Commonwealth it also provided a solution to the vexed problem of how to pay for the war in Ireland itself represented a tremendous bonus; the London Adventurer entrepreneurs who had underwritten the campaign being offered 10 million acres of expropriated land, with additional allotments also being offered to demobilised soldiers in lieu of back-pay.

The interests of state and commerce were, thus, to be happily married. The entire island of Ireland was hastily surveyed and its estates divided. The chief planner of all this, Physician General to the army, Sir William Petty, unsurprisingly turned himself into a major Irish landowner in the process. However, other entrepreneurs also did very nicely for themselves often out of land speculation, or clearfelling the remaining forests: a tidy double-killing, short-term proceeds from the logging, long-term from the change of usage to pasture.[179] A process, in other words, quite familiar from any frontier. The vast majority of Irish land that was not already in English or Scottish hands now passed to the English.[180] There was, though, one significant hitch. As it turned out, there were relatively few new settlers to take advantage of all these opportunities, only perhaps some 12,000, and many of these, the big incoming landowners particularly, needed labour to work their new estates or to provide them with an income. If the old Irish ruling class had been definitively banished to Connacht or had gone into foreign exile of their own volition, the English in Ireland needed its people whether they liked it or not. Subdued, at least for the time being, they may have been, but the Irish were at least to be spared the full impact of Anglo frontier conquest and settlement visited on other 'natives'.[181]

In some ways quite similar, but in others rather different, the experience of the Gaelic Scots was also one of a genocidal potential and its avoidance. A significant number of the clans exploded out of their Highland eyries as the military van of the last great Jacobite attempt to retake the British state in what was commonly referred to as the '45. This was also, in their own more immediate terms, a final desperate effort to retain some last vestige of an already much disintegrated and politically emasculated tribal-based society against British state and societal encroachment.[182] The inherent weakness of the attempt and the military and political isolation of the participating clans did not, however, prevent their initial run-away lurch as far south as Derby, sparking off not only panic among the English ruling class but also a more populist and 'rampant Scotophobia'.[183] That the potency of these apparently irresistible and ferocious broadsword-wielding 'savages' was in fact little more than that of a paper tiger was proved at their last-ditch stand at Culloden where, faced with the field guns and grapeshot of a modern military machine they were systematically blown off the field.[184]

With the Highlanders irrevocably destroyed in military terms, this could well have been the moment when the British state went in for the kill, extirpating in so doing another 'never again' tranche of misconceived 'popish' treachery and rebellion memories – misconceived not least because most clans were actually Episcopalian, staunchly pro-royalist and hence seriously averse to the Jacobite cause. In spite of this the Hanoverian regime did teeter on the brink. High-placed figures in the administration such as the cultivated man of letters, and Lord Lieutenant of Ireland, Lord Chesterfield, urged a naval blockade to starve the Highlands to death. The military commander on the spot, the king's son, the Duke of Cumberland would have been only too ready to oblige, his own diligence in razing villages and executing without trial all rebel suspects already earning him the dubious sobriquet of 'Butcher' Cumberland. If the army's own desire for a military solution was in part a case of overcompensation for its largely inept bungling of the campaign as a whole, it undoubtedly did carry with it a significant groundswell of grass-roots support.[185]

That the state did not go down this exact path is perhaps testament to its insight that it could achieve its goals by other means. Take away the chieftains' hereditary juridical rights and replace them with the king's law; ensure that you have complete surveillance and control of the Highland region by building a thousand miles of military roads across its length and breadth, yet at the same time co-opt the chieftains themselves to your own interest by offering them a place at the capitalist's high-table; and the Hanoverians found that they could consolidate this last domestic frontier and trouble-spot without recourse to genocide. The trick, of course, lay in conceding something very permanent and substantial to the chiefs, a pay-off which would have hardly been conceivable in the zero-sum game of overseas conquest and settlement. By allowing the retention of their estates and the opportunity to participate in a more general Scottish economic take-off – its overseas commerce expanding by an astounding 300 per cent in the period 1750–1800[186] – the umbilical cord between Highland leaders and their people was irrevocably cut. Detribal-ised, dispossessed of hearth and home in the face of the incoming sheep, their children forcibly schooled in English language and custom, the only options for the majority of the residual Gaelic peasantry was to starve, submerge themselves as their English counterparts were also doing in the ranks of the industrial proletariat, emigrate to the new colonies, or accept a role in the greater scheme of things by providing their menfolk as 'tribal soldiers' in the new Highland regiments that the British state was busily manufacturing.

But if this is a case of how one particular genocidal process ended up being diffused in a mix of ethnocide, forced assimilation and – through the bizarre appropriation of the tribal tartan – as the basis for an entirely spurious reinte-gration of Highland culture as the touchstone of a new 'Scottish' adjunct to British identity,[187] how does it inform or relate to the wave of properly exe-cuted genocides perpetrated by Anglos in the Americas and Australia? The answer has an element of tragic irony in it. By letting them live to fight another day, so to speak, as the military cannon-fodder in its imperial advance, many Gaelic Highlanders became the often extremely patriotic cutting edge of British wars in these other parts. In the American theatre of the Seven Years War, for instance, some British commanders seem to have had the notion that their ferocity would be a suitable antidote to Indian warfare. What it actually meant, in practice, was that Highlanders were often in the forefront of battle 'and suffered the highest casualty rates among the Anglo-American forces'.[188]

Where the knock-on effects of Britain's exterminatory violence in the Gaeltacht were much more significant, however, was in the vast numbers of Irish, Scots, as well as Scots-Irish, who ended up in the Americas and antipo-des. Their arrival there was mostly a direct consequence of their catastrophic displacement back home. Substantial numbers of Irish were already being deported to the Americas in the 1650s as punishment for their involvement in the 1641 rebellion. Many hundreds of thousands more of these indentured labourers, i.e. temporary slaves, arrived throughout the seventeenth and eight-eenth centuries, though with the New World option closed to this traffic on the advent of American independence, transportation to the Australian penal settlements became the replacement destination. Not all such convicts were Irish or Scots, just as not all nominally free settlers arriving in Australia and North America in the late eighteenth and early nineteenth centuries were the human flotsam from the Highland Clearances. But the significant number of both these categories who were from the Highlands – and whose best hope for a future rested on their move to settle the yet unconsolidated frontiers – meant that it was they, more often than not, who were the 'white' front line in the encounter with these same frontiers' indigenous peoples. Brutalised by their previous experience, still looked down upon by their Anglo 'betters' as little more than savages themselves – the 'Scum of the Earth' and 'Refuse of Mankind', not to say 'like the Goths and Vandals of old'[189] – it was perhaps not that surprising that some of their number became serious native exterminators in their own right.[190] Nor is it surprising that, in so doing, they should be forerunners of what other displaced, dispossessed and sometimes genocidally threatened refugee peoples – notably Circassians in Ottoman Turkey, or later Eastern European *Volksdeutsche* brought under Nazi protection – were equally capable of committing. Indeed, in the case of the Irish and Scots, it may well have been an unwritten policy of state. As Colin Calloway notes, colonial authorities, perfectly aware of Scottish, Irish and Scots-Irish clan rivalries, blood feuds and Old Testament senses of justice 'steered Scots-Irish immigrants to the frontier, knowing they would provide effective defence against Indian attacks. Alternatively, they made excellent shock troops for the invasion of Indian lands'.[191]

But if this is a case of victims becoming perpetrators, there is an even more cogent case for arguing that the original perpetrators in the Irish and Scottish wars were not only able to extend their exterminatory skills to the killing of natives overseas (and sometimes from there back to Scotland and Ireland)[192] but in a more political sense develop from this domestic frontier experience procedures that, transferred to the Americas and antipodes, became the stock-in-trade ground rules for their further colonising programme. Francis Jennings, a leading scholar of the Anglo-Indian encounter on the eastern seaboard, describes these procedures as follows:

> 1) a deliberate policy of inciting competition in order, by division to maintain control; 2) a disregard for pledges and promises to natives, no matter how solemnly made; 3) the introduction of total exterminatory war against some communities of natives in order to terrorise others; and 4) a highly developed propaganda of falsification to justify all acts and policies of the conquerors whatsoever.[193]

2. Anglo Consolidation in the Americas and Antipodes

Transferring the Ground Rules:
The British in North America and the Antipodes

Jennings' charge is shocking not only in its own right but also because it stands in such marked contrast with repeated, official British and later US promises of non-violent assimilation of native populations on the basis of their consent. Is there, then, any basis for reconciling these two quite contradictory sets of ground rules, or is the accommodationist stance, as Jennings and others have argued, simply a case of hypocritical, double-faced cant?

Looking at early British settlement in America it should be quite clear that there was no genuinely sincere effort to absorb Indians into white culture. The obvious transmitter for such a process would have been the Church but, in marked contrast to the Catholic Spanish, or even French in the Americas, there is only limited evidence of Protestant evangelisation among the natives. Many of the early settlers in New England were, of course, devoutly Puritan, which rather conveniently excluded from their own parameters of moral obligation anybody who was not a member of the 'Elect'. This rather left the field of native proselytisation to the much more inclusivist Jesuits operating to the north in French Canada, or smaller continental sects such as the Moravian Brethren who colonised parts of Pennsylvania.[1] If amongst the settlers the Plymouth Brethren were, thus, the most absolute in putting a cordon of virtual untouchability around those they constantly referred to as 'savages' – an exclusivity, incidentally, in marked contrast to the Indian assimilative embrace of whites willing to join their communities[2] – Puritan anti-native hostility, racism and demonic projection strongly set the standard for the Anglo colonisers as a whole. Indeed, in so far as they were prepared to countenance the existence of Indians at all, it was very much in the spirit of the elder Richard Hakluyt's prescription, at the very outset of projected Virginia colonisation in

1585, for those who would be 'gentle and tractable'.[3] Put more realistically, this meant natives who proved that they were not dangerous to the colonisers and who were prepared to put up with any demand made upon them, including vacating their land and livelihoods without complaint and in return meekly accepting colonial authority – preferably as 'praying' Indians – like good children.

This does not mean that there were not periods of relative calm, even of co-existence and cultural interchange in what has been referred to by Richard White as 'the middle ground' between native and colonial societies.[4] But we ought to be wary of reading into this very much about the imperatives of either official colonial policy or some roseate alternative version of white man–red man accommodation. The ephemeral stand-off which White specifically highlights in an extended Great Lakes region – the *pays d'en haut* – was throughout most of the late seventeenth and eighteenth century a country where there were very few white men and almost no white settlements other than military forts and trading posts. In other words, just as was the case at the very outset of eastern seaboard colonisation, one of the things which kept direct conquest in check was that European interests in the region were directed towards making a financial killing from the fur trade – most particularly from beaver pelts for which there was an insatiable European demand – and not towards a more permanent agriculture-based settlement. Instead of seeking to dispossess the Indians, the fur trade entrepreneurs were dependent on them to trap the beaver, and to a significant degree went on needing them as extending coastal settlement pushed their field of operations west and northwards both towards and beyond the Great Lakes. The fact, moreover, that this commercial interest was initially contested by three major European powers, Dutch, English and French, none of which had the manpower or other resources with which to gain a monopolistic predominance, again, on one level, actually advantaged some of the eastern seaboard tribes. Able to bring their own military potential to these struggles, not only were the most astute of the tribes positioned to play the Europeans off one against the other but, even – most notably in the case of the powerful five-nation Iroquois confederation – hold the regional balance of power.[5]

These geo-strategic considerations and more particularly the military stalemate in what became the dominant Anglo-French contest for Eastern seaboard supremacy once the Dutch had retreated from it, certainly would appear to have provided a significant breathing space for the tribes to the west of the Appalachian watershed. In fact, even this apparent consolation hides deeper, and actually entirely ghastly realities. For one thing, as an increasing number of tribes became sucked into the demands – and enticements – of the fur trade, driving them to hunt further and further afield for a beaver that they were driving to the edge of extinction, they inevitably spilled over onto other tribes' traditional communal and hunting grounds.[6] This led in turn to a scope, scale, intensity and unrestrained violence of inter-tribal warfare never previously witnessed. Indeed, the introduction of European weaponry and, with it, European modes of warfare, turned these encounters increasingly into wars of extermination.[7] The hybrid communities of White's 'middle ground' were largely, in fact, made up of the vastly decimated, fragmented and entirely traumatised refugee remnants of mostly Algonquian-speaking tribes who had been persistently attacked by the Iroquois in the mid-seventeenth century in the latter's efforts to control the disappearing sources of beaver.[8] Displacement led to further mortality through epidemics: anything between 25 and 90 per cent of a number of these tribes are believed to have been wiped out by the early 1700s.[9]

True, in practical terms, further depredation and destabilisation was parried to some extent by the growing late seventeenth-century relationship between the French and the peoples of the *pays d'en haut*. The partial French protection and arming of these peoples meant that the Iroquois themselves began to diminish in numbers as Hurons and other tribes got their retaliation in. But the downside to this was that practically all tribes became beholden as military auxiliaries to either French – or British – patrons at a juncture when the eastern seaboard was becoming a touchstone in an increasingly globalised Anglo-French contest. The stresses in this situation were already becoming apparent in the 1720s and 1730s, when even the French, as a matter of *raison d'état*, launched their own attempted exterminatory campaigns against two peoples, the Mesquaki (Fox), in the Great Lakes region, and the Natchez, further to the south in Louisiana, in each case not only on the grounds of their suspected connivance with the British but, equally significantly, for their thoroughly aggressive efforts to be independent players in their own right.[10] By the time of the climactic Anglo-French struggle for the whole region, in the form of the Seven Years War, beginning in 1756, the possibility of any native people or alliance, the Iroquois included, being able to hold any sort of balance between, or against, the power of the European contestants had been effectively ruled out of the equation. Yet, despite the heavy backing of Indian tribes on behalf of the French, not least against the growing depredations of Scots-Irish and other 'Anglo' settlers beyond the trans-Appalachian watershed, it was the British who emerged entirely victorious. Complete control of the region, however, now posed a new problem for the British Crown. Instead of aiding and abetting the 'savages' in order to eliminate each other, would the Anglos themselves now have to take a more forceful hand in the procedure?

There was a paradox here. So long as the French were there as the main enemy, and British military capacity against them remained strictly limited, imperial Britain could hardly look upon the wipe-out of native American peoples whose menfolk might be engaged as surrogate soldiers, with equanimity. On the other hand, inciting tribes against each other – just as Jennings, with the Gaelic precedent in mind, has charged – had always been part of a battery of divide-and-rule tactics from the outset of English colonial conquest. The contradiction is glaring. Destabilisation of native relationships was built into the process of English settlement, including frequent use of tribes to fight and sometimes destroy each other. That this was possible at all, however, was also in critical respects a product of tribal chieftains' willingness to lend themselves accordingly.

Pre-contact native tribal society by its very nature was in a more or less permanent state of aggravation over the means and territorial range of subsistence, with its usually nearest neighbours. The apparently unsullied but in military technology terms well-endowed European incomers appeared to provide a way out of the impasse to any tribal leadership seemingly astute enough to take up the assistance proffered. What ensued was from an English standpoint – not least in the early years, given their relative demographic and territorial weakness – a perfectly logical method of picking off their native opponents one by one, and from the opposite perspective, a usually rather temporary tribal gain followed by a searing recognition – nearly always too late – that they had been fatally wrong-footed.

When, thus, as one early example, the Narragansetts in the 1630s eagerly allied with the newly created Puritan Connecticut colony to cut their historic Pequot enemies down to size, they seem to have been quite at a loss, not to say utterly traumatised when the English proceeded to all intents and purposes to try and *wipe out* the Pequots.[11] The burning of several hundred mostly women and children at the Pequot fort at Mystic in May 1637, seems to have particularly rankled and upset those Narragansett warriors present at the act. Women and children up to this point had nearly always been spared in Indian warfare.[12] The effect was dramatically to turn their leader, Miantonomi, into a powerful advocate of Indian tribal solidarity, an attempt cut short, ironically, by his being shopped to the English by a rival sachem, leading to his 1643 assassination at the colonialists' behest.[13] When many Narragansetts were finally, some thirty years later, to join with other disaffected tribes in the area, in a belated struggle *à outrance* against the New England colonies, the resulting King Philip's War, as it came to be remembered – after the English name for the Wampanoag leader, Metacom – became a general Indian catastrophe. 'Not above a hundred men (are) left of them who last year were the greatest

body of Indians in New England' wrote a jubilant Puritan leader, as the colonists turned the annihilatory tables on their adversaries.[14] It was true. Overall,
the tribes of southern New England by direct or indirect trauma, starvation
and enslavement as a result of the war may have collapsed by as much as a half
to two-thirds – or some 8,000 people – that is, on top of ongoing demographic devastation created through pandemic waves of smallpox and other
diseases already rampant through European contact.[15] Indian lands in southern New England henceforth were ripe for the white man's taking. Yet again,
ironically, the remnants of the Pequots, and some other Indians peoples, both
'praying' and heathen, and from breakaway groups who had taken the field
with Metacom, stood by or fought *with* the English.[16]

American native history would be subsequently littered with examples of
tribes who would do the white man's bidding, offer their menfolk as trackers,
scouts and warriors in the Anglo cause and then pay the price.[17] In the antipodes, the story would be very similar, the severity of the Tasman aboriginal
attacks on settlers in the 1820s being countered, in part, by 'friendly black'
trackers expressly brought in for the purpose from the mainland. The litany
would continue with the crushing of concerted aboriginal resistance on the
1840s frontiers of New South Wales, Victoria and Queensland by now-
uniformed troopers from other tribes, while this itself would only be the
prelude to an even more systematic exterminatory policy undertaken in
Queensland through a specially formed and equipped Native Mounted Police.[18]

The use of native people against native people in the Americas and antipodes would thus seem to highlight a particular weakness of tribal society and
culture in the face of concerted nation-state agendas either in their domestic or
colonial forms. The way that, more recently, Kurdish clans have been used by
Iraqi and Turkish states against one another, with catastrophic results, would
seem to endorse this general rule.[19] However, we could also choose to read this
apparent failing in an entirely different way. The very fact that in all these
instances states have had to engage tribes to fight other tribes, very often *after*
having tried and failed to defeat them themselves, suggests that the statist
subjugation of native adversaries is very far from some foregone conclusion –
even where the latter may be seriously depleted in numbers through starvation, displacement and disease. Indeed, one might argue the point further by
proposing that the very ethnographic diversity of tribal societies and hence of
the very special ecological and spiritual relationship of each to a particular
landscape and habitat will ensure that their communal defence of what they
consider theirs will be unusually desperate and tenacious, to the point where it
may even narrow the gap in the contest between themselves and their technologically and epidemiologically better equipped settler-conquerors.

It is exactly in *this* situation that we have the explanation for so many acts of exterminatory violence in the modern north American and antipodean experiences. Far from liquidating all their native adversaries with insouciant ease or encouraging them into submission with syrupy promises of protection and good governance, the Anglo conveyers of a Manifest Destiny found themselves repeatedly floundering against one native opposition after another; each playing by different rules, fighting their military engagements in totally unconventional ways and often seeming to have the capacity to run rings round the whites. Even worse, there were specific moments when, instead of taking the bribe and fighting other tribes, Indian nations did what they were supposedly incapable of doing and took to the field in common cause against the British. Reeling as the latter did from the great Algonquian rebellion of the *pays d'en haut* in 1763, their charges of savage conspiracy, treachery, deceit – and in the person of Pontiac, a mercurial but sinister leader – are surely proof enough, if additional proof is needed, that beneath the exterior of arrogant triumphalism lurked an intrinsic self-doubt which could only fully manifest itself in projective form.[20] But then, the threat of disintegration was more than simply psychological. It rested, as Dirk Moses has so astutely and cogently emphasised with regard to Australia, upon a *moment* – or perhaps more accurately still, the term should be *moments* – of acute crisis when the colonial advance or its consolidation really did seem either directly endangered or stymied by the active response of *particular* tribes or tribal groupings in a given region.[21] The resources such tribes could bring to bear in such a dynamic, objectively speaking, could not do anything but temporarily halt the colonial advance. Nevertheless, given the perpetrator mindset, such challenges were often sufficient for principles of accommodation to be temporarily put on hold or even more aggressively thrown out of the window altogether in favour of a massive exterminatory overkill.

Indeed, it is remarkable in the degree to which over a period of nearly 300 years, the same scenario is played out time and time again. Whether on coastal shore, distant prairie or desert interior, both north America and Australia witnessed essentially the same native–settler dynamic: first contact in which there were tentative and strained efforts at co-existence; mounting native resistance to increasing and insupportable settler depredations; a redoubled settler determination to seize absolute territorial control; an ensuing crisis leading to a genocidal explosion; finally an aftermath in which any surviving remnant of natives either retreat elsewhere or are allowed to exist as subjugated dependents on the margins of the now established and victorious white society.

The scenario began almost right at the beginning, in the very opening decade of the seventeenth century, with the first properly established Virginian colony of Jamestown. Initially entirely dependent on the powerful Powhatan chiefdom for food and hence sheer survival, ambiguous, sometimes friendly, but always close encounters gradually gave way to a spiral of violence and counter-violence as the English repeatedly broke solemn promises, seized land, corn and natives and committed a range of atrocities. The once-accommodating local peoples grouped together in the Tsenacommacah federation, not surprisingly, retaliated by attempting to turn off the food supply and keeping the colony hemmed into its riverine toehold. Ultimately they had insufficient success. Even so, this deteriorating relationship only finally came to a head fifteen years after the founding of the colony when the Tsenacommacah finally rose up in an attempt to destroy it.[22] They slaughtered 347 – or something around one-third of its inhabitants – but in turn provoked a much more powerful English determination to rid themselves of their neighbours. Indeed, a number of commentators have observed the almost palpable sense of relief and satisfaction with which its governor and council now set about exterminating the Tsenacommacahs *and* further surrounding tribes.[23] With the assistance of the several hundred official troops at their disposal, they hunted down the Indians as if they were animals, using specially trained bloodhounds for this purpose, burnt their villages, crops and canoes, poisoned to death hundreds more with wine offered at a fabricated parley and sold into slavery in the West Indies all those they had caught who had not otherwise been shot, hacked, burnt, or torn to death. This total war against the Tsenacommacahs was pursued until 1632, by which time there were so few of them remaining – there had been perhaps as many as 100,000 on the eve of Virginia colonisation – that it was considered 'no longer worth the time and expense of tracking them down and killing them'.[24]

Only a few years later, the same basic pattern would be repeated further north along the New England coast to the Pequots, Narragansetts, Wampanoags, Mohegans, Nausets, Nipmucks and other native peoples who had the misfortune to be in the line of the encroaching Plymouth, Massachusetts and Connecticut colonies.[25] In the period 1711–17, the emphasis would dramatically shift once more to southerly shores, as this time the new colonies of the Carolinas, both north and south, would join forces – engaging Cherokee and other tribes as auxiliaries for the purpose – in an almost identical series of exterminatory wars versus Tuscaroras, Catawbas, Yamasees and Guales.[26] There were some survivors from these as well as many other Indian peoples, the Tuscaroras fleeing north into Iroquoia, and those able to flee south into the

Florida swamps beyond the immediate reach of the colonists coalescing as a new 'Seminole' nation.[27]

If this suggests that each of these exterminatory assaults were not total – in the sense that the English did not set out to kill every last Indian – they were nonetheless archetypal examples of the phenomenon in the way that each emanated from a crisis at a breakpoint in an ambitious developmental shift. In Virginia the shift from very early on was one of trading for furs to cultivating tobacco, implying extensive settlement and land change. In New England there was no single cash crop as catalyst so long as the Indians could be encouraged to hunt for beaver pelts for European markets. Anxiety about the Pequots, then the Narragansetts, filling the power vacuum in an area recently vacated by the Dutch certainly provided an additional source of tension but here again it was primarily the supercession of the fur trade, or more critically, by the 1670s, its collapse – as the beaver and other animal numbers went into catastrophic freefall from overhunting – which precipitated a much more focused and accelerated colonial drive to purchase or seize Indian land. Thus, by this date – if not before – New England land was being firmly treated as if it were itself capital, whose value to the settlers lay not in the cultivation of foodstuffs for their own immediate needs but as an improvable asset with which to produce saleable 'commodities' to be traded on the international market.[28] In the Carolinas again opportunities not just for settlement but for agri-business-style development founded on indentured or black slave labour – an expansionist policy given a boost by none other than Cromwell on lines markedly similar to Irish and West Indian 'plantation' programmes – similarly provided the critical ingredients for conflict with the natives and hence for a genocidal chain reaction.[29]

By the mid-eighteenth century, factors were coming seriously into play that would contain this ongoing scenario. Weighed down by the costs of almost perpetual conflict with the French – which, falling unduly on the now thirteen colonies would be a critical factor galvanising their own imminent secessionist rebellion – the British ability to sustain the momentum of conquest and settlement in their western hemispheric empire seemed to falter critically at the very moment when French defeat and withdrawal from its north American parts had been assured.[30] The ferocity of Pontiac and related Indian rebellions from the Great Lakes to Alabama appeared to take the British unawares. In the wake of the uprisings, in October 1763, the proclamation by George III solemnly repudiating control of territories west of the Allegheny and Appalachian mountains, and thereby in effect recognising Indian national self-determination beyond these boundaries, again seemed to confirm that the British had drawn a line on expansion further westwards.[31]

Had the British ability to exterminate the natives ground to a halt? Had they gone soft on natives? The immediate answer is a resounding no. One of the last acts of Lord Jeffrey Amherst, the dramatically unsuccessful British commander-in-chief with responsibility for countering Pontiac's forces, was to issue orders for a peace parley to be negotiated as a subterfuge by which to infect the Indians who were present there with smallpox. A subordinate hit upon the possibly original but otherwise crass idea of distributing gifts of blankets as the vehicle for this biological onslaught. The ensuing and rapid spread of the disease is believed to have killed some 100,000 Ottawas, Mingos, Miamis, Lenni Lenâpés and other peoples.[32]

The longer-term answer if more mixed, however, is hardly less damning. Having been evicted from their north American possessions, bar Canada, in the American War of Independence of 1775–83, much of the British direct settlement effort turned to the more temperate regions of the southern hemisphere, particularly the antipodes. Here, again, at the furthest periphery of their colonial march, in New Zealand in 1840, the British seemed to put a line under their previous exterminatory forays against native peoples by signing a treaty at Waitangi with the North Island Maori chiefs, which guaranteed the Maoris title to their lands in return for the surrendering of their overall sovereignty to the British. Cynically, one might argue that the reason for this was very much akin to the Ohio Valley scenario of the early 1760s: the British, having been fought to a standstill by the ferociously martial Maori, conceded to an ostensible *modus vivendi* with them while aiming to pursue their forward movement by stealth, legal chicanery, and through the usual epidemiological route.[33] As things turned out, outstanding Maori success in mounting continued and adaptively innovative military resistance to Anglo encroachment not only slowed up land confiscations well into the 1860s but even led to British anthropological reassessments of their adversaries, at the height of this era of racial classification, in order to denote the Maori as 'Aryan' – in other words as worthy opponents![34]

The moving of the goalposts aimed at removing the Maori from that rung of irreclaimable savagery – where, for instance, Australian aborigines were deposited by elite and demotic Victorian observers alike – represents an extraordinarily dubious accolade, not to say a highly ironic one. Yet if Maori skills in violence were obviously responsible for their political and cultural survival, a more charitable interpretation of British colonial policy, after the loss of their American empire, alternatively might emphasise the impact of a vocal and forceful liberal, humanitarian lobby upon it. After all, at their goading, the British state abolished the slave trade in 1807, finally girded its loins to abolish actual ownership of slaves in its own domains in 1833 and proceeded, through its command of the high seas, to attempt unilaterally to stamp out its trade elsewhere.[35]

The focus of abolitionists, meanwhile, almost naturally proceeded to the treatment of native peoples in Crown colonies, the British and Foreign Aborigines Protection Society being founded in 1836 to put a stop to native extermination, with evidence of its political clout clearly signalled the following year with the creation of a House of Commons Select Committee of Inquiry. Its remit, amongst other things, was to investigate the decline of the Tasmans and other Australian aboriginals. The committee report concluded that the cruelty of individuals among settlers was particularly to blame for this state of affairs and recommended that colonial authorities needed to be much more vigilant in stamping out abuses, including unlawful land seizures.[36] In the wake of its findings, Sir George Gipps, inaugurated in early 1838 as governor of New South Wales – at a time when the territory was in throes of frontier conflict with aboriginal tribes – proceeded to try and legislate for aboriginal protection and to bring British law to bear against malefactors. The first fruits of this clean broom materialised later that year when a group of eleven white stockmen, who had kidnapped and then massacred a known twenty-eight quite harmless aboriginal men, women and children, were put on trial for the offence. Seven were subsequently hanged.[37] Though their treatment was greeted with an outpouring of popular outrage, and was seen as a case of imperial interference in Australia's domestic affairs, the new metropolitan wisdom that the indiscriminate killing of aboriginals would not be countenanced ostensiblyseemed to be mirrored in colonial policy on the ground. For instance, two years after the creation of the independent colony of Queensland in 1859, repeated complaints regarding alleged atrocities committed by its Native Police, and more particularly reports of a serious police massacre, south-west of Brisbane, led to a state parliamentary government inquiry. It was duly recorded that the Queensland government 'could not countenance the indiscriminate slaughter which appears on more than one occasion to have taken place'. It also led to reprimands directed at 'the inefficiency, the indiscretion and the intemperate behaviour of some of the Officers'.[38]

The trouble with all this sort of high-minded rhetoric, however, was that it carefully covered up not only what was really happening in the Australian outback but the driving forces behind it. The stockmen convicted of the 1838 Myall Creek massacre who claimed in mitigation that they were simply doing what others had done in the colony many times before and that they were certainly not aware that they were 'violating the law', had more than a point.[39] Just weeks before the Myall Creek events there had been an equally if not more serious incident not very far away in the same Gwydir River district, this time involving uniformed mounted police sent in pursuit of marauding Namoi, Weraerai and Kamilaroi people who had killed a number of stockmen. The resulting 'collision' had led to a massacre in which possibly seventy, and possibly many more aborigines had been gunned down.[40] Yet despite Gipps' earnestness to investigate this Waterloo Creek incident, the inquiry lapsed and was eventually shelved.[41] By the time of the Queensland inquiry, moreover, two decades later, the whole thrust of colonial *practice* had changed. It was not that the personnel in colonial state governments, or more critically those over-seeing them in the London Colonial Office, did not know what was actually happening to aborigines in conflict with settlers and police – indeed, reports of massacres were common fare in Australian newspapers of the period. Instead, they simply turned a 'pragmatic blind eye'[42] to such incidents, accepting that the great majority were either not notified to the relevant authorities or administratively 'lost' – especially though not exclusively where they involved non-uniformed participants – or alternatively were written up in such a way, most particularly where policemen were involved, in order to justify their actions and/or obfuscate their actual murderous outcomes.[43]

In a sense nothing had changed since the early days of the Crown coastal penal settlements founded in the late eighteenth and early nineteenth centuries. Killings of aborigines certainly had not been officially countenanced then either, but 'characteristically small scale, scattered and sporadic' conflict[44] had been the norm ever since whites had begun venturing out to make claim on a continent interior that prior to European settlement had supported an estimated 750,000 aboriginals in perhaps 300 to 500 clans.[45] As in America, with the Proclamation Line, there were some initial Crown efforts to put limits on these settler encroachments and thereby dampen the basis for such confrontations. By the 1820s, however, this policy had been comprehensively abandoned and free settlers were being encouraged to farm large tracts in the outback being also assigned convicts as stockmen for the purpose.[46] It was in effect the same story as in offshore Tasmania but writ large. Australia's initial potential for the British lay in its apparently limitless supply of grazing land. It was this, in terms of its relationship to an emerging global market-place, which was the great spur to immigration. However, while the some 200,000 European incomers between 1832 and 1850[47] were themselves a highly significant index of the accelerated development of the continent, it was the fantastic number of accompanying or bred *in situ* sheep which was the real catalyst to white–aboriginal conflict. Indeed, what brought this to fever pitch from the 1830s onwards – unlike in America – usually involved really quite small numbers on the former side. In 1860, for instance, in a wide swathe of frontier between southern Queensland and south Australia there were still only an estimated 4,000 whites, mostly stockmen often living in acute isolation from one another on remote sheep stations. But the fact that these frontiersmen had gobbled up some 400 million hectares of land for their 20 million sheep – in Queensland, indeed, by the early 1860s, the frontier was estimated to be inexorably advancing by some 200 miles each year[48] – which provides the primary catalyst for white conflict with the continent's indigenes.

As in Tasmania, driving out the traditional wildlife upon which the aborigines depended was disastrous enough. What was worse on the mainland was the general climatic rigour and hence inhospitability of the continental interior, focusing attention for man and beast alike on access to its precious rivers, creeks and springs. As soon as Europeans sought undivided control of these water courses for their thirsty and too numerous ovines any possibilities of a *modus vivendi* with the natives was effectively voided. The aborigines could either sedentarise on the margins of European settlement and see their societies implode, move on further into the waterless interior and starve, fight with other clans over remaining fertile country, or stand their ground and resist. The moral universe of these deeply egalitarian peoples involved concepts of reciprocity and sharing which were fundamental to their sense of social order and stability. Thus, the sexual hospitality of aboriginal women to white settlers was one aspect of an attempted accommodation which, fatally misunderstood and sacrilegiously abused by the incomers, was prone to lead to lethal disputes and reprisals on both sides.[49] Even then, as Henry Reynolds has argued, aboriginal efforts to find some basis for co-existence are evident in the frequent time lags, sometimes as much as a generation, between the arrival of the whites and a descent into exterminatory conflict.[50] That these flashpoints occurred in different places and at different times, however, practically provides a map of the expansion of the Australian frontier. Centred on Tasmania in the late 1820s, their epicentre moved to the north-eastern corner of New South Wales in the late 1830s, and further north into the south Queensland country of the upper Brisbane Valley and Darling Downs in the 1840s.[51] Yet evidence that, at critical moments in this ostensibly inexorable advance, the aborigines proved dangerous and effective resisters to it is attested to by this editorial extract from Queensland's leading newspaper:

> During the last four or five years the human life and property destroyed by the Aboriginals in the North totals up to a serious amount ... settlement on the land and the development of the mineral and other resources of the country have been in a great degree prohibited by the hostility of the blacks with undiminished spirit.[52]

This was in 1879, a juncture at which, in the parallel expansion of the United States, the remaining independent Indians had been to all intents and purposes pulverised into submission. The comparison is remarkable enough. What makes it all the more so in the Australian case is the extreme discrepancy between Anglo views of aborigines as the lowest and most contemptible form of humankind, practically to the point where they were not considered human at all, and – as the editorial amongst others acknowledged – the 'cunning' ability of these same 'black savages', despite their complete lack of resources or modern weaponry, to so completely throw the imperial agenda into disarray. This is not to overstate or romanticise the case. Aboriginal guerrilla resistance using spear, fire and even sorcery, allegedly, not only was responsible for the deaths of possibly as many as 2,500 settlers and thousands more of their beasts but 'at times appeared to threaten the economic viability of pioneer industries – squatting, farming, mining and pearling' to the point where it 'emerged as one of the major problems of colonial society'.[53] The discrepancy proved explosive, and as with so many similar cases, one which could only be resolved – and mentally relieved for the party with the overwhelming power – by recourse to campaigns of mass exterminatory assault.

These explosions, following the standard contours of settler–native encounter, nearly always came at times and in locations where the struggle for land and resources had reached its acute point of crisis. Hence its shifting terrain, and with it the possibility that after the killers' work had been done there might still be some aboriginal clan members left as destitute survivors. The number of direct aboriginal deaths from a century and more of this dynamic of conflict is put at something in the region of 20,000.[54] In other words – here as in the Americas – the role of genocide *per se* in the destruction of native society did not operate as an autonomous factor but only 'within a broader matrix of forces that bore down with cumulative effect'.[55]

What, however, does make these Australian *moments* of genocide particularly noteworthy – if not in themselves that unusual – is not only the bizarre disjuncture between their regular reportage in the local and national press and official denial, or more accurately silence on the matter on the part of the authorities, but the peculiar lengths to which the latter were prepared to go to give the *appearance* that such 'extra-judicial' killings would not be tolerated and that the pacification of hostile tribes would rather – somehow – proceed by due legal process. The sophistry might be pursued by claiming that when stockmen took it upon themselves to go out on horseback and hunt down aborigines or poison them in scores with what was quaintly called 'death pudding' – the Kilcoy station massacre, north of Brisbane in 1842 being the most reported case of the latter – they were acting entirely off their own volition and thus were outside the law.[56] Retrospectively one might even pursue this tack and argue that because this was the behaviour of individual settlers and not the conscious or intentional act of either British crown authorities or colonial state, 'genocide' would be an entirely inappropriate description for it. Or, perhaps more accurately, it ought to be understood, as Alison Palmer has posited, as a particular category of societal (not state-led) genocide.[57]

The problem with this line of reasoning, unusual events such as the prosecution of the Myall Creek massacre notwithstanding, is not only that there was generally nothing to stop settlers taking the law into their own hands but that it was more often than not persons in positions of administrative or judicial authority who gave the green light, or even led the assaults. It was, after all, New South Wales Governor Brisbane in August 1824, in response to fierce aboriginal resistance in the zone of settlement around Bathurst, up-country from Sydney, who declared a state of emergency, entitling the constabulary to enlist settlers as supernumerary policemen and send them against the natives – very much like the duly authorised ranger units in California – to go and do their worst.[58] The American parallel is noteworthy. An attack on property, or the killing of a white Australian frontier stockman or family of settlers often resulted, in this way, in the instantaneous mobilising of a retaliatory posse. In the Port Curtis area along the Queensland coast, some decades later, it was the Commissioner of Crown Lands who led a party of squatters in retaliation for the killing of two of their number. Several hundred of the Gin Gin tribe are said to have been gunned down on Paddy's Island, near Fairymead, as a result.[59]

Certainly, the authorities created for themselves a major credibility gap by these sort of responses. In the United States, recognising Indian adversaries as sovereign nations, at least, gave to the authorities the justification that they were engaged in war and therefore could proceed accordingly. No such excuse, however, existed in the Australian case, given that from the very outset the aborigines were deemed as having no intrinsic ownership of any particular territory though the corollary to this was that they were also from that moment technically treated as British 'subjects' and therefore, supposedly, entitled to the same justice before the law (whether they understood it or not) as the white man.[60] It was not simply the fact that this dubious, indeed ludicrous entitlement did not and could not operate in practice within the bounds of a society in which both bar-room and genteel parlour opinion was practically of one mind in its assumption that the only solution to the aboriginal question lay in its 'extermination'.[61] Rather, the official conundrum lay in the fact that repeated acts of aboriginal resistance made a complete travesty of the legal sophistry in the first place. One might attempt to counter their resistance by declaring martial law, thus identifying aborigines as common criminals who had placed themselves beyond society's bounds – as had been the case with the Bathurst 'disturbances' – but if one repeatedly had recourse to this extreme measure it rather too blatantly exposed the lack of civil order in the colonies not to say flouted their own official rule-books to the point of bringing them into disrepute.

The ultimate answer to these problems was provided through Queensland's 1859 separation from New South Wales. What the new government of the state hit upon as the solution to the dilemma was a very simple expedient: *institutionalise* extermination through the creation of a special counter-insurgency force, but do it in secret, 'off the map' and through orders entirely separate from the normal rules of engagement required of the regular uniformed police.[62] In itself, the creation of native mounted police was not new. The southern colonies had created such forces in the 1830s and 1840s primarily in order to keep the frontier peace and, ironically, to prevent settler retaliation getting out of control. Distant and massive Queensland, two and a half times the size of Texas, was not only a more authentic frontier society for much longer but, not unlike 1850s California, a more obviously radical one in the sense that it was run almost entirely by, and for, the benefit of its pastoralist and mining elite. The California parallel thus is very clear. The duly authorised Queensland government and state officers, as magistrates or district land commissioners, had a primary interest in protecting their own exponentially expanding investments.[63] The Native Police Corps became the covert instrument of this design.

Officered by white men, the aboriginal rank and file of the Corps were recruited from distant clans, and very often from jail, it being made clear that this would be to where they would return if they did not perform as expected. The troopers, in other words, were themselves consciously demeaned and brutalised, not least through frequent floggings, by their usually – though hardly surprisingly – thuggish white masters. Officers and men, however, were in effect given carte blanche to go out and pursue 'niggers' far into the bush and indiscriminately shoot them down – often quite regardless of whether a particular tribal group had been responsible for an alleged wrongdoing or not – with the rape of cornered women inevitably being one unofficially sanctioned perk of these operations. Indeed, the only rules were to incinerate the bodies and keep quiet.[64] The equipping of the force in the 1870s with Snider carbines and, a decade later, with Martini-Henry repeating rifles, undoubtedly amplified their efficiency and capacity. The lethality of native police as well as vigilante raids, for instance, is attested to by the way four significant central Queensland peoples, the Jiman, Wadja, Kairi and Darumbal, were reduced through massacres to small groups.[65] Indeed, the killing continued, especially in the north of Queensland, through into the early twentieth century, the estimated tally of 10,000 Queensland aboriginals exterminated – half the continental total – speaking for itself.[66] Yet these fatalities, most of which were at the hands of the Corps, were omitted from all official reports, even though news of them inevitably leaked to the press and so, too, to the colonial administration in Whitehall. In return, the Queensland government, both in its own 1861 inquiry and in response to later allegations made against it, remained adamant in its rebuttal of any improper conduct. All that had taken place, it insisted, was a series of 'dispersals', another classic euphemism to add to the language of modern genocide denial.[67]

However, if there were questions asked, both in the colonies and the metropolis, and 'Christian' voices raised protesting against the treatment of natives in British Australia no more than in British America, did anybody dare propose that the only logical alternative was to halt the colonisation programme itself?

> Right or wrong we are in Australia, and we may take it for granted that we mean to stop here. That being the case, it is to strain a gnate [sic.] and to swallow a camel to pretend to hesitate on conscientious scruples about taking such measures as are necessary to secure our safety in doing so ...[68]

In other words, if one wanted the land then one should not get squeamish about the methods by which one came by it. In fact, on this score, the actions of the Queenslanders gave to the British colonial state grounds for having their cake and eating it. It is a paradox that the frontier became a more violent place after the Crown withdrew its army from frontier operations in 1838, insisting instead that the Australian colonies organise their own border police to deal with aboriginal disturbances.[69] By exterminating the natives not at one remove, but twice-removed, while at the same time making it invisible, Queensland effectively gave to the Colonial Office in London the freedom to claim that such behaviour had nothing to do with official native policy but was the result of abuses committed by rogue administrators, insubordinate junior police officers or unruly settlers.

However, any such mitigating plea should itself be seen as transparently weak in the light of the British state's quite conscious devolution of powers to Crown-appointed governors, or contracted companies, since the very outset of its overseas expansion. Here again, one could argue that circumstances in some key respects served to undermine the tight rein of its direct supervision of native affairs. When the United Colonies precipitated themselves into the exterminatory violence of the King Philip's War, the Crown's attempts to arbitrate through Sir Edmond Andros, its consciously imperial-minded appointee to the governorship of New York, led to his summary rebuff at the hands of the New Englanders, resulting, in turn, not only in New York's becoming an asylum for native refugees from the conflict but in Andros' pursuit of a native American alliance with the powerful Iroquois, a primary aim of which was to keep the ambitions of the United Colonies in check.[70] The paradox is that if Andros' actions underscored the degree to which autonomous self-governing companies and colonies were seen as a thorn in the side of the Crown's wider agendas, the longer term consequences, not least in the light of the traumatic secession of the thirteen colonies a century later, were viewed as a mistake never again to be repeated. In order to maintain ultimate control over colonial governments in Australia, London was ultimately more than willing to settle at the price of non-interference in their internal policies.[71]

If this thereby points towards a British state culpability for genocide in Australia in the sense of turning a blind eye to, for instance, Queensland's 'dispersal' programme, even this does not really get to the heart of the issue. Appalled the humanitarians may have been by an increasingly racist thinking in the outback, where aboriginal men, women and children became 'niggers', 'gins' and 'piccaninnies' devoid of rights and completely unprotected from settlers who chose to go out and do a bit of 'snipe-shooting',[72] but there is also evidence that the values of the colonial experience began seeping back to shape and transform ideas of empire in the colonising metropolis itself.[73] True, as Keith Windschuttle argues, 'The colonial authorities wanted to civilise and modernise the Aborigines, not exterminate them'.[74] And, yes, there were colonial officials who genuinely attempted to prevent violence and bring settler malefactors to book.[75] The problem was that these good intentions were at odds with the very colonial project itself. Gipps and the Colonial Office do-gooders were yesterday's men very quickly for the simple reason that the motor force driving colonial settlement was developmental.

After all, antipodean colonisation was an integral product of the emergence of the domestic British nation-state with all the issues of economic and demographic transformation which this implied, not to say the urgency to find a new framework of existence for the millions of Irish and Scots and also an English and Welsh peasantry-turned-rural-proletariat dislocated in the process. But by the mid-nineteenth century more than simply emigrationist pushes and pulls were driving Australian territorialist expansion. Potentially huge profits from Australian mines in the far reaches of Queensland or Western Australia, and from the production, processing and sale of beef and lamb for far-flung international markets, had become the primary goad to the colonial occupation and settlement of an entire continent and, with it, of the final liquidation of whatever residual aboriginal life, liberty and livelihood remained. What had begun as a seemingly benign, implicitly anti-genocidal native policy thus became not just a *failed* policy but actually took on its reverse nightmare image; the very logic of non-negotiable, not to say accelerated, land seizure and conquest in the face of aboriginal resistance inevitably forcing Crown colonial good intentions into a cul-de-sac from which they could only be extricated through explosions of extreme, exterminatory violence.[76]

Such a trajectory, of course, was already significantly prefigured in the Anglo-controlled Americas. Certainly, by the late eighteenth century a new and innovatively capitalist British polity, despite its moments of acute domestic crisis, was not only coming together as a coherent whole but, particularly through the thirteen colonies of its north American empire, offering hope for that part of its excess population who could not be absorbed in its protean industrial and urban development. For the settlers, here as in Australia, there could be no limits or boundaries placed on expansion. On the contrary, if natives resisted the colonisers, then logic dictated that the British state had an absolute responsibility to use force not to protect the former but to secure the life and liberties of the settlers themselves. Having led a militia army against the intensely obdurate tribes in the upper Ohio River valley in 1774, the British commander, Lord Dunmore, spelt out the settlers' position thus:

> they do not conceive the Government has any right to forbid their taking possession of a Vast tract of Country, either uninhabited, or which serves only as a Shelter to a few scattered tribes of Indians [sic.] Nor can they be easily brought to entertain any belief of the permanent obligation of Treaties made with those people whom they consider as little removed from brute Creation.[77]

George III's Proclamation Line forbidding further westward advance at the expense of the tribes was clearly beginning to rankle in the exteme. The British Crown's excuse was that, in the context of ongoing struggle with the French and the scale of debt recently incurred in the Seven Years War, the dangers of overreach needed to be tempered by restraint. The fact that for settler patriots the apparent shouldering of the Crown's fiscal burden in the form of additional taxes for their own colonies' defence – in spite of the truth that their tax burden remained remarkably light compared with the home country – came at a juncture when the French threat, not least through their expulsion from Canada and hence the primary geo-strategic brake on British westward expansion, had been removed, proved a volatile mix. In 1776 the thirteen colonies erupted into full-scale revolt against British rule.[78]

The fighting in the ensuing war was extremely violent and punctuated by repeated atrocities, especially on the frontier lands between the areas of settlement and Indian country: 'whites killed Indians, Indians killed whites, Indians killed Indians, and whites killed whites in guerrilla warfare that was localised, vicious and tolerated no neutrals'.[79] Yet while losses on the insurgent side were very heavy it is perhaps significant that the British state did not resort to the sort of genocidal assault previously employed against Irish and Jacobite Scottish rebels. On one level this would appear quite singular. The war, in fact, did have some critical ingredients for genocide; not least a popularly based secessionist movement which had allied itself with Britain's mortal enemy, France, and the real threat that this posed to Britain's imperial – not to say domestic – prosperity, security and prestige. In addition, the very success of the Americans in the field, particularly in their use of guerrilla tactics, with all the psychological as well as physical humiliation for the British which this entailed, provided just the sort of potential one might expect for a massive retaliation against unarmed non-combatants. As the British position became more desperate, the high command certainly did seek to unleash Indian wrath against settler communities, if first and foremost as a propaganda tool with which to terrify the insurgents into surrender. And there were certainly a number of such Indian atrocities, the ritual mutilation and then burning at the stake of Colonel William Crawford by Delaware Indians, at Sandusky, in March 1782, looming particularly large in the American imagination then and in succeeding generations. What Americans were prone to forget was that this particular incident involved a quite conscious Delaware revenge for the wholesale massacre of a community of entirely peaceful, if not friendly Moravian-converted Delawares by Indian-hating American militiamen at Gnadenhutten just weeks earlier.[80]

While, moreover, intense frontier fighting between guerrillas loyal to the British cause and American counterparts produced their own bitter legacies,[81] for the most part there seems to have been genuine British confusion about taking fire and sword to the wives and children of a colonial population whose elite, certainly, were perceived in their behaviour and attributes not as savages but rather as a mirror-image of the British self.[82] More to the point, perhaps, their ability to act as such against 2.5 million opponents who were fighting from their own territory and who, in resource terms, were considerably advantaged against the British (who had to bring in all their supplies by sea and ultimately were forced to sue for peace) made a resort to genocide, if not impossible, then certainly implausible.

Where one might say that exterminatory warfare was a facet of the War of Independence was in the campaigns launched quite explicitly at the behest of

General Washington, the American supremo, against allegedly hostile Indian nations. The burning of cornfields, which were not just of material but also of spiritual sustenance to many Indian peoples, had always been par for the course in colonial raids. 'Make smooth work as you go ... cut every Indian cornfield, and burn every Indian town',[83] exhorted one American commander against opposing Cherokees in 1776. But the campaigns into Iroquois country three years later, under General Sullivan and other commanders, seem to have involved much more conscious, systematic efforts to use the occasion of many – though certainly not all – of the Iroquois federation siding with the British, as a pretext for a war of extirpation. As Sullivan's troops thus prepared to invade Iroquoia his officers drank to the coming expedition, on 4 July 1779, with the toast 'Civilisation or death to all American savages!'[84] They concentrated on the death.

In what would become known as the Squaw War, an Onondaga chief later recalled that 'the invaders put to death all the women and children, excepting some of the young women, whom they carried away for the use of their soldiers and were afterwards put to death in a more shameful manner'.[85] In addition, orchards were hacked down, funeral sites smashed and looted, two score of towns put to the torch and every last sheaf of corn to the tune of possibly a million bushels, burnt or carried away. With starvation in sight, in what turned out to be one of the coldest winters on record, it is hardly a wonder if epidemic started to set in amongst survivors who fled to squalid refugee camps and British forts. More than half the Iroquois peoples are believed to have perished in the conflict.[86] If this was not War Type Two *as* genocide, it is very difficult to imagine at what other point that Rubicon could be conceivably crossed. It was Indians, above all, who suffered catastrophic losses as a result of the War of Independence. But in a sense this critical watershed in the exterminatory history of north America was also a prelude to what was to come. Because of the several-cornered struggle between different European parties for control of the northern part of the continent and equally because Indians themselves, through diplomacy and military resistance, had kept the Anglo advance in check, they still remained in 1783 – despite all their disasters – the dominant element on the the continent west of the Appalachians. All that was about to change as, finally and unequivocally, 'the Revolution elevated the acquisition of Indians lands into a national policy'.[87]

The United States: Towards the Final Frontier?

The departure of the British from the north American scene – bar Canada – underlined the reason why the majority of Indians had supported them in the war and not their opponents. It was not – as we have seen – that the British in America were not capable of exterminating Indians, but simply that as a colonial power rather than an unadulterated national one, they lacked the accelerated drive to regional territorial aggrandisement, resource maximisation and settlement which was the hallmark of their successors. The famous lines of the New York newspaper editor, John L. O'Sullivan – 'It is by the right of our manifest destiny to overspread and possess the whole of the continent which Providence has given us for the development of the great experiment of liberty and federative self-government entrusted to us'[88] – may not have been uttered until 1845 but they were implicit in the American self-image, and agenda, from the very start. In this sense it was not that Americans as conscious nation-builders were so very different from their original British sponsors or forebears: simply that they were more focused in their ambitions and more attuned to the possibilities for wealth creation, power and grandeur specifically realisable from it.[89] It was these possibilities and opportunities, wedded to the overtly democratic but also individualistic principles laid out in Jefferson's Declaration of Independence – providing one was white – which in the course of the nineteenth century were to provide the primary stimulus for millions of European immigrants to set their sights on the United States, rather than, say, the also expanding British neo-Europes. What had been the 2.5 million inhabitants of the thirteen colonies, nearly all living within one hundred miles of the eastern seaboard in 1776, had by 1900 become the 76 million spread in the federally unified forty-five states from the Atlantic to the Pacific.[90] If any one factor on its own can explain the cumulative disasters facing the still surviving north American native peoples in this period it would, thus, have to be this demographic one.

Linked to it, of course, was the drive for land. The sheer weight of population pressures building up in the east were enough to ensure that the British Proclamation Line was dead in the water, if not from its very inception, then certainly from the advent of the new republic. But, equally important for settlers heading westwards from the Appalachians across the Cumberland Gap was the knowledge that a Congress committed – at least in principle – to the original Jeffersonian vision of a nation of independent yeoman farmers, would honour that commitment not only in terms of cheap land but guaranteed title to it, met through statute. Even when these ideals were clearly being superseded by more agri-business-style imperatives, the interests of the homesteader were very far from sidelined, as is evidenced in the relentless statistical record. By 1774, despite the Proclamation Line, there were already 50,000 European settlers west of the Appalachians,[91] with the heaviest pressure on Indian territory in the upper Ohio Valley and its tributaries. Here the white population literally swamped the indigenes in the first decade of the nineteenth century, jumping from 4,500 at its outset to over 23,000 at its end.[92] It was true that Europeans remained a marginal element west of the Mississippi, at this juncture. Indeed, until 1845, there were fewer than 20,000 whites living across the great river.[93] Yet thirty-five years later, in one trans-Missourian state alone, Nebraska – which had only received admittance into the Union in 1867 – there were already half a million white inhabitants. In the eastern half of this state, moreover, by this stage, nearly all of these incomers were within twenty miles of a railroad.[94]

This critical conjuncture between settler-acquisition of land and a communications infrastructure enabling them to deliver their produce to some wider, domestic – but, of course, increasingly trans-continental – market adds yet a further pointer to how the fate of the Indians was heavily determined by the fast-track nature of American state-building. The enormous federal state revenues generated from sales and speculation in land were in turn pumped into subsidies for commercially built roads, canals and railroads which rapidly spread from the eastern seaboard to the western frontiers. Indeed, by the late 1860s those frontiers by any standard infrastructural index had ceased to exist. Telegraph linked California with the rest of the Union in 1861; there were already by this time overland mail and stagecoach routes and, in 1869, the laying of the last section of the Union Pacific – only seven years after its initial authorisation by Congress – thereby completing the much anticipated coast-to-coast continental railroad connection.[95] Communication links stimulated vast capital transfers to the virgin territories, which enabled the rapid extraction of their plant, animal and mineral resources. These, in turn found their way back to newly established processing centres at the eastern termini of the railways. As the natural resources depleted, so the basis for native subsistence collapsed with them.

Of course, it was never altogether quite as straightforward as that. Take a key index of the impact of this massive commodification of nature: the near-extinction of the bison. In the early 1860s, prior to the joining of the Union Pacific and Central Pacific railway lines, there were still an estimated 13 million of these great beasts on the great central plains of the continent, providing for a seasonal migratory pattern for the adjacent tribes whose physical and spiritual sustenance to a significant degree depended upon them. Yet, in so far as their relationship with the bison was concerned, the native encounter with the white incomers had not been for all of them, initially at any rate, entirely negative. Access to horses and then rifles increased the range and scope of their hunts – indeed many of the farming peoples on the eastern fringes of the plains 'abandoned their fields and villages and took to hunting full-time'[96] – while for some powerful tribal groupings such as the Lakota (Sioux), selling hides to the American Fur Company, which from the 1830s could ship them down the Missouri by steamboat, provided a lucrative income with which to buy both more rifles and other Western goods, especially alcohol.[97]

The problems seriously began to arise, very much like the earlier depredations of the beaver, when the bison numbers began to collapse. Inevitably, the consequences were particularly deleterious for weaker tribes who found their access to their traditional hunting grounds often lethally blocked by others who wanted to monopolise the herds that were left. If these threats to a traditional culture and economy were catastrophic enough, once the whites intervened directly in the bison 'business', in the early 1870s, it spelt the end for the autonomous existence of *all* Plains Indians. With railways to transport the hides to an eastern tannery which could then turn them into commercial leather without the intensive process traditionally undertaken by the Indians themselves, and with a new weapon, the .55 calibre Sharp rifle, with which to exponentially increase the kill-rate with no danger to Anglo marksmen at all, the decade saw the bison population plummet by a million a year to nearly zero.[98] Hardly surprisingly, the price of hides similarly spiralled downwards to 50 cents a robe, while bison bones crushed for fertiliser sold for a mere $5 a ton.[99]

Was all this undertaken with malice aforethought to the surviving autonomous tribes? In other words, can we discern in this process a genocidal intent? The immediate answer would have to be negative. It was simply the workings of an entirely mechanistic, commercially orientated culture which treated nature as an item to be legitimately asset-stripped by whoever had the wherewithal to accomplish it and then, when that was completed, move on to some other usage for the land, now suitably parcelled up as real estate. Certainly, in this view, the Indians were economic casualties but only in the same way that were English tenant farmers who could not compete in the commercialisation of traditional agriculture. Moreover, from a utilitarian standpoint, the sweeping away of the bison from the plains and their replacement by new herds of cattle, pigs and sheep provided sustenance for many more mouths than the region could traditionally feed. Consider a centre like Chicago; the most important terminus for livestock coming from the mid-west region. With stockyards set up to slaughter prodigious numbers of animals on a conveyer-belt system – 200,000 hogs a day – and with the development of refrigeration enabling carcasses to be sent not only by rail throughout the United States but even by ship abroad, this rapidly expanding city became an obvious magnet for immigrants seeking work in its burgeoning processing and packing industries.[100] By the 1870s and 1880s these were, moreover, no longer the 'standard' Anglo, Germans or Irish stock who had been the migrant backbone of the first half of the century, but part of a much vaster influx of eastern and southern Europeans.

The dominant utilitarian-cum-capitalist ethos of American nation-building, thus, did not carry a vindictive virus against the Indians *per se*, simply a sense that they should not be allowed to impede what was considered the necessary, proper and legitimate utilisation of the resources around them. And that their relatively sparse occupation of the land should not be an obstacle to the far greater number of incomers who could maximise production from it. Yet it is easy enough to see how this apparently 'neutral' or indifferent *homo economicus* stance could be readily merged with prevailing – and of course entirely antipathetic – cultural notions and prejudices to produce an altogether more bleak and sinister outlook for the natives. As Andrew Jackson endeavoured to spell it out:

> The tribes cannot exist surrounded by our settlements and in continual contact with our citizens. They have neither the intelligence, the industry, the moral habits, nor the desire of improvement. They must necessarily yield to the force of circumstance and, 'ere long, disappear.[101]

If such a statement fell just short of an unequivocal declaration of exterminatory intent, it certainly conveyed a general American wish-fulfilment that the Indians would do the right thing by somehow conjuring themselves into non-existence. Whether the protagonist was an inveterate Indian-hater and killer of the ilk of Jackson,[102] or the likes of the self-proclaimed advocate of Indian life, the artist, George Catlin, himself intent in the 1830s on putting that life on canvas before it disappeared, the message was identical: the Indians wouldn't be around for very much longer.[103]

In this, of course, we come back to the fatal nexus between the Anglo-American drive to rapid state-building and genocide. Repeated incantations to the effect that the natives of north America would, like the aborigines of Australia, simply fade away in the face of those 'more vigorous, robust and pushing than themselves'[104] failed to materialise. And this in spite of the horrendous, often intentionally introduced epidemics, which continued to decimate the tribes.[105] Far from being able to say that they were 'smoothing the dying pillow' – another outrageously lame sophistry enabling American, like Australian, leaders to *imagine* that they were making the last days of almost extinct peoples more comfortable – no such ready-made and convenient solution actually presented itself.[106] Whether pragmatically accommodationist to US demands, or for outright resistance, the majority of natives were intent on staying where possible in ancestral homelands and, as a rule, refusing to be intimidated into moving by an increasingly overwhelming *force majeure*. Worse, from the very outset, in the 1780s, US state-builders were in a serious double bind as to how exactly to tackle the problem. On the one hand, removing natives from land contiguous with American territory was a practical necessity for the simple reason that, very much like the Commonwealth in Ireland, warrants for land – i.e. land which did not belong to the state – was the only immediate recompense, in lieu of payment, that the Continental Congress could offer those who had been militarily mobilised in the War of Independence on its behalf. On the other, Congress, and its successors, were ostensibly duty-bound by the precedent of *jus gentium* followed by the British – though significantly not in Australia – to recognise the Indian nations as sovereign entities. In 1787, this seemed to be enshrined in the US Ordinance on the North-West Territory, the very region earmarked for immediate expansion:

> the utmost good faith shall always be observed towards the Indians, their land and property shall never be taken from them without their consent: and in their property rights they shall never be invaded or disturbed, unless in just and lawful wars authorised by Congress.[107]

The statement in itself, however, provides an important insight into the schizophrenia of the official American position, not to say the chicanery and deviousness which would subsequently proceed from it.[108] Knox as chief architect of the Ordinance, after all, was hardly proposing that the Indians should continue in possession of their homelands in perpetuity. The issue at stake was purely and solely a matter of the most effective mechanism by which they could be made to part with their lands in an orderly fashion and, in such a way, too, that no aspersion would be cast on the honour of the new nation-state. On this latter score, America's self-image in the eyes of the world was already clearly a matter of some import and sensitivity. In 1793, for instance, Knox warned one of the generals out in the field, the suitably nicknamed 'Mad Anthony' Wayne, not to extirpate the tribes with which he was then engaged as this would besmirch 'the honour and future reputation of the country'.[109] America, just as Britain before it, had to guard its external reputation by making its native policy a national federal matter and thereby putting a brake on the more blatantly exterminatory behaviour of its constituent parts.

The problem was that this whole notion was based on a presumptuous false-hood. The only reason the Ordinance had been entered into in the first place was because the Indians – despite having been unceremoniously dumped by their ostensible British allies – had repudiated the series of fraudulent treaties which the commissioners of both federal government and individual states had attempted to foist on them, and gone on successfully fighting. By the time they had been forced to sue for peace again, at the Treaty of Greenville in 1795, everybody in government was privately agreeing that continuing prom-ises to respect Indian land rights had 'little real meaning'.[110] Jackson most honestly represented the leadership's real position when he confidentially wrote to President Monroe – albeit more than twenty years later, in 1817 – stating that the Indian treaties were absurd, the Indians themselves nothing more than dependents of the state which, in turn, had the right to take their hunting grounds and dispose of them as it saw fit. Monroe in response agreed, throwing in his own halfpennyworth that, unless the Indians became civilised, they would become extinct.[111]

So here in a nutshell was the consistent dilemma of the American govern-ment throughout this entire period. It needed, in Reginald Horsman's words, a *deus ex machina*,[112] a benign ingredient which would solve the problem of direct physical extermination and thereby let successive US presidents and their cohorts off the hook. The supposed solution was, as we have already seen, the entirely spurious one that Indians would become sufficiently, but not too much, civilised to see the error of their ways, and so, sell up. In the supposedly most humane version of this fantasy – that promulgated by Jefferson – they would even be allowed to intermarry with whites and participate in the fruits of American wealth-creation. But Jefferson, no less than any other American leader, required their tribal disintegration and hence their vacating of the land.[113] Jackson, a much more consummate operator, greased many more tribal palms, and cajoled and threatened his way to US control of millions of acres of fertile Indian territory primarily in the rich south, providing, of course, amply for his own unquenchable thirst for real estate in the process.[114]

Where this approach failed, he went to war. This was the real let-out clause and by its own admission, the only legitimate way the federal government could seize Indian land, until Congress finally overthrew even this pretence, in 1871. Indeed, given a native obduracy which continued to hold Anglo west-ward advance in check for what amounted to decades, it thus made good sense to make life so intolerable for the tribes that they, themselves, would ulti-mately have no recourse but to make war on the United States. Towards this end, recognising the Indians as sovereign nations directly served an entitle-ment under international law to expropriate lands as a right of war. Muddled and schizophrenic the policy may have remained, but at least recognition of the Indians as nations gave the federal authorities – in a manner rather distinct from the covert stratagems employed by the Anglo-Australians – the ostensible opportunity to manipulate and or coerce their way towards a 'legitimate' (sic.) native dispossession. They could go on making treaty after treaty with the tribes, solemnly promising to guarantee the inviolability of their land for all time, plus the offer of payments and annuities for whatever they did 'voluntarily' cede (plus enforcement of the treaties against settlers and mining prospectors who violated them), knowing full well that these pledges had no worth save as that of a holding operation. As soon as government policy was ready to renege on the these paper arrangements, and the actually rather small peacetime US army in position to use *force majeure*, the screws could be suitably tightened, war would result, while all along Congress could claim that its hands were clean and that its policy remained one of native accommodation.

Yet there remained an overriding conundrum; a critical flaw in this agenda by subterfuge. This lay in the ongoing premise that outright extermination was avoidable by dint of there always being somewhere else 'out there', somewhere, in Washington's words, 'in the illimitable regions of the west',[115] to which to deport either 'voluntary' native migrants, or defeated ones. From the time of the first government-commissioned exploratory surveys to the far west, in the early 1800s, most famously that of Lewis and Clark, a critical part of their cartographical remit was to find exactly such a trans-Mississippian territory for this purpose.[116] The idea of deporting the remaining Indian tribes in the east was hardly something new. Nor was it a marginal or elite agenda. In the Carolinas, for instance, it was the popular will 'even at the start of the American revolution'.[117] By the mid-1820s, all manner of plans were afoot to resettle the tribes either east or west of the Mississippi, preferably in some single designated territory, under United States' protection, even to the point – in the removal bill drafted but not introduced under James Adams' presidency – to disintegrate their tribal identities and 'encourage an eventual amalgamation of all the tribes into "one mass"'.[118] The full recognition that this would be their likely fate had already driven the nativist millenarian and pan-tribal tendency amongst the remaining embedded eastern seaboard peoples towards heights of desperate, last-ditch resistance in support of the British war against the United States in 1812–14.[119] By this juncture, however, the demographic and political-military balance had turned decisively against them. Described by Gregory Dowd as 'more a severe aftershock rather than a seismic rift', Jackson's leading role in the bloody extirpation of the revolt – including the turning of Upper Creek country, the epicentre of the rebellion, into 'a charnel house' – ensured that the systematic implementation of any future

deportation agenda could no longer be effectively stymied by native resistance.[120] Certainly, glimmers of Indian unyielding determination – with or
without outside assistance – remained, most particularly in the form of the
Seminole struggle in the Florida swamps, and that of the Sauk-Fox confeder-
acy, led by Black Hawk, in the Great Lakes region in the 1830s.[121] On the
other hand, no barrier to westward expansion, nor threat to a now 15-million-
strong 'white' nation firmly set on the elimination of all its Great Power competitors within its imagined range, was now going to stand in the way of the
United States.

Jackson, more than any other figure, represented this more clearly enunciated purpose. Elevated to the presidency in 1828, with mass popular support,
an act of Congress legitimising compulsory Indian removal quickly followed.[122] With it voluntary native migration, the paper-thin rationalisation of
the Jeffersonian tendency, was effectively dumped. But it was not just rapacious southern whites eager to lay their hands on Creek and Cherokee land
who were behind the new dispensation. Jackson now also significantly carried
with him a northern humanitarian lobby which gave its blessing to the Act on
the grounds that it was safer for the Indians to be removed than suffer the
vices and predatory violence of the white man.[123] In other words, removal was
now being justified as an Indian *survival* policy and practical *alternative* to
genocide.[124]

The immediate result, in the eight years of Jackson's presidency, was the
mostly forcible removal of nearly 46,000 Indians, by the army, to new 'homelands' across the Mississippi, in what was now designated as a 'Permanent
Indian Frontier'.[125] These included fiercely resisting Seminoles, cleared from
the Gulf Coast at a staggering cost of $10 million to the US treasury, not
because of any agricultural value to be gained from the Florida swamps where
they were entrenched, but because Jackson remained obsessed that their
removal would deprive the British or Spaniards of utilising them in any supposed campaign of imperial restoration.[126] The administration's intention in
all this may not have been overtly exterminatory. Yet it was little short of it in
practice. The series of mismanaged and bungled US army-organised 'reloca-
tions', aided and abetted by contractors keen to make their own 'killing'
through the provision of inadequate food and supplies, became known as the
'Trail of Tears'. As a result many thousands of Cherokee, Choctaw, Chickasaw,
Creek, Seminole and other native people died of exhaustion, trauma and ultimately epidemic disease on the long and arduous march, sometimes in the
most terrible winter conditions.[127]

*

Once more, this was not a terminus in a native tragedy but a further station on a genocidal highway. The US state aspiration to find a basis for Indian survival as opposed to extermination founded on a vast tract of the interior which 'white' Americans would not want, or need, was shown to be wanting in the very nature of the removal exercise itself. As soon as the survivors were 'resettled', one-half of its very premise was rather too obviously exploded. Far from the great plains being limitless, the deported tribes now found themselves bottled up in clearly designated parcels, in effect cheek by jowl with the region's already incumbent indigenes. A sustainable independent existence for all of them based on its limited natural resources – after all, whites often referred to it as the Great American Desert – was clearly implausible. The only option thus, was for both the incomers, and increasingly the incumbents too, to place themselves in the hands of the federal administration, and accept whatever political economy it devised for them.[128]

The instrument of this new policy was the reservation system. This was essentially a gridwork of defined and demarcated tribal territories, with large chunks vacated by the plains Indians to make space for the incomers and with a series of cash-payments and annuities for all ceded lands – whether in the plains region, or lost under the terms of the Indian Removal Act – to be paid out to each tribe, by the federal government, through its Bureau of Indian Affairs. The system, in other words, while – as in its 1851 Treaty of Fort Laramie formulation – claimed to represent a restatement of Indian 'nation' sovereignty, in practice was the exact opposite: a scheme for the enforced dependency of the tribes upon the state, closely monitored and supervised by a bureau agent on each reservation. Even at its best, through the individual efforts of agents to promote assimilation through schooling and sedentarisation, and to keep the inter-tribal peace, it was little more than a vehicle of a social and political control administered, since 1849, by a technically civilianised agency never in reality far from the interests and diktats of the War Department. At its worst, of course, it was the very model of all modern state native administrations: an utterly corrupt, patronage-ridden 'spoils' system in which men, like Superintendent Henley in California, were very much the norm rather than the exception. The result was that the tribes were repeatedly defrauded not only of supplies and funds which kept them quite literally from starvation's door, but also of millions of acres of land of their last remaining inheritance.[129]

However, to focus attention on these individual system abusers, fixers and manipulators, in an important sense is to miss the point. Even with model agents – and there were a great many of these, particularly high-minded Quakers after the implementation of a radical cleaning-out of the Bureau in

1868 – the system retained its inbuilt toxicity. The federal administration could itself turn on or off funds and supplies at will, if the tribes proved recalcitrant, or it could call out the army if they openly showed defiance. That this sort of denouement was actually inevitable and that it was the reservation system itself that provided the catalyst for the final staccato sequence of genocidal moments on the north American continent is implicit in the prosaic fact that no sooner had the system been created than it had become redundant.

Again, simple statistics explain why. Between its inception and 1842, the United States had acquired by 'fair' means or foul 442,866,370 acres of Indian land which it proceeded to sell in the public domain for $1.25 an acre.[130] Even at such knock-down prices the revenue bonanza which this created not only for the state, but for private speculators – the two, through congressmen, senators and their cronies often being quite synonymous – not only thus acted as the primary engine to US development but provided an unquenchable voracity for more of the same. All this, of course, was at native expense. Nevertheless, no sooner had the 'new' Permanent Indian Frontier been created than all manner of businessmen, settlers and chancers were hastening to cross it and extract whatever wealth from it, flora, fauna, mineral deposits or future potential that could be realised. And all, if possible, at minimal cost to themselves. The British Crown, the best part of a century earlier had for reasons of colonial expediency attempted to put a halt to such vaulting ambitions. For the US – no more than the sum-total of its democratically elected parts – such an eye to the main chance was something that it could not, nor desired to, resist. In other words, the second part of the premise upon which the territorially based genocide avoidance strategy was supposed to work – namely by providing a genuine protective safe zone for its residual first peoples – was flatly contradicted by the polity's intrinsic conception of what belonged transcontinentally to itself. Everything! From the end of the war with Mexico in 1848, its final vanquished competitor en route to this goal, the trans-Mississippian region was rapidly parcelled up into a batch of new or prospective states of the Union.

The speed of this process ensured that any expectation on the part of the reservation-interned natives that they might ride the storm, even accommodate in some way on honourable terms to the New Order simply did not exist. Some, of course, like the Omaha of Nebraska, and the Cherokee before them, did attempt this pacific course, reinventing themselves as 'good' Indians. But though it won them American admirers and staved off the continued enforced deportations visited on many other tribes, it made very little difference in terms of demographic sustainability.[131] Repeated cycles of starvation and vulnerability to death through mass epidemic was the prevalent condition among nearly all the tribes in these twilight years. That so many chose to go down fighting is hardly surprising. Yet if this last very 'macho' image of proud warriors of the plains struggling in one last glorious apotheosis against impossible odds is today the one we prefer to remember, it is actually an image which deflects from the darker realities of a genocidal process.

When the 3,000 or more Santee Dakota (Sioux) rose on the Minnesota River in 1862, in the first of a wave of Indian insurrections that were to punctuate the closing of the frontier during the following two decades, it was not some considered revolt to overthrow or halt the American advance, but an entirely desperate and actually rather knee-jerk reaction to quite intolerable conditions in an already very heavily settled area. Literally imprisoned on a narrow sliver of reservation entirely surrounded by rapidly encroaching farms, the Santee had not received their annuities that year and had been thrown back for literal survival on an unscrupulous but agency-appointed trader who inflamed a deteriorating situation further with the much publicised comment that if the Indians were hungry they ought to eat grass, or their own shit.[132] The Santee uprising, thus, classically prefigured all the native acts of resistance of this latter period; an insurrection of the disposessed, with no cards in their favour and no chance of success.

It is interesting, then, to consider the American reaction to it. With this in mind it is worth pausing for a moment to recall that the creation of the United States had required its nation-builders to see off some genuinely serious challengers and competitors. There had been the British who had attempted a failed come-back in the war of 1812–14, the French who had bailed out through the Louisiana Purchase, the Mexicans who had lost 300 million square miles of territory in the 1846–8 war, and finally the attempted secession of the southern slave-owning Confederate states who, through the ensuing civil war of 1861–5, really did have the potential to tear the Union asunder. Certainly, in this latter context, the Santee uprising does take on a particular significance as it exploded at the very moment of near-catastrophe for the Union as a result of the disastrous second Battle of Bull Run, thus inciting classic 'genocide-ingredient' rumours that it must be part of some sinister Confederate conspiracy. Not only in days of the uprising was Minnesota Governor Ramsey telegraphing the secretary of war in Washington that 'the Sioux Indians have risen, and are murdering men, women and children', but the insurrection was being reported as being 50,000 strong, encompassing Winnebagos, Ojibwas as well as Sioux; that 500 settlers had been killed and 50,000 more were in terrified flight.[133]

It was, in short, the Irish uprising of 1641 all over again; a case of panic buttressed by vastly inflated casualty figures, the spectre of the bloodthirsty, rampaging 'savages' tearing away at the seams of civilisation, and finally the promise, on this occasion made by the man put in charge of the military response, John C. Pope – the recently vanquished general at Bull Run – 'to utterly exterminate the Sioux'. They are, he said 'to be treated as maniacs or wild beasts, and by no means as people with whom treaties or compromises can be made'.[134] In fact, far from being some adversary of gargantuan proportions the starving insurgency was put down with relative ease, if great brutality, by the massive combined forces of the military and hastily organised Minnesota militia. But the discrepancy itself highlights the mindset of perpetrators now vengefully baying for some final exterminatory solution.

That this was partially averted or, more accurately, sidelined in the case of the surviving Santee, was partly due to the fortuitous intervention with President Lincoln of an outspoken Episcopalian bishop, in itself a reminder that the American public arena contained a multiplicity of competing and contrasting voices. Of the 303 Santee men summarily sentenced to death – though chained together with many more in the cattle pens at Mankato – only 39 were executed (despite this being the largest single mass execution in US history), while the remaining 2,000 other survivors were deported to barren reservations in Nebraska. So, too, were 3,000 neighbouring Winnebago who had not been party to the uprising at all. In Nebraska both peoples continued to starve to death in droves.[135] Their former lands, of course, were impounded 'as "reparation" for expenses incurred by the state in annihilating them', chief pickings naturally accruing to Governor Ramsey, the American Fur Company entrepreneur, Henry H. Sibley – suitably appointed by Ramsey as Minnesota militia general – and other assorted friends.[136]

The Santee episode, however, was no isolated aberration any more than was the cry of 'exterminate or banish' eructed by angry Minnesotans.[137] Throughout the west – in the midst, remember, of a seriously manpower-depleting civil war – army units, volunteer regiments and local vigilantes were galvanised into action against any tribe which was not where it was prescribed to be on an agency-run reservation, or deemed, in some other way, to be interfering with the march of progress. The mobilisations were accompanied by dire threats and warnings, primarily, of course, for the ears of eagerly thankful fellow American men and women. Colonel 'Kit' Carson, operating against Navajos and Apaches in the Department of New Mexico, charged that those who did not comply would be considered as hostile and 'treated accordingly'.[138] His commanding officer, Brigadier General Carleton, went one better in explicitness and ordered that only women and children were to be taken prisoner, males 'to be slain whenever and wherever they can be found'.[139]

The commanders were generally as good as their words, though rarely discriminating in gender terms. At the Bear River, on the Idaho–Utah border in January 1863, California volunteer cavalrymen decided to teach Shoshoni and Bannock tribes a lesson for daring to disrupt actually illegal Mormon settlements in the area, with a massive retribution which left hundreds dead. The massacre was accompanied by systematic mutilation of the corpses that did not prevent the local Mormons celebrating it as 'an intervention of the Almighty'.[140] Carleton, coming to the assistance of supposedly hard-pressed settlers further south, worked on a different approach to bring the actually almost entirely quiescent Navajo to heel, ordering his subordinate Carson to corral the Navajo's sheep and systematically destroy their peach-tree orchards. Suitably bludgeoned into submission, three columns, totalling nearly 5,000 people, began their 'Long Walk', a mini-replay of the Cherokee 'Trail of Tears', in early 1864. From their Arizona mountains and valley homes they trudged in freezing conditions to Bosque Redondo, a desolate scandal of a reservation – more accurately, simply a large concentration camp – where they too, alongside their traditional tribal enemies, the Mescalero Apaches, died in hundreds through degradation and psychic collapse.[141]

This was not, of course, the end of it, the Sand Creek massacre being very much a copy-cat affair; at least if the editorials of Denver's *Rocky Mountain Star News* are anything to go by. The paper's publisher-editor, William N. Byers, was in early 1863 applauding the recent Californian onslaught on the Shoshoni as an inspiration which he openly proposed should be the basis for a similar programme of extermination against the Cheyenne of Colorado.[142] The only problem was that this tribe, under the leadership of Chief Black Kettle, was at this very time going to inordinate lengths to rein in its own young hotheads and make itself as harmless as possible. As so often, behind the media-fanned hysteria about Indian atrocities were more venal interests. With Carleton in Arizona and New Mexico it had been his actually misplaced conviction that the territories constituted 'one of the richest gold countries in the world … millions and millions of wealth'.[143] In Colorado it was the ambitions of men like Byers, Chivington and Governor John Evans who not only wanted the territory elevated to that of statehood but saw the Cheyenne – who had quite correctly renounced sale of their traditional hunting grounds as a swindle – as the main obstacle to a financial killing once those lands were brought within the public domain.

The ensuing attack on the Cheyenne encampment by Chivington's Colorado volunteers in November 1864 was in itself not unlike previous, or future massacres. Up to 500 people were slaughtered, accompanied, as one bashful American writer has put it, by 'certain atrocities' by which he means the women, pregnant or otherwise, were raped, disembowelled, scalped and sexually mutilated in almost every conceivable manner, though often not before having seen their babies' brains bashed out.[144] Three salient aspects, however, make Sand Creek more broadly significant. Firstly, the village was known by Chivington to be under martial sanction, the Cheyenne chiefs having two months earlier negotiated, through another officer, that it should serve as a *de facto* internment camp in what was now reluctantly conceded by the Cheyenne to be the kernel of a reservation area. Secondly, the perpetrators put their accomplishments on public display, a deliriously received victory parade through Denver providing the opportunity for them to bedeck their horses, uniforms and other accoutrements with the various bodily parts – mostly female genitalia – that they had garnered as trophies.[145] Thirdly, there was such an outcry when news of the massacre and its aftermath reached back east that the federal government was forced into a series of investigations.

The outcome of these, however, is equally noteworthy. Unlike the one isolated example made in Australia when the Myall Creek perpetrators were brought to justice, there was no equivalent for those responsible for Sand Creek. There were simply a number of government fulminations and a failed attempt to file charges against participating officers who had stolen horses. Very much like the less sophisticated defendants at Myall Creek, however, Evans and Byers counter-charged that what had been done at Sand Creek was perfectly consistent with their polity's native policy, correctly pointing out that '"Eastern humanitarians" had no moral standing from which to condemn Coloradoans, since they themselves were comfortably ensconced in Indian-free states ... by employment of exactly the same methods'.[146] Their accusation was more than apposite, not least because in the aftermath of Sand Creek the federal authorities made no attempt to change general course whatsoever. If anything, the situation deteriorated.

Of course, there was now a genuine if entirely asymmetrical dynamic to drive the conflict onwards. Having seen or heard not only American broken promises but also the atrocities they were capable of committing, those Indian tribes still able to escape their clutches, or put up a fight, did so. Settlers, miners, railroad surveyors and workers, sometimes even military units sent out to liquidate them, paid the penalty. On a handful of notable occasions, most famously at the Little Bighorn in 1876, whole army detachments were wiped out.[147] The problem for the natives with these – by their nature very ephemeral – successes, was that they also tended to push American public opinion and policy more and more in the direction of 'total' genocide. One expert commentator has averred that using the term 'in the conventional under-standing of the word is nonsense', claiming that 'no more than a tiny proportion of the white population of the United States, mainly in the West, ever advocated such a measure' and that 'no government official ever seriously proposed it'.[148] What we have been at pains to labour here, however, is that in the Americas, as in the antipodes, the potential for genocide did not emanate from a clear and straightforward government policy *per se*, but out of a fevered imagination as to native capacity, though one often equally shared by 'Anglo' elite and *demos* alike.

Certainly, accounts of native violence against the white man were repeat-edly painted in much blacker and more sinister hues than their actual record merits. In the main period of the overland wagon trains to the far west, between 1840 and 1860, for instance, it has been estimated that not only did Indians kill fewer than 400 migrants but the vast majority of these were not at the hands of plains Indians – i.e. those with the alleged reputation for murder-ous intent – but by natives on the western side of the continental divide. Even then, many of these fatalities came about through misunderstanding, often when starving natives approached the wagon trains seeking food.[149] That most of the killings on these dangerous trails were the work of white outlaws is also conveniently forgotten. So, too, is the fact that even when later, Cheyenne, Kiowa, Lakota, Arapaho, Apache, Comanche, Modoc and Ute were all on the warpath, the tangible threat they presented to the completion of the state agenda was negligible.

What matters, however, is the way the threat magnified in the American mind into some dreadful chimera, almost in direct proportion to their state's political determination to carry through the final phase of frontier consolida-tion. Far from the ending of the civil war providing the opportunity for a pause, to take stock of the situation, the Union set itself on an accelerated leap towards its own completion. From this, massive violence against the natives *was bound to result*. The commitment alone to the 1862 Homestead Act, which gave away 160 acres free to any settlers who planted themselves on 'virgin' land for five years, implying millions of acres of native dispossession, was pro-vocation enough.[150] So too were repeated federal promises to protect miners who were flooding onto reserved native land. Nevertheless, the primary goad to conflict was arguably the trans-continental railroad link, the national project *par excellence*. Just as the army had made the protection of the western trails across Indian land its domestic priority in the wake of the Fort Laramie treaty, so, similarly, in the late 1860s, it was the Central and Union Pacific lines leading to their projected nexus at Promontory, Utah.[151] Thus, any native attempt to sabotage these projects was likely to be viewed by the War

Department as a direct attack on the state. With the three leading civil war Union commanders, Grant, Sherman and Sheridan in key positions with which to determine the course of the state's post-war Indian response – with Grant, indeed, as US president from 1868 – the likelihood of this leading to some final and comprehensive military solution to the native question would seem, in retrospect, rather plausible.

Subsequent pronouncements emanating from these leading players, plus the actions of US soldiery in the field in the late 1860s and early 1870s, certainly would lend weight to the view that the official, time-honoured, if entirely two-faced federal policy of Indian accommodation was about to be jettisoned in favour of something more akin to that being opined by the likes of Chivington, Evans and Byers.[152] The Indian treaties were declared redundant, Sheridan authorised a conscious extermination of the remaining bison (and, where appropriate, horses too) to starve intractable tribes into submission, while the sweeps of 'hostile' country were now mostly undertaken by regulars rather than volunteers. Major massacres followed. General Custer, who would be slain at the Little Bighorn, attacked and razed a Cheyenne village on the Washita River in the winter of in 1868, in a close rerun of Sand Creek. Hundreds of miles further north on the Marias River in January 1870, a cavalry force rode into a peaceful Piegan village and slaughtered 173 people, mostly women and children, the majority of whom were prostrate with smallpox, supposedly, though utterly nonsensically, claimed Sheridan, in retaliation for raids carried out 600 miles away by the Cheyenne.[153] Meanwhile, a year on in Tucson, Arizona, a town notorious for its scams to swindle local Camp Grant reservation Apaches out of government rations, two private citizens demonstrated that there was still room for a grass-roots input into such actions. Leading a party of Mexicans and Papago Indians onto the reservation, they proceeded to give its inhabitants the full Sand Creek treatment, hacking and clubbing to death 144 of their number, only eight of whom were men. The *Denver News* responded by extolling the raid, lamenting only that the number killed had not been doubled, while Eastern demands for a trial led to a five-day hearing at the end of which it took precisely nineteen minutes for the jury find the ringleaders not guilty.[154]

Considered in a broader hemispheric context, of course, one might argue that turning the residual American 'west' in this way into an unadulterated free-fire zone failed to reach the level of systematic extermination being visited simultaneously on its southern cone natives. The 1870s certainly marked the final phase in Argentina's push to clear its great open pampas of Araucanian, notably Tehuelche Indians who had been holding up the Spanish advance in the region for centuries. Significantly, it was that critical Latin American sea change; the shift from Spanish colonial empire to a cluster of competing, set-tler-elite led and boundary-obsessed nation-states, which provided the emotional and material stimulus for this renewed surge forward and with it for the slaughter of more 'Latin American Indians in the nineteenth century … than in the previous three centuries of Spanish rule'.[155] Charles Darwin in his famous trip on *The Beagle*, in search of the origins of life on earth, had wit-nessed this exact death-dealing opposite in its early stages when, in 1832, he had visited General Rosas and his troops on the ill-named Colorado River. Vis-ibly shocked by what he saw, Darwin confirmed in his voyage report that Rosas' aim was to put an end to the pampas Indians, the Argentinians closely liaising with their opposite numbers on the Chilean side of the border in this early example of bilateral state coordination in the pursuit of genocide.[156] Four years later, Darwin would have more to lament when *The Beagle* arrived in Tas-mania.[157]

Paradoxically, one of the factors radicalising Argentinian policy was the fear that their Chilean neighbours would ultimately take advantage of an Arauca-nian virtual 'state within a state' to push their own claims to territory which Argentinians believed was rightfully theirs. The problem was that, for all Rosas' confidence that the extermination programme could be completed in three summer seasons, the Indians actually continued to hold Argentinian expansion in check for nothing less than the next four decades. And this was despite the fact that immigration, settlement and agri-business pressures were building up in the country just as they were in the United States. Indeed, Argentina's political, not to say military reputation was at stake. The state's ultimate resort to the floating of a bond loan – shades, of course, of Cromwell's Irish campaign – with each bondholder receiving 2,500 hectares of pampas on the successful completion of what was now christened the 'Con-quest of the Desert' rather underscores its acute desperation.[158] However, with the experienced military commander and Minister of War, Roca, directly in charges of proceedings, the new Remington rifle to facilitate it, and all manner of exhortations from President Avellaneda as to its role in 'the great work of civilisation', the complete eradication or subjugation of Indians south of the Rio Negro was duly, if belatedly reported as completed, in 1885.[159] With sur-viving Tehuelche women 'voluntarily' married off to soldiers and incoming settlers, there were, by 1914, estimated to be only one hundred pure-bloods remaining. By these same measures, a contiguous people, the Puelche, had similarly arrived at the edge of extinction.[160]

Was this sort of blanket destruction of the last nominally free tribes pre-vented in the United States because ultimately Sherman and Sheridan, unlike Argentina's generals, had their hands tied? Because, despite their ostensible desire to put the rhetoric of extermination into tangible practice, there was still a sufficient and countervailing humanitarian sentiment to outweigh and restrain them? It is certainly true that at the critical moment when the proposed transfer of the Indian Bureau back to the clutches of the generals at the War Department was deemed to be a formality, news of the Piegan massacre so outraged eastern opinion that the transfer was cancelled.[161] It is also true that President Grant was swayed by this sort of groundswell to reform the Bureau itself and appoint new and principled reservation superintendents whom, he hoped, would also be the agents of his so-called 'peace policy'. Yet what all this tells us is not so much that genocide was consciously rejected as that its aims were ultimately achieved by other means.

The accommodationists who coalesced, in the early 1880s, as the Mohonk reformers or 'Friends of the Indian' and who sought to resolve the Indian 'problem' by detribalising the native and turning him instead into an individual property-holder who would think and behave like any other 'modern economic man', in getting their agenda accepted, through the 1887 Dawes General Allotment Act, served a fundamental US interest to perfection.[162] Not only by breaking up the residual reservations into multiple individually owned tracts of land did they dramatically accelerate the dissolution of native life and lives, they also ensured that a huge acreage, considered surplus to native requirement, came onto the market, where it was suitably gobbled up over the next less than fifty years to the tune of 60 million acres, alongside a further 27 million acres sold by destitute Indians to whites.[163] Even, however, as Dawes was being debated, the very last native resisters, the Chiricahua Apaches were being brutally cattle-trucked to incarceration in Florida – an ironic case of deportation against the natural grain of Indian immiseration – far away from their south-western desert homes and with the loss of all their lands and chattels.[164] The federal state had not gone soft on natives. But perhaps more tellingly, the obvious explanation for the avoidance of general extermination was because there was no more perceived need for it. The sheer pace at which its frontier had been closed by the greatest industrial state of modern times had brought the American state-builders everything they desired and, in so doing, made the recourse to further genocide an irrelevance.[165]

From this standpoint, one might expect to see what came thereafter as the start of a fresh, new non-genocidal chapter in the history of native–white relations. Yet to assume such a paradigmatic shift would be critically to ignore the location of actual genocide within the broader framework of a genocidal process. The white relationship to the surviving natives in America, as in Australia, has not fundamentally changed since the last quarter of the nineteenth century. The ultimate issue at stake is still, as it has always been since the beginnings of the encounter, one of control of land and resources, a control which from the perspective of state and dominant society demands that the native *qua* native should be forever politically powerless, utterly economically dependent, and broken. In these terms, the consistently stated, legalistically framed liberal answer to the problem, namely assimilation, accommodation and citizenship simply serves to deflect attention from the precise realities on the ground.

It is no accident today that in these two fabulously wealthy countries the life expectancy and life opportunity of their indigenous peoples is as deplorable as in the very poorest of the third world. For the situation to be any different and for – individuals apart – there to be any serious social, occupational, or educational mobility amongst aborigines, or native Americans, would be to imply a new relationship of power, and with it also a new dynamic in which the land and its assets would once again be open to contest. The very possibility even of apology and limited restitution, indeed, has led, in recent years, to a notable neo-conservative backlash in Australia. With so many geo-strategic and corporate interests, both here and in the USA, residing on today's residual native lands – including the whole panoply of nuclear testing sites, missile sites, 'sacrifice' belts of mass open-cast mining and processing, not least of uranium – such a redrawing of the lines would be, in effect, to acknowledge some fatal weakness, or flaw, in the process by which the modern settler state arrived in the first place.[166]

Is this why, even after the native 'savage' had been utterly pulverised, the Anglo psyche remained still in thrall – not to say terrified – of its potency? So much so that when a few hundred starving and freezing Lakota, in the last days of 1890, defied the government prohibition on a new messianic 'ghost dance' movement amongst Indians, which promised a return to the old days – with the bison, without the white man – if only they danced the dance, the federal authorities responded by sending 3,000 men of the Seventh Cavalry, replete with Hotchkiss cannon, onto their Pine Ridge reservation to quell them?[167] Or that ten days after this last great ignominious Wounded Knee massacre was perpetrated, L. Frank Baum, in his editorial, was still pleading for the army to 'finish the job' by exterminating all Indians?

TWO
Enter the Nation-State

3. The Vendée – A Paradigm Shift?

Roads Sown with Corpses

On the 21 January 1794, or what – under the recently inaugurated republican calendar brought in by the Jacobin-dominated National Convention – had become Duodi, of the first decade in the month of Pluvoise, Year 2, the revolutionary French state launched its 100,000-strong Army of the West, in a twelve-column pronged assault on the Vendée, a maritime region south of the Loire.[1] It was a year to the day since the Jacobin regime had guillotined the former French king Louis XVI, though it is not clear whether the timing of the Vendéan campaign was itself an intentionally commemorative act. What is clear is that in the months following the regicide, this otherwise rather marginal, rural backwater had been transformed into the core of the counter-revolutionary opposition to the republic. Peasant, populist, yet deeply conservative, the Vendéan insurrection was, however, catalysed as much by the regime's self-proclaimed atheism and its physical assault on Catholicism and Catholic priests as it was by its sweeping-away of the Bourbon dynasty. When the Jacobins added insult to injury by demanding that peasant sons be conscripted into the army to defend what would have seemed to them quite alien, not to say blasphemous, values and notions against the threat of pro-royalist foreign intervention, scratch resistance in the Mauges *bocage* of the Vendée quickly turned into a widespread peasant crusade. For a time it seemed that it would not only engulf the whole of western France but, linking up with the British fleet in the Channel, might strike a direct and fatal blow at the republic's metropolitan centre.

In fact, the Vendéan threat to the revolution proved short-lived just as that of serious British intervention proved a chimera. With its strategic advantage lost early on, and once properly checked at the fateful battle of Cholet in the Mauges heartlands, in October 1793, the insurrection disintegrated into La Virée de Galerne, a rag-tag and inchoate winter retreat involving anything between 50,000 and 100,000 Vendéan men, women and children across the

Loire.[2] Here at Savenay, near Nantes, just before Christmas, the rout by the Army of the West was not only total but in turn led to one of the most atrocious single massacres in the whole of French history. General Westermann, the republic's commanding officer at the battle, however, reported his achievement to his political masters at the Convention, in rather more upbeat terms:

> The Vendée is no more ... I have buried it in the woods and marshes of Savenay ... According to your orders, I have trampled their children beneath our horses' feet; I have massacred their women, so they will no longer give birth to brigands. I do not have a single prisoner to reproach me. I have exterminated them all. The roads are sown with corpses. At Savenay, brigands are arriving all the time claiming to surrender, and we are shooting them non-stop ... Mercy is not a revolutionary sentiment.[3]

Westermann's efforts — for which he would be appropriately dubbed 'the butcher of the Vendée' — however, proved only to be a prequel to the main action. If the aim at Savenay had been to destroy and exterminate the Vendéans in battle, then the operational plan devised and implemented by General Louis Marie Turreau in January, as he himself explicitly informed the Committee of Pubic Safety (CPS), the Jacobin regime's most senior executive and policy-making body, was to ensure the systematic elimination of the entire population of the region.[4] Over 100,000 troops were assigned to the task, including cavalry and accompanied by artillery.[5] For his part, Turreau attempted to be as good as his word. From a start-line on its eastern fringes, his six divisions divided into twelve flying columns — the *colonnes infernalles*, again another darkly appropriate term — were to work their way westwards, village by village. At each, all the inhabitants were to be rounded up and then liquidated. Turreau's orders ruled out exemptions from this intent, regardless of whether individuals had, or had not, participated in the rising. There were offers of pardon made but these only as a ruse to get people to surrender. Opportunities of escape, too, were drastically curtailed as Turreau had built into his plan military frontier posts around the designated target region, including along the Loire. Most importantly of all — and this needs to be spelt out — distinctions with regard to age, gender or illness put no inertial drag on the killing spree whatsoever.[6]

If anything the opposite was the case. Given the impact of the previous year of war on the area, the Vendée's social profile in January 1794 was bound to be heavily skewed towards women, children, old and sick people. These, then, were the vast majority of those dragged out of their homes and usually bayoneted, bludgeoned or literally crucified to death, thrown into barns or churches where they were burnt alive, or lined up before pits which they had been forced to dig themselves, before being executed by firing squad. Yet the lack of menfolk to protect them and perhaps the commonly held perpetrator conviction that it was they, the Vendéan women, who had been instrumental in fomenting the insurrection in the first place as well as supposedly giving their (lascivious?) support to the local clergy, which provided the goad or, more exactly, excuse to turn these day-by-day massacres into a truly misogynous, sado-erotic *promenade*.[7] Certainly, the leadership of some columns more than others seems to have provided the green light for their soldiers' full, unadulterated enjoyment of these activities, as well as for the looting which went with them, accounts of the campaign repeatedly highlighting General Grignon's second column and Cordelier's fifth as the most zealous, but with Cordelier's chief lieutenant, Crouzat, appearing to defeat all competitors in the sadistic stakes.[8]

Yet, paradoxically, as so often in such instances, the participants' total immersion in the gratification of their most base instincts proved to be somewhat at odds with the 'higher' interests of the state. For one thing, Turreau hardly could afford to see his military forces disintegrate into an orgy of violence, particularly in a campaign which was originally, if quite unrealistically, scheduled for completion within six days.[9] For another, more was at stake than simply killing all the Vendéans. The assault on the region was also intended as an asset-stripping enterprise, the final recorded tally of confiscated goods: 46,000 farm animals, 153,000 hundred-weight of grain, 111,000 pounds of various metals, a vast catalogue of other items, including fifty children's shirts, all being realised for the benefit of French nation-state building and the revolutionary cause.[10] Yet if this provides an insight into the very modern bureaucratic thoroughness of the *Commission civile et administrative*, its task, operating in the train of Turreau's columns, could hardly be smoothly accomplished until the complementary task of extirpation had itself been thoroughly and speedily expedited.

The perpetrators' problem in the Vendée, thus, turned on the logistics of killing. How could one isolate and then liquidate a whole population, efficiently and rapidly, without creating an enormous health hazard for perpetrators and surrounding populations alike? And how to do it in a way that would not distract the killers from moving on to their next task? The new invention of Monsieur Guillotine might represent the latest state of the art in terms of efficient execution but while it might endure as a potent symbol of revolutionary justice, it was hardly adequate as an instrument for streamlined mass murder. Shooting people, of course, was always an option, if on the one hand, you could round up or capture sufficient numbers, and, on the other, you had the will and authority to do so. Marie-Pierre Francastel, CPS *représentant-en-mission,* and hence the government's chief enforcer north of the

Loire, ultimately did not flinch from this prospect in the wake of Savenay when he had some 2,000 prisoners and suspects gunned down without trial near Angers.[11]

Much urging for this exemplary action came from Jean-Baptiste Carrier, Francastel's historically more infamous opposite number south of the Loire. Carrier was also responsible for shootings both before and after Savenay but was challenged too, simply by the sheer number of half-starved and ill Vendéan and other captives with which he had to deal. Already, by the late autumn of 1793, there were an estimated 10,000 of them clogging up the prisons in Nantes, his key operations centre, already suffering absolute crisis conditions through the influx of refugees from the fighting in the country-side.[12] With no further room to house the prisoners temporarily in this Atlantic port, better known for its slave trading, Carrier and his subordinates on the spot had to experiment and improvise as best they could. There was urgency too, a real fear that epidemic would spread from the captives to captors. Commandeering the large flat-bottomed barges, otherwise used for incarcerating blacks until they were transported to the Americas, presented itself as one solution to their problem. Towing these down to two points, Pont-de-Ce and Auricle, on the Loire, droves of prisoners were herded onto them by night, where they were sunk and then refloated for serviceable reuse on further nights.[13]

These *noyades* (drownings) certainly showed a potential for effective disposal of large numbers of people. And are, indeed, a foretaste of a much more extensive killing-by-drowning programme employed in Black Sea operations by Committee of Union and Progress 'enforcers' during the Armenian genocide of 1915.[14] However, the apparent novelty of the Nantes *noyades*, and the subsequent martyrology which has gone with them, has rather tended to exaggerate their importance in the context of the Vendée as a whole. Certainly, narratives of concentrated mental torture of the victims; mothers being taunted with news that their babies were about to undergo 'patriotic baptisms'; adult men and women being stripped naked and tied together in what were voyeuristically described as 'republican marriages' cannot be firmly discounted.[15] Nor does the probability that the majority of the victims were actually priests detract from the vicious and ugly luridness of their demise. Ironically, however, the *noyades* did not solve Carrier's people-logjam, any more than his more fanciful suggestion that arsenic ought to be put down the wells of the Vendée – only a sound idea if the aim was to kill perpetrators and victims alike.[16] The historian Reynauld Secher's estimate of 4,800 deaths by *noyades* is almost certainly an overestimate.[17] As for Antoine Rossignol, the *sans-culotte* general's intervention at the time that the answer lay in further research and development – the chemist, Fourcroy, was charged with devising 'fumigations, mines to destroy, put to sleep, or asphyxiate the enemy' – this proved to be a proposal, its ominous portent notwithstanding, which did not make it beyond the drawing board.[18]

However, the importance of the above litany lies surely not in the efficacy of *noyades* or other more fanciful methods of extermination *per se* but in the fact that such things were being considered at all. And this from the governing regime of a new republic whose very *raison d'être* was founded on the entirely revolutionary concept of the liberty, equality and fraternity of *all* its recently enfranchised citizens, the people of the Vendée included. The fact that an exterminatory intent both overturns and utterly contradicts what Patrice Higonnet would refer to as 'an ontological absolute',[19] thus, must beg entirely fundamental questions. How did – indeed – how could this arise? More specifically, in what circumstances did it happen? And, perhaps to get down to the nitty-gritty of the conundrum, how genuinely comprehensive and all-embracing was the intention? Was this really about all the people of the Vendée – men, women and children – or only those who, in some fundamental way themselves had transgressed against the regime?

Let us leave some of the bigger questions, at least for a moment, to consider some of the more immediate chronological and contingent aspects of the issue. For these may determine whether what we are dealing with here, as already inferred, is a case of authentic and genuine genocide, or not. Can we, for instance, locate a moment when the republic commits the resources and personnel at its disposal to an annihilatory response to the insurrection? Is this, perhaps, on 1 August 1793 when the Convention issues its *terre brulée* decree, committing it, point by point, to the systematic torching of whole villages, flour stores, mills, farms, woods, hedges, heath and brush, throughout the enemy region? The decree is certainly heavily reminiscent of the 1652 Cromwellian proclamation to the Irish declaring its commitment to turn rebel areas into free-fire zones, though, similarly, the Convention's pronouncement seems to contain a get-out clause, in this case in its commitment to evacuate women, children and the old 'in keeping with humanitarian considerations'.[20] Even then, high-level talk that the destination of these spared survivors might be Madagascar hardly sounds like a reprieve in the light of of similar wish-fulfilments hatched by Nazis, and others, for the 'solution' of the Jewish 'problem' in the mid-twentieth century.[21]

Then again, could one make a case for 1 October being the crucial breakpoint? It is on this occasion when Barère, a leading figure in the regime, stood before the Convention and declared that the nation's safety and salvation demanded the extirpation of the brigands before the end of the month.[22] But then there had already been much hot air expended in this way, alongside all the various laws and decrees going back to the outset of the rebellion in the spring, repeatedly promising the death penalty without trial for all 'rebels'. Rhetorical promises of extermination were one thing, but at the beginning of October the Vendéans' self-styled Catholic and Royal Army of Saints had not only yet to be defeated but had just given a mauling to republican forces. Carrier, who in his repeated expostulations that he would rather see France turned into a graveyard than fail in her regeneration,[23] was another – like Barère – whose bark could be said to be far ahead of his ability to bite.

Except, of course, that after Cholet, Carrier's threats were hardly empty. When the island of Normoutier, fifty miles to the south-west of Nantes, was 'liberated' from the rebels in the early winter, it was upon Carrier's explicit instructions that all of the resisters 'regardless of sex' were slaughtered.[24] But if this would suggest a definite shift from a republican commitment to extirpate to both a capacity and an ability to so do from here on, looking to Carrier as the primary vehicle of this intent does not entirely satisfy, not least given that he was recalled to Paris in February 1794 just as the Vendée massacres were getting properly underway. 'Quantitatively and qualitatively' Turreau's violence is of an entirely different order from that of Carrier, is Arno Mayer's verdict.[25] It is also the correct one. The genocide *qua* genocide begins not in the course of the utterly brutal crushing of the insurrection – a process we certainly do associate with protagonists like the highly ideological Carrier and also with professional generals including Kleber and Westermann – but in its aftermath, when the genuine threat to the regime from the Vendée no longer pertained.

The key moment, thus, when the genocidal process, building up all through 1793, actually takes off, is with the very specific plan put forward to the CPS by Turreau himself, on 17 January 1794. To his immediate subordinates he commanded, 'All rebels, with or without arms are to be bayoneted: the same should apply to the women, girls, children … nobody is to be spared. The villages, farms, woods and indeed anything which will burn are to be put to the torch.'[26] On paper one could argue that this was simply a more explicit rendition of Barère's various threats proclaimed since the previous summer. The difference now is that it was being put forward as a systematic plan of military campaign. Clearly, on this occasion there was no get-out clause. That option had been proffered by General Kleber, just ten days earlier. In it, while proposing a programme for the pacification of the Vendée, Kleber had clearly proposed the need to maintain the confidence of the population and to ensure the discipline of the troops, the implication being that non-combatants would

not be harmed.[27] Kleber's proposal stands in marked contrast to that of Turreau. Yet it was the former which was rejected, the latter accepted by the CPS.

Certainly, at this crucial breakpoint, Turreau's urgent requests for formal,
written authorisation for his actions, including that of the extermination of
women and children, received no CPS reply. Only when he was already well
into his campaign, in early February, did word come from one of the Committee members, Carnot, that the general's actions were indeed authorised and
that his job was to continue with them.[28] As Jean-Clément Martin, the leading
non-polemical historian of the Vendée has pointed out, CPS responses to Turreau repeatedly failed to clarify the regime's exact position. These responses
are at times very ambivalent, neither explicitly authorising the killing of
women and children but also not condemning it outright either.[29] But the
weight of evidence clearly implicates the regime. If the CPS had wanted part
of the population spared, it would have appointed Kleber, not Turreau, to the
task in the first place. If it had had any qualms about the latter's plan as it
began to be implemented it would have contacted him post-haste. Further
représentants-en-mission were in fact sent out by the CPS to the Vendée but not
to reprimand Turreau's actions but closely to 'coordinate the means of exterminating the Vendéans'.[30]

There was, of course, also an aftermath. Turreau's wildly optimistic schedule
of six days to complete his mission, ground down into month upon month of
killing. Even in its own terms, far from being the undiluted success it had
promised, it failed to extinguish entirely revolt in the Vendée itself, while its
annihilatory zeal arguably fanned the flames of the Chouan guerrilla-style
rebellions emerging in neighbouring Britanny, Normandy and Anjou. Indeed,
the region was inflamed to such an extent that it forced Turreau's successor,
General Hoche, to negotiate, in early 1795, not only for the return of the
Vendée's still surviving deported inhabitants but the region's reintegration
into the republic on terms which largely conceded to the insurrectionists' original grievances.[31] Such retreats from full-blown remits of mass murder are the
repeated legacy of genocidal or post-genocidal regimes which have been forced
to concede partial failure or defeat.

Yet there is no evidence from the time to suggest that the CPS baulked at
Turreau's exterminatory plan. He himself was relieved in May 1794, not on
humanitarian grounds to prevent further atrocities but because his programme was clearly becoming counter-productive, while his troops were
increasingly needed to parry external threats on France's eastern borders. Yet
throughout these many months the Army of the West, supported by the
state's civil arm, continued in its exterminatory zeal unrestrained, without any
sign of revoking Turreau's original orders, or amnesty to the Vendéans

themselves. Indeed, even after Turreau had left the scene the massacres were perpetuated by his subordinates, right up to the overthrow of the CPS, and with them of the ultra-Jacobin regime, on 9 Thermidor/27 July 1794. And, despite all the revolutionary blood-letting which accompanied the high months of the Jacobin Terror and Thermidorean counter-terror – one casualty of which was Carrier – Turreau not only survived but was actually complemented by the president of the military council for the performance of his duties worthy of a soldier and citizen. In later years, this feted general would go on to become an imperial baron and Napoleonic ambassador to the United States.[32]

The effects of his campaign, however, speak for themselves. There is certainly much dispute over exactly how many of an estimated Vendéan population of 800,000 were killed in the genocide-specific months of January to July 1794. Often quoted figures of 250,000, even of half a million may say more about the need of some to invest what happened in the Vendée with the sanctity of religious martyrdom and sacrifice than about actual reality.[33] Even so, if *only* some 14 or 15 per cent of the Vendéan population died, translating, perhaps, in one very careful estimate into 130,000 deaths all told, this is an extraordinary figure.[34] Certainly, scores of parishes in the Vendée lost more than a third of their population in this period, with the effects of the scorched-earth policy such that many market towns still remained uninhabited in 1800.[35]

*

However, if the purpose of this exercise has been to argue that the anatomy of Turreau's campaign – as based on the very considerable extant documentary evidence available – points very clearly towards how it should be defined, it is equally significant in the degree to which, especially in France, describing it as 'genocide' continues to excite ample measures of consternation, controversy and downright denial. Ironically, back in 1794, the killing activities of the CPS – and not just in the Vendée – gave rise to the coining of a new term, 'populicide',[36] an important precursor to 'genocide'. Yet today those scholars who would repeat the latter charge would not only have to compete with those who would refute or resist it but themselves be accused of dubious scholarship or worse, unsavoury political agendas.[37] It is worth pausing, then, for a moment to consider some of these charges and counter-charges for, in a critical way, they provide a window not only onto the Western liberal approach to the broader phenomenon but also onto one of its intrinsic flaws.

At the heart of the problem is the fact that we are considering an event that emanates from the French Revolution, and thus, as Douglas Johnson reminds us, by definition assumed to be 'a boon to humanity in general, to which all right-thinking people' are 'rationally and morally bound to subscribe'.[38] Or to put it more prosaically, this time with an emphasis on its protagonists, you normally don't go around denigrating the 'good guys' and claim 'that those who plant "trees of liberty" ... rapidly make of them the gate-posts to prisons and to death-camps',[39] unless you are coming at the subject from some extremely entrenched illiberal, right-wing or even fascistic position. To go further and speak the names of Robespierre – or by the same token Cromwell – in the same breath as a Stalin or a Pol Pot, or even suggest that the former two, in their ideas or political actions, were the intellectual or philosophical forebears of the latter pair, would, similarly for some, either suggest very bad history or an attempt to yoke that history to some teleogically driven political agenda.[40]

It is striking then, that latter-day defenders of the Maximilien Robespierre-led Jacobin regime of 1793–4, have been as ready to invoke the term 'totalitarianism' as have its detractors. As if by framing the political debate thus, one has a ready-made formula for either confirming or dismissing the idea that what took place in the Vendée was genocide. It would follow from this that in the detractors' camp would be those who see in the Jacobin, particularly Robespierrean attachment to Rousseau's concept of the 'general will', the authentic origins of totalitarianism, or at the very least totalitarian democracy,[41] while, in the latter camp, Robespierre remains always the champion of freedom and of the dignity of man, an opponent of the death penalty and, above all, a politician motivated in his actions not by a desire for blood but for a universalist moral regeneration founded on the guiding principles of the Enlightenment.[42]

However, what if this often fractious debate is a case of looking at the problem in the wrong place, or possibly in the wrong way? It is certainly true, for the record, that the leadership of the archetypal regime we tend to think of as 'totalitarian', namely Soviet Russia, certainly in its early post-1917 manifestation, had a certain predilection for imagining the Jacobins as protean versions of themselves, always anxious, incidentally, that the former's Thermidorean fate would not be visited on their regime.[43] But this tells us a lot more about their mindset, or that of some of the more enthusiastic Marxist historians of the French Revolution, than its does about the Jacobin leadership. Robespierre and his chief lieutenant Saint-Just were not propelled by notions of class war, nor were they economic state planners of the Soviet variety. The actions which they appeared to take in this direction, notably the prohibitions on free trade, and the September 1793 'General Maximum' controls on the price of food-stuffs, indeed, were not conscious policy but intentionally ephemeral emergency measures designed to counter a food crisis, and thereby – in the midst of general war – keep the revolution afloat. One might go on from this to argue similarly that 'the Terror' – the whole panoply of CPS-instigated executions and killings over and beyond those perpetrated against the Vendée – were, again, not in essence, a conscious design but, rather an entirely *reactive* response to the exigencies of increasingly menacing internal and external threats to the regime's survival.[44]

But if, then, the Jacobins' credentials as 'true' totalitarians (whoever they are) are suspect – Robespierre and company arguably having a good deal more in common with their liberal Girondist predecessors than anything remotely communist[45] – while we can also find mitigating circumstances explaining their unpremeditated resort to violence, two further questions must necessarily arise. Firstly, if one begins from a liberal, albeit radical-liberal premise, does this act as a, if not *the*, all-important brake on one's perpetration of genocide? Secondly, turning the question back in on itself, how much are those whom we think of as 'totalitarian', born or nurtured that way, and how much do they become forced into this mould through the overwhelming task of political and social transformation that they set themselves?

We have already reviewed a persistent English, British colonial and American tendency to genocide in notable tandem with the evolution of these states toward liberal, even democratic credentials. And, of course, in further parallel with their startling, avant-garde surge towards a modern, powerful, industrially based nation-state coherence. If particular moments, 1649, or 1776, represent important watersheds in this process, the picture would certainly be incomplete without adding 1789, if anything *the* founding moment proclaiming the advent of the modern age. And if, in this moment, we have the paradigmatic shift from a traditional world-picture still inert under the *Ancien Régime* sway of a neo-feudal-cum-clerical hierarchy towards one which proclaims as its goal the emancipation of man's potential on the basis of his liberty, equality and fraternity, then it is in the radical and, one might add, quite logical extension of this aspiration under the Jacobins, that we find its most tangible concretisation. It is under them, after all, that the revolution's reforming goals reach their zenith: in which slavery is abolished, the state de-Christianised, education made secular and free, welfare in the form of embryonic old-age pensions, state hand-outs for the poor and unmarried mothers introduced, foreign trade nationalised, efforts made even to make the discrepancy between rich and poor less blatant. All this, moreover, is debated and ratified through a democratic constitution.

But what this also surely tells us is that the most dramatic processes of modernisation do not travel in separate compartments from genocide. They are, as Zygmunt Bauman correctly infers, part and parcel of the same 'modernising' process.[46] The fact that Robespierre, Saint-Just and the other intellects of the CPS are individuals whom we might recognise as radical liberals or even, in a more contemporary setting, as 'a fine department of Western Civilisation',[47] ought not to deflect us from this reality. Nor from the attributes that they share not only with a Cromwell, Washington, or Jefferson but also with a Himmler, Lenin or, for that matter Pol Pot. All of them, whether founding fathers of the modern liberal world, or their entirely antithetical would-be over-throwers, are protagonists of regimes which, against the grain of what normally would have been possible, have set out to reformulate the social organism, or body-politic in a quite unprecedented fashion. In this framework a terminological split between 'liberal' as opposed to 'totalitarian' is largely irrelevant. Indeed, it makes 'liberal' or 'modern' a quite false refuge in which to defend Robespierre and his associates from the charge of Vendéan genocide.

However, terminology has also been employed in another way to obviate or lessen the accusation; by claiming that what happened there does not deserve such an egregious appellation. On one level, this is a simply another avoidance tactic for those who decline to see their liberal or radical heroes being bracketed alongside more generally recognised mass murderers. Yves Ternon is interestingly one distinguished French scholar of modern genocidaires, willing to play this card. Ternon argues that it is unproven that Robespierre, or the CPS, were directly responsible for the Vendée killings, the weight of guilt thereby falling more firmly on Turreau and the two *représentants-en-mission*.[48] This is a rather curious opinion when, not only have we seen above that explicit orders did emanate from the centre to these functionaries, but that the idea of such a campaign being conducted by them without the absolute say-so of the CPS – at a juncture when it was demanding both absolute and very pedantic oversight of all its military and civilian operations in the field – was quite inconceivable. More pointedly, however, while Ternon does not dispute that dreadful killings were perpetrated in the Vendée, he casts doubt on these being an authentic genocide by the simple technique of denying the existence of a genuine Vendéan people.

Actually, in the terms of reference he offers, Ternon is both consistent and correct. The administrative department of the Vendée had only been created by the revolution itself, in 1790, out of parts of three contiguous *Ancien Régime* provinces. As for the CPS usage of the term '*Vendée militaire*', during 1793, this applied to a much wider zone of insurrection spanning some 10,000 square kilometres in parts of four departments of which the Vendée was only one.[49]

Nor was there anything about either of these four collectively, or the Vendée specifically, or for that matter the Mauges district at the core of the rebellion, which might notably differentiate their populations from other surrounding ones either in ethnic, religious or even political terms. Indeed, in many ways, the Vendée was archetypically what rural France was all about, a close-knit series of micro-societies, made up largely of peasants and weavers, geographically remote from the heartlands of the revolution and culturally and mentally, without doubt, a million miles from its metropolitan and urban power-houses. Certainly, there have been some notable efforts to develop this theme by seeking to isolate socio-economic or religious factors which might explain why large elements of the Vendéan population might have been more alienated by the revolution than elsewhere.[50] But what all these arguments really do is reinforce the degree to which this area was very traditional, pietistic, very attached to its local *curés* – not least in their role as intermediaries with *Ancien Régime* authority in what was actually a very under-administered region – and thus extraordinarily antagonised when 'townies' started to come in, throw their weight around and attempt to move all the time-honoured communal goal-posts. One has here the essence of a classic countryside versus metropolis argument, one that when push came to shove – 'push' being the demand on priests to swear allegiance to what appeared to be a brazenly atheistically secular regime; 'shove' being the demand that the young men should present themselves as cannon-fodder for it – the Vendée was catapulted over the precipice into open rebellion.

Nevertheless, while this may explain the very strong grass-roots underbelly to the insurrection, it does not add up to a Vendéan collectivity. Not everybody in the region was equally carried along with the rebellion, the towns remained loyal to the government, while, in the wake of Turreau's columns, the post-Jacobin director's attempt to counter the continuing guerrilla-style insurgency by recruiting some home-guard units was at least partially successful.[51] In the light of some of the massacres, this is itself hardly surprising. At the outset of the Vendée rebellion in March 1793, a brief orgy of anti-republican violence left anything up to 500 mutilated and battered to death in the little pro-Jacobin town of Machecoul, most of these simply local citizens. Other captured towns suffered similar depredations.[52] Indeed, throughout these critical months and years of post-*Ancien Régime* struggle for the control of French state and society there was always plenty of 'White' terror to complement 'Blue' terror; and it was hardly confined to this single region. The revolutionary state found itself having to stamp out violent armed opposition in no less than sixty of its eighty-three newly created departments, mostly in the period of the CPS emergency. In the winter of 1793–4, for instance, at the highpoint of its onslaught on the Vendée, military units under CPS direction in the Midi were similarly exacting summary justice on 'federalist' opponents, thousands being lined up against walls and shot, notably in the Lyons and Toulon *mitraillades*.[53]

It is this kaleidoscopic picture of civil war perpetrated by Frenchmen against other Frenchmen, a veritable war *franco-français*, which leads Ternon – and many others – to aver that the Vendée, therefore, cannot possibly be a case of genocide. Many historians may, thus, concede that the state's retribution was worse here than anywhere else but equally refute that this was motivated by any ethnocidal animus, or systematic attempt to exterminate a 'Vendéan' ethnic group.[54] But this, of course, is to miss the point wilfully. The enactment of genocide does not require the existence of a 'race' of 'Vendéans', or 'kulaks', or for that matter 'Jews'. All it requires is that a state regime *in its own mind* comes to the conclusion that a community, however it chooses to define it, is both separate and dangerous and on that basis determines to *biologically* liquidate it. Certainly, the Jacobin regime in particular committed executions and massacres across the board. However, nowhere, except in the Vendée, do we have an example of it setting out to wipe out an entire community systematically with a longer-term view to repopulating the territory with its 'own' loyal followers.

By the same token, the fact that the regime attempts to do so here, largely without abstract musings about the nature of the Vendéans, or some deep-seated hatred towards them, is largely irrelevant as to whether what happens is genocide or not. Barère may have been screaming blue murder against the Vendée, trotting out all the usual genocidal vocabulary about cancers on the political body of France and so on,[55] but this is only from the high summer months of 1793. This was after the rebellion had broken out, after the atrocities at Machecoul, after the Vendéans had made common cause with more powerful emigré opponents of the regime, not to say with the wider international constellations of forces that genuinely had the capacity to destroy it. For the nearly four years prior to this the people of the region had been embraced within the same framework of citizenship: that is, entirely on the same terms as everybody else. This would thus seem to point to a genocide whose wellsprings are essentially *situational* or more pointedly, as Donald Sutherland has argued, simply part of 'the dialectic of revolution-counter-revolution'.[56]

Certainly, in terms of explanation this does leave us with a problem. Where is the motivation to exterminate a whole regional population, regardless of whether they have participated in the insurrection or not? Should we treat the determination of the CPS to avenge itself on the Vendée as an entirely reactive response to the threat that the latter itself had posed but otherwise – *contra* the view of chief genocide accuser, Pierre Chaunu – without premeditated malice or ideological predisposition?[57] This is not entirely far-fetched. After all, the circumstances of 1793–4 are both entirely extraordinary yet exactly the sort in which genocides can and *do* occur. A newly implaced, entirely revolutionary yet fragile and insecure regime was battling against a massive foreign military coalition ranged against it, plus many more internal oppositions, and against the background of almost complete economic and fiscal collapse. No wonder, if in this sustained state of emergency its protagonists began to be completely carried away by the notion that there was some huge international conspiracy arraigned against them.[58] The more real the threat – and there is no doubt that throughout much of 1793 the Vendée threat was very real – the more overblown and paranoid their response became. On the wider scene, remember, this regime was seeing enemies everywhere, a situation which would actually reach its high-water mark *after* the destruction of the Vendée, with the law of 22 Prairial (10 June 1794), which effectively deemed *anyone* liable to the death penalty on suspicion alone.[59] If the trajectory specifically towards a *Vendée-vengée* – the revenged Vendée – came almost from out of the blue, and accelerated very fast before finally exploding into a murderous frenzy of sustained energy release, is this not all indicative of a regime in absolute crisis, not to say free-fall?

However, if this is a description of a genocide perpetrated by a regime which has lost its rag in a particularly grand and phobic way, there is some critical ingredient here which is surely missing. In fact, albeit indirectly, and certainly paradoxically, there is an 'ideological' warning sign written all over this affair that not only points us towards that ingredient but which, equally importantly, links the thought processes of the perpetrators to the latter-day refuters of the Vendée as genocide. The sign is provided by the notion that the French Revolution *qua* revolution is indubitably virtuous and good. Hence, there must be something intrinsically at fault with its contemporary or retrospective opponents who deny it that value. In which case, as far as the Vendéans are concerned, genocide becomes *not* genocide, or at very least something rather less than that, because the 'victims' are themselves to blame. They are not killed because they are poor, benighted 'savages' standing obdurately yet irredeemably in the way of progress but, in some ways, for a more heinous crime still. At least one could say that the 'savage' is absolved of direct guilt by dint of being brought up in a culture that, through physical distance, could not be directly amenable to the civilising impulse. But no such quirk of geographical misfortune prevented Vendéans from embracing the full societal benefits of citizenship to which they were, in any case, fully entitled. Indeed, like other French peasants, they were – at least in principle – peculiarly advantaged beneficiaries of the anti-feudal decrees that, having been inaugurated by the revolution, paved the way for a significant land redistribution in their favour. The fact that, in practice, Vendéan peasants were largely marginalised from this process was certainly not a case of intentional vindictiveness on the revolution's behalf.[60] However, the point is that, unlike the aboriginal in the Americas or antipodes, whose place in the modernising scheme of things was firmly on the sidelines, here the status of the Vendéan was firmly intended to be within the nation-state's universe of obligation. This made his (or her) refusal to acknowledge its virtue all the more one of misguided but wilful transgression.

How entrenched that Vendéan transgression is seen to be is summed up in the word revolutionaries, such as Barère, repeatedly invoked to describe their Vendéan adversaries: 'fanatics'.[61] And what is the basis of their fanaticism? It is their unswerving devotional reverence for a supposedly outmoded and bankrupt set of cultic superstitions, iconised through the scapulary which the fighters in 'the Royal and Catholic Army of Saints wore … around their necks together with the badge of the sacred Heart and Cross in flames'.[62] We can, thus, imagine here similar paroxysms of bewilderment and vituperation which English Puritans might have felt against their Irish foes in the 1640s and 1650s. The difference then, of course, is that it was two versions of essentially the same religion which were pitted against one another, with a definite ethnic component thrown in for very good measure. What makes the wellsprings of the Vendéan genocide distinct – and, arguably, more shocking – is that the animus, at least in so far as it was about ideas, emanates entirely out of a conflict between secularism on the one hand, religiosity on the other. The argument between Protestant and Catholic in the mid-seventeenth century may not have seemed bridgeable then, but the distance between the two positions cannot ultimately be compared with the entirely, mutually contradictory worldviews encapsulated in the struggle for the Vendée. A traditional, ordered, hierarchical society founded on religious faith and confessional unity versus the demands of the secular, universalist, integrated nation-state, one and indivisible: here was the essential clash upon which turned the hegemonic world as it had been and the hegemonic world as it would be.

With the revolutionary state–Vendéan communal dynamic constructed in terms of such binary opposites, proponents of the revolution at the time, and their latter-day more unquestioning defenders, have thus been able to present Vendéan insurrection not only as illegitimate in its own terms but also, teleologically, as an egregious precursor to anti-Dreyfusard, Pétainist, Poujadist and other rightist tendencies deemed as worst enemies of French modernising liberalism. With rightists themselves, particularly from the 1870s onwards, weighing in with their own efforts to appropriate the Vendée as a great symbol of Catholic martyrdom,[63] it is hardly surprising if historians trying to interpret its 'moment' of insurrection in something other than one-dimensional, moralising terms have had an uphill struggle.[64]

But then much is at stake here. If this is the first contemporary genocide, as Secher maintains, or even the first ideological genocide, as Chaunu more forcefully insists, how should historians seek to locate it within the broader range of the phenomenon?[65] As already suggested from previous chapters, the supposition that this is a first cannot be easily sustained. Other cases, at least of proto-formation are evident most notably in the Irish sequence in 1651–2, where, as in the Vendée, the turn to systematic people-extermination grew out of the virulence of a War Type Three struggle, reinforced by religious dogma as well as powerful geo-strategic imperatives. But, then, if much was at stake for the revolutionary states engaged in both these dynamics, colonial–native encounters on the Anglo-American frontier also evinced the ability, repeatedly and persistently, to turn into totalised warfare with zero-sum results.

Having said that, the Vendée is not, in any sense, a colonial genocide. In terms of political geography it is clearly a European, continental event. In the way in particular it pits a regional community at socio-economic and cultural variance against a self-consciously nationalising and modernising regime, it seems to have distinct resonances of genocides we associate with the twentieth century, in the first instance most obviously within a European or near-European frame rather than any of the places which, through the rise of the West, were becoming the metropolitan peripheries. Is it, therefore, a harbinger of what, in the popular mind, are the 'great' genocides of the modern era, a foretaste of what Ittihadists, Nazis and Soviets would do in order to push through their radically transformative, state-building agendas? There is only one problem for the historian here. The Vendée is dramatically isolated in time from these other events. There is no obvious, specifically modern state-building parallel until close to, or during the course of the First World War. This rather perverse, even pedestal-like, singularity would seem to demand further examination. If, as will be argued, it is the emergence of nationalism in its revolutionary French manifestation which is the underlying, truly paradigmatic issue here, then the long-term legacy of this shift – even where this may lead, paradoxically, to some 120 years of absence of genocide on the European continent – still needs to be worked through. This is a matter for the following chapter.

In the interim, what we need to consider now is the distinctive factors which made a Vendée possible. As what happened in the west of France in the

1790s was clearly synchronous with, for instance, genocidal moments in the American-Indian struggle, we cannot treat this event as archetypal of modern genocide as a whole. On the other hand, if we were to ground our search in conditions peculiar to the European domestic scene, rather than in its overseas expansion, might we not have the basis for understanding a particular and rather significant strand of this emerging phenomenon? Nevertheless, this still leaves us with the problem of hindsight. If our whole focus is on what came afterwards, in the twentieth century, our whole approach will necessarily be skewed towards the issue of ideologically driven state formation (or reformation) arguably catalysed by the coincidence of war and revolution.[66]

Alternatively, however, should we not, at least in the first instance, be looking backwards, towards a much longer and continuous tradition of state coercion against peasant grievance, and more especially religious heterogeneity? The Vendée, on the one hand, can be represented as a typically premodern peasant *jacquerie*. On the other, its fervent religiosity is a particularly recognisable feature we can cross-reference with a whole range of national, regional and local revolts which repeatedly rocked pre-modern Europe. Historians are largely in agreement, at least, that the critical catalyst to the Vendéan explosion was religious.[67] What makes it startling different from anything which had come before is that the Vendéans were attempting to defend the religiously conventional and mainstream against a regime which was avowedly, and very vociferously, antithetical to it. The world had been turned upside down. But what, then, of the world of pre-1789 Europe? In order to get at the origins of an apparently novel toxin we need to dig down to some deeper roots.

Precedents, Religious and Otherwise

A perplexing question for all historians and, indeed, anybody interested in the nature of contemporary globalised society is why it was that it was not the most historically entrenched or advanced civilisations which made the dramatic breakthrough to modernity and, thus, subsequently led this process, but a handful of relatively puny and geographically rather marginal, Western societies. Examination of this phenomenon inevitably must centre on discrepancies between political-ethical systems in the empires or cultures of China, India and Islam, which were essentially monolithic and authoritarian, by contrast with European ones which allowed space for the emergence of a more autonomous, even individualistic development. The eventual resulting take-off of capitalism in the West, however, did not lead – as one might perhaps expect – to state disintegration but rather to an increasingly close nexus between capital and modern nation-state formation.[68]

It is a paradox of this situation, then, to note an obverse relationship. Purveyors of the pre-modern Western belief-system, i.e. papally sanctioned Christianity, represented a literate, high tier of society akin to the clerical or clerical-administrative castes, or elites, who either ruled, or gave social direction to the general populace, in Eastern civilisations. As such they were, in critical ways, similarly separated, insulated or at one step removed from their *demos*. Yet, at the same time, the institutional penetration by Christian clerics of the social and cultural milieux of ordinary people in the Latin West acted as a major drag on any grass-roots tendencies towards religious heterodoxy.

That the pre-Christian underbelly of European society was no less diverse or multi-faceted than elsewhere is evidenced by the wide range of religious practices and creeds, including Judaism, accommodated by the Roman empire.[69] Chinese imperial governance similarly allowed for a syncretistic mix of religious ideas from diverse sources. Brahmin-led India was thoroughly pluralistic. Even Islam, despite its strict monotheism, was able to tolerate both a wide variety of heterodox interpretations, as well as Christians and Jews, in its midst. As a result, when Eastern Christian orthodoxy was politically submerged, from the mid- to late medieval period onwards, under Turkish or Tatar hegemonies, the one thing that was definitely not expunged was its spiritual existence. On the contrary, under Ottoman rule in particular, Eastern Christianity survived, and arguably thrived, alongside not only an often bewildering range of Muslim and Jewish mainstream and schismatic groupings, but alternative Christian ones too.[70]

However, such state-sanctioned religious diversity would have been quite inconceivable in the western and central European lands embraced under the Latin Catholic Church. While, thus, class-based urban revolts and peasant *jacqueries* were extirpated with the same brutal if ephemeral efficiency as employed by state rulers everywhere – a fate also awaiting any proto-national revolts who could not find the military wherewithal to make good their case – the all-out, systematic and prolonged extirpation of them by Christian rulers was usually especially reserved for cases where the revolts aligned themselves with heterodox religious tendencies. Such tendencies rarely appeared in social or political isolation. Nevertheless, it was to them that the medieval and early modern European body-politic was most seriously and persistently allergic.[71] If one were seeking a pattern of genocidal-style behaviour, pre-dating the advent of modernity and within, rather than at the margins of, the European context, it is to here that one would be required to concentrate attention. But, in doing so, one would pose some further perplexing questions. Did this religious issue leave a lasting legacy when Europe reinvented itself in its modern and essentially secular guise? If so, what does it tell us about a thought system which appears to contain within it both the potential for individualism and open enquiry and a marked, even genocidal aversion to criticism or deviance?[72]

The subject would be a book in itself. The short answer to what is clearly a contradiction may have something to do *both* with the nature of the thought system and the social and political context in which it became so firmly embedded. A historical clue is, perhaps, on offer from the period when Christianity itself became the subject for intense state-sponsored persecution, the great third century martyrdoms of great numbers of its adherents by a spate of Roman emperors, culminating in Diocletian's declaration of it as a *religio illicta* in AD 304.[73] Rome, as we have noted, was markedly latitudinarian when it came to individual beliefs; what it did demand from its free populace was unswerving loyalty. However, Christianity with its evangelical claims to holding the key to personal enlightenment and future salvation for *all* humanity, regardless of ethnic background or social status, not only implicitly cut across the issue of political authority but in its wider message carried with it profound implications for the conduct and organisation of society. In conditions of acute and unrelenting political and socio-economic crisis for the empire, it is hardly surprising if its rulers responded by declaring anathema upon the creed just as the Roman Church itself would do when, under similar crisis conditions, its leadership would be repeatedly confronted by questioning sectaries and schismatics. If these, then, were classic circumstances for the paranoid scapegoating of an 'out' group for all society's woes, the only difference with fourth-century Rome was that the state then proceeded to arrest the process by attempting to graft the religion onto itself as a strategy for its own survival.[74] That this, in fact, came too late to prevent imperial disintegration, however, does nothing to diminish the power of the thought system that, now duly institutionalised as the official religion of the West, adapted itself perfectly well to the new political reality of small or medium-sized aristocratic-led feudal kingdoms, principalities or city-states which gradually emerged out of the debris of empire, or, in the Germanic lands, beyond its historic borders.

If in this we have a thumbnail sketch of the historic emergence of the 'West' we also have the conditions for the tension between liberty and uniformity. Papal Rome might have aspired in principle to the idea of a politically coherent, supra-territorial Christendom but found that it could best serve the aspiration by providing, through its army of clerics, standardised spiritual, legal and administrative support services across political geographical boundaries. In this sense 'Christianity kept Europe together'[75] while remaining at one critical remove from a dense social fabric that, particularly in a number of more advanced regions, from c. AD 1000 onwards, was displaying marked and dynamic growth in trade, proto-industrialisation and urbanism. Yet if this points to a European trajectory in which localised political autonomies and liberties, in the interstices of feudalism, dovetailed with the emergence of independent classes and, in turn, to a spirit of intellectual and more grass-roots questioning and even dissent, territorial princes generally shared with the Church a disquiet at anything that might undermine the maintenance of order, discipline and social control.

Medieval Europe might still be a long way off from the eighteenth-century absolutist desire for *un roi, une loi, une foi* but, even in what were usually fragmented and often very fluid territorial units, held together by dynastic marriages or the spoils of war, rulers already had a strong vested interest in uniformity.[76] The desire then might only have been to be more fiscally efficient so that they could carry on fighting wars. With almost incessant military competition generally recognised today as the motor driving European polities towards the sort of administrative centralisation (and technological innovation) we associate with modern state-formation,[77] the Church continued to provide more than simply the inter-state codes of conduct regulating both war and its diplomatic conclusions. It also provided an overall umbrella under which the warring parties could still, nevertheless, think of themselves as part of the same culturally homogeneous 'society'. Even when this illusion was utterly shattered by the sixteenth-century arrival of Protestanism, it did nothing to encourage the majority of rulers to be more responsive to religious heterogeneity. On the contrary, with some notable exceptions, the potential in this direction arguably diminished, and not least in most self-proclaiming Protestant states, which sought to utilise their now territorially 'nationalised' Churches as vehicles for the inculcation of state-determined social, linguistic and educational norms among their subject populations.[78]

The Catholic–Protestant schism, however, highlights two more general aspects of the pre-modern European picture particularly relevant to this discussion. The first is that different, even finely tuned interpretations of the Christian message carried with them the possibility for varied, even quite radical reshapings of the social and political organism. Not only, thus, did Protestantism facilitate state-formation but particularly in its Calvinist version, it acted as an important vector for the acceleration of capitalism.[79] Yet a late twelfth- or thirteenth-century Europe which might have gone down an earlier heterodox route, that of the dualist Cathars, with their gnostic emphasis on personal inner enlightenment (not unlike elements of the original pre-Roman Church), anti-materialism, anti-authoritarianism, belief in the equality of men and women, and vegetarian lifestyle, arguably would have been quite drastically different again.[80] It is this, of course, which explains why temporal and spiritual authorities were usually so ready to close ranks against the heterodox and brand them as pernicious and dangerous heresies. Always arising in conditions of acute social, demographic and economic crisis such sects not only offered counter-cultural alternatives to the Christian mainstream but usually were able to fashion their own parallel ecclesiastical organisations. Whether these on their own could represent a real challenge to the hegemony of Church or State is highly debatable. But in the history of genocide or proto-genocide it is not the reality but the perception that counts.[81] And while the institutional Church was able to absorb into its embrace some of the socially more radical religious tendencies emerging on its margins – notably the thirteenth-century Franciscan and Dominican mendicant orders – the truly heterodox found themselves not simply beyond the pale of the medieval universe of obligation, but denounced and dehumanised as the cohorts of the devil and agents of the anti-Christ.

One might assume that genocide would have been the logical follow-through. But the situation was rarely quite so simple. This brings us to our second generalising point about these pre-modern European intimations of genocide. There were implicit brakes preventing the assault on heresy turning into a wholesale extirpation of communal populations. Partly, this was for the simple reason that the Church claimed a universal monopoly on the truth and with it on the path by which humanity in its totality – both the living and the dead – would be ultimately, according to its own lights, redeemed and saved. With a historic mission to save souls, the Church thus had a vested interest in persuading the misguided to recant and return to the fold. To have gone for the alternative option of massacring everyone tainted by heretical association would not only have placed impossible logistical demands on the Christian 'magistrates' who would have been required to accomplish it, it also would have done nothing either for the Church's immediate credibility, even less its long-term agenda.

However, just to confuse the picture there was also a further complicating variable. When the Duke of Alba's Habsburg army rampaged through the Netherlands to stamp out the Calvinist heresy in the late 1560s and 1570s – culminating in the 1576 sack of Antwerp – its officers certainly did not stop to ask if anybody would like the opportunity to recant.[82] Indeed, once a pre-modern army was given this sort of carte blanche, the chance of its turning into a series of unrelenting and indiscriminate massacres, regardless of the victims' beliefs, was all the more probable. But if this certainly represented at the very least a genocidal potential, its full implementation could also be arrested if confronted with a serious political-military opposition. When the Duke of

Orange broke ranks with the Spanish Habsburg regime in the Netherlands to become the kernel of political military resistance to it, his ability to protect Protestants in the wake of Alba's advance was initially not very great. But at least it enabled dissenters to flee to his emerging power-base north of the Scheldt.[83] In France, in this same period, the threat of state-led persecution of Protestant Huguenot communities was similarly partially alleviated – disasters such as the great St Bartholomew's Day massacre of 1572 notwithstanding – through the intervention on their side of the Bourbon princes of the blood, along with other leading aristocratic families.[84] In thirteenth-century Occitania it had been the counts of Toulouse, and for a brief period, the crown of Aragon, fulfilling a similar military role vis-à-vis the Albigensian Cathars.[85] Two centuries later, the Hussite movement in Bohemia, an important precursor of Lutheran Protestantism, turned to the Czech nobility for help, in so doing saving itself from almost certain liquidation at the hands of Roman pope and German emperor.[86]

The message of these examples would seem to be that without significant political-military support, heterodox movements were doomed to a bloody, even genocidal foreclosure. Those too radical for any princely authority to come to their assistance, such as the sixteenth-century Anabaptists caught between the ire of both Lutherans and Catholics, were thus the ones who were likely to suffer the most.[87] The Taborites, on the radical fringes of the Hussite movement, certainly seemed to buck this trend by their own extraordinary grass-roots mobilisation, and the good fortune of having Jan Žižka, a brilliant military tactician, at hand.[88] On the other hand, repeated Taborite and Hussite victory in the field – carrying in its wake, and not unlike the Vendée, its own propensity for rampaging atrocity[89] – itself highlighted the dangers of success. The more protracted and violent the conflict became, the more it was likely to intensify the hegemonic power's projective frustration and hence determination to see its anti-heretical agenda pursued to the bitter end. Against the Hussites, the papacy declared a crusade, as two centuries earlier, had another pope against the Albigensians.[90] In these terms, political-military resistance did not in itself prevent the possibility of physical annihilation, it simply held it in abeyance until such time as the heretics' powerful allies could be bought off, smashed in battle, or simply encouraged to ebb away.

The vulnerability of heterodox movements, moreover, was often amplified by the very fact that what may have begun as communal conflicts in a given territory quickly spilled over into neighbouring ones, or possibly attracted the interests of outside state rulers who could see the potentiality for wresting overt political advantage from them. France may have been initially reluctant to come to the papacy's assistance against the Albigensians, but once it became clear that involvement provided the most favourable route by which French control could be extended over the Languedoc, its extirpatory zeal against heretics – and indeed anybody who stood in its path – was ensured.[91] Three hundred years later, Spain was to intervene in the French wars of religion not only to uphold the Catholic faith but to keep France weak. On the obverse side, both the French and English would intervene on the Dutch behalf and against the Spanish in the Netherlands, not out of any particular sympathy for the Calvinists but for reasons of urgent *realpolitik*.[92]

The danger for religious minorities in these much larger inter-state struggles was not simply that it turned them into political pawns, to be potentially wiped off the chessboard as the players' game-plan evolved, but it also, paradoxically, reinforced both elite and popular assumptions of them as dangerous 'foreign' bodies in their own right, quite willing to act as stooges, or agents of a country's mortal enemies. In these actually rather modern terms, where a group's supposed religious attributes ended and its political ones began became rather blurred. What is significant for our discussion, however, is the degree to which this external element in the equation was played out time and time again. In the context, moreover, of an early modern geo-strategic picture in which the major authentic political-military danger to Christendom came not from Protestantism but from the Ottoman empire, the alleged threat clearly extended to groups who were not technically heretics at all but by implication, or inference, somehow associated with the Turks. Nomadic Roma for instance – their very appellation as 'gypsies' suggested (quite erroneously) that they had come from Egypt – were widely suspected in the fifteenth and sixteenth centuries of being Ottoman spies. The accusation was entirely unsubstantiated. Nevertheless, from 1497 onwards it led successive Holy Roman emperors and other rulers to expel them from their territories.[93]

At least persecuted Roma had the ability to move on either to remote districts where they would not be apprehended, or to other territories where the ban was less than zealously administered. By contrast, Muslims and Jews, the two significant, sedentarised non-Christian populations of the Iberian peninsula, suffered the full brunt of mainstream Christian paranoia about Ottoman fifth columns throughout the late fifteenth, sixteenth and early seventeenth centuries. Of course, the very fact that there were practising non-Christians at all in the supposedly religiously uniform Latin West had a certain anomalous quality about it. In Iberia, it was particularly a legacy of the hundreds of years of Muslim political dominance before Islamic power had waned in the face of the revitalised Christian kingdoms of the north. Even so, there had been moments in time, after the shift in the Christians' favour was already underway, when relative international calm and trading opportunities had signposted the possibilities for not simply peaceful co-existence but even a marked degree of cultural interchange between all three religions. Best characterised by the situation beginning in late eleventh-century Toledo, under nominal and then more direct Castilian proprietorship, something of this same cosmopolitan *convivencia* had enabled the Albigensian flowering *alongside* Catholicism and a significant medieval Jewish population, in twelfth-century Languedoc.[94] Even at the height of the Habsburg-led Catholic struggle with both Ottomans and Protestants, a multiculturalism embracing Jews, Protestants and Calvinists, plus Eastern Orthodox and Armenian Gregorian, as well as scattered Muslim groupings all under the aegis of a Catholic crown in Poland-Lithuania, proved that, given the right conditions, Christian tolerance was not impossible.[95] But then not only was this a period when Poland was politically and economically powerful, it was also one step removed from the struggle with the Ottomans.

The problem is that these positive examples are all exceptions to the rule. Earlier centuries of Christian reconquest in Iberia, and also in southern Italy, had for the most part *not* led to compromise or accommodation with now subjugated Muslim (and Jewish) populations. The very fact that the Iberian *reconquista*, from the mid-eleventh century onwards, was proclaimed and sanctioned by the papacy as a crusade, itself represented a very particular warning sign. Like the drive to capture Muslim-held Jerusalem, not to say the onslaught on the Prus, the Iberian crusades were spearheaded by militant, entirely militarised Christian orders. True, communal annihilation did not follow. Indeed, a skein of hope was kept alive through the promise to Muslim and Jewish communities who now came under, for instance, Castilian or Aragonese sway, that both their security and their judicial autonomies, allowing the free practice of their religion, language and culture, would be vouchsafed.[96] This was the principle. The practice could be very different. In 1248 the entire Muslim population of Seville was expelled without compensation, and their properties allocated to the rich and the powerful amongst the conquerors. In Sicily, fifteen years earlier, 20,000 Muslims were punished for participation in an anti-imperial revolt by deportation to Apulia on the Italian mainland. In both cases 'loyal' Christian populations were imported to replace them.[97] In both, too, the fear that the deportees would act as a Trojan horse for a Muslim return, should they have been allowed to stay, acted as a powerful goad for these early instances of European ethnic cleansing. Similar anxieties would weigh with the Russian tsar, Ivan Grozny, after his capture of Tatar Kazan in the 1550s,[98] and again in the Habsburg creation of the Croatian military frontier with the Turks – the Krajina – less than a century later.[99] The tendency would reach its culmination in the most drastic and certainly most blanket expulsions of this early modern era. In 1492, in the wake of the Spanish capture of Granada – the last remaining Muslim kingdom in the peninsula – the entire practising Iberian Jewish population – possibly as many as 150,000 people were disgorged overseas. However, between 1609 and 1614, arguably double that number of Moriscos, nominally Christianised Spanish Muslims – again an entire communal cohort – suffered this same fate.[100]

Temporal distance may make it difficult to identify or empathise with the scale of these man-made catastrophes. A communal group by turns accused of collusion with North Africans, Egyptians, the French, the Turks, pirates, Lutherans and other Christian heretics, thousands of Moriscos were to pay with their lives as they were set adrift, or drowned, or murdered on hostile shores. The physical and psychic suffering of the survivors, the majority forced to adapt as best they could to an often marginalised and unwelcome existence in the Maghreb, is immeasurable.[101] Yet if the Moriscos were ultimately the casualties of some larger international calculation in what was, in the shape of the Ottoman–Habsburg struggle, the superpower political-cum-ideological confrontation of its time, such a conclusion fails to address the fundamental problem. Expulsion was enacted – one step short of outright extermination – because the Spanish state was seemingly unable to find a *modus vivendi* with a section of its indigenous population that was religiously, culturally and socially different.[102]

Two caveats are in order here. The first is that technically Spain, as a political entity, existed neither in 1492, nor for that matter, in 1609. Unification around the dynastic connection, through marriage of the crowns of Aragon and Castile remained notional and when seriously attempted in 1648, met with fierce resistance from autonomous regions that rightly saw this as an attack on their traditional liberties. What this tells us, however, is that the drive to a religious, even an ethnic uniformity on the Iberian peninsula, considerably *preceded* that towards the formation of a centralised state. Secondly, and as an important corollary to this, the very fact that the existence of Jews and Muslims within this emerging framework should be conceived of as anomalous or superfluous at all is very telling. Neither marginal 'savages' nor for that matter 'wayward' heretics, these communities were utterly in the mainstream of Spanish life: industrious, commercially adept, notably cosmopolitan and, particularly in the Muslim case, agriculturally sophisticated far in excess of their Christian counterparts. Their long-term value to 'Spanish' development was out of all proportion to their numbers. Even so, demographically speaking, their numbers, particularly that of the Moriscos, were also significant, especially in the all important, agriculturally rich province of Valencia, where 160,000 of these 'Christianised' Muslims made up an estimated 34 per cent of the total provincial population.[103] A Spain which continued to embrace both them and the Jews undoubtedly would have developed in a markedly different way over the following centuries, especially when we know with hindsight that its dramatic imperial surge in the sixteenth century, carrying with it aspirations to European, even global, hegemony, was followed by an equally precipitous decline towards acute political weakness and economic poverty. Neither Spain nor Portugal would be in the van of the rise of the industrial, capitalist West.[104]

Yet in their medieval and early modern strategies for dealing with Jews and Muslims, these countries, far from being out of kilter with a more general western European tendency towards cultural homogenisation, were rather at its cutting edge. The Spanish Christian kingdoms particularly attempted, at different moments or in different places, both forced segregation and forced encapsulation. At Murcia, in 1266, for instance, in contravention of their legal rights, the Muslims had a wall built round them, separating them from their Christian neighbours. If this was, at the time, considered an extreme measure, all manner of regulations to prevent social and, more pointedly, sexual intercourse between the two communities were promulgated. As always in such matters, it was cases of Muslim men having relations with Christian women which were most harshly punished, though another perceived cause for stern penalty was the employment of Muslim nannies for Christian children.[105] The nature of the regulations certainly suggest underlying anxieties about religious apostasy. But they could equally be interpreted in terms of fears regarding some more insidious bodily, even racial contamination. The authorities attempted to resolve the issue once and for all, in the decades after the conquest of Granada, by forcing all Muslims *throughout* Spain to convert, a policy followed up very rapidly with an all-out assault on their daily culture. Moorish costume was forbidden, as was the veil for women in public places, Arabic was outlawed, Spanish made compulsory as were Spanish – Christian – names. Moriscos were even required to leave the doors of their homes open for public view.[106] Steven Katz has not been alone in describing these enactments as a conscious and systematic case of 'cultural genocide'.[107] Certainly, the Moriscos' response, from their last quasi-autonomous bastion of the Alpujarras, was one last desperate and disastrous act of revolt, an event that brought in its wake not only 'a vast orgy' of indiscriminate and disorganised killing perpetrated by protagonists and opponents alike, but a green light from Philip II for the region to be looted and ransacked at will, with Morisco survivors then being largely dispersed to other regions of the kingdom.[108] Though the long pause between this 1568 catastrophe and the final 1614 expulsion is itself evidence of contradictory tendencies within the state's Morisco policy – to say nothing of an imperial overstretch making an organised programme of removal well-nigh impossible – for its ultimately triumphant political-cum-religious homogenisers the 'never again' pretext for an unadulterated extrusive solution had been clearly signalled.[109]

With the Jews, however, Spanish policy took on a slightly different but no less disturbing turn. Prevented from a strategy of forcible conversion by the dictates of canon law, so many Jews were nevertheless baptised in the wake of the murderously ubiquitous grass-roots pogroms against them in 1391, that it has been estimated that, a century later, there were many more of these *conversos* in Spain than there were practising Jews; possibly some 300,000 compared with 200,000.[110] Translated into occupational categories this also meant that a sizeable proportion of the Spanish urban, commercial population were by this time of Jewish background, a situation which could only be exacerbated, in the eyes of the old Christian Spanish, in 1492, when at least one-quarter of the remaining Jews opted for conversion as the only available alternative to compulsory expulsion.

That one should use the term 'exacerbated' at all to describe this state of affairs, on one level, ought to be treated as grossly inappropriate. Christianity's self-styled mission was avowedly to save the Jews from the supposed wickedness of their ways. Collective encapsulation of so many, however, seems to have brought with it a serious psychological displacement for many Spanish 'old' Christians with regard to their 'new' brethren. It was understandable, of course, that they might be distrustful of those who had converted out of the sheer necessity of safeguarding lives and livelihoods. More pathological, however, is the way that many 'old' Christians were unable to let the matter rest there through letting assimilation take its natural course but rather chose to bring a wholly negative attention to the descent of fifth- or sixth-generation *conversos* by lambasting them, instead, as '*marranos*' – which was commonly assumed to mean 'pigs', a striking inversion of a Jewish culinary prohibition.[111] If, certainly, some of this could be put down to defending vested interests, particularly in areas of Church and State administration against a new class of often ambitious and clever entryists, what made it much more obviously phobic was the beholder's sense that inside each one of these 'new' Christians there really lurked an intrinsic crypto-Jew whose presence, thus, at the heart of Spanish Christian society, represented a pernicious and even mortal threat to its social, moral and even biological fabric.[112]

The Jews – A Special Case?

The charge, of course, is a strikingly familiar one. *The* Jews, under cover of assimilation and, or conversion, organising a creeping takeover of *echt* society, has been a recurring and core leitmotif of anti-Semitic paranoia, right through to the 'un-German situation' which supposedly characterised Weimar in the twentieth century. In sixteenth-century Spain the anxiety took such hold that it led increasing numbers of 'old' Christian families to resort to geneaological tables to prove their *limpieza de sangre*: their purity of blood.[113] But if this racialisation of the issue represented both a novel and ominous departure, the Jewish 'problem', as perceived by the Spanish, was hardly exclusive to them. On the contrary, it was at the core of Christian Europe's monolithic inability to cope not only with the idea of the 'other' but, equally signficantly, any 'other' which had its own alternative, authoritative and – as far as Christianity was concerned – dissenting voice.

Yet it was also clear that the Jews were a special case. A very special case. The fact that there were Jews at all in Christendom was testament enough to that. Spread in a multitude of European-wide communities, their social, cultural and economic existence, though displaying marked geographical diversity, was, in overall terms, in sharp contrast with the dominant norms of the feudal-military Christian mainstream. Nor was this entirely the result of Christian persecution. Diaspora Jewry's own great legal canon, the Talmud, nourished a thought system tailored to conditions of post-exilic powerlessness and ubiquitous minority status – any semblance of Jewish political-territorial existence having crashed with the Roman defeat of the Judean revolt in AD 70 – which enabled them to survive on the social margins of Europe's rural-based majority while often providing very necessary intermediary services to it. Medieval Jewry, in short, even where the majority of them continued to be very poor, nevertheless displayed aspects of a nascent proto-capitalist middle class at a juncture when, at least in principle, capital formation was not yet acceptable as an economic philosophy. Indeed, one might go further and argue that the Jews, more than any other single group, offered a glimpse into a very different sort of Europe, not only entrepreneurial and bourgeois but also non-territorial and genuinely cosmopolitan.[114]

The position of Jews inevitably poses an enigma as to why pre-modern Christian rulers allowed a Jewish existence through grants of localised judicial self-rule in the first place. The answer is complex, paradoxical and historically deeply embedded. In other words, it is largely outside the scope of a study on genocide in the age of the nation-state. But its fundamental aspects are too critical to be entirely skimmed over here.

On one level, one might argue that there is no mystery. The status of the 'Jew' was one of pariah. Hence, Spain and Portugal's expulsions, far from being against the conventional grain, instead could be represented as the logical if overdue culmination of a process of state-sanctioned removals which had been gathering apace in western Europe for a number of centuries. If the Jews, in Cecil Roth's words, were 'the first Europeans',[115] they were, by 1600, most likely to be eastern or south-eastern Europeans, the most advanced west European countries – the ones with the most developed commercial urban centres – having, by this time, more or less disgorged themselves of their Jewish presence. The fact that no sooner had this enforced west–east migration been more or less completed than, on a much more voluntary basis, it began to be reversed is, of course, an indication of a very different socio-economic and cultural climate which was beginning to emerge in the west. Indeed, the very founding of tolerated, if small, Jewish communities in port cities such as Bordeaux, Amsterdam and Trieste, is evidence enough of a potential new European orientation founded not on religious dogma but on commercially driven opportunity.[116]

That this new, clearly modernist, spirit was also state sponsored was most clearly demonstrated with Cromwell's permission for Jews as Jews to re-settle in England in the 1650s, after nearly 400 years of state-enforced absence. Yet a century on from this watershed event, this arguably most openly freethinking and religiously dissenting country in Europe threw out a parliamentary bill for their naturalisation – that is, that Jews might be treated like other Englishmen – with a quite extraordinarily vituperative animus. One opponent, for instance, thought it relevant to draw up a mammoth list adumbrating the vile characteristics of contemporary Jewry's *biblical* forebears. They were:

> rebellious, gainsaying, stiff-necked, impenitent, incorrigible, adulterous, whorish, impudent, forward, shameless, perverse, treacherous, revolting, back-sliding, idolatrous, wicked, sinful, stubborn, untowards, hard-hearted, hypocritical, foolish, sottish, brutish, stupid, ungrateful ...[117]

The list goes on. And on. Another writer with a desire to inject a broader historical sweep to the general denunciation reminded his audience that:

> The Writers of all Ages ... have born Witness of the cruel and implacable Malice the Jews have born against Christians; as by solemnly cursing them every day in their Synagogues, by raising Persecutions wherever they could in all Times against them, by stealing, and torturing, and oftentimes crucifying Christian Children, never professing to keep any Terms of Civility, Truth or Honesty with Christians; but always doing them all the Mischief in their Power, and murdering them by all the Tortures they could devise, by Thousands.[118]

There are actually only two things unusual about these otherwise entirely standard trans-European portrayals. One is that the actual number of Jews in Britain in 1753 was insignificant except in London and a handful of maritime towns. The other is that that the last time when there would have been a real target for these entirely regurgitated anti-Semitic motifs would have been back in the thirteenth century, when there had last been practising Jews in England. But then such constructions do not require the presence of the authentic object to ensure their longevity. That, in a sense, is provided by the sheer nastiness of the stereotype itself, an image of a people who are supposedly not only extremely unwholesome but both wicked and very dangerous with it. Jews kill people, particularly children, without compunction. It is Christians, in other words, who are their victims and who ought to be afeared of Jews, certainly not the other way round. But, if this is the case, this simply reinforces the condundrum: why did pre-modern Europe, which, as we have already noted, found itself almost incapable of tolerating even the most minor religious difference, tolerate in its midst these most odious of all bogeymen?

The conundrum goes back to the very origins of Jewish–Christian relations. Yet it also remains essential to an understanding of the dominant European mindset and hence of its particular animus against this specific people, even after the retreat of organised state-inculcated Christianity. Perhaps the conundrum is most pithily encapsulated in two terse lines of the late fourth-century Christian opinion former, and later patriarch of Constantinople, John Chrysostom: 'I hate the Jews, because they violate the Law. I hate the synagogue because *it has* the law' (my emphasis).[119] Christianity, in other words, suffered a double-bind when it came to the Jews. Founded in a Jewish-Palestinian milieu, led by a Jewish leader, with Jewish disciples, even as it changed tack and, by degrees, attempted to divorce itself from its Jewish legacy, Christianity remained manifestly an offshoot of Judaism. In the context of the Roman empire, in which many of its would-be converts must have found it difficult to distinguish between it and its parent religion, it clearly needed some way of simply clarifying the distinction. Worse, in an atmosphere of anti-Jewish feeling in the wake of successive Judean and diasporic insurrections against Rome, it desperately needed to distance itself politically. The solution to this early life crisis was to proclaim a version of its origins, articulated in the Synoptic gospels, and more particularly the Gospel of St John, which turned the Jews into the bad guys in the story, with full responsibility for the death of Jesus, their proclaimed messiah (*Christos*). As he, moreover, was, by this juncture, also being posthumously regarded as the human embodiment of God, Jews hence were not simply Christ murderers but equally God murderers.[120]

It followed that the Jews were the enemies of all that was good, virtuous and 'Christian' in mankind; the original and authentic enemies of the people. But the problem for Christianity was that it was unable to blot out the other side of the equation: the Jews were not only the 'chosen' God bearers – the alleged legitimacy of Jesus as messianic saviour being grounded in Old Testament prophecy – but were essential to the whole teleological process by which all mankind arrived at the moment of general resurrection and salvation. Eschatologically speaking, Christianity could not do without the Jews. They might be stiff-necked sinners in their refusal to acknowledge the true faith but that made their collective conversion all the more not simply a *sine qua non* but the vital ingredient announcing the arrival of the millennium: the thousand-year reign of Christ on earth. If Chrysostom, St Augustine and others articulated some of the early blasts in an increasingly virulent yet elite tradition of anti-Jewish discourse, the *Adversus Judaeos*, the Church also, by the terms of its own Christology, knew that it could not sanction the death of the Jews, but, on the contrary, was obliged to protect their persons.[121]

The long-term tension lies in the contradiction. If Jews are such a significant but malicious force in the world, they must do things that are manifestations of their wickedness. And if that is the case, how can honest Christians stand by and acquiesce? But the contradiction can also be read in an entirely different way. If Christianity is founded on the promise of its messiah's imminent return to earth to save mankind, its ongoing failure to deliver would make the doubting Jews, after all, the carriers of both reason and truth and Christianity, hence, a massive hoax. 'It is hard to evade the conclusion', argues R. I. Moore, writing of the twelfth century, 'that the urgent and compelling reason for the persecution of the Jews at this time … was that they offered a real alternative and therefore a real challenge, to Christian *literati*'.[122]

Historians of anti-Semitism generally agree that the theological diatribes against the Jews did not seriously translate into a pattern of open violence until this very period of dramatic European social and cultural crisis and change. The crisis also brought with it increasing doubts among many of the sophisticated and freethinking elements of the population about the efficacy of the central core of Christianity's ideas and ritual practices.[123] It, equally, might have been mediated by a growing corpus of Jewish advisors, and above all financial administrators, utilised, protected and privileged in their roles by the leading formative states of the Latin West. It is in this very context, proposes Moore, that one begins to see the formation of a persecuting society organised and directed by a Christian clerical elite against all those elements in society which it denounces as deviant, heretical and impure. But in that society the most comprehensive campaign of denunciation is reserved for its most 'formidable social and intellectual' competitors.[124] Thus, there was the rapid emergence at this juncture of a strong counter-current which would project the irrational back onto the Jews, and which would give rise to a whole series of lurid accusations against them, including the ritual murder and/or crucifixion of children, accompanied by cannibalism, and of the desecration of the Host, the most sacred and sacrificially potent element in the act of the Christian Eucharist.[125] There is no doubt that these phobic projections developed a broad grass-roots appeal, and that the consequences for the Jews themselves could be devastating. From the onset of the crusades, in 1096, when the numerous Rhineland Jewish communities were set upon by itinerant bands allegedly en route to the Holy Land and – through direct slaughter or flight – almost completely extirpated, a pattern of popular anti-Jewish violence was set in motion.[126]

However, to explain these outbursts as a simple matter of xenophobic scapegoating of the obvious outsider every time things went wrong, or disasters such as the Black Death struck, would be to miss the point just as it would be to lay responsibility for these acts entirely at to the doors of the most thuggish or under-class elements of society. Direct physical violence might be officially abhorred by the upper reaches of the ecclesia but it was no more than the flip side of an emerging web of legal enactments promoted by itself and aimed at freezing the Jews out of mainstream political and economic activity, as well as 'normal' social, sexual and cultural exchange. If this was all part of a long-term exercise in what Steven Katz describes as transforming the 'Jews' into 'metaphysical markers, ontological principles, eschatological abstractions',[127] the more immediate and urgent aim was to stymy the threat of a perceived intellectual and moral contamination. The Church, thus, had no interest in disputing popular anti-Semitic tales of sado-erotic orgies. On the contrary, in encouraging the image of Jewish deviancy, not to say quintessential evilness, lay medieval Christianity's most trusted defence mechanism against its greatest fear: that of unmasking.

Yet, if this necessarily required collective Jewish demonisation, it also carried with it an escalating logic. If Jews, by their murder of Christ and the barbaric mutilation of little children were evil, then by the same token the forces of good clearly lacked the wherewithal with which to combat and resist them. In earlier centuries accusations of Jewish 'international' collusion with external forces such as the Arabs, or even the Vikings, however fanciful, were at least grounded in real political events.[128] By contrast, as Jews in the later middle ages became increasingly powerless, the degree to which the powers inversely attributed to them became entirely fantastical, chimerical, superhuman and ultimately supernatural is interesting. Ritual murder, or the poisoning of wells, might be the most obvious physical manifestations of their ability to cause hurt and mayhem, but it was the invisible powers behind these acts of sabotage that really mattered; powers worked through medicine, astrology, alchemy, necromancy and other forms of magic which ultimately proved their true master as Satan.[129] A conservative rationalist of the stature of the mid-thirteenth-century Dominican theologian, Thomas Aquinas, might attempt to put the ecclesiastical brakes on these sort of paranoid fantasies and calumnies – not least by speaking out against mob violence and forced conversion. But Aquinas' own insistence on the sinful wickedness of Jews *since* Christ's crucifixion, by their continued rejection of him, pointed to an incurability of condition – shared in the more general persecuting milieu with the depraved likes of lepers and homosexuals – which logically seemed to demand a collective punishment in perpetuity.[130]

Protestantism, more than two centuries later, would do nothing to soften these core accusations. Admittedly, Luther briefly moderated his tone, though less as it turned out because of his approximation to the more tolerant ideas of contemporary humanists and much more because of his own eschatological wish-fulfilment that imminent mass Jewish conversion would prove him right in the face of his papal detractors. Disabused of this notion by leading German rabbis, Luther's subsequent diatribes against the Jews not only placed them alongside the pope and the Turks as the three most dangerous enemies of Christ's kingdom at the still supposedly imminent end of time but were couched in language as vitriolic and ugly as anything in the annals of anti-Semitism.[131] Politically febrile Jews might have been but the threat that they allegedly posed remained not only in their physical behaviour and actions towards Christians but above all in a belief system which denied Christ. But then, at least, the failure of conversion enabled Protestant states to keep Jews at one remove from the body-politic through separation into ghettos or even more plausibly through expulsion. Once, however, they were in one's midst *masquerading* as Christians there was no knowing where the contagion would stop.

It was this sort of visceral fear that also gave a new lease of life to the workings of the Inquisition in Spain in the early sixteenth century and so to the rapid escalation of the number of alleged crypto-Jews burnt at the stake in acts of *auto-da-fé* in this period. The Inquisition itself was not new, having been authorised by Pope Gregory IX in 1232 as a body for the rooting out of the Cathar heresy. What was notable about its dramatic, specifically Spanish reinvigoration, was two-fold. One was its remarkable longevity; the powers of Inquisition remained in force until the early nineteenth century. Second, was the wide social and ethnic diversity of its victims in the two most active centuries of its operation, alleged Judaisers rapidly being superseded by Moriscos, Protestants, 'sodomites', though also, tellingly, foreigners of all descriptions.[132] Yet, if this represents an early modern variant of 'Reds under the beds' anxieties, in other words, if it was as much about social and sexual deviance undermining the bonds of self-proclaimed legitimate society as anything purely political, this kind of moral panic was hardly confined to a Habsburg super-power in crisis. It was in this same sixteenth- and seventeenth-century period that accusations of witchcraft, arguably the last great pre-modern outburst against the heterodox, became a truly endemic and chronic feature of European society. And these charges were on both sides of the Protestant–Catholic divide.

The Crushing of the Deviant

The very wide geographical spread of witchcraft accusations made in both urban, though more particularly rural, localities across Christian Europe, and over a significantly long timescale, has ensured that no consensual historical explanation of the phenomenon exists. The problem, moreover, that to modern observers the accusation appears as primarily a statement about the irrational, even hysterical fears of the accusers, rather than the accused, throws the precision of empirical analysis into further doubt. Whereas it is possible to consider groups such as Jews, Roma or even, up to a point, Cathars or Anabaptists as discrete communal entities, no such case can be made for 'witches'. On the contrary, while there might be criteria for how to spot a witch available, for instance, in the infamous witch-hunters' manual, the *Malleus Maleficarum*, of 1486, their application could as easily lead to the charge backfiring on the accuser, him or herself. This does not make, however, for an entirely arbitrary or stochastic victimisation. The charge of witchcraft was nearly always levelled against those considered in some respect deviant from accepted social norms, usually as made by neighbours, or others, in close proximity to the accused but always judged and dealt with by a town or district's political, clerical and judicial elite. The frequency – though one should add not exclusivity – of economically marginal, older single women and widows amongst those so charged is thus quite striking, not only in its own terms, but in the parallels it throws up with anxieties about other 'outsider' groups.[133]

Like Jews, or more particularly crypto-Jews, for instance, the objective reality of the 'witches' political and social powerlessness is thus replaced or more accurately inverted in the projected image as one of hidden or occult and thus all the more supernaturally potent powers. 'Witches' gained their alleged power though collective consorting and fornication with the devil. Orgiastic sexuality and peverted ritual necessarily followed in these *sabbats*, as did nocturnal visitations in which children were killed and cannibalistically eaten and their body parts used for the production of further items of black magic. The tropes are so familiar that it is hardly surprising that a papal bull of 1409 instructed an inquisitor to seek out fleeing Jews, Waldensian heretics and those responsible for witchcraft practices, as if they were all in some way linked together.[134]

As Robin Briggs and others have recently emphasised, how far one can read into witchcraft accusations some clear, underlying political or socio-economic causation is less measurable. Witchcraft accusations tended to come from the grass-roots; they were often pursued by particularly zealous, sometimes self-appointed witch-hunters rather than state authorities *per se*; nor did they notably lead, as was often until quite recently assumed, to the targeting and execution of *particular* traditional, female occupational healers such as midwives.[135] And this despite all the transparent misogynism of the *Malleus Maleficarum*. On the other hand, there is evidence to suggest that the spasmodic flurries of witchcraft mania *were* part of a more generalised and heightened sixteenth- and seventeenth-century state onslaught on popular 'superstitions' or what had come to be perceived as socially undesirable or criminal. These happened to include the sometimes esoteric if primitive knowledge associated with white magic, healing and pain relief that were primarily practised by rural women, handed down orally from mother to daughter over the generations but which were neither amenable nor accessible to the control of clergy or magistracy. None of these practices had mattered so much in the centuries when Christianity was a thin overlay of social, behavioural and ritualistic norms. In a Europe politically and socially dominated by the prolonged Reformation versus Counter-Reformation struggle, the Church-cum-State, whether Protestant or Catholic, however, was much less likely to accept any challenge to its monopoly of social control, or accede to a plurality of 'natural' wisdoms, grass-roots or otherwise.[136] That in cases of alleged witchcraft the magistracy was also often able to draw to its investigations the regular involvement of physicians, in other words of another peer grouping with supposedly systematised medical knowledge at odds with traditional neo-pagan or heterodox practices, also speaks volumes for the way political, professional and clerical elites were beginning to line up as a body behind 'rational', state-supported terms of reference against the socially deviant and the heretical.[137]

Perhaps, more tellingly, the high-water mark of genuine witchcraft panics, between the 1580s and 1640s, can be located quite noticeably in regions where the ideological and political-territorial contest between the Reformation and Counter-Reformation was itself at its most intense, and/or, in middling or still underdeveloped states where moves towards state consolidation and centralisation remained fiercely disputed. It is precisely in this political geography of crisis encompassing the area of the so-called Spanish Road – the Habsburg artery running along a gauntlet of unstable small states through the Franco-German and Rhenish borderlands on the one hand – the various duchies of south-west Germany, the Swiss Confederation, the kingdoms of Scotland, Denmark and Sweden on the other, which most obviously succumbed to witchcraft hysterias and trials in their most intense and undiluted form.[138]

Given the broader ubiquity of the witch phenomenon in the Europe of the period, however, and the way that what in previous ages had been part of a fabric of localised and hence largely mediated communal conflict, became reworked and reclassified into the ultimate diabolical heresy, could one not argue – albeit with the benefit of hindsight – that this is actually the final and crucial phase in the hundreds of years of effort by European Christian elites to assert their total authority against religious heterogeneity or cultural difference as they strove to streamline their social organisms towards the interests of a national, or proto-national statehood? Or put another way, fighting the heterodox, even where powerless within, simply became the necessary adjunct to fighting very real theopolitical enemies without. Yet if this is a statement which simply iterates that the crisis of the seventeenth century was a culmination of processes which had been building up for a long time, the outcome of which was the extremely painful birth-pangs of a European-centred modernity, this still raises the question of whether the centuries of assault on the heterodox or marginal which went with it amount to a parallel prehistory of modern genocide. Alternatively, do they contrarily provide evidence for a basic continuity that makes an irrelevance of distinctions between the modern and pre-modern?

A single, straightforward, let alone comprehensive, answer is not available. We have already, in the two preceding chapters, proposed that the onslaught on the Americas and antipodes provides one critical arena in the thrust towards the modern in genocide. Its victims, however, were clearly regarded as on the outside of civilised society and hence in ethical as well as political terms 'savages' beyond the pale. But such labelling was in practice very much more difficult to apply to European-domiciled Jews, or Jewish *conversos*, Moriscos, or even Roma, on the one hand, 'witches' (for want of a better appellation) or those, for instance, who embraced the Cathar creed, or Anabaptism, on the other. The very fact that all of these very different entities (witches, of course, a confabulated one) were living within the boundaries of Christendom, often for generation upon generation, meant they were all in some intrinsic way part of its familiar social and cultural make-up. Jews and Moriscos might upset the ideal picture of a streamlined Christian uniformity but whitewashing them out of the picture was highly problematic when these groups could point to precedents of juridical privileges or state protection from earlier centuries. Roma, however precarious and transient their existence often was, were exceptionally adept at surviving at the social and economic margins of the sedentarised norm. As for the heterodox, and other sundry transgressors, these were hardly individuals or collectivities socially or culturally divorced from the mainstream at all, but simply wayward sheep of whom holy mother Church wished nothing better than to have them returned to the fold. All of this suggests implicit if diverse brakes on the recourse to state-led extirpatory violence against minority communities.

Yet it is also clear in the emerging crises of the medieval and early modern periods the degree to which critical policy-making or opinion-forming elements in European state-societies felt deeply and persistently threatened by such communities. Objectively speaking, this has to be viewed as primarily a matter of elite perception, when it is equally evident that none of these groupings were endowed with the sort of territorial base, let alone underlying socio-economic support systems, with which to mount serious political-military challenges to the hegemonic order. This does not mean that such things never happened. Utter desperation – the revolt of Alpujarras – or eschatological fervour could trigger such eruptions. When, in an example of the latter, an Anabaptist insurrection overthrew traditional oligarchic rule in the Westphalian town of Münster in 1534, inaugurating a sixteen-month reign of communistic, not to say polygynistic, *dis*-order, it led to a torrent of denunciatory propaganda emanating from far and wide, adumbrating not just the savagery but the leading role of the devil in the insurrectionists' purpose.[139] The effect was remarkable if only in the way it had Catholic and Protestant princes lining up *together* to quash the regime. But if Münster was unusual in the manner in which it did genuinely, if very ephemerally, rock the traditional order, what is noteworthy is the frequency, depth and intensity with which other entirely quietistic, pacific or non-threatening communities were equally accused of the same sinister intent. Indeed, much more so than native resisters on the colonial frontiers, politically impotent outsiders in the heartlands of Europe were repeatedly invested with quite inordinately limitless and even cosmic powers.

There are ingredients here which certainly do provide linkage if not directly with genocide then certainly with aspects of a modern genocidal mentality. For instance, the hidden, unseen powers attributed to Jews and Roma in medieval times not only carried through into the mindset of Nazi accusation but they kept much of the traditional linguistic baggage still in tow. Binary opposites of good and evil, light and darkness, concretised and made visible by reference to specific acts of sado-eroticism, or cannibalism, have been as prevalent in the pages of the Nazi paper *Der Stürmer*, as they were in sixteenth- and seventeenth-century chapbooks or almanacs.[140] However, one should be wary of treating any of this, whether in the primitive world of yesteryear, or the supposedly demon-free milieu of modernity, simply as a question of a manipulative, instrumental propaganda. Then as now, the propaganda fails to mask the underlying, essentially psychopathological nature of the anxiety. The idea of bodily possession by the devil, so central to the witchcraft accusation, in this sense is only a particularly striking variation on a theme of creeping contagion, corruption and contamination of both the individual and the social organism. That this again, in the past, always required the involvement of the diabolical – thereby explaining and rationalising how socially subordinate Jews, witches or heretics were able to acquire such malevolent powers – has simply been more contemporaneously updated, usually minus the figure of Satan, in some other all-encompassing, omnipresent but invisible conspiracy.

More tellingly still, the notion that the accused could through these powers attack 'the delicate fabric of communal and personal life', 'impair health and cause plagues … make men impotent and kill children' and also in so doing 'directly affect the course of history, to rebel against Heaven and undo Christendom'[141] underscores the degree to which pre-modern societies were as prone to conditions of acute ferment and fluidity as their more modern, arguably more agenda-driven counterparts. Yet the blame for apocalyptic crisis, whether in 1096, or 1918 – two critical years particularly for German Jewry – never fell on 'outside' groups purely out of thin air. And it is in this, of course, that we have to confront an ongoing paradox. Heterodox sects, 'gypsies', Jews, Muslims, independent women, were always the potential victims in times of crisis by dint of the power they did possess: *the power of difference*. Clearly there are matters of degree here. Not only is it doubtful whether peasant midwives steeped in folklore represented a coherent alternative world-system in the same ways as, say, Judaism, but the danger perceived to come from them only arose at a given point in European development. If, thus, comparatively speaking, anxieties about 'witches' may have been more ephemeral and possibly not so deeply embedded in Europe's cultural milieu as anxieties about Jews – contentious as this proposition may itself be – what both they and our other examples share in the context of Christian uniformity is the genuine potency of the alternative. Nor, by the same token, was anxiety about such challenges restricted to given sections of the mainstream. The amenability of the masses to elite mobilisation against the accused in retribution for some alleged moral or physical sabotage – in other words, crisis conditions that state elites found it impossible to control – was quite as plausible as the unwillingness of the authorities to intervene in the face of communal rampages against ethnic outsiders or social transgressors.

Yet if these aspects point to a cultural consonance between elites and at least elements of broader society with regard to given outgroups – aspects, that is, which would offer some basis for continuity into the modern period – it is less easy to determine whether the follow-through translates into given instances of genocide. Having very haphazard data on numbers of fatalities is certainly part of the problem. For instance, anything between 30,000 deaths and a proposed upper limit of 200,000 offered by Steven Katz as a direct result of witchcraft accusations in the entire period from 1400 and 1750,[142] is clearly a rather wide margin. But even if it could be proved that the actual number was at the lower end of this spectrum this would not in itself exclude a case for genocide. What we need to know for confirmation of this particular type of mass murder is that in some given region, or even locality, agents of the state undertook a systematic policy aimed at physically eradicating whole communities so accused. What we are actually confronted with, however, is a great many people – men as well as women – being targeted and sometimes judicially murdered as alleged witches in their *individual* capacities.[143] Certainly, within a generally very dispersed geographical pattern of killings, there were significant clusters of mass hangings or burnings which included many related family members. Witches could end up in this way as a sort of 'self-defining group' through the imputation of witchcraft being passed on from generation to generation. But there is little or no evidence that families were automatically targeted as such, while there is substantial data to show that significantly large proportions of the accused were acquitted, or punished or humiliated, without being killed.[144] This would be consistent with the way authorities primarily carried forward their onslaught through judicial trials and inquisitions not only against 'witches' but in Spain against crypto-Jews, in southern France against Cathars, and elsewhere against other cases of deviance or heterodoxy. Such mechanisms, however, even where they include torture, are very far from ideal instruments for a policy of genocide. Not only are their efforts far too protracted, time-consuming and pedantic, they also assume the possiblity of the 'victim' avoiding death through confession, recantation or acquittal.

This is not to suggest that there could not be very real physical explosions of violence against 'outgroups', the extirpation of the town of Béziers by a papal army in 1209 during the Albigensian wars, being often cited as one notable example.[145] Interestingly, however, this very type of explosive mass killing does not lend itself well to an explanation of systematic genocide either. Béziers was a case of the besieging soldiery being given free rein after the town had refused to surrender, a practice far from uncommon in the middle ages. As a result, its citizens, both Cathars and Catholics, mostly Catholics, in fact, were put to the sword. Certainly, this does not preclude the argument for a more general policy of genocide against Catharism which, after all, was extirpated in this period. But again we simply do not know the degree to which this was successful because of repeated extermination of communities. What we do know is that it was the hard-core leaders, the *perfecti*, who were particularly targeted by the Inquisition while the great mass of their followers were allowed to recant.[146] In other worst cases, notably the sixteenth-century onslaught on the Anabaptists, historians have been loth to offer estimates for the numbers of dead. What is clear is that communities of Anabaptists, such as the Mennonites, seem to have survived by adopting a notably quiescent and pacific posture.[147]

Here again we need to be cautious, as survival of a group is no evidence that at some stage genocide was not committed against it. After all, while Jews for most of their diasporic existence were not subject to the sort of perpetual persecution claimed in lachrymose readings of their history,[148] there clearly were moments, especially in the medieval phase, when latent antipathies against them spilled over into direct extirpatory violence. This would once again be consistent with the nature of genocide were it not for the lack of evidence which would nail the medieval state as its instigator and organiser. Physical attacks on Jews tended to come from below, not from above. Indeed, there is evidence in some such cases that attacks on Jews or other such specially 'protected' groups, including lepers, were intended as indirect attacks on the power of the Crown itself.[149] Certainly kings and princes might be responsible for systematic legal discrimination and, in the most egregious cases, mass expulsion. But a state-led genocidal process generally stops short at this point. If the Jews were anathema to the dominant medieval European mind, just as misogynism was intrinsic to it, this did not translate into any single unadulterated case of either state-sponsored gynocide[150] or Judeocide. Nor is there *sufficient* evidence to suggest that conflict between the state and other heterodox groups led to the former taking an unambiguous lead in sustained, exterminatory assaults of this kind; at least not in Europe.

There is a case to be made for this in Japan, primarily in the decade after 1614, when the Tokugawa shogunate banned Christianity for not dissimilar reasons to the justifications European Christian states deployed against heresy. Brought into the country by Jesuit missionaries who had accompanied mostly

Portuguese traders in the mid-sixteenth century, some 250,000 or 300,000, of Japan's 20 million people, including elements of the military *samurai* caste, were estimated to be among its flock by 1614.[151] In a Japanese setting, however, Christian teaching implicitly contradicted not so much the country's quite syncretist religious system but the much more important tenets of loyalty and obedience demanded by the Bakufu, the ruling military 'curtain' government. It was thus the Christian potential as a political challenge – a fifth column – which excited intense Bakufu animosity at a critical juncture when it was attempting not only to consolidate central power against the feudal might of regional *daimyo* but also to regain a total monopoly of its important foreign trade against European, especially Portuguese competitors. Thus, whether imagined or real, Christians were perceived as a collective enemy working in the interests of foreign powers and against a Japanese state developing a coherent, authoritarian-driven, national agenda. Some thousands of men, women and children were burnt or crucified as a result in mass public executions, though how many thousands, exactly, remains a matter of dispute.[152] Certainly, as in Europe, recantation was possible, a course that, despite continuing persecutions, enabled the ongoing existence of a crypto-Christian population, especially in the south of the country.

A New Tolerant Dawn?

However, if an early seventeenth-century Japan, utterly obsessed by the dangers of Western penetration – at least in part through the agency of alleged domestic proxies – offers an important signpost to genocide in the age of the nation-state, what is perhaps most striking about Europe in the latter half of the century, is the contrasting degree to which it seemed to be moving away from this genocidal potential. Rather significantly, the tentative way forward was provided by an attempt at resolution of Europe's religious tensions at an international level. The Treaty of Westphalia of 1648 brought to a not quite conclusive end the previous thirty years of warfare which had torn central Europe apart, largely destroying in the process its prosperity, infrastructure and vast swathes of its population. The conflict had been about much more than religion; Westphalia's purpose, above all, being an attempt to find some overarching framework within which competing European state territorial aspirations might be held in some sort of peaceful balance. At one level, this hope proved quite illusory, combinations of states repeatedly going to war with one another through to 1815. Nevertheless, the Westphalian concept of Europe as an amalgam of independent, equally sovereign polities – regardless of their diverse Catholic, Calvinist or Lutheran stamps – did have the effect of reinforcing pragmatic interests as the primary impetus for state policy, both domestic and foreign. The contrary tendency towards a unified and religiously uniform Christendom had been effectively quashed with Habsburg political-military collapse in the final years of the Thirty Years War.[153] The result was hardly the inauguration of the secular state. But it did appear to assist in the subordination, if not cancellation, of the idea of a European religious mono-culture. The logic of the situation pointed to a normative religious pluralism in domestic relations too. A situation, indeed, where George Shiffner, a typical eighteenth-century English gentleman might quite comfortably intone that: 'Men of different opinions worship God in their own way ... we are to respect them in their different manner of worship ... the existence of an Omnipotent God whose Providence over-rules all events is the universal belief of all People of whatever denomination.'[154] And this was enunciated only a few decades on from the most intense and often brutal English government-assisted persecution of both Catholics and dissenters.

The era of the Enlightenment had arrived. Or had it? On the other side of the Channel, any notion of a benign, upward trajectory towards toleration being just temporarily put on hold by some mistaken but otherwise ephemeral government reaction had, at the very least, to contend with the events of 1685. The efforts of France's Louis XIV towards the creation of a genuinely centralised, strong state, under his own personal control, was not in itself at odds with Westphalian tenets but rather its logical extension. Legal, adminis-trative and fiscal reorganisation in the interests of a single, absolutist dynastic ruler so that he (occasionally she) could more readily monopolise and mobilise all the resources of his, or her, sovereign territory or territories for the more efficacious and robust fighting of war, were, indeed, a typical aspiration – with some notable exceptions – throughout the Europe of the *Ancien Régime*. The aspiration assumed the erosion of traditional feudal and clerical privileges. But with its mercantilist emphasis on acquiring wealth for the state's *dirigiste* development, rather than for the glory of God, centralisation of worship could be assumed to be not simply superfluous but even idiosyncratic.

Not so with Louis, who identified two prime – *religious* – enemies. First were the Jansenists, an austere, reforming sect just about within the frame of the Catholic Church. Second were the Protestant Huguenots, at something up to 1.75 million people, an entirely more significant and influential if minority element within the French population, especially in the west and south of the country. Economically diverse, though with significant urban concentrations among the artisanry and bourgeoisie, the Huguenots hardly represented a serious political threat to Louis as they had to his predecessors of a century earlier.[155] During the widespread disturbances of the *Fronde* at the outset of his reign, in the 1640s and early 1650s, they had remained markedly quietist. Earlier still, the Edict of Nantes, in 1598, had guaranteed their freedom of worship and jurisdictional autonomy in given areas, in itself an important reminder that France was both a frontrunner and innovator in the field of religious compromise and toleration.[156]

The reversal of this tendency, however, proved that *raisons d'état* could run decidedly counter to historical wisdom or economic good sense. But, then, the accelerating onslaught on the Huguenots from the late 1670s was not purely the whim of one over-mighty Gallican ruler, anxious to mend his bridges with the papacy. The policy was popular. The hundreds of decrees aimed at drumming the Huguenots out of guilds, schools, the professions and public life, the prohibition of key elements of their religious practice itself, not to say the forced billeting of soldiers on those of their number who refused to convert – the so-called *dragonnades* – could not have been carried out without the zealous support of at least a significant part of the dominant population.[157] In turn, local violence – legal, physical and cultural – was encouraged. Indeed, when this policy, after several years of build-up, reached its culmination with the 1685 revocation of the Edict of Nantes and, with it, the outlawing of the Protestant faith in France, it signalled an open season for anybody wanting to attack Huguenot property, churches and cemeteries or to terrorise, torture, commit rape, or other atrocities, on Huguenots themselves. No significant state crisis had catalysed this policy. It was simply an agenda that demanded complete religious homogenisation. The consequences were as great as anything in the comparable Spanish assault on Jews and Moriscos. While thousands of Huguenots abjured, and thousands more tried to survive by going 'underground', a minimum of 200,000 – and possibly many hundreds of thousands more – fled into exile.[158]

But at least these refugees had somewhere to go. What was France's loss was others' gain; notably Brandenburg, the Netherlands, Britain and her north American colonies.[159] These countries were, of course, Protestant, but no longer exclusively, or at least, uniformly so. All increasingly displayed the ability to turn a blind eye to the existence of sectarians and Catholics in their midst. Even Jews, the key bell-wether of a country's practice of religious freedom, were to greater or lesser degrees, tolerated, though usually in quite small numbers. In all these cases, however, pragmatic considerations as to what these groups could contribute to the common weal – in the Huguenot case a great deal – largely overruled religious bigotries. There was no general English onslaught on *native* (as opposed to Gaelic) Catholics during the Jacobite scares of 1715 or 1745. More pointedly, in the American colonies, where adherence to the concept of religious freedom and to an ethos of individualistic self-help were in principle, if not always in practice, a *sine qua non* for entry and settlement, a wave of Huguenot refugees either succeeded or joined additional waves of Calvinists, Quakers and Catholics, or were themselves succeeded by significant numbers of Mennonites, Moravian Brethren, and other Christian sectaries, in search of a less perilous environment than that of traditional Europe.[160]

These positive developments would tend to suggest that diverse religious beliefs – at least religious beliefs on their own – by the mid- to late eighteenth century were, *contra* Louis XIV, no longer taken to be fundamentally destabilising threats to the political or social fabrics of the emerging, most advanced Western states. Indeed, the leading luminaries of this high Enlightenment era were working hard on how they might eliminate religion from the equation altogether. Nowhere was this more so, ironically, than in post-Louis XIV France. Here with Voltaire's vituperative and relentless attacks on the clergy as the chief obstacle to man's untrammelled progress, and Montesquieu's almost cultural relativist observations on the nature of other non-European societies, the French *philosophes* were very much in the van of an increasingly secularised way of thinking that looked forward to human fulfilment on the basis not of dogma or doctrine, but of reason. True, there was no consensus on how this critical tool of the scientific revolution would translate into an actual political or social agenda. All that essentially linked the *philosophes* together was the notion – belief might, ironically, be the more appropriate term – that the application of reason was the key to unlocking man's potential on earth. And that this, in turn, might at last genuinely enable him to make of it the best of all possible worlds.[161]

Certainly, there could be no obviously utilitarian role for an established Church in such a quest. But, by the same token, nor could their be a differentiation between men on the basis of their given culture, race or religious disposition. The implication was not only entirely universalistic, it was also – at least initially – markedly optimistic to the point of utopianism. Freed up from a received Church-sanctioned wisdom which began man's history at the point of his fall, the Enlightenment was in effect offering an alternative prelapsarian starting point in order to propose not only that men, all men, might be entitled to something better but that they might actually arrive there through a process – to use a very Enlightenment term – of their 'regeneration'. This could be to the point where, continuing with this *de rigueur* vocabulary, they might even become 'happy'.[162] Jefferson and his fellow drafters of the 1776 American Declaration of Independence, themselves deeply imbued with Enlightenment values, were famously besotted with the pursuit of happiness.

Their European counterparts were prone to use the term with equal abandon. In 1785, for instance, the prestigious Royal Society of Arts and Sciences in Metz announced an essay competition entitled 'Are there means for making the Jews happier and more useful in France?', a formulation which assumed a Jewish deficiency on both counts. The question might have been totally loaded but, at least by its own standards, it did start from the premise that the subject matter was redeemable. Like the gypsies, that other much despised 'out' group, Enlightenment thinking was full of schemes and stratagems that would recover their apparently dormant humanity from beneath their supposed waywardness and, thereby, return them to the social mainstream.[163]

This assumption that man's intrinsic natural humanity was what ultimately counted and that this represented the key to future human progress remained an important and recurring motif in Enlightenment thought. But it was the Genevan, Jean-Jacques Rousseau, that most problematic and arguably most significant member of its intellectual pantheon, whose development of the theme matters most. Rousseau was certainly not unusual in looking to the 'noble savage' of the Americas and elsewhere as his true model. But while actual 'savages' were being busily massacred by other Europeans, it was he who translated the argument that the Europeans were, in so doing, destroying their own single best hope into a form of political creed. It was, argued Rousseau, the men living in the most civilised societies who actually were the ones most shackled, enslaved and hence unhappy. Reversing the trend and thus putting them back on a path towards progress, happiness and so to human perfectibility required refinding not so much the natural condition possessed by the savage but certainly his natural liberty. If this was at the heart of Rousseau's 1755 *Discourse on the Origin of Inequality*, seven years later, in the *Social Contract*, he postulated how this might be practically applied to the issue of governance. Sovereignty in Rousseau's ideal state would be vested in the general will. In other words, in a situation where men freely and equally came together in the interests of the welfare of the entire community, they would act, accordingly, as one. By such a combination, Rousseau proposed, not only could men 'unify and control the forces already existing' but they could also create 'a totality of forces sufficient to overcome the obstacles resisting them, to direct their operation in a single impulse and make them act in unison'.[164]

Here was a very potent conception indeed. By operating through the general will, men might not only give their existence a meaningful social utility but take it forward towards something entirely better. A firm riposte to the entirely contrary and implicitly static notion propounded by the seventeenth-century English philosopher, Hobbes, that men were driven by the barbaric realities of nature (and the likelihood of their killing each other in it) to forego their sovereignty to a strong ruler who would keep the peace between them; Rousseau's proposition also suggested a strongly dynamic inference.[165] Implicitly, it looked forward to a sovereign state where the sum-total of the participants' unified actions would be greater than the sum of their individual parts. In other words, there would be significant material benefits accruing from everybody's participation in the general will. Yet Rousseau did not envisage a venal motive as the basis upon which his political community would work. On the contrary, for Rousseau (as also for the German Enlightenment philosopher, Kant), men would participate for ethical reasons: because they were enlightened moral beings. It was this ethical dimension, indeed, which would hold the general will together and prevent it from collapsing into discord and anarchy. Individuals who disagreed with aspects of the contract would demur to the majority because they would recognise that they had erred in their assessment of the wider communal interest. Because enlightened men were moral, it followed that their public actions would also be disinterested.

How they would arrive at this moral state of enlightenment in the first place, or, more cynically put, how they would leave aside their complex humanity to become consistent and hence one-dimensional altruists, is less discernible. From the commanding heights of the mid-twentieth century many commentators, notably Jacob Talmon, lambasted Rousseau's democratic vision as the authentic intellectual founding-stone for the century's great experiments in totalitarianism.[166] It is certainly disturbing that Rousseau's concept of a new, or more accurately, regenerated type of man, whose embrace of the general will would come out of his sense of communal public spiritedness, has more than a passing resemblance to Stalinist, fascist, Ba'athist and other dreams of monolithic conformity. But it is only so because of the vast irony involved. Rousseau's starting point, after all, is with the *individual* unbound; whose consequent immersion in public life is made possible through his – or her – personal liberation from feudal and ecclesiastical hierarchies, and with it from the weight of social conventions. It was the very consonance between these revolutionary ideas and the way they seemed to be acted out in practice, with the actual overthrow of the powers of Church and aristocracy, in August 1789, which made his vision so incredibly popular. It was not just Robespierre who went around clutching his copy of the *Social Contract* to his breast, endlessly spouting the merits of regeneration, civicness and virtue. Nor he alone who spoke of 'the general will' as if it were some 'tangible, visible object'.[167] Rousseau himself may have been dead eleven years but if anybody informed the great revolutionary slogan *liberté, égalité, fraternité*, it was he, just as he did the new National Assembly's first great act, the Declaration of the

Rights of Man and the Citizen, with its pronouncement of sovereignty in the people.

The Nation – By Way of Rousseau

The Declaration did something more to catapult Rousseauesque rhetoric onto an entirely new plane. When the author of the *Social Contract* wrote about the people as a collectivity he used the entirely abstract, unemotive, not to say rather clumsy term, 'general will'. Yet in the preamble to the Declaration this same idea appears in an altogether more intoxicating guise as 'la nation une et indivisible'. The term 'nation' is hardly present in the *Social Contract*, as one would perhaps expect from a restless cosmopolitan operating in an intellectual milieu whose other participants equally prided themselves on their own cosmopolitan or even internationalist credentials. Obversely, the notion of a more populist attachment to the nation – British, French, Dutch and so on – while not novel in its ability to elicit emotional or even mystical arousal, certainly up to this point lacked secure ideological underpinnings. In the Declaration, however, man's inalienable and sacred rights as derived Rousseau-like from his natural being are firmly bound to the social context – the nation – in which they make a collective sense.[168] This is demonstrated by a national assembly that goes on to create a national flag, a *fête nationale*, a national anthem, national cult, and so on.[169]

But if the nation is derived from nature and hence, in the words of another of its key revolutionary protagonists, the Abbé Sieyès, 'exists before all' and 'is the origin of everything'.[170] where are its boundaries and who exactly its members? The answer as given by another of the revolution's spokesmen, the Abbé Volfius, unfortunately brings us no closer to clarification. 'The true *patrie*', he declared, 'is the political community where all citizens, protected by the same laws, united by the same interests, enjoy the natural rights of man and participate in the common cause'.[171] Tautology aside, even the word nation is avoided here. Of course, this would be quite normal in the early phase of the revolution, the very term nationalism apparently not being used before its coinage by another abbé, Barruel, in 1798. However, if '*patrie*' with its connotations of native homeland or hearth offers a quite plausible localised setting for the enactment of a Rousseauesque sovereignty, the scaling up of that context to a territory the size and population of France would quickly make of Volfius' definition a thoroughly implausible proposition. Either Volfius had not taken into account the certainty that there would be multitudes of French inhabitants who would not share the interests of the revolution and so be unwilling to participate in the common cause, or he had turned a blind eye to this because he knew that to do otherwise would show up the contradictions in his formula. There is, of course, a further possibility; that Volfius could not bring himself to *imagine* that there might be groups of people who, looking the benefits of the nation squarely in the eye, might still choose to reject it.

Could such people exist? It was not just French revolutionaries who found such an idea almost incomprehensible. A few decades later, John Stuart Mill, the British political philosopher and stout defender of the rights of the individual, could write as follows:

> Nobody can suppose that it is not more beneficial for a Breton or a Basque of French Navarre to be ... a member of the French nationality admitted on equal terms to all the privileges of French citizenship ... than to sulk on his own rocks, the half-savage relic of past times revolving in his own little mental orbit, without participation or interest in the general movement of the world. The same remark applies to the Welshman or the Scottish highlander, as members of the British nation.[172]

Mill's comment is ominous on two accounts. First, is its strident linkage between the idea of the nation and progress. To cut oneself off from the latter by dint of some quirk of linguistic or cultural distinctiveness makes no sense. Indeed, Mill seems to be taking it for granted that groups who might arguably possess attributes enabling them to conceive of national self-determination in their own right should naturally – and voluntarily – forfeit this possibility because of their 'primitiveness' compared with, for instance, the more 'advanced' French or British mainstream. In other words, the loss of distinctiveness is the price worth paying if it means entry into modern civilisation. Yet Mill seems to be compounding the injury not only by implicitly accepting a territorial definition of the *patrie* founded on some process of state formation which precedes the ideology of nation but also one in which the practice of sovereignty must necessarily follow and be determined by its ethnically dominant group. Mill, of course, is not ruling out the right of participation for other groups. He is simply stating that this participation will be in already predetermined parameters.

A much more jaundiced awareness of the implications of such theorising are, however, offered by Lord Acton, another latter-day British commentator on the revolution, writing in 1862. Not only, in marked contradistinction to Mill, does Acton deny any benefits to be had from the French conception of nationality, but its 'fictious unity' – the general will – Acton claims to be only a cover with which to crush 'all natural rights and all established liberties for the purpose of vindicating itself.'[173] Even worse:

By making the State and the nation commensurate with each other in theory [nationality] reduces practically to a subject condition all other nationalities that may be within the boundary ... According, therefore, to the degree of humanity and civilisation in that dominant body which claims all the rights of the community, the inferior races are exterminated, or reduced to servitude, or put in a condition of dependence.[174]

In this discrepancy of opinion between the liberal Mill and the conservative Acton, we are thereby presented with some possible, basic contours of an ongoing dispute as to whether the ideology of nationalism is in itself responsible for – at the very least – the potentiality for genocide. For the optimistic but thoroughly utilitarian Mill, the general will is not the issue so much as the greater good, the danger to social or ethnic groups out of synchronisation with this general process being obviated by the essential beneficence of the project itself. By contrast, Acton's entirely pessimistic reading that nationalism is really about the overruling of diversity in favour of a state-determined uniformity can do no more than hope that the worst scenarios which may develop from this will be constrained by the 'humanity and civilisation' of those in charge. It is noticeable that both commentators, however, consider the most likely point of fracture within the ideologised nation-state to be with regard to its minority ethnic communities. This thus questions the degree to which any implied connection between nationalism and genocide brings us any closer to an explanation of what happened in the Vendée.

Assessing the Culpability of the French Revolution

A first plausible defence of the Rousseau-inspired protagonists of 1789 might be that what they were attempting to create was a new *conceptual* community, not an ethnic or racial one. In this sense, Acton's accusations against it, in so far as they relate to some attempt of a dominant group to subvert the liberties of a subordinate one, is no more nor less valid than for his own beloved hybrid British nationality. Indeed, the founders of modern France were, at least initially, much more overtly universalist and cosmopolitan in their actions than either their 1688 British, or 1776 American counterparts, and not least in the way that they rapidly conferred French citizenship on a small galaxy of foreign champions of liberty.[175] Having stated that, however, what is equally striking is that while the French revolutionary discourse appears to be all about the rights of the citizen, the framing of those rights are entirely embedded within the context of an already prescribed nation. Article III of the Declaration of the Rights of Man and Citizen reads: 'All sovereignty resides essentially in the

Nation. No body, no individual can exercise authority which does not explicitly emanate from it.' Article VI may go on to affirm the rights of the male (but not female) citizen to participate in the formation of the general will but again this is offset and arguably immediately nullified by the duty of each man to respect it.[176] Thus, if in the Volfius rendition of the 'true *patrie*' there is an implicit assumption not so much about the benefits of liberty as about the requirements of conformity, in the Declaration itself the civic obligations and duties of the individual to what is actually the nation-cum-state are quite explicit.

Again, there is nothing here, as Eric Hobsbawm approvingly has noted, to prevent or deny anyone living within the boundaries of France – whether Gascon, German-speaking Alsatian or Bordeaux Jew – from the full entitlement of their citizenship rights,[177] though one might add that the onus would now appear to be on each and every one of these to return the compliment by speaking, thinking, acting, dressing and generally conducting themselves as Frenchmen. A more coruscating assessment, doubtless echoing much of the sentiments of Lord Acton, however, is provided by Liah Greenfield. The real point, she proposes, is that, unlike in England, where the political culture genuinely started with the 'idea' of the individual, in France it is the other way round: 'the dignity of the whole that restored dignity to those who claimed membership in it ... The liberty of the nation that constituted freedom of the individuals ... the nation from which authority emanated, and empowered ... individuals.'[178]

Whether viewed positively or negatively, what one cannot avoid, however, is the extraordinary novelty of the revolution's conception of the state as a social organism. For centuries all Europeans, with the exception of Jews, Muslims and those who consciously put themselves beyond the pale as religious and social dissidents, had taken their cue for correct behavioural conduct, and its social meaning, primarily from the Church, with added gloss provided by the generally accepted dictates associated with their position within a class-based hierarchy. The primacy of the state in countries that had gone down the Protestant path had not fundamentally changed this situation except that such states henceforth more overtly delegated the task of socialisation and the values that went with it to their 'national' Churches. However, with the revolution's definitive dismantling of the old corporate society in France, by legal enactment, and with it the separation of Church from State (a process partial in its accomplishment on the former score, non-existent in its achievement on the latter in the much more evolutionary post-1688 British parallel), the historic *mediation* through which rulers enjoined social-cultural values as well as political-legal requirements upon the mass of the population simply disappeared. There was now simply 'state' and a mass of atomised individuals. If mediation between the two through aristocrat and curate had been made redundant at a stroke, arguably so had that which might alternatively operate either through extended family and kinship groups, or through regional and local power-brokers. These were, in other words, entirely uncharted waters. They were also ones, however, which gave to those with executive power an unprecedented and – because it was uncircumscribed by the idea of God – entirely arbitrary sanction with which to determine nationally whatever social norms and moral values they saw fit.

There is a further tremendous paradox here. For the previous two centuries conscious state-centralisers, either theorists of the ilk of Bodin and Hobbes, or practical exponents such as Louis XIV himself, had been denied the comprehensive achievement of their generally more limited political goals by these same intermediary powers which the revolution had now abolished. Yet, in doing so, those most earnest in proclaiming the blow as one struck for liberty were actually also the ones most critical in laying the groundwork for state centralism. We do not have to doubt their Jacobin, libertarian credentials, nor their self-exculpation as merely 'guides' (to use Rousseau's terminology), seeking to interpret the 'general will', to confirm this. Nor, even, at the high point of CPS rule, the sincerity of Robespierre's argument that this 'despotism of liberty' was an entirely ephemeral emergency measure.[179] Simply by acting out the notion of national sovereignty, the revolutionaries had stumbled upon a mechanism for social control far beyond the wildest dreams of *Ancien Régime* absolutists.

How far this was dependent on a conscious attempt to displace God in favour of an overtly secular religion of nationhood is not entirely material here. Jacobin revolutionary efforts to create a theistic Cult of the Supreme Being were not ultimately successful.[180] Nor was Christianity pronounced a traitor to be expelled from the nation, as happened with its sacred authority on earth, the king. That said, without Louis to fulfill the function, the idea of nation was henceforth clearly being offered not simply as an alternative 'source of identity and focus of social solidarity'[181] but itself as a sacred abstraction to be worshipped and obeyed. If, in this way, it followed that the nation had superseded religion as the organic gel binding society together and, as its alpha and omega, that which gave to its members a deep and spiritually profound meaning – even to the point of feelings of redemptive fulfilment – everything that *the state* did to turn this ideal into practice became not simply allowable but necessary.

But the other societal side to this equation is equally striking. Vast numbers of ordinary French inhabitants were not only drawn to this highly charged national proposition but were even willing to lay down their lives for it. How else could the revolution have mustered a grand *levée en masse*, a genuine people's army in double quick time, or, even after years of war and cannon-fodder depletion, still supported Napoleon's 1813 mobilisation to the tune of 1,300,000 men?[182] By this time, of course, bureaucratisation of the process had become well entrenched, while waning enthusiasm for relentless war, reflected in large numbers of deserters, suggested the degree to which state coercion was maintaining the myth of the nation-in-arms. There was, too, the fact that these were hardly normal conditions but one of sustained emergency – at its highpoint from the summer of 1792, when the Duke of Brunswick launched a combined Austro-Prussian army across the French border, through to the autumn of 1793, when the Vendéan insurrection was effectively parried – which could have resulted in the revolution's complete defeat and collapse. Yet the very fact that it did not fall apart owes everything to the hundreds of thousands of Parisian *sans-culottes* and their provincial *fédérés* prepared to rally to its defence and so back the Jacobin clubs most ready to take decisive, ruthless and dictatorial action on the nation's behalf. It was this shift to a more hard-line, radicalised interpretation of the revolution which in turn, of course, began tearing it apart in the wave of fratricidal killings of both 'Blue' and 'White' terror. That said, the sheer numbers who put their persons at the disposal of the CPS as impromptu, unpaid bureaucratic recruiters for its administrative and military efforts, as its policing, information-gathering and surveillance agents, and finally – in the form of the some 40,000 cadres in the hastily organised *armée revolutionaire* – as enforcers of 'the Maximum', expropriators of hoarded food and general harriers of anyone considered guilty of *incivisme*, lend credence to the proposition that the drive towards the accumulation of dictatorial state powers was carried forward with much demotic acclaim.[183]

In other words, willingness to up the ante and support more radical measures came because enough people saw the revolution as *theirs*. It was their *ça ira*, their *Marseillaise*, their *patrie*. For those who felt this way, the revolution was indistinguishable from the 'nation'. Nor can those who identified with it and became its most fervent protagonists be simply dismissed – as nineteenth-century detractors such as Taine would have it – as some amorphous crowd of bloodthirsty scum, criminals and hooligans. They were by and large respectable, often self-employed if not middle class, literate and politically committed,[184] the very social types who, beyond France, would be the standard purveyors of the national idea in their own countries. This, of course, makes our French prototypes no less capable of mass atrocity and killing. In the heightened climate of near-hysteria and panic following the Duke of Brunswick's dire warnings to take 'exemplary and eternally memorable revenge' on the revolutionary populace should his forces be opposed, or harm come to the French royal family, it was the revolutionaries, in September 1792, who unleashed a first great wave of reactive, grass-roots massacres. Collective 'enemies of the people' could be as much determined and assaulted by those who believed themselves to be the quintessential people-nation as their elite guides.[185]

Even then, Acton's later fears that it would be ethnic groups who would be most vulnerable to the new national equation were neither borne out at this point, nor at any significant juncture in the ongoing process of French nation-state formation. Basques, Bretons or Alsatians, were neither specific targets of demotic revolutionary violence, nor excluded, at the legislative level, from the embrace of citizenship. True to its conceptual foundations, the new France, instead, demanded their loyalty through linguistic and cultural assimilation. The same was also true for the c.40,000 Jews residing in France, the vote by the National Assembly, in September 1791, favouring their emancipation appearing to dramatically confirm the sincerity of the revolution's universalist credentials.[186]

Perhaps, however, we can discern an important caveat for the future here. French Jewish emancipation was a first in European history. But the manner in which it actually came about was suggestive of an emerging grey zone in the theory of nationalism. Not only was this evident in the very fact that Jewish citizenship had to be debated at all, rather than being conferred automatically according to the logic of the Assembly's own Declaration of Rights but in the equally glaring anomaly that some Jews were considered more acceptable as citizens than others, the already highly assimilated Sephardi Jews of the Bordeaux area receiving full rights in advance of, and with much less fuss than the much larger number of their ethnographically quite distinct Ashkenazi brethren in Alsace. Similarly, while the Jews' loss of their traditional corporate status was arguably quite consistent with a revolutionary agenda to make every citizen equal before the law,[187] the attempt by Napoleon, more than a decade later, to apply specific, utterly exceptional, and actually highly coercive conditions on the terms of that citizenship contradicted this logic entirely. The proposals, submitted to two bodies of Jewish lay and rabbinical leaders, convened at the emperor's pleasure, in 1806 and 1807, were, in effect, a recipe for the biological dissolution of French Jewry, quite blatantly so in the unrealised proposal that for every two endogamous marriages in the community there should be one intermarriage. These efforts were followed up, in 1808, with a further series of decrees requiring Jews to take French rather than Hebraic names, to submit compulsorily to military service – other Frenchmen could provide a replacement – and most significantly of all, in placing a series of

quite focused geographical and occupational restrictions on the Alsatian element, greatly impeding their freedom of movement and ability to make a
living. By these means, the national state was in effect signalling that ethnicity
could be an impediment to full inclusion in it when linked to social norms of
acceptable or desirable behaviour, as determined by itself. The point was hammered home in further directives requiring local authorities to screen Jews and
provide statistics on the incidence of usury (sic.) and begging among them.[188]

What exactly, then, were the ground rules for those who would be
embraced within the nation, or left out, or for that matter held at arms length,
if not ultimately ejected? If citizenship could be qualified for sections of the
indigenous population on the grounds that that they were failing to live up to
the expectations placed upon them with respect to the general will, actual foreigners might find their position even more precarious. In the scare climate of
1792–3 the cosmopolitan embrace of the outsider rapidly gave way to feelings
of intense suspicion and xenophobia. There was no doubt that much of this
charged atmosphere emanated from the projected fears and anxieties of ordinary people. What matters here is the way the CPS seized upon them in its
first great tranche of repressive legislation in March 1793, to confirm the status of foreign residents as definitively beyond the national pale. True,
foreigners were given the opportunity to be cross-examined by a *comité de surveillance* in whichever town they lived and, where they succeeded in convincing
it of their civic virtue and loyalty to France, to remain rather than be banished;
but not without a price. Government measures, even though not widely
applied, demanded that these lucky ones wear an armband on which the name
of their country would be inscribed, together with the word 'hospitality'.[189]
The precedent was an ominous one and not just for its resonances of the yellow star Jews in Nazi-occupied Europe would later be required to exhibit on
their clothing. Nearly eighty years after the revolution, at the outset of the
Franco-Prussian war, 80,000 Germans living in France would practically all be
expelled.[190] The CPS again had not only stumbled across an instrument for
determining who was in and who was 'outside' the confines of the nation but
more pointedly had found a very serviceable implement with which future
governments might stoke the fires of popular anxiety and animosity against
the 'outsider'.

The problem was that, once started down this route, the new nation-state
model was well positioned to embrace in its 'patriotic' anger almost any category of person that it chose, whether living within or without the country. Or
the state could simply invent such categories. The surveillance committees
were, after all, empowered to investigate *anybody* suspected of malice against
the regime, whether foreigner, emigré, aristocrat or other citizen. But what

exactly constituted malice, or sabotage, or the undermining of morale – all attributes which supposedly linked these alleged fifth columnists to foreign, royalist or other emigré conspiracies – remained a matter only for the regime's determination, albeit aided by a demotic voice emanating from the Parisian sections and Jacobin and Cordelier clubs. Yet, when these latter *enragés* took it upon themselves to storm the prisons in Paris and elsewhere in September 1792, in search of 'Austrians in French dress',[191] their revolutionary fury was hardly limited to *political* suspects alone. Indeed, some 70 per cent of the esti-mated 1,400 people massacred in the Parisian prisons in this five-day period – more died outside and beyond the metropolis – were 'common thieves, prosti-tutes, forgers, vagrants and the like'.[192] In other words, their victimhood had nothing to do with any supposed counter-revolutionary potential they pos-sessed but was entirely a function of their *social* marginality.

How convenient, suggests the historian Brian Singer, to have this petty criminal underclass with 'no clear place within the social order' as the revolu-tion's eternal scapegoats.[193] But if the rough justice meted out against them highlights the way in which popular frustrations and anxieties in times of crisis are often directed against those deemed socially undesirable, deviant, or disor-dered, the Jacobin regime – once, in the wake of the September massacres, it had taken a firm, formal and monopolising grip on the execution of state vio-lence – did not shrink from both recasting and broadening such 'outsider' categories as if they were political. A year on, in September 1793, for instance, at the apotheosis of the counter-revolutionary moment, it 'declared suspect all who had befriended tyranny, federalism and counter-revolution by deed, word or by way of personal relations'.[194] Superficially, this decision might appear as if the regime's quarrel was only with genuine political adversaries. The only problem was that by this time anybody who did not agree with it, or failed to identify with its values, was effectively beyond the law and so outside the nation. As Tallien, an apostate from radical Jacobinism, caustically quipped: 'the only foreigners in France are bad citizens'.[195] Worse, the fact that the decree implicated families or, indeed, anybody connected by social or sexual contact with the accused, effectively reified the opposition into a biological monolith.

*

Finally this brings us back to the Vendée. There was no doubt that a sizeable portion of Vendéans had risen against the regime, or approved of the rising, at a juncture when the CPS could justifiably claim that *la patrie* was in genuine danger. In this sense, the insurrection was an act of collective treason which could expect in return no more mercy from the state than that of any previous regional or peasant revolt. But then what made the Jacobin response to the Vendée so quantitatively and qualitatively different from all of these? How was it that the commonplace and vicious brutality that we normally associate with the retributive quelling of insurrection in pre-modern Europe was translated here into a policy agenda of *unlimited* elimination?

Partly, as has been suggested, it was grounded in circumstances of sustained state and societal emergency associated with 'total' war. Straining all its resources and manpower to parry the political-military threat on its frontiers, the revolutionary French state was hardly going to negotiate with those consciously intent on wrecking its foundations from within. If the Jacobin response to the Vendée's insubordination should be treated, therefore, as an archetype of modern genocide, it is not because the state in this instance had nothing to fear from its peasant adversaries; nor because, as with Nazis versus Jews or Roma, the perceived threat was essentially a product of a fevered, collective imagination but rather, for exactly the opposite reason. The 'cumulative radicalisation' of the Jacobin response was in key respects a direct product of the very ongoing and successful resistance which the Vendée offered. Completely outside Parisian authority throughout the high summer months and into the autumn of 1793, there was nothing more the Jacobin state could fear than that the insurrectionist region would survive long enough for its example to be replicated elsewhere, in a second Vendée. Here, then, was not only its spur towards 'getting its retaliation in' before it was too late but an incitement to accelerate towards the finishing line, as a stark 'never again' warning to other recalcitrant regions who might be minded to do the same. No wonder, given all the other challenges which were stacked against it at this juncture, that this crisis-ridden regime began exhibiting not simply frantic but overtly paranoid behaviour towards the scratch peasant-people army pitted against it. No surprise, either, that its frustrations at the nature of this War Type Three dynamic were, by degrees, translated into something all the more unforgiving and geared towards retribution for retribution's sake.

Having said this, however, putting the onus for what happened in the Vendée, on those, who, when all is said and done, were its victims, is not simply unsatisfactory, it is incomplete. It may sound entirely paradoxical to say that the Vendée became the *Vendée-vengée* – the revenged Vendée – at least in part because of the idea of the revolution itself. But let us remind ourselves of the principled aspiration at its very heart. The protagonists of 1789 had wanted to unshackle all men from what they saw as the tyranny of hierarchy, embedded in the *Ancien Régime,* in order to make men's lives happier and more fulfilled. There was certainly no exact programme as to how this was to be accomplished – even its most coherent pursuit in the little more than a year of Jacobin emergency lacked anything akin to a blueprint. Nevertheless, a practical implementation of the universalist ideals of the Enlightenment was – whether one was Jacobin or Girondin, Brissotin or Hébertist – the revolutionaries' common goal. What they equally expected in return from the people of France was gratitude. This, after all, in their eyes was the road not only to the betterment of the French condition but the signpost to the regeneration of all mankind. One, indeed, in which Frenchmen themselves would be honoured as essential bearers of a *mission civilisatrice*. What they received, instead, from the Vendéans, was not simply an ingratitude in the face of this momentous opportunity but a desire to revert to their former condition. A desire demonstrated in the most passionate and violent terms.

From the revolutionary perspective, therefore, Vendéan contumacy was not simply the most outrageous *incivisme*, it flew in the face of reason. It followed that the Vendéans' behaviour was deeply and disturbingly unnatural; and hence unnational. Their guilt on this score was proven, chapter and verse, by the way they had put themselves at the disposal of the party of the executed king, a king who had transgressed against the nation by aligning himself with foreign powers. Outside nation, outside nature; his legal execution by the sovereign people's appointed guardians was, proclaimed Robespierre, not simply 'a measure of public safety', but 'an act of *providence nationale*. Louis must die because *la patrie* must live'.[196] But if this was now the ultimate higher good, then, by the same token the Vendéan attempt to overturn the follow-through and with it to negate the very sacrifices which the revolution felt it had made on the people-nation's behalf, became the ultimate act of wickedness.

Again, to posit that underlying the revolutionaries' rationalisations for their actions in the Vendée was an inherent Manichaeism may sound not simply preposterous but even grotesque when the Jacobin regime was so clearly and earnestly attempting to divorce the political – and social – life of France from religious strictures. It was the Vendéans, after all, who had self-consciously fashioned themselves into a crusading army, acting on behalf of Christ's kingdom, against an ungodly and vile aberration of a republic. On this level, the inversion, if not complete collapse of the traditional norm, where state authorities came to the assistance of religious orthodoxy against the deviant or dissenting, is itself noteworthy. But to what extent was the revolution, still perhaps unknowingly, playing according to these same ground rules, simply under the guise of a terrestial millenarianism? One perceptive recent commentator thinks this is the exactly the case. 'The revolution', suggests Frederic Cople Jaher, 'substituted the nation for the body of Christ as the fundamental affiliation of the French people. Citizenship, not Christianity, determined membership of the civic nation'.[197] As a result the term Anti-Christ may be missing from the Jacobin charge-sheet against the Vendéans. But the sense that, in willingly allying themselves with the king's party, they had been transmuted into a cohort of demons ranged aganst the forces of light, is fairly unmistakable. The only essential difference was that their irredeemable blasphemy and sin was against a man-made millennium whose ritual was that of the 'cult of reason', whose incantation had become 'progress', and whose sacred text none other than Rousseau's *Social Contract*.

Is this, then, simply proof that nothing had really, fundamentally, changed? That the revolution for all its innovation could not but restate *Christian* Europe's embedded tendencies towards individualism on the one hand, social and cultural conformity on the other? Yet clearly this will not suffice. Something had fundamentally changed. There could be no going back to religious sanction as the authoritative foundations of the sovereign state. The state's legitimacy now rested on man, and man's reason, not God or faith. But in that case, what moral restraints prevented its national political leadership from doing whatever they saw fit? Priests and prior rules were finished with. Society, in effect, had become a tabula rasa to be moulded and manipulated to whatever greater good the new breed of secular millenarian prophets demanded of it. And if a group of people within the territorial boundaries of this national sovereign entity were found to be wanting, or to have transgressed against its higher goals, or, worst of all, rejected its basic tenets, what *in principle* now prevented their complete eradication? Pity? Clearly not in the case of the Vendée.

It returns us to our fundamental paradox. The French Revolution was the paradigmatic shift in the emergence of the modern world. It brought human rights, citizenship, and a new civic framework for the law. Alongside 1688 and 1776, it was the starting point for liberalism, parliamentarianism and democracy; ideals to which millions of people would subsequently rally. Though ultimately few would willingly lay down their lives for these abstract notions, let alone the legal and political institutions which were built upon them, they would for the underpinning idea: the idea of the nation. The cunning of the revolution had been to give vast numbers of French men – and women – regardless of their class background, a sense of a self-consciously equal and fraternal belonging. It had done so by redefining sovereignty as vested in themselves, appearing in the process to make the *feeling* commensurate and compatible with the *institution* of an already pre-existent state. That sense of nation–state oneness could only be enhanced by the conditions of relentless crisis in which it was forged, the external military threat ramming home the message that Frenchmen were all in this together, equally sharing in the burden and sacrifice of national service. But, by the same token, this image of a societal organism with 'a single, smooth surface'[198] could have no room for regional or local difference. There were no special cases where religious practice, or cultural idiosyncrasy could merit exemption.

Above all, there could be no polite indifference to any collectivity which begged to differ with the prescript or, worse, acted on this, by putting itself outside or beyond the authority of the national state. Unlike with Christian Europe, where the possibility of return to the fold was always implicit in a forgiving script for the heterodox or deviant – and where even admission into the fold was in principle available for the infidel Muslim or the Jew – the example of the Vendée seemed to point instead towards a new secular order, where persistent, collective disobedience in the face of state diktat could only be answered in the most absolute and zero-sum of terms.

4. The French Model, its Discontents and Contenders

The New Dispensation

The French Revolution had created the essential model for the new type of modern state that would come to proliferate around the entire globe. Centralised organisation and standardisation were of its essence. Implicitly, if not explicitly, the prescription was coercive. Long-term sustainability, therefore, could only be bought by making the population, or at least the majority of them, feel that they were part of it. The carrot was nationalism.

Two elements specifically arising from this model are important for our broader discussion here. The first relates to the direct experience in which the Gallic nation-state was forged. Simon Schama has called it a 'militarised nationalism'.[1] Twenty-three years of almost perpetual war by the French against most of the rest of the European state family had demanded a controlled and efficient mobilisation, coordination and planning of manpower resources as never before. Of course, this was far from being entirely novel. The repeated, often persistent warfare between European states under the *Ancien Régime* had already ensured high levels of state militarisation and bureaucratisation. But the degree to which the new French model, operating from a base line of fiscal and social collapse in 1789, was dependent upon the *equalisation* of its citizenry, can hardly be overemphasised, most obviously in terms of the *levée en masse*, in order to sustain its war effort and survival.

If the external threat to the existence of a sovereign France was the primary catalyst to its truly national formation, the problem here, however, is that it was the French state, rather than the French nation, whose interests were most likely to be advanced by these contingencies. A much increased bureaucracy – from 50,000 administrators at the outset of the emergency to something in the region of a quarter of a million at its Napoleonic end[2] – was one result. But the imperative to fight and win total wars over such prolonged periods effectively ushered in not just a limitless bureaucrat's dream but also one for technocrats too; what William H. McNeill refers to as to the creation of 'a command technology',[3] aimed at the production and delivery of the most up-to-date weaponry and ordnance. Even then, without rapid communications linking up the metropolis to its outlying regions and borders, advanced military hardware was as good as useless. War, or the threat of it, provided the primary stimulus towards the infrastructural modernisation of France which – within a century – would see the country criss-crossed by standardised railways, roads, docks, bridges, postal services and, as it came on stream, telegraphic communications. Legal, fiscal and administrative harmonisation all fell in line behind these state imperatives.

Almost without realising what it was doing, France had set in motion the prototypical engine for rapid development which any society determined to survive in the modern world would be required to follow. Certainly, an industrially revolutionising Britain was already much ahead of France, according to economic wisdoms of a more laissez-faire variety. The USA, too, with a constructed political space geared towards enabling unfettered exploitation of human and natural resources in entrepreneurial interests, was equally focused on capital formation as the appropriate bedrock for a massive industrial take-off. If France, ultimately, was more *dirigiste*, more interventionist than either of these, it was in part because it had much more ground to make up. All three states, moreover, had suffered bruising military encounters with either, or both, other parties in the high revolutionary years. None was likely to ignore the close inter-relationship between economic modernisation and state security. What made France different, was that it was very much the political preconditions of state-formation, from the 1790s, which provided it with the wherewithal to target state expenditure on infrastructural overhaul in the following generations. If in terms of relative economic output it lagged behind the other two,[4] there is no doubt that in terms of coherence and system, France took its place alongside Britain and the United States as an advanced Western polity, and, as such, as 'a reference society' for how to undertake the transition to modernity.[5]

If this, certainly, was the assessment of outsider commentators, on the one hand keen to tap the source of the West's accelerating industrial and military power and, on the other, alarmed at the prospect of their own societies falling prey to it, there still remained an enigma. How did all this change not simply tear the social fabric apart? Caustically, one might argue that in the drive to empower the state there was precious little room for ordinary people. Far from liberating them, it intruded far more into the private domain than it had ever done under the *Ancien Régime*. Indeed, a whole tier of state-created institutions

– prisons, police, hospitals, asylums and so on – which we particularly associate with advancing nineteenth-century polities, as most devastatingly examined in the work of Michel Foucault, were transparent state attempts to socialise the majority or 'sequester' those who deviated from its norms.[6]

The conundrum would seem to be answered in the continuing efforts of Western leaderships, the French again in the van, towards coaxing, cajoling and inculcating into their populations the notion that the state was not really the issue at all but the nation. They – the people – were the nation, it belonged to them, indeed within it they were all one united being. 'In a free people language is one and the same for all', pronounced the CPS in 1794, in one early, apparently innocuous, not to say beneficent, example of the state's programmatic agenda.[7] It might, in practice, take more than a century to have the 90 per cent of mostly peasant dialect-speakers literate in a standard French,[8] but this linguistic homogeneity in the long run mattered far more in the nationalisation stakes than any attempt to create a uniform but impersonal legal code or, even in terms of state employment, the hundreds of thousands of bureaucrats to administer it. It brings us to our second point about the nation-cum-state model. From the time of the revolution onwards, the French state genuinely worked hard at the encapsulation of all its members, with a ubiquitous curriculum of education as its most critical and effective instrument. By bringing a standardised, text-book French – and so with it all the symbolic paraphernalia of revolution, culture and history – into a compulsory classroom, generations of French children would be emotionally swept up in the feeling of national belonging as if it were perfectly normal and natural. It was enough for the Arab commentator Rifa'ah Rafi al-Tahtawi, living in Paris and other European capitals throughout much of the 1830s and 1840s, to pronounce that the source of Western 'progress and strength' lay not in their technological and entrepreneurial achievements *per se* but in their patriotism. If only his own society could grasp this instrument, he postulated, it would be the 'means to overcome the gap between the lands of Islam and Europe'.[9]

However, if other societies were prepared to buy into this potential, does this mean they were prepared to ignore its dark implications? To call the French model 'totalitarian' might be to blur the distinction with twentieth-century police states. Nevertheless, its agenda was certainly 'totalising' in its intent. Moreover, how could one avoid or ignore its consequences in the Vendée, that part of France which had refused encapsulation?

European Consequences – Especially German

There is, of course, one plausible rejoinder, the implication of which would be to repudiate the problem. That is, treat the Vendée as an aberration. Thus, rather than being a critical watershed in the emergence of modern genocide, we might view the events of 1793–4 as an isolated one-off occurrence, in a remote region of France, brought about by quite extraordinary, contingent events and without any obvious parallels in contemporary history. Or, perhaps, on a slightly different tack, accept that, while the Vendée is representative of a transitional phase in European history, it is not in itself indicative of some more deep-seated relationship between modernity *per se* and mass violence.[10] Such an approach would be supported by the fact that no genocide occurred on the European continent for at least a century and a quarter after the Vendée. Even then, similarities to Nazi exterminations of Jews, Roma, and others, are not easy to discern. Nor is comparison with the Stalinist destruction of peasant populations from the late 1920s onwards, particularly self-evident given that the Jacobin onslaught on the 'peasant' Vendée left France's rural majority not only largely undisturbed but long-term beneficiaries of the revolution. One might carry the counter-charge a stage further by noting that even when it came to ethnic populations, the inclusivity of liberal notions of citizenship strongly militated against genocidal outcomes either in France itself or in countries that adopted its nationalising formula. The result might be strong tendencies towards the enforced assimilation of minority populations but no evidence of exterminatory agendas beyond that. The fact that in the most obvious test of this trajectory, namely the nineteenth-century process of Jewish emancipation in western and central European countries, such enactments were met by the vast majority of recipients with a fervent determination to acculturate to national norms, values and loyalties, would seem to highlight not the coercive aspects of the nation-state project at all but rather, *à la* Mill, the social and economic benefits that it conferred.[11]

Of course, one should be wary of inferring a general rule from a single example. More pointedly, by the 1870s or early 1880s, the Jewish case could hardly be taken as an untroubled and conflict-free process of absorption. Even in France, where encapsulation appeared to be already well advanced and where the Jewish population was a mere 0.2 per cent of the whole, an emerging wave of popular anti-Semitism found voice in the press and new political movements before it finally exploded into the Dreyfus affair, the major *cause célèbre* of the 1890s.[12] If then we take, as many political commentators do, the increasingly precarious Jewish situation in Western societies as a bell-wether of their more general health,[13] then the sanguine view that European national development, emanating from the French revolutionary experience, lacked either an inbuilt or long-term toxicity, may require some cautious re-evaluation. Certainly, we can say, without proviso, that the nineteenth-century creation of additional nation-states in western and central Europe did not produce any single example of a descent into acute genocidal process or genocide. Yet all that may tell us is that the potentiality remained latent and that all it required was the conditions associated with another massive crisis, such as that produced by the First World War, to become manifest. Nor did this preclude knock-on effects of the gathering pre-1914 storm being exported elsewhere – with a series of genocidal, or other mass exterminatory outcomes – as we will consider in the next chapter.

Nevertheless, the very fact that the Vendée was succeeded by a long absence of genocide in Europe would seem to demand – not unlike that other *longue durée* of historiographical consideration, 'the long eighteenth century' preceding the French Revolution – an explanation as to how it is that political and socio-economic conditions can both keep a tendency in check, yet, on the other hand, ensure that it does not go away. Closely linked to this is a need to explore what happened to the French revolutionary idea of the nation itself. There is no basic mystery on this latter score. Over the course of the next century, as it was adopted by other societies, the idea underwent a series of mutations into more virulent forms. En route, it also faced two key ideological challenges, one in the form of racism, which practically threatened to take it over, lock, stock and barrel, while another, Marxism, to a greater or lesser degree, sought to subvert its basic premise. However, the very fact that these challenges had the opportunity to emerge in a long period of tumultuous change *yet* precarious stability, would also seem to underscore that any attention to the domestic situation in specific countries cannot be divorced from the wider international framework of the post-revolutionary epoch. Indeed, the retardation of Europe's general drive to nation-statehood after 1815, may hold the key to both its avoidance of genocide in the nineteenth century, and its catastrophic impact on the twentieth.

*

The eventual defeat of Napoleon Bonaparte, by the sixth European coalition of counter-revolutionary powers, certainly stymied all incipient and actual moves to create a series of nation-states in the French image. From the Congress of Vienna in 1815 through to the Italian war of 1859 – in which another Bonaparte, Louis Napoleon, led a renewed French military challenge to the settlement's chief Habsburg beneficiaries – the concert of European powers successfully held in check major territorial shifts while also, at least in part, turning the political and cultural clock back to the clergy-backed absolutism of the *Ancien Régime*. This is highly significant on two accounts.

In the first place, it left Central European bourgeois elites – the people who had been most aroused and enthused by the impact of the national idea during the years of French revolutionary sway – politically high and dry. Whether francophile or francophobe in their reactions to Napoleonic dominance, their sense of empowerment and participation in the affairs of community and state, which the revolutionary interregnum had made possible, was, after 1815, seriously closed off. This was not in itself disastrous. For the next three decades, the suppression of liberal ideas, press and comment by authoritarian regimes taking their cue from the arch-conservative Austrian chancellor, Metternich, also acted as goad for the perpetuation of radical and necessarily revolutionary oppositions.[14] Their moment finally came in 1848. This 'springtime of nations', when the spirit of the French Revolution converged with demands for national self-determination across the face of Central Europe, clearly marked a critical watershed in Europe's political recasting. But this was at least as much because, in immediate terms, these revolutions all failed. The result was that not only were German and Italian unification, in particular, held up for another critical ten, if not twenty years, but when these processes did finally come to fruition it was neither with liberal nationalists genuinely at the helm, nor according to a script obviously based on their understanding of national self-determination. True, the sense of being onlookers rather than protagonists was softened in the Italian case both by the exploits of the republican Garibaldi and by the ascendancy of the liberal moderniser, Cavour, in Piedmont-Savoy. But this could neither disguise that what took place, after 1861, was monarchist Piedmont's statist absorption rather than national consolidation of most of the rest of the Italian peninsula, while leaving outside the new polity significant Italian-speaking populations still within the Habsburg domains.[15]

The consequences of this lack of synchronicity between state and nation formation would be serious and long-lasting enough in the Italian case. They would be altogether more pronounced and profound in Germany. Its part-amalgamation, albeit with the title of German 'reich' under the aegis of a traditionally reactionary and authoritarian Prussian Hohenzollern dynasty, for a start – in an ironic inversion of Italian unification – left out all the German speakers under Austrian Habsburg rule. This exclusion was, historically, all the more idiosyncratic when one considers that the Habsburgs had for centuries been the one point of continuity around which a dense patchwork of independent medium, small, or Lilliputian German polities had been figuratively held together under the virtual reality of the Holy Roman empire.[16] When this had been finally dissolved, at the 1815 Congress, in favour of a somewhat more compact thirty-eight-unit German confederation, the fulcrum of power still firmly resided with Catholic Vienna, not Protestant Berlin. The whole complex mid-century dance of ruthless *realpolitik,* by which Bismarck wrested Austrian power in the Confederation to the Prussian interest, was to culminate in the war of 1866 and, thereby, to the creation of a 'lesser' Germany minus Austria. The latter's own search for territorial compensation, in the form of eastern imperial aggrandisement, was a displacement from this sequence of events of some pertinence to the final chapter of this volume. Meanwhile, Bismarck's further recourse to Clausewitzian war against France, not least in order to bludgeon the remaining notionally autonomous south German states into Prussian subservience, confirmed the new *kleindeutsch,* federal but otherwise definitively Berlin-dominated prescript. If this was supposed to be a nation-state, it was categorically not one either founded on some pre-existing political entity, as in France, or one made holy again by some mimetic revolutionary conjuring trick involving notions of popular sovereignty or the general will. On the contrary, whereas post-1789 France presented a polity where nation and state were conceptually fused, the post-1871 German situation was one where an 'imagined community of nationhood and the institutional realities of statehood were sharply distinct'.[17] To add insult to injury – for avowed nationalists – the discrepancy would be hammered home in forthcoming years by Bismarck's repeated refusal to be guided by any specifically national intentions in the pursuit of state policy, or any attempt to 'rationalise government actions through a coherent ideological commitment to the overriding legitimacy of national sovereignty'.[18]

As has been cogently and persuasively argued, by David Blackbourn and Geoff Eley, none of this, in itself, provides grounds for assuming a peculiarly distorted path to German development, or that the place of the bourgeoisie – the core 'national' class within it – was notably weak compared with other 'reference' Western societies. Far from being in thrall to Junker aristocrats, and super-industrial magnates, the middle classes undoubtedly helped mould a pre-1914 German culture which was brimming over with musical and literary societies, learned institutes, gymnastic and sporting clubs, with a refined sense of itself as a *Rechtsstaat* – a society founded on the rule of law – and with an educational excellence the envy of the world.[19] Equally robust in the parliamentary arena, the liberal tendency hardly crumpled in the face of reactionary challenges. For all its implicitly anti-democratic statism and militaristic superstructure, imperial Germany presented a complex, highly sophisticated and, as another commentator has put it, plural and polymorphous state, albeit in critical respects both very similar and very different to Britain, or France.[20] That said, at the bottom line, one might equally, persuasively argue for an essential congruity of modern *state* formation between at least Germany and France. Both ultimately were products of politically organised military mobilisations in the face of major inter-state conflicts, and both attempted to give to their peoples, through this prism, a heightened sense of who they were, and who they were not. Moreover, if, in the German case, this was all grist to the Hegelian notion that the individual's highest duty was to sacrifice *himself* in the collective national struggle forged in war, this was hardly more than what was expected of Frenchmen under Napoleon, while the insistence of Prussia's leading latter-day theoretician, Marshal von der Goltz, that the German army itself should be 'the school for the nation', was again little more than an articulation of what the French had been doing on this score since the 1790s.[21]

Yet, there was a difference. Unconditional subservience to the diktats of a Prussian, aristocratic-led army of the Reich was not entirely the same thing as service within a French military suffused with the memory (albeit false in the case of the Vendée) of the revolutionary and universalist *levée en masse*. However robust and heterogeneous imperial Germany's civic life may have been, it could not claim these same legitimising national credentials. To what extent the crucial moment of blocking off was 1871, or 1848, or earlier still may depend, of course, on the degree to which one is seeking some deeper historical clue to the origins of Nazism. Whether, as with Liah Greenfield, the clue lies with particular eighteenth-century frustrations of the 'educated class', the *Bildungsbürgertum* and the nationalisation of their *ressentiment* at the impact of Napoleonic occupation, or, as with Fritz Stern, in some peculiarly virulent strand of cultural pessimism brought about by a horror of encroaching materialist modernity,[22] the ongoing mismatch between the idea of the nation and the reality of the state – however difficult it may be at times to quantify – is nevertheless a fundamental feature of Germany's late nineteenth-century cultural baggage. As articulated by Theodor Georgii, president of the influential gymnasts' movement, there was, on the one hand, 'the German empire of our *hopes* and *dreams*' and, on the other, 'the *real* German empire'.[23]

Certainly, the discrepancy itself is built entirely around a paradox. What was created by a coalescence of political, economic and military factors in 1871, after all, was an extremely powerful state at the heart of Europe. Yet it was one that, from the perspective of the nation, could only be perceived as something artificial, unfinished, not to say completely unanchored in any deeper cultural or historical unity.[24] Some commentators, such as Stern, have read into this an estrangement on the part of much of the educated class, amounting to a conscious turning away from the political arena into a much more interior world.[25] This is debatable. There is little or no evidence of a post-1871 flight from public life and certainly not the degree of alienation which dogged the post-1918 Weimar republic. But erstwhile liberals were undoubtedly left with a bitter aftertaste of unfulfilled potential. It was a grudge that ran all the deeper because of its apparent implications for the country's long-term future in the broader world.

This, however, brings us to our second point about the long-term geopolitical significance of the 1815 settlement. Could it be that German cultural and national anxieties of the late nineteenth -century period only really make sense within the context of Germany's arrested political and economic trajectory as against the more general nineteenth-century rise of the West? Or, to put it more bluntly, was it the fact that Germany had arrived late? The span of one, or possibly two whole generations when she 'might have been' were the same critical period when the premier league of nation-states, Britain, France and the United States had been taking good advantage of their early arrival to make their most dramatic leaps forward on the world stage. By the 1850s, Britain's supremacy as the industrial 'workshop of the world', was acknowledged everywhere. All the world wanted British goods, so all the world had to bend to Britain's economic philosophy of laissez-faire, or what the Germans called *Manchestertum*. The French, not to be outdone, were also industrialising rapidly. Certainly, there was no foreseeable chance of their overtaking the British. But what they lacked in this department they were more than prepared to make up for in terms of military punch. With Louis Napoleon at the helm, the middle years of the century, indeed, looked set for a repeat of recent Gallic dominance not only in Europe but also in significant other parts of the globe. At least the United States seemed to lack such imperial ambitions and, anyway, for four critical years from 1861 to 1865, was both absorbed and hobbled by its own spectacular civil war brought on by the secession of its southern states. But this brief interregnum only heightened the degree to which a post-bellum America would, in the sheer momentum of its modernising surge, have the profoundest impact of all on the German and broader European condition. With its interior opened up – by, as we have seen, repeated recourse to genocide – fuelling in turn the basis for a massive commodification of its combined agricultural product, an entirely market-driven economy was both positioned, and, through technological advance in shipping, capable of dramatically undercutting the Europeans with goods which they had traditionally grown or produced themselves.[26]

Objectively speaking, of course, none of this should have mattered one iota to the new post-1871 Germany. Indeed, the initial industrial gap between

Germany and the frontrunners may have actually proved beneficial as, reaching nation-statehood on the cusp of a new wave of technological breakthroughs, Germany was able to respond with injections of capital and labour not so easily transferable, for instance, in Britain.[27] Germany's organisation and science were advanced, its ability to deploy them in military terms clear from its conclusive military defeat of France in 1870. Moreover, the indices of German industrial output, in following decades, were proving that Britain's marginal industrial lead would soon be overtaken. Not only by 1900 was Germany clearly in the premier league, but its ability to keep pace with the society most obviously making the long-term running, the United States, was more than plausible.[28] In short, there was nothing inherent in the time-lag which determined that Germany's political or economic independence would be circumscribed, nor that its position in world affairs, like that of other nation-states of older vintage, such as Sweden, or the Netherlands, would, of necessity, have to be subservient or subsidiary to some select club of forerunners.

The long-term legacy of 1815, thus, boils down to what one might call a case of relative deprivation. A sufficiently large number of German people *felt* that they their 'nation' had been denied its proper birthright by dint of a set of political decisions and cultural influences which, they charged, had emanated, if not been imposed, from outside. This is not to say that whole sections of German society were not genuinely marginalised, or at least knocked off balance, by the general post-1870 intrusion of mass-produced goods or, more specifically, by the flooding of cheap American grain onto regional and local markets. Tradespeople, artisans and shopkeepers, the traditional *Mittlestand* of German society, were all adversely affected by this major economic shift, as were landowners, farmers and rural communities at large. But, then, this trend was very far from exclusive to Germany, nor were the resentments which went with it.[29] Everywhere in the advanced European polities, including Britain and France, there were major political realignments to the left and the right, as liberalism took the blame.[30] It was, indeed, ironic that the depression hit at a juncture when liberal governments were belatedly extending the franchise to a mass constituency, thereby fuelling the potential for a political backlash at the very moment of the ideology's emerging weakness. Certainly, the onset of political anti-Semitism on the continent, either in the platforms of existing parties, or in entirely new political formations, dates from this incipient period of mass democracy. One might even go further and argue that a politics of hate had been arrested up to this point only by a liberal conceptualisation of citizenship that kept the common man 'passively' at one remove.[31]

However, if this signified that political elites, henceforth, had to be more attuned to the demands of the *demos* – even in Germany where the political system was still determined top–down through the kaiser rather than bottom–up through parliament – what made the German situation arguably different was not just the spread of frustration and alienation to the educated bourgeoisie, professional circles, opinion formers and policy makers; after all, France after 1871 was also a notably embittered and increasingly polarised society, but the more pronounced manner of its articulation. It was an articulation, or perhaps more a series of articulations that, far from isolating Germany's cultural response as unique, is all the more important because of its mimesis in societies *looking to it* for guidance and leadership.

The Path of Radical Nationalism

The growing and increasingly charged contemporary debate about the origins and spread of nationalism is not our main concern here. Certainly, Ernest Gellner's persuasive instrumentalist view that the phenomenon can only be understood within the framework of the culturally homogenising needs of modernisation, that effectively begins with the French Revolution,[32] has had some serious contenders. Anthony Smith, in particular, has pointed out that Gellner's thesis fails to explain the spread of separate nationalisms amongst culturally subordinate groups – highlighting the problem of which comes first, the nation or the state – while resting his own more obviously primordialist case on the ubiquity of pre-existing, pre-modern *ethnies*.[33] If, thus, the spread of modern nationalism, according to Smith, cannot be understood without reference to myths of common ancestry and shared historical memories of ethnic communities the world over, the problem of how this has been transmitted so successfully into the building blocks of modern nationalisms still remains.

Another influential book on the subject, Benedict Anderson's *Imagined Communities*, as its title implies, does not share the solidity of Smith's ethnic starting point.[34] Nevertheless, Anderson's emphasis on the importance of the revolution in print-capitalism does offer a cogent explanation on the processes involved. By providing a secular literature in standardised vernaculars, print-culture offered the vehicle for a shared sense of belonging among people geographically remote from one another, even across political boundaries in different states where they might be required to converse publicly in languages different to their own. Given, moreover, that in most traditional societies, literacy was generally restricted to educated elites, the market-driven tailoring of this vernacular media to their particular interests, or habits of consumption, ensured that this new type of conscious self-identification would, as it was transmitted to broader sections of the same linguistic population, follow the contours already set and developed by these avant-gardists. Cultural nation-building, in short, had the potential to develop wherever there was a monolingual market not just for newspapers but also for novels, plays, poetry and non-fictional media, especially historical studies and folklore. And it proved, in the process, that nation formation could start to happen before being called into existence on the orders of the state, *à la mode française.*

Whether, thus, ethnic communities were, or were not, the progenitors of nations before the French Revolution, it is the idea of their timeless or at least historically deep existence thereafter, as promoted by cultural nationalists themselves, which concerns us here. The potential for toxicity inherent in the notion was, as we have seen, hardly below the surface in the avowedly civic and assimilationist version promulgated by the French. What is noteworthy about the German national ideology, by extension, is the way it turned the idea of ethnic community into a 'primordial, self-evident and irreducible'[35] certainty and a thoroughly closed and exclusive one at that. Legally speaking, the principle of *jus sanguinis* – citizenship on the basis of a a person's descent – was actually a common Roman-derived heritage in both societies. But, as Rogers Brubaker has demonstrated, while French parliamentary debates in the 1880s on the status of immigrants were able to steer a course towards the somewhat safer and more inclusive shores of *jus soli* – citizenship on the basis of the place of one's birth – German debates on the same subject, as they finally crystallised just before the First World War, went entirely in the other direction.[36] There remains a question mark, of course, as to how much implicitly, if not explicitly, this outcome was bound up with a wider mentality of national disenchantment and disappointment associated with the moment and manner of a state creation in which 10 million (Austrian) Germans were left out of the state, while several other non-German peoples: Danes in North Schleswig, French in Alsace-Lorraine, above all 2.5 million Poles in east Prussia, found themselves within it.[37] Certainly, a very pointed corollary to the effective debarring of immigrants from the national community, in the 1913 law, was the positive embrace of *Auslandsdeutsche* – Germans living abroad – as eligible for citizenship. Was this statement of ethno-national solidarity against the 'others', in some deeper sense a compensatory mechanism for the perceived national failure of 1871? Or does the problem actually go deeper still: that behind the utterly schizophrenic amalgam of hubris at military victories, contempt for those who been defeated, injured national pride and obsessive fears of geo-political insecurity, lay an altogether more searing recognition that, having arrived at a destination of national greatness, Germans could not but be in the shadows of the Western avant-garde?[38]

On an entirely practical and rational level an answer to the problem had already been provided earlier in the century by the political economist, Friedrich List. Seeing the future for a united Germany in the shape of the rapid industrial development of Britain, List, in the 1830s, had developed an economic programme that, he argued, would take Germany there. Crucially, this proposed that there could be no closing of the gap so long as Germany followed the dominant laissez-faire philosophy of the day. Indeed, in rejecting this approach as nothing more than a recipe for the perpetuation of British advantage, List, in effect prior to Marx, promulgated the first modern theory of unequal development.[39] In setting out his own alternative – an independent *national* economic programme of prioritised state protectionism – he also, inadvertently, offered a major piece of advice for all future radical state builders, including genocidaires. If one was going to get nowhere under the international (or at least hegemonic) rules of the game, then one would have to make up one's own rules, or at the very least reshape the existing rules according to one's own desiderata. List's critique, thus, implicitly involved a complete rebuttal of the then current notion that, simply by becoming a nation-state, the problem of national inequality would go away. On the contrary, the very fact that the modern world was now in a state of constant dynamic flux ensured that any ideal of a 'brotherhood of nations', as held, for instance, by the Italian republican, Mazzini, simply could not work in practice. Indeed, in the face of the forerunners' continuing advantage, only by a subordination of economic considerations to a *Weltanschauung* – an ideology which linked history and society to a programme for future politically determined economic development – could national integrity be guaranteed.[40]

However, if List's programme was essentially scientific and technocratic, and entirely lacking the racist undertones or Volkish hocus-pocus so prevalent in the general turn of nineteenth-century German radical nationalism, it is still noteworthy that he based his philosophy, without question, on the primacy of the nation. For List, as for the great eighteenth-century German ethnologist, Johann Gottfried Herder, before him, the *cultural* nation was a given, linguistic difference its primary marker, and, as founded essentially in nature, the only genuine framework within which an individual's self-realisation and freedom were possible. This conception, in essence, was not so different from that of Rousseau. The critical difference was List's hard-headed and thoroughly modern assessment of the nation's prospects. In a world where 'giants and dwarfs, well-formed bodies and cripples, civilised, half-civilised and barbarous nations' were all competing, the task of making one's own stronger so that it could genuinely participate in the 'universal society of the future' thus became the single purpose of politics.[41] By implication, List was saying that only those nations who made the transformation to industrial strength would survive, while those who failed would disappear. By extension, he was also postulating that only territorially significant states had the possibility to accomplish this task. List's conception of the future Germany is actually that of a central European mega-state – a *Mitteleuropa* – and thus one to which smaller nations within its bounds would either have to bow or suffer forcible encapsulation. List did not consider what the consequences of such denationing might be, or what might happen if such nations tried to resist. Liberal and constitutional his conception of the greater German nation-state might have been, but it was equally predicated on the assumption that only strong, successful, advanced states had the right to such fulfilment.

List, among Germans, was hardly alone in these views. Karl Marx might have approached the whole question of underdevelopment from an entirely different standpoint, but, viewing the spread of the national contagion to the east in the ebb of events in 1848, he wrote:

> Apart from the Poles, the Russians, and, at most, the Turkish Slavs, no Slavic people has a future, for the simple reason that all the other Slavs lack the primary historic, geographic, political and industrial prerequisites for independence and viability.[42]

Nor was Friedrich Engels, Marx's great associate in the communist project, a solitary voice when, a little earlier, he had ranted against the oppression of the German nationality, claimed the reconquest of German-speaking areas on the left side of the Rhine as a matter of national honour, and 'the Germanisation of Holland and Belgium ... a political necessity'.[43] A sense of injured national pride clearly troubled all manner of Germans. And whatever their ideological proclivities, all, to greater or lesser degrees, consoled themselves with the proposition that only so-called 'historic' nations, like themselves, had the right to existence. But in the wake of 1848, with List himself dead two years and with programmes for a solution to their dilemma no nearer to concretisation – however cogent these might have been on paper – the need felt by many, particularly educated Germans for some more obviously emotional release from their frustration represented an arguably much more ominous tendency.

It was in the idea of the 'Volk' – the people – according to George Mosse, that idealistic yet disaffected Germans found their solace and hope.[44] In terms of the history of ideas, Mosse confirmed that much of the interest in this subject can be traced back to Herder and his critical explorations of traditional folklore and culture. In many ways this was typical of the classificatory research that we associate with the Enlightenment. Where Herder parted company with its mainstream wisdom was in his refusal to concur with the idea that different cultures were simply staging posts en route to some universal civilisation. Herder did not discount the importance of exchange and cross-fertilisation or, for that matter, conflict in the creation of national cultures. But he did refute any notion of national hierarchy, preferring to extol instead, in the words of Isaiah Berlin, the idea 'that different cultures could and should flourish fruitfully side by side like so many peaceful flowers in the human garden'.[45] This, then, was a philosophy of nation – with or without the state – which still basked in the tolerant and optimistic sunshine of the Enlightenment.

The emerging nineteenth-century Volkish movement, however, was hardly interested in the diversity of humankind for its own sake. On the contrary, it was thoroughly ethnocentric and anti-pluralist. It was also, on another level, deeply anti-modernist. It might be particularly espoused by student fraternities, university professors and literary gurus[46] – in other words by those among the most educated elements of German society – but it placed itself in marked opposition to followers of the French positivist, Saint-Simon, who assumed that the application of a rational *méthode systématique* at the behest of a new order of technocrats, administrators and other professionals, could resolve all the problems associated with man's age-old struggle with nature. By contrast, instead of attempting to denature man, the Volkists believed that only by thoroughly giving themselves up to it could they connect with their genuine primal selves. Again, this aspiration had a distinctly Rousseauesque feel to it, except that the Volkists had no interest in the noble savage *per se*, only in a very particular rendition of it; a *homo teutonicus,* the supposed original German who had inhabited the great northern forests in the distant past. Find the ur-German and one found not simply oneself but the meaning of life. Unlock the inner mystery, the 'essence' which was contained therein and one would also unlock 'the source of his creativity, his depth of feeling, his individuality, and his unity with other members of the Volk'.[47] This, then, was what the movement's acolytes meant by the term. It was a case of returning to one's mythic roots, not only in order to achieve personal enlightenment but to make pure and whole a collective body which, allegedly, had been sullied and degraded by centuries of outside influence and interference.

But for the Volkists, of course, this was not any national group that had been denied its balance and harmony. The ancient Germans had not been simply great and good and strong, they were exceptional. It said so – or at least that is how it was interpreted – in the great ancient sagas, the *Edda* and *Nibelungenlied* republished in endless nineteenth-century editions as imbibed by millions of avid German readers. Even more potently, it seemed to be historically grounded in the work of the important Roman historian Tacitus. Here, in *Germania*, his apparent eulogy to an undefeated foe, was evidence of a people who had not submitted but had fought back, destroyed Roman armies in the process, and kept their freedom intact. Why? Because, said Tacitus, they had maintained their physical, moral and spiritual purity – they had not mixed with other tribes.[48]

One might, of course, argue that the repeated recourse to this sort of historical good press, or that of the Teutonic Knights, another Volkish favourite, with all the blood and guts of battle implied, was no more, nor less, harmful than a lot of twentieth-century interest in militaria. By the same token, the German sagas have much in common with openly Manichaean and mystical restatements of more recent times, such as Tolkein's immensely popular *The Lord of the Rings*, while the Volkist obsession with the relationship between man, landscape and the cosmos, the efforts of some of their number to turn the 'Christian' Jesus into a sort of pagan sun-god, or the fascination of others with the occult, is perhaps no more cranky or kinky than contemporary New Ageism. If the latter, indeed, does have some distinct parallels with the Volkish movement in its particular appeal to some of those most intellectually and emotionally alienated from Western materialism,[49] what makes Volkism considerably more disturbing is its specific context.

The Volkish movement was, at source, a by-product of the romantic reaction against Enlightenment rationalism and the impact of urban and industrial development, tendencies which were not exclusive to Germany. However, its more forceful impact there – in a country otherwise steeped in Enlightenment learning – arguably had a great deal to do with particular strands of cultural pessimism and political disappointment shared by large sections of a self-consciously idealistic and educated elite. Volkism offered a way round their frustration by retelling the German story not only as its listeners wanted to hear it, rather than as it actually was, but with the promise that, by following its prescript for moral behaviour and tangible action, the nation could be finally redeemed. Or to put it another way, in order to invent a myth of a German 'golden age' to counteract a debased present, it had to 'forget' all those pieces of empirical evidence which inconveniently contradicted it. The French philosopher, Ernest Renan, astutely had picked up on this anomaly in his important 1882 essay 'What is a Nation', when he wrote:

> Forgetting, I would even go so far as to say historical error, is a crucial factor in the creation of a nation, which is why progress in historical studies often constitutes a danger for [the principle of] nationality. Indeed, historical enquiry brings to light deeds of violence which took place at the origin of all political

formations. ... the essence of a nation is that all individuals have many things in common, and also that they have forgotten many things.[50]

In fact, applied to Germany, Renan's generalising analysis was only half-correct. Not only did the Volkish movement positively revel in the violence, it was also able to draw on at least some established and famous historians such as Treitschke – Germany was, after all, the nineteenth-century power-house of the new scientific study of history – to make good its case. Indeed, with the imprimatur of leading scholars and literary figures in a society where they counted for a great deal, Volkish ideas, both before and after the 1871 water-shed, were able to enter the school curriculum, become central to the burgeoning youth movements and student fraternities, infiltrate part of the Protestant Church, and became quite prevalent in the quality press.[51] By a roundabout route, therefore, not just nationalism but a much more virulent and uncompromising version of it, seeped into the *thinking* of a modern self-consciously rationalistic, scientistic, precision-orientated German society. It certainly also gained the attention and sympathy of political and court circles, including, after his accession in 1888, Kaiser Wilhelm II himself.[52]

Moreover, in the person of the composer Richard Wagner – at least as acclaimed by his disciples – Volkish Germany even attained its own prophet.[53] The only problem was that in practically the entire output of his self-styled music-dramas, the Volkish self-image could only be sustained by focusing on an obscure and hence largely unverifiable, if not entirely mythic, past. If, however, that was the case, then what of the present? Consider Wagner's last, possibly most prophetic opera *Parsifal* – first performed in the same year that Renan's essay was published – as emblematic, then the Volkish answer would seem to be that Germany's uniquely ordained mission as defender of Christendom (or simply of goodness?), lost in the mists of time through physical contamination with impure bodies, could only now be restored through a long and painful process of intense and collective self-purification.[54] But against whom or what? Moreover, if this prescript was being seriously offered as a recipe for Germany's national development, how could it possibly square with the civic conception of inclusive citizenship grounded in the dominant French and Anglo-Saxon models?

The answer is that it could not. The Volkish principle offered nationality and hence citizenship only to those who were 'organically' and 'integrally' of its 'blood' and 'soil'. Others who lived in Germany but lacked a German soul and, as such, the physical and spiritual connectedness to the age-old rhythms of its landscape, were not simply misfits but, by their very presence, tainted the Volk's sense of its own collective well-being. This, then, was not simply a highly exclusive conception of nationhood, its mythic-cum-mystical self-explication reflected its angst-laden, not to say paranoid underpinnings. Necessarily, its ideal German type demanded an anti-type. And while there were a clutch of ethnic minorities within Germany, particularly Poles, who could be suitably lambasted, the anti-type role was specifically reserved for 'the Jew'.

We have already seen the long history of phobic anxieties directed against Jews in Christian Europe. The recrudescence of these feelings in a more secular age might suggest that nothing very much had fundamentally changed. Certainly, the rise of Volkish anti-Semitism confirmed that blaming the Jews remained the most readily available outlet for elements of a dominant society, which to a significant degree had lost their moorings. The critical difference now was that Jews were, by legal and political right, entering into the mainstream. Indeed, Germany provided a particularly clear example of the degree to which many were availing themselves of these new-found opportunities, not only to acculturate and even to a more limited degree physically assimilate, but also to involve themselves as fully as they could in the cultural, commercial and even political life of the country. It is this Jewish association with the modernising direction Germany appeared to be taking which particularly drove Volkists – and others – to apoplectic and vituperative denunciation. Not for the last time the cry went up that Germany was undergoing *Verjudung*: 'Judaisation'. And that this 'takeover', while it was taking place under the noses of *echt* Germans was, nevertheless, being accomplished by stealth and conspiratorial stratagem.[55] Not only did the accusation significantly link German Jews with *Manchestertum*, in other words with an economic philosophy inimical to the Listian programme of independent development, it also claimed that Jews *qua* Jews, both inside and outside Germany, were operating their own grand, anti-national design.

An early literary rendition of this theme was Hermann Goedsche's 1868 novel, *Biarritz*, in which thirteen sinister, even supernatural elders of Zion are espied in the Jewish cemetery in Prague secretly plotting to enslave the peoples of the world. Through capitalist control of the stock-exchanges and factories, on the one hand, and the fermenting of revolutionary unrest of the masses against Church, aristocracy and Crown, on the other, the elders see their dastardly plans coming close to fruition. With its sensationalist *frisson*, *Biarritz* can justly be seen as a precursor of the sort of formulaic science-fiction plot more recently associated with the cult American television series, *The X-Files*.[56] The problem is that the original piece of fictional make-believe was increasingly to become the progenitor, in pre-First World War years, of accounts which portrayed these conspiratorial machinations as fact. Eventually, with *The Protocols of the Elders of Zion*, true believers would have a narrative assuring them that the takeover was imminent, the final twist in the plot being a scheme to blow up the national capitals of the world by a network of underground railways if the Gentiles did not capitulate to the conspirators' demands[57] But en route Germany produced a whole series of supposedly serious scholarly works raising the alarm. There was Wilhelm Marr, otherwise best known as coiner of the term 'anti-Semitism', with his 1879 prophecy *Jewry's Victory over Teutonism*, closely followed in 1880 by Karl Eugen Dühring's *The Jewish Question as a Problem of Racial Character and its Damage to the Existence of Peoples, Morals and Characters*. Ten years on there would be Hermann Ahlwardt's *The Desperate Struggle between Aryan and Jew*, while possibly the most influential of all these renditions, *The Foundations of the Nineteenth Century*, written, in 1899, by Houston Stewart Chamberlain, the British-born German-naturalised son-in-law of Wagner, failed only in its title to dissemble its explicit anti-Jewish message.[58] These works were not marginal to the German publishing scene. They were mainstream and extremely successful. So too were the great number of Volkish novels, with their cast of ugly, mischievous or swindling Jews as appropriate antithesis to the kind, hardworking but often browbeaten German man or woman of the soil yearning for an end to the materialist, urban yoke which the cosmopolitan, rootless, above all, denatured Jew also represented. Morally deceived, financially cheated, sexually abused; even putting racism to one side, all the essential ingredients for what nineteenth-century Germans felt most embittered about, yet crucially most feared as aspects of their own inner condition, were being carefully stacked up into a lurid but potent, projected image.[59]

Yet despite all these feverish nightmares of degradation and emasculation, a Volkish antidote, in the form of a radical, ethnically based transformation of society, was not translated into the direct actions of the imperial German polity. In this we are presented with another paradox. The state certainly did flex its muscles and pick a fight with a cohesive religious community but *not* with the Jews. Indeed, the fight it got into had much more of the Vendée about it; minus the ultimate recourse to exterminatory action. Even so, the parallels between this first post-1871 assault on an internal, supposedly enfranchised community within the nation and French events eighty years previously, cannot and should not be ignored. The actions involved Bismarck's overtly belligerent efforts to bring all Catholic institutions, funds, foundations and above all, (mostly Jesuit-run) schools firmly under state control. Catholics made up some one-third of the population, particularly in the west, east, and south of the country, where Blackbourn has characterised them as being the German equivalent of a 'British Celtic fringe'.[60] The majority of them viewed Bismarck's efforts as an unadulterated and unwarranted assault on themselves as a collectivity. Their reaction could not have been helped by the tendency of most (Protestant) liberals fervently to support the state on the grounds that Catholicism was intrinsically backward, decadent and corrupt and an inertial force holding back their ignorant and cowed flock from the benefits of modernity and progress.

Cast in such Manichaean terms (indeed, the term *Kulturkampf* – culture war – coined by Rudolf Virchow, the leading left liberal and figure in the fledgling science of anthropology[61] quickly stuck), it is also hardly surprising if the conflict quite rapidly developed its own dynamic, hard edge. As the state strove to enforce its will, locking up priests, closing down churches, violently dispersing crowds, Catholic localities responded with heightened organised mobilisation, intensified devotional – and emotional – solidarity and a structured passive resistance behind which, argues Blackbourn, the potential for a more violent, physical resistance remained mostly latent.[62] Even so, the particular defence of local priests, who were largely viewed by their congregations not as representatives of a archaic old order but rather as tribunes 'against a privileged new order which was perceived as a threat to land and small property',[63] makes the comparison with the Vendée groundswell uncannily apposite. Again, as in the Vendée, self-styled liberal modernists responded with a whole tranche of insinuations about priestly manipulation of women and children, in the former case with the inference of sexual manipulation hardly below the surface, with a public rhetoric in which fighting Catholic institutions was likened to taking on 'phylloxera, Colorado beetle and other enemies of the Reich'[64] and, finally, with an increasing willingness to use the iron fist. Indeed, in response to crowds gathering in the Saarland town of Marpingen after local reported sightings of the Virgin Mary – again an extraordinary statement in itself about the actual manifestation of Catholic dissent – the local secular authorities called in the troops.[65]

That the state's persecutory nastiness and zeal ultimately stopped far short of a Vendée is not in dispute here. There were no massacres at Marpingen, or elsewhere. In the end, moreover, Bismarck backed down, Catholic intransigence was channelled into a political opposition – the Centre Party – which in turn ultimately became an integral element in Wilhelmine and post-Wilhelmine state and society. But again, neither should we dismiss the *Kulturkampf* as essentially some red herring. On the contrary, the potential for state–communal violence was very real, not least because it was the first test of the *Machtstaat* attempting to map out its programme of modernising social homogenisation. In the face of Catholic obduracy a whole communal segment became, instead, *Reichsfeinde*, 'enemies of state'. That this also carried with it the inference of being a Trojan horse, a fifth column ready and willing to act on behalf of defeated Austrian and French Catholic states intent on their own revenge and also a genuinely if highly beleaguered international Catholicism in the shape of the papacy, tells us much about the fragile, even vulnerable mindset of the new German state even in the wake of its outstanding military triumphs. A state, incidentally, which was quite capable of transferring its anxieties – and with it its hatred – to another communal target, the social democrats, and with them, by inference the working class, once the *Kulturkampf* had been unceremoniously ditched.

But was any of this indicative of a German ethnic nationalism becoming the guiding principle of state policy? Can we perceive its hand when, in 1885, Bavaria – one of the Reich's constituent states – introduced identity papers and other draconian measures designed to curtail an influx of Roma from an increasingly destabilised Balkans? Or when this appeared to be extended to native-born Roma as well as other itinerants – the *Jenische* – with the ominous 1899 establishment of the *Zigeunerzentrale*, a Central Office for Gypsy Affairs in Munich's police headquarters?[66] Arbitrary expulsions of Roma certainly followed, as they did against other unwanted traders and immigrants. *Ostjuden* – Eastern Jews – would be particular targets in these *fin-de-siècle* round-ups as were Galician Poles, many of whom arrived for seasonal or longer-term work alongside the Jews at eastern border stations, notably at the major Austrian crossing point, near the town of of Oswiecim, or Auschwitz.[67] This specifically Prussian policy reached its crescendo between 1883 and 1885 when 32,000 such foreigners, two-thirds of them Poles, were summarily deported in what has been described as 'an action unprecedented in nineteenth-century Europe during a time of peace'.[68] Certainly, even putting aside the obvious, later, Jewish, resonances here, the wider attack on Poles at this juncture, including Bismarck's legislation to curb spoken Polish in schools and public places in Prussia, was sufficiently harsh for another modern commentator to discern the appearance of 'a *national* intolerance aimed at a homogeneous nation-state'.[69] Taken together, Bismarck's attempts to keep foreign Poles out and his successors' efforts to suffocate Polish existence within – most notably in the form of a 1908 law allowing for property and land expropriation in predominantly Polish areas of West Prussia and Posznan in the interests of 'strengthening Germandom' – could be seen as a hardly disguised thin end of a consciously xenophobic and *Germanising* agenda.[70]

Paradoxically, as with the *Kulturkampf*, whether we require an overtly ethnic antipathy in these acts to see the beginnings of a genocidal reckoning is debatable. In fact, Bismarck's own coercive policy against the Poles was largely dictated by traditional political calculations regarding Polish loyalty to the state and not national imperatives. Even so, the very fact that Poles were being treated as a powerful and, through the Catholic connection, international col-

lectivity with the capacity hence to pose an internal threat to state security –
casting them in the role of mortal *Reichsfeinde* as a result – is quite in line with
other similar cases that have evinced the potential for genocide. At the time, it
was certainly recognised as completely in violation of Polish citizenship rights
within the state and thus of *Rechtsstaat* principles. As a result the policy was
vilified at home and abroad.[71] That said, one could actually go further and
argue that if Bismarck's end-goals remained essentially Machiavellian, his successors' championship of a German colonisation programme on Prussia's
eastern frontiers, the corollary to the 1908 law, which in turn was trumpeted
as the necessary antidote to a perceived *Drang Nach Westen* – the swamping of
the German east by Slavs and Jews – was a quite conscious attempt to 'appropriate the slogans of a conservative, Volkish German nationalism'.[72]

Yet, for all the institutional discrimination practised against Poles in the
pre-1914 period, not only did the last pre-war German chancellor, Bethmann-
Hollweg, consciously put a brake on use of the expropriation law, in spite of
Volkish outrage, but a steady increase in Polish seasonal immigration after the
mid-1880s expulsions underscored the way that economic necessity continued
to take precedence over political agendas.[73] More to the point, there is no evidence to suggest that the Wilhelmine state actually ever considered
reconstructing itself on purely ethnic lines. In this sense it remained with its
Poles, its Danes, its Alsatians, singularly akin to the French model. And,
indeed, with its more permanent migrants, actual numbers of foreign residents – a large numbers of whom were Jewish – tripling, from 430,000 in
1890, to some 1,260,000 in 1910.[74] Nor was there any overt state-sponsored
discrimination or persecution of Jewish incomers, or Jewish citizens, as there
was in this period in Russia and Romania. The Dreyfus affair might be evidence of a Western society teetering on the brink but by comparison
Germany's state record remained unblemished. Despite increasingly vocal and
raucous calls for anti-Jewish legislation from the marginal anti-Semitic groupings both within and without the Reichstag, there was, before 1914, no
rescinding of the Jewish emancipation completed with the creation of the
Reich in 1871.[75]

If, then, German radical nationalism, except in its less immediately toxic
Listian form, remained unrealised as a policy of state – and this in spite of the
fact that it clearly infected important sections of society – what is its significance for the study of genocide, other than the obvious linkage between
Volkish ideas and the emergence of Nazism? Concentrated focus on this single
relationship, however, is in danger of ignoring the degree to which Volkist-
style ethnic idealisation, and the extremism which went with it, became an
inspiration for national movements far beyond the frontiers of Germany. In

the first instance, this was for the simple reason that it was the obvious model for any would-be nation, or more accurately self-styled national elite who wanted a state but lacked one. Or possibly, as in the case of Turkish nationalists, it influenced national elites who already had a state but wanted an entirely different one. As most would-be claimants (by inference at this stage mostly European or near-Europeans) were, until the late nineteenth century, in one or other of these aggrieved categories, and were likely to remain there so long as the then international order more or less prevailed, some form of integral, ethnically based nationalism thus provided the only hope for the legitimisation of their case. It did so, moreover, by proposing that underdevelopment, or the lack of a modern industrial base, represented no just cause for the denial of their self-determination. On the contrary, as their claim to statehood was founded on supposed ancestral institutions from a deep tribal past, the components enabling them to demonstrate the free exercise of their national sovereignty were already implicitly in place. All one needed was to prove, as in Ziya Gökalp's reiteration of the ethnic formula, the existence of 'a society of people who speak the same language, have had the same education and are united in their religious and aesthetic ideals – in short those who have a common *culture* and religion'.[76]

In a vacuum this might sound innocuous enough. Indeed, reshape some of these basic ingredients to read 'shared historic memories' and 'a myth of common ancestry', while adding 'historic homeland' for good measure, and one has all the essential ingredients for what Anthony Smith would generically define as nationalism.[77] The problem with the conception is that if one attempted to create a Europe, let alone a global community of nation-states on this basis, the demands for recognition would be almost endless. Even a nineteenth-century proponent of nationalism, such as Mazzini, could not envisage more than twelve such entities on the continent.[78] Attempt to reformulate it on genuinely ethnic lines and one would have scores. They would be seriously competing states at that, as practically no ethnic community could make an actual, or for that matter historic, claim to any territory without encountering one or possibly several counter-claims. In an eastern Europe – not to say Near East – where, under imperial aegis, diverse, religious and ethnic communities had co-existed and intermixed with one another for centuries, the unleashing of this new more radical, myth-infused variant of nationalism could be nothing short of disastrous.

Yet, let loose and then taken to its logical conclusion, the ramifications and consequences of nationalism were predictable enough. George Mosse has somewhat caustically noted that 'the rise of modern nationalism entailed a competition as to which of the peoples of Europe had a greater love of freedom'.[79] Equally, however, this could easily translate into *sacro egoismo*: 'the egotistic pursuit of the interest of one's own group, even if it involves the disregard and abuse of another', the former, moreover, always being deemed '"sacred" and hence morally self-sufficient'.[80] Or, to fundamentally ground the issue, freedoms of other nations count for nought if they happen to be sitting on what one considers to be one's own sacred land. The small problem of where this 'sacred' land begins and ends or indeed any practical issues which might arise are *ipso facto* ruled out in the face of the mythic claim. Nineteenth-century historical science was perfectly well aware, not to say much obsessed, through the concept of *Völkerwanderung*, that different tribes – or proto-nations, as nationalists preferred to view them – had migrated from region to region in the not so-distant past.[81] The detail, however, tended to be lost on those already convinced that, by planting themselves on the historic soil on which their supposed forebears had lived, they were recovering an ancient birth-right.

Before 1914, state-led attempts to supplant Polish peasants with German ones in West Prussia and Pozan proved notably unsuccessful, not least because Germans were increasingly migrating from the land in these regions into the industrial towns.[82] After the First World War, young Volkish enthusiasts of the German Artaman Society attempted to redouble these efforts by setting up agricultural colonies, mostly on Germany's eastern frontiers. At least as central to their philosophy and programme, however, was the intention to push these frontiers much further east, an intent that could only be realised at the expense of millions of the region's Polish and Lithuanian inhabitants. No matter, thought the Artaman leader, Wilhelm Kotzde, in 1924: 'Either we will go to the East, as our ancestors did once before in the twelfth century, or we will be erased as a people from world history'.[83] It was exactly this sort of unhealthy combination; national self-glorification and redemptive promise on the one hand, wounded pride and forebodings of nemesis on the other, which already by the late nineteenth century was becoming the dominant feature of radical nationalism.

Repeatedly, and morbidly, looking back to the violent struggles of the ancient or medieval past, in which phalanxes of 'civilised' Teutons fought hordes of 'primitive' Slavs, the difference now was that the expected replay was being welcomed as a final solution to national dilemmas. The concept of *Vernichtungskrieg* – annihilatory war – even found its way into the vocabulary and planning of the German high command.[84] But while here it was supposedly limited to notions of military engagement, its wider application to whole peoples was implicit in the aspirations of radical nationalists.

Nor were only Volkish Germans its enthusiastic supporters. While late-Wilhelmine organisations such as the Pan-German League, and the Eastern Marches Association, could fantasise about grand drives to the east, linking the German state with scattered *Volksdeutsche* communities in a sea of Slavdom, their Slavic adversaries were quite as capable of viewing the process in reverse, Pan-Slavism dreaming of the incorporation of Slavonic groups, like the Sorbs (Wends), isolated from their 'brethren' in the German west.[85] In the same way, not long after, advocates of pan-Turanism, or pan-Arabism, would equally draw for themselves maps of huge mega-states linking all the peoples of their own supposed kind.[86] Yet each and every one of these dreamt their dreams of national transcendence and world-historical mission at the expense of all those *other* peoples who just happened to belong to some different cultural or linguistic group – whether living in isolated enclaves or whole compact regions – astride their territorially all-encompassing visions. In short, radical nationalism was becoming habituated to the idea of violent competition and struggle between peoples as if this was both normal and inevitable. It might be, for the moment, played out primarily in the heads of those most enthused by its message but its portent was one of neither compromise nor mercy.

Race Enters the Picture

It was ironic, then, that this avowed picture of 'how things actually are': of entire peoples and nations fighting and obliterating one another, should appear – at least to some – to receive endorsement from the most important and sensational scientific breakthrough of the nineteenth century: Darwinism.

Charles Darwin's theory of evolution, as finally published in 1859, ran under the full and striking title: *On the Origins of Species by Means of Natural Selection: Or the Preservation of Favoured Races in the Struggle for Life*.[87] It offered a working explanation of change in the history of the natural world. In this sense it was not directly about man at all. But, of course, it was about man – man in nature[88] – and for all those going back to Rousseau who wanted to embrace that idea rather than simply tame it, or avoid it, it was dynamite.

Enlightenment natural history had been mostly preoccupied with the task of classifying the globe's flora and fauna, as if its existence were static, immutable, timeless and ordered. But the research of those, like the late nineteenth-century French palaeontologist, Cuvier, who had highlighted the mass extinction of mammoths and other species, pointed to an entirely different picture.[89] Unless one started from the Christian premise that this was simply proof of God's intervention in the 'Great Flood', one was left with the problem of how and why it was that whole ranges of species existent in the fossil record were now extinct, while others appeared to survive to the present, or, indeed, had been superseded by entirely new forms. The search for an evolutionary explanation did not begin with Darwin – or the more modest but equally cogent Alfred Russell Wallace[90] – but it was Darwin's theoretical conclusions that were almost universally hailed by the contemporary scientific establishment as the answer. And not just by scientists; Marx, for one, was so taken with the parallels between Darwin's entirely materialist explication of natural historical development and his own dialectical interpretation of human history that he had proposed to dedicate to Darwin the English edition of his own magnus opus, *Das Kapital*.[91]

It was Darwin's description of a constant life or death struggle for survival, both between individuals within a species, and between species themselves, in what, by implication, was a hostile environment, which really struck home in the mid-Victorian mind. The processes of individual adaptation and modification and their role as key transmitter of species transformation over eons of generational change, at the heart of Darwin's theory, counted for much less in this respect than the idea that what this was really all about was the strong making good and the weak, or febrile, going to the wall. It was actually not Darwin at all but his compatriot social scientist and philosopher, Herbert Spencer, who popularised the term 'the survival of fittest' but this was almost unanimously taken up as a short-hand for what Darwin had actually himself meant.[92] Slippage into social Darwinism: namely the application of this selective reading to human society, was, in this context, quite inevitable. The anarchist Peter Kropotkin's alternative and later reading, that Darwin's theory could be taken to infer the importance of social *cooperation* within many species, had few takers.[93] Not only was 'God … dead', as the great German philosopher, Friedrich Nietzsche, concluded but, according to Ernst Haeckel, nature was now shown up for what it was; a brutal, pitiless battleground with man as no exception from it.[94]

It was, indeed, through Haeckel's entirely unwarranted monistic efforts to turn Darwin's theory into a mystical truth about the nature of the entire universe that the *Origins* developed a broad and enthusiastic following in *fin-de-siècle* Germany.[95] Contemporaneously, through the work of the zoologist-turned-political-geographer, Friedrich Ratzel, it was also more specifically attuned to now almost standard Western assumptions about race. Ratzel argued that at the heart of the Darwinian theory was the necessarily violent struggle between species for territory within which to survive and prosper. Applied to human populations, Ratzel concluded, it was this search for what he termed *Lebensraum* – living space –the title of his 1904 book on the subject, which determined that the 'lesser' races, by which he meant, for instance, native American and African people, would have to make way for 'stronger' European, more specifically, 'Aryan' ones. Ratzel vacillated in his writings over whether the allegedly more febrile races in this supposed global struggle would simply die out on contact with their more vigorous and dynamic contenders, or would have to be physically driven out, or even exterminated.[96] Others, and not just German writers, were much more forthright. In the same year as the publication of Ratzel's volume, America's leading psychologist and educator, G. Stanley Hall, proclaimed in his own major two-volume opus:

> Never, perhaps, were lower races being extirpated as weeds in the human garden, both by conscious and organic processes, so rapidly as to-day ... this is inevitable and not without justification. Pity and sympathy, says Nietzsche, are now a disease, and we are summoned to rise above morals and clear the world's stage for the survival of those who are fittest because strongest .... The world will soon be overcrowded, and we must begin to take selective agencies into our own hands. Primitive races are either hopelessly decadent and moribund, or at best have demonstrated their inability to domesticate and civilise themselves.[97]

Here, then, an ostensible scientific authority interpreted through a philosophical prism – itself distorted for the sake of convenience – was being offered as an almost religious sanction for people-extermination. It was not, though, one might note, from some rabble-rouser on the margins of society but from a highly influential establishment academic at the heart of one of the world's leading nations. Yet Hall's comments were not singular. Sentiments such as these were by this time being regularly trotted out by Western opinion formers and policy makers without irony or shame. Not only with social Darwinism as an essential feature but with the added ingredient, paraded as a given scientific fact, that race, by definition, involved hierarchy and that, as a result, as one Australian scientific publication from this period put it 'to the Aryan ... belongs the destinies of the future'.[98] Again, however, as with Darwinism itself, we need to be wary of making an automatic equation between the study of race and *racism*.

The study of race – ethnology – was, at least initially, a perfectly legitimate branch of the Enlightenment's grand classification project of nature and closely linked to infant comparative anthropological and philological research pioneered by many of the same people. Others like Cuvier, Lamarck, and Linneus came to the subject from more biologically grounded backgrounds, foreshadowing Darwin's own 1871 classic, *The Descent of Man*. All these proponents were interested, to greater or lesser degrees, in divergent characteristics within the human species and, hence, with the natural historical origins and evolution of mankind.[99]

The problem was that these interests almost invariably got mixed up with all sorts of cultural baggage, including religiously based mantras and prejudices leading to an often distinctly hierarchic system of racial classifications. For instance, in the 1790s, the Göttingen professor Johann Friedrich Blumenbach not only propounded a five-group typology but also insisted that the supposed European 'Caucasian' grouping – the term itself had abundant biblical and Greek classical overtones – was several rungs up from the Mongoloid, Negroid, and others. Blumenbach came to his loaded conclusion by analysing different skulls, a process developed independently in the same decade by the Dutch painter and anatomist Peter Camper who, too, propounded that this provided the key to the 'ideal' human type, but added that cranial measurements also offered a guide to the moral and aesthetic qualities of each human being. It was a short step from this to Franz Joseph Gall's notion that intellectual as well as moral differences were inherent in the shape of people's heads. The more, thus, one conformed to the supposedly archetypal 'Caucasian' skull, the more one could claim, on the basis of Blumenbach's craniology, Camper's craniometry, Gall's phrenology, to be physically stronger, mentally more adept, emotionally more robust – as well, of course, more beautiful – than the others.[100] A century on, the more perspicacious observers of such race theory, like the French humanitarian, Jean Finot, were not only denouncing it as entirely subjective claptrap but as a convenient alibi for the most ugly aggression in Africa and elsewhere.[101] Yet over and beyond its obvious utility for politicians and demagogues, the general acceptance of the theory among wide swathes of educated Western society was not just a convenient function of powerful societies lauding it over the natives in distant climes.

Differentiating people on the basis of gradations of skin colour, and other physical attributes, as a tool whereby a dominant group legitimises its social control over other groups is very old in history. It is certainly not exclusive to Europeans. One only has to look at the caste system in India to note its longevity and invidiousness.[102] As for Europeans, the – albeit ephemeral – Spanish obsession with *limpieza de sangre* as a not very successful way of keeping former Jews out of the establishment suggests that racial notions preceded European conquests in the New World and beyond. Once in the Americas, however, while interbreeding with native Indians and black slaves was endemic, a highly complex twenty-three-part categorisation of the offspring was carefully developed in New Spain to keep the 'lesser breeds' of mulattos, quadroons, octaroons and the rest squabbling among themselves for place while ensuring that the 'white' establishment remained thoroughly in control. In the French Caribbean colony of Haiti – the largest single eighteenth-century market for the European slave trade – the point was made even more emphatically with a 128-part division of the gradations: an individual with 127-parts white to one part black still being considered 'coloured'.[103] Paradoxically, the very reality of miscegenation rather suggests that these extremely hierarchical, not to say baroque, categories were more honoured in the Latin American breach than in the practice and, hence, hardly comparable with, for instance, the much less complex but much more tightly institutionalised and heavily policed framework of racial categorisation and hence sexual separation – apartheid – sustained throughout much of twentieth-century South Africa.[104] The point being laboured here, however, is that none of these discriminatory systems need racial theory *per se* to sustain them, any more than southern whites in the United States – long after its abolition of slavery – necessarily needed a system to sustain their hatred of 'blacks'.

Instead, what all these examples have in common is a functional construction of alleged discrete racial distinctions in order to defend the cross-generational monopolisation of economic and political control of, or access to, resources by the some – usually a minority – while depriving it to the rest – usually the many. Necessarily, to work effectively, it has to be backed up by strict, even draconian enforcement and/or a series of deeply embedded cultural assumptions which either prevent or penalise movement across the constructed racial boundaries. In other words, it needs a framework much more akin to apartheid South Africa than its Latin American parallels. Yet, even in this more virulent former case, where the language of degradation and even dehumanisation was always highly manifest, this is not a racism imbued with notions of mass people-extermination. On the contrary, while its upholders may have held their 'racial inferiors' in utter contempt and ensured that their often short lives were ones of unmitigated misery, the system also remained normally dependent on their numerical – if not individual – perpetuation in order to provide labour for its needs.[105]

The emergence and development of the sort of European racism which we specifically associate with the nineteenth century and which finally came to full fruition with Nazi programmes of genocide, did not set out, however, from these essentially functional premises. On the contrary, its wellsprings have little directly to do with material issues at all. Étienne Balibar gets close to its core in his definitional summary. Racism, he says is:

> a philosophy of history, or more accurately a *historiosophy* which is the consequence of a hidden secret revealed to men about their own nature and their own birth. It is a philosophy which makes visible the invisible cause of the fate of societies and peoples: not to know the cause is seen as evidence of degeneracy or the historical power of evil.[106]

Certainly, it is the case that droves of geneticists, anthropologists, racial hygienists, population scientists and psychiatrists strove to play handmaiden to racism and give it the stamp of scientific legitimacy. Yet none of this was able to offer an empirical grounding or logical explanation for the much-vaunted superiority of Nordic Aryans only, like radical nationalism, which ran closely in parallel or in tandem with it, a dubious gloss for what in practice amounted to a secular salvationist faith to compensate for the perceived failings of the real world. This may sound distinctly odd given that race theory came so thoroughly into its own at the apotheosis of European imperialism. But then, perhaps this may also explain why, at its schizophrenic heart, was an archetypal anti-type which was neither one nor an amalgam of subjugated colonial peoples, so much as – transmuted into the racist parlance of 'Semite' – the age-old mythic European outsider and 'enemy': the Jew.

Of course, constructing whole natural histories and genealogies of racial superiority could be directed against any outsider group with which one might find oneself, or claim to find oneself, in conflict, or competition. And it could be built on almost any grounds whatsoever. Whilst, thus, in the wake of the Franco-Prussian war, German 'race' scientists were ascribing their victory to the long 'Bronze Age' dolichcephalic skulls which proved their civilised origins and also incidentally their historical triumphs (sic.) over more primitive 'short' brachycephalic Finns, Slavs and others, their French counterparts, such as Jean-Louis Armand de Quatrefrages were busily propounding that the Prussians were not really 'Germans' at all but themselves brachycephalics of bastardised Finnish, or of Finno-Slavic descent, hence explaining their supposed tendencies towards meglomania, barbarity and degeneracy.[107]

It was, indeed, in this word degeneracy that we get to the nub of the new racist ambivalence and dilemma. This is all too evident in its leading gospel, Arthur, comte de Gobineau's *Essay on the Inequality of Human Races,* written between 1853 and 1855. Superficially, the French aristocrat's work can be read as a great paean to the superiority of the 'white' Aryans, by which he meant the descendants of ancient Indo-Europeans who had settled in northern Europe in the distant past.[108] Putting aside the common error of confusing linguistic families with racial types, what is actually most significant about Gobineau's work, however, is its acute pessimism:

> Societies perish because they are degenerate ... The word degenerate when applied to a people means ... that the people no longer had the same intrinsic value as it had before, because it has no longer the same blood in its veins, continual adulterations having gradually affected the quality of the blood.[109]

In this single statement, the great proponent of race seems to be dismantling the whole edifice. Race does not and cannot exist, except in the most fluid, ever-changing forms, because human groups have always tended to mix with one another. Yet instead of accepting this at face value as a normal aspect of the human condition, Gobineau treats it as evidence of some terrifying historical catastrophe. Inter-group miscegenation spells doom for the better peoples, in the form of physical and cultural degeneration. The only antidote is a return to the immutable Utopia of the past, where the Aryans lived in a supposed unadulterated purity. This is not a doctrine of racial victory but of unmitigated fear.[110]

It is noteworthy then, that Gobineau's creed came to the fore, not when it was written, but in the 1870s and 1880s, after the key watershed of the Franco-Prussian war, the consolidation of the European nation-state system and, with it, the full advent of modernity. It was in this period that race, combined with social Darwinism, came more obviously to provide a way out, a soothing balm, a panacea for so many of those who felt disorientated in the face of the new realities, had lost their moorings, or simply did not like the way society was going. In other words, for all those individuals and groupings already most attracted to radical nationalism.[111] Though not exclusively. Race would also develop a following among those, like Gobineau's key disciple, Georges Vacher de Lapouge, who would call themselves socialists, with the added assurance that this was *not* hocus-pocus but authentic science. What the 'scientists' – Lapouge included – were actually putting on offer, though, was a reflection of racism's followers' own deepest insecurities and wish-fulfilments, dressed up as a mix of 'racial anthropological jargon and a mystical sense of social destiny'.[112]

What is most frightening about this post-1870s social Darwinist–racist nexus, however, is its predilection to articulate everything in terms of zero-sum bloodbaths. And, indeed, as in the writings of Lapouge himself, to predict it as a welcome inevitability. To avoid 'going under' – the race theorists' ultimate catastrophe – they imagined a series of apocalyptic race wars in which 'our' kind, because they were clearly stronger, more virile and martial *Übermenschen* would wipe out the 'others' – the *Untermenschen* – and, thereby avoid the danger of race mixing. The only problem was that if the 1871 test of modern war was anything to go by, the most martial and virile of one's own were at least as likely to be eliminated on the battlefield as one's opponents, and, by this same chop-logic, provide ample opportunity for lesser but more fecund races – the Chinese were a particularly persistent fixture in the racist incubus – to exploit the weakness. Such arguments ought to have simply shown up the contradiction in the essential race premise. All they actually did was drive the

Lapouges and Chamberlains to invoke the urgency for some more final, comprehensive exterminatory solution.

Their real angst was not about distant or even close-at-hand foreigners. In the wake of 1871, Germans and French certainly had reason enough to hate each other, while dire warnings of a Chinese 'yellow peril' swamping the civilised West certainly remained an aspect of the racist's nightmare scenario long after Gobineau had voiced his own anxieties on this score.[113] However, the threat of mongrelisation, as those like Chamberlain called it, leading to an inversion of Aryan victory through degeneration into emasculated febrility, was mostly projected onto social and ethnic groupings much closer to home. The perceived menace, indeed, was already penetrating deeply and pervasively into the fabric of Western society itself. It is worth pausing for a moment to consider elements of this accusation as propounded by late nineteenth- and early twentieth-century policy makers and opinion formers, not least because they were to become so significant, later on, in Nazi programmes of racial hygiene.

The primary element arguably, or at least superficially, did not involve a racial categorisation at all. Nor was it voiced solely by race theorists but by a whole range of Western establishment professionals, including medical elites who believed they had identified parts of their population whose alleged mental or physical condition were held to be a burden on the financial and institutional resources of the state and hence were allegedly dragging the rest of the nation down with them.[114] Who exactly these problem people were, remained then, as now, nebulous in the extreme. Certainly, they included all those incarcerated in mental asylums, or homes for the physically disabled. Traditional attitudes towards these unfortunates, who were often cared for by religious societies, were largely neutral, on the solid grounds that these people had no personal control or responsibility for their condition. A shift, however, began to occur at the *fin de siècle* with the appearance of a strand of theorising within criminal anthropology which linked mental deficiency with habitual criminal tendencies.[115] Equally disturbing but much more widespread was a hardening of attitudes towards the indigent poor. Here was a whole class of society allegedly sponging off the rest, or living by more direct criminality, while – to cap the insult – breeding like rabbits or flies. The terminology for these people, lumpens, dregs, underclass, may have changed, but not the persistent vitriol of their 'betters' against them. The best thing to do with them, proposed the leftist social reformers, Sidney and Beatrice Webb, in a famous 1909 minority report on the reform of Britain's Poor Law, was to commit them to semi-penal detention colonies.[116]

There undoubtedly was a problem – mass poverty. One which through the rapidity of mid- to late nineteenth-century capitalist-fuelled economic change, precipitated a vast exodus of unskilled or more often deskilled labourers from the countryside, matched by a parallel explosion of urbanisation. As a result, political and social elites throughout western and central Europe came face to face as never before with great masses of people who, without regular employ-ment, or basic state provision were dislocated, destitute and inevitably dirty. This last element was rather significant. Increasingly overcrowded in the most squalid and often fetid quarters of the growing cities, the poor's association with the great outbreaks of typhus, cholera and smallpox – which naturally did not respect the boundaries of more genteel residential areas – also coin-cided with an emerging and genuinely important series of medical-scientific breakthroughs as to the nature and transmission of infectious diseases. 'Horror of marauding, parasitic cockroaches, lice, and bedbugs', notes Paul Weindling, 'reached a fever pitch from the 1890s'.[117] Unsanitary housing conditions were, of course, breeding grounds for the lice and so for the potentially fatal bacilli which they carried. Just as poor nutrition, poor hygiene and lack of sunshine vastly increased the likelihood of stunted or deformed physical growth, so too did they produce proclivities to mental lassitude and illness, not to say higher infant mortality. Clearly, all this was an inertial drag on the health of suppos-edly advanced and extremely wealthy nations, as medical officers, for instance, found to their shock when recruiting, and, more often than not, rejecting as entirely unfit, volunteers for the British army at the time of the Boer War.[118]

There was, thus, an obvious answer to the problem: state intervention to support and nurture the poor, state regulation to protect them from occupa-tional and environmental hazards. Yet, even as a new breed of often socialist-minded, government-appointed social planners and public health experts were quick to confirm that poor environmental conditions were what bred problem people and not vice versa,[119] the notion that it might be something in their hereditary, genetic make-up which made them that way, was equally perva-sive. Genetics was the trump card of the race theorists, the science which seemed to prove that Darwinism really was about 'the survival of the fittest' and, as its flip-side, that if you interbred the malformed, febrile or criminal with the strong, intelligent and beautiful it would be the former which would always win out in succeeding generations.[120] But there was obviously some-thing entirely contradictory here. If, as Darwinism argued, it was always the strongest, or more accurately the *most appropriately adapted* individuals in a spe-cies who were destined to succeed and reproduce themselves, either it followed that there was nothing to worry about, as nature would take its course, or alternatively, that the race scientists had got it wrong and those that they claimed were weak and criminal were actually the ones who were cleverest and strongest.[121] The argument for scientific intervention to select who should be bred, or bred out of the nation certainly was the closest race theory came to becoming accepted Western mainstream wisdom in the pre-1914 period. Indeed, its case, arguably, was as strongly represented amongst the would-be state planners who looked forward to a socialist Utopia as amongst their more obvious counterparts on an authoritarian right.[122] But in both cases, it was supported, not because it was an example of logical, value-free science but, on the contrary, because it most closely reflected the domestic social anxieties of scientific, literary and political elites.

As early as the 1860s, many years, indeed, before Gregor Mendel's near-contemporary findings on inherited 'recessive' characteristics in the common green pea became the accepted starting point for the study of genes, the influential Italian-Jewish criminal anthropologist, Claude Lombroso was postulating that at least 40 per cent of hardened criminals were actually throw-backs to man's more primitive and savage ancestors. Because they were born 'organically fitted for evil, atavistic reproductions not simply of savage men but even of the fiercest animals',[123] there was no point, Lombroso thought, in attempting to be compassionate. Let them loose on society and they would cause havoc. One obvious solution, he proposed, was mandatory capital punishment.

Interestingly, Lombroso, in his stark inversion of the idea of the noble savage – and with it of Rousseauesque optimism – nevertheless considered himself, and was considered by others, to be a thoroughly enlightened socialist who was simply offering a rational formula for cleaning up society in order to make it safer. Some turn of the century Lombroso acolytes thought that the 'born [sic.] criminal' was so closely linked to questions of biological deficiency, that insanity and criminality ought to be treated under the same state legislative roof.[124] But start down this dubious track and where would one finish? An emerging eugenicist-type discourse was already postulating the merits of sterilisation and not just for habitual criminals, the incurably insane and for violent sex offenders, but also for epileptics, alcoholics, people suffering from syphilis, tuberculosis and cancer, not to say in the view of the German criminal psychologist, Hans Gros, all 'violent, ineducable and intractable young people'.[125] But if this was actually to happen, would it be all, or only some of these categories which would be 'cleaned up'? And who, moreover, would decide?

At the turn of the century, Darwin's clearly brilliant cousin Francis Galton believed he had the answer: it would be he and other qualified university-based geneticists who would make these decisions. Certainly, his Laboratory for National Eugenics (originally founded as the Eugenics Record Office in 1904), and his equally prestigious *Journal for Racial and Social Biology* did not openly proclaim mass sterilisation or euthanasia for 'inferior types' *per se* as did Lapouge in France.[126] Rather, the language of Galton's eugenics was one of 'positive' selective breeding and 'population management' for the overall betterment of the racial stock. Galton's message, however, was equally fervently promoted by his acolyte, the 'biometrician' Karl Pearson who was less coy about trumpeting the need to breed out the country's 'lower stocks' in order to keep up a high pitch of 'efficiency' in its struggle for existence with both inferior and equal races.[127] Similar ideas were also receiving high-level support – and with it serious funding – elsewhere. Though the Kaiser Wilhelm Institute for Anthropology, Human Heredity and Eugenics in Berlin – a key player in Nazi racial hygiene – was not actually established until 1927, the groundwork for a German state-sponsored Galtonian-style research establishment was already underway in the 1900s.[128] As for the United States, substantial endowments, not least from the humanitarian-orientated Carnegie Institution, ensured that its Eugenics Record Office, at Cold Springs Harbor, was up and running with 'an army of research students' as early as 1904.[129] With an International Federation of Eugenics Organisations linking these and other research centres together, the new scientific apostles of what the British called 'national efficiency' were clearing gaining respectability and kudos by leaps and bounds.

Certainly, at this stage, few were prepared to go publicly on record as the German polemicist Adolf Jost, in 1895, had done, to propose that the state had the right to terminate the individual lives of those it deemed a burden on society.[130] The nearest the pre-war West came to this, in practice, was the legislation, beginning in 1907, in a growing number of US states, mandating them to sterilise handicapped people and criminals.[131] Even so, what the practitioners euphemistically were referring to as 'negative' eugenics was beginning to infiltrate into a more popular discourse in the idea of the lethal chamber.[132] And if some of the eugenicists themselves were too bashful to spell out what they had in mind, others were prepared to be much more forthright. Introducing the subject by way of science fiction, for instance, in his 1898 best-seller, *The War of the Worlds*, H. G. Wells has a London survivor of the Martian attack expostulate:

> We can't have any weak and silly. Life is real again, and the useless and the cumbersome and mischievous have to die. They ought to die. They ought to be willing to die. It's a sort of disloyalty, after all, to live and taint the race.[133]

Another celebrated English novelist, D. H. Lawrence, writing ten years later – albeit privately – was even less oblique:

> If I had my way, I would build a lethal chamber as big as the Crystal Palace, with a military band playing softly, and a Cinematograph working brightly, then I'd go out in the back streets and bring them in, all the sick, the halt and the maimed; I would lead gently and they would smile me a weary thanks; and the band would softly bubble out the Hallelujah Chorus.[134]

Lawrence and Wells were, in effect, proposing a truly grand September massacre, the only difference being that it would be carried out in a more orderly and systematic fashion by government authorisation. Wells, one of the most popular novelists of his day, certainly returned to the subject repeatedly and unashamedly. Indeed, in the last chapter of his *Anticipations*, written in 1902, he looked forward to a future world state – the New Republic – where the quest for Utopia had been resolved not only by eliminating the weak and undesirable but inferior races too; all 'those swarms of black, brown and dirty-white and yellow people, who do not come into the new needs of efficiency'. Included also would be one other group, 'the alleged termite of the civilised world, the Jew'.[135]

Wells had let the eugenicists' cat out of the bag. The social question was not distinct from the race question: it was perceived as part and parcel of the *same* problem.[136] The Irish repeatedly found themselves the domestic butt of this equation in popular as well as scientific Victorian discourse.[137] It was, thus, a dubious consolation if anthropologists found them not to be on the lowest rung of human worth: a position clearly reserved for 'dark-skinned … unclothed and unclean, promiscuous and brutal … savages'.[138] For the best white stock to breed with these types, however, was, according to German eugenicist research of the period, to court disaster for it would indubitably lead to 'a pauperisation of the genetic traits of the superior … race'.[139]

At the supposed cutting edge of this research was the young Freiburg anthropologist, Dr Eugen Fischer, the man who later, as both director of the Kaiser Wilhelm Institute and rector of Berlin University, would freely give his prestige and scholarly imprimatur to Nazi *Mischling* policy on Jews, gypsies and other undesirables.[140] The term *Mischling* was, in fact, already in common German currency when Fischer first set about considering race mixing, in the mid-1900s though at this stage primarily with regard to black–white miscegenation. Ironically, in his 1913 study, 'The Rehoboth Bastards and the Bastardisation Problem in Man', based on field research in German South-West Africa in the immediate wake of arguably the first genocide of the twentieth century, he did not find the evidence that he was seeking. There was a further irony, too, possibly lost on Fischer, that the Rehoboth had remained loyal to the colonial power throughout the latter's exterminatory campaign. That notwithstanding, Fischer deferred to the already fixed view of Professor Felix von Luschan, the leading German ethnological 'expert' on *Entmischung* – racial de-mixing – that the degenerate physical and psychological attributes of the inferior race would always reappear generations down the line, however much those future offspring only interbred with other whites. Fischer's conclusion, that there should be no further colonial race mixing, was, thus, not only no surprise, it was already, for some years, standard German colonial policy – albeit more in the breach than the practice.[141]

However, Fischer's pre-1914 focus on colonial *Mischlinge* did not mean that it had no relationship to, or bearing on, attitudes to Jews and Roma before the advent of Nazism. As the voluminous works of Sander Gilman testify, an alleged degeneracy in the form of, amongst other things, ugly, nasally dominated physiognomy, flat-footedness, not to say generally poor build, plus constant illness and lassitude, including tendencies towards acute neuroticism and hypochondria, were part and parcel of the dominant medical-eugenics discourse on Jews at the *fin de siècle.* Interbreeding with them, it was constantly reiterated by such authorities, could only perpetuate these Oriental, semi-Asiatic features, a fear all the more prevalent in the wider literature of the period because intermarriage was actually growing apace.[142] There was something else too; Jews were not only diseased – tuberculosis being specifically identified as 'Jewish' – but were also associated with the spread and origins of disease. Typhus, which was particularly feared, might actually be on the wane in the decade after 1900, but repeated calls in Germany for the eastern borders to be sealed in order to prevent its spread were linked to the repeated charge that it was itinerant foreign workers, Poles, gypsies and above all *Ostjuden* who were its chief carriers.[143] Indeed, bacteriology seemed to be not only at one with race hygiene in this respect but with a broader public opinion that charged migrant Jews not only with carrying lice on their filthy bodies and soiled clothes but being parasitic and pathogenic vermin, if not death-dealing microbes themselves. As the leading Volkish publicist and anti-Semite, Paul de Lagarde, put it in 1887: 'One does not negotiate with trichinae and bacilli: trichinae and bacilli are not chosen to be educated, they are exterminated quickly and as thoroughly as possible'.[144]

From the race perspective, however, there was again just one small problem with this analysis. Bacilli, lice and other vermin might be disgusting but they were clearly far from weak or pathetic. On the contrary, they were not only multitudinous and resilient but clearly extremely powerful with it. If Jews really were like them, then any ensuing 'race' struggle was, at the very least, going to be with an evenly matched foe. Indeed, could it be that, like a particularly virulent strain of pathogene, the Jews might actually win? Loathing, implicit in the racist's anti-Semitic image, thus, much more starkly than with any other racial stereotype, stood in schizophrenic tension with a kind of awe. It is clearly present in many novels of the *fin de siècle*, not least the most successful and famous one of all, George du Maurier's *Trilby*. In this, the scheming anti-hero, Svengali, may be a filthy and physically repulsive Jew but his mesmeric powers over the otherwise lacklustre 'white' beauty, Trilby, not only enable him to turn her, as if by magic, into a sensational diva but also, by implication, to take sexual possession of her innocent body.[145]

The idea of a Jewish racial potency could be ascribed to other areas too. Werner Sombart, an extremely eminent German economic historian, for instance, wrote something of a best-seller in 1911 – *Jews and Capitalism* – in which he proposed that the emergence of the latter had been brought about almost single-handedly by the former. Sounding almost adulatory in his verdict, Sombart proclaimed that 'Israel rises over Europe like a sun. Wherever it appears new life blossoms, while in the places that it leaves, everything that flourishes up to then withers and fades'. Only his subsequent comments affirming that Jewish superiority was a matter of blood and that this posed 'the greatest problem of mankind', belied his hyperbolic appraisal. The solution, Sombart argued, was to protect the inferior Germans by preventing miscegenation between the groups.[146] Nietzsche, another thinker notable for his refusal to buy into the straightforwardly anti-Semitic canon, had already, a quarter of a century earlier, pronounced that the Jews, if they wanted to, or were forced to, 'could right now have control and literally a stranglehold on all of Europe'. The point, however, insisted Nietzsche, was that they did not want to.[147]

It was left to Houston Stewart Chamberlain to turn Nietzsche's absurdly fantastical commentary on its head. Not only, said Chamberlain, was the history of the world a racial history, but it was one in which there were ultimately only two contestants which mattered. In this explication the Teutonic Aryans naturally represented everything that was honourable and worthwhile in mankind. The carriers of civilisation, bequeathed from the Greeks and Romans, they were also the only hope for the future, the one race that through the preservation of its inner purity and soul would be able to transform the external world into something of enduring beauty. Significantly, Chamberlain did not reject modernity, science or industry to reach these transcendent heights. What he did reject was these instruments finding their ways into the hands of the Jews who, Chamberlain prognosticated, would use them to accomplish their malevolent goal of global supremacy and, thereby, turn the world into something soulless and useless. For Chamberlain, thus, the supposed attributes of Jewish racial power were not to be taken lightly. Here was a serious, collective enemy, whose existence, governed by a set of supposedly iron, mechanistic laws, necessarily demanded the destruction of the 'beautiful saving Aryan' as the one obstacle in its path even if this meant mixing with the Aryan 'in order to produce a race of pseudo-hebraic *mestizos*, a people beyond all doubt degenerate physically, mentally and morally'.[148] This, then, was race theory offered as unashamed Manichaeism; not just a pretext for getting rid of what one did not like, but what one most feared.

Class – An Unlikely Contender?

If racists at the *fin de siècle* were prepared to go to enormous lengths to dress up their exterminatory salvationist nightmares and wish-fulfilments in pseudo-scientific clothes, at the very least the potential for this sort of approach was also beginning to become evident in a movement with an entirely different agenda: Marxist socialism. To utter Marx and someone such as Chamberlain in the same breath, or to propose that they might have a commonality in providing at least some of the intellectual antecedents to the genocidal trajectories of the twentieth century will, certainly in some quarters, be treated as nothing less than a pernicious blasphemy on the name of the great founding father of revolutionary socialism. After all, far from proposing that the future wellbeing of mankind be restricted to a chosen few on the basis of some spurious claim to racial or national superiority, Marx unashamedly propounded a secular, universal theory of human emancipation regardless of race, colour or creed.

This is not to deny that class struggles could not be dressed up in racial language. When, for instance, protagonists of the French Revolution, the Abbé Sieyès included, proclaimed, that the French nobility were actually not French at all but descendants of 'savage' Frankish – i.e. German – invaders who ought to be sent back as a body to the forests of Franconia, they were simply substituting one self-justificatory pretext for another.[149] Marxism, by contrast, did not appear to be responding to any such feeling of relative deprivation, nor, indeed, any other psychological anxiety caused by the advent of modernity, but rather to a very direct and tangible by-product of its primary driving force: the immiseration of vast numbers of ordinary people. As such, it offered a voice for all those seeking redress for the oppression, social injustice and poverty brought about by unrestricted capitalism. More specifically, in propounding not only a rational, historically grounded explanation for its causes but a redemptive prognosis for the ultimate unshackling of its social and economic chains, Marx arguably set himself up as the authentic heir of Rousseau.

That said, it is in these very utopian qualities that we can also discern a shared reservoir of ideas and concerns with Marxism's bitterest enemies. Balibar, for one, has commented on both the symmetry and complementarity of race and class theories as they developed in the nineteenth and early twentieth centuries, particularly in the way that both sought the achievement of a finalised, supranational universalism: the first by creating a hierarchy of nations, the latter by dissolving them.[150] Both also shared the same determination to read history in strictly teleological terms, looking back to the earliest origins of mankind in order to throw light on humanity's present condition but also, more extraordinarily, looking forward to some final resolution, an end to race or class struggle, and with it an end to history itself. Marx, of course, claimed to have rejected, *in toto*, any religious, mystical, let alone messianic terms of reference to reach his particular conclusions on the course this would take. Yet one can hardly avoid noting that his forecast of some final, irrevocable collapse of the present political economic system, heralding a 'withering away' of the state, has distinct parallels with the apocalyptic, millenarian tradition within the Judeo-Christian canon.[151]

Whether it was these expectations, or the claim to a scientific basis for his philosophy of history, or his own espousal of the necessity of theory being given practical application, which led generations of intellectuals, both in Marx's native Germany and far beyond, enthusiastically to adopt and espouse Marxism is certainly a matter for debate. There is no doubt that in advancing a theory – which he dubbed dialectical materialism – for how basic economic need operated as the primary motor force for historical development, Marx made a contribution to social sciences which closely paralleled Darwin's near-contemporary breakthrough in the field of natural sciences. Arguably better still, Marx was able to offer something absent in Darwin's evolutionary schema; the notion that human society was genuinely progressing. And not only that, but as society technologically advanced through what Marx called 'the means of production', so the resolution to human conflict became more imminent. But in this, of course, was Marx's dialectical sting. The social and political structure of a given time were a reflection not only of the technological sophistication of the means of production but of who controlled them. The engine of history, thus, was moved forward by the dialectical struggle between those who controlled the means, the ruling class, and those in antithetical – and necessarily 'underdog' – relationship with them. What made Germany and the wider Western world earth-shatteringly exciting, thought Marx, in his seminal writings of the mid-century, was the emergence of a new ruling class, the bourgeoisie, who were taking technological development further forward, and more rapidly than ever before. But as they did so, and as the world became subsumed by the market forces at the core of their capitalist system, so its internal contradictions would contain the seeds of its own destruction. Thus, as the crisis of capitalism became more acute, so too, argued Marx and followers, would the intensity of the struggle with the class spawned by capitalism itself; the industrial workers; the proletariat. It would all culminate when the monopolising tendencies in the capitalist edifice finally ruptured and control of the means of the production passed to the proletariat, the synthesis of human development, and, henceforth, the first classless society.[152]

It was neat and very optimistic; and also quite unlike the majority of arguments in the racist or ultra-nationalist camps, neither ambivalent nor hostile to modernity. On the contrary, Marxists embraced change, particularly industrial change. Even better for many disciples disengaged from, or entirely alienated by national or nationalist politics, orthodox Marxism had no place for nations in its schemata – let alone races – at all. Nation-states were simply part of capitalism's superstructure. The future would not belong to them but to an *international* working class. The fact that, in one important respect, this scenario closely mirrored race theory's own self-comforting conviction that at the end of the day 'our' side was bound to win because its interpretation of history said so, was necessarily ignored. So too was the close similarity between theories which, despite Marx's insistence on the role of human agency, had at their cores, not the role of the individual but 'world-historical' life-and-death struggles between *groups*. When all was said and done Marxism, like racism, was predicated on a social Darwinian, zero-sum view of the world in which 'our' side, or 'class', would overcome and the 'other' side, or class, would go under or conveniently disappear.[153]

But who exactly, for Marxists, were the adversary class and what if they did not disappear? What, indeed, if the crisis of capitalism failed to materialise properly? Or perhaps manifested itself in entirely unexpected ways? Second- or third- generation Marxist theoreticians tended, like Marx and Engels themselves, to be highly educated and invariably middle class in background, men, indeed, like Eduard Bernstein, who in the 1890s rose to become leader of the recently state-recognised German Social Democratic Party (SPD). Marxism allowed, indeed encouraged, the 'enlightened' elements of the bourgeoisie to throw in their lot with the self-styled progressive forces of history; without them, emerging Marxist-orientated parties like the SPD would either have been leaderless, or of a very different complexion. But, as a Marxist, Bernstein faced a dilemma. Marxist prophecy was not being borne out in practice. As he tersely noted: 'Peasants do no sink; middle classes do not disappear; crises do not grow ever larger; misery and serfdom do not increase'.[154]

Without the fulfilment of these conditions Marxist theory at the *fin de siècle* was in a fix. Indeed, it was predicated on the notion that, as the hold of capitalism became ever more universal and monopolistic, the ranks of those thereby proletarianised would swell to such an extent that they would end up facing a tiny *haute*-bourgeois minority. Not only was this highly convenient, come the expected revolution, but also rather necessary given that, in the here-and-now interim, it was not just the great bankers, business magnates and industrial captains whom Marxists considered as the 'enemy'. The bourgeois class, according to the critique, embraced a whole range of people, including a *petit*-bourgeoisie – in Germany, the *Mittelstand* – who themselves were notably vitriolic in their opposition to socialists of almost any hue and whom they equally saw as potential expropriators of their often meagre property and livelihoods. An equal measure of socialist contempt and distaste for them in return, thus, could only logically be tempered if they were absorbed into the proletariat. The same was true of those elements of pre-capitalist society, particularly the peasantry, whom Marx himself made no bones about lambasting as representatives of barbarism and 'the idiocy of rural life'.[155] Marxist predictions about the fate of these groups may have carried a certain plausibility in the years of the Great Depression. Yet thereafter, in the immediate years leading up to the First World War, none of them could be described either as notably residual or on their way out. Any more, for that matter, than the actually swelling ranks of the urban unskilled – the lumpenproletariat – another group which Marxist leaders either generally despaired of, or disparaged in terms hardly distinct from the damning verdict of the eugenicists.[156]

It left little choice, thought Bernstein, except to accept that the capitalist crisis was not imminent and that the role and purpose of the SPD in Germany, therefore, was to operate, if not in principle, then certainly in practice, as a *national* party – i.e. among other non-Marxist parties – engaging with both the state through parliament and the big industrial companies to improve the sectional interests of the workers in the here and now. This 'revisionism' was certainly heretical in the eyes of all those who clung to Marx's own prescript that class warfare precluded any compromise with the bourgeoisie, or its political superstructure. Nevertheless, for those who continued to accept Marx's dictum that the point was not simply to interpret the world but to change it,[157] the conundrum still remained, from whence would the signal for worldwide revolution come?

The potential answer – though one still very much on the horizon before the advent of the First World War – was itself distinctly revisionist. The break-through would not come from the most advanced industrial countries, Germany, France, Britain, or the United States: the countries, in other words, with the largest and most politically organised and powerful working classes, as Marx and Engels had predicted. It would come from the semi-periphery, from a state, or states, where, due to the nature of uneven development, capitalist formation was still in its infancy but where the birth-pangs associated with this process were producing extreme turbulence and state repression. But if this led to mass popular unrest, even a revolutionary moment, this could hardly conform to classical Marxist notions of a capitalist superstructure literally falling into the hands of a mass working class. On the contrary, if capitalism in any such country was still in its infancy, any basis for a *minority* proletariat attempting to take control on its own behalf would be distinctly premature, not to say in defiance of the historical dialectic as Marx understood it. *Unless*, perhaps, it could be demonstrated that this would indeed trigger mass proletarian uprising in the core capitalist countries.[158] Even so, in the interim, the logic of an initial forced seizure of power in any one country would be an invitation to a probably more extreme replay of the Jacobin scenario: increasingly draconian rule by a minority group under acute crisis conditions, beset by popular counter-revolutionary opposition from within, combined with the likelihood of statist military intervention from without. If this were the only way 'the inevitability' of worldwide proletarian victory could be assured, it could clearly only succeed through massive violence.

Interestingly, the use of violence as an instrument of revolutionary struggle was, at the *fin de siècle*, not something one particularly associated with the Marxist brand of socialism at all so much as with its key contemporary rival: anarchism. The emerging socialist movement, generally, was varied and divided, with emerging *Marxisant* parties among them hardly able to claim a monopoly of proletarian allegiance to themselves anywhere, except in Germany, where the attraction of the SPD lay, arguably, in its reformist tendencies. Anarchism certainly lacked Marxism's penchant for theory but it was also much less exclusive in its focus on the industrial working class while also much more geared towards spontaneous action; its avowed enemy being state oppression in all its manifestations. The result was not only strong followings in relatively less developed countries, like Spain and Italy, where it easily crossed worker–peasant divides, but also in repeated waves of terrorist attack and assassinations directed at leading establishment institutions and leaders.[159]

None of this could hope to bring down the state on its own. However, anarchism also partly spawned a more specifically industrial movement, syndicalism, which through the 1908 treatise of its leading French advocate, Georges Sorel – *Reflections on Violence* – also extolled the uses, indeed centrality of violence as an instrument for a more concerted form of internationalised revolutionary class-warfare consciously aimed at bringing down the bourgeois edifice. Significantly, Sorel's own starting point in his expositions on this theme was *not* as an anarchist but as a Marxist. 'The idea of the general strike was a translation into concrete terms of the Marxist apocalypse, and the sole real historical function of Marxism was to act as a instrument of war'.[160] Certainly, Sorel's ideas would not be openly espoused by revolutionary Marxists, not least given his increasingly antipathetic views on Marxist materialism or that his next port of call would be mystical nationalism.[161] Nevertheless, Sorel's embrace of violence as the motive force in history, combined with his exposition of a syndicalist elite who would operate like a religious sect both separate from and unbound by moral obligations to the rest of society – even while building around themselves a myth centring on their heroic self-sacrifice – was clearly attractive to frustrated or disenchanted activists on the periphery of both Marxist and anarchist movements. In Italy, one such Sorelian disciple was the leader of a nascent post-First World War fascism, Benito Mussolini.[162]

If, then, the emergence of the fascist tendency underscored Italy's uncertain or at least contested candidacy as a site for an authentic revolutionary yet proletarian Marxist takeover, Russia was another matter. Marx himself had blown hot and cold in his final years either as to its potential, or relevance.[163] On the other hand, by the time of his death, in 1883, Russia was already in the early stages of a traumatic, state-led industrial take-off that was spawning a relatively small but significant working class. It also, equally importantly, had already witnessed decades of populist- or anarchist-inspired terrorist action, the advocates of which had no qualms about provoking increased state repression. Indeed, it was part of their design; late nineteenth-century groups like Narodnaya Volya – the People's Will – predicated their actions on the belief that it would incite draconian counter-measures on the part of an entirely monolithic tsardom which, in turn, would spark off a general people's rising. Few of these activists worried about theoretical issues, such as what might happen *after* a successful revolution, given the empire's lack of a mature economic or political base.[164] Even less did they consider the probability that its many ethnic non-Russian peoples might chose to go their own way. Into this picture emerged, in 1898, a specifically Marxist-orientated revolutionary party, the Russian Social Democratic Labour Party (RSDLP) as well as one Vladimir Ulyanov – Lenin.

Lenin, who would rise in 1917 to be leader of the Russian Revolution and of the first modern communist state, was in key respects a typical Marxist intellectual, believing that his theoretical observations on the class struggle placed him squarely in its internationalist mainstream. Contrary to Bernstein, he argued that reformist tendencies within capitalism did not demand the retreat of orthodox analysis but, rather, an awareness that capitalism itself was going through a critical transition that, in turn, necessitated not a relaxation but rather a tightening up of party structure. Or, to put it another way, while Bernstein was seeking to put the revolution off to some distant date, Lenin was preaching its imminent arrival. But that still left the question of what seminal role could either the RSDLP or Russian working-class play in it, so long as capitalism in Russia remained insufficiently developed there. Lenin's answer, in his seminal 1902 pamphlet, *What is to be Done?* was to transform the party organisation into a highly centralised, militant and professional elite.[165] But what was the point of such an undertaking, unless the RSDLP was preparing for power?

Largely pre-dating Sorel's writings, radical opponents of Lenin's thesis were, nevertheless, quick to grasp its dangerous implications. They accused him of Blanquism, a reference to Sorel's critical compatriot precursor, the mid-nineteenth-century activist, Louis Blanqui, whose entire career had been dedicated to fomenting – what turned out to be abortive – *coups d'état* against a whole range of regimes. Blanqui's vision was one of an egalitarian, communistic version of Jacobinism. But in order to arrive there Blanqui propounded that the revolution came first, the people's support for it second. In other words, the fomenters of revolution themselves had to be, in the first instance, tightly disciplined conspirators and in the second, ready to maintain control against the inevitable counter-revolutionary backlash by dictatorial means. If Leninism was not a form of Blanquism dressed up in suitably Marxist attire, what was it?[166] Though, in 1902, he had not formulated any programme for exactly how it was going to be achieved, Lenin was in effect looking forward to a very Russian revolutionary seizure of power, by a tiny party that at best could claim to represent only a fraction of the population, in a larger society where orthodox Marxist analysis of conditions hardly applied. And, as further borne out in the fractious RSDLP Congress debates of the following year, where not even the future autonomy of non-Russian peoples – even where these themselves claimed to be represented by socialist Marxist parties – would be allowed.[167]

The Toxic Climate of the *Fin de Siècle*

Yet did any of this really matter? Lenin may have been a ruthless party operator, and nothing if not single-minded in his determination to see 'world-historical forces' harnessed and carried through to their 'inevitable' destination; regardless of the human consequences. But the idea that he, or a bunch of similarly outlawed *deraciné* intellectuals could proclaim themselves heirs-apparent to the Russian empire, let alone the custodians of human destiny, would have seemed, before 1917, utterly ridiculous. We may now look back on their 1903 London and Brussels Congress as a seminal moment in the fate of the twentieth century. Yet the fact that it had to take place under constant police interference and surveillance, far away from Russia itself and with such bitter disagreement among its participants – Lenin's declaration that he represented the Bolsheviks, the 'majority' among them being constructed on an entirely ephemeral agenda victory – not only seems to underscore how marginal these individuals were but also, arguably, how far removed they were from reality.

One might, of course, say the same for the equally fractious Young Turk conference held the previous year in Paris. It was noteworthy for its major split around the issue of centralised unity, or decentralised autonomy, for the Ottoman empire's ethnic component parts. Here again was an outlawed, revolutionary party far removed from the Porte's corridors of power, yet purportedly making momentous decisions on its behalf.[168] As for that adolescent painter *manqué*, Adolf Hitler, and his early thoughts on the future of the German race, he would be reduced a few years later to tramping the streets of Vienna.[169] If these were the men of destiny, whose heated organisational arguments, or personal musings, contained the seeds of future genocides, they were also still complete outsiders. This would seem to throw the weight of explanation for the great European, or near-European genocides of the twentieth century firmly onto the countdown to, or direct explosion of the First World War, events so cataclysmic that they would enable these revolutionary nobodies to become, still revolutionary, leaders of state.

The First World War, undoubtedly, was the great watershed in the process. But the genocidal trajectory did not begin here. These last two chapters have sought to show how deeply embedded its potential already was in the European, more specifically western European frame, even to the point where it held up a mirror to the nature and, one might say, peculiarities of its political-religious formation. Having said that, while clearly being put into operation primarily by Anglos on its peripheries, or further abroad, somewhat earlier, genocide did not fully and unequivocally crystallise on the continent of Europe

until the Vendée. In other words, the First World War was preceded by a critical prior watershed, the French Revolution, which in turn underscores the
linkage between genocide, the nation-state and the advent of a secular
modernity.

However, the transmission of genocidal potential between these two cataclysmic events is a more complex issue. It was certainly not carried forward
entirely or directly by politics *alone*. What the French Revolution had done,
instead, was set up a powerful new social, cultural as well as political model –
the nation-state – for how forward-looking societies might organise and
develop themselves. The model could be emulated or opposed, but not
ignored, not least because it became so closely associated with a laissez-faire
capitalism that gave to the model's avant-gardist leaders, France included, an
economic weapon which they could wield for both commercial and political
advantage on the broadest international stage.

In these terms, the Lenins, the Talaats, the Hitlers detestation of liberalism
and all it stood for, cannot be viewed in isolation. In critical respects this new
generation of ideological dissidents were *a* logical end-product of societal frustrations which had been building up for the best part of a century. Certainly,
they were not the *only* logical end-product, as evidenced in the fact that within
both the RSDLP and Young Turk movement themselves there were alternative
much more moderate and conciliatory programmes for attempting to ride
change. Equally, though, one might argue that the very fact that such uncompromising agendas were now being considered at all – with the further
implications for societal violence which they entailed – was simply an extreme
reflection of a more general hardening of a European-cum-Western societal climate at the *fin de siècle*. Paradoxically, as we will see more obviously in the next
chapter, such tendencies also pervaded the leading liberal nation-states. After
the American Civil War, the Franco-Prussian War, the Boer War, nothing
could any longer be taken for granted. The optimism of the Enlightenment,
and the idea of progress which followed from it might still be central to the
Western liberal ethos but, well before 1900, it was also being notably tempered by a much more pessimistic if widely accepted view that life for
individuals, classes, nations and races was dominated and determined by
unforgiving struggle and competition.

Such social Darwinian anxieties manifested themselves in a variety of ways,
all of which had as their source some aspect of modernity. A horror of urbanism and with it of the 'masses', led many intellectuals, in particular, towards a
Nietzschean-informed compensation in the notion that they were supermen
and all those hordes of lumpens and yellow men ripe for mass extermination.[170] Fears of disease might not prevent middle-class males from seeking

sexual gratification from lower-class prostitutes, yet it was from exactly this same 'gentleman' strata that calls to clean up the criminal poor and foreigners were at their loudest, and the craze for health and fitness through gymnastics and other 'manly' pursuits at its most obsessive.[171] Clearly such anxieties needed a public cover for private weakness, a talisman to make one feel brave, and something or somebody to blame. But when such anxieties were mixed with frustration and embitterment not just about one's own individual position or status but about the wider society of which one was part, the result could be altogether more virulent and toxic. Is it entirely coincidental that ideologies of organic nation, race and class all took such notable root in Germany, a country whose notably educated and literate strata almost continuously proclaimed from generation to generation – from the time of Napoleon right up to the onset of the First World War – such aggrieved injury? Or that the most obvious source of this grievance was the fear that Germany was going to be perpetually left behind in a social Darwinian world dominated by other more advanced nation-states?

Class and race theories of society might tackle the problem from vastly different perspectives but what they commonly shared, alongside ultra-nationalism, was the promise that the problem would be not simply overcome but transcended. Each, indeed, preached a redemptive message in which the nation-state was found to be an historical cul-de-sac, not to say an irrelevance. The fact, moreover, that in each case this was founded on the notion of a judgement of history, provided not just a certitude as to where one was ultimately going and, more importantly, a sense of liberation with it. True believers did not need the nation-state because they had something much better to look forward to. Whether one's preference was the Volk, the race, or the international brotherhood of man, one could subsume oneself within it and take this to be one's destiny. And curiously, despite the variance between an openly mythic ultra-nationalism and racism compared with an avowedly rigorous Marxist scientism, each predicated this future collective well-being on a version of historical inevitability, the key to which lay in man's evolution from his earliest origins.

Unravelling this key became the critical and urgent quest by which true seekers refound their innate freedom and in so doing made the leap towards utopian harmony and salvation. But getting there equally demanded understanding, confronting and finally overcoming what had denied this true path of progress in the first place. In a pre-secular age it would have been commonly called evil, a metaphysical factor with the power to infect people's minds, as well as harm their bodies. By the late nineteenth century it had transmuted into a much more tangible series of pollutants including degenerative disease, racial miscegenation and the contamination of money. Volkish, racist and class theorists all necessarily threw up human anti-types as representatives of these various mortal foes, though it was also curious the degree to which these were often familiar if more virulent reincarnations of earlier religious enemies. Not least there was enemy number one: 'the Jew'. Certainly it was not so blatant or central in Marxist antipathy as it was in much of the racist analysis, but Marx's own Jewish background proved no barrier to his own vitriolic diatribes against supposed Jewish responsibility for the bain of capitalism, nor to the insistent regurgitation of this theme by Marxists theoreticians, many themselves of Jewish background.[172]

These tendencies were, of course, not exclusive to Germany. In the decades after Sedan, the prevalence of racist and ultra-nationalist discourse in particular, and with it a notable populist upsurge in blaming the Jews for just about everything – a cry regularly joined by the French radical socialist left[173] – speaks volumes about the shattered confidence of the quintessential nation-state and the urgency therein for some compensatory mechanism. The mention already of Talaat, Hitler, or, for that matter, Lenin, further suggests the spread of these oppositional ideologies well beyond their core German or Western centres of origin. Yet this still leaves a conundrum. Nowhere in the Western world, or indeed beyond, were racist, ultra-nationalist or Marxist ideas translated into the pre-1914 policies of state.

This does not mean that a genocidal wish-fulfilment could not take on a very publicly ugly face. There was the infamous occasion, for instance, in the midst of the Dreyfus affair when a group of French military officers invited subscriptions for a proposal that a new type of gun be tried out on on the Jews of the country. More than a thousand other officers flocked to have their names added to the proposal, including four generals on active service and the then minister of war.[174] The repeated cry of 'death to the Jews' even provided the stimulus to the election of a populist city government in Vienna, though in practice the administration of Karl Lueger proved to have a bark much worse than its bite.[175] This is surely the point; the extreme parties did not make good in the pre-war years. In Germany, as in Austria, the anti-Semites might continue to rant and rave against 'secret Judah' but they proved largely ineffectual at the ballot box just as, in France, anti-Dreyfusard sentiment itself did not ultimately overwhelm liberalism. Similarly, for all the social turbulence and in spite of a growing labour movement in this era of emerging mass democracy, revolutionary Marxism remained politically marginal. Sorel's apocalypse failed to materialise, the writer Jack London's 1908 novel of an abortive proletarian struggle wiped out by corporate capitalists in a ocean of blood, remained a singular, if horrifying prophecy.[176] Only in the field of eugenics – and here only very tentatively – can we speak of any convergence between the new uncompromising ideologies and *state* implementation.

Clearly, there was a paradox here, or more accurately, a whole series. The new ideologies informed the cultural climate of the *fin de siècle* just as, in turn, they were a reflection of it. They expressed not only levels of anxiety and frustration with perceived failings of the nation-state, strongly held by significant, including opinion-forming sections of society but, more importantly still, they expressed a growing desire not simply to circumvent these failings through some new Zeitgeist, new dawn, new moral revolution, but utterly to transcend them. In this sense, the ideologies had more than something in common not only with traditional religion in its emergent enthusiastic phase but, more recently, with the supranational 'world-historical' aspirations of the French revolutionaries, especially the Jacobins. Like the latter, the genocidal potential inherent in these essentially anti-statist 'ethics as politics' visions would, paradoxically, only crystallise when they became wedded – and, in so doing narrowed – to the apparatus of state. But not yet. And not in France, or Britain, or the United States. Or, at least, not in their domestic policies of state.

With hindsight, we might trace the translation of our three key ideologies, racism, revolutionary Marxism and ultra-nationalism into the state politics of other countries, most obviously Germany, Russia and Turkey, only through discerning the particular traumas which these countries underwent in the prequel, actuality and then aftermath of the First World War. Certainly, some recent historians of Germany would even challenge this premise by pointing out that its pre-1914 nationalism was not of such a virulent variety as has often been portrayed[177] or, alternatively, that it was being firmly subordinated to a process of state-led political reform that was actually taking the country in a institutional direction more akin to that of France.[178] Correct or not, the new ideologies – here as elsewhere – were indubitably held in check both by the absence and avoidance of total European war. So long as the old Westphalian system of inter-state relations survived, the possibility of another ideologically driven Vendée remained remote, at least, that is, in a domestic European context. And here we meet a further, final aspect of our extended paradox. The system's survival was founded primarily not on the strength of nineteenth-century liberal nation-statism – in other words, the Western model – but on the dominance of *realpolitik* rulers in the critical Central European arena who were, at the very least, ambivalent towards the whole concept of the modern nation-state, and wanted to hold it at bay. At home, Metternich strove to quash nationalism, German or otherwise, while, in foreign affairs, his energies remained devoted to keeping the European state system in some sort of peaceful equilibrium. A more transitional Bismarck, admittedly, was prepared to manipulate German nationalism and go to war in the Prussian state interest but, like Metternich, he too remained wedded to an essentially reactionary, almost *Ancien Régime* version of the status quo.

The problem was that by the time of Bismarck any notion of being able to stand still and, hence, of fending off the forces of modernity, internally or externally, had well-nigh disappeared. The economic surge forward of the avant-garde states demanded rapid industrial development if late competitors, such as Germany, wished to stay in the race, and equally the ability to manage the emerging social forces thrown up by the very speed and intensity of a transformed milieu. For the first time, often ultra-conservative elites found themselves having to engage with the increasingly vocal representatives of a mass democracy through new parliamentary fora as well as being expected to deliver not just in straightforward materialistic social and economic terms, but in response to populist demands on issues ranging from immigration to the conduct of foreign and colonial affairs.

The inability of the old order to manage this new era of mass democracy effectively certainly represented a major contributory factor plunging Europe, in 1914, into the maelstrom of war. And, of all its contenders, Germany has been regularly cited by historians as the most paranoid in its fears not only of external encirclement but of social forces undermining it from below.[179] Even so, the recourse to a military solution to domestic as well as foreign relations problems came almost as second nature to all the old European ruling elites.[180] The problem was that this war would not and could not be fought according to some refined and, by definition, limited set of *Ancien Régime* rules but only as a totalised national struggle. All participants, in other words, whether they saw themselves as nation-states or not, would be required to mobilise along the lines that France had done from the outset of her revolutionary wars, in 1792, simply in order to survive. One did not need to be a self-proclaimed prophet, like H. G. Wells, to recognise the potential for mass people-killing both of combatants and non-combatants inherent in this situation. Nor that in the event of military stalemate or – worse – reversal, radicalised state leaderships might seek to harden the line, force the pace and even consider dispensing with whole layers of or groupings within their *own* population, simply in order to win through. As the war, by degrees, turned into a life-and-death struggle, so the ideologues' viewpoint, whether in patriotic support, or bitter opposition to the war, inexorably came closer to centre-stage. Yet there was an irony. If it required total war to make this ideological potential manifest on the European or near-European stage, the impact of liberal, nation-state Europe, in its pre-1914 high imperial phase, was already giving rise to genocide on a much broader, global canvas.

THREE
Empires in Advance:
Empires in Retreat

5. Ascendant Imperialisms

Introduction: Imperial Conundrums

The primary thrust of *Genocide in the Age of the Nation-State* is to propose that the origins and continued momentum towards the potentiality for genocide in the modern world has been intrinsically bound up with the strivings – albeit convoluted and often frustrated – of societies towards some form of national, territorially grounded coherence. Which rather raises the question of why the final section of this volume should be devoted to the subject of empires.

Nation-state and empire: the very terms suggest antithesis. The former is bound up with an idea of popular sovereignty as derived from, and vested in, a specific group of people. This does not necessarily assume their ethnic commonality. But it does assume the idea that that population willingly lives within the fixed and internationally agreed boundaries that separate it from other peoples – who are themselves citizens of different national states – while accepting the political rights and duties of the state which is *their own*. Empires, however, are not of themselves circumscribed by any such implications. They require no formal mandate from a general popular voice. They are not dependent on bonds of commonality. They are politically top–down. The very word empire is derived from the Roman term, *imperium*, meaning supreme power vested in the person of consuls, or an emperor.[1] And this latter term is itself nonsensical outside the idea and practice of supreme military command. *Force majeure* is, thus, the primary *modus operandi* of empire. More pointedly, its use is not circumscribed to a particular set of people. On the contrary, when we think of empires today we usually have in mind a metropolitan state – possibly peopled by a single homogeneous ethnic or cultural group – subjugating and then ruling over many other socially, ethnically or religiously diverse peoples with whom that state has little or nothing in common. As a result empires, whether existing in one landmass, or spread out across seas and oceans, usually entail territorially vast if not sprawling zones of hegemonic control.

In the past, empires may have attempted to justify such hegemony by claiming a sacral sanction from God, or the gods. This often fed further universalist pretensions in which some anointed emperor claimed a holy mandate with which to bring all those barbarian and savage peoples beyond the realms of civilisation into its beneficent embrace. Again, Rome, carrying with it the all-important notion of *pax Romana* has been the Western model and paragon, attracting emulators, not least in the dreams of the sixteenth-century Habsburg, Charles V.[2] But no polity today would openly make such claims. Or call itself an empire. Nor would any dare to. It assumes first and foremost violent conquest. Over and beyond being simply 'a mode of political oppression',[3] it also reeks of a broader economic system for the collective monopolisation as well as expropriation of wealth – or, in Marxist terms, of the surplus value – of whole regions.[4] In a world built on the sophistry of an international system of economically free and independent polities which are, also, the product of national self-determination, empire thus, would appear to be not simply a concept which is defunct but a practice which to all intents and purposes is inoperable.

Does this then mean that our thesis has got the wrong end of the stick; indeed, has got the whole thing wrong? That it is not authentic nation-states at all who are the true makers of genocide, but empires? Consider two of the worst offenders of recent times; Nazi Germany and Soviet Russia – to whom we will be devoting much of the next volume – and could one not argue that it is in their very attempt to pursue outmoded imperial agendas in a world increasingly moving into nation-state mode that their genocidal proclivities lie? Perhaps we might pursue this line of thought further by proposing that there is something peculiarly, if nightmarishly modern about their conceptions of empire, not least in a Hitlerian version, where vast swathes of subject people are not simply subjugated but slated for elimination to make way for some new homogeneous Aryan master race. But even so, could one not equally say that it is in the very bankruptcy of this tendency compared with the impetus towards an international order founded on liberal, democratic, implicitly tolerant nation-state values that one can perceive the clear road away from genocide?

Retrospectively, it would follow that the seeds of the mass genocides of the twentieth century should not be sought either in the underpinnings or actions of the truly avant-gardist nation-states but rather in the antiquated hulks of the surviving dynastic empires in their late nineteenth-century twilight years. And certainly, in the following chapter, we will be drawing an arc through Qing (Manchu) China, Romanov Russia, Ottoman Turkey and Habsburg Austria-Hungary with a view to discerning, if not the full-blown contours of our phenomenon, then certainly its potentiality. In some cases it was a devastating potential. Nevertheless, this line of thought is in danger of proceeding on the basis of a big assumption; namely that genocide is actually a function of empire and even intrinsic to its very nature.

Fundamentally at stake here are issues of continuity and change. There is no doubt that the four above-named continental empires were all, in different ways, massively out of kilter with the demands and tenor of a modern forward-looking world. But then world-empires of this type[5] had not only been around for millennia but, amongst organised polities, had tended to be the globally dominant norm. Nor is there particular evidence that empires *once established* were notable purveyors of mass violence against their subject peoples. On the contrary, if we consider the long-term tracks records of the Qing, Romanov, Ottoman and Habsburg, what in terms of continuity we would primarily discern are political policies and administrative practices, if not enabling, then at least allowing their diverse peoples to co-exist with one another, often even where this involved widely divergent cultures, not to mention social and economic habits.[6] This is not to suppose that these empires were necessarily reconciled to this reality, or positively perceived themselves as multi-ethnic or pluralistic polities. On the contrary, significant disjunctures in the way that, for instance, the Romanov regime behaved towards its non-Russian subject peoples in its final decades, compared with the much more strikingly benevolent path adopted by the Habsburgs in this same period, would rather suggest that imperial rulers were normally predisposed to view their subject populations with a mixture of mistrust, xenophobia and unadulterated animus.[7] Yet the very fact that *fin-de-siècle* Austria chose to strike out on a largely experimental as well as radicalised path towards what were by then being considered as its 'nationalities' while Russian animus towards its own simply became more pronounced, would suggest that what these empires were attempting to do, in their separate ways, was tackle something not only new but profoundly unsettling. In other words, the potential for toxicity lay not in the existence of these empires *per se*, but rather in the particular circumstances or conditions of unrelenting change to which they were being forced to react. Indeed, align late Habsburg and Romanov ethnic policies with the increasingly catastrophic Chinese and Ottoman behaviour towards their subject peoples, in this period, and one cannot but come to the conclusion that what each was doing was not simply responding to a series of unrelated internal exigencies but a single, relentless wave of *external* pressure which was threatening to engulf them all.

What was happening, of course, was a fundamental and apparently irreversible geo-political and economic shift in favour of the West. Or, as the world historian, William McNeill, has put it 'a self-reinforcing cycle in which its military organisation sustained, and was sustained by economic and political expansion at the expense of other peoples and polities of the earth'.[8] Though the process had been gathering pace for some hundreds of years, one critical index demonstrated that, by 1800, the entirety of Western industrial production was still insufficient to dislodge Chinese paramountcy in this field. Yet, sixty years later, two-thirds of industrial production was Western while, by 1913, no less than nine-tenths of it was so.[9] At stake here is not just the overwhelming of traditional craft practices by new industrial techniques. As the sheer volume of Western factory-made goods began to swamp indigenous markets, often at the point of the gun – another, this time military technological, index of the growing East–West disparity – massive deindustrialisation and social dislocation of formerly largely self-sufficient empires and regions, ensued. Notions of autarky and economic independence as ground rules governing state and societal organisation were similarly forced to the point of extinction. The Western-led global political economy had arrived, and with it, beginning around the 1870s – at least as as argued by Geoffrey Barraclough, a key exponent of the concept – a new era of *contemporary* history.[10]

However, the implied equation here – Western nation-states advance, Eastern empires retreat – in its straightforward, even zero-sum finality tells us both everything and nothing. If it were true it could only be true in part, for the simple reason that the nation-statist West, where it was not already heavily imperial by the time of our Barracloughian watershed, was rapidly becoming so. The obvious big difference between these Western empires and their Eastern counterparts was that, whereas the latter were land-based territorial extensions from an original core region, the former were usually distant overseas colonies acquired, at least at the first instance, by maritime, naval power. The result was that the new semi-detached empires of the West rarely evinced any of the territorial coherence or economic self-sufficiency which were normal to the condition of the historic variety, even while they were tangible confirmations of the global reach and power of their nation-state creators.

That said, the dichotomy between the two imperial forms was far from absolute or monolithic. Particularly when we further remember that Spain, once *the* leading avant-gardist in the rise of the West could, by the late nineteenth century, be considered primarily an *empire* itself in headlong retreat.[11] This did not prevent Spain making small territorial advances overseas on the cusp of the new contemporary era, alongside those also made by the Portuguese and Dutch, two further avant-gardists whose global power was by now also rapidly waning.[12] But the fact that all three of these states at the start of the twentieth century were still desperately holding on to a range of far-flung overseas possessions, rather than magnanimously dispensing with them, suggests that the idea or aspiration for empire was hardly the monopoly of some antediluvian Qing or Ottoman mindset. If, moreover, it could be argued that the Spanish, Portuguese and Dutch empires were themselves simply the residue of some earlier now outdated mercantile phase in the rise of the West, what is one to make of the mindset of Germany, the newest, most ultramodern, nation-state on the Western scene after 1870? Its self-proclamation, the following year, as a *Reich*, incidentally heralding the demise of imperial France which it had just signally defeated, rather underscores the fact that modernity was no barrier to those who aspired to dress themselves up in imperial clothes. Strangely, bar its various Danish, French, Polish and other smaller Slavic-speaking minorities, the notion of *Reich*, except as some wayward historical reminder of the medieval Holy Roman empire, seemed rather inappropriate and inept. But then Germany simply rectified the discrepancy, within a decade, by beginning to acquire its own overseas colonies, replete with native populations.[13] Another breakneck modernising newcomer on the global scene, Japan, followed a remarkably similar path. Of course, Japan at this stage was a long way off being recognised as part of the 'West', but its emulation of all things Western, and more particularly German, did not prevent it from 'restoring' or indeed vastly reinforcing the traditional powers of the emperor, nor embarking on its own expansionist drive on continental and offshore east Asia to underpin its worthiness to the imperial title.[14]

If German and Japanese cultural self-perceptions and ambitions thus serve to blur the distinction between modern nation-state and traditional world empire, at least these two latecomer states had the excuse that they had not commenced their drives to power with any prior promise to uphold the official Western rules of laissez-faire. By contrast, for decades France, Britain and the United States had all been forcefully proclaiming exactly this free trading commitment and, with it, their detestation of empire and all its supposed ills. Interestingly, none of this led Britain to disencumber itself of the still-significant acquisitions it held from its pre-1800 'first empire' phase of empire-building, nor prevented it from acquiring a whole new range of overseas, mostly tropical territories, even in spite of its commercial – and with it 'informally' political – predominance around the globe.[15] Overall, British armies were involved in no less than fifty major colonial wars between 1803 and 1901.[16] France, similarly, eager to compensate itself for its losses in the earlier period, was in practice bent on an even more overtly expansionist course. One, indeed, which actually accelerated under the republican successors to the officially designated empire of Napoleon III.[17] When, thus, a new global phase of

Western imperial acquisition really got under way, leading, between 1876 and 1915, to a quarter of the world's land surface changing hands and, with it, of course, millions of peoples,[18] it was these leading nation-states, not Japan or Germany, who were its principal promoters and beneficiaries. Clearly, something contradictory, even rather schizophrenic, was taking place in international relations if the states which were supposedly the most vociferously anti-imperialist were by degrees turning themselves into the most overtly and noisily imperialist. That still, one might argue, leaves us with the exception of the United States. Except that it does not. Putting aside consideration as to whether its primary nineteenth-century trans-continental expansion was really a form of imperialism anyway, the USA joined the Western mainstream, in 1898, when it annexed a clutch of formerly Spanish Caribbean and Pacific colonies.[19]

What then, to come back to the original conundrum, does all this tell us about the relationship between empire and the rising incidence of genocide, or at least genocidal potential, in the lead up to 1914? Strangely, bar Hannah Arendt,[20] there is a striking paucity of scholarly effort to interpret that relationship. We have already ruled out the possibility that the chief, or only, culprits were a bloc of traditional, backward empires compared with another coeval bloc of non-genocidal Western polities, for the simple reason that it is inaccurate. The most advanced nation-states were as ready to acquire vast non-metropolitan territories and the populations which inhabited them – with all the dangers that potentially might imply for those populations – as the old continental, or earlier maritime empires were as desperate to hold on to theirs. This does not mean that these various forms of empire were bound to converge into a single type. On the contrary, the modern advanced form was markedly novel and innovative in that it was not even founded on a *conception* of empire so much as a purely technological advantage which enabled nation-states a global reach with which to found new markets, resources and investments for their metropolitan centres.[21] Despite belated attempts at justification, in the form, for instance, of *la mission civilisatrice* or the 'white man's burden', the new nation-state driven empires, thus, did not attempt to claim some universalising – let alone religious – sanction for their expansion.[22] Nevertheless, if we are looking for a primary motor for an emerging pre-1914 genocidal pattern in *both* retreating and advancing varieties it is in the latter variety – and here we are in essential agreement with Arendt – that we must necessarily seek it. It is not, then, simply a question of whether the new empires were perpetrators of genocidal actions against the native peoples they directly encountered. There is also the question of the degree to which their political, economic as well as cultural penetration of the residual world empires – puncturing in the process the latter's sense of a discrete universal self-sufficiency, and forcing them into an entirely unequal interaction with the West – was bound to have indirect yet serious repercussions on these empires' own relationships with their subject peoples.

*

Let us consider this indirect impact first. In fact, there is one obvious arena in which the world empires felt directly threatened by the West's own imperial advance, namely in their frontier regions. As the planet became in a sense smaller, again through Western-led developments of steamship, railway, morse code and telegraph, so these often formerly remote and inaccessible recesses of traditional empire were not only rather rapidly opened up to the prying eyes of the outside world but in turn became potential foci for a predatory interest.

An emerging Western conception of the globe in its own image brooked no place for the traditional notion of frontiers at all. Frontiers denoted something unspecified and fuzzy, in other words in urgent need of tidying up. What British, French or German foreign offices wanted in their place were clearly demarcated borders between one sovereign state and the next, as verified by a standard, professionalised cartographic practice.[23] *Within* each such state, too, it was assumed that every hectare or acre of land would be mapped out, allocated, and then registered to a legal owner. There was always room and, indeed, encouragement in such a system for units of land to be moved from one legal owner to another as 'transferable parcels of real estate',[24] but it was all real estate none the less. The notion that some of the land might collectively belong to a family, kinship group, or community, by dint of it having been cultivated or alternatively left fallow in a particular way, or even shared in common by different groups of people, because this was the place they had always come at a particular time of year, to hunt, or to bring their livestock, or worship since time immemorial, held no water whatsoever within the terms of Western property law. If the West thus moulded the new parameters of what was acceptable, and what was not, not least by insisting on a state's territorial sovereign unity and indivisibility, it was hardly surprising if the weaker continental empires responded by striving with increasing urgency to consolidate fully within their realms those frontier regions whose very existence as such was being so persistently questioned.

However, one notable paradox in what followed was that the continental empires did not simply stop there. In their attempts to parry the threat of outside encroachment, they also expanded their territories. Or, at least, made attempts to do so. Russia was certainly in the van of this movement underlying its strident contention that it was not some second-tier yesterday's man but fully deserving of its status as a Great Power. Western rivals, especially the British, were prone to agree and looked on tsarist efforts to control the Caucasus and Central Asia with a century-long mixture of consternation and trepidation. Yet what they, the British, nevertheless dubbed 'The Great Game', was for the Russians a matter of deadly earnestness, largely motivated by the fear that, unless they took firm and forceful possession of those territories on their periphery to which they had not yet substantiated a claim, someone else more powerful than them would get there first.[25] Chinese moves, also in Central Asia, were conditioned by not dissimilar geo-strategic neuroses. The same was also true for the post-1867 Habsburg dual monarchy, in its more limited advance in the Balkans. Ottoman incapacitation at the hands of Western powers certainly stymied its efforts to join this competition but even this did not prevent one last dramatic bid for expansion, under the cover of general war in 1914, with, significantly again, the Caucasus and Central Asia as the desired prize.

The consequences of these developments at a geo-political level were serious enough. The old empires might be weakening, at least relative to the rising military and economic strength of the Western powers but this in itself could be said to have acted as the most powerful goad to these older empires to punch above weight, so to speak, in order to retain their places at the international system's top man's table. The problem was that the actual political geography of their efforts was bound to bring them into potential collision not only with one or more of the Western powers, but also with one or more of each other. The old playground adage about 'turkey' stepping on 'grease' (i.e. Greece) and breaking 'china' might be wrong in its particulars but it does express rather well the general idea. From the eastern great plateau regions of Sinkiang and Dzangaria, through the Central Asian steppes to the Caspian, beyond into the Caucasus, from there into Anatolia, and, finally, across the Bosphorus into the Balkans, may be a passage across discrete geographical zones, but taken together they could be equally viewed as a continuous chain along the spine of the Eurasian landmass. To understand the significance of this connection politically, however, a geological metaphor, might be more apt. Each of these regions in the nineteenth century was not unlike a series of interlocking fault lines on a major tectonic plate.[26] A small seismic shift on one fault, thereby, could be enough to spark off a whole series of after-shocks further down the plate. As an example, if Russia made moves to consolidate its hold over the north Caucasus, the knock-on effects might be felt in terms of Chinese reactions in Central Asia, Ottoman ones in both Anatolia and the Balkans, precipitating in turn Austrian and, again, Russian responses in this same Balkan region.

Again, it is significant that when this pattern looked as if it was going to spiral completely out of control, it was none other than the now leading Western players on the international stage who intervened to halt and then regulate it. The Congress of Berlin, of 1878, is justly famous – or perhaps infamous – as an attempt, on the Western players' part, to impose an internationally binding solution on Turkish and Russian warring parties with some considerable reference to the Westphalian balance-of-power model yet, at the same time, juggling new national realities in the form of statehood recognition for a clutch of former Ottoman Balkan subject peoples. The arrangement was certainly for the most part viewed triumphantly by Britain and France, and even more so by Germany, in the person of Bismarck as presiding adjudicator. They had, after all, not been parties to the recent cataclysmic Russo-Turkish war but had successfully ringfenced it, advanced their own territorial and commercial interests in the region, and at the same time had forced Russia, the aggressor, to concede nearly all the territories it had gained, Ottoman Turkey, the loser, to bow to major territorial amputation, and Austria, the other major interested party, to more or less agree with whatever Germany decided.[27]

There was just one problem. The 'Eastern Question', as the British politely called the struggles for the spoils of the Ottoman empire, was none other than one critical by-product of the more general global destabilisation whose first cause was the growing ascendancy of the Western states themselves. Any attempt to patch up or decelerate that destabilisation by some international conjuring trick determined by these parties could, thus, only serve to expose or actually exacerbate the position of those peoples in the weakened continental empires whose position, for geographical or historical reasons, was already vulnerable. Here, indeed, was the defining feature at the crux of the mid- to late nineteenth-century shift towards the potential of genocide, not only in the Balkans but in the entire interlinking zones of the Eurasian tectonic plate. In all these regions, the ethnic, cultural and religious composition of the inhabitants was heterogeneous and complex. Under relatively stable conditions in which the old empires themselves did not feel threatened, such ethnographic diversity, however, remained tenable. As already implied, traditional empires were inclined towards toleration – even where they were culturally ill-disposed towards particular groups – if only as an adjunct of what were often decentralised patterns of divide and rule. Take away this stability and the most immediate and likely effect was a much more pronouncedly aggressive state ethnic policy with particularly dire consequences for those who were perceived, correctly or incorrectly, as the protégés or proxies of Western or foreign interference.

This policy in itself did not necessarily require *nationalism* as an ingredient. If, for instance, we were to return to our potential Russian flashpoint in the north-west Caucasus, the shift from almost continual warfare there to something much more overtly annihilatory, in the early 1860s, seems to have had little to do with the intrusion of any modern national consciousness amongst the region's majority Muslim Circassians. An all-out tsarist drive against them, nonetheless, can probably be traced to anxieties that arose out of the Anglo-French invasion of the adjacent but increasingly – for the Russians – important Black Sea coastline in the recent Crimean war and hence to the strategic requirement to nullify the existence of any perceived hostile population to its rear.[28] Interestingly, and alarmingly, however, Circassian survivors of this genocide were almost entirely displaced to the Ottoman empire, where that regime chose to use them as a demographic counterweight against Christian populations, notably Bulgarians and Armenians, in Rumelia and eastern Anatolia respectively,[29] and at a juncture when not only were these indigenous peoples being equally viewed as proxies of outside, especially Russian interests, but where their emerging nationalist identifications *were* beginning to be a critical factor in a broader genocidal equation.

Thus, it would seem that what might begin as a state–communal crisis in one region could, displaced into one or more adjacent or near-adjacent ones, not only complicate other state–communal relations, but, through the interaction with these somewhat different political and social environments, also shape and transform something in the perception of both original perpetrators and victims towards one another. Certainly, the history of genocide in the north Caucasus did not end in the early 1860s but was repeated with new components of ideological baggage under the tsar's Soviet successors seventy or eighty years later. But while this may demonstrate the need for a diachronic form of investigation, to be pursued in a forthcoming volume, it is perhaps worthwhile to pause for a moment here to consider what today we remember of the wider nineteenth-century canvas. If contemporary Western society has an awareness of mass ethnic killings at all along our tectonic plate, it tends to be of massacres perpetrated against Armenians, primarily in Ottoman eastern Anatolia, in the mid-1890s. Even then, there is some doubt, especially in the light of the much more systematic and total Committee of Union and Progress (CUP)-directed drive against the Armenians in 1915–16, as to whether genocide is the appropriate term. Yet the fact that there is some residual awareness of these events and almost next to none of what happened to Circassians or Uighurs twenty or thirty years earlier also raises some further disturbing questions. Is the lack of contemporary newspaper reportage of what was happening in the Russian Caucasus, or Chinese Turkestan simply a function of these places being even more difficult to reach than the already quite inaccessible Armenian vilayets? Or is there a more sinister Chomskian type of explanation: that, despite being in a remote area, the atrocities committed by Muslim Turks against Christians in eastern Anatolia were reported in shocking detail, while those committed *against* Turkic Muslim peoples, in the Russian case by Christians, were of much less Western interest, or even, in some quarters, positively welcomed?[30] To make the query more obviously symmetrical, why, nearer to home, was a Victorian public so knowledgeable and indeed consumed with interest, in the mid-1870s, with news of the repeated massacre and rape of thousands of Bulgarian Christians in Macedonia and Rumelia and so totally oblivious to the possibly many more tens of thousands of Muslims in this area and beyond who suffered identical atrocities, not to say the *millions* thereafter who suffered successive waves of ethnic cleansing at the hands of Christian Bulgarians, Serbs and Greeks?[31]

Granted, we are in danger, at this point, of simply descending into an entirely futile polemic in which the sole aim of the exercise is to prove that 'our' people suffered more than 'yours'. Yet the very fact that the Western version of this line-up in the pre-1914 era was determined entirely on religious criteria – regardless of the worlds of difference between a Bulgarian peasant, or Armenian herdsman, and the man on the perennial Clapham omnibus – offers a rather good example of how what Samuel Huntington calls a clash of civilisations had potently intruded into an emerging modern geo-politics.[32] None of this diminishes the severity or horror of the atrocities committed against Armenians or Bulgarians. What it should do is remind us that neither of these events happened in some Ottoman splendid isolation. Indeed, the key to the Armenian disaster, in many ways, is to be sought in the internationalisation of the issue at the Berlin Congress, while the equally radical decision there to partition much of the remaining Balkan glacis of the Ottoman empire into supposedly national states, such as Bulgaria, throws the weight of responsibility for what happened in these regions, especially after 1878, heavily onto the dominant powers.

Of course, one cannot charge the Western powers with *direct* responsibility for the various acts of genocide along our tectonic plate. Through their hegemonic position, combined with normal statist self-interest, they simply helped create and possibly accelerate conditions in which genocide was likely to be an outcome. By giving to the Armenians, for instance, every incentive to see themselves as a separate nationality under Great Power protection, they in effect poured a bucket of poison into Turkish–Armenian relations, yet without any intention of coming to the rescue when the Turks predictably overreacted.

The whole point of Great Power diplomacy, after all, was to regulate their territorial acquisitions, or spheres of influence, in such a way that they would not collide with another and thereby become embroiled in intra-state war. Supporting the Armenian cause might be useful to one or more Great Power interests, there might even be those in high places genuinely motivated by a humanitarian imperative. However, the often convoluted diplomatic twists and turns which the Armenian question took, in the period to 1914, were always ultimately dictated by matters of *realpolitik*, not the immediacy of Armenian exposure to danger.[33] By the same token, the creation of nation-states in the Balkans, in 1878, had much less to do with Great Power enthusiasm for the extension of the national idea to the region *per se*. Rather, the assumption was that 'Balkanisation' would provide a group of pliant, client states whose stabilisation under Great Power aegis would also ensure firmer control over what remained of the Ottoman empire itself. In practice, this proved to be utterly misconceived, not least because the new states had every intention of asserting their genuine independence. Unfortunately, however, by supporting nation-statism in the first place in a region in which a multitude of ethnic communities were inextricably mixed, the dominant powers at Berlin inadvertently legitimised what would become over the next century the primary instrument of Balkan nation-building: ethnic cleansing.

*

If Great Power, and more specifically Western, responsibility for the potential of genocide from the Balkans through to western China was, thus, at one remove, what of the regions of the world where the Western imperial interest involved direct takeover? It is, perhaps, both ironic but also fitting that the Berlin Congress of 1878 should have been succeeded by a second conference in the German capital, again hosted by Bismarck, in the winter of 1884–5. Like its predecessor, this conference's efforts were geared towards regulation of international disputes but this time in order to avoid collision primarily between the British, French and Germans as they made direct and very rapid territorial acquisitions in a geographical arena quite distinct from the Eurasian landmass. Indeed, the possibilities for land-grab seemed so irresistible in this arena that it was already being dubbed the 'scramble for Africa'.[34]

   The contours of the new imperialism thus seem to offer a set of considerations entirely divergent from those facing the declining continental empires. Yet were the dynamism and virility of the one as opposed to the supposed lassitude and weakness of the other, the necessary prophylactics for the avoidance of genocide or rather the very agents likely to facilitate and even ensure it?

Logic would seem to dictate that the new imperialism's capitalist under-pinnings – the need above all to sell abundant quantities of Western goods, most obviously textiles, to captive markets – required the existence of large, sufficiently prosperous indigenous populations in order to buy them. This, in itself, would seem to have determined that wherever the Western imperial flag was planted, self-interest favoured the preservation of stable, life-supporting conditions. Even the more obviously predatory aspects of territorial acquisition, especially the monopolisation and extraction of resources, required the existence of a long-term, cheap, labour pool for its accomplishment. With relatively very few Western administrators or soldiers, for the most part, to enforce the imperial writ over large populations spread across huge distances, it hardly made commercial, let alone political sense to attempt to advance these goals by unadulterated terror and coercion. On the contrary, the whole thrust of the new situation rather tended instead towards the adoption of a technique practised for centuries, if not millennia, by the older continental empires: the perpetuation, or increased empowerment, of traditional local elites, albeit aligned to the parallel practice of divide and rule. In effect, this was asking the new imperial masters to become the very antithesis of what they were in their own domestic nation-state contexts: segmented polities dependent on local, authorised intermediaries in place of streamlined, centralised and institutionally uniform polities; diverse, multicultural and even pluralist societies in place of monocultural but unified ones.

There was a bizarre irony here. The old continental empires were increasingly seeing, and indeed discarding, these very arrangements as the elements acting as a drag on their ability to modernise and hence compete with the West. Yet it was these very pre-modern aspects which offered the most obvious life-line for Western nation-states, that were busily turning themselves into empires, to do so without recourse to perpetual mass violence. Of course, the bottom line for all empires was a military hegemony – in other words, a monopoly of violence – at the very least within the confines of their sovereign domains. And allied to some limited degree of central administrative apparatus and uniform legal machinery there could be significant pay-offs in this reality even for important elements of the subject populations. If empire equalled the guarantee of universal peace and with it not only personal security but greater intra-regional commerce and prosperity, in the process enhancing access to the better things in life, then empire might be seen as actually benevolent. It was this very sense of benevolence combined with the idea of imperial perpetuity that had enabled empire rulers throughout the ages to wrap themselves up in a certain mystique. Yet, particularly with the most culturally distinct and often geographically remote of subject peoples, this arrangement had always had something of a *quid pro quo* element to it: suitable subject obeisance to the emperor's new clothes, yet, in practical terms, government which reserved to the subjects' traditional leaders a sufficient degree of local autonomy and even a high degree of laissez-faire when it came to cultural and socio-economic practice.

It was the disintegration of these very arrangements in critical zones of geo-political contest, usually at the peripheries of the continental empires, that fuelled an increased potential for genocide on the cusp of the contemporary era. But the proposition here has also been that a lack of, or more conscious omission to engage in such arrangements in the newly acquired African and other territories of the advancing Western imperial powers would also have produced similar results. Did, then, the West get it right? The term genocide, where it appears in history books at all, with reference to the Scramble for Africa, is usually only reserved for one single case: the destruction of the Herero people, in German South-West Africa in 1904–5. But if this is, indeed, the only case, might we be forgiven for assuming, yet again, that we are thus dealing with an aberration? And, therefore, that it must follow that the late nineteenth-century Western imperial trajectory fundamentally diverges from that of its continental cousins?

Certainly, then, those at the helm of Western expansion sought to promote what they were doing as nothing less than an act of thoroughly altruistic benevolence. Without a hint of irony, the Berlin conferees of 1884–5, for instance, declared that their aim was 'to watch over the preservation of the native races and the amelioration of the moral and material conditions of their existence ... to educate the natives and to lead them to understand and appreciate the advantages of civilisation'.[35] Indeed, implicit in this statement was the view that Europeans had to intervene, either to put an end to barbarities and atrocities being inflicted on Africans by others, or which they were inflicting on themselves. Lurid images of mass mutilation, ritual sacrifice and cannibalism had certainly been the stock-in-trade of the European perception of Africa for centuries.[36] But when Europeans actually encountered the real thing it did not prevent them from being any the less shocked.[37] The mass nineteenth-century depredations perpetrated by Swahili and Arab slave trad-ers in the east and centre of the continent, indeed, elicited such moral outrage from a broad Western public that this cannot be discounted as a factor sway-ing the deliberations of 1884, or the 1889 Brussels Conference – the latter supposedly entirely devoted to the subject – in favour of intervention.[38] There is, certainly, a perfectly sound case for arguing that the really considerable mass killings and ethnic depopulations of central-southern Africa – the *Mfe-cane* – somewhat earlier in the century, were the product of an essentially indigenous, if innovative turn in the nature of some Bantu societies en route to their own particular conceptions of empire.[39]

The fact, however, that the issue of anti-slavery was consciously utilised by one of the new European empire builders, albeit an unlikely one, King Leopold II of the Belgians, as a successful smokescreen for one of the most voracious acts of asset-stripping in history – the conquest and hyper-exploitation of the natural and human resources of the Congo basin – rather suggests that beneath Western self-exculpation for colonial ventures lay a rather less pleasant mix of cant, self-deception, hypocrisy and convenient amnesia.[40] After all, hardly more than a generation prior to the 'Scramble', slaves had not just been the West's literal stock in trade from African shores but, in a broader world historical context, the ongoing atrocity upon which the West, at least in part, derived its short-cut to capital accumulation and global hegemony.[41] The statistics in themselves are devastating enough. Between 9 and 11 million Africans were transhipped over a more than three-century period to the Americas, the largest single forced migration in history.[42] An estimated 8 to 10 per cent are believed to have died from illness, neglect and maltreatment en route.[43] The severe attrition rate continued, however, once the survivors found themselves put to work in New World plantations and colonies, figures of 2 million deaths either during the 'Middle Passage' across the Atlantic or from 'seasoning' – the initial period of hyper-exploitation – being commonly cited.[44] In short, the accelerated power-surge of first the Spanish and Portuguese, then the English and French, was dramatically built upon the exhausted or discarded bodies of Africans as, before them, of native Americans. But does all this necessarily prove that what happened in Africa itself, from the 1880s onwards, was an inevitable sequel to the Atlantic slave trade, in much in the same way that authors like Stannard and Ward Churchill have charged that what was done to native Americans, after 1492, also follows a more or less continuous genocidal trajectory? Or should we perhaps see the expanded imperialism of the nineteenth century as the start of some new, more obviously modern breeding ground for the phenomenon as others, like Sartre and Lindqvist, have proclaimed?

Significantly, Sartre's starting point is 1830, the year of the French invasion of Algeria, leading to the imposition of 'an economic system of unequal exchange', accompanied by both massive land expropriations from the indigenous population, and the wholesale destruction of the region's traditional infrastructure. As only terror through perpetual massacre could realise these objectives, Sartre proposed that there was to be a natural affinity between genocide and colonisation.[45] Even were we to accept his rather loose definition of what constitutes genocide, however – a caveat of 'cultural genocide' being an element of his pamphlet-length case – his thesis would certainly seem to point to the overturning of the time-honoured and sustaining ground rules of traditional empire, founded on the preservation or bolstering of local intermediary elites. Actually, Sartre may well have something of a case in so far as Algeria is concerned, just as Lindqvist, in his own initial focus on the Congo, may have one too. The exterminatory lengths to which successive regimes were prepared to go in order to absorb the Algerian region into metropolitan France not only raises some doubt as to the uniqueness of the Herero genocide in the context of the imperial advance, but also invites comparison with genocidal 'pacifications' conducted by the continental empires in this period, notably that of the Russians in the north Caucasus. As for what Leopold's quite inappropriately named Congo Free State was attempting to achieve, it clearly lacked any effort to involve indigenous mediation, or conciliation. The subjugation of the Congo was accomplished by coercion and terror, pure and simple.

However, even if this did lead, in the Belgian and adjacent French parts of the region, both to the reducing of the majority of its peoples to a perpetual servitude, and, as a by-product of this, to repeated atrocity, possibly accounting – directly or indirectly – for 5 million deaths,[46] the colonial agenda here was still predicated on the continuing existence of a Congolese population, if only to provide extractive labour. In the case of Algeria, Sartre similarly acknowledges the French settlers' ongoing dependency on an indigenous 'subproletariat'. None of this would negate Lindqvist's contention that some Europeans seemed to have enjoyed killing Africans. Nor, necessarily, would it disprove his further contention that the new scientifically legitimised racism was as much to blame as sheer greed or power-lust. But, taking Joseph Conrad's great 1902 novel of the rape of the Congo, *Heart of Darkness*, as emblematic of modern Western imperialism as a whole, Lindqvist has gone much further by, in effect, inferring that the litany of murder he describes is genocidal *tout court* throughout the imperial advance, as well as, incidentally, the path that paved the way towards the Holocaust.[47]

If Lindqvist – or for that matter Sartre – is right, then the extermination of the Herero is, at the very best, the tip of the imperial iceberg. But what if they have taken worst-case scenarios and turned them into the basis for a rather overblown generalisation? For instance, what made Algeria an extreme case was the French intention to colonise and closely settle at least parts of it with Europeans. Given the arid nature of most of German South-West Africa, conditions were less ripe for such a concerted programme. Even so, they were sufficient for the Germans to consider a wholesale expropriation of the indigenous population in favour of white incomers. Indeed, the only areas of the continent where climate and soil conditions could support such extensive northern European colonisation were in the very northern littoral and a more extensive range in southern Africa, plus a few more limited temperate highland plateaux in east-central Africa. The parallels with the neo-Europes of particularly North America, Argentina and the antipodes are obvious. But even here we can take the analogies too far. There was no *general* exterminatory drive by Anglo imperialists in southern Africa as there was in north America. Black African demographic preponderance and, one might add, their – for the most part – all-important epidemiological resistance to European-imported diseases denied it.[48] Or to put the case more crudely: there were simply too many Africans to kill. Moreover, unlike in north America where the natives were largely dispensed with in terms of labour needs, in Africa they remained, again with some caveats with regard to the Boer republics, absolutely essential and fundamental to both colonial and more general imperial exploitative projects.

Could it be, therefore, that where a lurch into genocide did occur, the explanation does not lie in a simple correlation between it and the political geography of colonisation *per se* but also in something to do with the nature of the native response itself? Again, it would be logical to assume that resistance to the imperial advance would be strongest where the impact was most severe, an assumption which, by implication, would embrace the non-colonised Congo as much as it would those parts of Algeria or South-West Africa earmarked for European settlement. But again this carries within it too much of a generalising assumption about African or indeed any other set of societies. Not only were what the imperialists trying to achieve in widely divergent parts of Africa, in their specifics, quite different from each other, but native cultures and societies throughout the continent were far from being in essence the same, however much it might have been convenient for the Europeans of the time negatively to typecast them as such.[49] Economies ranged from the urban-centred to the hunter-gatherer, the commerce-orientated to the heavily sedentarised or pastorally self-sufficient. Polities ranged from notably cohesive and statist, if not imperial structures, to much more loose, though never quite so simply tribal or kinship based. All these operated within a broad spectrum of animist, Muslim or Christian belief systems, helping to mould in turn a myriad of quite distinctive social and cultural responses to each other, their neighbours, not to say intrusive outsiders. With this range of polities and economies, how could we possibly expect Africans to all respond to the Europeans' imperial projects according to some supposedly scientifically constructed template?

If the inference here is that the historical study of genocide, like every other historical study, has to take into account the human factor, just as it has to be on the constant lookout for all sorts of unexpected contingencies, does this not leave us with no particular rhyme or reason to the resulting catastrophes, let alone a sense of the bigger plot? Looking at the evolving interactions between the Herero, their indigenous neighbours and the Germans, there is certainly ample evidence for the importance of these human and contingent factors. And if the issue were reduced to them alone, then perhaps we could return to the rather comforting notion, thus, that what happened to the Herero was nothing ultimately to do with the intentions of empire but simply a tragic accident or mistake. That said, this analysis has been developed on the proposition that empires, despite their often inbuilt, usually self-interested and self-regulatory mechanisms for the avoidance of exterminatory conflict with subject peoples, can, under certain conditions, develop genocidal tendencies just as can nation-states. Indeed, it was exactly in the conditions of the nineteenth- and early twentieth-century transition from more traditional imperial-centred political economies to that of the new globally dominating national-centred ones that this danger became most acute. Paradoxically, it affected both main types of empires, the old retreating continental empires struggling to come to terms with the new hegemonic profile of Western nation-states just as it did the advancing empires which were themselves the outgrowths of this new nation-state phenomenon. Thus, though there is no one single ingredient explaining their common descent towards genocide, the bunching of the incidence in each from the mid-nineteenth century to the early twentieth century – *that is the period when the stresses of the global power shift were at their greatest* – is surely significant. But, of course, in a sense there was something else the advancing and retreating empires had in common. As they each attempted to adjust to the new global realities, even where, as in the case of the Western empires, these were largely self-made, it was particular subject peoples in each, usually in politically sensitive regions, who found themselves bearing the full brunt of the adjustment. The result, inevitably, was a dynamic of state–communal conflict that, unless it could find some suitable channel for dilution, was more than likely to lead to a crisis situation in which something was bound to give.

But to draw such conclusions we need to consider, at least in brief, the anatomy of the genocides in question. The obvious entry point for any discussion of the wider implication of the Western imperial advance must begin with the destruction of the Herero. It is around this case that the rest of this chapter revolves.

Annihilating 'the Revolting Tribes with Rivers of Blood and Rivers of Gold'[50]

The bald facts can be simply stated. In early January 1904, the 80,000-strong Hereros, the main tribal people in the centre of the twenty-year-old German colony of South-West Africa burst into open revolt.[51] Led by their paramount chief, Samuel Mahahero, they invaded white farmsteads and killed anything up to 150 mostly male, German settlers or soldiers. For a few, brief weeks, during which the Herero had the upper hand, the very continuation of imperial German rule in the territory seemed to be in doubt. In fact, despite the limited number of *Schutzgruppe* troops at the disposal of the governor, Theodor Leutwein, the Herero military advantage rapidly dissipated. On the other hand, Leutwein's failure to quell the uprising led the kaiser, Wilhelm II, in early May, to invoke his constitutional powers and appoint another man, General Lothar von Trotha, to take over military command of the operation. Von Trotha already had a ominous reputation for ruthless butchery, made in his crushing of the Wahehe revolt in German East Africa, in 1896, and for his part in the combined European operation against the Chinese Boxer Rebellion in 1900.[52] His appointment now, in German South-West Africa, represented a conscious sidelining of Leutwein – still civil governor of the colony – who believed he could still bring the Herero to heel by military means combined with the negotiation of a partial amnesty. Von Trotha, by contrast, was to state repeatedly that he had been given explicit orders by the kaiser not to negotiate but rather to 'crush the rebellion by fair means or foul'.[53]

Recent historical research has thrown doubt on whether this meant that von Trotha set out from the very outset literally to annihilate the Herero.[54] What is clear from the time of his arrival in the colony in June is that his aim, following the standard German military doctrine of the period, was to engage the Herero in a single battle of *military* annihilation.[55] This von Trotha rapidly proceeded to work towards. The colony was placed under a state of emergency and martial law while his 4,000-plus troops, also mostly arrived from Germany, were to be supported by machine guns and artillery for this supposedly final encounter. The battle took place in mid-August, when the main body of the Herero, an estimated 60,000 people, accompanied by their cattle flocks, found themselves ringed by the general's forces on the remote Waterberg plateau. The Germans proceeded to bombard the Waterberg for three days. When they had finished, a general massacre of those they found still alive ensued. Eyewitness accounts, both recorded in soldiers' letters, or provided by terrified members of the Berg Damara tribe, who contributed native levies for the campaign, offer a glimpse into this mass orgy of killing. Not only were there repeated machine gunnings and cannonades, but Herero men were slowly strangled by fencing wire and then hung up in rows like crows, while young women and girls were regularly raped before being bayoneted to death. The old, the sick, the wounded were all slaughtered or burnt to death. Nor were children spared, one account describing how men, women and children were corralled into a high thorn and log enclosure before being 'doused with lamp oil and burnt to a cinder'.[56]

The only problem for von Trotha, however, was that the battle of the Waterberg was not judged to be the decisive victory as intended and required. With his troops extended thinly round the plateau and with communication between them consequently confused, large numbers of the Herero were actually able to escape through a south-eastern gap in the general's ring, though in the direction of the waterless Omahake desert. There was actually no doubt that, in military terms, the Herero had been destroyed at the battle. But von Trotha's conclusive and crushing achievement – and the appropriate prestige to go with it – had been denied. He was, thus, left with the dilemma of whether or not to engage in pursuit of the survivors.[57]

The fact that he chose to do so, notes Henrik Lundtofte, led to a fundamental change in the character of German campaign.[58] For some six weeks after the Waterberg the Germans relentlessly pursued the Herero survivors into the Omahake, the latter's numbers rapidly dwindling through thirst and starvation, or through execution, in line with von Trotha's orders not to take prisoners. The pursuit was only brought to a halt when the Germans themselves became too exhausted. At this point, on 2 October 1904, von Trotha openly made public his intentions in the form of the now infamous *Vernichtungsbefehl*, or extermination order. This proclaimed that the Herero people were no longer German subjects, and – by implication – were guilty of capital crimes, including theft and the mutilation of wounded German soldiers. They were also charged with cowardice because they were no longer fighting. As if he were directly making a speech to the Hereros themselves, the order continued:

> All the Hereros must leave the land. If the people do not do this, then I will force them to do it with the great guns. Within the German boundaries, any Herero, whether found armed or unarmed, with or without cattle, will be shot. I shall not accept any more women or children: I will drive them back to their people or I shall shoot them. This is my decision for the Herero people.

Von Trotha signed the order: 'The Great General of the Mighty Kaiser'.[59] Almost simultaneously, von Trotha wrote to the chief of general staff, Alfred Graf von Schlieffen, stating that he intended to destroy the Herero nation, if not directly, then by other means, including expulsion.[60] In practice, this did now amount to complete physical extermination. The caveat, in a supplementary order to the *Vernichtungsbefehl* about not shooting women and children, was entirely illusory when expelling all Herero whatever their age or gender into the Omahake was effectively a sentence of death.[61] The water holes on the desert's western approaches had already begun to be sealed up and or poisoned in the weeks following the Waterberg pursuit. Now a 250-kilometre patrolled *absperrenungslinie*, or barrier line, was erected along it from north-west to south-east, with the expressed intention of driving the remaining Herero to an agonising death. Descriptions of vast numbers of putrefying bodies in the desert attest to this fate. A mere thousand or so survivors, including Mahahero, were able to cross the Omahake eastwards to the safety of British Bechuanaland. For those who turned back towards Hereroland, attempting in so doing to run the gauntlet of the blockhouse-guarded barrier line, there was no mercy.[62]

Certainly, two months on from the *Vernichtungsbefehl,* anxiety in the Wilhelmstrasse about its negative reception in Western capitals had literally forced the hand of an otherwise extremely reluctant kaiser to countermand it. But the decision had little impact on the man on the spot. Not only was von Trotha not relieved of his command, but, with the revolt now spread to the Nama peoples in the south of the colony – a direct consequence, in fact, of his extermination order – his self-justification for his unforgiving methods was, if anything, reinforced. In April 1905 he issued a second proclamation, this time aimed at the Nama, in which he warned them that they would suffer the same fate as the Herero unless they agreed to submit to the kaiser's mercy. 'This policy', he added, 'will go on until all such Hottentots have been killed'.[63] On-the-spot executions of suspects certainly continued for most of that following year. And by this time it had become largely indiscriminate, regardless of whether the victims were nominally hostile Herero and Nama, or members of the Berg Damara, the tribe who had fought alongside Germans at the Waterberg, or for that matter San – bushmen peoples living at the very margins of German control.

It is true that after the cancellation of the original *Vernichtungsbefehl* a form of counter-policy aiming at the incarceration, rather than extermination, of the enemy tribes was attempted in part. This was facilitated through the 'good offices' of the Rhenish Mission Society, the Protestant missionaries who had been busily Christianising the tribes in this region, even before the advent of German rule. Assuming that their lives might be spared, groups of starving, exhausted Hereros sought the missionaries' protection in this way. It made little difference. They were handed over to the German colonial authorities for internment in concentration camps where men, women and children were treated as slave labour, some for deployment constructing the Otavi railway, one of the original causes of the Herero revolt. As a result, though there was estimated to be nearly 15,000 Herero in the camps, by May 1906 their numbers continued to decline precipitously. Thus, when a census for the colony was taken in 1911 – nearly five years after the camps had been closed down – the Herero population was still struggling to maintain that 15,000 figure. Or, to put it another way, the tribe had collapsed to considerably less than one-quarter of its pre-revolt numbers. But if this, demographically speaking, was the most devastating of the results of the war in German South-West Africa, the other central and southern tribes hardly fared better. For instance, of 1,795 Nama, interned in the concentration camp on Shark Island, off Angra Pequena, in September 1906, 1,032 perished from cold and ill-treatment within seven months. Nearly all the rest were crippled. Indeed, the 1911 census reported only 9,800 Nama, *in toto*, in the colony, compared with an estimated 20,000 from before 1904. Even the neutral, or German-allied Berg Damara lost 10,000 in the conflict, out of their 30,000 total. Von Trotha's extermination policy may have begun with the Herero specifically in mind, but by 1906, when the 'pacification' of the territory had been more or less completed, an estimated 60 per cent of its central and southern peoples had perished.[64]

However, if all this certainly ought to confirm the scale and extent of the killing, from the viewpoint of historical analysis, it still leaves a lot of questions unanswered. Does responsibility really rest on the shoulders of a bloodthirsty, loose cannon of a general? Or on an equally monstrous, irresponsible if not entirely socially dysfunctional kaiser?[65] Or does this miss the point in that what happened in German South-West Africa was not some unique one-off occurrence but actually part of a broader pattern? Certainly, we can make some immediate comparisons. The sequence of genocidal killing is not unlike that of the Vendée, beginning with a War Type Three annihilatory battle which is then consciously succeeded by a much more systematic campaign to wipe out a whole, defeated and hence no longer resisting population. One can even find obvious parallels here in the way that Leutwein is overruled in favour of von Trotha, just as the somewhat more correct and cautious Kleber, in the Vendée, is replaced by the utterly fanatical Turreau. The fact that in the Herero case the perpetrators are Germans, however, inevitably raises a different set of questions about its relationship to the Holocaust. Should we thus view the events of 1904–5 primarily as a milestone, en route to the most systematic and relentless genocide in history, and, if so, does this provide evidence of a very peculiarly German recidivism?[66]

We have already noted the particular emphasis that the German military placed on the concept of *Vernichtungskreig* – exterminatory war – well before the advent of Hitlerism. However, to assume that the concept was always intended as something more than simply military engagement with opposing armies may be to misunderstand its original purpose as, for instance, compared with Wehrmacht practice on the Eastern front in the Second World War. That said, there is certainly one particularly chilling if equally ambivalent resonance of von Trotha's *Vernichtungsbefehl* at a critical point in the launching of the 'Final Solution'. On 30 July 1941, Himmler issued an oral command to the 2nd SS Cavalry Regiment operating in the Pripyat marshes region, close the central thrust of Operation Barbarossa, in which he stated: 'All Jews must be shot. Drive the female Jews into the swamp.' During the following two weeks the regiment, supported by *Einzatzkommandos* and police battalions, massacred, in this very limited area, some 15,000, mostly Jewish people, including women and children.[67] But while the problem of how to word a killing order which would include women and children is noteworthy in both instances, there is no evidence that either Himmler, or Erich von dem Bach-Zelewski, the SS general on the spot, were consciously emulating von Trotha.

Indeed, to go down this Holocaust-centric path carries further dangers of both distorting as well as isolating German actions in South-West Africa from the broader picture of imperial advance. After all, there were many elements in the German administration, particularly in the Colonial Office, as well as in German society at large who were resolutely opposed to the von Trotha approach. This includes one very central player too: Leutwein, whose whole governance of the colony from the time of his appointment, in 1889, had been consciously geared towards imitation of the British model of divide and rule.[68] But this itself would be to assume that Leutwein was incapable of using the iron fist, when we know that he repeatedly put down native resistance with uncompromising ferocity. It would also be to accept at face value that the British themselves were paragons of colonial virtue.

If none of this, therefore, adds up to a satisfactory, contextual explanation of the Herero genocide, perhaps we have no choice but to revisit those ingredients in the Western imperial advance most regularly cited as culprits for mass violence: racism and greed (or should this read plain capitalism?). Arendt certainly has characterised the new imperialism as a force that, fed by racism, while even operating beyond mere economic imperatives, took on an entirely unfettered and limitless propensity for violence.[69] Perhaps, if it can be found that these elements were particularly virulent, or rampantly out of control, with regard to the colonisation of South-West Africa we might be able to reach our destination.

Looking for Explanations

There is no lack of evidence to confirm that the full flowering of European racism, in the mid- to late nineteenth century, had a profound bearing on the treatment of newly disempowered or subjugated peoples caught in the throes of the Western imperial advance. Almost entirely gone by now was the Rousseauesque idea of the 'noble savage'. The very fact, moreover, that dominant voices in the emerging science of anthropology practically held it as an article of faith that the 'dark' or more pointedly 'lower races' were physically, mentally – and hence culturally – quite inferior to Europeans, carried with it the further assumption that whatever would be the fate of these peoples in the future, it would be one determined by their European or 'white' masters.[70] On offer, at best, seemed to be a situation not unlike that of the native Americans, where they would be treated as wards to be brought on, civilised and liberated from 'barbarous customs', as the declaration of the 1890 Brussels Conference smugly proclaimed.[71] At worst, as writers like Ratzel, or the influential Scottish anatomist and anthropologist, Robert Knox, pontificated with some relish, they would simply become extinct. W. Winwood Reade, an acolyte of Knox, in the newly formed and overtly racist London Anthropological Society, spelt out in his 1864 book, *Savage Africa*, how this would transpire. Africa, he predicted, would be shared out between Britain and France. The Africans themselves would dig the ditches and water the deserts. It would be the hard work which would lead to their probable extinction but Reade extolled his readers to 'learn to look at the results with composure. It illustrates the beneficent law of nature, that the weak must be devoured by the strong'.[72]

If this was European racist wish-fulfilment at its most grotesque, not to say a genuinely stark portend of the 1942 Wannsee Conference – where Heydrich would propose a work programme for an estimated 11 million European Jews 'in which doubtless a large part will fall away through natural reduction'[73] – there was, however, a problem. The Europeans still needed the 'lower races' for the imperial enterprise; if only to work for them. To treat the natives simply as an expendable item might lead to a situation where that work-force might 'collapse and disappear'. This was exactly the conclusion of the Belgian Colonial National Congress in 1924, after its anxious administrators in the Congo had ordered a population census of the region. The census found that at 10 million, the population was half of what it ought to have been; it was in danger of becoming 'a kind of desert'.[74]

Significantly, however, it was the very nature of the Western outcry at the persistent abuses and atrocities that had led to this situation over decades which also may require us to qualify the assumption that European racism was, to use a Goldhagen piece of terminology, a form of cultural cognitive model. On the contrary, the moral indignation which the English activist, E. D. Morel, was able to whip up on both sides of the Atlantic in support of his 1904-founded Congo Reform Association (CRA) rather suggests that there were strong countervailing tendencies in the Western cultural tradition which were deeply humanitarian.[75] Nor was all that was being written in this period about Africans racist. Mary Kingsley's popular and widely read *Travels in West Africa* (1897), for instance, not only described native societies as thoroughly coherent but denounced European self-proclaimed civilisers and missionaries alike as forces bound to wreck them.[76]

That said, the humanitarian lobby clearly had its limitations. It was highly paternalistic, as evidenced in the case of the Congo outcry by its willingess to follow the European Morel but not black American missionaries of the ilk of William Sheppard, who had been one of the leading exposers of King Leopold's atrocities. And with the exception of the perspicacious few, Morel included, humanitarians were largely unwilling to consider that colonialism and settlement – whether Belgian, German, British, or whatever – might actually be inherently incompatible with its lofty aims. Significantly, someone who did recognise the contradiction was Governor Leutwein in German South-West Africa. It was humbug and self-deception when social democratic deputies in the Reichstag, like August Bebel, spoke of the need for humanitarian principles in the pursuit of colonies, Leutwein insisted, when 'colonisation is always inhumane'. Thus, in his view, 'high-minded promises' given to the Hereros at the outset of German rule in order to get them to sign blank treaty forms, effectively giving away their sovereignty were nothing more than a diplomatic ruse, due to the German's 'weak strategic position at the time', while what followed was no more than a typical colonising situation where German settlers had simply helped themselves to African land and labour.[77]

Leutwein's frank and blunt appraisals for the benefit of the Colonial Office in Berlin in the late 1890s had put the finger on the essential point. Racism was an absolutely necessary bolster to the new European conquests, particularly in instances where their actual situation was relatively weak. Settlement, thus, could only be maintained and justified by constantly asserting to onself that the 'natives' were less than human and that they therefore deserved to have both their land and cattle expropriated and their persons humiliated and abused. Thus, even though they had been there hardly a matter of years, a petition to the Colonial Department from residents of the colony's nascent capital, Windhoek, complained that 'from time immemorial our natives have grown used to laziness, brutality and stupidity ... any white man who has lived among natives finds it almost impossible to regard them as human beings at all in any European sense'.[78] Few settlers, in fact, even bothered with the formality but simply referred to them as baboons.[79] Privately, Leutwein may have abhorred these attitudes and their inevitable consequences, the commonplace and, as he himself acknowledged 'barbarous' floggings, cheatings, rape and sometimes murder, by settlers of natives. Yet at the same time he maintained all this was unavoidable and did little or nothing to prevent it.

Moreover, while Leutwein may have had his reservations, the experts' view on the natives was hardly at odds with that of the settlers but simply dressed up in a more abstract and opaque terminology. Dr Richard Hindorf, for instance, writing an 1894 report on the economic utility of the territory, considered the Herero 'not a suitable and serviceable element of the population, nor could they play any part in the development of the colony'.[80] Paul Rohrbach, a rather more significant figure, who not only was head of the territory's settlement commission *after* the genocide but also later propounded views which influenced German government as well as more popular thinking on the Armenians, elaborated the Hindorf argument further in 1907:

> For a people, as for an individual, an existence appears to be justified in the degree that it is useful in the progress of general development. By no argument in the world can it be shown that the preservation of any degree of national independence, national prosperity and political organisation by the races of South West Africa would be of greater or even of equal advantage for the development of mankind in general or the German people.[81]

Rohrbach concluded that the only grounds upon which such inferior races could gain a moral right to exist would be by putting their land and persons at the service of the higher, white race. With such views representing the conventional wisdom, it hardly should come as surprise to discover that Eugen Fischer was at this same time conducting his anthropological field research in the territory, in order to prove (sic.) that miscegenation of white settlers with black women inevitably led to genetic decrepitude.[82] No surprise either to see the attitude of the war veteran who, in his 1907 memoirs, detailing his exploits could unashamedly include a picture with the following caption:

> A crate with Herero skulls was recently packed by the troops in German South West Africa and sent to the Pathological Institute in Berlin, where they are going to be used for scientific measurements. The skulls, whose flesh had been

removed by Herero women with pieces of broken glass before they were put in the mail, belong to Herero who were hanged or killed in action.[83]

All this should also certainly confirm that, when the Herero response to the years of colonial degradation finally exploded into open rebellion, the Germans in turn believed themselves to be fighting a race war which, in the words of von Schlieffen, could 'only be ended by the destruction of one of the parties.'[84] Race hatred may thus tell us a great deal about the conduct of the ensuing war. What it cannot do, however, for all its transparent mix of the vicious and the callous, is fully explain the descent into genocide in the first place. At stake is not simply the matter of other white non-German administrators, soldiers and settlers in colonies throughout Africa and beyond holding remarkably similar views without – necessarily – engaging in mass murder at the drop of a hat but the fact that Leutwein's whole programme was based on turning the Herero in particular into a pliant but continuing labour force. Indeed, however much they might have been considered as deficient and beneath contempt, even Rohrbach had to concede that actual extermination 'could be politically and economically disastrous'.[85]

*

So, if race alone is not quite sufficient an explanation, do we need to turn to our other nasty ingredient – greed – to complement or supplement it?

Greed as a descriptive term may seem a little coarse or even lame in the face of major economic processes that were rapidly transforming Africa, not to mention the wider world. Multifaceted these processes were, but greed nevertheless retains a certain pungent appropriateness for representing the drive not only to take more than one needs, but to ingest much more than one could easily or safely manage. Certainly, in the van of the Scramble for Africa were a whole cast of restless European adventurers driven on by the belief that beyond the next malarial swamp or mountain range, gold, diamonds or some other portable commodity would be awaiting them in such quantities that they would be fabulously enriched. Very much like the conquistadors of the Americas, with a similarly bloody-minded determination that nothing and no one was going to stand in the way of them claiming their prize. The psychopathology of some of the leading figures of this new breed is well attested. For instance, Carl Peters, the maverick, arrogant, sadistic, and quite extraordinarily narcissistic founder of the Society for German Colonisation, and leader of two early German military expeditions to east Africa, is often cited as just the sort of individual who would read native obduracy to his demands as a case of personal insult and unflinchingly respond to such supposed 'insolence' with brutality, beatings and murder.[86]

But something other than the wayward behaviour of inevitably rather marginal individuals may be needed to explain the broader connection between greed and a propensity to unmitigated mass violence. After all, as E. D. Morel noted of the atrocities committed in the Congo: 'given certain premises ... these deeds must of *necessity* take place'.[87] At least at the outset, a lack of serious venture capital let alone the guarantee of state support or protection for most of the adventurers' money-making projects may offer a partial clue as to how this came about. Again, we have a paradox here. Until it could be proven that diamonds, or gold, or some such wealth-creating resource, was on limitless tap, metropolitan investors generally fought shy of the adventurers' blandishments. Admittedly, this could change overnight, as happened after the discovery of diamonds on the West Griqualand frontiers of the British Cape Colony in the late 1860s.[88] By contrast, as late as 1913, by which time the equivalent of over £100 million had been invested in Germany's overseas empire – and diamonds and other mineral deposits had been finally discovered in South-West Africa – colonial trade represented a minuscule 0.5 per cent of Germany's total commerce.[89] This rather suggests that, with some notable exceptions, most new late nineteenth-century colonial companies began their trading lives vastly undercapitalised, infrastructurally weak, with little or no collateral, while operating quite literally out on a limb. To say nothing of constantly looking over their shoulders at some other, usually foreign competitor muscling in on what they perceived to be their patch. Yet practically in every case they did so in the full expectation that they were going to make massive profits.

All this points to ventures which were not simply high-risk, or founded on the notion of break or bust but forced to take short-cuts to gain their market-share, or even monopoly, at the expense of the native peoples on whose territories the supposed precious resource or resources lay. As the only obvious savings available came down to the cost of labour, it followed that traditional native middlemen would have to be dispensed with, while those who traditionally harvested the ground nuts, ivory, rubber or whatever, would have to be made to do so on terms which suited the global market-place orientated company, not the producer. This was tantamount to enslaving the producer population. Or, if that proved impossible, to importing some more pliable or easily coerced group to take its place. Moreover, once having gone down this draconian route, it was all but impossible to withdraw from it. Founded on terror, the only way to keep the population working was to apply more of the same. Capitalist imperatives similarly dictated that, once the profits did start rolling in, the best ways of ensuring good or even better dividends for the now increasing number of shareholders was to keep labour costs to an absolute minimum. Two questions, however, arise. Could this sort of profit-driven terror lead to genocide? And, if so, was it this, more particularly, which underlies our Herero tragedy?

There had been a case nearly three centuries earlier to suggest that genocide might arise as a direct outcome of an attempt to apply a resource monopoly. In the 1610s, the newly formed Dutch East India Company (VOC) had driven out its Spanish and Portuguese competitors from the Indonesian archipelago, similarly denied the English access, while proceeding to initiate its own monopoly on the purchase of cloves and nutmeg from its unique Indonesian source, the Moluccan islands, at rock-bottom prices fixed by itself. This meant not only the aggressive elimination of local Indonesian trade in these products but also the effective subjugation of the islanders who now came under Dutch 'protection'. In 1621, the indigenous population of the tiny Banda islands decided they no longer were going to participate in this system. At which point Jan Pietersz Coen, VOC's governor-general in the region, responded by having them all, to a man, woman and child, exterminated or deported as slaves or ethnic soldiers to other islands, with an entirely new indentured population shipped in from all over Asia to replace them.[90] Though there was no absolute repeat of the 1621 episode, other cases of non-compliance or active resistance against the monopoly, notably in Western Ceram in 1651, led to hardly less vicious punitive measures.[91] C. R. Boxer, the great doyen of early modern maritime history, dryly notes that 'it is arguable how much this spice monopoly benefited the Company commercially once they had achieved it'.[92] What is clear is that, once begun, VOC had no choice but to use constant military measures directed against the Moluccan population as a whole, in order to enforce their policies.

Similar trajectories can certainly be discerned in the process of the nineteenth-century Scramble for Africa. Sir George Goldie, who had wielded a number of small British companies into the much more powerful and royally chartered Niger Company in the 1880s, did not hesitate to quash with exterminatory zeal any indigenous uprising which challenged the Company's drive to monopolise the lucrative palm oil trade from the Gulf of Guinea region, in favour of a return to the status quo ante.[93] Though the number of whites remained minuscule in these tropical climes compared to the native population, medical advances enabling them to survive the adverse conditions and the use of a new, devastating but portable weapon, the Maxim machine gun, ensured that they were now positioned – at minimal outlay – to determine what natives produced and to whom they sold it, regardless of the local social and economic consequences. The importance of palm oil as a critical lubricant for European industrial production, as well as for the manufacture of soap, made societies in zones where it was produced particularly vulnerable to the Niger Company's strong-arm tactics, just as VOC's primary focus on spices had previously endangered the Moluccans and, from the 1890s onwards, an insatiable Western demand for rubber drove societies in tropical central Africa to the point of extinction.

We have already noted the spotlight thrown on King Leopold's operations in his own enormous private fiefdom, the Congo Free State (CFS), particularly through the efforts of Morel's CRA. With often poorly organised, under-equipped and understaffed concession companies operating under licence as cover for the king's effective trading monopoly of the region, and with his own voracity as a further spur to cash-in fast on the rubber boom so long as it lasted, the companies found themselves in effect given carte blanche to tap the wild rubber by whatever means available. In this they were ably assisted by the Force Publique, Leopold's paramilitary, native-recruited gendarmerie cre-ated for the ostensible purpose of maintaining law and order in the CFS.[94] Its actual role, however, was to ensure that the peoples of the Congo Basin did Leopold's bidding by going out into the jungle and tapping the vines and – where they failed to do so – to intimidate, whip and mutilate them back into line. The result was nothing short of catastrophic. Villages who succumbed to the regime's demands and hence to a relentless toil for an inevitably decreas-ing source of vines began to starve, while villagers who fled into the jungle to avoid the enforced labour became increasingly susceptible to smallpox, sleep-ing sickness and a range of intestinal infections. The combined effects of malnutrition and disease wiped out an estimated half million Congolese in 1901 alone.[95] As a result, whole regions covering thousands of square miles began to be depopulated.

Nevertheless, localised resistance was given short shrift. Week after week, Morel's campaigning paper, the *West African Mail*, was full of stories of Congo-lese men whose hands had been amputated for having failed to deliver sufficient rubber, or of abused and violated women and children held hostage to try and force their recalcitrant menfolk back to work. Moreover, cases which came to light, like that of the district commissioner of the Inongo region, Jules Jacques, who, on learning that the locals were killing the vines rather than tapping them, threatened that if they 'cut another single cane, I will exterminate them to the last man',[96] proved not to be the isolated ravings of a white man succumbing to 'tropical frenzy'. When, after putting fire and sword to village after village along the Aruwimi river, during the spring and summer of 1895 – with droves of their inhabitants decapitated – another district officer, Louis Leclerq, was awarded a bonus of 100 francs for his exceptional energy in putting down opposition and was personally congratulated by the governor-general.[97] In the relentless drive for profit in the Belgian Congo mass atrocity clearly had became an acceptable corollary for its masters. Nor was such behaviour confined to the CFS. In other parts of tropical Africa – as well as in the Putuyamo River region of Peru – there is substantial evidence that the period of rubber boom, in the 1890s and early 1900s, was equally disastrous and murderous for their inhabitants.[98]

Nor was the monopolisation of specific commodities the only basis upon which colonial Europeans might justify their exterminatory assaults. If what in the Congo was referred to as the *Lokeli* – the overwhelming[99] – may have been a very extreme case, imperialist exterminatory violence elsewhere on the continent could also be catalysed by more general economic factors. Take British-administered southern Africa, for instance. Here a general economic upswing, including conditions in which native Africans were able to accumulate capital from seasonal labour in the diamond mines of Kimberley, created, in turn, the possibility for those African societies which still remained nominally autonomous under British aegis to find a potential niche within which to survive and even compete in the Europeans' market-place.[100]

One such society was the 7,000-strong Hlubi people of Natal Province. Refugees in the 1850s from the *Mfecane*, their resettlement at colonial behest on 90,000 acres of fertile land beneath the Drakensburg gave them a notable opportunity, not unlike the Cherokee a quarter of a century earlier in the United States, to literally plough in their capital to agricultural development and produce a surplus which also undercut prices from neighbouring white farms. Not only thus, again like the Cherokee, were the Hlubi by the 1870s showing signs of prosperity, they were doing so while retaining – even enhancing under their Chief Langalibalele – their politico-economic independence. It was an independence that could not be allowed to last. The imperatives of neo-European settlement, as in the Americas, demanded that any remaining available land should be parcelled up as white-owned farms. The only role for the dispossessed natives on the farms was as working dependents on them. Accordingly, in 1873, the Hlubi were accused on quite trumped-up charges of insubordination – supposedly by refusing to register their firearms – provoked, thereby, into an unintended rebellion, hunted down and then shot out of hand by regular troops and settler volunteers. The colonists made sure the Hlubi had understood the magnitude of their sin. Their kraals were burnt, their old people, women and children smoked out of caves where they had gone to hide. Their land was then taken away, the tribe broken up, and thousands of men and women marched away 'to be handed over to settlers, as apprentices, hardly better than slaves'.[101] Members of the neighbouring Putini tribe, which had had nothing to do with the rebellion, were similarly attacked, shot down in their hundreds before suffering an identical fate of expropriation and virtual enslavement.

However, if the Hlubi of Natal, like the Brassmen of the Niger, or the Budja, Kuba and many other peoples of the Congo, all fell foul of the new European-imposed and unsubtly self-preferential system of market relations, there remains a question mark over the degree to which their respective denouements can, in the fullest sense, be deemed to be acts of genocide. There is no doubt that each suffered criminal mass killings. But they were killings nevertheless predicated on the colonist's assumption that this was the only way these native peoples could be made to do their exploitative bidding. At what point pulverising a people into acceptance of the fact becomes so total as to become indistinguishable from genocide, is certainly a moot point. But, if the primary driving force behind these actions is commercial gain, then we would be hard-pressed to read into the German economic agenda for South-West Africa any more extreme or radical demands than in these worst cases described above. Expectations of the finding of diamonds there associated with the first coastal purchases made by the entrepreneur-adventurer, Adolf Luderitz, around Angra Pequena, in 1883, proved at the outset entirely disappointing. It was a paradox that there were rich deposits, not only of diamonds, but of copper, iron, lead, zinc and uranium, but these either remained undiscovered, or lacking the capital for their significant extraction until *after* the Herero revolt. Certainly, the conjunction of these two elements did add a modest spurt to white settlement in the colony from 8,200 at the end of 1907, to 14,000 just two years later.[102] But the notion advanced by the East German historian, Horst Drechsler, that behind the extirpation of the Herero people lay the asset-stripping interests of metropolitan cartels does not easily dovetail with the fact that, in the 1890s, the German colonial office was so underwhelmed by the colony's prospects that it seriously considered handing it over to the British.[103]

Undercapitalisation in itself, of course, could be as easily read – as in the Congolese case – as a direct goad to the more ruthless exploitation of the indigenous peoples' labour potential. Leutwein's more limited programme of pre-1904 development certainly envisaged the country's interior becoming a series of large-scale cattle ranches, orientated towards the world market and run by a few hundred Europeans with the Herero, Nama and others doing the hard work. The plan took as given the wholesale sequestration of grazing land, as well as the transfer of flock from natives to incomers. This alone arguably represented the most severe form of structural violence that could be visited on a pastoralist economy operating at the brink of drought conditions and chronic competition with traditional neighbours. And Leutwein, as we have already suggested, was as ready as any other European colonial administrator to use direct physical violence in order to accomplish these goals. The problem was that he simply did not have the resources at his disposal to carry through the project alone. Instead, he was forced back onto the time-honoured colonial technique of divide and rule, in effect allying with Mahahero in order to seize lands and cattle controlled by other southern Herero chieftains, in the so-called 1896 'War of the Boundary'.[104] But the additional problem was that, if building up Mahahero as paramount chief was always intended as Leutwein's subterfuge by which to capture *all* the Herero lands and people for the German economic interest, then the strategy, at least until 1897, manifestly failed. The majority of the Herero were able adequately to sustain their own autonomous economy without entering into wage labour on the Germans' behalf, and thus did not sell the latter cattle in any great number, in turn preventing the sort of livestock-based take-off of a colonial economy of which Arthur in Tasmania, three-quarters of a century earlier, had been so proud. Indeed, German frustration at their own inability to change the situation is perfectly evident in repeated descriptions of the Herero in this period, notwithstanding the racist stereotyping, as a people of 'great meanness and a strongly developed arrogance' who, in the fight for their cattle are an opponent 'not to be despised'.[105]

This stalemate was finally broken, in 1897, with the arrival of an entirely independent contingency: rinderpest. The cattle plague has been described as one of a number of disasters of 'biblical proportions' striking Africa at the very apotheosis of European takeover.[106] Coming in the wake of a particularly strong El Niño climatic shift, which brought severe drought to all of southern and east Africa, the rinderpest killed an estimated 95 per cent of African tropical bovines.[107] While the Herero losses may not have been quite so great, for a people entirely wedded to a cattle economy it was indeed an absolute catastrophe both in actual physical and – equally importantly – psychological terms. Starvation was accompanied by a massive typhus epidemic, followed by a further plague of locusts. Ten thousand Herero are estimated to have died.[108] Sheer survival for those still living meant throwing themselves on the mercy of the Germans, whose own small stocks of cattle had mostly survived the rinderpest through vaccination and who were now positioned to buy up what remained of the rest and the land with it, at dirt prices. In a dramatic shift of fortunes, the few hundred German (or other European) ranchers had, by 1903, control of 3.5 million hectares, or approximately 25 per cent of Hereroland, with ownership of as many head of cattle as some 80,000 Hereros.[109] By way of stark contrast, increasing numbers of Herero found themselves in hock to unscrupulous and, by all accounts, particularly unpleasant German traders, and/or reduced to a thoroughly servile dependency on farms, or working for a pittance on now-emerging infrastructural projects, such as the railway from Swakopmund at the coast to Windhoek, the new German administrative capital.[110]

Lying technically within Herero territory and completed in 1903, the railway was emblematic of the new contours of German–Herero power relations. Mahahero's paper independence was proving valueless in the face of the proliferation of unpunished maltreatments, abuses and outright murders being committed by German settlers against Herero men and women. And while Leutwein, believing himself the very model of colonial moderation, promised to ease up on the Herero plight by cancelling their trading debts, the enactment of an ordinance to this effect in late 1902, by giving German creditors twelve months' grace with which to call the debts in, only exacerbated the situation further by enabling them, with the assistance of the colonial police, to simply collect cattle in lieu.[111]

The truth was that the Germans, Leutwein included, believed that they had finally got the Herero where they wanted them. With Mahahero himself, ostensibly, a suitably broken, drink-sodden puppet, Leutwein pressed ahead towards a final parcelling up of Hereroland. In October 1903, the building commenced of a further railway linking Windhoek with new copper mines at Otavi, this certainly controlled and backed by a German financial syndicate.[112] It aimed to slice diagonally across what Leutwein was now calling the Herero 'reservation' and came with typical, additional prerogatives to the syndicate, in the form of land and water rights surrendered by Mahahero. What Leutwein had not calculated upon was the Otavi project being taken as 'the last straw'[113] by the Herero, the call for general revolt – certainly egged on by more vociferous patriots – being made by none other than Mahahero himself. 'Let us die fighting rather than die as a result of maltreatment, imprisonment or some other calamity',[114] Mahahero had proclaimed as he attempted to involve Nama, half-caste Basters and the other indigenous peoples of the colony in a more general anti-imperialist insurrection. It was ironic that the Germans perceived a threat to their rule coming from some of these other more obviously truculent peoples, not the Herero. Leutwein's departure to the south, in January 1904, to quell a local revolt by the Bondelswarts, a Nama people – also caused by the threat of land seizures – was, indeed, the very spur and opportunity Mahahero grasped for making his own bid to throw off the German yoke. Yet it is equally significant how little the Germans understood as to why the Herero revolt had taken place at all. Their official 1904 inquiry put it down 'to the arrogance of the natives and to their confidence in the superiority over the Germans',[115] a statement which not only speaks volumes about the nature of imperial hubris but even more of the German incomprehension of the structural conditions which might drive people collectively towards the most utterly desperate response.

But without the ferocity of that response, we would be hard-pressed to locate our genocidal outcome. Undiluted economic rapacity supported by racist justification certainly were essential factors in a toxic mix, but only when ignited by the bitter pill of resistance of those who would become its victims can we discern, in the Herero case, the lethal mix which would engender genocide. Yet, if victim resistance is a factor, then how do we account for the many other examples in this period of anti-colonial revolt that we do not generally consider as genocide? Or, then, perhaps, is it our own perception which is skewed; that the issue is not how different the Herero extermination is from others, but rather how similar?

Fin-de-Siècle Colonial Revolt and its Consequences

Pushed to the wall by the territorial acquisitions, economic subjugation, or cultural contempt of the imperialists, indigenous societies, even where the odds were totally against them, often mounted desperate defences of their land, livelihoods and values. For the most intransigent – and usually geographically isolated – among them, the result could be an almost continuous 'total' warfare spanning generations. In Algeria, the various Kabyle tribes of the eastern mountain hinterland fought for over forty years to resist the French takeover. They neither gave nor received mercy, suffered repeated exterminatory massacres for their efforts and, after the defeat of the 1871–2 Muqrani revolt, were so physically exhausted and depleted that the French were finally able to carry through a massive expropriation of their best communal pastures, orchards and forests in favour of incoming *colons*.[116] Retribution for having dared to challenge French rule when the latter's back was turned to fight the Prussians at home undoubtedly also played a part; and so too, classically, did the commitment that 'never again' would the mountain peoples be allowed to stand in the way of the French colonial agenda. The result, assisted by the massive ratcheting up of taxes – which conveniently led to more forced land sales – was massive pauperisation and physical swamping. Paradoxically, one of few outlets available for the avoidance of clan starvation was for Kabyle menfolk to join the imperial French *Armée d'Afrique*, thereby replicating the fate of dispossessed Scottish Highlanders.[117] If the history of Kabyle resistance does not lead us to the near-absolute terminus we associate with the Herero, it does, however, provide us with the ground rules for a specifically French counter-insurgency which was undoubtedly sub-genocidal in nature.

Far away in the Pacific, for instance, the French mid-century invasion of New Caledonia, leading to the forcible dispossession of nine-tenths of the fertile coastal land from the native Kanaks, in favour of *colon*-run plantations, ranches and penal colonies, precipitated a great native insurrection, in 1878. Two hundred Europeans were butchered, leading, in turn, to demands from the settler mouthpiece, *La Nouvelle Calédonie,* for a war of extermination against *all* Melanesians. A sort of colonial Vendée ensued, with elements of indigenous island catastrophes, such as Tasmania and the Canaries, thrown in for good measure. At the head of the *colonnés mobiles* composed of colonial troops, settlers and local native auxiliaries, one Captain Rivière led a prolonged scorched-earth rampage through the centre of the island, burning hundreds of villages, systematically destroying their irrigation systems, killing the men and handing the women over as booty to the pro-French tribes. The Kanaks had a reputation as particularly ferocious head-hunters but, as the exiled communard, Louise Michel, noted, it was not the Kanaks but the Third Republic who gave 'lessons in canibalism'.[118]

Nor, when the chips were down, did the British prove any the less bloodthirsty. Dominating their imperial mindset far into the twentieth century were the Indian events of 1857, when thousands of ethnic soldiers – sepoys – had revolted against British East India Company rule, 'the only time in the century when a native army trained by Europe rose up against its masters'.[119] Lurid tales of the rape and murder of 'white' women and children, particularly emanating from one true incident at Cawnpore,[120] clouded the imperial response and turned the struggle into Britain's own overtly race war. The fact that underlying the largely inchoate and disorganised mutiny, were accumulated but serious resentments against the rapidly accelerating impoverishment of large sectors of native society, both rural and urban, in the wake of the country's opening up to free market forces, and that with this went the undermining – in Disraeli's words, no less – of 'laws and manners, customs and usages, political organisations, the tenure of property, the religion of the people', tended to be reflected upon by the colonial power only after the event.[121] At this point, company rule was replaced by direct Crown control with some belated efforts to conciliate Indian grievances. Clearly, there was no state or corporate intention to commit genocide, even in a limited sense against those elements of the population who had joined the mutiny – and on this score it should be noted that even the majority of the sepoys remained loyal. More to the point, in a sub-continent where the colonial commercial interest, as pursued by a relatively minuscule British administrative and business class, was entirely dependent on the acquiescence of India's populous millions, any policy of open, violent coercion – at least in already subdued regions – made no sense whatsoever. Yet what is striking about what happened in the wake of the recapture of the central-north Indian towns at the epicentre of the mutiny is just how prolonged, indiscriminate, utterly savage and repeatedly gratuitous was British vengeance. Indeed, with the repeated sewing up of Muslim soldiers in pigskin before their dispatch, or the tying of others to the mouths of cannon from which they were then blown to pieces, the supposedly sang-froid, stiff-upper-lip British military had clearly lost it.[122]

The response to the mutiny, thus, is significant for this discussion in its illustration of how violent resistance to colonial takeover or rule – particularly when that resistance appeared to the colonialists to come out of the blue, and even more the case when it was militarily successful – could so knock imperial self-esteem off its pedestal that it could lead in turn to a frenzied, if not fanatical counter-reaction in complete and total defiance of rational judgement. Of course, human history is so sufficiently littered with overreactions of this kind that one might be excused for assuming that it is simply a rather predictable if entirely egregious aspect of the human condition. Yet, towards the end of nineteenth and at the beginning of the twentieth centuries, the number of examples where the retributive extirpation of anti-colonial resistance veers towards the overtly genocidal is enough to demand somewhat closer inspection.

Back on the African continent, in 1879, when the martial but traditionally armed Zulu nation was consciously provoked into war by its annexation-minded British neighbours on the Natal borders, its complete elimination at Isandhlwana of a 1,600-strong modern, technologically equipped military force sent against it precipitated in turn a much more systematic scorched-earth campaign by the British army, the aim of which became 'the destruction of the economic foundations of Zululand'.[123] In the immediately preceding years, British efforts to extirpate any hint of native independence in South Africa had seen their ruthless scotching of insurrections by the Gcaleka-Xhosa and Ngquika of the Transkei, the mixed-race Griqua along the Orange River, as well as the Hlubi.[124] With Zulu resistance, however, threatening to spark off insurrections by yet other tribes, and thoroughly inflamed by the disaster at Isandhlwana, British efforts against the Zulu were ratcheted up to such a degree of total war that one astute writer has asserted that 'genocide came close to being adopted as official policy'.[125] The Zulus' complete military defeat, at Ulundi, followed by the surrender of their King Cetshwayo, may have saved them from this worse fate. Perhaps, this has something also to do with the fact that they were nominally independent and, thus, at least initially, perceived by the British as genuine, even legitimate military adversaries. Nearly twenty years later, when the Ndebele and Shona peoples broke into open revolt to reassert their lost independence against the recently imposed rule of the crown-chartered British South Africa Company (BSAC), no such mitigating circumstances were deemed permissible by the latter.

The Umvukela and Chimurenga uprisings of 1896–7 have been described as the first genuine wars of independence in sub-Saharan Africa.[126] Their insurrections thus stand as significant precursors to those launched by the Herero and Nama, though it is not just the spatial and chronological proximities between the two series of events which offer striking parallels.[127] As in German South-West Africa, the revolts in British territories – that the BSAC were already, in 1890, calling Rhodesia after the company's founder, Cecil Rhodes – were precipitated by a very similar set of factors and circumstances. Corporate chicanery which parcelled up land and mining exploration rights in the BSAC interest through entirely fraudulent undertakings offered to the Ndebele chief, Lobengula, was one obvious similarity. With encroachment on traditional grazing land came the usual economic subjugation and political emasculation. It was also no coincidence that a major precipitant to the revolt was the El Niño-linked drought that in turn provided the seedbed for the massive locust and rinderpest plagues which arrived in Matabeleland and Mashonaland a year before they struck German South-West Africa. As in the latter case, it was the combination of colonial oppression and overwhelming environmental disaster that seems to have provided the most critical ingredients driving these pastoral-cum-peasant societies towards total insurrection.

The parallels, with some notable divergences, however, arguably go further than that. Conquistador-like in their cupidity, the hotch-potch of BSAC pioneer settlers and mercenaries who began encroaching on the Shona and Ndebele lands from 1890 assumed rights of ownership where none existed – Rhodes' 'state' had no legal basis in international law – while also labouring under the entirely mistaken belief that they were to become imminent beneficiaries of gold and other fabulous mineral wealth. It was this early failure to realise its fantastic goals that underscored the extreme tenuousness of the BSAC enterprise.[128] Moreover, unlike in South-West Africa, where the imperial state intervened to pull company chestnuts out of the fire, Rhodes' remaining options were between abandoning the whole project and attempting further perilous overreach. He opted for the latter, engaging in a whole series of covert stock-exchange orientated manipulations to keep the BSAC afloat while at the same time creating a new 'front' company that, in committing itself to open up the wider region through the extension of two railways from the already gold-rich Witwatersrand and from the coast at Beira, seemed to offer the prospect of delivering further huge latifundia-style land grants to potential investors.[129] As in Hereroland, and as so often in the modern world, railway lines were proving to be more than simply emblems for the loss of indigenous independence, but in their very creation the very fuse-wire leading to genocidal explosions.

Equally significant, in comparative terms, is the role played by the Ndebele and Shona themselves. After all, these were not weak and pathetic African societies waiting passively to be wiped out but actually rather vigorous ones, alive to the impact of European encroachment and straining every sinew to meet the challenge. Jan-Bart Gewald has written of the Herero as a people who, from as early as the 1860s, were attempting to transform themselves from a strongly decentralised, transhumant, pastoralist society into something much more centralised, even urbanised, and in which 'political concepts and structures ... drawn from outside sources' were appropriated and transformed to these needs.[130] But such transformations were not peculiar to the Herero. Nor was Samuel Mahahero in any way unique when he sought to use the Germans as *his* proxies in order to extirpate rival chiefs and consolidate his power.[131] Lobengula similarly sought to manipulate the British interlopers, rather than the other way around. Coming from a background which was literally bathed in blood – Lobengula was the son of the fearsomely ruthless chieftain, Mzilikazi, who had broken away from the Zulu nation some fifty years earlier, in a notable spin-off from the *Mfecane*[132] – the Ndebele kingdom was itself the product of a recent, bloody conquest. And this, in turn, made the Ndebele's neigbours, mostly notably the Shona peoples, whose kin had been massacred, displaced, or subjugated in the process, intensely suspicious of Lobengula's encouragement to the BSAC to go and take control over Mashonaland.

Paradoxically then, if Lobengula's primary strategy – like that of Samuel Mahahero – was to ensure and perhaps even extend his own people's political and territorial integrity by displacing confrontation with the Europeans onto another native community, the aim of the BSAC, in the person of Dr Jameson, Rhodes' special 'on the spot' emissary, was to find any excuse to wreck it. Not least was this because the whole BSAC enterprise was running out of time – and money. Jameson's moment came in the summer of 1893 when Lobengula's warrior *impi*, believing themselves still to be entitled to go on cattle-raids into now BSAC-occupied Mashonaland as they had previously done, perpetrated a massacre of a group of Shona in full view of a BSAC fort. The occasion became a pretext for Jameson to carry out his own military strike on Lobengula's Bulawayo kraal, Maxim-gunning down large numbers of

Lobengula's warriors in the process and leading, thereby, to the defiant suicide of Lobengula and the *de facto* extension of Chartered Company rule over Matabeleland as well as Mashonaland. There followed wholesale land expropriations in favour of white settlers and companies.[133]

However, all this should confirm that we are under no requirement to paint the victims – at least not their leaderships – as one-dimensional plaster-cast saints when what we are actually dealing with are political actors striving for survival, and even advantage. The history of Shona–Ndebele relations should also make clear why the possibility of a joint revolt was not plausible any more than it was in the case of the Herero and Nama, peoples whose proximate dependency on tightly contest grazing lands, particularly in times of drought, provided grounds enough for conflict, even putting aside all the complications arising from the impact of an outside third party. Could one speculate, indeed, that in the 1896 and 1904 sequence of events, both Shona and Nama respectively stood initially but consciously by when European guns were turned on their Ndebele and Herero neighbours because, after all, what they had always most wanted was the military emasculation of their traditional enemies? Only when they realised that the European response was not so much emasculation as extermination were they precipitated into their own desperate 'national' insurrections. Certainly, in retrospect, we can see in the unwillingness of these peoples to unite or at least coordinate their military strategies – notwithstanding in the 1904 instance Mahahero's plea to the Nama to join the resistance – an utterly fatal flaw. Even so, on their own, the intial momentum of each of these separate revolts suggested sufficient capacity to drive both BSAC and German South-West African enterprises into *irretrievable* positions.

It is in this tantalising possibility that such forces of native resistance might have not just thrown a spanner into the works of imperial projects but actually forced them into retreat that we can locate the moment in which colonialism had the potential to produce genocide. In 1896, as again in 1904, two relatively weak, overextended, yet arrogantly ambitious, colonial projects were in the business of accelerating their drive towards a rapid financial return on their initial capital outlays, even though their actual control of territory, resource and people remained tenuous. Each enterprise could only proceed by the starkest actual as well as structural violence, ratcheting up the attack on the traditional social fabric and livelihoods of the conquered peoples, confiscating their cattle, imposing taxes and, thereby, forcing whole populations into entirely degrading wage labour subservience. Thus, the societies on the receiving end were more than aware that they were staring into the abyss, that once the railways and roads were laid, their autonomy and integrity would be gone and that this was their one and only last chance to break free. Just as in the

Herero uprising, so in the Umvukela, the Ndebele people seized their moment when the colony's forces of 'law and order' were elsewhere, in this instance having almost all entirely vacated the territory in Jameson's notorious but abortive raid on the independent Boer Transvaal. And, just as in 1904, they struck out at isolated rural farmsteads, with the critical difference that, with no orders from a Samuel Mahhahero to target *only* the male soldiers and settlers of the occupying power, the killing was quite indiscriminate. With some 200 white men, women and children, not to mention many more of their black servants massacred,[134] the European towns besieged and the price of BSAC shares on the stock exchange in free-fall, would it have been any wonder if Rhodes' response had been one of annihilatory vengeance?

So, why do we not think of succeeding events, in 1896, as akin to the genocide against the Herero? The simple answer is because they were not – at least not quite. After a typical bout of murderous retribution, Rhodes, as BSAC supremo, suddenly changed course, offered amnesty to the Ndebele and a spurious promise to end their grievances, while the Crown, forced to intervene with imperial troops for the BSAC's urgent assistance, gave no special punitive mandate to Sir Frederick Carrington, its appointed commanding officer. Certainly his operating instructions stand in marked contrast to those of von Trotha's *Vernichtungsbefehl:* 'clemency was to be shown to the wounded, women and children are not to be injured and prisoners are to be taken whenever possible'.[135] When it came to putting down the more bitter and protracted Shona revolt it is acknowledged, even by Zimbabwean commentators, that the real demographic blow came not from the armed struggle itself but from the ensuing influenza epidemic.[136]

Are we, therefore, to assume that the British, faced with the potential loss of a colony kept a somewhat cooler head than their German counterparts or that, save for Rhodes, his shareholders and assorted adventurers, did not feel quite so much was at stake? Perhaps so. The only problem is that on the ground the evidence points to a response at marked variance with Carrington's ground rules for 'civilised' warfare, particularly when it came to the Shona. Rather like the predominant German racial characterisation of the Herero as a people without the martial spirit with which to mount an effective rebellion, the Shona were similarly derided by the British as degenerate cowards who would not dare to challenge BSAC rule[137] and who, certainly, would not prove worthy warrior adversaries in the guise that the British painted their obviously more truculent Ndebele neighbours. When, however, the Shona's decentralised network of local communities proved these racialised notions to be utterly and stupidly fallacious, with a tenacious guerrilla struggle which lasted far into 1897, long after the much more centrally organised Umvukela had collapsed, the British campaign developed contours markedly resembling that of von Trotha. There was, of course, the 'standard' pacification techniques, in the form of a systematic scorched-earth policy – the burning of homes, the killing of cattle, the destruction of standing crops and food stocks – designed to drive the population towards starvation. But when these methods failed to bring about their capitulation, imperial troopers and Jameson's men alike simply resorted to dynamiting the caves in which the extended family groups of the Shona had taken refuge. Nobody knows how many men, women and children died in this final holocaust of the Chimurenga; Lawrence Vambe, writing from the perspective of family tradition handed down over the generations, says it was thousands.[138]

And, yes, there were survivors to suffer the misery of a particularly brutal, nasty and, one might add, fearful post-pacificatory colonial rule in Rhodesia. It was similar to the case (with the exception of the 1,000 who had escaped with Mahahero across the Omahake) for the residue of Herero, Nama and other south-central Namibian peoples in the aftermath of the kaiser's war, before the overthrow of German rule by the British Union of South Africa in 1915 brought both new opportunities and restatements of old colonial oppressions.[139] In this sense, arguably what we are dealing with here are military responses to colonial revolt that dramatically overreacted rather than conscious policies of people-extermination.

*

However, the fact that the *fin-de-siècle* epoch *repeatedly* produced colonial overreactions of this sort actually may provide an important insight into the ugly dawn of a twentieth century we more readily recognise as genocidal. What also happened in this period in Japanese-occupied Korea, or the US-'liberated' Philippines, or, for that matter, the Dutch-controlled East Indies, were not simply the inevitable outcomes of unequal military engagements between traditionally armed local (or even imperial) societies and the new – or not so new – maritime-based, technologically modernised ones whose hegemony was now being asserted on a global scale. Of course, this was the moment when the fundamental power shift that had been building up for 300 or possibly 400 years did, at the very least, reach a first level of culmination. Global power was now very much in the hands of those Western societies – or in the single case of Japan, those non-Western societies – who had aligned themselves to the Western statist model and who had developed a sufficient industrial base to deploy advanced military technologies to go with it. But if this ensured that War Type Two or Three conflicts between advancing empires and national or proto-national resisters were bound to be asymmetrical and one-sided affairs, this in itself cannot explain why, to paraphrase a line from Henrik Lundofte's perceptive study on the German *radicalisation* of its Herero struggle, the low threshold between total war and genocide in the colonies was easily crossed.[140] If military superiority translated into easy victory then rather the opposite was true. Either colonial insurrections should have folded on the first impact of Western long-range guns and thereby saved a lot of lives, or desisted from the effort in the first place.

Of course, there were plenty of instances where, despite the acute social, economic and cultural trauma which the imposition of Western hegemony was producing, societies did not revolt.[141] This was true even in some cases where the colonial power was constantly looking over its shoulder in expectation that this would happen and which, consequently, was always preparing for the worst. In British India the fear of another 1857, for instance, was such a fixed motif in the official mind of the Raj that it could lead to the creation of an entirely fictive uprising where there was actually none. This led, in 1919, to arguably the single most egregious episode in British imperial history, the cold-blooded gunning down of over 1,000 people at an entirely peaceful rally, at Amritsar in the Punjab. At least 300 died though the culprit, one Brigadier-General Dyer, continued to be feted by large sections of imperial society as 'the Saviour of the Punjab'.[142]

Yet, twenty years earlier, when anything between 3 and 10 million Indians, particularly Gujaratis, died in the great famine of 1899–90,[143] there had been no uprising. The immediate cause of this catastrophe was another series of monsoon failures brought about by another effect of the late-1890s extreme El Niño-Southern Oscilllation (ENSO). But rather like – from the much smaller demographic base – the equally apocalyptic Irish famine of the late 1840s, real responsibility lay with the refusal of a British imperial government to relax its doctrinal commitment to the principle of laissez-faire, thereby allowing grain exports from a relatively drought-free (or in the Irish case potato blight-free) region or province, while millions in neighbouring ones starved.[144] In itself, the Indian famines, and those that befell much of northern China, south-east Asia, the Brazilian *sertão* and the horn of Africa, as well as its southern half, ought to stand as a necessary reminder, or corrective, that the serious mass killing perpetrated by the hegemonic ascendancy of the West, at the *fin de siècle*, did not come out of the barrel of a gun but from from the much more chronic structural violence which emanated from the creation of its world market. For this one should read Mike Davis' devastating exploration of the subject.[145]

If sheer exhaustion in the wake of mass starvation combined with heavy policing may, in part, explain why colonies such as Ireland, or India, did not necessarily pass, at critical moments of crisis and demographic collapse through a sequence of revolt followed by genocide, there were plenty of other crisis spots in the emerging third world where this potential was much closer to being realised. Perhaps, again, a significant factor in these cases may have been that these were often societies that were not yet fully integrated into a colonial structure, as were an Ireland or India, but latecomers to its embrace, or, then again, outlying regions which, though nominally absorbed into imperium or even nation-state, in practice had remained until a late stage peripheral to its economic dictates, or on the margins of the state rulers' political vision. This does not mean that when the full impact of colonialism came, indigenous pauperisation and consequent social distress was any the less acute – simply that these societies were sometimes able to draw upon quite fresh memories of an intact social fabric as well as on deeper cultural traditions of an independent autonomy with which to mount their insurrectionary challenges.

On the obverse side, however, what is equally significant is the degree to which colonial regimes repeatedly misread these danger signals. This could have been founded on straightforward racist arrogance, at a time when Western imperialisms were displaying some of its most extreme manifestations, including assumptions that the 'natives' would be too cowed, or stupid, or disorganised to even contemplate rebellion or, as in the American case in the wake of the Spanish-American war of 1898, because they had really convinced themselves that the indigenous response to their arrival would be one of eternal gratitude.[146] The key mismatch, however, is in the almost complete mental unpreparedness on the part of the colonial authorities to recognise and understand what they were encountering. The sheer audacity of weak, third-world societies to rise up against the greatest, most militarily well-equipped and sophisticated powers on earth was unnerving enough. The fact that these movements seemed to be able to draw on untapped and unseen reserves of energy, even when half-starved, and to go on fighting completely against the odds, seemed, further, to defy logic. Worst of all, if these really were authentic movements of people-power struggling for freedom, then *la mission civilisatrice* – in other words, the whole pretence upon which the advancing empires rested their justification to be in far-away lands – would be shown up to be the meretricious lie that it was. In a critical sense, therefore, the annihilatory physical violence unleashed by the colonial military in these situations was preceded by what one can only describe as a form of psychic self-violence. The potency and resilience of native resistance came too close to the imperialists' knuckle; it too obviously controverted the assumed reason upon which the new world order of the *fin de siècle* was being built.

Underlying unreasoned late-imperial responses to insurrection, thus, were often quite deep anxieties about the nature of the forces they were facing. Is it not significant that the Shona spirit-mediums associated with the Mwari cult, held to have played an instigating role in the Chimurenga, were specifically executed by drumhead military courts,[147] or that Leutwein blamed the Nama uprising on an enigmatic but supposedly fanatical black prophet, named Sheppert Sturmann, who was avowedly doing the rounds of the continent, preaching pan-African resistance?[148] What was beyond the ken of the imperial mindset was always denounced as the machinations of fanatical madmen intent on wrecking peace and good order. But what if the various messages being preached gave to the insurrectionists a sense of their own special power? The 'maji', the 'magic' water that spirit-mediums, led by an ordinary peasant refugee, Kinjikitile, claimed would protect their followers from imperial bullets may not have worked in the face of the machine guns of imperial *Schutzgruppe*, but this did not prevent clan after clan, from very different peoples, joining the entirely trans-tribal Maji-Maji rebellion against German rule in vast swathes of southern and western Tanganikya, in the summer of 1905. As in South-West Africa, so, for a moment, here too, it looked as if native power armed with spears and cap guns was equal to, if not stronger than, that of its imperial adversary.[149] Even put on the defensive the african tribes waged guerrilla warfare for months into 1906, ultimately only being defeated by a conscious systematic military-induced famine, throughout the region.[150] Perhaps as many as 250,000 to 300,000 people died, including an estimated half of the Vidunda people, more than half the Matumbi, and three-quarters of the Pangwa.[151]

But if liquidating whole populations, not to mention laying waste to vast tracts of their homelands, was the only way colonial officers and administrators could sleep easily in their beds, perhaps they were not so invincible after all. Kinjikitile and his acolytes had promised not just a sweeping away of colonial rule but a millenarian new order in its place. Further to the north, in the Sudan, a different cultural version of this same message, this time expressed through a resurgent and militant Islam, seemed, for the best part of two decades, to achieve just that. Not only was this Mahdiyya instrumental in ejecting Anglo-Egyptian rule in 1881, and replacing it with a revolutionary theocratic polity, but it also continued, quite astoundingly, to keep the British at bay – despite this being at the height of their advance – until an imperial army led by Lord Kitchener stormed Omdurman, the regime's capital, in April 1898. Kitchener's was a classic War Type Two campaign, predicated on starving the supporting population into submission and annihilating the 'dervish hordes' in a notably one-sided battle facilitated by 1 million bullets and 3,500 shells.

Thousands of enemy wounded were shown no mercy.[152] Certainly, for all its racist nastiness, the campaign did stop short of outright genocide. Yet the spectre of Muhammad Ahmad ibn' Abdullah, the charismatic religio-military leader who had declared that he was the expected Mahdi, 'the divine leader chosen by God to fill the earth with justice and equity',[153] and who had led the Sudanese anti-colonial revolution at its outset, continued to haunt British and, indeed, practically all the colonial powers thereafter.[154] With horrible consequences.

In 1906, for instance, in the village of Satiru, in Sokoto province of north-west Nigeria, another self-styled Mahdi led a violent peasant rebellion against British rule. The rebels brutally killed three British officials and more than two score of their black soldiery in the process. Lord Lugard, however, the high commissioner for the region, did not stop to assess the situation, or to consider negotiation. Only isolation of the rebels, followed by their 'annihilation' – his words – would suffice, a policy pursued à outrance, without regard to disentangling the innocent from the guilty, or the men from the women and children. Two thousand were mown down by his troops, the village razed and any survivors then executed, 'their heads cut off and put on spikes'.[155] Lugard claimed, correctly, to be acting on the direct authority of the British Crown. There was no inquiry into his actions.

Another administrator-cum-military man with similarly robust views of millenarian-tinged Islamic *jihaddiya* was J. B. van Heutsz, appointed governor-general of the Dutch East Indies in 1904, after years out in the field attempting to quell rebellion in Aceh, a Muslim sultanate at the extreme eastern edge of Sumatra. The war in Aceh, actually, had been going on for decades with negligible success for the Dutch. However, von Heutz, and G. C. E. van Daalen, the officer appointed soon after as the new military governor of Aceh, decided it was time for a more thorough 'clean-up operation'. Van Daalen's methods proved him to be the nearest the Dutch could offer in the von Trotha mould. In addition to the usual scorched-earth pacification strategy his assaults on enemy villages offered no quarter or distinction between men, women and children. All were slaughtered. The atrocities committed on his orders found their way eventually into a little book entitled, *How Civilised Netherlands Brings about Peace and Order in Aceh in the Twentieth Century*. The litany certainly shocked elements of the Dutch press and public and facilitated van Daalen's resignation. But, like von Trotha who, for his pains, was very publicly decorated by the kaiser, van Daalen received similar honours and plaudits from the Dutch government for his 'services and courage'. The only difference was that the Achinese refused to give up their struggle and so, unlike the Herero, did not receive the full brunt of exterminatory retribution which the Dutch military had intended for them.[156]

Aceh's ability to defy imperial might in this sense stands as something of an exception to the rule. The one thing imperial states could not allow in their midst at the *fin de siècle* was a counter-culture – and indeed counter-political economy – that successfully and resiliently went its own way while, at the same time, offering the threat of its 'bad' example to neighbouring communities. In the modernising, positivist Brazil of the 1890s, the jewel in the crown, in other words, of (until 1889) the former Portuguese empire, a messianic but otherwise quietist Christian commune at Canudos, in the remote drought-ridden north-east, had army after army sent against it for exactly these reasons. The problem was that on each occasion these well-armed expeditions kept being liquidated by the entirely scratch forces of the defenders, and, at each turn, thereby adding to the potency of this primitive, ramshackle but highly communitarian 'New Jerusalem' and of its ageing prophet, Antonio Conselheiro. The effect was to inflame utterly the new, transitional but markedly uncertain Brazilian republic and to ensure that the war against Canudos would become a war of extermination. When the fourth and final expedition was sent against the mud walls of the city, in July 1897, it was massively supported by modern artillery but even then took three months to accomplish its goal. According to its modern chronicler, Robert M. Levine, the final assault involved an orgy of killing. 'Children had their skulls smashed against trees', while wounded *conselheiristas* were either 'drawn and quartered or hacked to pieces limb by limb'.[157] The vast majority of its thousands of inhabitants were slaughtered in this way. Some hundreds of surviving women and children were evacuated to the Bahian coast where – not unlike later survivors of the Armenian genocide – they were absorbed as servants, sexual chattel or, arguably more fortunately, as full family members of perpetrators or bystanders. Perhaps at least as significantly, however, every last trace of the 'holy city' of Canudos was utterly and systematically erased by the Brazilian army 'as if it had housed the devil incarnate'.[158]

The incubus of supposedly crazed fanatics upsetting a rational, incontrovertibly correct path of progress produced genocidal results on the Asian continent too. In Korea, in the early 1890s, the bogey was the secret, millenarian Tonghak, literally 'Eastern Studies' or 'Eastern Learning Society', which was able to mobilise over 100,000 peasant rebels in the southern Cholla provinces around its overtly egalitarian, anti-Western, anti-Christian but also markedly anti-Japanese platform. Japan had at this stage not yet wrested direct control of this quasi-independent but technically Chinese tributary state. However, Japan's 'civilising' influence, over and above all of the other interested imperial parties, was already well advanced, not least in its preferential contract for the export of Korean rice to its home market. Most of this came from Cholla, the peninsula's traditional granary. Yet, by 1894, El-Niño drought conditions as well as insupportable domestic taxation was producing famine in the region. The final straw that broke the camel's back was the unrelenting continuation of the rice exports in the midst of this misery. The Korean government, unable to counter the insurrection, called for Chinese assistance which in turn provoked direct Japanese intervention, thus leading to a direct Sino-Japanese confrontation in which the Chinese went down in spectacular defeat.[159] The Tonghak, however, did not succumb to the Japanese, or to the traditionalist Korean ruling classes who sided with them but rather fought on in classic guerrilla style until their adversaries resorted to 'a systematic extermination of their civilian base'.[160] Again, hundreds of thousands of peasants were directly killed or died from the after-effects of the Japanese scorched-earth campaign.

In China the millenarian undertones of revolt in this same decade mixed even more forcefully with a virulently bitter but perfectly comprehensible xenophobia. Though again, there were equally catastrophic results for those who encountered the Western imperial reaction. China, of course, was one of the great traditional world empires but one which, by the 1890s, was showing distinct signs of febrility, if not complete disintegration in the face of a Western penetration which had been gathering pace over a period of decades. Natural disaster had also taken its toll. Millions had died in the El-Niño induced sequence of famine in 1876–8, particularly in northern provinces such as Shanxi. But when a further equally devastating wave of floods, followed by drought and famine, began again to ravage northern China from 1897 onwards, popular blame was much more readily directed towards the alleged evil influence of foreigners on China's sense of balance, harmony and *feng shui*.[161] In fact, the famine arrived at a particularly critical moment when the pace of foreign encroachment was rapidly accelerating. In the following year Germany and Britain negotiated new spheres of influence in China, entirely over the heads of the imperial Qing court in Beijing, while the other powers hurried to pick up what other prizes they could lay their hands on. The Western cultural assault on traditional Chinese belief systems was also in rapid and unchecked advance, at this juncture, with Protestant missionary activity, in particular, enabled by diplomatic treaty, consular protection and financial incentives to converts.[162] Most tangibly of all, Western inroads into the Chinese market were a matter of unfettered *political* advantage, imports of cheap cotton goods without tarrifs wrecking domestic competition and plummeting China's own formerly strong balance of trade into massive deficit. Without sufficient revenues, the empire could not properly function; with railways – the primary vectors of the European advance – traditional canal- and land-based routes and trading foci were simply bypassed or fell into desuetude.

The famine reached its peak in the spring of 1900. It was surely no coincidence that this was also the moment when the great Boxer Rebellion had its explosive take-off. It carried with it, one might add, the seeds of China's own potentiality to commit genocide. The Boxers targeted native Christians, foreigners and often rich Chinese who had failed to share their grain stocks. This, then, was a social and cultural as well as political revolution. And it was, undoubtedly, consciously violent. Even so, while the movement may have begun, rather like the Tonghak, as one or more secret sects practising esoteric magic and martial arts – immunity to bullets after 100 days of training was one of the Boxer claims[163] – it was quickly able to mobilise as a broadly based national movement of independence eventually even taking with it the Qing court in one last gasp of imperial leadership. In the ensuing assault on everything foreign, Chinese Christians were slaughtered in their thousands along with scores of European missionaries, the German minister in Beijing assassinated and the foreign legation quarter – along with all those who had taken refuge in it – besieged.[164]

Retribution, however, proved more violent and terrible still. Setting out to relieve the legations, an International Expeditionary Force of eight foreign powers bore down on Beijing with an annihilatory zeal. Hundreds of thousands of innocent as well as combatant Chinese are estimated to have been killed or executed in the expedition's exterminatory drive. Moreover, in revenge for the killing of his diplomat, the kaiser personally ordered the commander of the German force, Field-Marshall von Waldersee to emulate the carnage of Attila. His men, Wilhelm proposed, in a notorious public speech made at von Waldersee's Bremerhaven embarkation, should act like Huns.[165] They dutifully obliged, even though by the time they had arrived on the scene in September 1900, the legations had already been relieved by the other 'national' units. The ability of Russians, French, Japanese and British Indian troops to act out the sort of sado-erotic fantasies the kaiser clearly had in mind, however, is attested to in the thousands of Chinese women and girls raped en route to Beijing, not to say the thousands more women in the capital who were to throw themselves down wells to escape a similar fate.[166] Rescued diplomats and missionaries were truly staggered by the scale of the ensuing military-perpetrated carnage, not to mention the looting which went with it.[167] Von Waldersee – technically supreme commander of this 'international' relief force but bereft of a liberating role by over a month – attempted to redress the balance in the autumn, by sending his German troops on repeated

punitive expeditions into Beijing's hinterland where they razed villages, massacred villagers and largely turned a blind eye to their commander's own
paper orders *not* to kill women and children.[168] One of the most brutal participants in these killing sprees was none other than Lothar von Trotha.

In this case might we not cast blame for the subsequent bloodbath perpetrated by von Trotha in South-West Africa on a particular military 'type':
individuals like Lugard, Captain Rivière, von Waldersee or von Trotha himself,
with a known altogether bloody-minded attitude to native insubordination,
acting in different circumstances of colonial of neo-colonial crisis in which
their invariable response – of their *own* volition – was to take the most egregious course of action? Such an interpretation would certainly have the
convenient side-effect of exonerating metropolitan governments who were
clearly a long way away from the scene, not to say powerless to dictate to 'the
man on the spot' the correct textbook response. It would also arguably diminish the charge of genocide, as what we would be dealing with would not be
considered policies of state so much as the aberrant behaviour of autonomous
– even rogue – commanders who were off the government leash, not to say
completely out of control.

Certainly, there are some grounds for arguing that in many of the most brutal *fin-de-siècle* pacifications of colonial revolt, tensions did arise between home
administrations and commanding officers in the field. Von Trotha's overtly
genocidal campaign, for instance, was finally reined in by German chancellor
von Bülow, strongly supported by his colonial office when it became clear that
the campaign was damaging Germany's reputation abroad.[169] Lugard's act of
'butchery' at Satiru similarly had Winston Churchill, then under-secretary of
state for the colonies, straining to accept that such things could be done in the
Crown's name. Even so he had to accept that this was the case.[170] This was
part of the problem. Military officers who happened to carry out systematic
exterminations were rarely unauthorised in their positions and often had been
appointed exactly because of their utterly uncompromising and unmerciful
reputations. Von Waldersee's drive for revenge against the Boxer Rebellion,
after all, was as a result of a personal order from the kaiser. It was the kaiser
again who had appointed von Trotha to undertake a similar vengeance against
the Herero. Yet if this tells us much about European, including German
political-military establishments of the period, even then it does not tell us the
whole story. Again, in Germany, public opinion, aided and abetted by the
press, worked itself into a lather in 1900 over the 'crimes unparalleled in the
history of mankind'[171] which it was claimed the Boxers had committed. If this
conveniently put the Chinese *as a people* beyond the 'legal community of civilised nations',[172] how much more was this the case with regard to the Herero,

when the atrocities against German settlers in the spring of 1904 began to be reported in the metropolitan press? One must certainly be cautious in assuming that every shade of German opinion responded by baying for negro blood. In the Reichstag the Herero-Nama war actually encountered stiff resistance from the Social Democrats.[173] On the other hand, by encouraging and mobilising chauvinist sentiment quite openly around the destruction of South-West African peoples, in what was specifically dubbed the 'Hottentot election', von Bülow himself found that he had the perfect tool with which to win a massive electoral victory, in December 1906, over his anti-colonial opponents and slash the Social Democratic presence in the Reichstag by nearly a half.[174]

This would seem to confirm that a public endorsement for exterminatory colonial warfare did exist at the *fin de siècle* – at least in part. It would also suggest that this was predicated on the popular assumption that colonial regimes had the right to do this on the grounds that colonial peoples were innately, racially *inferior* to their conquerors. Yet both for military men on the spot, and for their adoring publics back home, the real weakness in this assumption was radically exposed in circumstances exactly such as that of the Herero revolt, the Boxer Rebellion or the struggle in the Philippines against US annexation. As soon as an insurrection effectively challenged the colonial edifice, the racist prop underpinning it was as good as useless. A pattern of *fin-de-siècle* genocidal or sub-genocidal reactions to revolt was, thus, not simply a series of coincidences. It represented a pattern of almost predictable responses by various colonial regimes in the face of their greatest fear – that they would be shown to be not the all-conquering, invincible masters after all.

The period from the 1890s onwards, moreover, provided a very particular context in which these underlying anxieties had the potential to trigger genocidal outcomes. In 1896, the Italians, in their own belated effort to muscle in on the African scramble, went down to a disastrous and utterly humiliating defeat at the battle of Adowa, at the hands of an Abyssinian army itself reeling from famine conditions. As a result, not only did an authentic African empire retain its independence, against the grain of the general European carve-up of the continent, it also signalled the possibility that indigenous forces might be able literally to smash colonial agendas.[175] But if this was allowed to happen it might equally mean that an imperial competitor might seize advantage from another's failing. Kitchener, thus, *had to* crush the Mahdiyya, in the Sudan, not only because it was an affront to British rule but also because the alternative was to allow the French to extend their control from west Africa and, possibly in the process, block off British access to the strategic headwaters of the Nile. By the same token, in southern Africa, the Mashona and Matabele *had to* be crushed because without a grip on their lands, the supposed 'real enemy' – the independent 'white' alternative to the British in the region, the Boers of the Transvaal and Orange Free State – would still have the option to expand to the north and, thus, at least in the minds of obsessive imperialists like Rhodes, remain a potent menace and obstacle to dreams of a British-controlled Cape to Cairo railway. But the 'lessons' of such weakness, for those who saw them as such, were already quite evident. The Chinese failure to act quickly and decisively against the Cholla insurrection had seen Japan take Korea; Spain's abject failure to quell the Cuban rebellion had similarly precipitated American intervention and effective supercession.

Colonial powers, thus, had to prevail in their struggles against native resistance, not only because of their own sense of racial worth, but because of their much deeper anxiety that failure would expose them as decadent and febrile in the eyes of their competitors. There was, of course, something utterly schizophrenic in this mindset. In this very period, these same leading world states were busily constructing or more accurately restating an international set of guidelines, codified in the two Hague conventions, of 1899 and 1907, which supposedly created a framework for 'civilised warfare'.[176] In this the conventions were a testament to the residual ability of the Great Powers, in the lead-up to 1914, to still work together. However, it was also quite transparent that the rules of civilised warfare as laid out – whatever one thought about the flimsiness of the very conception – only applied to conflicts of a War Type One nature and so were inapplicable to situations where the adversary turned out to be non-uniformed and, thereby, 'illegitimate'. While, thus, on the one hand, the leading powers proclaimed themselves to be purveyors of a humanitarianism even when it came to warfare, on the other, they unanimously exempted themselves, in total, when it came to the colonial context, on the simple grounds that necessity demanded otherwise. The contradiction was even more glaring when it came to efforts to ban particularly nasty weapons. At the 1899 convention, for instance, the British successfully objected to the outlawing of the recently created dum-dum bullet claiming that nothing less would stop 'savages' such as the Mahdists in the Sudan.[177]

Quite classically, therefore, one obvious way of deflecting responsibility for the colonialists' own highly 'uncivilised' response to native rebellion was to blame the victims. Or, alternatively, to cite precedents which everybody understood to merit an extraordinary response. Or there again, to claim that this particularly civilised country would not normally entertain such behaviour but in the circumstances had no choice but to *borrow* some of the less pleasant methods one associated with one's less 'civilised' competitors. The American response to insurrection in Cuba and the Philippines illustrates these apologia rather well. Having forcibly taken possession of these Spanish dependencies in

1898, an incoming military-cum-civilian administration simply could not understand why, instead of being gratefully welcomed as liberators, their arrival simply fanned the flames of anti-colonial insurrection.[178] In both instances, moreover, the Americans were frustrated by the gaping discrepancy between their racial stereotypes of savage, servile, childlike – and even effeminate – *mestizo* populations obediently doing what their former Spanish, and now American, masters required of them and the nature of an enduring and tenacious grass-roots resistance.[179] In Cuba, the nightmare was certainly amplified by the historic memory of the great slave rebellion led by Toussaint L'Ouverture in the neighbouring French island of San Domingo.[180] If black slaves equipped with little more than their wits and ingenuity could defeat whatever Napoleon, the Spanish, or the British could throw against them, why could not Cuban ex-slaves do the same, 100 years on? Worse, the Cuban insurrection offered an even more potent notion, a united 'nation in arms' *regardless* of racial origin.[181] Such a nightmarish spectre had American liberators straining every sinew to detach traditional 'white' business and landowning elites, including recent Spanish incomers, from the black and mulatto masses. If this policy of divide and rule ultimately succeeded in isolating the rebels while delivering the island – along with its sugar crop – as a significant client state, the strategy worked much less well in the Philippines.

As in so many other similar cases, insurrection here was fanned by the effects of drought, rinderpest and the already accelerating drive by land-owing elites, in the midst of these catastrophes, to re-orientate food production to US- and British-controlled global markets. The Philippines rebellion, thus, closely paralleled the Cuban in the sense that it was as much a social peasant revolution against the monopolisation of wealth and power by the rich, as it was a political revolution against Spanish rule. And it was no coincidence that at its epicentre was the big sugar island of Negros. Economic self-interest, aligned to the usual *fin-de-siècle* fears that if they failed to take the archipelago other imperialist vultures – notably Germany or Japan – would do so, were, thus, key factors encouraging a blatant US annexationism. In turn, this ensured that the already incipient and bitter struggle of the *pumulayo* – the common people – against the rule of both the Spanish and the land-owning *hacenderos* would now take on an even more all-encompassing national character. Paradoxically, the fact that the conflict was spread over a number of islands, where localised strategies of guerrilla resistance quickly became the norm, also added to the US failure to nip the opposition in the bud. It was not long before the secretary of state for war, Elihu Root, was announcing that the army would have to resort 'to the methods which have proved so successful in our Indian campaigns' while, hardly less euphemistically, one of the US commanders on the ground, Brigadier-General Samuel Young, was urging the necessity for methods employed by 'Spanish and other European nations'.[182]

What Young, of course, was obliquely referring to was the intended strategy for defeating the Cuban rebels favoured by General Weyler, the Spanish general sent to put an end to the insurrection in early 1896. This had involved cutting off supplies and support to the rebels in their Oriente and Caruaguey heartlands, by moving beyond scorched-earth tactics towards the 'reconcentration' of entire rural populations in camps close to Weyler's military fortifications. Here, supposedly, they could be monitored and constantly supervised. But not only did this legitimise the creation of free-fire zones in an ostensibly depopulated countryside, it also had the effect of condemning the camp population – given the complete lack of resources or facilities – to starvation and mass epidemic. Bottled up in these conditions at least 100,000, and possibly as many as 400,000 – possibly half their number – died.[183] Was this strategy consciously genocidal? Again, arguably not, in the sense that there is no evidence that Weyler set out to conduct an exterminatory campaign against the *whole* population of Oriente and Caruaguey. Whatever we call it, however, when the programme got under way in the latter half of 1896, it certainly drew outrage from the American press who dubbed its creator, 'butcher Weyler'.[184]

However, when faced with a similar inability to quell the populist wing of the Phillipines insurgency, three years later, the US military command, under General Arthur MacArthur, and then, more markedly still, under his successor General Adna Chaffee, followed much of Weyler's prescript with equally, if not more devastating results. Back at home, attention was slow to focus on an emerging litany of American atrocities, though when General Jacob H. Smith, commanding officer on Samar, threatened to turn the island 'into a howling wilderness' and to shoot all males over the age of ten in reprisal for the near destruction of a US unit there, east-coast press denunciations did become a critical factor in his subsequent court-martialling and retirement.[185] But if this provides some paltry evidence that military massacre – or at least the threat of it – was liable to some very mild reprimand when perpetrated by serving officers of a Western democracy, the example of 'Hell Roaring' Jake Smith, as he became known, tends to deflect attention away from a much more systematic exterminatory policy being conducted elsewhere in the Philippines campaign.

As Glenn Anthony May has pointed out, despite Smith's terrifying rhetoric, there was no *general* campaign of assault on the civilian population of Samar, whereas what General Franklin J. Bell was achieving – operating more or less simultaneously in the Batangas and Laguna provinces of south-western Luzon – was exactly that.[186] Here again, the problem for the invaders was the tenacity and resilience of a local millenarian-inspired grass-roots movement of resistance led by a brilliant native general, Miguel Malvar. The failure to defeat Malvar was to goad Bell towards a 'textbook' version of Weyler's reconcentration programme, a parallel not lost on the more perspicacious of the US press.[187] Even so, the ensuing population collapse in the two provinces did not come from the 'reconcentration' policy *per se*, so much as from the scorched-earth sweeps of the countryside that accompanied it. In just one such operation in southern Batangas in January 1902, for instance, 1,400 tons of rice and palay, along with hundreds of bushels of corn, were burnt, while 6,000 houses were razed and hundreds of farm animals slaughtered.[188] Thus, while *only* an estimated 11,000 Filipinos may have died in the camps,[189] the systematically induced policy of famine of late 1901–2, along with the epidemiological effects – rampant, of course, in a tropical zone – of malaria, cholera, measles, various enteric disorders, as well as other contagious diseases on a population which was already massively debilitated and traumatised, forced Malvar – faced, as one author of the resistance has put it, 'with the prospect of genocide' – to sue for peace.[190] It was this military-organised and developed destruction of food supply, accompanied by naval blockade which broke the resistance through expending swathes of Filipinos, rather than the ugly threats from Smith, or even the egregious human rights violations organised by the US administration at one remove, through the mobilisation of auxiliary native forces. This was true, even given the latter's role, in the words of another US general, in 'exterminating the Goo Goos'.[191] From a base population of about 7 million, it has been suggested that the death toll may have been as high as 1 million.[192]

Of course, American methods of counter-insurgency were neither particularly shocking nor even novel when compared with those applied by her imperial competitors. By the same token, German pacification techniques in South-West Africa were not remarkably out of kilter with those of the British, Spanish, or French. Everywhere, at the *fin de siècle*, and on the explicit authorisation of metropolitan governments, the iron-fist generals, the ones who were prepared to contemplate radical solutions to colonial insurrections, replaced those who operated by the book. Weyler replaced Martinez Campos in Cuba, as von Trotha replaced Leutwein in South-West Africa, just as Kitchener replaced Roberts in neighbouring South Africa, as the British sought to finally overcome the independent Boers.

In this final instance, in a classic case of double-standards, a substantial element of the British chattering classes *were shocked* when news came out of Kitchener's concentration camps. Ostensibly defeated after two years of bitter War Type Two struggle against the might of the British empire, the Boer response to the loss of their republics, in the summer of 1901, was to begin a last-ditch guerrilla-style insurgency from the veldt. Kitchener's response was nothing if not draconian, though, in the broader context of British and more general colonial campaigns of this period, not particularly extraordinary. To defeat the guerrillas implied denying them their support base, resources and population. This meant indiscriminately burning down Boer homesteads, impounding or destroying their livestock and standing crops and, most significantly in terms of systematised modern warfare, using barbed-wire fence lines to divide up the 'enemy' countryside into a grill work, or 'steel chequerboard', each section being guarded by a concrete blockhouse. Kitchener's aim was to immobilise, isolate and either capture or eliminate the commando – Boer male combatants. But the strategy also involved denying them the assistance of non-combatants – in other words, their wives and children. The result was the forcible removal of the latter – whether in fact their menfolk were out fighting on the veldt or not – to 'camps of refuge' along the main connecting railway line between Cape Colony and the two Boer republics.[193]

It has been argued that as the veldt had become an extremely dangerous as well as inhospitable free-fire zone, removing the Boer families to a place of greater safety had a certain humanitarian logic to it.[194] Out on the veldt Kitchener's scorched-earth policy was working; in the camps starving non-combatants were at least likely to be fed and also spared being caught up in the counter-insurgency drives of his mobile columns. Even accepting, however, that large numbers of internees arrived in the camps already half-starved and debilitated, rations, along with other sanitary facilities, proved entirely, if not intentionally, inadequate. As a consequence, epidemics of typhoid, dysentery and particularly measles began killing the internees, especially the children, in droves. By October 1901, mortality, calculated as an annual rate, had reached 34 per cent. Indeed, out of a camp population of c.111, 000 'whites' and over 43,000 of their coloured servants and retainers, some 26,000 to 28,000 of the former died, with fatalities among the black population estimated at anything between 14,000 and 30,000.[195] The Boers believed this was a conscious policy of extermination against themselves, i.e. genocide. Ironically, it was well-placed British observers on the ground, and their support committees back home, who raised a public storm of indignation. They also picked up on the similarity with Weyler's *reconcentrado* system, anglicising Kitchener's version in the term 'concentration camp'.[196]

Yet there was a paradox here. Partly because of the metropolitan outrage at Kitchener's 'methods of barbarism',[197] when the British government, at the end of the day, offered peace terms to their defeated adversaries, not only did this include the offer to reinstate the self-government of the Boer republics, including their full linguistic and civil rights – albeit within a British Union of South Africa – but it also offered compensation to the surviving commandos and to their families for the damage to their property and farmsteads, as well as interest-free loans to help towards their reconstruction. Defeat for the Boers, thus, did not entail outright extermination, nor collective dispossession and degradation but rather a degree of contrite amelioration.[198]

What a contrast, then, with the complete lack of compensation to the blacks who had been equally interned and died in the camps, let alone in the denial of civil or political rights for the majority black and coloured population of South Africa as a whole. Or, indeed, with the continuing British colonial retribution to further black rebellions in southern and eastern Africa in subsequent years. There were no great outbursts of indignation or charges of barbarism when over 3,000 Zulu, goaded into a pale imitation of the Umvukela and Chimerunga by the introduction of a poll tax in Natal in 1906, were mercilessly gunned down by colonial troops. There was only a flurry of abusive protests from colonial whites, not only in South Africa but also from far-away Australia and New Zealand, telling the Colonial Office in London to mind its own business when it queried self-governing Natal's exterminatory response.[199] Nor were there apologies or compensation when thousands of square miles in the fertile 'white' highlands of Kenya, traditionally farmed by, among others, Nandi, Kikuyu, Embu and Kisii people, were, in this same period, traversed by a new railway and forcibly handed over to British and Indian settlers in order to cultivate *arabica* coffee and sisal cash crops for the world market. Instead there was only further 'pacification' which led to thousands of native defenders massacred and to another expostulation of the word 'butchery' from Churchill – as he had done on learning of Lugard's annihilation of the population of Satiru.[200]

Is it too cynical, then, to propose that racism was the critical ingredient which not only prevented a popular outcry against the potential extermination of native black or yellow peoples in revolt, but which ultimately saved the white Boers? Yet even then it is clearly not quite so simple. To defeat the Boers, Kitchener did not blanch from using essentially the same annihilatory instruments – starvation of whole populations *in situ*, deportation of non-combatants to reservations or camps, divide and rule to ensure the enemy killed each other, or were killed by other ethnic parties mobilised and armed for the purpose – as did all the other colonial powers in similar crisis situations. On the obverse side, moreover, there were always some voices – including some rather unlikely ones, such as Churchill – who were prepared to dispute the extermination of blacks in British colonies just as, in the Reichstag, there were Germans who protested against the extermination of the Herero, or Pangwa.

Signficantly, however, genuine protest movements against human rights violations in the colonies – with the single exception of the Boer case – only really took on a head of steam when it was a case of the pot calling the kettle black, that is, when the wrongdoer was the colonialist in a competitor country, not one's own. We thus have the rather unedifying spectacle of the British in South Africa getting into a lather of indignation over the destruction of the Herero, only to become considerably more circumspect with the advent of the Nama insurrection, when it looked like this might jump borders and ignite a more general African struggle against white domination in the Cape.[201] Then, again, with the advent of the First World War, the South African Union produced a report, or Blue Book, on its now enemy German neighbours, which clearly and persuasively enumerated not only the circumstances which had caused the Herero and Nama revolts, but all the German abuses against the surviving populations that had followed. Technically disallowed the ownership of livestock or land from 1905, and banned from living together in tribal groups, the only legal existence available to them from this time was on the basis of German-provided identity papers, or passes, which gave them the right to labour as and where determined by their colonial masters. In short, the Blue Book made it unequivocally plain that the survivors of the genocide were enslaved prisoners, that colonial South-West Africa was a police state and that its German administration was unfit to rule.[202]

Yet what did British South Africa do, once it had defeated the colony, taken it over and repatriated many of its German settlers? It not only set about reimposing the main features of its predecessors' discriminatory rule in order to deliver the best lands and extractive resources for its own settlers and entrepreneurs – and this in spite of the promises made under its post-war League of Nations mandate to, amongst other things, restore the native lands of the Hereros and others[203] – but, even more remarkably, it adapted the main features of the German pass law system of surveillance and control throughout South Africa. In so doing, the contours of one perpetrator polity's post-genocide paranoia eventually became integral to another state's post-1948 model of racial segregation and structural violence: apartheid. The blatant hypocrisy of this volte-face would be exemplified in the appreciative post-war accolade offered by the South African prime minister, Jan Smuts, to the former German rulers of South-West Africa. Their 'successful and conscientious work', he extolled, would in the future 'materially help in building an enduring European civilisation on the African continent which is the main task of the Union'.[204] With these words the Boer commando general who had witnessed the full horror of Kitchener's retributive war against his people not only signalled the degree to which he had already been co-opted into the workings of the British colonial system but of his further willingness to let bygones be bygones when it came to Britain's former German enemy.

This was providing, of course, that it was clear that it would not be any white man who would be paying the bill. In 1926, when the legislative assembly in Windhoek demanded that all official and library copies of the Blue Book be excised and destroyed, the South African government duly acquiesced.[205] But then four years earlier it had already proven its essential affinity with the German colonial mindset. Faced with a rebellion from the Bondelswarts, the very Nama people who had sparked the Herero uprising in 1903, it sent in the police, armoured vehicles and the airforce. What were the Bondelswarts protesting about? A dog tax! In other words, a state mechanism for completely denuding a society which had already suffered the most egregious litany of deportations and deprivations of its last remaining asset – its hunting dogs – with which, even at the absolute margins, it was still attempting to maintain an autonomous existence. Speaking of the airforce operation, the German consul-general in South Africa warmly noted: 'Through the lavish use of bombs, they have speeded up the process of wiping out the bands.'[206]

Even so, the operation could not compare with von Trotha's campaign. With *only* some one hundred bedraggled male insurgents killed in 1922, the aerial bombing was sufficient to smash the rest of the Bondeslwarts people into complete submission. There had been no decision to go on killing the people to the bitter end, as von Trotha after the Waterberg eighteen years earlier had determined upon. In this critical respect 'The Great General of the Mighty Kaiser' had managed to outdo all of his nearest rivals and challengers. But only by a relatively small margin; and more because he had committed his thoughts to an infamous order rather than because of any particularly extravagant exterminatory zeal. After all, not only had many more died in the destruction of the Maji-Maji but, in collective terms, the mortality among many of the Tanganikyan peoples was as great if not greater than that visited upon the Herero, Nama and Berg Damara. But then, who much remembers Governor Graf von Götzen, the architect of the campaign in German East Africa?

Operating with many fewer *Schutzgruppe*, considerably less money and appreciably less self-aggrandisement, von Götzen achieved essentially the same results by an entirely more effective but much less spectacular strategy than that initially adopted by his South-West African counterpart: starvation.[207] Of course, though, ultimately this too became von Trotha's route to the extermination of the Herero after the direct killing associated with the

Vernichtungsbefehl had been rescinded. In this way, physical annihilation of recalcitrant and troublesome peoples could still proceed apace without the obvious evidence of vast numbers of bullet-ridden or mutilated bodies for all the world's press to ogle and report. It was not, in the world of late-colonial modernity, that an advanced technology of killing had become insignificant or unimportant. It was simply much better if one could reach one's desired goal at one remove, through letting loose 'friendly' native auxiliaries to do the real dirty work. Or dividing up the rebel hinterland into sectors and zones where you could get on with your business, preferably unseen. Or, then again, removing the active male 'enemy's' support population to out of the way camps or reservations where, crowded in, you could then ensure their plummeting numbers simply by failing to provide adequate food, shelter or sanitation.

All this carried risks of media exposure, as Weyler and Kitchener found to their cost. But if you could keep the killing essentially hidden and 'off the map', while keeping prying newspaper reporters on-side, preferably by feeding them with stories of the atrocities committed by the insurgents, then the whole profile of one's actions could be justified to the outside world – as indeed to oneself – as rational, legitimate and civilised.[208] To have suggested anything else, that, for instance, one intended to exterminate the very people earmarked as the lowly proletariat who would service one's colonies, would have made no sense whatsoever.

And that, of course, is at the heart of our problem. Colonial genocides made no obvious sense. Yet the collective refusal of many native peoples to accept the terms of the new order, even when they were supposedly completely subjugated and submissive, sometimes so threw imperial regimes off their balance that they ended up doing things that they had never consciously planned. This is not to excuse them in any way. In fact, it simply magnifies the innate exterminatory potential in all of them. One might argue that Wihelmine Germany displayed these tendencies most glaringly in a period when its *Weltpolitik* drive towards a self-justificatory, even paranoid compensation for its latecomer status as a front-rank power was most in evidence. However, such state and societal neurosis – and hence weakness – was far from being the monopoly of this one overreaching global predator. All the leading, and not so leading, world powers at the *fin de siècle* were hitched to the notion of imperial conquest and expansion with the consequence that none of them found themselves able to cope *psychologically* with its serious insurrectionary repudiation by colonial peoples. Compounded, moreover, by the additional anxiety that an inability to quell such uprisings would not only be interpreted as weakness by their competitors but, in so doing, handicap their chances for contending position in the ongoing global race, these empires in advance, all, at various times resorted to the most extreme violence. True, once the insurrections had been crushed, so the direct killing usually stopped. In this respect, many of these campaigns remained partial, or sub-genocidal. And with the general consolidation of the advancing empires by 1914, the likelihood of repeat performances also diminished.

However, the fear of failure, or perceived failure, also remained an enduring legacy. One final example is Italy, that notable latecomer to the imperial race. Its attempt to conquer Abyssinia had already been covered with ignominy. Its later 1911 effort to wrest Cyrenaica and Tripoli – modern-day Libya – from the Ottoman empire proved equally humiliating, when it came up against a wholly unexpected resistance from its indigenous Arab as well as Turkish state adversaries. Notionally, the invasion led to incorporation of the provinces into the Italian empire. In practice, the insurrection in Cyrenaica continued for the next twenty years. Worse, the real force bolstering resistance were the Sanusi, a militant dervish order who had not only proclaimed *jihad* – holy war – against the infidels but also inevitably brought in their wake fears of another Mahdiyya. Certainly, the Sanusi helped weld the disparate and internecine Bedouin tribes of the region into a coherent and coordinated *national* resistance.[209] They were also typically uncompromising in the defence of their country, the Italians soon after their invasion, publishing a long propaganda list of their 'crimes', including the crucifixion of a number of captured Italian soldiers.[210] As with all the imperial conquerors, the ritual mutilation and murder of their men in uniform sent the Italians seriously over the psychological edge, they having seemed to have forgotten, in what V. G. Kiernan aptly describes as 'the peculiar imperial squint' that it was they who were doing the invading as well as most of the atrocities.[211] Hundreds, and possibly thousands of Bedouin were shot in reprisal.[212]

The abiding problem for the Italians, however, was that, after the interregnum of the First World War, whatever they sent in the form of armoured cars and aeroplanes against the Sanusi, they could not scotch them. With defeat looming and the desired retribution unobtainable, the new fascist regime of Benito Mussolini decided, in 1928, that it was time for radical action. Italy's own military hard-man, General Graziani, was appointed to the task. As vice-governor of the region, from 1930, he acted as would have a Kitchener, or a Weyler, rounding up all the hill tribes and placing them, suspect or not, in vast barbed-wire enclosures on the desolate Marmarica plateau. Appalling conditions and lack of adequate food did the rest. Out of an original population of some 225,000 inhabitants in the region, at least 60,000, and possibly as many as 100,000 perished.[213] By 1931, however, the rebellion was crushed and Cyrenaica at last made ostensibly clear for Italian agricultural colonists to, in Graziani's words, 'till and make fruitful this ancient Roman soil'.[214] It was a hundred years since the French invasion of Algeria had begun the advancing empires' sequence of modern colonial genocide.

6. Declining Powers

Further Imperial Conundrums

Italy's 1911 grab for Cyrenaica should act as a reminder that the old, great continental empires were themselves not immune to the direct territorial depredations of the jumped-up and new. How serious such an impact could be is amplified by the knowledge that the Italian action sparked off a further round of Balkan land grabs initiated by ex-Ottoman states in the region and, in addition, an intensification of Great Power rivalries which led to one final culminating catastrophe – the First World War. Throw oneself headlong down this precipitous slope and one might find oneself confronted at its bottom with the genocidal realities of the twentieth century. In other words, with the actions of driven states struggling to cast off the encumbrances of the traditional world order in order to survive in the new. Yet, at the last gasp of the old, the empires that had been at its core were themselves still capable of producing genocidal or, at the very least, sub-genocidal manifestations of their own.

Rarely, however, were these manifestations direct consequences of brazen land grabs such as Italy's. Indeed, rarely did new imperial conquest proceed by direct assault on the old empires at all while there were still smaller less powerful fish to be gobbled up. Italy's efforts were those of an untutored and careless latecomer. On the other hand, they were also hard evidence of what old empires such as the Qing, or Ottoman, had been fearing for the best part of a century: that the West's aim was to so chip away at their territorial and economic power-base that one day they would simply fold. Or, as in the case of Russia and Austria-Hungary, that they would fall so behind in the modernising stakes that they too would go under.

Placing Romanov and Habsburg empires alongside the Qing and Ottoman, of course, offers so many obvious dissimilarities as to render this potential grouping quite inoperable. The former were not only recognised culturally, and in terms of values, as part of European 'society' in ways that the latter were not, but also as part of the dominant international 'system' to which

again the latter, by the late nineteenth century, were deemed essentially subservient.[1] There again, the relative strengths of Austria compared with Russia
are matters of dispute. Russian industrialisation certainly seemed to be growing at such a pace that, by the *fin de siècle*, other leading powers, such as
Britain, were viewing it as a potential contender for the top of league. This
was a view ostensibly corroborated by the extent of Russia's territorial acquisitions and continuing appetite, until, perhaps, its disastrous 1904–5 war with
Japan for the fruits of Manchuria and Korea seemed to suggest its inherent
weaknesses.[2] At least Austria, lagging behind in terms of tangible territorial
gains, could claim that it had made genuine efforts to create a passably democratic *Rechtsstaat*. Moreover, unlike Russia, it was a state that had attempted to
accommodate, rather than suffocate, its ethnically and religiously diverse populations.[3] Put all these aspects of administrative, legal and political difference
on the table, before even considering the wide-ranging ethnic and social con-
stituencies of each empire, and one would have a powerful case for arguing
against further comparison.

However, looked at through the prism of of an inexorably encroaching global system – as most obviously represented by the economic and political
interests of the advancing nation-state-cum-empires – and a picture of *some*
commonality does emerge. It is one of ruling state elites literally obsessed with
the need to assert or reassert their traditional authority throughout the
breadth of their sovereign realms and, more particularly, of the need to do so
in remote regions either historically at one remove from the empire's direct
control or, indeed, contiguous with, but technically outside, their own territory. In their varying efforts to consolidate these outlying frontiers thus lurked
a common set of imperial anxieties that, if they did not assert their authority,
other powers would, if only to use the regions as potential launching pads
from which to strike at the empire's very own heartlands.

In a critical sense these anxieties were not new at all but the very imperatives which kept empires alert and militarily prepared. Since time immemorial
they had been prone to clash with one another at the points of their territorial
intersection. What was distinctly new was the context in which this was now
happening. No longer were traditional imperial rulers independent actors
responding to the dictates of their self-contained and self-sustaining concepts
of *imperium* but, rather, ones trying to fend off largely uncontrollable forces
operating at a seemingly global level. It was, of course, highly ironic that the
resulting imperial collisions rarely involved direct military confrontation
between the old and the new great powers. Russia's conflict with Japan was
predicated on the mistaken notion that the latter was not a great power.
Italy's attack on the Ottoman empire was in its directness exceptional. Never-

theless, by exposing how vulnerable the realms of the Sublime Porte were to frontal assault, the Italian action illuminated not only Ottoman neuroses but also Austrian and Russian ones. It was these two empires, after all, who became most agitated over the potential vacuum opened up in the Balkans as Ottoman control there collapsed in the wake of the Cyrenaica invasion. And it was they who vied with each other to fill it.

But what of the indigenous populations in these regions of dispute? How did they respond to being treated as part of an imperial vacuum? Significantly, in the Balkan crisis of 1912, what Austria and Russia most keenly failed to appreciate was the degree to which Balkan political leaderships themselves expected not simply to be taken into consideration in the final territorial outcome but to be its *primary* determinants.[4] And this was regardless of the geopolitical interests, or security of Russia, Austria or anybody else. Admittedly, the Balkans were critically different to other points of crisis along the tectonic plate of our retreating empires by dint of the simple fact that their populations in much of the Balkans were already organised – willingly or unwillingly – into internationally recognised post-Ottoman nation-states. And when four of these states, Greece, Bulgaria, Serbia and Montenegro, seized the initiative, without reference to either Russia or Austria, to launch an assault on the Macedonian remains of the Ottoman empire in Europe, it was loyal Muslim populations who were the main victims of the wave of mass ethnic cleansing and sub-genocidal atrocity which followed.[5]

If this, thus, represents a sobering reversal of the 'normal' imperial scenario in which insurrectionary populations were the ones threatened with genocide, it also highlights – albeit in its most crystallised form in the Balkans – a notable ingredient in the genocidal potential of the retreating empires largely absent in that of their advancing competitors. In both types, autonomous or quasi-autonomous communities who happened to be in the way of imperial agendas were naturally vulnerable to assault, and worse. Even more so if they chose to resist or actively rise up against imperial rule. Indeed, one could argue that the danger ought to have been more acute in the retreating empires, simply by dint of the fact that they were more crisis-ridden and hence more driven to achieve their objectives, whatever the human cost. In fact, in practice, the perception of crisis within the advancing empires largely determined that their genocidal behaviour was actually remarkably similar. However, what was rarely discernible in these advancing empire examples were situations where insurgents could turn – or, at least, thought they could turn – to another imperial power for assistance. Finding themselves in the interstices of imperial collisions, the opportunism in supplicating the rival of one's nearest enemy to be one's protector and friend was self-evident. Again, acting as a proxy of some greater power in return for political survival and security was hardly novel, but in a time-honoured tradition. The striking modernity of the situation only really lay in the increasing self-awareness on the part of communal insurgents within traditional empires that they were people with a *just cause* and that other powers ought to support them *for this reason alone*. Indeed, the notion could ultimately crystallise, as it did with the revolutionary movements among Ottoman Armenians, as a demand for a no-strings-attached foreign intervention – even involving powers who were at one remove from the imperial confrontation – simply because, on *humanitarian* grounds, it was always right and proper to do so when Armenians were being abused, tortured and killed.[6]

Certainly, one could find instances where rival powers were prepared to use a humanitarian justification as a smokescreen for military intervention in another empire. In 1877, for instance, Russia launched an all-out invasion of the Ottoman Bulgarian provinces on the grounds that it could not stand idly by while its fellow Orthodox co-religionists were being wantonly massacred by bands of Muslim *bashi-bazouks*.[7] Russian intervention not only turned the pattern of massacre on its head – it was indigenous Muslims who were the recipients of Russian and Bulgarian mass reprisals – but also led, indirectly, to the recognition of the Bulgarian and other Balkan states at the Congress of Berlin.[8] The insurrectionary formula thus initiated by the Bulgarians seemed to be: foment an insurrection – even if you know it is going to fail and lead to massive bloodshed among your own base population – publicise the ensuing atrocities as broadly as possible on the world stage and then wait for public outrage to translate into a direct and punishing response.[9] The only problem was that the premise was false. Whatever heat was emitted as a result of moral indignation, the historical record suggests that only cynical *realpolitik* calculations brought tangible and effective intervention. The effect of hitching oneself to the language of the rights of man and of self-determination, thus, did not in itself improve an insurrectionary ability to gain outside support. What it did, instead, was confirm in the minds of imperial rulers the already festering notion that communities in revolt were either stooges, or fifth columnists of interfering and malevolent outside powers intent on sabotaging state agendas. Worse, the very notion thrown up by Bulgarian insurrectionists, and others, that they were speaking on behalf of whole 'national' populations could only feed the countervailing imperial retort that if such entire populations were behind the insurrectionists then they should be dealt with accordingly.

Such blanket prescriptions brought the conflictual state–communal dynamics of retreating empires much closer to the ground rules of twentieth-century genocidal warfare. On the other hand, such potential remained held in partial check, paradoxically, by more traditional, pre-modern facets of empire. For instance, Armenian political parties might seek to articulate a historical meta-narrative of national unity on both sides of the Ottoman–Russian border, but blurred linguistic and cultural boundaries at the localised level between Armenians, Kurds and other peoples was simply one of many factors confounding the aspiration. In remote rural areas, in particular, people remained held together by extended family, clan or – if nomadic – tribal ties, whatever their ethnic origin. As such, even attempts to demarcate on grounds of religion could sometimes prove mistaken.[10] The fact may not have stopped Muslim clerics from encouraging their congregations to attack Armenian Christians in their churches after Friday night prayers, in the sequence of 1890s massacres.[11] Chinese massacres two decades earlier in Turkestan were clearly directed against Muslim communities, as were Russian massacres in the Caucasus a decade earlier still. Even when it came to the War Type Two confrontation between Austria-Hungary and Serbia, in 1914, Catholic versus Orthodox enmities certainly played their part.[12] On the other hand, the manufacturing of a national, or even national-religious enemy – either on the part of the state or a would-be national movement – clearly ran into the buffers so long as heterogeneous populations thought of themselves in essentially local terms, remained unaware, or uninspired, by their supposed national identity, while remaining bound to other groups *across* ethnic and religious divides, by allegiances founded on traditional clientship, lineage, or on other forms of social, economic and cultural exchange.

As we have suggested, this certainly did not prevent retreating empires, or their insurrectionary adversaries, from attempting to cultivate a sense of group solidarity on the one hand, and ethnic or religious hatred on the other. Yet even here, the results tended to represent something of a cross between Western borrowings and elements of a more traditional *mentalité*. An utterly authoritarian tsarist Russia, for instance, always particularly in times of crisis, made much of the sinews which held together *nas narod* – our people – and was even prepared to play to the grass-roots tune of *russkiy*, the Russian people, when it suited, compared with the wholly more imperial and statist conception of *rossiyskiy*.[13] Yet never, in the nineteenth century, did a distinctively Russian nationalism fully crystallise, only the rather more nebulous, if highly charged slavophile idea that all – particularly orthodox – Slavs, whether they lived inside or outside the bounds of the tsarist empire, were carriers of some special mission to the world and that this mission might be taken forward politically under the leadership of Russia.[14] What this pan-Slavic universe might mean for all the various peoples in its midst who were neither

Slavic nor orthodox was never quite spelt out. Which was probably just as well. Like another pan-national idea from which it rather obviously borrowed – that of pan-Germanism – the idea worked magnificently well in the heads of romantically inclined intellectual enthusiasts but was prone to founder as soon as one attempted to translate it onto an ethnographic map. The very idea of such a map setting out the ethnic composition of a state or empire, province by province, represented a notable nineteenth-century departure.[15] Even so, how the many hundreds of thousands of German speakers, for instance, living in pockets of rural or urban settlement far to the east and south east of either the German or Austrian empires, would be seamlessly joined together in one unitary whole, could only be imagined if you blanked out all the millions of other peoples, clearly evident from such maps, who were not Germans. There were, moreover, very few Volga German peasants (where they were aware of it) who were enraptured with the idea, if only because they had to live alongside other Slavic peasants.

There were, of course, plenty of urban German-speaking intellectuals who were so enthused, often especially when they did live, or perceived that they were living, cheek by jowl with non-Germans. One can trace something of these urges, in part, to tangible domestic sources of conflict particularly in an Austrian empire where both the rise of local ethnic nationalisms, particularly of Czechs and Poles, and the job-seeking migrations of these and other non-German peoples into former bastions of metropolitan Germanism had direct mid- to late-century social and economic knock-on effects.[16] Pan-Germanism, like pan-Slavism, however, might also be seen as a form of compensatory cultural *ethnie*-ism among those elements of society – most obviously those same sufficiently educated, print-reading classes – who felt particularly aggrieved by political failure on the wider world stage. David Saunders, for instance, has linked the positive literary reception for what often is viewed as the bible of a specifically Russian pan-Slavism – Nikolai Danilevskii's *Russia and Europe* (1869) – to feelings of humiliation in the wake of Russia's disastrous showing in the Crimean war. Significantly, Danilevksii's theory of a Slavonic 'cultural-historical type', reeking, suggests Saunders, of an 'ill-digested Darwinism',[17] contains exactly the sort of self-adulatory message which was typical of a racist-informed late Western imperialism. Indeed, the fact, again, that Germany provides the one example where the notion of an innate superiority to rule over other peoples is manifested both in continental and overseas versions – doubtless in turn interacting with one another – is itself noteworthy. However, if this confirms that the proponents of the pan-German tendency, like their pan-Slav cousins, were able to spatchcock integral nationalist and scientific racist elements to their positions and, in so doing, replicated the general contours of the dominant Western mindset, what the former, paradoxically, lacked was the ability to translate their agendas into tangible practice. While, thus, Western empires were able to conquer distant, exotic lands, pan-German or pan-Slav aspirations largely festered in the realms of quasi-messianic fantasy wish-fulfilment, despite the object of their desires being territories usually contiguous with Romanov, Habsburg or Hohenzollern domains and with which they claimed some deeply historical, ethnic-cultural connection. In a curious way the social and political frustrations of the ideologues thereby provide an insight into the psychological wounds, particularly of Austrian and Russian empires, whose sense of constraint, if not weakness, on the broader world stage threw them into aggressive confrontation with each other at their respective European peripheries. That said, neither pan-Slav nor pan-German ideologies officially informed Russian or Austrian foreign policy. Nor did they motivate the vast majority of their ethnically and religiously mixed populations.

The discrepancy between idea and reality should have been even more stark when it came to pan-Turanism. A latecomer ideology which again clearly borrowed from its Slavic and German counterparts, the notion of a state which joined up all the Turkic-speaking peoples throughout the Ottoman empire *and* central Asia, while at the same claiming for them a unique historic role as the transmitter of civilisation from China and Persia to Europe, sounded very much like the dream-child of embittered intellectuals in need of a restorative tonic in the face of Ottoman woes. Which it was.[18] In terms of practical politics it should have been a complete non-starter. Putting aside the non-Turkic peoples who might stand as obstacles to its aspiration including, at the *fin de siecle*, the majority in the Ottoman empire itself, it could only, in broader geo-political terms, tangibly succeed by invading the southern regions of the Russian empire – the home of the majority of non-Ottoman Turks. Its unfeasibility should have been its saving grace. In fact, in 1914, the new nationalising CUP regime attempted to prove the contrary, ringingly declaring war, with the statement that 'the ideal of our nation and our people leads us towards the destruction of our Muscovite enemy, in order to obtain thereby a natural frontier to our empire, which should include and unite all branches of our race'.[19] It was the Ottoman Armenians who took the full brunt of the message.

If Ottoman Turkish actions at the onset of the First World War therefore might suggest that pan-nationalism was the culminating explosion of toxic tendencies which had been stacking up in all the retreating empires, it still does not quite explain the genocidal moments which had already rocked all of them – bar Austria-Hungary – in the preceding sixty years. *Fin-de-siècle* Chinese nationalists, after all, also had some proclivities towards a pan-national ideal in the form of pan-Asianism. Most keenly promoted by the Japanese, and with a straightforward agenda to link up all the independent Asian peoples in order to defeat and then kick out the European imperialists, the movement, like pan-Turanism, and arguably the others too, remained a distinctly minority creed, with or without the leading turn-of-the-century Chinese nationalist, Sun Yat-sen, as one its supposedly leading advocates.[20] Nor had it even appeared when the Qing were busily exterminating Muslim Uighurs in the Chinese far west in the 1870s. Perhaps China did not need such a rationalisation when its own understanding of imperial mission was already so deeply rooted. Maybe it did not need anything other than an overwhelming sense of encroaching catastrophe if it did not scotch the Muslim insurgents for once and for all.

Certainly, this does not require us to discount the intrusion of modern elements into the pre-1914 genocidal equations of retreating empires. The Ottoman appeal to pan-Islamism, under Abdulhamid II – an undoubted factor in the Armenian massacres of the 1890s – for instance, was not simply a restatement of traditional Islam. It was a quite conscious attempt to activate bonds of Muslim solidarity worldwide, in support of the last remaining Islamic empire, as it succumbed to quite obvious external threats to its socio-economic as well as political fabric. As Dominic Lieven aptly comments, 'Resurrecting the caliphate and stressing its international role was a means of paying back the European empires in their own coin'.[21] It is a paradox, therefore, that while Armenians, perceived as the arch-agents of foreign encroachment, were direct victims of pan-Islam's domestic appeal, Muslim Circassians and Uighurs might have benefited from its more forceful and tangible Ottoman assertion abroad, particularly if Abdulhamid had become sultan a decade and a half earlier than 1876.

Pan-Islam, however, did not presuppose killing all Ottoman non-Muslims, or even necessarily all Armenians. So long as the empire remained predominantly multi-ethnic – and, as recently as the 1850s, Muslims had constituted only 44 per cent of population, with Turks a smaller percentage[22] – sultans had had to grapple with this reality, whether they liked it or not. Nor did any of them – not even Abdulhamid – contemplate the abandonment of the traditional millet system of Christian and Jewish self-governance: how else could an imperial mosaic of distinct societies be regulated without destroying the imperial polity altogether?[23] By the same token, even the most radical of Abdulhamid's Armenian revolutionary adversaries were hesitant about demanding complete secession of the Armenian heartlands – the so-called six vilayets of eastern Anatolia – from the empire, when they knew full well that, even on the basis of their own probably inflated estimates, their compatriots there constituted less than 40 per cent of the population.[24] And then, of course, what would have happened to all the other Armenians spread in communities throughout the empire if such a programme had been implemented? Despite all the mass killings of the 1890s, and mass refugee flows which emanated from them, nobody yet was publicly prepared to articulate compulsory deportations or population exchanges of entire peoples. Moreover, if you started down this road with one 'national' community, where exactly would you stop? So long as the empire – however residual – remained as such, with both its ruling and adversarial communal elites committed to its perpetuation rather than transforming it, or alternatively fragmenting it into something else, an inertial drag on full-blown genocidal policies of state seemed implicit.

Even with completely differing specifics, the same essential principle should have applied to China, Russia and Austria-Hungary. Just as in the case of the advancing empires, so in the retreating ones, genocide militated against their long-term security, stability, well-being and economic sense. Yet, just as the destruction of the Herero was not a single aberration among advancing empires, neither was that of the Armenian massacres among retreating ones. Indeed, the points of interconnection would seem even more revealing in our latter example, with the possibility of tracing a sequence and pattern along our geo-political tectonic plate. And in this, surely, we have our basic commonality. Not simply in a vicious dynamic of conflict in which communal groups in insurrectionary mode, national or proto-national, found themselves pitted against the full weight of imperial polities who, nevertheless, saw these insurrections as threats to their *raisons d'être*. But in an overarching international political framework which not only was critical – albeit always at one remove – in triggering these conflicts in the first place, but also in helping to create a broader climate of paranoia and fear where anything other than the most maximalist, exterminatory resolution became almost inconceivable.

The remaining part of this final chapter seeks to outline these cases with a view to charting some of these interactions. It needs to be reiterated that they were not identikits resemblant in every way. A recently incorporated province in the Chinese empire is not the same thing as a recently created Serb state with an international imprimatur. An externally directed War Type Two directed against the Serbs by Austria in 1915 clearly involved different contours and parameters to the War Type Three launched by the Ottomans against its internal Armenian community in the 1890s. An emerging modern national consciousness in both Armenians and Serb struggles is not detectable as a significant ingredient in the struggles of the Muslims of the Caucasus, or Dzangaria, even if all these cases involved exterminatory 'total wars'. However, perhaps in charting the distinctions geographically – if not quite chronologically – from east to west, we might be able to bring into focus more closely those emerging elements from which, after 1914, a modern form of 'total' genocide would fully crystallise.

Crushing Muslim Revolt in China's Far West

To highlight the destruction of a revolt at the furthest extremities of the Chinese empire in the 1870s, when, over the previous two decades, there had been so much *more* killing in its heartlands may seem somewhat odd. In terms of sheer scale nothing in the nineteenth century, not even the *Mfecane*, could compete with what the Taiping uprising and its eventual extirpation produced. How many millions died directly, or indirectly, in this and the plethora of other rebellions against Qing rule in this period is largely conjectural. Modern guestimates suggest that the net result was a population which plummeted from around 410 million in 1850 to 350 million in 1873.[25] Moreover, in the most general terms, these various outbursts were all part of a pattern in which imperial weakness, in the face of foreign inroads into Chinese commerce and trade at mid-century, produced broadly similar results. Less imperial port revenues resulted in heavier and heavier direct exactions on the populace, which produced, in turn, a subsequent loss of legitimacy giving rise to great peasant rebellions which forced the court in Beijing to turn to the foreigners to help put them down. Of course, this weakened the empire even further. The very fact that Taiping emerged as a populist counter-system to the Qing, based on a millenarian Christian cult – albeit a highly bastardised one – rather suggests that one did not need to look to the imperial periphery as a source of destabilisation when Christian missionaries were so busily playing their part in loosening the gel of imperial authority up and down the Yangtse.[26]

The geo-political significance of the far west for China, however, combined with the fact that it involved ethnically and religiously distinct populations from that of the dominant Han, rather obviously links the extirpation of rebellion here to the exterminatory actions of the Russians in the Caucasus and Ottomans in eastern Anatolia. Certainly, ethnic distinctiveness on its own cannot explain why in this case, or the others, the empire struck back against insurrection in such an overtly and relentlessly punitive manner. After all, distrust and disdain were the normal lot of most ethnically subordinate communities in the traditional empires. This was particularly true in China, where the only route to inclusion and acceptance was via a complete and utter sinicisation. To stay all or in part on the outside was to confirm that one was

Yi-ti, by implication someone who was not just foreign but animal-like and uncivilised. To be, by contrast, *Hsia*, 'great' or 'magnificent' and thus part of the domain of the Middle Kingdom, according to dominant Confucian tenets dating back to the fifth century BC, precluded any sharing of one's civilised social space with such barbarians. Any attempt to do so could only lead to the overthrow of virtue and, with it, cosmic order.[27]

While these conceptions were not strictly racist, in the sense that peoples could and did voluntarily integrate with the Han, the name of the great second century (Christian era) dynasty which became synonymous with civilised Chineseness, they did highlight the great horror of contamination which contact with barbarians was deemed to pose. The historical complicating factor rests in the fact that these very same peoples played an overwhelmingly disproportionate role in the history – and destiny – of the Middle Kingdom. They may never have represented much more than the current 6 per cent of its total population but they inhabited 60 per cent of its claimed surface area.[28] More keenly still, when it came to the north and north-western steppe lands where a plethora of nomadic pastoralist Mongol and Turkic peoples were dominant, it was not so much the great dynasties who subjugated them at crisis moments but, rather, they who rode into the sedentarised, urbanised and populous Han plains to seize power for themselves. The Qing (or Manchu) the very last of the Chinese dynasties, from 1644, were themselves usurpers of this kind. Sinicised they may have become but it did not prevent them from having their own acutely sensitive antennae trained on the borderlands in the fear that one day it might be themselves on the receiving end of some other truculent set of interlopers.

The problem was that no sooner had the Qing firmly got into their dynastic stride than a further but this time quite novel set of complicating factors intervened in the form of the European powers. Keeping the steppe peoples at arm's length had for centuries involved treating them as tributary buffer states and, bar placing a Chinese garrison in the key towns along the main trading routes, largely letting their traditional elites run their own affairs. Chinese Turkestan, for instance, had been one such buffer state since the seventh century. The signing of the Treaty of Nerchinsk with the Russians in 1689 dramatically brought this time-honoured policy to an abrupt end.[29] In itself determining the boundaries between Russia and China at a remote Manchurian intersection was not such a major event. What made it so momentous was the fact that China was entering into bi-lateral relations with other 'foreign' (and thus also barbarian) powers at all and thereby conceding not only to their presence but also to their *modus operandi*. Having done so, China henceforth effectively had no choice but to jettison the whole conception of buffer zones and to reorganise itself instead as a unitary state with clearly demarcated boundaries.[30] In turn this presupposed the acquiescence of non-Han peoples on the outer peripheries to direct rule. Or, failing that, preparing for their resistance.

It was not, then, that the new geo-political realities led to the replacement of the old imperial fear about the steppe tribes riding in from the outlands, with a newer one in which the Europeans themselves did it in a more mechanised way. Rather, it simply amplified the primary neurosis by making the Chinese anxious that unless they took a firm hold of these outer provinces the Europeans would do so, if not necessarily by taking them directly, then by exploiting their peoples as instruments or props for their own nefarious designs. By the late nineteenth century the Chinese peripheral scene was becoming rather crowded in this way. The British reached out to the Tibetans, the French to the much persecuted hill peoples in Yunnan, while later on, the Japanese, having defeated the Russians, would make a special point of promoting the notion of Manchurian autonomy.[31] However, more than anywhere else in the Qing official mind, the spectre of foreign interference focused on what the Russians were intending, or doing, in the furthest reaches of Chinese Turkestan, in the area known as Dzangaria.

At a distance of some 3,500 miles from Beijing, what was so important about this extraordinarily remote and inhospitable high altitude steppe and desert region was its passageway through the Pamir mountains, the Dzangar Gate or Gateway of Nations. Control of this strategic asset brought with it, at one remove, control not only of the oases along the silk routes of Central Asia but also of the Mongolian flank from which the most devastating of the invasions of the Chinese heartlands had been launched in the thirteenth century. It is surely no coincidence, therefore, that one of the most singularly out of sight people-exterminations in modern history, the Qing destruction of the Dzangar tribe, came at the very juncture, between 1757 and 1759, when Russia's own advance into Central Asia was rapidly accelerating in this direction. If the Russians had taken the Gate and, south of it, the Illi river, they would in effect have been able to stand astride Central Asia on the Chinese side of the watershed. The destruction of an estimated 80 per cent of the 600,000 strong Dzangars, and the obliteration of their very name,[32] at the behest of the Chinese general, Zhaohui, certainly represented an extraordinarily unmerciful Qing response to an insurrection which, if it had taken off and carried other of the Mongol and Turkic peoples of the region with it, might have threatened the Qing imperium, as had the great pan-tribal confederation of Genghis which had destroyed the earlier Ch'in imperium, five centuries earlier. Thus, on one level, the Dzangar genocide can be seen as a most fearful and awesome case of a state apparatus 'getting in its retaliation first' against an apparently recognisable competitor whose emerging, increasingly centralising, Buddhist-orientated exercise in its own state-formation resonated with dread, historical precedent.[33] But if, in this sense, the liquidation of the Dzangars was firmly embedded in the fears of the past, the Qing signal to the Russians that China had prior rights east of the Dzangar Gate also marked the Middle Kingdom's entry into the world of modern Great Power neuroses.

Of course, in the context of its time, one might be forgiven for arguing that the Qing drive into Turkestan hardly represented an anxious empire at all but one on the crest of a wave. No Western empire of the period could have conceived of, let alone achieved, a land-based military conquest at such distance from its home base. The imposition of direct rule on the whole Turkestan region, now renamed as Sinkiang, or 'new territory', indeed, represented the high-water mark of Qing territorial expansion. However, the problem was not simply the genocidal moment of its achievement; it was the knock-on effect. Ruling Sinkiang as a remote frontier colony was not unlike– albeit on a much larger scale – that of the British in Tasmania. Certainly, in an entirely depopulated Dzangaria, it was possible to set up penal and other military colonies as a seed-bed for future, full scale colonisation. There was an irony, too, in that the Kalmyks – like the Dzangars a western Mongolian nomadic steppe people, but one displaced from their homelands on the Volga by Russian imperial advance far to the east – were one of the groups invited in for this purpose.[34] In this way, under the martially imposed, special jurisdiction of the Qing themselves, rather than their empire *per se*, the future of both incomers and indigenes appeared to be being organised according to a tightly regulated prescript.[35] There remained, however, the problem of all the other peoples in the wider and, indeed, very much vaster region of Sinkiang. If the British in Tasmania considered the aborigines as savages who could neither be digested nor properly assimilated into civilised society, the Qing took an equally acerbic view of the Turkestani ethno-cultural mosaic, the most demographically significant element of which were the Turkic Uighurs. In fact, for the colonisers, this negativity was far more laden. For one thing, there was no prospect of the inhabitants 'disappearing' on Tasman lines; they were far too numerous for that.[36] Even more seriously, with the majority Muslims – in other words, buttressed by their own coherent and unifying thought system theoretically transcending the very sedentary versus nomad, town versus tribal divisions through which the empire might have maintained a colonial divide and rule – they presented a genuine cultural and, hence, political obstacle to the Qing game-plan quite absent in the Tasmanian case.

It was not just that Islam was a different creed, it was one whose entirely alternative vision of the world confounded Confucian notions of hierarchic order and harmony. Worse, as one that was militantly proselytising (as well as legally grounded), it threatened to infect the Han themselves. Millions had already embraced Islam.[37] Incorporating Sinkiang rather than keeping it at arm's length could only exacerbate this perceived contamination to the body-politic further and at a time when the external threat was magnifying exponentially. Under the Ming, the Qing's predecessors, there is, in fact, evidence of a relatively tolerant and benign policy towards Muslims.[38] Under the new regime, however, a policy aimed at circumscribing Islamic practice, most particularly through interference with legal custom, reflected a much more belligerent statist approach. This combined with heavy taxation – resistance to which was provided by more militant Muslim orders such as the Naqshbandi, – and the result was a more generalised Muslim insurrection which, when it broke out in the early 1860s, extended far beyond the boundaries of Sinkiang.[39] Indeed, available evidence suggests that the longevity and resilience of the rebellions in provinces such as Kansu, Ninghsia and Shensi, much closer to the Chinese heartlands, may have produced both Muslim and non-Muslim death tolls far higher than in Sinkiang itself.[40]

What, thus, makes the state–communal dynamic specific to Sinkiang particular to this discussion is neither the nature or scale of resistance *per se* nor even necessarily the degree of ensuing state counter-violence – in fact the Chinese commanding general Tso Tsung-t'ang put down the Uighur insurrection with comparative speed compared with the years he laboured to this end in Kansu – but, rather, the way it brought together into a genocidal matrix, elements which were indicative of a much wider pattern of imperial empires in retreat. Here, at an outer but nevertheless highly sensitive frontier of empire, an accelerating momentum, particularly notable after 1831, towards the segregation and/or outright expropriation of indigenous peoples by the state, in favour of a concerted and systematic programme of 'loyal' re-settlement by Qing, Han and others, precipitated an Uighur-led bid for independence in southern Sinkiang. It came about at a juncture, the final years of the Taiping turmoil, when the empire's abilities to counter it effectively were at their weakest. Quasi-messianic Islamic religious fervour, as we have already suggested, played a critical role in mobilising and concretising the insurrectionary cause, just as it had done against the French in Algeria, and the Russians in the Caucasus. And finally, that all-important factor, the involvement of foreign powers, proved central and critical to the outcome.

Again, the role of the Russians looms large; but not just the Russians. When Yakub Khan, a religious-cum-political leader from Khokand – that is, from the Russian side of Turkestan divide – took the leadership of the incipient revolt, in 1865, it was to the Ottomans that he obviously turned, and from whom he received the promise of support. This doubly confirmed the revolt's Islamic credentials. Yakub Khan may have been previously domiciled in Khokand but his lineage belonged to that of the *khojas* who had ruled southern Sinkiang as the khanate of Kashgaria before Chinese incorporation, and whose legitimacy rested on their claimed descent from the Prophet and his followers.[41] In re-establishing the *de facto* independence of the khanate, Yakub's victory was one to be greeted by the whole Muslim world. However, if the Ottomans might have liked to have wrested some advantage from this situation, the gaping Chinese realisation that the region might be lost forever to their rule came when both the British *and* Russians started courting the khan in earnest. Back in 1851, China had already had to concede a treaty to the Russians that allowed them to trade freely at Illi and set up a consulate there. These commercial concessions were soon extended to Kashgar, among other places. Russian economic leverage, leading to a notable expansion of its trade in Sinkiang thus already seemed to be a harbinger of a Russian superseding of China in the region. In 1872, the Russians certainly did not stop to ask the Chinese permission to establish full commercial relations with the Khan. The British followed suit the next year.[42] But then the Russians had already occupied Illi in 1871, offering to the Chinese only the feeble and transparent excuse that they were doing so to safeguard the place against Muslim attacks until Chinese imperial authority could be re-established. Nobody expected this would happen. The leading Chinese diplomat Li Hung-chang, noting that 'The neighbours are growing stronger and stronger, while we are getting weaker and weaker',[43] proposed that the only thing to do, in the circumstances, was abandon Sinkiang altogether. Signalling that the Chinese empire had been trumped (just as it would actually be by the Japanese in response to the Tonghak insurrection in Korea twenty years later), he was effectively acknowledging Chinese febrility and – in not so many words – inviting the British and Russians to fight it out for what remained of Chinese central Asia.

Thus, unlike in some other cases where colonial insurrection was met with a swift and ruthless explosion of retributive fury, the Qing court, even had it wished to respond in this manner, could not. Not only was a military expedition to Sinkiang impossible when there were rebellions closer to home but there was a whole faction at court, with Li Hung-chang their most vociferous spokesman, who argued that the most imminent threat to imperial integrity came from the European powers launching a *coastal* invasion. Paradoxically, too, when it came to a final forcing of the issue in favour of a military campaign against Kashgar, the only way it could be mounted in the face of near-bankruptcy of the state was by going cap in hand – for the first time in imperial Chinese history – to Western bankers to raise a huge loan.[44] Nevertheless, that the faction which favoured reconquest finally won out largely hung on the arguments of its chief protagonist, Tso Tsung-t'ang:

> If Sinkiang is not secure there will be unrest in Mongolia; then it is not only Shensi, Kansu and Shansi which will be disturbed, it is also the sleep of the nation's capital. Furthermore, the present situation is even worse than before. The Russians are expanding daily ... from west to east their territory borders our frontier for thousands of miles. Only in the central section do the Mongolian tribes more or less function as a buffer zone ... We have to make early preparation to face this fact.[45]

It was Tso who was appointed by the court in 1875 to crush the putative khanate. The elevation of a Han to reconquer a territory which had been, up to this point, an exclusively Qing domain, represented a small revolution. There is little information in Western sources on how exactly he conducted his campaign. The main available commentary, by Wen-Djang Chu, is much more focused on Tso's undoubted feat of transporting and supplying his 60,000-strong army far from its home base than with its direct results. Certainly, Tso does not appear to have been in the same category as a von Trotha, in the sense that he began with no specific programme of extirpatory violence for its own racist, or bloodlusting sake. One might add that Uighur demography and political geography made such an all-out genocide implausible, though not – given the Dzangar precedent – impossible. That said, both Tso and his court backers in Beijing were of one mind that the reconquest of southern Sinkiang had to be so total that it would ensure a Chinese control of the province for all time.[46] And Tso was nothing if not systematic. The extirpation of the khanate involved a conscious effort to eliminate or emasculate entire urban and rural communities and clans which stood as obstacles to the Chinese new order in southern Sinkiang. This was accomplished either by direct massacre, or wholesale mass deportation. A similar largely autonomous wave of insurrection by T'ungkan, partially sinicised Turkic Muslims who had earlier been resettled in the north of the Sinkiang, met the same fate. Perhaps as many as a million people overall died as a direct or indirect result of the Chinese campaign.[47] In the more significant southern rebellion, with Yakub Khan taking his own life and the pacification complete, Sinkiang was, thereafter, incorporated as a normal province of China in 1884. No longer was its status that of special colony. On the contrary, consolidation was intended as the basis of its full integration as part of Han polity and society. Only continuing imperial weakness and distance could actually hold the darker, underlying implications of this long-term agenda in check.

At the time, however – bar the Russians – it is interesting just how upbeat and positive European consuls in Beijing were about the bloodbath. As John

King Fairbank puts it, they were 'impressed with China's evident ability to slaughter Muslim rebels and checkmate Russian imperialists', the latter a reference to the 1881 Russian climb-down over her continuing occupation of the Illi valley when faced with a direct Chinese confrontation.[48] It was as if the feat of military genocide had forced the West to reconsider its normally contemptuous evaluation of Chinese virility and prowess. Indeed, the extermination of Yakub's khanate, and so many of its people, could be said to have provided the necessary bona fide for China as a great power, prepared not only to fight for her position as such but using the same means as everybody else.

Asserting Russian Control in the Caucasus

China's successful assertion of her hegemonic position in the far west may have been considered as a striking blip by Western observers more prone to view her as a febrile and decadent empire in terminal decline. The view, however, did not generally extend to tsarist Russia. On the contrary, for most of the nineteenth century, if any one political image brought the British particularly out in a sweat, it was that of the Russian bear. And if anything proved to them the point that Russia was not in the same declining category as China, it was the degree to which the former was advancing not only at the latter's expense but all across the Eurasian landmass. Rarely, in the process, did this make central Asian peoples, who might have been less than happy about actual or potential Chinese tutelage, automatically plump for Russian protection. And this in spite of Russia's not very convincing argument, in 1881, that they needed to retain part of the Illi valley to safeguard Sinkiang Muslim refugees who had fled there.[49] We have already seen that, over a century earlier, anything up to 150,000 Buddhist Kalmyks had fled their ancestral steppe lands between the Black and Caspian seas to far-away Dzangaria and Mongolia, rather than accept tsarist subjugation. Over two-thirds perished in the effort, many at the hands of their old Muslim, Turkic nomadic rivals, the Kazakhs. Yet when the Kazakhs were themselves in turn so overwhelmed by Russian settlement at their expense, many of the survivors of their belated, bloody but abortive 1916 uprising fled into Sinkiang.[50]

The pace, manner and scale of Russian colonisation eastwards invites obvious comparison with the corresponding US 'domestic' imperial surge westwards. Proceeding over a much longer time-frame, and without any supporting programme of industrialisation to give it bite, it was, though, also fuelled by excess peasant populations pushing out into what were perceived as 'virgin' lands ripe for settlement, as well as by similar rationalisations as to why the land belonged by right to them, and not to the natives.[51] The Russian movement, too, reached its culmination between the 1820s and late 1860s. True, its transcontinental reach did not have a railway to go with it, until the Trans-Siberian was begun in the 1890s, but this only marginally suggested a sluggish great power. Equally tellingly, native resistance was stamped out at least as quickly as anything the Americans could organise.

Stephen Shenfield has cited a number of such encounters where the Russians came perilously close to genocide. In addition to nineteenth-century localised Kazakh uprisings, in the face of the expropriation of traditional grazing lands where the response involved repeated massacres, Shenfield considers much earlier tsarist campaigns in eastern Siberia, notably against the Yakut tribes along the river Lena in the 1640s, and equally murderous expeditions against Chukchi, Koryak and Kamchadal peoples in the Kamchatka peninsula, in the late 1690s.[52] Having stated these examples, however, Shenfield considers what happened in the north-west Caucasus in the early 1860s – or perhaps more specifically what happened to particular Circassian tribes here – to be much more systematic attacks on whole populations, and in his view, an unequivocal case of genocide.[53] This rather raises the question: what made for this exception?

The answer would seem to lie with some rather familiar, imperial ingredients. One was a simple matter of geography. Controlling Siberia, or the distant Pacific to the east, was all well and good but hardly conferred the same benefits as access to the Black Sea to the south. Control of the latter provided year-round warm water ports and hence the possibility of trading potentially limitless Ukrainian grain with burgeoning European markets. Markets equalled money, money provided the motor to the sort of state-led industrial takeoff which Russian finance minister Sergei Witte at the end of the nineteenth century, believed would stave off from the Romanovs the same neo-colonial fate as had befallen the Qing and Ottoman empires.[54] Ironically, Witte, as the great proponent of the Trans-Siberian railway, believed its ensuing east–west trade would also assist Russia in its efforts to overcome its perceived handicap. But for all these dreams and their calamitous consequences, in the form of the 1904 encounter with the Japanese in Manchuria, when it came to serious geo-politics, the Russian south normally took precedence over the Russian east.

So we arrive at our Caucasian crossroads. Whereas the drive to the Pacific had actually been largely completed by the turn of the seventeenth century, the Russians did not take the strategically important Crimea, on the Black Sea, until 1783. All the way to this goal they had had to overcome obdurate resistance from Turkic peoples – the remnants of the Golden Horde that had

once ruled Muscovy as a client state itself – and, even once arrived on the Crimea, the Russians anxiously looked to their flank, the great Caucasus range
beyond the sea of Azov, rimming the eastern Black Sea shores. In short, firm
consolidation of the Black Sea region as a major state-building asset also
required securing control of the Caucasus. The result was what has been
described by one commentator as 'the defining event for the Russian empire in
the nineteenth century', or put more soberly, 'the longest military operation
which either the Russian empire or the Soviet Union has yet experienced'.[55]

On one level, therefore, the drive to genocide in the Caucasus could be said
to be closely tied up, firstly, with an inbuilt sense of Russian frustration at having arrived in the south too late to take full advantage of it in the international
power game, and, secondly, at finding themselves faced with the most serious,
obdurate and pervasive resistance there. By the 1850s, not only had the Russian army garrisoned 200,000 of its troops in the region, but it had already
taken tens of thousands of casualties.[56] It would not be until 1864 – actually a
full century on from its first attempts at conquest – that Russia could claim
that it had properly secured the north Caucasus. The very fact, moreover, that
this signal failure was due to a grass-roots, clan-based resistance, very much
along the lines that the French encountered in Algeria, may go some way to
explain the regular litany of atrocities that punctuated the struggle. Indeed,
the Russian similarity here with its French counterpart is very striking. Both
faced tribal insurgencies fuelled by Muslim, sufi-inspired militancy. Both
oppositions were led by brilliant politico-religious guerrilla warriors: the amir
Abd el-Kader in the Kabyle, the Dagestani Avar imam, Shamil, in the Caucasian equivalent. In each case, their resistance successfully blocked the imperial
advance for at least two decades in the mid-nineteenth century. And each in
turn led to the imperial attacker resorting to increasingly desperate and unforgiving tactics, including scorched earth, the use of other tribes to act as 'dirty
war' proxies, as well as mass, indiscriminate reprisal.[57]

Yet paradoxically it was neither the half-million-strong Dagestanis, nor
their equally intransigent Chechen neighbours, who suffered the full brunt of
nineteenth-century Russian wrath and vengeance in the Caucasus, but an
entirely different ethnic and linguistic grouping. The Dagestani and Chechen
homelands were on the eastern side of the Caucasus, closer to the Caspian Sea.
By contrast, those of the some 2 million Circassians populously straddled the
Black Sea coastline and its mountainous littoral much closer to the Russian
naval bases in the Crimea. The fact that there were a lot of them is significant.
After the Armenians and Georgians, the Circassians were the largest Caucasian ethnographic grouping with a common, strongly held identity and hence
the critical prerequisites for nationhood. On the other hand, their notably

anti-hierarchical, clan-based structure lacked any tendencies towards centralised, administrative unity.[58] It was not, then, that the Circassians were
earmarked for more severe treatment simply on account of their organised
political threat to Russian suzerainty or, for that matter, for their martial
resistance, when they had actually been less prominent on this score than
other mountain peoples. Nor, even, was Russian racial contempt for them as
'Asiatic' or 'Tatar' savages exceptional, given that this was the standard Russian view of all the Caucasian tribes.[59] Then again, nor was it because the
Circassians were 'fanatical' *jihaddiya*-obsessed Muslims when their credentials
on this score were actually notably pragmatic and recent.

However, herein lies one obvious clue to their particular vulnerability. In
the face of Russian encroachment on their territory, these formerly Christian
mountain peoples had gone over *en masse* to Sunni Islam in the eighteenth century, in an effort to solicit the protection of the Ottoman empire, as well as the
then still-surviving Crimean Tatar khanate. The effort had been to no avail –
with hindsight the Circassians might have done better to join their steadfastly
Christian Georgian neighbours in looking to the Russians themselves for protection. What this episode should remind us, however, is that the Caucasus
was not just some extraordinary ethnographic mosaic with its up to fifty different ethno-linguistic groups, some Muslim, some Christian and some
holding onto older religious traditions still. It was also, to cite the Caucasus
expert, Paul Henze:

> the key to the defence of the Islamic world, a land bridge between two seas, a
> link between two continents, open to the vast Eurasian steppe to the north,
> highroad to the Fertile Crescent to the south ... a region where cultures have
> crossed and clashed for millennia.[60]

One might add that this historic geo-political frontier, in which competing
empires sought alliances among indigenous peoples and vice-versa to defend
and advance their respective interests, was dominated, in the immediate
period before the intrusion of the Russians, by the Persians and Ottomans.
However, by the early nineteenth century, Persia was no longer a factor in this
equation, while the relentless Russian advance to the borders of Ottoman
suzerainty – and indeed beyond – was literally grounded in the creation of the
Georgian Military Highway through the heart of the mountains. Here,
though, lies the critical element in the unravelling of the Circassian tragedy.
The road had been completed before the Russians had secured mastery of the
Caucasus. In so doing, it made the Ottoman-dependent Circassians – in the
Russian official mind – 'dangerous enemies well to the rear of the Russo-
Ottoman front line'.[61] But if this in itself exposed them to the charge of being

potential – and in the light of their recent history – traitorous fifth columnists with a direct interest in sabotaging Russian expansion, it was actually the mid-nineteenth-century vulnerability of the Russians themselves, in the Black Sea region, which provided the tsarist state with its overwhelming self-justification for the comprehensive liquidation of the Circassians.

In 1854, Britain and France had come to Ottoman assistance against an allegedly renewed threat of Russian invasion – the last one had been in the 1830s – and proceeded to mount a joint invasion of the Crimea. From the Allied viewpoint the ensuing military campaign had been something of a fiasco. From the Russian standpoint, however, it was a complete disaster. An inability to defend its own territory, leading ultimately to the capture of her premier Black Sea naval port, at Sevastopol, has been considered, ever since, as the wake-up call for Russia's new tsar Alexander II to set the empire on a fast-speed programme of social and economic modernisation.[62] But in immediate terms the 1856 Peace of Paris seemed to be more a statement about Russia's international demotion to a ranking on a par with a subservient China, the most important clauses of the treaty being those neutralising her Black Sea ports and in effect giving carte blanche to the British, the hegemonic naval power of the period, to strike at them with impunity whenever it chose.[63]

With the Ottomans (and for that matter the Persians) in hock to a globally supreme Britain led by a notably bellicose prime minister, Lord Palmerston, who made no pretence about his desire to 'rollback' – to use a later American piece of terminology – the Russians from both the Caucasus and the Black Sea, it is hardly surprising if the Russian official mindset, in return, became increasingly haunted by what the British, or even the British combined with an aggressive Napoleon III-led France, might do next.[64] Significantly, the same obsession about an Anglo-French attack seems to have taken a hold on the Stalinist leadership in 1940. And with the same geographical focus, too: the northern Caucasus.[65] So the argument went: if the Western powers could foment rebellion here – as they were rather adept at doing in their more general imperial guise – and use the Caucasian mountain peoples as their proxies, they would not even need to intervene directly.

There was, of course, a terrible irony, in all this. While post-war tsarist anxiety about the vulnerability of its Caucasian flank translated into a decision approved by Alexander himself in 1860 to deport the entire Circassian population, the latter's pleas for help from the Ottomans and Britain actually fell on deaf ears. Indeed, there was a double irony involved here. During the 1830s and 1840s, there had been some covert British operations aimed at opening up supply lines to Circassian insurgents and even Shamil.[66] During the Crimean war itself, moreover, Britain had been urged by an influential observer of the region, Baron von Haxthausen, to give the rebels full backing on the grounds that – apart from the British themselves – they were the only obstacle to a Russian advance.[67] British prevarication on this score leading to the open abandonment of the Circassians in the Peace of Paris and beyond, according to one 'Great Game' scholar, may have thereby deprived 'the Turks and the British of their most valuable potential allies within the Russian empire'.[68] Paradoxically, however, it did nothing to soften the now blanket Russian charge that the Circassians were active and malicious agents of enemy foreign powers.

If this further suggests that the various Circassian tribes were protagonists in their own fate, catastrophe might still have been averted by a tsarist policy which tempered justice with mercy. 1861, the year when the new 'cleansing' operation began to be put into preparation, after all, is more generally and, arguably, justifiably remembered as one of those great *annus mirabilis* years in modern Russian history. Not just because it brought the emancipation of the serfs. It was also a great year of hope and expectation, one in which it genuinely looked as if Russia was going to turn itself from an Asian despotism into a modern liberal state governed by the rule of law, on the western European model. For a brief moment, even amongst the empire's non-Russian subject peoples – not far short of half its population – intellectuals read into watchwords of the new regime such as *glasnost*, openness, and *sblizhanie*, rapprochement, the belief that they would be encouraged at last to participate in the empire's new order and in which there would be a genuine place for them within it.[69] Even for the Jews, the minority traditionally held at the furthest arm's length by tsarism – as well as in the greatest contempt and suspicion – it looked for a time as if opportunity really might beckon; one critical observer, Hans Rogger, for instance, noting that Jewish access to public office, for a time, actually outdistanced that of their co-religionists in many supposedly more advanced Western states.[70] That said, most if not all of these expectations were to be dashed, not least with the bloody suppression of the national uprising in Congress Poland in 1863, and the consequent turn towards a much more conscious and thoroughly coercive russification.[71] Perhaps this only underscores the point that any non-Russian anticipation of a new *modus vivendi* was built on the entirely false premise that a liberalising modernisation, in itself, could provide the necessary communal safeguards against the threat of tsarist state violence against its subject peoples.

However, it is doubtful that the contours of catastrophe in Circassia were ever accessible to the dictates of *glasnost* or *sblizhanie* in the first place. Passing hopes that that the tsar's orders would allow the tribes to resettle as collective groups under their own political and religious leaderships or, indeed, his own reception of a delegation of tribal chieftains, in September 1861, did nothing to budge the regime from its deportation agenda.[72] The only problem was where exactly was one going to relocate up to 2 million people? There was very little land available in the immediate Caucasian region. Moreover, the whole point of the operation was to replant and consolidate this section of the frontier hinterland with loyal Cossack, Greek, or Georgian settlers. (The fact that this was largely unsuccessful is beside the point.) Even assuming that the Circassians had meekly accepted the tsarist diktat, this would have either meant a potentially lethal American native-style exodus to some distant and insupportable terrain in the empire's remote interior, or 'voluntary' and hardly less awful emigration – already before 1858 acceded to by some 200,000 Circassians – to the Ottoman empire.[73] In the circumstances – amplified, as in so many of our other imperial examples, by a series of natural disasters and epidemics that brought mass livestock and human death in their wake – it is hardly surprising that the majority of those still *in situ* chose diehard resistance; or that the Russian response should have rapidly escalated from one of vicious ethnic cleansing into one of outright extermination.

The commanding officer with responsibility for the deportation, General Evdokimov, was, after all, operating in a long line of Russian Caucasus commanders – General Ermolov, Count Vorontsev, Prince Bariantskii – who in many ways had all taken their cue from Tsar Nicholas I's 1829 directive that the only methods for dealing with Caucasian insurgents were either pacification or extirpation.[74] For the thirty succeeding years of almost unremitting warfare in the region the consequences had been a siege strategy against the insurgents, in which the destruction of livestock and crops were the intended instruments of starvation and demoralisation of their supporting populations, in which vast areas of forest were felled in order to create free-fire zones, and in which hundreds upon hundreds of villages were razed, accompanied by terrorist reprisal and atrocity directed against their inhabitants.[75] The covering justification had always been military necessity. The issue now, however, was no longer simply military (at least not in traditional sense): much larger geopolitical imperatives had entered into the equation. Indeed, the decision-making and directives for the new thoroughgoing and systematic policy of demographic conquest of the Caucasus were coming from the highest reaches of the war ministry, in St Petersburg itself.[76] Evdokimov, as its faithful servant, was certainly not given carte blanche to exterminate *all* the Circassians, any more necessarily than in a different context, and with regard to a different people, forty years later, was von Trotha. The Russian war ministry agenda was mass deportation. Even so, as participating officers, such as Rostislav Fadeev made perfectly and publicly clear after the event, Evdokimov recognised that the only way a general Circassian capitulation to the policy could be achieved was if a 'significant portion' of the population was exterminated first.[77]

This policy of conscious exterminatory terror, once put into effect, clearly began to produce results. The major Shapsegh and Abadzakh tribes, overwhelmed by massacre and starvation submitted to deportation, followed by the notably intransigent Ubykh soon after. Sheer *force majeure*, however, failed to quell the resistance of a number of smaller coastal tribes – the Pskhu, Akhtsipsou, Aibgo and Jigit[78] – the result being that, by 1864, two years after the commencement of this campaign of final solution, the contours of a renewed but classic Russo-Caucasian stalemate were becoming all too familiar. The evidence, thus, is of a specifically Russian example of cumulative radicalisation towards genocide, ending up with an attempt to trap the remaining free tribes in a sort of Caucasian Waterberg – the small but strategically important Khodz valley – though, on this occasion, minus the loophole of Omahake-style exit through which they might still escape. In May 1864, the Russian battle-plan was initially repulsed with heavy losses. However, the military response was to bring up heavy artillery which proceeded to bombard the valley from every direction, over several days. Reported Shauket, a Circassian chronicler of the battle and ensuing massacre:

> men and women were slaughtered mercilessly and blood flowed in rivers, so that it was said that the 'bodies of the dead swam in a sea of blood'. Nevertheless, the Russians were not content with what they had done but sought to satisfy their instincts by making children targets for their cannon shells.[79]

Another Circassian chronicler attests that every man, woman and child in the valley was killed. Neither the exact manner in which they died, nor how many of them were involved is entirely clear. What is clear is that this massacre marked a definitive terminus in the Russian campaign and that within days of it the military authorities were setting about their programme of ejecting the surviving Circassians for once and for all. Modern guestimates suggest that anything between 500,000 and a million Circassians were involved in this, 'first of the violent mass transfers of population which this part of the world had suffered in modern times'.[80] The words of Paul Henze are resonant, for the survivors were not deported to Siberia or Central Asia but across the Black Sea, to the Ottoman empire. Indeed, the death of so many of them by drowning – as overcrowded, possibly intentionally spiked barges[81] sunk off the coast at Trabzon and Samsun – would be an eerie foretaste of what would happen to equally large numbers of Armenians in 1915. And, as with the latter catastrophe, so with the Circassians: the very act of violent, traumatic dislocation, in the first instance, followed by the complete lack of sustenance, shelter or sanitation thereafter, ensured spiralling numbers of fatalities through starvation and epidemic. Yet even if this constituted the visible fall-out from a conscious programme of ethnic cleansing, it still does not, in Shenfield's view, take into account – even accepting the some 200,000 pre-1858 'voluntary' emigrants, and another 120–150,000 others, resettled in the Russian empire – all of the shortfall from a Circassian pre-conquest population of 2 million. Shenfield's own conclusion is that anything between 1 and 1.5 million Circassians perished either directly, or indirectly, as a result of the Russian military campaign and their subsequent forced removal.[82]

Yet if this is disturbing enough, there are two, possibly three other aspects of the Russian drive against the Circassians which are equally and possibly momentously significant. The first represents a notable shift on the issue of the state's monopoly of violence. Martial attributes, plus the right to bear arms for tribal societies, had always represented primary symbols of their independent status. Empires historically, particularly in their frontier regions, had more often than not accepted the fact and devolved military power accordingly. If this effectively gave to tribal groups a right to be a law unto themselves, in the context of the sort of nation-state modernisation – not to say social and cultural homogenisation – practised by Britain and France, such lifestyle was not only deemed as inadmissible but entirely anachronistic. Not quite, of course. Employment as tribal soldiers firmly under the control of state, and with some of the residual privileges of their traditional existence, was still a possibility, and, indeed, was a mechanism operated with a considerable degree of success by the British with their Highland regiments, the French with their *zouaves*, and, of course, most notably the Russians themselves with their Cossacks.[83] But if such tribally based groupings could not be co-opted in this way, or could not be disarmed, the Circassian example seems to suggest most starkly how the upshot might be complete elimination.

In pursuance of a modernising programme which would bring the empire if not into line, then at least into competitive contest with its Western rivals, tsarism, in the 1860s, was effectively signalling its willingness to go down this genocidal route. As has been searchingly illuminated by Peter Holquist, this clearly intermeshed with an entirely new state emphasis on 'population politics' in which an instrumental violence furthered statistically informed, political-demographic imperatives.[84] It also fed into another developing tendency, in which officers from different European armies learned through the relevant manuals, or even direct, officially mandated observation from the military science and practice of their competitors, and sought to apply them to their own domestic-cum-colonial circumstances. What the French general staff, did, for instance, in the Algerian Kabyles could, thus, be equally acceptable and translatable in the Caucasus, in the hands of like-minded Russian commanders all too eager to emulate them.[85] In this way, not only was a programme of ethnic cleansing-cum-extermination, as conceived by the late-Romanov state, perceived as entirely compatible with one of liberal modernisation; equally noteworthy was the general lack of outrage, either in Russia or abroad, at the outcome. Indeed, it was as if what was happening in the northern Caucasus somehow did not register in the metropolitan public mind. Was this because Circassians, after all, were perceived as nothing more than semi-oriental savages off the cognitive and actual map, or – to use Helen Fein's parlance – because they had never been embraced within the universe of obligation of Russia, or any other 'civilised' society? Perhaps, the very fact that, often, Circassian clans, alongside those of other north Caucasian mountain people, were remarkably egalitarian, was simply something (though one might have thought it would have elicited a degree of admiration) which was just too difficult for more 'organised' polities to handle. Whatever the reason, that the destruction should have taken place with hardly a murmur of domestic or foreign disquiet, at the highpoint of pre-1917 Russian liberalism, is extraordinary.

Finally, there is one highly tangible aspect of this catastrophe which suggests that the fallout from Circassia also had serious long-term consequences. We do not know if tsarism intended to use the event as a tool with which to destabilise its Ottoman neighbour. What we do know is that in exporting some half million starving, traumatised and sick refugees across the Black Sea to a neighbouring empire not only entirely lacking the basic facilities or long-term infrastructure to receive them but itself reeling from its own structural inadequacies in the modernisation stakes, this was a result.

The Ottoman State Wreaks Vengeance on the Armenians

This does not mean, however, that the road from the attempted destruction of one ethno-religious group of people, on one side of the Caucasus in the 1860s, to an entirely different group, on the other, in the 1890s, is a straightforwardly linear one. Perhaps it would be more accurate to suggest that what we are considering here is one particularly important trunk road with a large number of intersections with other important ones.[86] The consequence for our particular study is a paradox. Even though analysis of the Armenian massacres still awaits a thorough modern study and is hardly a subject that has been considered in detail by historians,[87] nevertheless, compared with the disasters which befell the Circassians – let alone the Chinese Turkestani – this is an event which is just about present on the radar screen. The paradox, thus, lies in the fact that because we have some considerable material evidence, and hence historical awareness of it, one might argue that the effect has been to magnify the singularity and hence importance of the 1890s mass killings in Ottoman Anatolia, while – possibly inadvertently – diminishing their significance within the broader canvas of imperial mass atrocity at the *fin de siècle*.

How this has happened is passingly instructive. The 1890s massacres were a prequel and, arguably, a staging post to the full-scale genocide of 1915. And in a contemporary context of Turkish state – and societal – denial of this latter event, it is hardly surprising if the whole subject continues to excite fierce passion and controversy. The result, however, sometimes appears as one of a single life-and-death contest between two peoples, in which the Armenians are all cast in the role of conspiracy-minded terrorists intent on the destruction of Ottoman state and society, or alternatively, the Turks are portrayed as bloodcurdling killers intent on the mass murder of this particular people.[88] True, other peoples sometimes have been allotted secondary roles in this Punch and Judy cast, the Kurds, in particular, often being treated as one especially nasty set of troublemakers and Ottoman bully boys.[89] The overall impression, however, tends to be one in which all the many other ethnic and religious communities of the empire are essentially relegated to the margins of this main dispute, while the behaviour of foreign powers is portrayed as essentially a reactive one to the manifold disasters befalling the Armenians.

Yet, perhaps significantly, this same highly charged tunnel vision also seems to have informed and amplified the actions of various critical players at the time. By all accounts, it appears that Abdulhamid really was obsessed with the notion that the Armenians as a people posed a genuine and extraordinary threat to the Ottoman body-politic.[90] Equally, Western observers on the spot, and their public audiences at home, were adamant that the massacres were the entire fault of this singularly wicked and despotic sultan-caliph. Front-page newspaper reports, outraged correspondence, public protest meetings, demands for direct intervention, including one from the recently departed Prime Minister Gladstone, not to say the actuality of contingency plans drawn up by the admiralty for this eventuality, were all symptoms of Western outrage.[91] And in this case it was from a country, Britain, which was supposed to be the Ottoman state's chief patron.

The very intensity of this contemporary reaction, however, would also seem to demand some further scrutiny. After all, the initial epicentre of the massacres was in a particularly inaccessible mountain region of eastern Anatolia and, thus, as remote as the northern Caucasus. Could it be, therefore, that Westerners were already predisposed to take a more particular interest in the affairs and welfare of the Armenians, over and above that of most other Ottoman communities, and that this predisposition itself actually became a critical vector in the deteriorating relationship between Armenians and Ottoman state in the last decades of the nineteenth century? If this is so, could it even be that the sultan's exterminatory onslaught on them can only really make sense within the context of an empire in rapid political and social retreat in the face of Western – as well as Russian – encroachment; the attack on Armenians thus being the next best thing to attacking that foreign encroachment itself? From both sides of the equation the inference would seem to demand an answer to the question: why the Armenians? But perhaps considering the massacre-sequence in itself might help unravel the degree to which the international dimension was intrinsic to it.

The true massacre dynamic began in the high summer of 1894, with an authentic insurrection in the remote Sassun district, west of Lake Van, at the core of the historic Armenian heartlands. The uprising, however, was very localised and may have been ignited as much by immediate demands and depredations emanating from encroaching Kurdish *aghas* as from any intention that this should signal the opening shot in some general Armenian revolt. However, on the other side, though Kurdish irregulars – the infamous Hamidiye regiments – were certainly involved in its extinguishing, so too were the official military instruments of state, including a considerable number of regular units of the Ottoman Fourth Army Corps backed up by several batteries of artillery. The Ottoman response, in other words, far from being an *ad hoc* one, involved some degree of logistical preplanning leading to twenty-four days of what Vahakn Dadrian has called the first modern instance of Ottoman state-organised mass murder against Armenians in peace time.[92]

There followed an immediate outcry from European consuls, missionaries, and other observers on the spot. Reports rapidly accumulated of what had happened and what they suggest is a picture of perpetrators, both in and out of uniform, being provided with carte blanche to do as they pleased with their victims. Mass rape, before killing, figures prominently in these reports as do extensive descriptions of other gratuitous and viciously cruel atrocities. Certainly, in the upshot there was no age or gender discrimination as to who was killed, conservative estimates suggesting 8,000 men, women and children perishing in this initial phase.[93] Significantly, however, while the European diplomatic consensus seems to have been that the massacres had been unprovoked, 'prepared in advance', 'carried out programmatically' and on 'secret orders emanating from the Palace',[94] Abdulhamid at the height of the massacres not only repudiated these claims in person to the British ambassador, Sir Philip Currie but weighed in with his own counter-charge. The Armenians, he proposed, were up in revolt 'with the object of exciting European sympathy' so that they might 'obtain from the government concessions and privileges'. More to the point, he suggested, they were receiving 'encouragement from British officials'.[95]

These entirely contradictory interpretations of the cause of the conflict were now to play major roles in its further escalation. The leading European powers leant on the sultan to form a commission of inquiry into the events at Sassun. This consisted primarily of the Porte's appointees who, after considerable vacillation, as well as the suppression of evidence, declared that the Armenians were themselves to blame, thus confirming the state's view that it had no case to answer. This, however, led to its British, French and Russian consular delegates repudiating these findings in favour of their own damning verdict on Ottoman responsibility. On the strength of this, the European powers now – in May 1895 – proposed a package of reforms for the six so-called Armenian vilayets. These, amongst other things, included turning them into a single administrative unit with a European-appointed permanent control commission to oversee their management. Under further pressure – a statement in itself of Ottoman state weakness – these were set to be implemented, in October 1895.[96]

On 30 September there was a major Armenian demonstration through the streets of Constantinople, the ostensible aim of which was to present a petition to the Porte supporting the reform programme. In fact, it had been in preparation for months, with its organisers' ulterior motive being to demonstrate to the European embassies in the capital that Armenians expected their concerted backing for the full implementation of the programme. Whether part of the demonstrators' agenda was, thereby, to provoke massive state violence, with a view to bouncing the Europeans into direct intervention on their behalf, is non-proven. But even Dadrian notes that this was the first time in Ottoman history that a non-Muslim minority had dared to confront the central authority in this way, not to mention on its very doorstep.[97] Add to this the fact that the organisers were none other than the Hunchaks, the most overtly revolutionary and unashamedly terroristic of the Armenian parties, and a more charitable view of the demonstration seems hardly plausible.[98] What is not in doubt is that, after their post-Sassun hiatus, the 30 September events ignited the massacres again on an entirely grander and more widespread scale.

At the demonstration itself some 2,000 demonstrators, many of whom were armed with pistols, knives and other weapons, were met by a carefully prepared, equally lethally armed counter-demonstration which was quickly able to get the upper hand, thanks to police and army assistance. The hunting down of Armenians in the streets of the capital, particularly in the poorer quarters, continued over the next several days.[99] However, the Hamidian regime in effect having given the 'mob' the green light to kill with impunity, the anti-Armenians cudgels were now taken up – quite literally – in all the main Armenian population centres in the east. Beginning in Trabzon, on 8 October, the killings ebbed back and forth across all of eastern Anatolia as far south as the Aleppo area, before culminating in one particularly grizzly assault in Urfa, at the end of December, in which not only was there a general massacre in the Armenian quarter but some 3,000 people, who had taken refuge in its cathedral, were burnt to death when it was torched with kerosene.[100]

The Urfa 'holocaust', certainly on one level, highlights the specifically religious charge of these massacres. Sanction – indeed encouragement – to participate in the killings regularly emanated from local Muslim leaders. Nor was it just *softas* – young religious students or *medrese* drop-outs – both of whom had played such a prominent role in the Constantinople pogrom, who were the most eager respondents to the call. The regular involvement of quite respectable tradespeople suggests a high degree of popular mobilisation and support for the massacres, even though, in these ethnically mixed towns, this would have meant confronting people who would have been known and respected as customers, workmates, neighbours, and even friends. As just one example: in Aintab, in late November, it was the butchers and tanners of the town, who, to cries of *Allah Akbar*, broke into, or fired Armenian homes, cut down the inhabitants with their cleavers and hatchets, and proceeded to continue to murder in this fashion for a whole day, only stopping for midday prayers.[101] This willingess of Muslims to mutilate and rape, loot and kill Christians who, like Jews, were traditionally accorded in Muslim polities the guarantee of their *dhimmi* status – in other words their safety and the right to practice their religion in peace under Muslim tutelage – must invite comment.[102] The fact that this transgression also could involve a highly symbolic act of sacrilege against a Christian sacred site which, under sharia law, was specifically off-limits to Muslims, is equally noteworthy.

Debate, however, remains as to the degree to which this was attack on 'all' *dhimmi*. In Diarbekir province, for instance, Nestorian Christians were also collectively assaulted, while, on the other hand, Protestant and Catholic Armenians had better chances of being spared where the protection of Western diplomats or missionaries was visible. However, this did not prevent an assault on the American Protestant mission in Harput,[103] underscoring the charge, certainly made against *all* Armenians – whether belonging to the mainstream and traditional *Ermeni* millet or of its breakaway rivals – that their specific sin lay in having had 'recourse to foreign powers'. It was the assumption, thus, that Armenians had opted for their own sectarian interest and hence, in renunciation of their *dhimmi* privileges, which ordinary Muslims read as a forfeit of their right to Ottoman protection. In the same way, it was their heinous transgressions against the understood Ottoman order of society which equally were taken as a justification for the actions of ordinary Muslim folk – as a 'religious duty and a righteous thing' – to violate Christian body and space. This, at least, was the explanation the chief dragoman of the British embassy gave in his assessment of both specific events at Urfa and the more general wave of massacres.[104]

This brings us back again to the other side of equation. As the dragoman himself stated, what the Armenians – or more accurately their revolutionary parties – had been trying to do since *before* Sassun was to draw outside imperial powers, especially Britain, towards a direct intervention on their behalf. By themselves they completely lacked the wherewithal to foment a successful secessionist insurrection. Indeed, the best the various Hunchak and Dashnak 1895 uprisings throughout a significant number of Armenian communities could hope for, in military terms, was a situation where, instead of being over-whelmed by their attackers, they might be able to hold them off. The point is, however, that, like the Bulgarian revolutionaries in 1875–6, the whole pur-pose of these quite desperate efforts was finally to galvanise the British, French, Austrians, Germans, and Russians, into action. Despite all their best efforts, though – bar one dead letter of a collective ambassadorial note of pro-test – no intervention materialised.

The third and ultimate wave in this massacre sequence, this time in August 1896, was thus catalysed by one last, and one might say utterly lunatic, effort to force the Great Powers' hands. It was not the Hunchaks but their revolu-tionary competitor, Dashnaksutiun, who were the instigators on this occasion, seizing the all-important Constantinople headquarters of the Imperial Otto-man Bank: the seat of foreign, especially British and French dominance over the economic life of the Ottoman empire. At least the interlopers' demands were succinct: grant autonomy for the Armenian provinces under European protection or see the bank with its 150 hostages blown sky high. Ambassado-rial intervention averted this *scandale*, the terrorists being allowed to make their escape on a French embassy boat. This time, however, both *softas* and thugs were unleashed onto the streets of the capital with even more abandon, while the police and army stood by. An estimated 6,000 men, women and children were bludgeoned and hacked to death in the ensuing days of blood, in what Christopher Walker describes as a carnival-like atmosphere. Indeed, in two districts, Kasim Pasa and Kilidj Oglu, mostly populated by poor migrant workers, the Armernian population was virtually annihilated.[105] Ironically, as a result, European troops did make a Constantinople appearance but not to help Armenians, only to safeguard the lives of their own respective nationals.

*

Simply considering the contours of these mass killings, on their own, confronts us with critical distinctions from the other cases we have reviewed in this chapter to date. Whereas, for instance, the Circassian killings were confined to a compact territory more or less identical with these peoples' heartlands, the domestic diasporic relationship of Armenians to theirs, almost on its own, determined that the 1894–6 pattern would not be the same. The killings – at least post-Sassun, were also markedly urban and, while not all such Armenian town quarters were equally affected – some, notably port communities such as Smyrna, with strong European presences, being spared altogether – some of the most serious massacres, as we have seen, took place in the full metropolitan glare of European embassies and foreign media attention. Indeed, the very fact that there may have been an element of conscious design in this, rather suggests a regime that was intent on making an extremely forceful point not only about its attitude towards the Armenians but about its relationship to the outside world.

However, if we can discern intent in the mass murder of at least a substantial part of this specific ethnic community, are we not dealing with a genocide? It is interesting in the degree to which most serious scholars of the subject baulk at this prospect. Undoubtedly, an aspect of this revolves around an anxiety that 'elevating' the events of 1894–6 to the title will detract from the totality of the 1915 genocide, when this itself still remains contested in some quarters. Another, possibly less articulated concern is that the rather obvious dynamic between Armenian revolutionaries and state, in both the lead up to, and actuality of the former sequence, may somehow undermine the victims' credentials. The correct rejoinder to this hesitation should be, of course, that Herero armed insurrection, or that of Circassians, Uighurs or others, did not preclude reactions which were genocidal.

Could it be, however, that the rather staccato sequence of killings carried out in significant part by the 'crowd' do not actually add up to an exterminatory intent on the part of the state? Robert Melson, in an important comparative study seems to be of this opinion, arguing that Abdulhamid had not formulated or implemented policy along these lines. He concludes that even the term 'partial genocide' is an inappropriate one.[106] Yet, paradoxically, Melson is in complete agreement with authoritative contemporary observers, such as the German orientalist, Johannes Lepsius, who averred that the rampages of Hamidye irregulars, or town pogromists, did not appear out of the blue but involved careful, thought-out coordination between local civil and military authorities.[107] Melson, in fact, is in no doubt that the sultan's executive role in all this was critical; the only thing he disputes is that his intention was to wipe out *all* Armenians. Yet, as we have seen elsewhere in our gamut of imperial genocides, such mass extermination was rarely planned as grand design but rather snowballed and radicalised, as communal resistance to state agendas itself turned more violent and desperate.

Certainly, by late 1896, the sequence of Armenian killing had run a course, even leading, as Melson correctly notes, to state and community attempting to resume some sort of uneasy relationship with one another. Extraordinarily, such post-genocide truces do happen even where the death toll and devastation are as great as in this case. While estimates on the number of fatalities diverge widely, between a low of 50,000 and a high of 300,000 – figures themselves not assisted by further wide discrepancies on Ottoman Armenian population assumptions of the time – Lepsius' contemporary verdict of not less than 100,000 dead probably gets us as close as we are ever likely to get to the true figure.[108] However, this, of course, is only one index of a genocide, and its aftermath. In addition, to between 2 and 12 per cent of of the Armenian population who had directly lost their lives in the atrocities,[109] thousands of others had had to abandon the hundreds of villages which had been destroyed in the assaults, or found that their ancestral lands had been wrecked beyond repair, or expropriated. Some 645 churches and monasteries, too, had been razed, or turned into mosques, while large numbers of their congregations had been forced to convert to Islam, at the point of a sword.[110] Many more traumatised survivors had simply fled across the Russian border, or were to emigrate elsewhere. All this points to a consciously and systematically organised campaign, aimed at eroding the Armenian social and institutional base to such a point that it could no longer effectively function within a broader *political* equation.

That this did not succeed – at least not in the Ottoman state mind – rather suggests that the 1894–6 massacres should be treated, albeit retrospectively, as a transitional phase in an evolution towards total genocide. Indeed, of all the *fin-de-siècle* mass killings in the global arena, these are the ones that most evince the transitional quality of this period. Certainly, as we have already remarked, one feature which seems to have ratcheted up the scope and scale of these particular killings was the unusually high level of grass-roots mobilisation. Pitting ordinary Muslims against ordinary Christians, the active participation of large numbers of Circassians, Tatars, Laze and Turkomans, in addition to Kurds and Turks, would also suggest a series of latent ethnic conflicts. Match these up with other earlier murderous attacks on Ottoman

Christians, in which the state played no direct role, most notably Kurds against Nestorians – also in the eastern Anatolian region – in the 1840s,[111] and Druze against Maronites in the Lebanon a decade and a half later,[112] and one might be forgiven for assuming that traditional cultural antipathies were at the root of our genocidal causation.

The weakness with this formula, however, lies in its one-dimensionality. As Ussama Makdisi has authoritatively demonstrated, the vicious sectarian violence of the Lebanese mid-century conflicts, far from being primordialist in character, was actually a product of a Western-informed transition to modernity in that region.[113] By the same token, while we do not have to accept at face-value overly rosy assessments of historic Christian–Muslim relations in eastern Anatolia,[114] we can still be struck by the contrast between the centuries of symbiosis between Sassuni Armenian herdsmen and their Kurdish neighbours and the way this zone of interaction was transformed into the very heartlands of the 1890s Hamidye onslaught.[115] Even when it was over, some of the more perceptive Kurdish commentators, associated with the externally published journal *Kurdistan*, denounced the Hamidye units for terrorising settled Kurds as well as Armenians, and urged instead that the two peoples should continue to 'walk hand in hand'.[116] Moreover, when, in 1902, a congress of Ottoman liberals convened in Paris to demand equal rights and local self-administration for all the empire's subjects, its delegates, again, included Kurds and Armenians, as well as Circassians, Greeks, Turks and others.[117]

These aspects of inter-ethnic cooperation would seem to mitigate against any generalising assertion about some inbuilt hostility between Armenians and other Anatolian peoples while throwing some considerable onus on the regime itself, as the key manufacturer of ethnic violence. However, this still remains too easy an explanation. It assumes that actually diverse Muslim populations were pliant and suggestible to whatever hate message the regime might concoct. It further implies that the Ottoman empire contained within itself some deeply held hatred or mistrust of this particular millet. But this is very far from correct. While acute hostility may have fuelled Abdulhamid's abiding obsession with them, this was very much a product of its time. In quite recent decades, the Armenian community had been considered, of all the non-Muslims of the empire, *millet-i sadika*: the most loyal and trustworthy. And in significant part this was because it was considered *to lack* any political threat.[118]

An indigenous Caucasian-Anatolian people whose history of independent nationhood dated to late Roman times, with the emergence of a church, liturgy and written language separate from the dictates of either Catholic Rome or Greek Orthodox Byzantium, the Armenians, and their historic homelands, had come firmly within the orbit of Turkish Muslim empires – though with the exception of a small though significant area under Persian, later Russian domination – since the high middle ages. This certainly ruled out any return to political independence and under long centuries of Ottoman rule determined a clearly subordinate place within a two-tier system of Muslims and *dhimmi*. But this neither interfered with Armenian-Apostolic religious and communal autonomy, which was guaranteed under millet arrangements, nor did it preclude the active participation by Armenians in the political life of the empire. Ottoman government and administration, right to its very end, were in fact filled with Armenians, often to the very highest level.[119] Moreover, alongside Greeks, and to a lesser extent Jews, Armenians played a dominating role in the empire's trade and commerce. True, any overt emphasis on these tendencies, or on the Constantinople-based *amira* – the Armenian mercantile and administrative elite – obscures the degree to which the social and economic life of the vast majority of the community's peasant population in the east was, by the nineteenth century, in marked deterioration. However, such structural inequality – not peculiar, of course, to the Armenians – on its own, cannot undermine the fact that, through into the middle years of the century, Porte–community relations remained generally sound. In this period, for instance, growing numbers of urbanised, educated Armenians were proud to identify with Ottomanism, the new mid-century notion of a common citizenship regardless of ethnic or religious background, while the state itself was prepared to back a programme for greater democratisation and secularisation of millet affairs, even though the resulting 1862 Armenian National Constitution arguably took the community in a more overtly nationalist direction.[120]

So, if, as Gerard Libaridian argues, Armenians had been 'an integral part of Ottoman society for many centuries',[121] what, by the 1890s, had turned this situation not just sour but potentially genocidal? The simple answer would be the impact of Russia. A more complex but also more accurate one would be a series of internal and external interactions in which the genuinely advancing empires also played catastrophic if less overtly proactive roles.

*

The Russian advance to the Crimea and Caucasus, as we have already suggested, had direct consequences for the human geography and demography of its Ottoman neighbour. Waves of Tatar, Circassian, Chechen and other *muhajirs* (Muslim refugees) may have changed the ethnic composition of Anatolia as a whole, by a factor of one in ten.[122] The position was even more marked in eastern Anatolia, where large *muhajir* numbers were intentionally settled by the Ottoman authorities. To what extent ethnicity on its own, thereby, became a factor in deteriorating inter-communal relations on the plateau is debatable, it was, after all, already an ethnographic hotch-potch. But in a period where, in the ebb of a series of epidemics, the general population rose by 50 per cent in a matter of decades, competition for land and resources became intense.[123] This particularly mattered for those Ottoman Armenians who staked their national future on their demographic preponderance in the region, while in more immediate terms it also had a deleterious impact on Armenian lives and livelihoods. In 1862, for instance an Armenian rebellion at Zeitun may have been in part ignited by the resettling of Crimean and Nogai Tatars in the vicinity. The Cilician mountain town was certainly an unusual Armenian centre, noted for its Montenegro-like semi-autonomy and militancy. Certainly, its violent response was not at this juncture replicated in Armenian communities elsewhere.[124] However, if the Zeitun episode was isolated, the problem of Armenian demographic embattlement in the region was actually amplified and exacerbated by the Russians – not at one remove, but through their direct intervention.

Ottoman frontiers had been retreating in the face of Russian *force majeure* since the late eighteenth century. But further clashes, from the late 1820s, led, for the first time, to a series of direct, if ephemeral, Russian occupations of much of Ottoman eastern Anatolia. These invasions, in turn, exposed Armenians as potential supporters and proxies of the Russian interest. The Russians, of course, were Orthodox, not members of the Apostolic Church, but this did not prevent them offering themselves as protectors of their fellow – Armenian – Christians. What this meant in practical terms, however, was that every time there was a Russian advance into the region, there was a flow of Muslim refugees out of it and, every time the Russians withdrew – under pressure from the other Great Powers – large numbers of Armenians left with them.[125] This arguably had the beneficial effect of substantially augmenting the Armenian population on the Russian side of the border – eastern Armenia. But it also determined that Armenians living on the Ottoman side – western Armenia – increasingly looked to the Russians both as guarantors of stabilisation and against further demographic haemorrhage. When, thus, in 1877 the Russians invaded again, as a second front in their Bulgarian campaign, and this time under a general, Loris-Melikov, who was himself an ethnic Armenian, they were actually petitioned by the patriarchal head of the Armenian millet in Constantinople, for assistance. One of the things which was expressedly requested was a guarantee of security from Kurds and Circassians, a stipulation which actually appeared as Article 16 of the 1878 Russo-Ottoman peace treaty of San Stefano.[126]

This was a defining moment. The leadership of the Armenian millet had ostensibly cut itself loose from its subordinate but, nevertheless, contractual relationship with the Ottoman empire and had turned instead to an empire which was an Ottoman enemy, in order to gain an improvement in its domestic circumstances. In turn, that enemy empire had promised to support the requested reforms – in effect an Armenian-administered, local self-government programme, on the Lebanese model – and not to evacuate its troops in the region until the Ottomans had implemented the reforms. As is well-known, further intervention by the other Great Powers at the subsequent Congress of Berlin diluted these provisions by insisting on an immediate Russian withdrawal. Nevertheless, the general principle was maintained: Abdulhamid was expected by the new Berlin treaty's Article 61 (a famous inversion of San Stefano's Article 16), to carry out the reforms. The Armenian question had been internationalised – whether, or not, anybody was actively prepared to come to the Armenians' assistance.

Equally important, however, is the context in which this occurred. The main aim of San Stefano had been to create a large autonomous Bulgaria that, while nominally under Ottoman suzerainty, would effectively be a Russian satellite. In its actual invasion of the Danubian province in support of this agenda, moreover, the Russian military, supported by its Bulgarian national clients, had quite consciously purged whole districts of their Muslim inhabitants. Indeed, if one takes into account further expulsions, or 'voluntary' evacuations, of Circassian and Laze populations from the Caucasus and Black Sea region, in this same 1877–8 sequence, the number of refugees created as a result may be as high as 1.5 million, of which at least 0.5 million remained permanently displaced.[127] This rather raises the question of whether this same sort of coercive manipulation of populations in eastern Anatolia may have been envisaged by the Russians, in order to promote an autonomous Armenian client province.

However, even with a growing Armenian population in the six vilayets posited, in 1882, as numbering 1,630,000,[128] a Bulgarian-style expulsion of Kurds, Circassians and others, would seem highly implausible. The Bulgarian ethnic cleansing had begun from a position of numerical dominance; by contrast, the Armenians were only the most numerous of several communities on the plateau, and then less than 40 per cent of the total.[129] Nevertheless, post-1878 Russian and more general Great Power discussions on the reorganisation of the region did not baulk at its administrative reformulation 'along ethnographical lines'.[130] Indeed, redistributions of populations and their separation into homogeneous groupings, primarily to keep Kurds out of Armenian areas which the latter considered theirs, were a major element of the proposed 1895

Great Power reform package which the control commission was meant to implement.[131]

More to the point, the possibility that under Russian, or even Great Power aegis a Bulgarian solution at the empire's western frontier could be similarly manipulated into play at its eastern one, provided a powerful goad to national-ism minded Armenians. Was it just coincidence that the Dashnak party, founded at Tiflis, in Russian Transcaucasia, in 1890, had its closest external ties with IMRO, the Macedonian revolutionary party that, in the wake of the Congress of Berlin's refusal to countenance a Greater Bulgaria, had committed itself to a struggle for independence within that part of the Balkan region restored to Ottoman control?[132] Dashnaksutiun, like its slightly older, bitterly antagonistic Hunchak rivals, might in practice only represent a tiny fraction of Armenian society – and most of these not even in eastern Anatolia – but their separate agendas shared a common desire to foment a revolutionary situation out of which an autonomous, or entirely independent Armenia would emerge.[133] Few observers have had particularly kind words for either party in this period. Whatever they might have said about the necessity of a self-liberating revolutionary struggle, their tactics of incitement, terrorism and assassination were clearly intended to provoke a massive Hamidian backlash on the Bulgarian model and, thereby, bring about foreign intervention. And, like their Bulgarian *komitadji* exemplars, they had scant concern for the price in blood which would be paid by the rest of the Armenian population.[134]

The one thing the revolutionaries did achieve, however, was a completely disproportionate response from the Porte. All the available evidence suggests that the sultan and his closest advisors were, by the early 1890s, utterly and obsessively convinced that the Armenians *as a people* were now seeking a seces-sion from the empire along Bulgarian lines, that the powers themselves were deeply mired in this supposed conspiracy, and that their joint demands for domestic reforms were nothing more than a subterfuge 'like holding one's beard in one's left hand and cutting one's throat with the other'.[135] Paradoxi-cally, the Hamidian state lacked the state-controlled manpower, resources or expertise with which to effectively isolate the revolutionaries and not least in an eastern Anatolia – the main centre of their operations – still only tenuously under central control. What it opted for instead was a contracted-out cam-paign of blanket terrorisation in this remote region, in which local players were positively encouraged to loot, rape and kill Armenians, under the state's authority, and with an effective promise of impunity from prosecution.

Mobilisation of this kind had already been extensive in the late 1870s, when Kurdish tribes had been given leave to carry fire and sword to Armenian vil-lages, in reprisal for their supposed support of the Russians.[136] The method was in effect indefinitely extended into the following decade, with nomadic clans increasingly wintering their flocks on Armenian agricultural land and pasture and demanding protection money from villagers for the joy of it.[137] Not only did this attrition-style, scorched-earth strategy bring mass starvation to whole districts, it also carried with it the threat of endemic violence. It is surely also noteworthy that it was the most marginal, impoverished and embittered elements of society who were successfully mobilised for this purpose, certainly not sedentarised Kurds, or their rich *aghas* but poor nomads, plus, of course, great numbers of Circassian, Tatar and Laze *mujahirs*.[138] In 1891, moreover, the opportunities for rapine and pillage which this policy allowed were not only given a more official sanction, with the organisation of the tribal participants into the eponymous Hamidye regiments, but ratcheted up a gear with the distribution to them of British-imported Martini-Henry rifles, an entirely new range of lethal weaponry.[139] Having said all this, before 1895, there was no intended programme of genocide as such; only a particularly sustained and ugly repression of the Armenians in their central heartlands, firstly by way of teaching them a lesson for attempting to engage outside interest and, secondly, as a rather unsubtle instrument for denying the revolutionaries grass-roots support. The fact that it had rather the opposite effect confirms that the spill-over into mass killing came out of a further intensification of this state–communal dynamic.

According to modern commentators, the Hunchaks considered both the Sassun rising, which they had helped to foment, as a 'great victory', as well as the bloody Constantinople demonstration of the following year.[140] The irony was that if the name of this game was foreign intervention then the least eager party for it, in the mid-1890s, were the Russians. Having decided at this juncture that the route out of their own imperial weaknesses lay firmly in eastern, Manchurian adventures, their usual machinations in Ottoman affairs were very much on hold. Nor were Armenian revolutionary efforts likely to make them change their mind. Foreign insurgency might all be well and good when it served tsarist interests but when, transparently, it was aimed at creating a single Armenia on both sides of the Ottoman–Russian divide, it was hardly likely to be treated – particularly in the markedly reactionary St Petersburg of this period – as anything other than yet one more radical socialist or *narodnik* movement intent on the destruction of the Romanov empire itself.[141] But then, perhaps, the Russians were no longer the perceived instrument of Armenian liberation anyway. Judging by his own exchanges with their ambassador, it was the British, in 1894, with whom Abdulhamid believed the Armenians were in cahoots.[142] If this were the case it would add one further dimension to our already complex picture of Armenian catastrophe in the vortex of imperial collisions.

*

At the Congress of Berlin, Russia's efforts both to create a greater Bulgaria, and a *de facto* autonomous Armenia, were reined in by the other Great Powers united in their anxiety that the Ottoman empire should not be turned into a febrile adjunct of the Romanov one. The concern seems somewhat odd when we remember that they were also quite unashamed in their haste to parcel up great territorial lumps of it in their own interest, the British, for instance, awarding themselves protectorate status over Cyprus while, four years after Berlin, unilaterally doing the same for Egypt. In fact, the only issue at stake at Berlin was not one of Ottoman integrity *per se*, but simply how best its territorial and economic assets could either be divided – or alternatively managed – so that everybody else was satisfied that they had got their rightful due. Having thus removed most of the Balkans from the empire, the European powers opted for management of the remainder on the grounds that 'it was easier and more profitable to dominate the empire's market through privileges and concessions from a single centralised Ottoman administration'.[143] Britain, it is true, also had very particular imperial reasons for wanting to keep the Ottoman edifice afloat. To this effect, not only were the outer symbols of Ottoman sovereignty to be maintained, albeit in a reduced territorial space but even, in critical ways, made more effective, Britain again being prime promoter in mid-century of the important programme of Tanzimat aimed at a major overhaul of Ottoman administrative and governmental functions. As a result, on the eve of Abdulhamid's elevation to the sultanate, the empire, for the first time, had a Western-style constitution and, with it, the provision of equal rights, at least on paper, for all its inhabitants, regardless of race or creed.[144]

Significantly, neither the new sultan's dumping of the constitution in favour of a return to personal rule, nor the state bankruptcy which had preceded this, overly alarmed the British, or other interested parties. Certainly, having a sultan who conformed to the Western stereotype of an oriental despot was to be deplored but his scope for independent action was already severely circumscribed. Fighting repeated defensive wars against the Russians, as well as domestic insurgents, while at the same time trying to meet Tanzimat's modernising goals, determined that the Ottomans were effectively in hock to European bankers. With the state's bankruptcy, they simply took over supervision of Ottoman state revenues, in the form of a public debt commission.[145] And with the empire already flooded with foreign products as a result of having been forced to acquiesce to free trade, any chance of an independent industrial-style catch-up with the now hegemonic Western forces on the world stage was well-nigh impossible. Add to this the system of capitulations, which enabled the citizens of specified foreign powers to trade in the empire exempt from state interference and taxes (bar import and export duties, which after 1881 would also fall under the supervision of the debt commission), and it is clear that the Berlin Treaty was simply an affirmation of an already existing reality. The Ottoman empire, like the Qing, had become a neo-colonial one, with its future economic and infrastructural development almost entirely dependent on what its British, French, German and Austrian overseers determined for it.

However, indirect control of the empire, favourable as this was for the Western powers, also brought with it the need for commercial agents and intermediaries on the ground. And it is here that we can begin to see the contours of a Western–Armenian nexus emerging – and with it, of its dangers. The Armenian business class, of course, were not the only potential trading partners. Throughout the centuries of Ottoman dominance in the Near East, trade – both at an international and domestic level – had been almost exclusively in the hands of elements of the Greek, Jewish, as well as Armenian millets. Indeed, so long as the empire had remained strong, this situation had suited the Ottoman system rather well. It had ensured that those most entrepreneurial elements of society contributed substantially to its fiscal health while not interfering with a dominant communal space, nor a military and landowning primacy held by Muslims. It may have even helped stabilise broader Muslim–non-Muslim relations.

To speak of an occupational division of labour, may, it its true, distort an overall picture of Ottoman Armenian life and livelihood very far from the comprador caricature of many Marxist, modernisation, dependency, and world-system theorists.[146] By the nineteenth century, however, with Ottoman trade increasingly gravitating towards the Western interest, it was inevitable that many indigenous entrepreneurs would take full advantage of the benefits that went with it, the most obvious of these being capitulations.[147] As these entitled non-Muslim traders to apply to foreign consulates both for protection and passports, immunity from Ottoman taxation also followed. The destabilising effect is obvious. At a time when a desperately retreating empire was both attempting to create bonds of a common Ottoman citizenship and stem its fiscal haemorrhage in order to fend off some of the most egregious aspects of its neo-colonial servitude, critical, if minority, non-Muslim elements of its population were becoming increasingly associated with exactly this tendency.

Why this charge of disloyalty particularly stuck to the Armenians, however, is related to two other features of their nineteenth-century profile which somewhat puts them apart from Jewish and Greek Orthodox millets, while giving them some commonality with both Lebanese Maronites, and Nestorian Assyrians, whose position, as we have noted, was also becoming increasingly untenable in this period. The first feature clearly had a religious dimension. A critical vector in the nineteenth-century Western penetration of the Ottoman empire was the unfettered way in which Catholic and Protestant missionary organisations, whose home bases were either in western Europe or north America, were able to set up their schools, hospitals and other projects, under consular protection.[148] Insulting, of course, to the very concept of the Islamic state, any missionary success, in terms of proselytisation, would be further evidence of the inability of traditional religious leaderships – whether Muslim or non-Muslim – to command continuing authority and legitimacy with their respective populations. In this sense, Christian missionary activity wherever it operated always did so, consciously or unconsciously, as the advance guard of the imperial wave. But it also tended to be most successful where there was already a weak link, where an ethnic community or social group was already strongly alienated from the broader polity or society. Interestingly, in China, it was the Muslims of the north-west, given their hostility to Han rule, who the missionary societies identified as one group particularly susceptible to their message.[149] In the Ottoman empire, the Jews generally looked to their own increasingly powerful Western co-religionists for support, while the Orthodox could always count on Russian protection.[150] The Orthodox patriarchate was also notably authoritarian, not taking kindly to emerging 'national' splits within the millet, let alone challenges from outside interlopers.[151]

This still left the historically most embattled Christian communities of the empire, the various Monophysite 'eastern' churches, the Maronites, and the Armenians themselves, under whose millet all these others were traditionally, if entirely nominally grouped. Of these, the Maronites – while they did not generally embrace Catholicism – were more than eager to accept Catholic protection, not least because this so often went in tandem with French commercial opportunities for their more entrepreneurial elites in the Syrian littoral.[152] There were no such abundant economic carrots for the extremely isolated and impoverished though 50,000-strong Nestorian community, in the east Anatolian region of Hakkari, when British and American missionaries stumbled upon them, in the 1830s. Nor was there any particularly obvious reason why they should abandon their ancient rite in favour of Protestantism. On the other hand, being told by the missionaries that they were the latter-day descendants of the ancient Assyrians – a classic case if there ever was one of a racially informed Victorian wish-fulfilment – and that they would soon be playing a commanding role in the 'spiritual regeneration of the east', must have been very exciting. Few in the Hakkari community became Protestants but the majority were more than happy to accept the schooling, medicine and access to the outside world offered through what was eventually and grandiloquently to become 'The Archbishop of Canterbury's Mission to the Assyrian Christians'.[153]

In sheer terms of scope and scale, however, the Protestant missionary projects to the Assyrians in this period were dwarfed by those that catered for Armenians. But then many more Armenians were proactive in their embrace of Protestantism just as large numbers, before them, had already become Catholics. This exodus from the Apostolic creed was so large, in fact, that the Ottoman state had to accommodate it with the creation of separate Catholic and Protestant millets.[154] Cynically, one could argue that this foreign missionary success had everything to do with Armenian opportunism, especially amongst those who were already members of the commercial classes, or aspired to be. After all, if one wanted to be an agent for a Constantinople or Smyrna-based English or French firm, knowing their language was imperative and the best way to achieve it was to go to a French- or English-speaking missionary school, or college. But if this was logical enough, the Armenian orientation towards a Western re-Christianisation was also matched by a second exceptional feature: the degree to which, as an entirely self-willed process, Armenians embraced a more general Westernisation – whether as members of the Apostolic Church, Protestants, or Catholics. Indeed, of all the peoples of the empire, Armenians earlier, more fervently, and in larger numbers, took on European lifestyles, ideas and values.[155]

The result was clearly paradoxical. In an empire in terminal decline, dramatically reflected in the acute breakdown of the social fabric in the eastern region where the majority of impoverished Armenian peasants lived, these same conditions also favoured the creation of an increasingly bourgeois, upwardly mobile Armenian society in the towns and major cities. Their high degree of literacy, education, not to say cosmopolitan sophistication, in turn produced a major Armenian cultural revival – the *Zartonk*.[156] It was doubly paradoxical that with the forging of a new more consciously modern sense of Armenian national idenitity on the European model came radical politicisation. It was from young, secularly educated Armenians, particularly in the western metropolises, many of whom had studied abroad – or if from the Russian side, at universities there – that the revolutionary parties were able to draw significant numbers of recruits to their increasingly nationalistic cause. A cause whose fuel, in the 1880s and 1890s, even though often at one remove, was the desperate plight of the eastern heartlands.

Here in turn were the essential ingredients of Western support. Given the overtly racialised European portrayals of non-Europeans at the *fin de siècle*, we would not expect Armenians to be necessarily viewed by Westerners in admiring terms. The image of the male Armenian as an unscrupulous and cunning Levantine trader was certainly a common British and American stereotype of this period.[157] The fact that some Armenians were also terrorists should also hardly have appealed to the respectable, middle-class, evangelical opinion from which, in these countries, the Armenian cause drew its most solid partisanship. Significantly, however, this potential blot on the copy book was largely overlooked, in favour of the more narcissistic notion that, as the Armenians were really 'Europeans of the East' – in other words a mirror image of themselves – their actions were clearly self-defensive and hence entirely justifiable.[158] Some of these same sentiments had extended to the Bulgarians, both in the lead-up to and during the massacre-sequence of the 1870s. But with the Armenians they were, arguably, even more intense. Certainly, Gladstone on his accession to the British premiership, in 1880, made no bones about his feelings. 'To serve Armenia', he said, 'is to serve civilisation'.[159]

What was so disastrous about this 'humanitarian' sympathy vote, however, was that it simply added grist to the mill of the growing conviction among key sections of Muslim-Ottoman society that the Armenians – and other Christians – were simply stooges of some Western or broader foreign conspiracy to dismantle the empire. The comment made to a Turkish official by the Kurdish Shaikh Ubayd Allah, in 1881, is particularly revealing: 'What is this I hear: that the Armenians are going to have an independent state in Van and that the Nestorians are going to hoist the British flag and declare themselves British subjects?'[160] Four years earlier, at the onset of the Russo-Turkish war, this important Naqshbandi leader had already made up his mind on the matter by declaring *jihad* and proceeding, of his own volition, to attack Armenian villages. It was ironic that one of the factors which aroused the shaikh, and others like him, was the recent loss of Kurdish autonomy within the empire, at the hands of a would-be centralising Ottoman state. The Kurdish emirate of Botan, the last genuine manifestation of the old order, had ceased to exist in 1847. It was doubly ironic, then, that one of the key factors precipitating *its* demise was British and French pressure to have the emirate punished for its attack on the Hakkari Nestorians, four years earlier. The Kurdish assault had been nothing if not utterly murderous, with possibly as many as 10,000, or one-fifth of Hakkari's entire population being slaughtered.[161] But equally significant in this 'first major conflict between native Christians and Muslims in modern times',[162] was the Kurdish justification for the action on the grounds that the Hakkari religious leader, the Mar Shamun, had arrogated to himself a power 'he had never had before' and, one might add, with the assistance of American missionaries.[163] Similar indignations can be discerned in the even more murderous Druze attacks on the Lebanese and Syrian Maronites, though in this case with the French firmly in the role of *eminence grise*.[164]

The common denominators in these separate explosions of communal violence are rather self-evident. First, there is the accusation that Christians, or more arguably specific groups of Christians, were increasingly and flagrantly flouting their understood place within the Ottoman order of society for sectarian reasons and, in so doing, depriving Muslims of theirs. Implicit in this charge are resentments and jealousies at the apparent material betterment of those who were supposed to be subservient, while the position of their social betters was apparently deteriorating: in other words an acute case of relative deprivation.[165] Secondly, there is the conviction that the resulting breakdown of the social hierarchy was calculated to benefit Christian foreigners. Thirdly, that if this process was left unchecked, it would result in the dissolution of the empire. As the state, moreover, was proving largely ineffective and incapable on this score, there was no choice but for traditional sources of local power to take matters into their own hands.

This finally brings us back to Abdulhamid, and the much more obviously organised massacres of the 1890s. These were not simply a series of grass-roots initiated pogroms but involved the conscious mobilisation of the available machinery, resources and manpower of state. They were also clearly intended as a message both to the Ottoman populace at large, and to the outside world, that the red sultan, in his capacity as personal head of state, would not tolerate any further intrusion on the integrity of the empire. The aspiration to create 'a separate Armenia'[166] – whether a delusion or not – had in Abdulhamid's mind severed any Armenian call on Ottoman protection or mercy. At least as significantly, however, his ensuing onslaught on them, particularly with the second radicalised phase of killings, in 1895, was as much a shot over the bows of the European powers and a warning to them not to interfere with the course of events even if this, according to Lepsius, threatened 'the risk of a general rising in Europe'.[167]

Here then, paradoxically, was not only the attempted reassertion of a strong, independent Ottoman state in the face of foreign diktat – most obviously represented by the Great Power reform programme for Armenia – but one that was legitimised by significant sections of Abdulhamid's own Muslim populace. Indeed, the very fact that so many were willing to participate in the killings points to the emergence of a new type of societal solidarity – and identity – within the late Ottoman state. Consciously and vociferously Islamic, it appeared to both eschew the sinews of multi-ethnic tolerance that had

traditionally held Ottoman society together – a society indeed 'where "difference" instead of "sameness" was paramount'[168] – as well as the more modern,
essentially 'colour-blind' concept of citizenship promoted under Tanzimat.
Instead, it drew a marked distinction between those deemed loyal to sultan,
caliphate and empire, and those perceived as suspect. The criteria were religious. Nevertheless, what was being promoted, or at least imagined, was in
essence modern. A Hamidian proto-citizen was one who had passed the test of
loyalty. He (or she) was certainly not *any* Muslim but specifically an Ottoman
Muslim who supported the sultan in his programme to preserve the integrity
and unity of the empire. Suspect groups might still be embraced within this
identity if they could be made to conform. The attempted (but ultimately
unsuccessful) state campaign to coerce the 'heretical sect' of Yezidis in the
1890s into becoming 'proper' Muslims is a case in point.[169] Significantly, the
campaign was conducted at the same time, and in the very same region, eastern Anatolia, as Armenians were being massacred. It was a case of intended
encapsulation using violence for the one group; detachment, decimation and
removal, by using even more extreme and systematic violence, for the other.

True, none of the these events would have been likely to have come to pass
as they did, without the personal fears and imaginings of Abdulhamid. But
what is particularly noteworthy is the degree to which these fears and imaginings were shared by large sections of the 'core' populace: a sense of acute
victimisation at the hands of interfering foreigners, combined with an even
more acute sense that this was all leading to an imminent state and societal
dissolution, in the interests of outside powers. Conspiracy and paranoia were in
the air and the Armenians – whether revolutionaries, or entirely innocent, as
the vast majority were – paid for them in the most terrible coin. And yet, in a
critical sense, their scapegoating was the outcome of something more than
simply a state–societal nexus against a perceived, if largely confabulated internal threat. Rather, the violence of the anti-Armenian expression was
symptomatic of a retreating imperial entity battling, both in its head *and* in
reality, against the demons unleashed by the new world order. Which brings
us to our one final example of a once-great empire, equally overtaken by its
own obsessive sense of persecution, in the face of the hegemonic forces.

Austria versus the Serbs –
The Touchpaper for Global Conflagration

Placing the Austrian assault on the Serbs, in 1915, in the same referential frame as the genocidal killings committed by our other three retreating empires, in a cognitive sense must represent a departure, at the very least. The chronological coincidence with the totalising genocide which befell the Ottoman Armenians in that same year, is rarely if ever considered, in itself, even though the net result – by the end of the First World War – was the death of an estimated one-quarter of Serbia's 4.5 million population, with a staggering 800,000 of this death toll non-combatants.[170] Even according to our own terms of reference there are some obvious disjunctures. Armenians, Circassians and Uighurs were all technically subjects of the empires that murderously attacked them. The attack on the Serbs was primarily an attack by one internationally recognised state upon another, even if this was undoubtedly a War Type Two assault; in other words, by a first state which considers itself legitimate against a second which it purports to be illegitimate.

Actually, there is *some* evidence to suggest that the Dual Monarchy assault extended beyond this, to the nearly 2 million Serbs who were subjects, indeed citizens, of Austria-Hungary itself.[171] In the wake of the assassination of the Austrian heir, Archduke Franz Ferdinand, in June 1914, there were round-ups of ethnic Serb nationalists especially in the recently annexed province of Bosnia-Herzegovina. Additionally, there was the forcible 'evacuation' of some thousands of Bosnian Serbs, from its eastern borderlands with Serbia.[172] The potential for further radicalisation was clearly also evident in an army decree at the outset of fighting which allowed it to take hostages on *both sides* of the Hungarian-Serbian border, and to execute them where it deemed it a matter of military necessity. There followed not only mass executions of men but wholesale massacres, village burnings and accompanying atrocities around the Serbian border town of Sabac, some of which were graphically, not to say spine-chillingly recounted by the leading American reporter, John Reed, and in reports by Austrian socialist observers which led at least one of them to conclude that the Habsburgs were intent on conducting an anti-Serb 'race war'.[173] That said, no mass deportation of Austrian or Hungarian Serbs on the Young Turk model ensued, nor any general – as opposed to localised – mass executions as were visited first on the Armenian intelligentsia, then on its soldiery serving in the Ottoman army, and finally on the mass of the Armenian populace. In fact, in spite of some considerable evidence of maltreatment and wholesale desertion, ethnic Serbs continued to serve in the Austro-Hungarian army throughout the war, constituting, alongside Croats, nine out of every one hundred members of its personnel. As such, Serb soldiery could not but be major elements in the Habsburg campaigns to smash and then liquidate the Serbian state.[174]

These rather contradictory elements clearly mitigate against a clear-cut charge of genocide against Austria-Hungary, at least on the basis of *domestic* ingredients. An assault on a frontier peoples within one's own state – the case with each of Uighurs, Circassians and Armenians – is not quite the same thing as an attack on a dominant ethnic population in a neighbouring one. There is a further caveat, too. The Habsburg empire may have been founded on not dissimilar notions of autocratic rule to its Qing, Romanov and Ottoman counterparts, just as it was sustained through a very definite military tradition, which cohered, guaranteed and, indeed, gave meaning to the empire of Franz Joseph. Religion, similarly, was central to its historical identity, the centuries of Habsburg title to the Holy Roman emperorship, and its actual role as defender of Christendom/Catholic Europe against both Ottoman threat and Protestant heresy, equally underpinning its claim to divinely appointed mission as keenly as anything caliphate, Holy Russia, or Middle Kingdom could muster.[175] Yet, if all this spoke of a very traditional pre-modern *imperium*, Austria's gradual transformation into a neo-democratic *Rechtsstaat* suggested a political and social evolution much more akin to the Western model. Of course, territorially straddling a great mass of middle Europe as far east as parts of the present day Ukraine brought with it a richly diverse ethno-religious composition which precluded any possibility that it might turn itself, bar radical social engineering, into a classic nation-state. The two politically dominant groupings, after the *Ausgleich*, or Compromise of 1867 – the Germans and the Hungarians – could together only account, in 1910, for a mere 44 per cent of its population, figures which, as Dominic Lieven notes, correspond exactly with those for the Russian primacy in the tsarist empire, and the Muslim in the Ottoman (albeit in the latter case sixty years earlier, when it was still territorially more intact).[176] The key difference is that, whereas avoidance of the multi-ethnic dimension in these latter two empires was maintained largely through personalised despotic rule, until 1917 and 1908 respectively, Austria, by giving its genuine commitment to equal legal and political rights for all of its subjects, as part of its *Ausgleich* restructuring, was forced – whether it liked it or not – to accommodate it. And, paradoxically, even more so under war conditions. Indeed, Austria's absolute dependency on the cooperation of its various peoples was underscored, in 1914, by a military mobilisation in which getting on for half of its total fighting force were ethnic Slavs: men who, by a pan-Slavic logic, should have been fighting with the Russian enemy.[177]

Of course, much has been made of the piecemeal nature of Habsburg efforts at appeasing these various communal interests while doing nothing to create a genuinely coherent multi-national framework of state. Stern critics have railed against a form of governance which was acknowledged, by its very actors, as a continual exercise in 'muddling through'. Count Taaffe, the Austrian prime minister, from 1879 to 1893, even defined political success 'as keeping all the nationalities of the Monarchy in a condition of even and well-modulated discontent'.[178] The brakes on efforts at modernisation – if only of the army – were quite palpable. Hungarians in their half of the empire simply ignored the Austrian lead and attempted to force subject Slovaks, Croats and Romanians to accept Magyarisation.[179] This was, quite paradoxically, much closer to the nation-state prescript. But in the empire as a whole it could not have succeeded, if only because on the Austrian side of the Dual Monarchy divide there were the Czechs to consider. Keeping them, the most organised, combative and overtly nationalist of the Slavic peoples on side proved a thoroughly time-consuming, costly and losing battle.[180]

Having said all this, what is, nevertheless, remarkable about the Habsburg empire, in its final, ostensibly decrepit Dual Monarchy dotage, is the degree to which these multiple inter-ethnic tensions and conflicts were contained. Nationalist frustrations were spent in endless, pointless debates in the Austrian parliament. Lueger's vitriolic anti-Semitic polemic, from the heights of the Vienna mayoralty, was essentially that: polemic. Jews generally felt safe and secure both within the metropolises and the empire at large. So did Muslims, a situation hardly replicated in the new Balkan nation-states to the south. It was absolutely true that Austria-Hungary was shot through with internal contradictions, vastly over-bureaucratised, beset by high-level feuds and intrigue and ultimately dependent on the single person of the gerontocratic emperor to hold it all together. Perhaps his imperial insignia *Kaiserlich* and *Königlich*, as the writer Robert Musil sardonically suggested, provided the key to what his farflung realm really was – 'Kakania' – a heap of excrement.[181] Yet Kakania also had citizenship, a high degree of internal peace, social progress, even the public space for the theoreticians of its own legally recognised Marxist party to dream up and publish schemes for creating a genuinely post-imperial Danubian confederation of nationalities.[182]

If we are searching, then, for the source of Austria's *fin-de-siècle* political angst then trawling through her *Innerpoltik* or more accurately, her *Innerpoltik* in splendid isolation, will not bring us to our destination. Austria's relationship to the outside world – and again, more accurately, her geo-political relationship – is an entirely different matter. Certainly, domestic and foreign policy at the best of times can never be easily divorced from each other. For instance, the decision to effectively hand over half the empire to the Hungarians, albeit under the single headship of Franz Joseph, would never have been seriously contemplated until the empire's defeat by Prussia in 1866. Indeed, the last great internal crisis of empire, in 1848–9, in which a Hungarian national movement had attempted to secede from it, had been drowned in Magyar blood.[183] The 1867 *volte face* was, thus, entirely the result of the military conclusiveness of the Habsburg debacle, at the hands of her more modernised and efficient Prussian adversary, leading, in turn, to a relinquishment of Austria's presiding control of the other German states which she had effectively exercised since the High Middle Ages.

The experience brought the Habsburgs face-to-face with the acutely late nineteenth-century conundrum facing all Great Powers at their moments of crisis. How do you demonstrate to the world that you are a Great Power and have control of your own destiny? The standard, contemporary answer was self-evident: colonial-style territorial expansion. As everybody who counted was already clearly already a long way down this route, nothing else could suffice. A programme of internal modernisation and neo-democratic reform might add grist to economic development, indeed, in the Hungarian case enough head of steam had been generated by 1906, that it had become the second fastest growing economy in the world.[184] The problem was that commitment to this *alone* would have simply confirmed Austria as a medium-sized, second-rate power. Which, of course, is exactly what the empire now was. Instead, the emperor's new clothes were intended to dissemble this central truth in a bid to reassert the Dual Monarchy's place at the top table. Limited modernisation and liberalisation, as much as anything, thus served the pragmatic need to adopt and adapt instruments from the toolbox that had clearly enabled Western states to become the international frontrunners. In the same way, co-option of the Magyars – the most aggressively go-ahead people of the realm, bar the Germans themselves – served similar goals. Nothing, however, could hide the stark fact that the Habsburg empire was, actually, a retreating empire. And one that, like the others along our tectonic plate, was attempting a break-out from its constraints through an agenda which – by exposing further its inherent weakness – could only magnify the chances of a catastrophic outcome. That Austria should find itself at all at the western terminus of our unstable Eurasian series of fault-lines is equally, even portentously significant. Bereft of its historic, firmly middle European fulcrum, lacking anything more than a pocket navy with which to emulate Western, extra-European ventures and with an outlook on the world which was nothing if not continental, the only obvious direction for its expansion was in a southern, and more specifically south-eastern direction. In other words, across another historic European divide into the Balkans, and with it, into a largely culturally alien world of Islam and Orthodoxy.

None of this was entirely new territory for the Habsburgs. Their seventeenth- and eighteenth-century rollback of the Ottomans from Hungary had been followed through with some dramatic if ephemeral advances into the Balkans, followed, again, by a long period of stand-off on what became an Austrian military frontier with the region. Any new advance thus carried with it the possibility of a renewed imperial collision with the Ottomans, though also with the Russians, as they sought too to exploit Ottoman weakness. Yet what is so striking about the disaster of 1914 is that this was not brought about by a fatal encounter with another empire but with a *nation*.

*

Serbian independence had been given its international imprimatur at Berlin in 1878. The seemingly inexorable rise of this aspiring Balkan Piedmont not only appeared to parallel the decline of its northern imperial neighbour but to lead to a conflict of interests between the two that would ultimately blow up in Austria's face. In theory, however, Serbia was a poor and backward country easily manipulable to the Habsburg interest. As late as 1901, Austrian foreign minister, Goluchowski, could sum up Serbia's situation thus:

> Politically in complete disorder, financially on the verge of bankruptcy, militarily quite insignificant and weak, this country lies so much within our power that it will always be dependent on us.[185]

This assessment, however, perhaps tells us as much about the fixed and narrow way Austria wanted to understand Serbia as about some of its emerging realities. It was certainly true that this post-Ottoman polity, like the Balkan region as a whole, when compared with the Habsburg European heartlands, was remote and undeveloped. Almost entirely agrarian and seriously impoverished, the majority of its inhabitants were traditionally illiterate peasants, or mountain people, often prone to extended family or clan feud, vendetta or, in the *longue durée* of Ottoman decline, large-scale brigandage. Political liberation from Ottoman rule, similarly, in no way freed either Serbia, or its neighbours, from their economic and demographic realities, the attempt to soak up their increasing rural manpower into a single burgeoning state sector – the army – failing to halt population pressures on the land.[186] With any hope of more stable industrial development, or administrative modernisation, inevitably heavily dependent on European credit, technical expertise and goodwill,[187] it was clear, thus, that the relationship of a Balkan state, such as post-1878

Serbia's to a neighbouring giant, like Austria-Hungary, was likely to be not so very different from that of colonised Africans to their European masters. Indeed, that this is exactly what was imagined in Vienna was already signalled a generation before Goluchowski when another Austrian foreign minister, Andrassy, had dismissed all Balkan peoples 'as wild Indians who could only be treated like unbroken horses, to whom corn should be offered with one hand while they are threatened with a whip with the other'.[188]

The problem for the Ballhausplatz was that the young Serb state increasingly behaved as if it had not understood its role in this script. This became particularly evident, just two years after Goluchowkski's 1901 prognosis, when a bloody army coup removed Serbia's entirely corrupt – but from Austria's viewpoint extremely pliant – puppet, Alexander Obrenovic, and instituted a regime change which started looking more like a Hunchak-led Armenia might have done had it gained independence. A couple of years later, Belgrade negotiated a customs union with neighbouring Bulgaria, without consulting Austria, and, when the latter retaliated to this impudence by closing its Serbian border, had the further audacity *not* to keel over and beg for mercy. On the contrary, far from providing evidence of an Austrian economic stranglehold on the country, the ensuing 'pig war' highlighted the Serbian ability to find other markets for their primary export product, adding further to Ballhausplatz apoplexy by purchasing artillery from the French, rather than the Austrians as, again, they were supposed to do.[189] Relatively speaking, Serbia remained poor. But dreams of its own special mission to unite the South Slav peoples into a Great Serbia increasingly infiltrated into the life of the nation, not least through one aspect of its domestic agenda clearly in evidence in this period – its primary school curriculum.[190]

Thus, far from Austria having a controlling influence on the life of a client and entirely subservient neo-colonial state, the immediate years prior to the First World War were ones in which it seemed to be the Serbs who were turning the tables on Austria itself and infecting ethnically related people within its boundaries with Belgrade's own territorially aggressive agenda. Most of this perceived spectre was actually completely confabulated. After war had been declared in 1914, Serbia might have proclaimed its war aims to be the liberation and unification of all its oppressed Serb, Croat and Slovene brothers,[191] but there is very little evidence to suggest that large numbers of these peoples, within Austria-Hungary, were queuing up to join a Serb-led *risorgimento*. On the contrary, pre-1914 Yugoslavism was essentially a rather pragmatic project internal to the empire. Being effectively governed by Belgrade had very little or no support amongst the various Croat or Serb political parties within the south-eastern provinces of Austria-Hungary, and it was the imperial authorities who – entirely counter-productively – succeeded in part-promoting the idea through a thoroughly manufactured conspiracy trial.[192] This, however, only materialised in the wake of a major political crisis for the Habsburg state, centring on the one ostensible piece of evidence that it was an advancing empire: Bosnia.

*

The Austrian version of the German *Drang Nach Osten* was actually predicated both on avoidance of direct conflict with either Russian or Ottoman empires, or of direct military conquest. Assuming continuing Ottoman retreat from the Balkans, Austrian policy, until 1908, mostly sought to come to an understanding with the Russians over the spoils, most optimistically in the hope that the latter's ambitions would concentrate on empire-building far away, at China's expense. In fact, there was a real Austro-Russian conflict of interests in the Balkans, the result of which was that their diplomatic relations mostly operated on a spectrum from bad to worse. But while the unilateral Russian attack on the Ottomans in 1877 brought these relations to an all-time low, the new post-war order, determined by the genuinely Great Powers at Berlin, also brought with it an ostensible silver lining for Austria. She was rewarded with control of the Ottoman province of Bosnia-Herzegovina, both for her non-involvement in the war, and as a balance to a Russian-sponsored, autonomous Bulgaria.

The new acquisition, in fact, carried with it substantial dangers for the empire, not least, in adding another 1 million or more Slavs to her rule.[193] Divided as they were by religion and historic culture, with the Bosnian Croats Catholic, and the Bosnian Serbs Orthodox, these two groupings, nevertheless, had a language in common and, thus, a basis for enthusiasts among them to project the notion of national oneness. To which, of course, one might also add the substantial Muslim population of the province, who were also Serbo-Croat speakers. In particular, for the Hungarians, who controlled most of the imperial territory contiguous with Bosnia, the potential nightmare was not, however, just one of a localised national rendezvous. The Hungarian territories across the Bosnian northern and western boundaries were inhabited mostly by Croats who also happened to be notably restive under authoritarian Magyar rule, while Bosnia's eastern flank was bounded by a Serbia which, from its very inception, regarded the province as part of its historic patrimony.[194] Add these ingredients together and the consequences of the Bosnian acquisition might begin to look less like the basis for a benign imperial advance and more like an impending imperial dismemberment, on post-Ottoman lines.

All this, however, was brushed aside by Franz Joseph in his firm conviction – and, one might add, his wish-fulfilment – that Bosnia-Herzegovina was going to be the key to the empire's rejuvenation.[195] In complete contrast to the Hungarian nightmare scenario, Bosnia, in this version, represented not only a building block of empire but a launching pad for its neo-colonial extension across the whole Balkan peninsula, as far as the Aegean port of Salonika. To arrive at this destination, Austria began to busy itself, in the post-1878 period, with planning and financing a network of strategic railways leading back from the port through the Balkans to the Danubian heartlands. In this way, too, Austria sought to lay a firm economic hand on the Macedonian rump of the Ottoman empire in Europe, all the way to Constantinople, while signalling also a prior claim on the territory in the event of any future political development in the region. Paradoxically, Austro-Serbian antipathies centring on Bosnia might have gone on simmering indefinitely if it had not been for events here in Macedonia. What took place in the early 1900s represented not simply a precipitous unravelling of the 1878 Great Power neo-colonial arrangement for the entire Ottoman empire but produced, in its wake, a small earthquake along our broader Eurasian tectonic plate, with ultimately calamitous results for more than simply the Serbs.

Again, it was the actions of revolutionaries, in this case, IMRO, who precipitated the wider crisis. While their efforts to goad a renewed Great Power intervention on their behalf, through first terrorism and then, in 1903, the staging of a classic Balkan-style insurrection, did not produce the desired results – on the contrary, there followed frantic Austro-Russian efforts, in particular, to shore up the 1878 status quo for fear of involving themselves in a further stand-off – the insurrection catalysed all the other interested local parties, Greeks, Bulgarians, as well as Serbs, to intervene, albeit indirectly through their own covertly supported guerrilla-band proxies.[196] The problem was that Macedonia, and adjacent Thrace, were not just strategically important as well as ethnically contested, they were also by Ottoman standards the richest and – relative to their size – the demographically most important parts of the sultan's remaining empire.[197] The result was that the Ottoman army fought back here with a particular ferocity, turning increasingly, in the process, to the employment of the sort of annihilatory counter-insurgency tactics which, as we have seen, had become an all-too familiar feature of *fin-de-siècle* colonial warfare elsewhere.[198] In turn, this 'dirty' war brought to the fore one of its most successful practitioners, a young major named Enver bey who, like many Ottoman army officers serving in Macedonia, also happened to be involved in the clandestine, anti-Hamidian Ittihad (CUP) party. Enver appears to have had no specific plans to topple the sultan. However, in an extraordinary turn of events in the summer of 1908 – precipitated particularly by the rumour that at a meeting between the Russian tsar, Nicholas II, and British king, Edward VII, it had been agreed to jettison the Macedonian status quo in favour of a new and imminent carve-up of the region[199] – Enver launched an insurrection against the sultan aimed, at least in part, at pre-empting these Great Power machinations.

The CUP takeover of power, in Constantinople, and its most horrendous consequence in the form of the 1915 Armenian genocide will be a subject for considerable discussion in the next volume. What concerns us here is the direct knock-on effects of these 1908 developments for Austro-Serb relations to the north. The obvious signal that the Ottoman army revolt had succeeded was Abdulhamid's resurrection of the shelved constitution of 1876. Indeed, for one extraordinary moment when Turks, Greeks, Armenians and Jews embraced each other on the streets of Salonika and Constantinople, it seemed as if all the problems of the empire, including inter-ethnic strife and potential secession, had been resolved in revolutionary fashion. The euphoria did not last long. But so long as it did, it threw the whole Austrian game-plan for the Balkans into jeopardy, especially because Bosnia-Herzegovina was still technically part of the *Ottoman* empire. As such its newly entitled citizens might conceivably vote for their reincorporation within it,[200] and, thereby, remove the main prop upon which Austria's Balkan sphere of influence had been predicated. Much worse, by again throwing into question the very provisionality of the 1878 agreement, it might even give landlocked Serbia another chance to declare its interest in the province and, with it, an opening to the sea. The Ballhausplatz hurried to pre-empt this spectre, hastily constructing a series of Balkan diplomatic manoeuvres designed to isolate Serbia and more generally neutralise the malodorous effects of what Austria now intended – the annexation of Bosnia-Herzegovina.[201] It was this event which is generally recognised as the starting point in the series of ensuing Balkan crises which would ultimately bring Franz Joseph's empire face to face with nemesis. And, thus, with it, the Great Powers and their entire imperial order.

But should we treat the October 1908 annexation as the aggressive first move of a cocksure empire with radically new expansionist plans, or the frightened knee-jerk reaction of a spent monolith – indeed a classic 'strong–weak' state – staring into the abyss? As so often, it is in the very contradiction that we may be able to glean critical ingredients of the ensuing dialectic. Russia, certainly, was in no doubt that the annexation was an act of aggression against itself, claiming that the arrangement privately entered into between Austrian and Russian foreign ministers the previous month – in effect for a further repartition of the Ottoman empire – had not included Russian acquiescence to the Austrian plan. Russia threatened war, only to back down in the face of Austria's own sabre-rattling. But this itself was less to do with Austrian confidence and more to do with the knowledge that the German kaiser had promised Vienna full military support if Russia should attack. With the tsar already bruised and humiliated as a result of his recent Japanese defeat, getting back at the Austrians for spoiling Russia's renewed Ottoman agenda now took on an entirely vindictive aspect. One consequence, indeed, was a series of Russian diplomatic efforts to bring the Serbs and Bulgarians together in an offensive alliance directed at Vienna.[202]

The paradox was that if this spoke volumes for a Russian state pathology, its own aggressive behaviour could only feed that of Austria's. But, again, there was a further paradox. If it was convenient for Austria to see behind the actions of little states a much nastier arch-manipulator, the actions of the little states themselves appeared to carry their own menace. When, thus, in the autumn of 1912, Bulgaria and Serbia decided *not* to make plans against Austria but to join with Montenegro and Greece for a direct military assault on the Ottoman empire, it was the most straightforward statement imaginable that these states were not going to be anybody's puppets but were going to carve out their nations' future boundaries irrespective of Great Power plans or anxieties for the region, let alone the ethnographic realities on the ground. That, from the Great Power standpoint, these upstarts were clearly off the leash and out of control could only be further confirmed when Bulgaria proceeded to fall out with its erstwhile allies over the Macedonian spoils, precipitating an even more bloody and quite overtly genocidal second Balkan war the following year.[203] Austria might have enjoyed some small *Schadenfreude* from this sequence as it effectively detached Bulgaria further from its Russian orbit, Sofia already having willingly declared its independence from Ottoman suzerainty in 1908 in eager support of Austria's annexationist subterfuges. But this could hardly compensate for Austria's fears regarding a Serbia which, in the space of months during 1913, had not only doubled its territory but jumped from a land of nearly 3 million inhabitants to one of nearly 4.5 million.[204]

Minus Bosnia, however, Belgrade felt cheated of its birth-right and of its 'chosen' destiny. Worse, its political and military elites feared that the Austrian annexation had been part of a wider strategy aimed at liquidating Serbia altogether. They had a point. Austrian contingency plans for a preventive war against Serbia, already in existence at the time of 1908 crisis, were predicated either on the state's partition, or complete incorporation into the dual monarchy.[205] That such an agenda could be contemplated at all rather suggests the degree to which Austrian high political circles had come to their own worst conclusions about the threat which Serbia seemingly posed to the empire. 'We have got either to annihilate Serbia, or, if we cannot do that, to learn to love it', quipped one analyst.[206] Loving Serbia was out of the question, not least with elements of Belgrade's military themselves consciously stoking unrest in Bosnia via nationalist groups such as 'Young Bosnia', who not only demanded union with Serbia but were willing to incite the cause through revolutionary terrorism akin to the Armenian model. But the overtly doom-laden, alternative forecast could also have been deftly circumvented if moderate spirits in Vienna had paid a good deal less attention to the bravado of the minority of immature Bosnian hotheads prepared to point Mausers at Austrian officials, and much more to the notable quiescence of the vast majority of the Serb, Croat, not to mention Muslim populations within the annexed province. The last group, in particular, all too aware of the mass atrocities the Serb army had committed against their Albanian co-religionists in Kosovo in the 1912–13 wars, propounded loyalty to Vienna as the very cornerstone of their politics.[207]

The problem was that, in the climate of intensifying mutual distrust and paranoia which characterised the post-1908 domestic as well as international scene, it is not difficult to see how an overworked Austrian political mind could have conjured up a careful trail of conspiracy leading straight back to Belgrade behind every act of 'Young Bosnia' sabotage. The situation was hardly helped by the fact that behind those who would become the Sarajevo plotters, there was, indeed, the 'Black Hand', a secret grouping in the Serbian war ministry whose purpose was the Serbian encapsulation of Bosnia, as a prelude to its acquisition of the empire's entire south Slav domain. Vienna's most fearful nightmare thus came to the fore at the very juncture when its Balkan *advance* seemed to be the only make-or-break basis upon which the empire's Great Power standing could still be assured. Is it any wonder, then, that it was Conrad von Hotzendorf, the Austrian chief of staff, and Vienna's most uncompromising advocate in favour of Serbia's destruction, who became the pivotal player in the disaster which was to follow?[208]

The immediate denouement is well known. The timing of Franz Ferdinand's arrival in the Bosnian provincial capital to lead annual army manoeuvres was, to the Serbs, about as provocative an act as imaginable. The day, 28 June was the most potent and symbolic date in the Serbian national calendar, marking the anniversary of the battle of Kosovo in 1389, the field of Blackbirds, in which a retreating medieval Serbian empire had gone down to a final – if, for nationally-minded Serbs, compellingly heroic – defeat at the hands of the Ottomans.[209] It was ironic that the archduke's visit elicited only positive responses from Bosnia's Muslim population and little or no opposition from most of its Serbs and Croats. In Serbia itself, however, the visit was taken not only as a conscious insult but as a harbinger that the Ottoman tutelage of the recent past was about to be replaced by an Austrian one in the very near future. It was doubly ironic, then, that the aim of Gavrilo Princip and his isolated group of Bosnian compatriots was not to provoke Austrian invasion through the archduke's assassination but, on the entirely mistaken assumption that he was the prime author of Austrian forward policy, to prevent it![210]

Misreading the tea leaves was not itself particularly unusual in a *fin-de-siècle* world where assassination of senior figures of state was two a penny and also where, as one later Yugoslav commentator reminds us, if slightly incorrectly, it represented 'a part, albeit an inevitable one, of the political reaction to the imperialist policies of great powers in the colonies'.[211] But if Black Hand's sponsored assassination was premised on the exact opposite of what Armenian and Macedonian terrorists had been trying to incite for decades – namely Great Power intervention – by the same token, Vienna's eagerness to use the occasion as a *casus belli* rather suggests the lengths to which it was prepared to go in order to be avenged on the Serbs. After all, Vienna knew almost from the outset that the Belgrade regime *as a whole* had not been implicated in the assassination. And von Hotzendorf, for one, clearly understood that Vienna's ensuing ultimatum to Belgrade would make Austria responsible not just for a third Balkan war but for a conflict which would suck in all the Great Powers. The key problem for Austria's decision makers was that to have opted *not* to go to war would have been 'an open confession of weakness'.[212] This was at the heart of its conundrum and with it of the entire edifice of Great Power politics at the *fin de siècle*. An empire's international prestige was at stake. The only way, apparently, that it could be recovered was by taking out its frustration, recrimination and ire, on a whole communal population. Von Hotzendorf attempted to do so by committing practically the entire Austrian reserve to the assault on Serbia, exposing in the process Austria's eastern frontiers to the possibility of Russian attack. The gamble proved disastrous. The military knock-out blow against Belgrade failed. Russia's subsequent advance highlighted Austria's absolute dependency on her German ally.[213]

With imperial hubris turning to humiliation, the Austrian response to the Serbs could only be that very familiar one we have encountered so many times in *colonial* struggles elsewhere: overkill. Of course, the Serbs were not the Shona, the Herero, or Nama, nor for that matter the Armenians, the Uighurs, or the Circassians. They were organised as a recognised independent state with a large if poorly equipped army and, technically, the backing of powerful Russian, British and French state-empires. The last two even landed troops in (by now Greek-controlled) Salonika in late 1915, in a bid to support their belea-guered ally. But whether these factors appreciably affected the Austrian desire for an entirely retributive and 'punitive expedition' against the Serbs[214] or for their collective projection of them as treacherous, native insurgents is doubt-ful. In the wake of the first major military encounter on Serbian soil at the battle of Cer Mountain in August 1914, in which the Austrians were roundly defeated, the Serb army recovered villages where not only had the men been summarily executed but their womenfolk and children also mass butchered after rape, or other gratuitous abuse.[215] All the way along the ensuing battle-line, Reed reported a repeated spate of such atrocities.[216] Clear as to what would be their fate if Austria actually won, the Serbs thus fought back as did all the other *communal* groups we have observed; as a total people struggle and as if this was literally a matter of collective life and death.

Nemesis came in the autumn of the following year. Having fended off the Austrians for more than twelve months, a combined three-army assault of Austrians, Germans and Bulgarians – the last now also a member of the Cen-tral Powers, partly in revenge for Serbian treachery in the previous Balkan war – finally tore the guts out of the Serbian defensive line. Abandoning both Bel-grade and countryside, the ensuing winter retreat over what were appropriately called the Accursed Mountains, to the relative safety of the Albanian coast, has been described as not so much the march of a withdrawing army but of an entire nation.[217] Signficantly, exact numbers of fatalities are not known. Certainly, out of a total of 650,000 fighting men in the Serbian army, only 150,000 were regrouped on the British-controlled island of Corfu, in February 1916.[218] But while this does not take into account those captured or left behind, it also fails to consider the large numbers of civilians who also took part in the retreat and who, equally, were violated or massacred – in signifi-cant part by Albanians, also taking their revenge for Serb atrocities in 1912–13 – or who died through starvation, exhaustion and deprivation. Though clearly quite distinct, in critical respects, this mass, death-dealing population movement shares features in common with the near-simultaneous Armenian disgorgement, at the hands of another member of the Central Powers, Otto-man Turkey.

This, however, was not the end of the Serbs' wartime travails. With military defeat came the extinguishing of their national independence, the country being occupied and demarcated as either Austrian or Bulgarian, pending Cen-tral Power victory in the overall Great Power contest. For Serbs in the Bulgarian zones – that is, in southern Serbia, or northern Macedonia – this meant, in effect, forced renationalisation as Bulgarians. For those in the Aus-trian zone, it also involved an extremely draconian and vicious occupation rule. Some 50,000 Serbs are estimated to have been deported to concentration camps in Austria-Hungary in these years. In both zones there were repeated mass executions of civilians.[219] It was the sort of attack on the foundations and fabric of national life to which Raphael Lemkin, a world war later, would put the name 'genocide'. It was also a vivid foretaste of what would happen in that war, not only in occupied Serbia but throughout eastern Europe, under the aegis of the Austrian-born Adolf Hitler.

*

Austria-Hungary was once famously described by Karl Kraus, one of its most acerbic but perceptive observers, as the 'research laboratory for world destruction'.[220] More recently, historians of the calibre of James Joll seem to have corroborated the implication from a different perspective by suggesting that the monarchy's headlong plunge into war may have been intended as a means of escape from insoluble internal difficulties.[221] Yet the killing had begun at the territorial periphery of the empire, in a region with a critical interface with the outside world. Out there, in contested territories to which advancing and retreating empires laid claim, or simply onto which they desperately clung, in their increasingly frenetic bids to maintain place in the global race for position, local societies and communities frequently had taken the full genocidal brunt of these efforts. Genocide, as yet, had hardly offered its potential as a symptom of the crisis of the domestic national polity. That, however, was about to change dramatically. As all the empires plunged into the vortex of the First World War, taking with them their core populations, the need to win through, and not go under, offered a green light to anybody willing to offer radical solutions. The 1914–18 catastrophe, of the West's ultimate making, was also about to give rise to a new, entirely more potent urge to genocide.

Notes

1 European Conquerors and Sundry 'Savages'

1 Quoted in Mark Cocker, *Rivers of Blood, Rivers of Gold, Europe's Conflict with Tribal Peoples* (London: Jonathan Cape, 1998), 178.

2 Quoted in David E. Stannard, *American Holocaust, the Conquest of the New World* (New York and Oxford: Oxford University Press, 1992), 126; Ward Churchill, *A Little Matter of Genocide, Holocaust and Denial in the Americas: 1492 to the Present* (San Francisco: City Light Books, 1997), 244–5.

3 Quoted in Mark Mazower, 'After Lemkin: Genocide, the Holocaust and History', *Jewish Quarterly*, 156 (Winter 1994/5), 6.

4 See Alfred W. Crosby, *Ecological Imperialism: The Biological Expansion of Europe 900–1900* (Cambridge: Cambridge University Press, 1986).

5 Churchill, *Little Matter*, 132. See also Francis Jennings, *The Invasion of America, Indians, Colonialism and the Cant of Conquest* (New York and London: W.W. Norton and Co., 1976), 17–20, for a further biting critique of Kroeber.

6 Churchill, *Little Matter*, 132–5.

7 See Stannard, *American Holocaust*, appendix 1, 'On Pre-Columbian Settlement and Population'. Henry F. Dobyns, 'Estimating Aboriginal Populations: An Appraisal of Techniques with a New Hemispheric Estimate', *Current Anthropology*, 7 (1966), 395–416.

8 Woodrow Borah and Sherburne F. Cook, *The Aboriginal Population of Central Mexico on the Eve of the Spanish Conquest*, Ibero-Americana no. 45 (Berkeley: University of California Press, 1963); idem., 'The Aboriginal Population of Hispaniola', *Essays in Population History: Mexico and the Caribbean* (Berkeley: University of California Press, 1971), vol. 1, 401–3.

9 Bain Attwood and S. G. Foster, 'Introduction', in idem., eds, *Frontier Conflict, the Australian Experience* (Canberra: National Museum of Australia, 2003), 5; Cocker, *Rivers,* 177–8.

10 John H. Bodley, *Victims of Progress* (Palo Alto, CA: Mayfield, 2nd edn, 1982), 40, notes a decline from 5,000 to 111 in this thirty-year period, i.e. an extrapolated 98 per cent loss.

11 Julian Burger, *Report from the Frontier: The State of the World's Indigenous Peoples* (London: Zed Books, 1987), 37. See also Cocker, *Rivers*, 179, for similar

catastrophes befalling the Kanaks of New French Caledonia and Maori losses in New Zealand. Also David E. Stannard, *Before the Horror, the Population of Hawai'i on the Eve of Western Contact* (Honolulu: Social Science Research Institute and University of Hawai'i Press, 1989), 69–75.

12 Noble David Cook, *Born to Die, Disease and New World Conquest, 1492–1650* (Cambridge: Cambridge University Press, 1998); William H. McNeill, *Plagues and Peoples* (London: Penguin, 1979), chapter 5, 'Transoceanic Exchanges, 1500–1700', for the broader context.

13 Steven Katz, 'Quantity and Interpretation – Issues in the Comparative Historical Analysis of the Holocaust', in idem., *Historicism, the Holocaust and Zionism* (New York and London: New York University Press, 1992), 119.

14 Stannard, *American Holocaust*, xii.

15 Ibid., 85. See also Tzvetan Todorov, *The Conquest of America, the Question of the Other*, trans. Richard Howard (New York: HarperPerennial, 1984), 133: 'If the word genocide has ever been applied to a situation with some accuracy, this is here the case.'

16 Churchill, *Little Matter*, 151–7.

17 Tony Barta, 'Relations of Genocide: Land and Lives in the Colonization of Australia', in Isidor Wallimann and Michael Dobkowski, eds, *Genocide and the Modern Age* (Westport, CT: Greenwood Press, 1987), 237–51; A. Dirk Moses, 'An Antipodean Genocide? The Origins of the Genocidal Moment in the Colonisation of Australia', *Journal of Genocide Research*, 2:1 (2000), 92.

18 See Lawrence Keeley, *War before Civilisation* (New York and Oxford: Oxford University Press, 1996), for this thesis. Having said that, the prevailing anthropological-cum-archaeological wisdom is that, *contra* H. G Wells' *Grisly Folk* (1922), genocide does not provide an explanation for the extinction of Neanderthal hominids, whom *homo sapiens* gradually replaced in Europe over 15,000 years, nor informs critical interactions between palaeolithic hunter-gatherers. I am indebted to Prof. Clive Gamble from the archaeology department, University of Southampton, for his communication on this issue.

19 Cocker, *Rivers*, chapters 4–6. See more particularly Todorov, *Conquest*, 139–43, for details of *conquistador* violence.

20 Todorov, *Conquest*, 134–9. More generally Charles Gibson, *The Aztecs under Spanish Rule* (Stanford, CA: Stanford University Press, 1964); L. B. Simpson, *The Encomienda in New Spain* (Berkeley: University of California Press, 1966).

21 For a specific example see John Hemming, *Red Gold, the Conquest of the Brazilian Indians, 1500–1760* (Cambridge, MA: Harvard University Press, 1978), 440–3, for the Manau revolt on the Amazonian frontier of the 1720s. Also Nicholas Robins, 'Genocide and the Great Rebellion of 1780–1782 in Upper Peru' (unpublished paper for the International Association of Genocide Scholars conference, University of Minnesota, June 2001), for a case in reverse, that is, of an attempted genocide of Spaniards by millenarian-inspired Indians. See, however, Henry Kamen, *Spain's Road to Empire, the Making of a World Power, 1492–1763*

(London: Allen Lane, 2002), 126–7, for corroboration on the primary point of issue here.

22 Claude Lévi-Strauss, *The Elementary Structures of Kinship*, trans. James Harle Bell et al. (London: Eyre and Spottiswoode, 1969), 46.

23 See François Hartog, *The Mirror of Herodotus, the Representation of Other in the Writing of History*, trans. Janet Lloyd (Berkeley and Los Angeles: University of California Press, 1988); Edith Hall, *Inventing the Barbarian, Greek Self-Definition through Tragedy* (Oxford: Oxford University Press, 1989); Anthony Pagden, *The Fall of Natural Man; the American Indian and the Origins of Comparative Ethnology* (Cambridge: Cambridge University Press, 1982), chapter 2, 'The Image of the Barbarian'.

24 See for instance, John Fairbank, ed., *The Chinese World Order: Traditional China's Foreign Relations* (Cambridge, MA: Harvard University Press, 1968), 2; Frank Dikotter, *The Discourse of Race in Modern China* (Stanford, CA: Stanford University Press, 1992); W. G. Beasley, *Japan Encounters the Barbarian: Japanese Travellers in America and Europe* (New Haven, CT, and London: Yale University Press, 1995). Also more generally Catherine H. Berndt and Ronald M. Berndt, *The Barbarians, an Anthropological View* (London: Pelican Books, 1973), chapter 2, 'Barbarians and Savages'.

25 From the Old French *sauvage* and Latin *silvaticus* 'belonging to a wood'.

26 Keith Thomas, *Man and the Natural World* (New York: Pantheon, 1983), 134. More generally on this theme see Richard Bernheimer, *Wild Men in the Middle Ages: A Study in Art, Sentiment and Demonology* (Cambridge, MA: Harvard University Press, 1978).

27 Cocker, *Rivers*, 13. See Richard Stotkin, *Regeneration through Violence, the Myth of the American Frontier, 1600–1860* (Middletown, CT: Wesleyan University Press, 1973), esp. chapter 2, 'Cannibals and Christians: European versus American Indian Culture', for considerable development of this theme.

28 Quoted in Wilbur R. Jacobs, 'The Fatal Confrontation: Early Native–White Relations on the Frontiers of Australia, New Guinea and America – a Comparative Study', *Pacific Historical Review*, 40 (1971), 300.

29 Quoted in Alan Moorhead, *The Fatal Impact, an Account of the Invasion of the South Pacific 1767–1840* (London: Penguin Books, 1968), 150.

30 Ibid., 105–6. Also Lyndall Ryan, *The Aboriginal Tasmanians* (Sydney: Allen and Unwin, 2nd edn, 1996 [first published 1981]), chapter 2, 'European Visitors 1642–1802', for further narratives of European 'native' observation, more specifically in Van Dieman's Land.

31 Pagden, *Fall*, 98–9, and more generally chapter 4, 'From Nature's Slaves to Nature's Children'.

32 See Karen Ordahl Kupperman, *Indians and English, Facing Off in Early America* (Ithaca, NY, and London: Cornell University Press, 2000), 2. More generally see Bernard W. Sheehan, *Seeds of Extinction, Jeffersonian Philanthropy and the American*

Indian (Chapel Hill: University of North Carolina Press, 1973), chapter 1, 'Environmentalism'.

33 Berndt and Berndt, *Barbarians*, 45. For some of the potential directions these 'exotic' constructions could take in the European mind, see Claude Rawson, *God, Gulliver and Genocide, Barbarism and the European Imagination, 1492–1945* (Oxford: Oxford University Press, 2001), esp. chapter 2, 'The Savage with Hanging Breasts: Gulliver, Female Yahoos and Racism'.

34 E. B. Tylor, *Primitive Cultures* (New York: Harper and Bros, 1958 [first published 1871]), for the classic rendition of the argument; George W. Stocking, Jr., *Victorian Anthropology* (New York: Free Press, 1987), chapter 6, 'Victorian Cultural Ideology and the Image of Savagery (1780–1870)', for commentary.

35 Quoted in Moses, 'Antipodean Genocide', 94. See also the almost identical comment by Reb. Braim, the early Anglican clergyman of Hobart, quoted in Jacobs, 'Fatal Confrontation', 299.

36 Berndt and Berndt, *Barbarians*, 20.

37 See William Cronon, *Changes in the Land: Indians, Colonists and the Ecology of New England* (New York: Hill and Wang, 1983), 56–7 and 77–9 for commentary on Locke's 1690 *Two Treatises on Government*. On Locke, see also Sheehan, *Seeds*, 26–7.

38 The view of one Australian pioneer quoted in Jacobs, 'Fatal Confrontation', 297.

39 Jennings, *Invasion*, 71.

40 James Wilson, *The Earth Shall Weep: A History of Native America* (London: Picador, 1998), 49.

41 Colin G. Calloway, *The American Revolution in Indian Country, Crisis and Diversity in Native American Communities* (Cambridge: Cambridge University Press, 1995), 55.

42 Stannard, *American Holocaust*, 234–5; Jennings, *Invasion*, 82, 135–6, who nevertheless notes the problems and contradictions of this early usage. See also Richard Tuck, *The Rights of War and Peace, Political Thought and the International Order from Grotius to Kant* (Oxford and New York: Oxford University Press, 1999), 47–50, for the humanist origins of this legal concept.

43 Bodley, *Victims*, 63–4. Also see R. H. W. Reece, *Aborigines and Colonists, Aborigines and Colonial Society in New South Wales in the 1830s and 1840s* (Sydney: Sydney University Press, 1974), 168–9.

44 See J. Lewis Hanke, *All Mankind is One: A Study of the Disputation between Bartholomemé de Las Casas and Juan Ginés de Sepúlveda in 1550 on the Intellectual and Religious Capacity of American Indians* (Dekalb: Illinois University Press, 1974), for more on this debate. Also Todorov, *Conquest*, 'Equality of Inequality', for sharp commentary.

45 See Pagden, *Fall*; 65–80; J. H. Parry, *The Spanish Seaborne Empire* (London: Penguin, 1973), chapter 7, 'Rights and Duties', esp. 125–7.

46 Quoted in Gregory H. Nobles, *American Frontiers, Cultural Encounters and Continental Conquest* (New York: Hill and Wang, 1997), 130. For the full text see

Theda Purdue and Michael D. Green, *The Cherokee Removal, a Brief History with Documents* (Boston and New York: St Martin's Press, 1995), 70–5.

47 Nobles, *American Frontiers*, 129.

48 See Anthony F. C. Wallace, *The Long Bitter Trail, Andrew Jackson and the Indians* (New York: Hill and Wang, 1993), chapter 4, 'The Trail of Tears', for a succinct summary.

49 Nobles, *American Frontiers*, 130. Robert V. Remini, *Andrew Jackson and his Indian Wars* (London: Penguin, 2001), chapter 13, 'Andrew Jackson versus the Cherokee Nation', for full details.

50 Bodley, *Victims*, 63–4.

51 See Sheehan, *Seeds*, for the full development and nemesis of this line of argument.

52 Quoted in Moses, 'Antipodean Genocide', 94.

53 Churchill, *Little Matter*, 245.

54 Wilson, *Earth*, chapter 10, 'Kill the Indian, Save the Man', for acute commentary.

55 Moses, 'Antipodean Genocide', 94.

56 See Reginald Horsman, *Expansion and American Indian Policy 1783-1812* (East Lansing: Michigan State University Press, 1967), chapter 4, 'The Aims of the New Government'.

57 William G. McLoughlin, *Cherokee Renascence in the New Republic* (Princeton, NJ: Princeton University Press, 1986), xix. McLouglin's is the most comprehensive and definitive study of the subject.

58 Ibid., 337–48, on black slaves; chapter 14, 'Politics and Economics', on the emerging Cherokee economic take-off.

59 Quoted in Jacobs, 'Fatal Confrontation', 306. In return the Cherokees' native Creek neighbours dubbed white Georgians as '"Ecunnaunuxulgee" – people greedily grasping after the lands of the red people'. See Calloway, *American Revolution*, 20.

60 Quoted in David Svaldi, *Sand Creek and the Rhetoric of Extermination, a Case Study in Indian–White Relations* (Lanham, MD: University Press of America, 1989), 84.

61 Gregory Evans Dowd, *A Spirited Resistance, the North American Indian Struggle for Unity, 1745–1815* (Baltimore and London: Johns Hopkins University Press, 1992), 120–1.

62 McLoughlin, *Cherokee Renascence*, chapter 19, 'Rebellion against the Constitution, 1827'.

63 see Svaldi, *Sand Creek*, 84–8.

64 See Armstrong Starkey, *European and Native American Warfare, 1675–1815* (Norman: University of Oklahoma Press, 1998), for Indian superiority in the conduct of frontier warfare.

65 Dowd, *Spirited Resistance*, xiii–xv.

66 Starkey, *Warfare*, 144–9. Churchill, *Little Matter*, 211–13, describes the American defeat on the Wabash, proportionate to the numbers of soldiery involved, as 'the worst loss the United States army has ever suffered'. See also Dowd, *Spirited*

Resistance, chapter 5, 'A Spirit of Unity'; Alvin M. Josephy, Jr., *Patriot Chiefs, a Chronicle of American Indian Resistance* (New York: Viking, 1958), the latter a useful, if romanticised compendium of key moments in Indian nativist resistance.

67 Dowd, *Spirited Resistance*, 118–20.

68 See, however, the excellent study by Henry Reynolds, *The Other Side of the Frontier, Aboriginal Resistance to the European Invasion of Australia* (London: Penguin, 1968).

69 Julie E. Carr, '"Cabin'd, Cribb'd and Confined": The White Woman of Gippsland and Bugalene', in Barbara Creed and Jeanette Hoorn, eds, *Body Trade: Captivity, Cannibalism and Colonialism in the Pacific* (New York and Annandale, NSW: Routledge and Pluto Press, 2001),167–79. Also Svaldi, *Sand Creek*, 45–57, for an interesting exploration of these tropes in historical literature especially with regard to Francis Parkman's classic 1915 work *The Conspiracy of Pontiac*.

70 See Frank Lestringant, *Cannibals, the Discovery and Representation of the Cannibal from Columbus to Jules Verne*, trans. Rosemary Morris (Cambridge: Cambridge University Press, 1997), for the increasingly negative Enlightenment version of the savage cannibal. See also the extended commentary in Rawson, *God*, 24–55; Creed and Hoorn, *Body Trade*, for eighteenth-century as well more recent discourses on this theme.

71 Calloway, *American Revolution*, 294–7, for the alleged Indian murder and scalping of Jane McCrea in 1777, which provided the nascent United States with its archetypal narrative of native savagery. However, as Starkey, *Warfare*, 30, points out, scalped victims sometimes survived to tell their tale while beheading proved a much more obvious atrocity committed by both sides in American warfare.

72 James Axtell and W. C. Sturtevant, 'The Unkindest Cut, or Who Invented Scalping?', *William and Mary Quarterly*, 3rd series, 37:3 (1980), 451–72, and Starkey, *Warfare*, 30–1, for attempts to adjudicate on the specific issue of scalping, plus Churchill, *Little Matter*, 178–88, for a rather convincing demonstration that atrocity of this kind escalated at the behest and practice of the invaders.

73 Geoffrey Plank, *An Unsettled Conquest, the British Campaign against the Peoples of Arcadia* (Philadelphia: University of Pennsylvania Press, 2001), 33–4.

74 Churchill, *Little Matter*, 177–8.

75 Svaldi, *Sand Creek*, 291.

76 Quotes from Stannard, *American Holocaust*, 120; Churchill, *Little Matter*, 150. Anthony F. C. Wallace, *Jefferson and the Indians, the Tragic Fate of the First Americans* (Cambridge, MA: Harvard University Press, 1999); Horsman, *Expansion*, chapter 7, 'The Ambivalence of Thomas Jefferson', for more on the yawning gap between Jefferson's humanitarian rhetoric and his presidential policy.

77 See Dowd, *Spirited Resistance*, throughout, for an exploration of the relationship between native messianic prophecy and the politics of resistance.

78 Stannard, *American Holocaust*, 114. Again see Slotkin, *Regeneration*, chapter 3, 'A Home in the Heart of Darkness: The Origin of the Indian War Narratives

(1625–1682)', for extended commentary on the nature of New England Puritan projection.

79 Quoted in Dee Brown, *Bury My Heart at Wounded Knee, an Indian History of the American West* (London: Vintage, 1991), 86–7.

80 Slotkin, *Regeneration*, 558.

81 see Svaldi, *Sand Creek*, 58–70, for a discussion of Samuel George Morton's 1839 *Crania Americana*. See also Reece, *Aborigines*, 85–94, for the British colonial turn to phrenology in the late 1830s to explain Australian aboriginal cultural and intellectual inferiority and deviance.

82 Svaldi, *Sand Creek*, 73, 62.

83 Barry Holstun Lopez, *Of Wolves and Men* (New York: Dent, 1978), and Peter Coates, '"Unusually Cunning, Vicious and Treacherous", the Extermination of the Wolf in United States History', in Mark Levene and Penny Roberts, eds, *The Massacre in History* (New York and Oxford: Berghahn Books, 1999), 163–83, for more on the perceived wolf–savage connections.

84 Jennings, *Invasion*, 146; Svaldi, *Sand Creek*, 'White Rhetoric and Native Americans', 328–35. More broadly, Roy Harvey Pearce, *Savagism and Civilisation: A Study of the Indian and the American Mind* (Baltimore: Johns Hopkins University Press, 1965); Slotkin, *Regeneration*.

85 Svaldi, *Sand Creek*, 188.

86 Quoted in Churchill, *Little Matter,* 151.

87 Peter Heather, 'The Huns and the End of the Roman Empire in Western Europe', *English Historical Review*, 110:435 (1995), 4–41, for further discussion of this theme.

88 Eric Christiansen, *The Northern Crusades, the Baltic and the Catholic Frontier 1100–1525* (London and Basingstoke: Macmillan, 1980), 73.

89 Richard Fletcher, *The Conversion of Europe, from Paganism to Christianity 371–1386 AD* (London: HarperCollins, 1997), for a thorough study of the subject.

90 Ibid., 487–8.

91 Christiansen, *Northern Crusades*, 34.

92 Ibid., 38.

93 Michael Burleigh, 'The Knights, Nationalists and the Historians: Images of Medieval Prussia from the Enlightenment to 1945', *European History Quarterly*, 17 (1987), 46–9.

94 See Fletcher, *Conversion*, 501–2, Bartlett, *Making*, 98–100, for further comment on the Livlandische Reimchronik.

95 Christiansen, *Northern Crusades*, 104.

96 Bartlett, *Making*, 297.

97 Ibid., 211.

98 See Michael Burleigh *Germany Turns Eastwards, a Study of Ostforschung in the Third Reich* (Cambridge: Cambridge University Press), 6; Anne Applebaum, *East to West, Across the Borderlands of Europe* (London and Basingstoke: Papermac, 1995), 16.

99 Burleigh, *Germany Turns*, 6.

100 Crosby, *Ecological Imperialism*, 79–103, for more on this whole episode.

101 Ibid., 80.

102 Ibid., 83.

103 See Parry, *Spanish*, 19.

104 Quoted in Crosby, *Ecological Imperialism*, 99.

105 The debate about whether the term genocide is applicable to the broad Austral-asian context has become intense. See Ann Curthoys and John Docker, 'Introduction, Genocide: Definitions Questions, Settler Colonies', *Aboriginal History*, 25 (2001), 1–15. See also the nine other widely divergent articles in this special issue appropriately entitled 'Genocide?: Australian Aboriginal History in International Perspective'. I am indebted to Dirk Moses (himself a contributor) for a copy of this edition. However, it is notable that while comparative genocide scholars assume the specifically Tasmanian case to be one of unmitigated geno-cide, the majority of Australian experts are considerably more circumspect. In the first category see, for instance, Leo Kuper, *Genocide: Its Political Use in the Twentieth Century* (New Haven, CT, and London: Yale University Press, 1981), 40; Helen Fein, 'Genocide: A Sociological Perspective', *Current Sociology*, 38:1 (1990), 11; compared with Ryan, *Aboriginal Tasmanians*, 3; Moses, 'Antipodean Genocide', 103, in the latter. In terms of historiography, these interpretations represent the median way between the very dark picture as initially painted in Clive Turnball, *Black War, the Extermination of the Tasmanian Aborigines* (Mel-bourne: Lansdowne Press, 1948), and the whitewash offered by Keith Windschuttle, *The Fabrication of Aboriginal History*, vol. 1: *Van Dieman's Land, 1803–1847* (Sydney: Macleay Press, 2002), now at the epicentre of an ongoing controversy sparked by his wider published denials or specific repudiations of set-tler violence against aborigines.

106 Ryan, *Aboriginal Tasmanians*, 58; John Connor, *The Australian Frontier Wars, 1788–1838* (Sydney: University of New South Wales Press, 2002), 24, 69, for wider British geo-strategic anxieties with regard to the Australian continent.

107 Ryan, *Aboriginal Tasmanians*, 73–81; Robert Hughes, *The Fatal Shore, a History of the Transportation of Convicts to Australia 1787–1868* (London: Collins Harvill 1987), chapter 11, 'To Plough Van Diemen's Land', for details.

108 Ryan, *Aboriginal Tasmanians*, 14.

109 Ibid., 51–7; Moorhead, *Fatal Impact*, 212.

110 Hughes, *Fatal Shore*, 415–17.

111 Cocker, *Rivers*, 138–9; Hughes, *Fatal Shore*, 415–16.

112 Ryan, *Aboriginal Tasmanians*, 83.

113 Hughes, *Fatal Shore*, 394.

114 Cocker, *Rivers*, 139.

115 Ibid., 144. See Reynolds, *Other Side*, 136–7, for further Australian instances where the accusation was made. More generally Ryan, *Aboriginal Tasmanians*, 92–7, for the strategic success of aboriginal attacks.

116 Hughes, *Fatal Shore*, 416.

117 Ibid., 417.

118 Moses, 'Antipodean Genocide', 98.

119 Moorhead, *Fatal Impact*, 212, quoting John Glover, artist's son and settler.

120 Hughes, *Fatal Shore*, 394, for more on O'Connor.

121 Connor, *Frontier Wars*, 93.

122 See Reece, *Aborigines*, chapter 2, 'Christianity and Civilisation'.

123 Hughes, *Fatal Shore*, 394–5.

124 Ibid., 420.

125 Connor, *Frontier Wars*, 93–101, for a full assessment.

126 Cocker, *Rivers*, 157; Ryan, *Aboriginal Tasmanians*, chapter 9, 'From Conciliator to Captor'.

127 That said, Ryan, *Aboriginal Tasmanians*, chapter 17, 'The Tasmanian Aborigines have Survived', makes a remarkably strong case for the emergence of the new mixed-race aboriginal community in the wake of the original community's extinction.

128 See Russell McGregor, *Imagined Destinies: Aboriginal Australians and the Doomed Race Theory, 1880–1939* (Melbourne: Melbourne University Press, 1997); Stocking, *Victorian Anthropology*, 'Epilogue: The Extinction of Palaeolithic Man'.

129 See Lynwood Carranco and Estle Beard, *Genocide and Vendetta, the Round Valley Wars of North California* (Norman: University of Oklahoma Press, 1981), 8–14, for the Yuki; Also Sherburne F. Cook, *The Conflict between the California Indians and White Civilisation* (Berkeley and Los Angeles: University of California Press, 1976), esp. 171–2.

130 Stannard, *American Holocaust*, 142.

131 Carranco and Beard, *Genocide,* 102–4. Much of the rest of this narrative is drawn from this source. For a good summary of the Yuki case study, largely, however, drawn from Carranco and Beard, see also Frank Chalk and Kurt Jonassohn, *The History and Sociology of Genocide* (New Haven, CT, and London: Yale University Press, 1990), 197–9.

132 Carranco and Beard, *Genocide*, 56.

133 Ibid., 75. Also Cook, *Conflict*, 289–94.

134 Carranco and Beard, *Genocide*, 84–91.

135 Ibid., 322.

136 Ibid., 92.

137 Ibid., 82.

138 Quoted in Churchill, *Little Matter*, 187–8.

139 Carranco and Beard, *Genocide*, 63, 160–1, including use of strychnine against grizzly bears too; Coates, 'Unusually Cunning', 171; Hughes, *Fatal Shore,* 417.

140 Carranco and Beard, *Genocide*, 114.

141 Ibid., 90, 92–3. The issue of the $40,000 worth of damage to Hastings' property in the form of stock, which the Indians had allegedly caused, was itself a com-

plete lie as his *total* stock in the area was only estimated at $32,000. For the O'Connor parallels see Hughes, *Fatal Shore*, 418.

142 Carranco and Beard, *Genocide*, 97.

143 Ibid., 126.

144 Ibid.,127–42; Wilson, *Earth*, 228–37. More generally, see Cook, *Conflict*, part 3, 'The American Invasion, 1848–1870'.

145 Carranco and Beard, *Genocide*, 138.

146 Patricia M. Limerick, *The Legacy of Conquest, the Unbroken Past of the American West* (New York and London: W.W. Norton and Co., 1981), 260–2; Stannard, *American Holocaust*, 144–5.

147 Carranco and Beard, *Genocide*, 141.

148 Bodley, *Victims*, 40.

149 Carranco and Beard, *Genocide*, 138.

150 Linda Colley, *Britons, Forging the Nation 1707–1837* (London: Pimlico, 1994), for the classic work on this theme.

151 Jennings, *Invasion*, 7.

152 See Rawson, *God*, 81. A notable example, for instance, with interests in both Irish and Virginia 'plantations' was Francis Bacon. See Anthony McFarlane, *The British in the Americas, 1480–1815* (London and New York: Longman, 1994), 34, n. 29.

153 Nicholas Canny, *Making Ireland British, 1580–1650* (Oxford: Oxford University Press, 2001), 48. See additionally Andrew Hadfield, 'Briton and Scythian: Tudor Representations of Irish Origins', *Irish Historical Studies*, 28 (1993), 390–408, and also Hartog, *Mirror*, 3–19, for the Herodotian origins of the Scythians as archetypal 'other'. Paradoxically, many Scottish Highland emigrants to Australia in the nineteenth century appear to have treated the aborigines as Scythians, though in some cases, with an admirable twist that the Scythians were a 'great race'. See Don Watson, *Caledonia Australis: Scottish Highlanders on the Frontier of Australia* (Sydney: Collins, 1984), 94.

154 Quoted in Peter Berresford Ellis, *Hell or Connaught! The Cromwellian Colonisation of Ireland 1652–1660* (London: Hamish Hamilton, 1975), 127.

155 Tremayne, 'Notes on Ireland 1571', quoted in Nicholas P. Canny, 'The Ideology of English Colonization: From Ireland to America', *William and Mary Quarterly*, 30 (1973), 584.

156 Rawson, *God*, 80, and idem., *Order from Confusion Sprung. Studies in Eighteenth Century Literature from Swift to Cowper* (London: Allen and Unwin 1985); 130–2, 141–3, for Elizabethan commentaries on Irish cannibalism.

157 Canny, 'Ideology', 588.

158 See Bruce Lenman, *England's Colonial Wars, 1550–1688* (London: Pearson, 2001), 1–2.

159 See Canny, *Making Ireland*, 23.

160 Canny, 'Ideology', 587–8.

161 Canny, *Making Ireland*, 43, considers Spenser the undoubted author of the 1596 text. Rawson, *God*, 232–3, also takes this as a given. A distinctly minority but interesting opinion, however, is offered by Lenman, *England's Colonial Wars*, 118–20, who disputes the attribution to Spenser, favouring Sir Walter Raleigh, the much more obviously violent and predatory Irish and American plantation *entrepreneur*, as the likely culprit.

162 See Canny, *Making Ireland*, chapter 1, 'Spenser Sets the Agenda'.

163 Rawson, *God*, 232–3; Canny, *Making Ireland*, 50–1.

164 Canny, 'Ideology', 579.

165 See Eric Richards, *The Highland Clearances, People, Landlords and Rural Turmoil* (Edinburgh: Birlinn, 2000), esp. 312–13, for confirmation on this point of issue.

166 See on this score Richard L. Rubenstein, *The Age of Triage: Fear and Hope in an Overcrowded World* (Boston: Beacon Press, 1983), esp. 34–59, 120–7, and a shorter rendition of the same argument in 'Afterword: Genocide and Civilisation', in Walliman and Dobkowski, *Genocide*, 284–98. Rubenstein's thesis is that the relationship between genocide and modernity can be traced back to the new economic relationships arising out the English enclosure movement and the displacement of a hence superfluous peasantry overseas to new colonial habitats including Ireland and Australia. Rubenstein's thesis, not least the way he builds population and land pressures into the framework, is an interesting and cogent piece of lateral thinking. But while Rubenstein provides important insights into some of the preconditions for genocidal processes in the modern world, the argument is insufficient to explain the dynamics of genocide *per se*.

167 See, for instance, Canny, *Making Ireland*, 165, where he notes that Spanish intervention on behalf of the Munster uprising of 1598 brought home to Queen Elizabeth and her advisors the real possibility 'that England's interest in Ireland would be obliterated, and that Ireland would become a satellite jurisdiction of the Spanish monarchy'.

168 Ibid., chapter 8, 'The Irish Insurrection of 1641', for the most comprehensive and incisive analysis.

169 See Robin Clifton, '"An Indiscriminate Blackness"? Massacre, Counter-Massacre and Ethnic Cleansing in Ireland, 1640–1660', in Levene and Roberts, *Massacre*, 109–14.

170 See James Scott Wheeler, *Cromwell in Ireland* (Dublin: Gill and Macmillan, 1999), 83–8, 94–100.

171 Ibid., 6. Wheeler here refers to the mortality figures estimated by the English army's physician general in Ireland, Dr William Petty, who asserted that 616,000 Irish out of a population of not quite 1.5 million perished from sword, plague, famine, hardships and deportation from 1641 to 1652. Other authors including Ellis, *Hell*, 9, 25–6, and more recently Ian Gentles, *The New Model Army in England, Ireland and Scotland 1645–1653* (Oxford: Oxford University Press, 1992), 353–4, 357–64; and Charles Carlton, *Going to the Wars: The Experi-*

ence of the British Civil Wars 1638–51 (London: Routledge, 1952), 241, n. 3, offer these or very similar figures.

172 John Brewer, *The Sinews of Power, War, Money and the English State 1688–1783* (London: Unwin Hyman, 1989), 47.

173 Gentles, *New Model Army*, 353–4.

174 Wheeler, *Cromwell*, 213.

175 Ibid., 5. Coote's landowning and manufacturing interests were in Connacht, Ulster and Leinster. Other notably exterminatory commanders, Roger Boyle, Baron Broghill and Sir Hardress Waller all had substantial Munster interests to recover and secure. In a slightly different vein was Morrogh O'Brien, the first Earl of Inchiquin, of part-Gaelic ancestry. Inchiquin, who fought on different sides throughout the wars from 1642 is reported, however, always to have put his own interests first. See also Canny, *Making Ireland*, 172.

176 Ellis, *Hell*, 25–7

177 Lemkin, *Axis Rule*, 79. See also Volume I, *The Meaning of Genocide*, Chapter 1, 43–4.

178 Ellis, *Hell*, 50–1

179 Ibid., 210–18 for Petty's critical role. Karl S. Bottigheimer, *English Money and Irish Land: The 'Adventurers' in the Cromwellian Settlement of Ireland* (Oxford: Oxford University Press, 1971), for a full analysis.

180 Wheeler, *Cromwell*, 229–30, notes that whereas Catholics owned some 59 per cent of Irish lands in 1641 (some 11 million out of 20 million acres) this had fallen to 22 per cent by 1660.

181 Ellis, *Hell*, chapter 1, 'The Settlement', for a broad analysis.

182 See Jeremy Black, *Culloden and the '45* (London: St Martin's Press, 1997), for a recent account.

183 Allan I. Macinnes, 'Slaughter under Trust: Clan Massacres and British State Formation', in Levene and Roberts, *The Massacre in History*, 144.

184 John Prebble, *Culloden* (London: Penguin, 1967), for a full assessment of the battle-massacre.

185 See Bruce Lenman, *The Jacobite Risings in Britain 1689–1746* (London: Eyre Methuen, 1980), 'The Aftermath of the '45'.

186 Colley, *Britons*, 123, who also notes that the 300 per cent growth rate compares rather favourably with England's 200 per cent in the same period.

187 See Simon James, *The Atlantic Celts: Ancient People or Modern Invention?* (London: British Museum Press, 1999), 48–9; Hugh Trevor-Roper, 'The Invention of Tradition: The Highland Tradition of Scotland', in Eric Hobsbawm and Terence Ranger, eds, *The Invention of Tradition* (Cambridge: Cambridge University Press, 1983), 15–41.

188 Starkey, *Warfare*, 49.

189 Nobles, *American Frontiers*, 103–4.

190 For the specific role of the Scots-Irish, most infamously in the 1763 extermination by the so-called 'Paxton Boys' of the entirely pacific Christianised Conestoga

Indians of Lancaster County, see Kevin Kenny, *The American Irish, a History* (Harlow: Longman, 2000), 37–8, and more broadly Richard White, *The Middle Ground, Indians, Empires and Republics in the Great Lakes Region, 1650–1815* (Cambridge: Cambridge University Press, 1991), 340–1. The Paxton Boys seem to have been particular purveyors of the proposition that the only good Indian is a dead one. For partial Australian parallels see Watson, *Caledonia Australis*, esp. 165–7, where Watson describes the Warrigal Creek massacre of some one hundred to 150 of the Brautauolong people of the Gippsland region of south-east Australia – itself reputedly one of the largest single massacres in Australian frontier history – as 'certainly a very Scottish affair' perpetrated by a self-styled 'Highland brigade'.

191 Calloway, *American Revolution*, 20.
192 Stannard, *American Holocaust*, 102–7.
193 Jennings, *Invasion*, 212–13.

2 Anglo Consolidation in the Americas and Antipodes

1 J. H. Kennedy, *Jesuit and Savage in New France* (Hamden, CT: Archon Books, 1970); Dowd, *Spirited Resistance* has repeated references to the eighteenth-century missions of the Moravian Brethren, particularly the seminal role of the Rev. David Zeisberger.

2 See, for example, John Demos, *The Unredeemed Captive, a Family Story from Early America* (New York: Alfred A. Knopf, 1994).

3 Quoted in Jennings, *Invasion*, 75. For more on Hakluyt's observations on the Eastern seaboard Indians see Kupperman, *Indians*, esp. 47–51.

4 White, *Middle Ground*.

5 See Francis Jennings, *The Ambiguous Iroquois Empire: The Covenant Chain Confederation of Indian Tribes with the New England Colonies* (New York: W.W. Norton, 1984). Also Robert A. Goldstein, *French–Iroquois Diplomatic and Military Relations 1609–1701* (The Hague: Mouton, 1969).

6 White, *Middle Ground*, 150–1; Cronon, *Changes*, 97–107, for the wider, including ecological impact.

7 See George T. Hunt, *The Wars of the Iroquois: A Study in Intertribal Trade Relations* (Madison: University of Wisconsin Press, 1940), esp. 66–87. Jeffrey P. Blick, 'The Iroquois Practice of Genocidal Warfare', *Journal of Genocide Research*, 3:3 (2001), 405–29, for a more recent assessment. Also Starkey, *Warfare*, 20–3.

8 White, *Middle Ground*, chapter 1, 'Refugees: A World Made of Fragments'.

9 Ibid., 41.

10 See Charles J. Balesi, *The Time of the French at the Heart of North America, 1673–1818* (Chicago: Alliance Française Chicago, 1992), chapter 9, 'The Fox Wars', chapter 10, 'The Chickasaw Wars'.

11 See Jennings, *Invasion*, chapter 13, 'We Must Burn Them', and Russell Bourne, *The Red King's Rebellion, Racial Politics in New England 1675–76* (New York: Oxford University Press, 1990), chapter 2, 'The Battle that Shaped New England's Mind: The Pequot War of 1637', for blow-by-blow accounts of the Pequot war.

12 Jennings, *Invasion*, 151–2; Kupperman, *Indians*, 223.

13 Kupperman, *Indians*, 235–9; Jennings, *Invasion*, chapter 17, 'Outrageous, Bloody and Barbarous', on English fears throughout the eastern seaboard of a general Indian uprising against *all* the colonies.

14 Quoted in Churchill, *Little Matter*, 177.

15 Bourne, *Red King's Rebellion*, 36; James D. Drake, *King Philip's War: Civil War in New England 1675–76* (Amherst: University of Massachusetts Press, 1999), 1–4; Starkey, *Warfare*, 80–8, for different assessments of casualty figures and the extent of the Indian catastrophe. Also Wilson, *Earth*, 74–7, on the preceding epidemiological devastation.

16 See Drake, *King Philip's War*, esp. 14, for a provocative thesis on this score, characterising the war as a 'civil war' in an ethnically mixed yet discrete region.

17 See for instance, Thomas Dunlay, *Wolves for the Blue Soldiers: Indian Scouts and Auxiliaries with the US Army* (Lincoln, NB, and London: University of Nebraska Press, 1982).

18 Mary Mackay, 'Captors or Captives? The Australian Native Mounted Police', in Creed and Hoorn, *Body Trade*, 47–65 for the physical and psychological impact of engagement on the participants themselves. Also Reynolds, *Other Side*, 103–4; Moses, 'Antipodean Genocide', 99–103.

19 David McDowall, *A Modern History of the Kurds* (London: I.B. Tauris, 1997), 354–7.

20 Francis Parkman, *History of the Conspiracy of Pontiac* (New York: Book League of America, 1929); Wilbur R. Jacobs, 'Pontiac's War – a Conspiracy?' in idem., *Dispossessing the American Indian, Indians and Whites on the Colonial Frontier* (Norman and London: University of Oklahoma, 1985), 83–93, for commentary.

21 Moses, 'Antipodean Genocide', 103. More recently, Henry Reynolds, *An Indelible Stain? The Question of Genocide in Australian History* (Ringwood: Viking, 2001), 130, also supports this analysis

22 See Kupperman, *Indians*, chapters 6 and 7, 'Incorporating the Other', and 'Resisting the Other', for background and analysis.

23 Jennings, *Invasion*, 80; Svaldi, *Sand Creek*, 2–3.

24 Churchill, *Little Matter*, 165–7.

25 S. F. Cook, *The Indian Population of New England in the Seventeenth Century* (Berkeley: University of California Press, 1976), for a concise overview of tribes and their demise.

26 Churchill, *Little Matter*, 200–1; Remini, *Andrew Jackson*, 10–20.

27 J. Leitch Wright, Jr., *Creeks and Seminoles, the Destruction and Regeneration of the Muscogulge People* (Lincoln, NB, and London: University of Nebraska Press,

1986), for a key study of new identity formation out of the fragments of exterminated peoples.

28 See Cronon, *Changes*, 76–9.

29 See McFarlane, *British*, 108–11, 115–19, for wider relationships between settlement and overseas trade.

30 Fred Anderson, *Crucible of War, the Seven Years' War and the Fate of Empire in British North America* (New York: Alfred A. Knopf, 2000), 503–6.

31 Ibid., 566–71; John Oliphant, *Peace and War on the Anglo-Cherokee Frontier, 1756–63* (Basingstoke: Palgrave, 2001), for slightly different interpretations on the degree to which the British were bounced into the Proclamation by Indian resistance. See also Jacobs, *Dispossessing*, chapter 9, '1763 – Year of Decision on the Indian Frontier'.

32 Elizabeth A. Fenn, 'Biological Warfare in Eighteenth Century America', *Journal of American History*, 86:4 (2000), 1554–8; Churchill, *Little Matter*, 154.

33 See for instance, Crosby, *Ecological Imperialism*, chapter 10, 'New Zealand'; Grant Morris, 'The Final Legal Frontier: The Treaty of Waitangi and the Creation of Legal Boundaries between Maori and Pakeha in New Zealand Society', in Lynette Russell, ed., *Colonial Frontiers: Indigenous-European Encounters in Settler Societies* (Manchester and New York: Manchester University Press, 2001), 119–33.

34 James Belich, *The New Zealand Wars and the Victorian Interpretation of Racial Conflict* (Auckland: Auckland University Press, 1986), esp. chapter 14, 'The Maori Achievement' and 300–25. Belich (291), significantly ranks the Maori military achievement as at least on a par with that of Shamil and Abd el-Kader. See Part III below, 'Empires in Advance: Empires in Retreat'.

35 McFarlane, *British*, 296–301.

36 Reece, *Aborigines*, 130–3.

37 Ibid., chapter 4, 'The Myall Creek Trials'.

38 Quoted in Moses, 'Antipodean Genocide', 101. See also Luke Goodwin, 'The Fluid Frontier: Central Queensland, 1845–63', in Russell, *Colonial Frontiers*, 114–16.

39 Barta, 'Relations', 245.

40 See Lyndall Ryan, 'Waterloo Creek Northern New South Wales, 1838', in Attwood and Foster, *Frontier Conflict*, 33–43, for careful assessment – in the light of different historical interpretations – as to what really happened at the Creek and the casualties resulting. See also Reece, *Aborigines*, 32–4; Connor, *Frontier Wars*, 105–12.

41 Connor, *Frontier Wars*, 113.

42 Goodwin, 'Fluid Frontier', 116.

43 See D. J. Mulvaney, 'Barrow Creek Northern Australia, 1874', in Attwood and Foster, *Frontier Conflict*, 44–51, for a good example of this double-think in operation, an aboriginal attack on a telegraph station which left two postal workers dead, leading to barely euphemistic newspaper calls for lethal retribution and the

chief commissioner of police for South Australia swearing in special constables for a raid in which 'a too close adherence to legal forms should not be insisted on' (46). How many aborigines were killed in this prolonged punitive expedition is a subject of speculation but no prisoners were taken. See also Raymond Evans, 'Across the Queensland Frontier', 66–7, ibid., on the gap between what was known and publicly articulated and what was officially suppressed as juridical evidence.

44 Henry Reynolds, The Written Record', in Attwood and Foster, *Frontier Conflict*, 79.

45 Evans, 'Across', 74–5, n. 25, for discussion of aboriginal numbers.

46 Connor, *Frontier Wars*, 55.

47 Moses, 'Antipodean Genocide', 96.

48 Ibid.; Evans, 'Across', 69.

49 Reynolds, *Other Side*, 70–2.

50 Ibid., 86.

51 Ibid. 84–5. Notes Alison Palmer, *Colonial Genocide* (Adelaide: Crawford House Publishing, 2000), 46–7: 'Historical records suggest that the killing of aborigines was particularly prevalent at the frontiers, the new areas of occupation'.

52 *Queenslander*, 15 February 1879, quoted in Reynolds, *Other Side*, 111.

53 Reynolds, *Other Side*, 111. Also 121, for estimates of white casualties. See additionally, Raymond Evans, Kay Saunders and Kathryn Cronin, *Exclusion, Exploitation and Extermination*: *Race Relations in Colonial Queensland* (Sydney: Australia and New Zealand Book Company, 1975), chapters 2 and 3, 'The Blood-Dimmed Tide: Frontier Violence and Aboriginal Resistance', and 'Musketry and Terror', for many Queensland examples of aboriginal resistance and counter-attack.

54 Reynolds, *Other Side*, 122.

55 Cocker, *Rivers*, 177–8. For instance, it might be noted that the collapse of the 750,000-strong aboriginal population of c.1780 to around 60,000 in 1920, was primarily the result of smallpox, measles and influenza. See Attwood and Foster, 'Introduction', 5.

56 Evans et al. *Exclusion*, 49–50. Evans notes that such examples of poisoning in North Queensland, were 'commonplace'.

57 Palmer, *Colonial Genocide*, 43.

58 See Barta, 'Relations', 244–5; Connor, *Frontier Wars*, 58–61. The resulting Bells Fall Massacre has been central to controversies surrounding Windschuttle's claims that such events were 'mythological'. See Keith Windschuttle 'Doctored Evidence and Invented Incidents in Aboriginal Historiography', 108–9; Tom Griffiths, 'The Language of Conflict', 142–3, and David Andrew Roberts, 'The Bells Falls Massacre and Oral Tradition', 150–7, all in Attwood and Foster, *Frontier Conflict*.

59 Palmer, *Colonial Genocide*, 57.

60 Reece, *Aborigines*, 168–9; Connor, *Frontier Wars*, 58.

61 See Alan Atkinson, 'Historians and Moral Disgust', in Attwood and Foster, *Frontier Conflict*, 115–19, for critical discussion.

62 Evans et al., *Exclusion*, 60. More generally, see his chapter 4, 'A Policy Tending towards Extermination'.

63 Palmer, *Colonial Genocide*, 48. Queensland is Palmer's key arena for a discussion of Australian genocide – see chapter 3, 'Queensland – a Case of Genocide'. In this focus Palmer mirrors Moses, 'Antipodean Genocide'.

64 Moses, 'Antipodean Genocide', 99–103. See also Mulvaney, 'Barrow Creek', 48–9, for the repeated lethal 'dispersal' over a twenty-year period of the southern Anmatyerre people, even though they appear to have no involvement in the Barrow Creek events; further suggesting that police revenge attacks in Northern Territory, as in Queensland, could be quite indiscriminate.

65 Evans, 'Across', 71, 64.

66 Evans et al., *Exclusion*, 75–8. See, however, Noel Loos, *Invasion and Resistance: Aboriginal-European Relations on the North Queensland Frontier 1861–1897* (Canberra: Australian National University Press, 1982), 190, who, basing his extrapolations on Corps punitive raids specifically in north Queensland estimates these figures to be far too conservative.

67 Palmer, *Colonial Genocide*, 51; Moses, 'Antipodean Genocide', 101.

68 Edward Kennedy, settler. Quoted in Evans, *Exclusion*, 65.

69 Connor, *Frontier Wars*, 119–21.

70 See Wilson, *Earth*, 112–13.

71 Palmer, *Colonial Genocide*, 8, 201.

72 Charles Heydon commentaries in the *Sydney Morning Herald*, here paraphrased from Evans, 'Across', 64–5.

73 See Heather Goodall, 'Authority under Challenge: Pikampul Land and Queen Victoria's Law during the British Invasion of Australia', in Martin Daunton and Rick Halpern, eds, *Empire and Others: British Encounters with Indigenous Peoples, 1600–1850* (London: UCL Press, 1999), 275.

74 Windschuttle, 'Doctored Evidence', 110.

75 See, for instance, Goodall, 'Authority', 260–79, on the 1840s Macintyre River district career of Richard Bligh, a commissioner for Crown lands.

76 See Jan Critchett, 'Encounters in the Western District', in Attwood and Foster, *Frontier Conflict*, 52–62, for an immaculate brief study of the dynamic of violence – its arrival, crescendo and diminution – at the local level.

77 Quoted in Starkey, *Warfare*, 114.

78 see McFarlane, *British*, chapter 9, 'Crisis of Empire', for background and commentary.

79 Calloway, *American Revolution*, 26.

80 Ibid., 294, 273; Dowd, *Spirited Resistance*, 85–7.

81 See Remini, *Andrew Jackson*, 14–17, for Jackson's personal and familial experience of this conflict. Also Starkey, *Warfare*, 135. On the loyalist side it is to be remembered that between 80,000 and 100,000 of them left the United States in

the wake of the revolution, mostly to Canada and the Caribbean. See McFarlane, *British*, 289.

82 Francis Jennings, *The Creation of America, Through Revolution to Empire* (Cambridge: Cambridge University Press, 2000), 210–12, for a valuable discussion of differences between British responses to the American revolution and Scottish Highlands insurrection.

83 Quoted in Calloway, *American Revolution*, 49.

84 Ibid., 297.

85 Ibid., 53.

86 See Wilson, *Earth*, 128–31; Starkey, *Warfare*, 124–5.

87 Calloway, *American Revolution*, xv.

88 Quoted in Wilson, *Earth*, 212.

89 See Jennings, *Creation*, for the argument of the nascent USA as a more aggressive clone of the Hanoverian empire.

90 Christopher Clark, 'How Did the United States Get so BIG?' (unpublished inaugural lecture, University of Warwick, 30 November 1999), 1.

91 Starkey, *Warfare*, 104.

92 Ibid., 155–6.

93 *The Wild West, the Way the American West was Lost and Won, 1845–1893* (London: Channel 4 Publications, 1995), 3.

94 David J. Wishart, *An Unspeakable Sadness, the Dispossession of the Nebraska Indians* (Lincoln, NB, and London: University of Nebraska Press, 1994), 187.

95 David Lavender, *The Penguin Book of the American West* (London: Penguin, 1965), 340–3, 348–50.

96 Wilson, *Earth*, 253.

97 Wishart, *Unspeakable Sadness*, 37, 48; Limerick, *Legacy*, 182;

98 Lavender, *American West*, 412; Robert M. Utley, *The Indian Frontier of the American West 1846–1890* (Albuquerque: University of New Mexico Press, 1984), 229.

99 *Wild West*, 22,

100 Daniel Pick, *War Machine, the Rationalisation of Slaughter in the Modern Age* (New Haven, CT, and London: Yale University Press, 1993),181–8.

101 *Wild West*, 3.

102 Remini, *Andrew Jackson,* chapter 1, 'The Making of an Indian Fighter', for the South Carolina roots of Jackson's anti-Indian antipathy.

103 Limerick, *Legacy*, 181–8, for more on Catlin.

104 Burger, *Report*, 39, quoting the Rev. Bishop Hale on Australia's aborigines.

105 See for instance, Bodley, *Progress*, 40, who notes the 85 per cent collapse in the population of Yokut and Wintun Indians as the consequence of a malarial epidemic introduced in the period 1830–3 by Hudson Bay Company trappers. The statistic equally translates into 75,000 deaths. If this was inadvertent, Churchill, *Little Matter,* 155, more pointedly reports the collapse of the Mandans from a population of some 2,000 to only fifty in the wake of a smallpox epidemic, fol-

lowing the June 1837 army provision at Fort Clark, North Dakota of blankets carrying the virus.

106 Watson, *Caledonia Australis*, 169.

107 Horsman, *Expansion*, 37.

108 See, for instance, Jennings, *Creation*, 280–5, for a suitably acerbic deconstruction of the meaning and long-term significance of the Ordinance.

109 Horsman, *Expansion*, 96.

110 Ibid., 102.

111 Remini, *Andrew Jackson*, 118–19.

112 Horsman, *Expansion*, 106.

113 Ibid., 112–13

114 Remini, *Andrew Jackson*, 180–2.

115 Horsman, *Expansion*, 6.

116 Wishart, *Unspeakable Sadness*, 1; Lavender, *American West*, 77–86, for more on the Lewis and Clark agenda.

117 Remini, *Andrew Jackson*, 16. Remini (vii), indeed, notes 'Americans during Jackson's lifetime tolerated and actively condoned removal'.

118 Wallace, *Long Bitter Trail*, 40.

119 See Joel W. Martin, *Sacred Revolt, the Muskogee's Struggle for a New World* (Boston: Beacon Press, 1991); Wright, *Creeks*, chapter 6, 'The Creek War, 1813–1815'.

120 Dowd, *Spirited Resistance*, 181, 187.

121 Ibid., 191–2; Wright, *Creeks*, chapter 9, 'The Defiant Muscogulges, 1835–42'.

122 Remini, *Andrew Jackson*, chapter 13, 'The Indian Removal Act'.

123 Sheehan, *Seeds*, chapter 9, 'Removal'.

124 Remini, *Andrew Jackson*, 280.

125 Ibid., 277. Overall, Remini (281), estimates that 81,000 Indians were relocated at US state behest in the period 1789–1839.

126 Ibid., 276. Wallace, *Long Bitter Trail*, 94, 99.

127 Different tribes caught up in the removal are estimated to have lost between 15 and 50 per cent of their number. See Russell Thornton, 'Cherokee Population Losses during the Trail of Tears: A New Perspective and a New Estimate', *Ethnohistory*, 31 (1984), 293. More generally Gloria Jahoda, *The Trail of Tears: The Story of the American Indian Removals, 1813–1855* (New York: Holt, Rinehart and Winston, 1975).

128 See Jane F. Lancaster, *Removal Aftershock, the Seminoles' Struggle for Survival in the West, 1836–1866* (Knoxville: University of Tennessee Press, 1994), for something of the impact.

129 Generally see Utley, *Indian Frontier*, 46, 133; Nobles, *American Frontiers*, 214–15; Wishart, *Unspeakable Sadness*, for a case study of the effects of the system on Pawnee and other Nebraska Indians.

130 Lavender, *American West*, 183.

131 Wishart, *Unspeakable Sadness*, esp. 118–24.

132 Nobles, *American Frontiers*, 217.

133 Ibid., 217.

134 Ibid., 218.

135 Churchill, *Little Matter*, 226.

136 Ibid., 227. Also Brown, *Bury*, 50–61, for Sibley and Ramsey's critical role in the origins of the insurrection, not least their massive defrauding of the Santees in the great bulk of ancestral lands purchased from them.

137 Brown, *Bury*, 65.

138 Utley, *Indian Frontier*, 83.

139 Lavender, *American West*, 378; Brown, *Bury*, 20.

140 Churchill, *Little Matter*, 227–8.

141 Brown, *Bury*, 14–36, for the whole episode. The Mescalero Apaches actually fled the reservation in November 1865. Through government commissions the surviving Navajos were given leave to return to their Canyon de Chelly homelands in 1868. See Utley, *Indian Frontier*, 83.

142 Svaldi, *Sand Creek*, 149–50.

143 Lavender, *American West*, 378.

144 Ibid., 381. Writing in the early 1960s – i.e. in pre-My Lai America – Lavender then claimed that 'controversy still rages over … motives and details' of an event that he describes as a battle. Lavender's is an extraordinary case of what today we would call 'going into denial'. See Churchill, *Little Matter*, 228–34; Stannard, *American Holocaust*, 132–3; Brown, *Bury*, 87–94, for the actual, gory details.

145 Churchill, *Little Matter*, 232–4.

146 Ibid., 235.

147 See James O. Gump, *The Dust Rose like Smoke: The Subjugation of the Zulu and the Sioux* (Lincoln, NB, and London: University of Nebraska Press, 1994), chapter 1, 'The Little Bighorn in Comparative Perspective'.

148 Robert M. Utley, 'Total War on the American Indian Frontier', in Manfred F. Boemeke, Roger Chickering and Stig Forster, *Anticipating Total War, the German and American Experiences, 1871–1914* (Washington, DC, and Cambridge: German Historical Institute and Cambridge University Press, 1999), 399.

149 Nobles, *American Frontiers*, 185.

150 Lavender, *American West*, 371.

151 Nobles, *American Frontiers*, 197–8. More generally, Lavender, *American West*, chapter 12, 'Clearing the Way, 1854–70', for the impact of road and railway development. Also Dowd, *Spirited Resistance*, 155, for a very comparable earlier Indian *casus belli*; the 1805 Treaty of Washington requiring the Creek to concede a federal 'horsepath' (sic.) – actually a twenty-foot wide road – across the heart of the Creek nation.

152 See Utley, *Indian Frontier*, 105, 123, 173, for examples of the rhetoric of extermination as a solution to the Indian problem from all three generals. Significantly, in his more recent essay, 'Total War', 399–400, Utley downplays this 'occasional rhetoric', arguing that it was never more than 'angry reactions to particular

events involving particular Indian groups' and certainly did not amount to an agenda.

153 Churchill, *Little Matter*, 240,

154 Cocker, *Rivers*, 220–1.

155 Richard Gott, 'Ploughing the Sea', review of Robert Harvey's *The Liberators*, *Guardian*, 7 May 2000.

156 Sven Lindqvist, *'Exterminate All the Brutes'*, trans. Joan Tate (London: Grant Books, 1998), 116; Alfredo M. Serres Güiraldes, *La estrategia del general Roca* (Buenos Aires: Editorial Pleamar, 1979), 168–80.

157 Moorhead, *Fatal Impact*, 213.

158 see Lindqvist, *Exterminate*, 116. Also Crosby, *Ecological Imperialism*, 301 on Argentinian population pressures.

159 Serres Güiraldes, *La estrategia*, chapter 4, 'La Araucanisation de la Pampa', and chapter 5, 'La Campana del General Roca'. Significantly, Serres Güiraldes' perspective on the campaign is one of an unadulterated Argentinian success story.

160 Bodley, *Progress*, 50

161 Utley, *Indian Frontier*, 133.

162 See Francis Paul Prucha, ed., *Americanising the American Indians, Writings by 'the Friends of the Indian', 1880–1900* (Lincoln, NB, and London: University of Nebraska Press, 1978).

163 See Limerick, *Legacy*, 195–200; Francis Paul Prucha, *The Dawes Act and the Allotment of Indian Lands*, ed. D. S. Otis, (Norman: University of Oklahoma Press, 1973 [first published 1934]).

164 Cocker, *Rivers*, 252–3. Significantly, Cocker (216), also notes that one reason for the draconian punishment of the Chiricahua Apache was because of the sheer cost in putting down the twenty-six-year resistance of Geronimo and other chiefs. Between 1862 and 1871 alone, $38 million was expended by the US army on its pacification campaign.

165 However, see Churchill, *Little Matter*, in which he argues that genocide does not halt with the closing of the frontier but should be understood as a continuum through to the present day. His view is based on a differing definition of genocide to that of this author, even though much of the tenor and substance of what is developed here owes a great deal to his work and that of like-minded advocates of the Indian and more general fourth-world cause. However, the point of issue, this author would hope, is not simply academic, and thus – as the quip goes – futile. At stake is how we seek to understand and put names to phenomena so that we can make sense of their meaning.

166 For more on these themes and issues, see especially Churchill, *Little Matter*, 'Cold War Impacts on Native North America'; Wilson, *Earth*, chapter 11, 'New Deal and Termination', and chapter 12, 'The New Indians'; Russell Thornton, *American Indian Holocaust and Survival: A Population History since 1492* (Norman: University of Oklahoma, 1987); Colin Tatz, *Aboriginals and Uranium and Other Essays*, (Melbourne: Heinemann, 1982); Heather Goodall, *Invasion to Embassy*,

Land in Aboriginal Politics in New South Wales, 1770–1972 (Sydney: Allen and Unwin, 1996); Bain Attwood, *Rights for Aborigines* (Sydney: Allen and Unwin, 2003). More generally, Burger, *Report*, chapter 10, 'Indigenous Peoples in Rich Countries'; James Wilson, 'The Original Americans: US Indians', *Minority Rights Group Report*, 31 (London: Minority Rights Group, 1976).

167 Brown, *Bury*, 416–45, for this final denouement.

3 The Vendée – A Paradigm Shift?

1 See Norman Davies, *Europe, a History* (London: Pimlico, 1997), 'Vendémiaire', 698, and appendix III, 1288, for the new French revolutionary calendar.

2 Peter Paret, *Internal War and Pacification; The Vendée 1789–1796*, Research Monograph, no. 12 (Princeton, NJ: Centre of International Studies, 1961), 49. See also Reynauld Secher, *Le Génocide franco-français, la Vendée-Vengé* (Paris: Presses Universitaires de France, 4th edn, 1992), 148–9, for the route of the retreat.

3 Davies, *Europe*, 705; Secher, *Le Génocide*, 150, for French original and details of the battle.

4 Secher, *Le Génocide*, 163.

5 Ibid., 170.

6 Ibid., 163–7.

7 See Michelet's retrospective accusations against Vendéan women, quoted in Claude Petitfrère, *La Vendée et les Vendéens* (Paris: Éditions Gallimard/Juillard, 1981), 74–5; Secher, *Le Génocide*, 172, for examples of specific atrocities against women.

8 See Secher, *Le Génocide*, 167–70.

9 Paret, *Internal War*, 558.

10 Ibid., 56.

11 D. M. G. Sutherland, *France 1789–1815, Revolution and Counter-Revolution* (London: Fontana Press, 1985), 221; Arno J. Mayer, *The Furies, Violence and Terror in the French and Russian Revolutions* (Princeton, NJ: Princeton University Press, 2000), 343, 352.

12 Mayer, *Furies*, 341; Jean-Joël Brégeon, *Carrier et la terreur nantaise* (Paris: Perrin, 1987), chapter 8, 'Les antichambres de la Mort', on the sanitary breakdown in Nantes, following from overflowing hospitals and prisons and leading to the creation of emergency burial pits.

13 Brégeon, *Carrier*, chapter 10, 'Les noyades'.

14 Lord James Bryce and Arnold Toynbee, eds, *The Treatment of Armenians in the Ottoman Empire: Documents Presented to Viscount Grey of Falloden*, Misc. No. 31, Command 8325 (London: His Majesty's Stationery Office, 1916), Testimony of Signor Gorrini, Italian Consul, Trebizond, 292–3.

15 Secher, *Le Génocide*, 152–3, recounting the witness Guillaume François Lahennec. That said, Brégeon, *Carrier*, 169–71, discounts both the sado-erotic stories

and stories of the mass drowning of children as counter-revolutionary propaganda and/or phantasmagoria.

16 Brégeon, *Carrier*, 284.

17 Secher, *Le Génocide*, 153. Brégeon, *Carrier*, 118, however, points out that there is no sound computation of how many died in this way. Estimates range from 1,800 to a more radical figure of 4,860 as carried by Secher.

18 Brégeon, *Carrier*, 284–85.

19 Patrice Higonnet, *Goodness Beyond Virtue* (Cambridge, MA, and London: Harvard University Press, 1998), 144.

20 Jean-Clément Martin and Xavier Lardière, *Le Massacre des Lucs, Vendée 1794* (Vouille: Geste, 1992), 33; Mayer, *Furies*, 336–7. For Irish parallels see above, Chapter 1.

21 See Simon Schama, *Citizens: A Chronicle of the French Revolution* (London: Viking, 1989), 789. The role of Madagascar, in Nazi and other state 'solutions', will be discussed in the next volume of this series.

22 Mayer, *Furies*, 337.

23 Quoted in Geoffrey Best, 'Introduction', in idem., ed., *Permanent Revolution, the French Revolution and its Legacy, 1789–1989* (London: Fontana, 1988), 14.

24 Mayer, *Furies*, 344–5.

25 Ibid., 346.

26 Secher, *Le Génocide*, 158 (quotation translated by M. Levene). See also the abridged version in Sutherland, *France*, 241.

27 Martin and Lardière, *Le Massacre*, 28.

28 Secher, *Le Génocide*, 158–9.

29 Martin and Lardière, *Le Massacre*, 31.

30 Sutherland, *France*, 241; Secher, *Le Génocide*, 159.

31 Mayer, *Furies*, 363.

32 Ibid.

33 Higonnet, *Virtue*, 52, interestingly uses the much-cited figure of 250,000 but without a source. The figure of 500,000 comes from Pierre Chaunu, the first person to charge genocide with regard to the Vendée in a *Le Croix* article, in June 1986, though in fairness to Chaunu his half a million figure, unsubstantiated as it may be, would seem to refer to all victims of the Jacobin massacres and terror *throughout* France. See his 'Avant-propos', in Secher, *Le Génocide*, 23.

34 Paret, *Internal War*, 68, quotes a contemporary source that he considers objective putting the figure at 159,000, which Paret himself has modified to c.130,000, thereby accounting for 15 per cent of the pre-revolutionary Vendéan population. Interestingly, the much more controversial thesis of Reynauld Secher, *Le Génocide*, 253, offers a minimum estimate which is smaller than Paret's, an overall computation of *not less* than 117,000 unnatural deaths (14.38 per cent) in the whole decade following 1792.

35 See Secher *Le Génocide*, section, 'Bilan'; Sutherland, *France*, 241.

36 See 'Genocides of the Early Modern Period', in Israel W. Charny, ed., *Encyclopedia of Genocide* (Santa Barbara and Denver, CO: ABC-Clio, 1999), vol. 1, 279.

37 See Steve Laurence Kaplan, *Farewell, Revolution, the Historians' Feud 1789/1989* (Ithaca, NY, and London: Cornell University Press, 1995), chapter 2, 'Credo and Crusade: Pierre Chaunu's Revised Revisionism', and also idem., *Disputed Legacies, the Historians' Feud 1789/1989* (Ithaca, NY, and London: Cornell University Press, 1995). *Disputed Legacies*, chapter 4, 'The Vendée Trope and Idée France', has a comprehensive review and assessment of the controversy. Also Douglas Johnson, 'The Twentieth Century: Recollection and Rejection', in Best, *Permanent Revolution*, 204–6.

38 Johnson, 'Twentieth Century', 232.

39 George Steiner, 'Aspects of Counter-Revolution', in Best, *Permanent Revolution*, 149.

40 Kaplan, *Disputed Legacies*, 93–5; François Crouzet, 'French Historians and Robespierre', in William Doyle and Colin Haydon, eds, *Robespierre* (Cambridge: Cambridge University Press, 1999), 268–70; Gwynne Lewis, *The French Revolution, Rethinking the Debate* (London: Routledge, 1993), 111.

41 See J. L. Talmon, *The Origins of Totalitarian Democracy* (London: Sphere, 1970). Also Kaplan, *Farewell, Revolution*, 42, for Chaunu's attempts to appropriate François Furet, the leading contemporary French historian of the revolution, in favour of this sort of linkage.

42 See William Doyle and Colin Haydon, 'Robespierre after Two Hundred Years', in idem., *Robespierre*, 6, on the role of the *Annales historiques de la Révolution française*, acting as the voice for the Societé des études robespierristes, founded by the trenchantly pro-Robespierrist scholar and Communist Party stalwart, Albert Mathiez. For an indication of his position – i.e. one in which Robespierre could do no wrong – see his *Robespierre, Terroriste* (Paris: La Renaissance du livre, 1921) and more recently George Rudé, *Robespierre, Portrait of a Revolutionary Democrat* (London: Collins, 1975).

43 Higonnet, *Goodness*, 328–32.

44 The essential argument of Mayer, *Furies*, and, of course, of many other historians who have sought to exculpate the revolution.

45 An argument which particularly runs through Higonnet, *Goodness*.

46 See Volume I, *The Meaning of Genocide*, Chapter 2, 101.

47 Michael Mann, *Sources of Social Power*, vol. 2: *The Rise of Classes and Nation-States, 1760–1914* (Cambridge: Cambridge University Press, 1993), 191.

48 Yves Ternon, *L'État criminel: Les génocides au XXe siècle* (Paris: Éditions du Seuil, 1995), 283–4. Also Martin and Lardière, *Massacre*, 31, for a similar line of argument.

49 Secher *Le Génocide*, 31.

50 See Charles Tilly, *The Vendée* (Cambridge, MA: Harvard University Press, 1964); Timothy Tackett, 'The West in France in 1789: The Religious Factors in the Origins of the Counter-Revolution', *Journal of Modern History*, 4 (1982), 715–45;

Claude Petitfrère, 'The Origins of the Civil War in the Vendée', in Peter Jones, ed., *The French Revolution in Social and Political Perspective* (London: Arnold, 1996), 339–58, for an excellent short summary.

51 Paret, *Internal War*, 67.

52 Schama, *Citizens*, 690–3, puts the figures at 500. Donald Greer, *The Incidence of the Terror During the French Revolution* (Cambridge, MA: Harvard University Press, 1935), 64, who has more carefully considered the range of revolutionary killings and counter-killings, puts the figure at between 300 and 400. See also Mayer, *Furies*, 335–6.

53 Greer, *Incidence*, esp. 38, 66–7.

54 Mayer, *Furies*, 367; Kaplan, *Disputed Legacies*, 97, for the views of François Lebrun and others.

55 Secher, *Le Génocide*, 156.

56 Sutherland, *France*, 219.

57 See Chaunu, 'Avant-propos', 23–4.

58 See for instance, Geoffrey Cubitt, 'Robespierre and Conspiracy Theories', in Doyle and Haydon, *Robespierre*, chapter 5; Sutherland, *France*, 250.

59 Sutherland, *France*, 242.

60 It was exactly this reality which led the great nineteenth-century historian of the revolution, Michlelet, to pronounce that the causes of the insurrection were 'enigmatic'. See Petitfrère, 'Origins', 341. However, also see Tilly, *Vendée*, chapter 7, 'Rustic Economics', who particularly notes that there was little gain for Vendéan peasants who were mostly leaseholders when the revolution heavily favoured land *ownership*, as well as Petitfrère, 'Origins', 350–1, who similarly points out that what the Vendée most sought was relief from taxation.

61 Secher, *Le Génocide*, 156.

62 Davies, *Europe*, 704.

63 See Jean-Clément Martin, *La Vendée de la mémoire, 1800–1980* (Paris: Éditions du Seuil, 1989).

64 See Johnson, 'Twentieth Century', 205–6.

65 Secher, *Le Génocide*, 24.

66 For instance, to apply the argument of Melson, *Revolution*, to the Vendée.

67 'Everything points to the fact that the mainspring of the Vendéan revolt was religious, and not social, or simply political'. François Furet, *The French Revolution, 1770–1814* (Oxford: Blackwell, 1992), 125.

68 This most significant of all issues of historical sociology carries with it a wealth of important literature. The critical writings on the subject, notably those of Max Weber and Karl Marx, have been mediated (or challenged) more recently through, amongst others: Anthony Giddens, *Capitalism and Modern Social Theory* (Cambridge: Cambridge University Press, 1971); Perry Anderson, *Passages from Antiquity to Feudalism* (London: New Left Books, 1974); Barrington Moore, Jr., *Social Origins of Dictatorship and Democracy* (London: Penguin, 1967); E. L. Jones, *The European Miracle, Environments, Economies and Geopolitics in the History of Europe*

and Asia (Cambridge: Cambridge University Press, 1981); John A. Hall, *Powers and Liberties, the Causes and Consequences of the Rise of the West* (Oxford: Blackwell, 1985); Mann, *Sources*; Kennedy, *Rise*, chapter 1, 'The Rise of the Western World'. See also most recently Kenneth Pomeranz, *The Great Divergence: Europe, China and the Making of the Modern World Economy* (Princeton, NJ: Princeton University Press, 2000).

69 See Peter Garnsey, 'Religious Toleration in Classical Antiquity', in W. J. Sheils, ed., *Persecution and Toleration, Studies in Church History 21* (Oxford: Blackwell, 1984), 1–28.

70 See Benjamin Braude and Bernard Lewis, eds, *Christians and Jews in the Ottoman Empire, the Functioning of a Plural Society*, 2 vols (New York and London: Holmes and Meier, 1982).

71 See Norman Cohn, *The Pursuit of the Millennium: Revolutionary Millenarians and Mystical Anarchists of the Middle Ages* (London: Paladin, 1970); Euan Cameron, *Waldensees, Rejections of Holy Church in Medieval Europe* (Oxford: Blackwell, 2000), for the broad sweep of medieval dissenting movements and their extirpation.

72 See Hall, *Powers*, chapter 5, 'The Role of Christian Europe', arguably, for the upside; R. I. Moore, *The Formation of a Persecuting Society: Power and Deviance in Western Europe, 950–1250* (Oxford: Blackwell, 1987), for the down.

73 W. H. C. Frend, *The Rise of Christianity* (Philadelphia: Fortress Press, 1984), chapter 13, 'Diocletian and the Great Persecution'; Stephen Williams, *Diocletian and the Roman Recovery* (London: B.T. Batsford Ltd, 1981), 182–3.

74 Fletcher, *Conversion*, 22–3, for a succinct statement of the new reality. More generally, see A. H. M. Jones, *Constantine and the Conversion of Europe* (Harmondsworth: Penguin, revised edn, 1972); Ramsay MacMullen, *Christianising the Roman Empire* (New Haven, CT, and London: Yale University Press, 1984); Frend, *Rise*, chapter 14, 'The Constantinian Revolution, 305–30'; Peter Brown, *The Rise of Western Christendom, Triumph and Diversity AD 200–1000* (Oxford and Malden, MA: Blackwell, 1996), chapter 2, 'Christianity and Empire'.

75 Hall, *Powers*, 123.

76 See Bartlett, *Making*, 220.

77 Kennedy, *Rise*, 25–32; Anthony Giddens, *The Nation-State and Violence* (Cambridge: Polity Press, 1985), 103–16; Charles Tilly, *Coercion, Capital and European States AD 990–1990* (Oxford: Blackwell, 1990), chapter 3, 'How War Made States and Vice Versa'.

78 See Peter Flora et al., eds, *State Formation, Nation-Building and Mass Politics in Europe, The Theory of Stein Rokkan* (Oxford: Oxford University Press, 1999), 144.

79 See Max Weber, *The Protestant Ethnic and the Spirit of Capitalism*, trans. Talcott Parsons (London: Routledge, 1992 [first published 1930]); R. H. Tawney, *Religion and the Rise of Capitalism: An Historical Study* (London: John Murray, 1926), for the classic English study.

80 There has been a recent explosion of popular books on the Cathars, rather suggesting a distinct contemporary appeal in their ideas. See Malcolm Lambert, *The Cathars* (Oxford: Blackwell, 1998); Malcolm Barber, *The Cathars, Dualist Heretics in Languedoc in the High Middle Ages* (Harlow: Longman, 2000), chapter 3, 'The Cathar Church', for clear and succinct historical accounts.

81 Moore, *Formation*, 151, notes, for instance, that 'the Cathar sects were *inflated* by commentators and inquisitors *into a vast and well-coordinated international organisation* with a culture, a theology and even a pope of its own. The promulgation of these *myths* justified and encouraged persecution' (my emphases).

82 Geoffrey Parker, *The Dutch Revolt* (Ithaca, NY, and New York: Cornell University Press, 1977), 178, describes the Sack, in which an estimated 8,000 were slaughtered, as a holocaust and 'one of the worst atrocities of the sixteenth century'.

83 See Henk van Nierop, 'The Nobles and the Revolt', in Graham Darby, ed., *The Origins and Development of the Dutch Revolt* (London and New York: Routledge, 2001), 48–66; Guido Marnef, 'The Dynamics of Reformed Religious Militancy: The Netherlands 1566–1585', and Henk van Nierop, 'The Nobles and the Revolt of the Netherlands: Between Church and King, and Protestantism and Provileges', both in Philip Benedict et al., eds, *Reformation, Revolt and Civil War in France and the Netherlands, 1555–1585* (Amsterdam: Royal Netherlands Academy of Arts and Science, 1999), 51–68, 83–98; and Pieter Geyl, *The Revolt of the Netherlands 1555–1609* (London: Benn, 1980 [first published 1958]), for the still classic study.

84 See Robert J. Knecht, *The French Civil Wars, 1562–1598* (Harlow: Longman, 2000), esp. 29–43; Jean-Marie Constant, 'The Protestant Nobility in France during the Wars of Religion: A Leaven of Innovation in a Traditional World', in Benedict, *Reformation*, 69–82, for the breadth of noble support for the Protestant cause in the provinces. Also Benedict's 'Introduction', 1–22, in the same volume, for comparisons and contrasts between the position of Huguenots and Beggars, and Natalie Zemon Davis, *Society and Culture in Early Modern France* (Stanford, CA: Stanford University Press, 1975), chapter 6, 'The Rites of Violence', for the sheer viciousness of atrocity in the French wars.

85 Barber, *Cathars*, 43–58.

86 John Martin Klassen, *The Nobility and the Making of the Hussite Revolution* (New York and Boulder, CO: East European Quarterly, 1978).

87 See Hans-Jürgen Goertz, *The Anabaptists* (London and New York: Routledge, 1996), esp. chapter 6, 'Heretics, Rebels and Martyrs', where the focus is on the Imperial Recess promulgated at the Diet of Speyer, 1529, which promulgated the death penalty for all Anabaptists.

88 H. Kaminsky, *A History of the Hussite Revolution* (Berkeley and Los Angeles: University of California Press, 1967), 366–83. Also Cohn, *Pursuit*, 205–22, and the older study by Frederick G, Heymann, *John Žižka and the Hussite Revolution* (Princeton, NJ: Princeton University Press, 1955).

89 I am indebted to Dr Henry Cohn, of Warwick University, for pointing out that the unvanquished Hussites went on the rampage in southern Germany, spreading terror.

90 Barber, *Cathars*, chapter 4, 'The Catholic Reaction'.

91 Ibid., 139; Lambert, *Cathars*, 136–41; Michael Costen, *The Cathars and the Albigensian Crusade* (Manchester: Manchester University Press, 1997), 150–60.

92 Geoffrey Parker, *The Grand Strategy of Philip II* (New Haven, CT, and London: Yale University Press, 1998), and idem., *Empire, War and Faith in Early Modern Europe* (London: Allen Lane, 2002), for the broad geo-strategic picture.

93 See Guenter Lewy, *The Nazi Persecution of the Gypsies* (Oxford and New York: Oxford University Press, 2000), 2. On broader Roma European migrations, Jean-Pierre Liegeois, *Gypsies, an Illustrated History* (London: Al Saqi Books, 1986), 38–47.

94 See Richard Fletcher, *Moorish Spain* (London: Phoenix Press, 2001), 134–44; Benjamin R. Gampel, 'Jews, Christians and Muslims in Medieval Iberia: *Convivencia* through the Eyes of Sephardi Jews', in Vivien B. Mann, Thomas F. Glick and Jerrilyn D. Dodds, eds, *Convivencia: Jews, Muslims and Christians in Medieval Spain* (New York: Braziller, 1992), 11–38, for cautious commentary on the strengths but also fragility of co-existence in Toledo and elsewhere in this period. Also Costen, *Cathars*, 34–51, for an emerging plural society in the Languedoc.

95 See Adam Zamoyski, *The Polish Way, a Thousand Year History of the Poles and their Culture* (London: John Murray, 1987), chapter 7, 'The Kingdom of Erasmus'; Norman Davies, *God's Playground: A History of Poland*, vol. 1: *The Origins to 1795* (Oxford: Clarendon Press, 1981), chapter 6, 'Antemurale, the Bulwark of Christendom'.

96 Anwar G. Chejne, *Islam and the West: The Moriscos, a Cultural and Social History* (Albany: State University of New York Press, 1983), 2–3.

97 Fletcher, *Conversion*, 323; Bartlett, *Making*, 179.

98 See Andreas Kappeler, *The Russian Empire: A Multiethnic History*, trans. Alfred Clayton (Harlow: Longman, 2001), 21–32. Kappeler cites a contemporary and official Russian chronicle of Kazan's capture which states: 'The tsar caused the women and little children to be taken prisoner, but all those who carried arms were put to death on account of their treason.' The two categories are themselves noteworthy. It would seem that the entire male population of the city of Kazan was put to death.

99 My former Warwick colleague, Dr Robin Okey refers me to a 1997 article by Mustafa Imamovic, in *Historija Bosnjaka* (Serbo-Croat), which argues that the c.1680 Habsburg takeover of the lands between the Danube, Sava and Drava led to the loss of the entire Muslim population c.115,000 people, or half of the total, either through forced conversion or flight.

100 See Steven T. Katz, *The Holocaust in Historical Context*, vol. 1: *The Holocaust and Mass Death before the Modern Age* (New York and Oxford: Oxford University Press, 1994), 111–16 and 573–5, for extensive bibliographies on the Jewish and

Morisco expulsions. Also Antonio Dominguez Ortiz and Bernard Vincent, *Historia de los moriscos, Vida y tragedia de una minoria* (Madrid: Biblioteca de la Revista de Occidente, 1978), 200, for careful assessments of the Morisco numbers killed and deported, which they estimate at 300,000.

101 Ortiz and Vincent, *Historia*, chapter 11, ' La diaspora morisca', for the dispersion and its effects.

102 See Andrew Hess, 'The Moriscos; An Ottoman Fifth Column in Sixteenth Century Spain', *American Historical Review*, 74 (1968), 1–25; Bruce Taylor, 'The Enemy Within and Without: An Anatomy of Fear on the Spanish Mediterranean Littoral', in William G. Naphy and Penny Roberts, eds, *Fear in Early Modern Society* (Manchester: Manchester University Press, 1997), 78–99, for slightly different emphases. Also Kamen, *Spain's Road*, 342–3, for the distinction between official policy and an often much more porous practice; especially in Spain's far-flung empire.

103 Chejne, *Islam*, 13.

104 See Ortiz and Vincent, *Historia*, chapter 10, 'Consecuencias economicas de la expulsion de los moriscos'.

105 Fletcher, *Conversion*, 323.

106 Chejne, *Islam*, 10; Ortiz and Vincent, *Historia*, 102–7, note the consequences in the rising number of Morisco cases coming before the Inquisition and those brought to *auto-da-fé*.

107 Katz, *Holocaust*, vol. 1, 572–7; Bartlett, *Making*, 241.

108 Fernand Braudel, *The Mediterranean and the Mediterranean World in the Age of Philip II*, trans. Sian Reynolds (London: Fontana/Collins, 1972), vol. 2, 791.

109 Ibid., vol. 2, 791–6: Ortiz and Vincent, *Historia*, chapter 8, 'Precedentes immediatos de la expulsion'.

110 John Edwards, *The Jews in Christian Europe, 1400–1700* (London and New York: Routledge, 1988), 34, though Henry Kamen, *The Spanish Inquisition, An Historical Revision* (London: Phoenix Giant, 1998), 23, disputes the actual figures, arguing that on the eve of expulsion there were no more than 80,000 Jews in Spain. Also Phillippe Wolf, 'The 1391 pogrom in Spain: Social Crisis or Not?' *Past and Present*, 50 (1971), 4–18, for analysis of the singularly countrywide 1391 massacres.

111 Claudine Fabre-Vassas, *The Singular Beast, Jews, Christians and the Pig*, trans. Carol Volk (New York: Columbia University Press, 1997), for a further exploration of this theme. Perhaps, significantly, Kamen, *Spanish Inquisition*, 10–11, n. 10, disputes this etymological foundation, proposing that a more likely origin lies in the notion of 'one who "mars" i.e. spoils the Christian faith'.

112 Kamen, *Spanish Inquisition*, chapter 3, 'The Coming of the Inquisition'; which is especially effective in scrutinising the degree to which the alleged Judaising 'danger' from *conversos* – leading to the 1480 creation of a full-time inquisition into the matter – was a consequence of administrative elite *perceptions*, not realities.

Also Henry Mechoulan, *El Honor de Dios, Indios, judios y moriscos en el Siglo de Oro* (Barcelona: Editorial Argos Vergara, S.A., 1981), 107–15.

113 Mechoulan, *El Honor*, 115–22; Kamen, *Spanish Inquisition*, 32–4. More broadly see Katz, *Holocaust*, vol. 1, 372–3, n. 244, for an extensive bibliography.

114 See Koppel S. Pinson, *Nationalism and History, Essays on Old and New Judaism*, ed., Simon Dubnow, (Cleveland and New York: Jewish Publication Society of America and Meridian Books, 1961), esp. Dubnow's 1898 essay, 'The Jew as a Spiritual (Cultural-Historical) Nationality in the Midst of Political Nations', 100–15; Yitzhak F. Baer, *Galut* (New York: Schocken Books, 1947); Abram Leon, *The Jewish Question, a Marxist Interpretation* (New York: Pathfinder Press, 1970), esp. chapter 3, for more on this line of thinking, the last in an albeit overtly materialist and hence controversial analysis based on the formulation of the Jews as a 'people-class'. More cautiously, the huge corpus of work by Salo Baron, including Leon A. Feldman, ed., *Ancient and Medieval Jewish History: Essays by Salo Wittmayer Baron* (New Brunswick, NJ: Rutgers University Press, 1972), chapter 8, 'The Jewish Factor in Medieval Jewish History', and chapter 11, 'Medieval Nationalism and Jewish Serfdom', also critically follows some of these contours.

115 Cecil Roth, 'The Jew as European', in idem., *Personalities and Events in Jewish History*, (Philadelphia: Jewish Publication Society of America; 1953), 30. I am indebted to Elisa Miles for this reference.

116 David Sorkin, 'The Port Jew: Notes toward a Social Type', *Journal of Jewish Studies*, 50:1 (Spring 1999), 87–97; David Cesarani, ed., *Port Jews, Jewish Communities in Cosmopolitan Maritime Trading Centres, 1550–1950* (London: Frank Cass, 2002).

117 Quoted in Frank Felsenstein, *Anti-Semitic Stereotypes: A Paradigm of Otherness in English Popular Culture, 1660–1830* (Baltimore and London: Johns Hopkins University Press, 1995), 14.

118 Ibid.,10.

119 Quoted in Katz, *Holocaust*, vol. 1, 259; Robert L. Wilken, *John Chrysostom and the Jews: Rhetoric and Reality in the late 4th Century* (Berkeley and Los Angeles: University of California Press, 1983), for Chrysostom's long-term influence on Christian anti-Judaic attitudes.

120 In this argument I closely follow the contours of the late Hyam Maccoby's thesis, expounded in *Revolution in Judaea, Jesus and the Jewish Resistance* (New York: Taplinger Publishing Co., 1980), and later works.

121 Mark R. Cohen, *Under Crescent and Cross, the Jews in the Middle Ages* (Princeton, NJ: Princeton University Press, 1994), 20–1, for the counterpoint between Chrysostom and Augustine on responses to the Jews. Also Katz, *Holocaust*, vol. 1, chapter 6, 'Medieval Antisemitism: The Process of Mythification', for a comprehensive analysis.

122 Moore, *Formation*, 150.

123 See Gavin Langmuir, *Towards a Definition of Antisemitism* (Berkeley and Los Angeles: University of California Press, 1990), 207–8, 333, for more on this compelling line of thought.

124 Moore, *Formation*, 151.

125 Langmuir, *Towards*, part 4, 'Irrational Fantasies', for details. Also Miri Rubin, *Gentile Tales, the Narrative Assault on Late Medieval Jewry* (New Haven, CT, and London: Yale University Press, 1999).

126 See Jonathan Riley-Smith, 'The First Crusade and the Persecution of the Jews', in Sheils, *Persecution*, 51–72; Kenneth R. Stow, *Alienated Minority, the Jews of Medieval Latin Europe* (Cambridge, MA, and London: Harvard University Press, 1992), chapter 5, 'The Crusades'; Robert Chazan, *European Jewry and the Third Crusade* (Berkeley and Los Angeles: University of California Press, 1987). See also Cohen, *Crescent and Cross*, chapter 10, 'Persecution, Response and Collective Memory', for the degree to which Christian Europe's irrational and demonising tendencies towards the Jews affected its treatment of them compared with the altogether more empirical, contemporary Islamic approach.

127 Katz, *Holocaust*, vol. 1, 263.

128 See Moore, *Formation*, 37. Also Allan Harris Cutler and Helen Elmquist Cutler, *The Jew as Ally of the Muslim: Medieval Roots of anti-Semitism* (Notre Dame, IN: University of Notre Dame Press, 1986), for the argument that it was perceptions of a Jewish ethno-religious alliance with external Muslim powers which was the primary catalyst to the medieval Western assault on its Jewry.

129 Joshua Trachtenberg, *The Devil and the Jews, the Medieval Conception of the Jew and its Relationship to Modern Anti-Semitism* (New York: Harper and Row, 1966); R. Po-chia Hsia, *The Myth of Ritual Murder, Jews and Magic in Reformation Germany* (New Haven, CT, and London: Yale University Press, 1988), 'Introduction, Ritual Magic and Murder', for full developments of this theme.

130 John Y. B. Hood, *Aquinas and the Jews* (Philadelphia: University of Pennsylvania Press, 1995), esp., 76, 108; Moore, *Formation*, 45–60, 91–4, for the growing representation – and persecution – of lepers and homosexuals as symbols of ultimate degradation. Also Nirenberg, *Communities*, chapter 2, 'France, Source of the Troubles: Shepherds Crusade and Lepers Plot (1320, 1321)', for a case study in which widespread rumours about a plot to poison Christendom linked Jews, lepers and a political Muslim conspiracy.

131 See Heiko A. Oberman, *The Roots of Anti-Semitism in the Age of Renaissance and Reformation* (Philadelphia: Fortress, 1984), part 3, 'Martin Luther: The Jews as Benefactors and Malefactors'; Martin Luther, 'Concerning the Jews and their Lies', in Jacob R. Marcus, ed., *The Jew in the Medieval World: A Source Book 315–1791* (Cincinnati: Sinai Press, 1938), 167–9.

132 See Katz, *Holocaust*, vol. 1, 373, n. 245; Kamen, *Spanish Inquisition*, esp. chapter 5, 'Excluding the Reformation'.

133 There is a wealth of literature on this subject for which, again, Katz, *Holocaust*, vol. 1, chapter 8, 'Persecution of Witches', provides an excellent bibliographical

summary. Recent significant and influential works include Lyndal Roper, *Oedipus and the Devil: Witchcraft, Sexuality and Religion in Early Modern Europe* (London: Routledge, 1994); Robin Briggs, *Witches and Neighbours, the Social and Cultural Context of European Witchcraft* (London: Fontana, 1997); Stuart Clark, *Thinking with Demons, the Idea of Witchcraft in Early Modern Europe* (Oxford: Oxford University Press, 1997).

134 Briggs, *Witches*, 32–3.

135 Ibid., throughout – for refutations on all these scores.

136 See Christina Larner, *Witchcraft and Religion, the Politics of Popular Belief* (Oxford: Blackwell, 1984), 137. More broadly, see Keith Thomas, *Religion and the Decline of Magic: Studies in Popular Belief in Sixteenth and Seventeenth Century England* (London: Penguin, 1971); idem., *Man and Natural World, Changing Attitudes in England, 1500–1800* (London: Penguin, 1984).

137 See Clark, *Thinking*, for a full exploration of this theme.

138 Briggs, *Witches*, 190–1; 328. Also H. R. Trevor-Roper, *The European Witch Craze of the Sixteenth and Seventeenth Centuries and Other Essays*, (London: Penguin, 1969), 156, who argues that witch trials multiplied where there was a Catholic reconquest of a formerly Protestant region. Also Brian P. Levack, *The Witchhunt in Early Modern Europe* (London: Longman, 2nd edn, 1995), 104, for a more nuanced analysis. Katz, *Holocaust*, vol. 1, 409, n. 23, adroitly adds: 'it was not Catholicism *per se* or Protestantism *per se* that explains the explosion in witch trials, but rather Catholicism or Protestantism in a specific, threatening theopolitical context'.

139 See Sigrun Haude, *In the Shadow of 'Savage Wolves': Anabaptist Münster and the German Reformation During the 1530s* (Boston, MA: Humanities Press, 2000); Cohn, *Pursuit*, chapter 13, 'The Egalitarian Millennium iii: Münster as the New Jerusalem'.

140 See, for instance, Dennis E. Showalter, *Little Man, What Now? Der Stuermer in the Weimar Republic* (Hamden, CT: Archon Books, 1982), esp. chapter 4, 'The Jew as Sex Offender', plus accompanying suitably scatological cartoons by Philip Ruprecht ('Fips').

141 Katz, *Holocaust*, vol. 1, 403, 430–1, speaking here of witches.

142 Ibid., vol. 1, 495–6.

143 Briggs, *Witches*, 8, argues that of his estimate of 40,000 to 50,000 executions, between 1450 and 1750, between 20 and 25 per cent were men.

144 See Briggs, *Witches*, 24–5; Levack, *Witchhunt*, 20–1.

145 See the inclusion of the Beziers episode in Chalk and Jonassohn, *History*, 117–20. See also Costen, *Cathars*, 123–5.

146 Barber, *Cathars*, 169–75; Emmanuel Le Roy Ladurie, *Montaillou, Cathars and Catholics in a French Village 1294–1324*, trans. Barbara Bray (London: Penguin, 1978), for the classic micro-study.

147 See Goertz, *Anabaptists*, 129. More generally, C.-P. Clasen, *The Anabaptists. A Social History, Switzerland, Austria, Moravia, South and Central Germany* (Ithaca,

NY, and London: Cornell University Press, 1972), for a study of Anabaptist adaptation and survival.

148 Salo Baron, 'Ghetto and Emancipation, Shall We Revise the Traditional View?', *The Menorah Journal*, 14:6 (1928), 513–26. Cohen, 'Persecution', in *Crescent and Cross*, for further commentary.

149 Nirenberg, 'France', in *Communities*. Also chapter 4, 'Lepers, Jews, Muslims and Poison in the Crown (1321)'.

150 Mary Daly, *Gyn Ecology: The Meta-Ethics of Radical Feminism* (London: Women's Press, 1979), for the charge; Briggs, *Witches*, 8, for the refutation.

151 C. R. Boxer, *The Christian Century in Japan, 1549–1650* (Berkeley and Los Angeles: University of California Press, 1951), 320–1.

152 Chalk and Jonassohn, *History*, 139, quote figures of 285,000, for the period 1587 to 1610 alone, i.e. before the major period of persecution began. Boxer, *Christian Century*, 360–1, however, had already suggested that these figures were based on a misreading of a Japanese text. Boxer himself estimated a minimum of 3,000 deaths with a maximum of between 5,000 and 6,000.

153 Kennedy, *Rise*, 51–2.

154 Quoted in E. N. Williams, *The Ancien Régime in Europe, Government and Society in the Major States, 1648–1789* (London: Penguin, 1970), 38.

155 Janine Garrisson, *L'Édit de Nantes et sa révocation, histoire d'une intolerance* (Paris: Éditions du Seuil, 1985), chapter 2, 'D'une confession et d'un autre', – for Huguenot seventeenth-century social composition – and chapter 4, 'Les protestants "seditieux ou mecreants"? 1630–1656'.

156 The 400th anniversary of the revocation not surprisingly produced a flurry of books on the subject of French tolerance and intolerance. See in addition to Garrisson, *L'Édit*; Elisabeth Labrousse, *Une foi, une loi, un roi, essai sur la révocation de l'Édit de Nantes* (Geneva and Paris: Payot, 1985), and Thierry Wanegffelen, *L'Édit de Nantes: une histoire européene de la tolerance du XVI au XXe siècle* (Paris: Le livre du poche, 1998), on broader issues of toleration.

157 Garrisson, *L'Edit,* chapter 5, 'L'etouffement a petites goulées 1657–1682'.

158 Ibid., 250. Garrison notes that figures on the number of exiles vary widely from a low of 50,000 to an extreme high of 3 million. Garrison's own conservative 200,000 figure stands in some juxtaposition to her further estimate (265) of some 600,000 to 700,000 abjurers, or more than 3 per cent of the French population, who mostly – superficially at least – knuckled down under the new homogenising order.

159 See, for example, Bernard Cottret, *Terre d'exil; L'Angleterre et ses refugiés français et wallons de la réforme à la révocation de l'Édit de Nantes 1550–1700* (Paris: Aubier, 1985); Jon Butler, *The Huguenots in America: A Refugee People in New World Society* (Cambridge, MA: Harvard University Press, 1983).

160 McFarlane, *British*, 180–1. See however, Jennings, *Creation*, 37–9, on the comparison between genuine religious liberty in Quaker-sponsored Pennsylvania compared with Calvinist Massachusetts but also the irony of the former being

bought – as always – at Indian expense. Further caution with regard to an ostensibly rosy picture of New World latitudinarianism might also be gleaned by considering the persecution and en masse flight of the Church of the Latter Day Saints – the Mormons – from Missouri and then Illinois to Utah in the 1840s. See Limerick, *Legacy*, 286.

161 For the general territory of the Enlightenment see Roy Porter, *The Enlightenment* (Basingstoke: Palgrave, 2nd edn, 2001); Norman Hampson, *The Enlightenment* (London: Penguin, 1968); Dorinda Outram, *The Enlightenment* (Cambridge: Cambridge University Press, 1995).

162 See Robert Mauzi, *Idée du bonheur au XVIIIe siècle* (Paris: Colin, 1960). Also François Furet and Mona Ozouf eds, 'Regeneration', in *A Critical Dictionary of the French Revolution* (Cambridge, MA: Harvard University Press, 1978), 785.

163 Paula E. Hyman, *The Jews of Modern France* (Berkeley and Los Angeles: University of California Press, 1998), 20. See Willems, *In Search*, 28–33.

164 Jean-Jacques Rousseau, *Discourse on Political Economy and The Social Contract*, trans. Christopher Betts (Oxford: Oxford University Press, 1994), 54.

165 This is not to deny either the debt Rousseau owed to Hobbes or the similarities in much of their analysis of the social organism. See Richard Tuck, *The Rights of War and Peace, Political Thought and the International Order from Grotius to Kant* (Oxford: Oxford University Press, 1999), 197–207.

166 Talmon, *Origins*, 3–6, 38–49.

167 Ibid., 91. See also Lynn Hunt, *Politics, Culture and Class in the French Revolution* (Berkeley, Los Angeles: University of California Press, 1984), for the way Rousseauesque language suffused the revolution.

168 Conor Cruise O'Brien, 'Nationalism and the French Revolution', in Best, *Permanent Revolution*, 28–30; Liah Greenfield, *Nationalism, Five Roads to Modernity* (Cambridge, MA: Harvard University Press, 1992), 172–7, for further discussion.

169 Virginie Guiraudon, 'Cosmopolitanism and National Priority: Attitudes towards Foreigners in France between 1789 and 1794', *History of European Ideas,* 13:5 (1991), 601.

170 Abbé Sieyès, 'What is the Third Estate?' (1789), quoted in O'Brien, 'Nationalism', 17.

171 Quoted in Hans Kohn, *The Idea of Nationalism* (New York: Collier-Macmillan, 2nd edn, 1967), 43.

172 John Stuart Mill, *Utilitarianism, Liberty and Representative Government* (London: Everyman edn, 1910), 363–4.

173 Quoted in Anthony Smith, *Myths and Memories of the Nation* (Oxford: Oxford University Press, 1999), 33.

174 Quoted in C. A. Macartney, *National States and National Minorities* (London: Royal Institute of International Affairs, 1934), 17.

175 Guiraudon, 'Cosmopolitanism', 591–5.

176 Quoted in Davies, *Europe*, 713–14.

177 See E. J. Hobsbawm, *Nations and Nationalism since 1780: Programme, Myth, Reality* (Cambridge: Cambridge University Press, 1990), 18–22.
178 Greenfield, *Nationalism*, 167–8.
179 O'Brien, 'Nationalism', 34–5.
180 Mayer, *Furies*, 142–59, for further discussion.
181 Greenfield, *Nationalism*, 166.
182 Giddens, *Nation-State*, 229. See also Hew Strachan, 'The Nation in Arms', in Best, *Permanent Revolution*, 49–73; Alan Forrest, 'Citizenship and Military Service', in Renée Waldinger et al., eds, *The French Revolution and the Meaning of Citizenship* (Westport, CT, and London: Greenwood Press, 1992), 153–68.
183 Richard Cobb, *The People's Armies* (New Haven, CT, and London: Yale University Press, 1987), 5–6. Also Theda Skolpol and Meyer Kestenbaum, 'Mars Unshackled: The French Revolution in World-Historical Perspective', in Ferenc Feher, ed., *The French Revolution and the Birth of Modernity* (Berkeley and Los Angeles: University of California Press, 1990), 20.
184 See George Rudé, *The Crowd in the French Revolution* (London and Oxford: Oxford University Press, 1967), 109–12, for this analysis.
185 Rudé, *Crowd*, 110–11; Cobb, *People's Armies*, 155–9; Brian Singer, 'Violence in the French Revolution: Forms of Ingestion/Forms of Expulsion', in Feher, *French Revolution*, 150–73, for critical commentaries on Rudé.
186 Paul R. Mendes-Flohr and Jehuda Reinharz, *The Jew in the Modern World, A Documentary History* (New York: Oxford University Press, 1980), 107, for the text of the National Assembly declaration.
187 Even this, however, has been a subject of debate within a specifically Jewish historiography. See Gary Kates, 'Jews into Frenchmen: Nationality and Representation in Revolutionary France', in Feher, *French Revolution*, 103–16.
188 See Frederic Cople Jaher, *The Jews and the Nation: Revolution, Empancipation, State Formation, and the Liberal Paradigm in America and France* (Princeton, NJ, and Oxford: Princeton University Press. 2002), chapter 4, 'The French Experience II: Napoleon and the First Empire', for penetrating and incisive commentary. More generally, Hyman, *Jews*, 45–50; Simon Schwarzfuchs, *Napoleon, the Jews and the Sanhedrin* (Boston, MA: Routledge and Kegan Paul, 1979).
189 Guiraudon, 'Cosmopolitanism', 595.
190 Geoffrey Best, *Humanity in Warfare* (New York: Columbia University Press, 1980), 231.
191 Schama, *Citizens*, 592.
192 Singer, 'Violence', 157–8.
193 Ibid., 158.
194 Talmon, *Origins*, 124–5.
195 Quoted in Rogers Brubaker, *Citizenship and Nationhood in France and Germany* (Cambridge, MA, and London: Harvard University Press, 1992), 47.
196 O Brien, 'Nationalism', 34.
197 Jaher, *Jews*, 96.

198 Singer, 'Violence', 163.

4 The French Model, its Discontents and Contenders

1 Schama, *Citizens*, 593.
2 Figures as quoted in Theda Skocpol, *States and Social Revolutions* (Cambridge: Cambridge University Press, 1979), 199, derived from a Clive H. Church *Past and Present* (1965) article.
3 See William H. McNeill, *The Pursuit of Power, Technology, Armed Force and Society since AD 1000* (Oxford: Basil Blackwell, 1983), esp. 278–85, for the late nineteenth-century acceleration of the tendency.
4 Paul Kennedy, *The Rise and Fall of The Great Powers* (London: Fontana Press, 1989), 215–16, for an assessment.
5 Mann, *Sources*, vol. 2, 237, referring to Richard Bendix's argument in *Kings or People* (1978).
6 See Michel Foucault, *Discipline and Punish, The Birth of the Prison*, trans. Alan Sheridan (London: Penguin, 1979), for the classic study. Norbert Finzsch and Robert Jutte, eds, *Institutions of Confinement: Hospitals, Asylums and Prisons in Western Europe and North America, 1500–1950* (Cambridge: Cambridge University Press, 1996), for Foucauldian-style development.
7 Quoted in Kohn, *Nationalism*, 92.
8 Eugen Weber, *Peasants into Frenchmen: The Modernisation of Rural France 1870–1914* (Stanford, CA: Stanford University Press, 1976), chapter 6, 'A Wealth of Tongues', and chapter 18, 'Civilising in Earnest: Schools and Schooling'. Weber (63) estimates that, even in 1863, about a quarter of the population were still unable to speak French.
9 Quoted in C. Ernest Dawn, 'The Origins of Arab Nationalism', in Rashid Khalidi et al., eds, *The Origins of Arab Nationalism* (New York and London: Columbia University Press, 1991), 5.
10 See Mazower, 'Violence', 1158–60, for discussion on changing attitudes of historical sociologists on this score.
11 Pierre Birnbaum and Ira Katznelson, eds, *Paths of Emancipation, Jews, States and Citizenship* (Princeton, NJ: Princeton University Press, 1995); Jonathan Frankel and Steven J. Zipperstein, eds, *Assimilation and Community: the Jews in Nineteenth-Century Europe* (Cambridge: Cambridge University Press, 1992), for more on this theme.
12 Peter Gay, *The Cultivation of Hatred*, vol. 3: *The Bourgeois Experience, Victoria to Freud* (London: HarperCollins, 1994), 79. More generally see amongst the wealth of literature, Stephen Wilson, *Ideology and Experience, Antisemitism in France at the Time of the Dreyfus Affair* (Rutherford and London: Farleigh Dickinson and Associated Universities Press, 1982); Eric Cahm, *The Dreyfus Affair in French Society and Politics* (London: Longman, 1996); Michel Winock, *Nationalism,*

Antisemitism and Fascism in France (Stanford, CA: Stanford University Press, 1998), part 2, 'The National Imagination and Anti-Semitism'. Also Hannah Arendt, *The Origins of Totalitarianism* (New York: Meridian, 1958), 46–50, and chapter 4, 'The Dreyfus Affair'.

13 See Arendt, *Origins*, part 1, 'Antisemitism'; Peter Pulzer, *The Rise of Political Antisemitism in Germany and Austria* (London: Halban, 1988); Michael Robert Marrus, *The Politics of Assimilation: A Study of the French-Jewish Community at the Time of the Dreyfus Affair* (Oxford: Clarendon, 1971); George Mosse, *The Crisis of German Ideology*; *Intellectual Origins of the Third Reich* (London: Weidenfeld and Nicolson, 1964); Shulamit Volkov, 'Antisemitism as a Cultural Code. Reflections on the History and Historiography of Antisemitism in Imperial Germany', *Leo Baeck Year Book*, 23 (1976), 25–46, for useful pointers on this score.

14 Elie Kedourie, *Nationalism* (Oxford and Cambridge, MA: Blackwell, 4th edn, 1994), 87–94, for both sides of the coin and some of the consequences.

15 Dennis Mack Smith, *Modern Italy, a Political History* (New Haven, CT, and London: Yale University Press, 1997 [first published 1969]), 'Section 1: Italy before 1861', for the standard study; Nelson Moe, *The View from Vesuvius: Italian Culture and the Southern Question* (Berkeley and Los Angeles: University of California Press, 2002), for a much more cultural reading, not least on Northern Italian imaginings of a backward and even barbaric Mezzogiorno.

16 David Blackbourn, *The Fontana History of Germany 1780–1918, the Long Nineteenth Century* (London: Fontana, 1997), 13–26, for an historical overview of the old system.

17 Brubaker, *Citizenship*, 4.

18 Geoff Eley, 'State Formation, Nationalism and Political Culture: Some Thoughts on the Unification of Germany', in idem., *From Unification to Nazism: Reinterpreting the German Past* (Boston, MA: Allen and Unwin, 1986), 72.

19 David Blackbourn and Geoff Eley, *The Peculiarities of German History, Bourgeois Society and Politics in Nineteenth-Century Germany 1780–1918, the Long Nineteenth Century* (Oxford and New York: Oxford University Press, 1984).

20 Mann, *Sources*, vol. 2, 320–1, 325.

21 Colmar von der Goltz, *The Nation in Arms: A Treatise on Modern Military Systems and the Conduct of War*, trans. Philip A. Ashworth (London: Hugh Rees, 2nd edn, 1906); Richard D. Challener, *The French Theory of the Nation in Arms 1866–1939* (New York: Russell and Russell, 1965); Richard A. Preston, Sidney F. Wise and Herman O. Werner, *Men in Arms, a History of Warfare and its Interrelationship with Western Society* (London: Thames and Hudson, 1962), chapter 12, 'The Nation in Arms and Napoleon'.

22 Greenfield, *Nationalism*, chapter 4, 'The Final Solution of Infinite Longing: Germany'; Fritz Stern, *The Politics of Cultural Despair: A Study in the Rise of the Germanic Ideology* (Berkeley and Los Angeles: University of California Press, 1974).

23 Quoted in Abigail Green, *Fatherlands, State-Building and Nationhood in Nineteenth Century Germany* (Cambridge: Cambridge University Press, 1987), 299, with Green's emphases.

24 See J. J. Sheehan, 'What is German History? Reflections on the Role of the *Nation* in German History and Historiography', *Journal of Modern History*, 53 (1981), 10; Brubaker, *Citizenship*, 13.

25 Stern, *Politics*, xxiv–xxv.

26 Kennedy, *Rise*, 193–203, 214–18, 228–34, for an overview.

27 See Knut Borchardt, *The Industrial Revolution in Germany 1700–1914* (London: Fontana, 1972), 11–12.

28 Kennedy, *Rise*, 254–60.

29 See Richard J. Evans, *Rereading German History 1800–1996, from Unification to Reunification* (London and New York: Routledge, 1997), chapter 2, 'Whatever Became of the *Sonderweg*?', for the retreat of the *Sonderweg* position among historians such as Hans-Ulrich Wehler, not least with regard to the centrality of the 1873–96 'Great Depression'.

30 See Norman Stone, *Europe Transformed 1878–1919* (London: Fontana, 1983), for a probing and lucid analysis of these changes.

31 Interestingly, Arendt's *Origins*, repeatedly refers to the 'masses', 'the crowd', and 'the mob', as the new political force ushering in the decline of the liberal nation-state and the consequent rise of anti-Semitism and totalitarianism.

32 Ernest Gellner, *Nations and Nationalism* (Oxford: Blackwell, 1983); also Hobsbawm, *Nations*, for a similar tack.

33 See Anthony D. Smith, *The Ethnic Origins of Nations* (Oxford: Blackwell, 1986) and amongst his other works, most recently, idem., *Myths and Memories of the Nation* (Oxford: Oxford University Press, 1999).

34 Benedict Anderson, *Imagined Communities: Reflections on the Origins and Spread of Nationalism* (London: Verso, 2nd edn, 1991).

35 Mark Hewitson, *National Identity and Political Thought in Germany, Wilhelmine Depictions of the French Third Republic 1890–1914* (Oxford: Clarendon Press, 2000), 252.

36 Brubaker, *Citizenship*, chapter 5, 'Migrants into Citizens, the Crystallisation of *Jus Soli* in Late-Nineteenth-Century France', and chapter 6, 'The Citizenry as Community of Descent, the Nationalisation of Citizenship in Wilhelmine Germany'. See also Yfaat Weiss, 'Homeland as Shelter or as Refuge? Repatriation in the Jewish Context', *Tel Aviver Jahrbuch für deutsche Geschichte*, 27 (1990), 200.

37 Brubaker, *Citizenship*, 125–6.

38 I am aware of the danger of reading too much in terms of some entirely singular, collective German complex here. Historiographically speaking, it certainly goes against a trend of recent years, particularly with regards to historians of Germany who have eschewed any form of master narrative in favour of cultural readings that accenuate 'fragmentation, difference and particularist parochialism'. See Bryan D. Palmer, *Cultures of Darkness: Night Travels in the Histories of*

Transgression (New York: Monthly Review Press, 2000), 4. The resulting insights have been multitudinous and genuinely enriching but could it be, as Palmer infers, that they also carry an understandable but perhaps misplaced tendency to avoid confronting a 'systematic centre of exploitation's and oppression's causality'?

39 Roman Szporluk, *Communism and Nationalism, Karl Marx versus Friedrich List* (New York and London: Oxford University Press, 1988), for more on this theme.
40 Ibid., 12.
41 Ibid., 117.
42 Ian Cummins, *Marx, Engels and National Movements* (London: Croom Helm, 1980), 37, quoting Marx, 'Democratic Panslavism', *Neue Rheinische Zeitung* (Feb. 1849).
43 Quoted in Szporluk, *Communism*, 128. Engels' own frustrations are even more evident in the following passage quoted in Cummins, *Marx*, 46: 'By the same right under which France took Flanders, Lorraine and Alsace, and will sooner or later take Belgium – by that same Germany takes over Schleswig; it is the right of civilisation as against barbarism, of progress as against stability ... This ... is the right of historical evolution.'
44 See especially Mosse, *Crisis*. Also Steven E. Aschheim, 'George Mosse at 80: A Critical Laudatio', *Journal of Contemporary History*, 34:2 (1999), 295–312, for assessment of Mosse's core writings on this theme.
45 Quoted in Szporluk, *Communism*, 90.
46 See Stern, *Politics*, on the seminal role of the writers, Paul de Lagarde, and Julius Langbehn, in these discourses.
47 Mosse, *Crisis*, 4; Also Greenfield, *Nationalism*, 368–71.
48 Mosse, *Crisis*, chapter 4, 'Ancient Germans Rediscovered'.
49 See Stern, *Politics*, ix, on this point.
50 Ernest Renan, 'What is a Nation?' (1882), in Geoff Eley and Ronald Grigor Suny, *Becoming National, a Reader* (New York and Oxford: Oxford University Press 1996), 45, and 42–55, for the full text.
51 See Mosse, *Crisis*, part 2, 'The Institutionalisation of the Ideology 1873–1918'.
52 Given the close examination of the kaiser's personality offered by John Rohl, the court's embrace of the most extreme ideologies and prejudices would be hardly surprising. See John C. G. Röhl, *The Kaiser and his Court: Wilhelm II and the Government of Germany*, trans. Terence F. Cole (Cambridge: Cambridge University Press, 1987), chapter 1, 'Kaiser Wilhelm II: A Suitable Case for Treatment?', and chapter 8, 'Kaiser Wilhelm II and German Anti-Semitism'.
53 See Paul Lawrence Rose, *Wagner, Race and Revolution* (London: Faber, 1992). On the seminal if, arguably, somewhat overstated role of Wagner in the contemporary era, see Jacques Barzun, *Darwin, Marx, Wagner, Critique of a Heritage* (New York: Doubleday Anchor Books, 2nd edn, 1958), esp. part 3, 'The Artistic Revolution'.

54 See notably Marc A. Weiner, *Richard Wagner and the Anti-Semitic Imagination* (Lincoln, NB: University of Nebraska Press, 1995), for Wagner's obsessions with sexual contamination and, closely linked to this, his hardly submerged anti-Semitism. See 185–97, 237–58, for evidence of these aspects in his dramaturgy, and more specifically in *Parsifal*. Also Friedlander, *Nazi Germany*, 87–9, for further valuable commentary.

55 See Steven E. Aschheim, 'The Jew Within: The Myth of the Judaization in Germany', in Jehuda Reinharz and Walter Schatzberg, eds, *The Jewish Response to German Culture* (Hanover, NH: University Press of New England, 1985), 212–41.

56 Cohn, *Warrant*, 38–41; George L. Mosse, *Toward the Final Solution, a History of European Racism* (New York: Howard Fertig: 2nd edn, 1985), 116–17; Daniel Pipes, *Conspiracy, How the Paranoid Style Flourishes and Where it Comes From* (New York and London: Free Press, 1997), for the somewhat more tendentious argument that modern-day conspiracy notions in the USA and elsewhere largely emanate from nineteenth-century theories linking Jews and secret societies.

57 Mosse, *Toward*, 118.

58 Ibid., 118–20.

59 Mosse, *Crisis*, chapter 7, 'The Jew';

60 David Blackbourn, *Populists and Patricians, Essays in Modern German History* (London: Allen and Unwin, 1987), 14. More generally, chapter 7, 'Progress and Piety: Liberals, Catholics and the State in Bismarck's Germany'.

61 Andrew Zimmerman, *Anthropology and Antihumanism in Wilhelmine Germany* (Chicago: Chicago University Press, 2002), 58, on Virchow's seminal role.

62 Blackbourn, *Populists*, 152.

63 Ibid., 153. However, see also Margaret Lavinia Anderson, 'The Kulturkampf and the Course of German History', *Central European History*, 19:1 (1986), 82–115, for the paradox here: namely the degree to which parish priests were indeed instrumental in creating a new form of lay, democratising, Catholic organisational solidarity, not least against the traditional, bishop-led ecclesiastical order.

64 Blackbourn, *Populists*, 149.

65 David Blackbourn, *Marpingen Apparitions of the Virgin Mary in Bismarckian Germany* (Oxford: Clarendon Press, 1993); Evans, *Rereading*, chapter 7, 'The Catholic Community and the Prussian State', for further commentary.

66 Lewy, *Nazi Persecution*, 5; Wim Willems, *In Search of the True Gypsy, From Enlightenment to Final Solution* (London: Frank Cass, 1997), 245–46.

67 Robert Jan van Pelt and Deborah Dwork, *Auschwitz, 1270 to the Present* (New Haven, CT, and London: Yale University Press, 1996), 54–61, on the town's pre-1914 border station role.

68 William W. Hagen, *Germans, Poles, and Jews, The Nationality Conflict in the Prussian East, 1772–1914* (Chicago: Chicago University Press, 1980), 132. See also Brubaker, *Citizenship*, 131–3, for more on the expulsions.

69 Brubaker, *Citizenship*, 130, quoting Oswald Hauser (with my emphasis).

70 Ibid., 132; Hagen, *Germans*, 183–90.

71 Hagen, *Germans*, 168.

72 Ibid.

73 Ibid., 197, 202, and more generally chapter 6, 'Capitalism and the Nationality Conflict: The Poznanian Economy and Population, 1890–1914'.

74 Brubaker, *Citizenship*, 118.

75 See Richard S. Levy, *The Downfall of the Anti-Semitic Parties in Imperial Germany* (New Haven, CT, and London: Yale University Press, 1975). This, of course, did not preclude Jewish anxieties about the future. See Friedlander, *Nazi Germany*, 78–9.

76 Heyd, *Foundations*, 63.

77 Smith, *Myths*, 13.

78 Davies, *Europe*, 814.

79 Mosse, *Toward*, 49

80 Quoted in Paul R. Mendes-Flohr, ed., *A Land of Two Peoples, Martin Buber on Jews and Arabs* (Oxford and New York: Oxford University Press, 1983), 16.

81 A search through the British Library pre-1975 Humanities catalogue found no fewer than seventy-two books, all in German, on the subject of the *Völker-wanderung*, the vast majority of them pre-1939 or pre-1914, and not surprisingly largely on the subject of German ancestral migrations. See also, however, Arnold Toynbee, *Mankind and Mother Earth, a Narrative History of the World* (Oxford: Oxford University Press, 1976), for a great British world historian who utilised the concept in length and depth.

82 Brubaker, *Citizenship*, 131–2. Hagen, *Germans*, chapter 6, 'Capitalism and the Nationality Conflict: The Poznanian Economy and Population, 1890–1914'.

83 Van Pelt and Dwork, *Auschwitz*, 79; also Mosse, *Crisis,* 116–20; Burleigh, *Germany Turns*, 22–32.

84 James J. Reid, 'Total War, the Annihilation Ethic and the Armenian Genocide 1870–1918', in Richard G. Hovannisian, ed., *The Armenian Genocide, History, Politics, Ethics* (New York: St Martin's Press, 1992), 21–52, for a revealing insight on this score.

85 Arendt, *Origins*, chapter 8, 'Continental Imperialism: The Pan-Movements'. For the impact of pan-Slavism on the Sorbs, see Gerald Stone, *The Smallest Slavonic Nation: The Sorbs of Lusatia* (London: Athlone Press, 1972), 2, who notes the 1883 description of the Sorbs as 'a little Slavonic island in a German sea'. See also idem., 19–31, for emerging post-1848 pan-Slavic tendencies amongst educated Sorbs themselves.

86 See for instance, Jacob M. Landau, *Pan-Turkism in Turkey* (London: C. Hurst, 1981); George Georgiades Arnakis, 'Turanism, an Aspect of Turkish Nationalism', *Balkan Studies*, 1 (1960), 19–32.

87 Charles Darwin, *On the Origins of Species by Means of Natural Selection: Or the Preservation of Favoured Races in the Struggle for Life*, ed. J. W. Burrow (London: Penguin 1968 {first published John Murray, 1859}).

88 See Stocking, *Victorian Anthropology*, chapter 5, 'The Darwinian Revolution and the Evolution of Human Culture (1858–1871)'.

89 See Lindqvist, *Exterminate*, 97–9. More generally, Dorinda Outram, *Georges Cuvier: Vocation, Science and Authority in Post-Revolutionary France* (Manchester: Manchester University Press, 1984).

90 See Alfred Russel Wallace, 'The Origin of Human Races and the Antiquity of Man Deduced from the Theory of "Natural Selection"', *Anthropological Review: Journal of the Anthropological Society of London*, 2 (1864), clvii–clxxxvii. Stocking, *Victorian Anthropology*, 96–102, for Wallace's distinctive contribution.

91 Michael A. Biddiss, *The Age of the Masses, Ideas and Society in Europe since 1870* (London: Penguin, 1977), 112. See also Barzun, *Darwin*, esp. 7–12, for parallels between Darwin's and Marx's materialism.

92 Gay, *Cultivation*, 41. The term 'survival of the fittest' may actually have been originally coined by Wallace. See Stocking, *Victorian Anthropology*, 101. Paul Crook, *Darwinism, War and History, the Debate over the Biology of War from the 'Origins of Species' to the First World War* (Cambridge: Cambridge University Press, 1994), chapter 2, 'The Age of Spencer and Huxley', however, for the linkages but also divergences between the conflict models of Spencer – and others – and evolutionary theory.

93 Peter Kropotkin, *Mutual Aid: A Factor of Evolution* (London: Freedom Press, 1987 [first published 1902]). Crook, *Darwinism*, 106–12, for commentary.

94 See Kurt Bayertz, 'Science and Aesthetics in Fin-de-Siècle Germany', in Mikuláš Teich and Roy Porter, eds, *Fin de Siècle and its Legacy* (Cambridge: Cambridge University Press, 1990), 280–1.

95 See Weindling, *Health*, especially the section 'Darwinian Demagogues', 36–48; idem., 'Darwinism in Germany', in David Kohn, ed., *The Darwinian Heritage* (Princeton, NJ: Princeton University Press, 1985), 683–730; Alfred Kelly, *The Descent of Darwin: The Populiarisation of Darwinism in Germany, 1860–1914* (Chapel Hill: University of North Carolina Press, 1981).

96 Zimmerman, *Anthropology*, 202–6; Woodruff D. Smith, *The Ideological Origins of Nazi Imperialism* (New York and Oxford: Oxford University Press, 1986), 146–52, for more on Ratzel.

97 Quoted in Stannard, *American Holocaust*, 245.

98 Frederick Farrar quoted in Evans, *Exclusion*, 14.

99 See Stocking, *Victorian Anthropology*, chapter 1, 'The Idea of Civilisation Before the Crystal Palace (1750–1950)'; H. F. Augstein, 'From the Land of the Bible to the Caucasus and Beyond, the Shifting Ideas of the Geographical Origin of Humankind', in Waltraud Ernst and Bernard Harris, eds, *Race, Science and Medicine 1700–1960* (London: Routledge, 1999), 58–79; Charles Darwin, *The Descent of Man and Selection in Relation to Sex* (London: John Murray, 2nd edn, 1882).

100 See Davies, *Europe*, capsule 'Caucasia', 734–35. In fairness to Blumenbach, Augstein, 'From the Land', 64, describes his theory as 'without a trace of contempt of

non-European peoples'; Mosse, *Toward*, 22, describes Camper, less charitably, as a 'pseudo-scientist'.

101 Gay, *Hatred*, 90.

102 Louis Dumont, *Homo Hierarchicus, the Caste System and its Implications* (London: Paladin, 1972), for the classic study. See also D. D. Kosmabi, *The Culture and Civilisation of India in Historical Outline* (London: Routledge, Kegan, Paul, 1965), for the early development of caste. Also more recently Ursula Sharma, *Caste* (Buckingham and Philadelphia: Open University Press, 1999).

103 See Peter Wade, *Race and Ethnicity in Latin America* (London: Pluto Press, 1997); C. L. R. James, *Black Jacobins, Toussaint L'Ouverture and the San Domingo Revolution* (London: Allison and Busby, 1989 [first published 1938]), 38.

104 See Rebecca Earle, "'Two Pairs of Pink Satin Shoes!!'": Clothing, Race and Identity in the Americas, 17th–19th Centuries', *History Workshop Journal*, 52 (2001), 175–95, for the porosity of race categorisation in this context. I am grateful to Dr Earle for our further discussion on this issue.

105 See Kuper, *Genocide*, 206–9.

106 Étienne Balibar, 'Racism and Nationalism', in idem. and Immanuel Wallerstein, *Race, Nation, Class, Ambiguous Identities* (London: Verso, 1991), 54–5.

107 Pick, *War Machine*, 93–5, and Stocking, *Victorian Anthropology*, 65, for the Swedish anatomist, Anders Retzius who invented the 'cephalic index'. See also Zimmerman, *Anthropology*, chapter 6, 'Anthropological Patriotism: The *Schulstatistik* and the Racial Composition of Germany', for Virchow's post-1871 efforts to measure the racial characteristics of 6 million German children.

108 Mosse, *Toward*, chapter 4, 'From Gobineau to Lapouge'; Arendt, *Origins*, 170–5, for commentaries.

109 Quoted in Pick, *War Machine*, 75.

110 Arendt, *Origins*, 171, notes: 'The most surprising aspect of the theory, set forth in the midst of the optimistic nineteenth century, is the fact that the author is fascinated by the fall and hardly interested in the rise of civilisations'.

111 See Weindling, *Health*, 109–10, for instance, for connections between Gobineau, the Pan-German League and Houston Stewart Chamberlain.

112 Pick, *War Machine*, 76.

113 Wilhelm II, however, may have the dubious distinction of coining the exact term. See Röhl, *Kaiser*, 203–4.

114 On the linkage between these tendencies, scientific and medical practice as well as political thinking and social planning see Weindling, *Health*, 80–101; G. R. Searle, *The Quest for National Efficiency, a Study in British Politics and Political Thought, 1899–1914* (London and Atlantic Highlands, NJ: Ashfield Press, 1990); Daniel Pick, *Faces of Degeneration, A European Disorder c. 1848–1918* (Cambridge: Cambridge University Press, 1989), esp. chapter 7, 'Crime, Urban Degeneration and National Decadence'.

115 Wetzell, *Inventing*, chapter 3, 'Criminology and Penal Policy, 1880–1914'.

116 Searle, *Quest*, 242. Desmond King, *In the Name of Liberalism, Illiberal Social Policy in the United States and Britain* (Oxford: Oxford University Press, 2000), 138–44, for more on the European background to the labour colony idea as a way of dealing with social problems, including vagrancy, unemployment and mental illness.

117 Paul Weindling, *Epidemics and Genocide in Eastern Europe, 1890–1945* (Oxford: Oxford University Press, 2000), 34.

118 Searle, *Quest*, 60.

119 See Weindling, *Health*, 76–80, for some of the more positive *fin-de-siècle* thinking; J. M. Winter, *The Great War and the British People* (Basingstoke: Macmillan, 1986), 8–18, for the hereditary versus environment debate in Britain.

120 Weindling, *Health*, 230–5, for the post-1900 consolidation of Mendelian science and its cross-fertilisation with notions of racial hygiene.

121 See for instance, Dan Stone, *Breeding Superman, Nietzsche, Race and Eugenics in Edwardian and Interwar Britain* (Liverpool: Liverpool University Press, 2002), 104, where he refers to a Karl Pearson lecture which 'began with the standard fear of the "over-fertility of the unfit" and the "lessened relative fertility in those physically and mentally fitter stocks"'.

122 See Michael Freeden, 'Eugenics and Progressive Thought: A Study in Ideological Affinity', *Historical Journal*, 22:3 (1979), 645–71; Diane B. Paul, 'Eugenics and the Left', *Journal of the History of Ideas*, 45:4 (1984), 567–90.

123 Lombroso, 'L'uomo delinquente' (1876), quoted in Stephen Jay Gould, *Ever Since Darwin, Reflections on Natural History* (London: Pelican, 1980), 226; More generally see Pick, *Faces*, chapter 5, 'Lombroso's Criminal Science'; Wetzell, *Inventing*, 29–31.

124 Wetzell, *Inventing*, 100–5.

125 Ibid., 104.

126 Crook, *Darwinism*, 83–7. See also Pick, *Faces*, 197–9.

127 Crook, *Darwinism*, 89.

128 Weindling, *Health*, 239–41, 430–3.

129 King, *In the Name*, 52. Also Weindling, *Health*, 232.

130 Michael Burleigh, *Death and Deliverance, 'Euthanasia' in Germany, 1900–1945* (Cambridge: Cambridge University Press, 1994), 12–13.

131 Stefan Kühl, 'The Cooperation of German Racial Hygienists and American Eugenicists before and after 1933', in Michael Berenbaum and Abraham J. Peck, eds, *The Holocaust and History, the Known, the Unknown, the Disputed and the Reexamined* (Bloomington and Indianapolis: Indiana University Press, 1998), 136.

132 Stone, *Breeding Superman*, chapter 5, 'The "Lethal Chamber" in Eugenic Thought'.

133 Quoted in Lindqvist, *Exterminate*, 79.

134 Quoted in John Carey, *The Intellectuals and the Masses, Pride and Prejudice among the Literary Intelligentsia, 1880–1939* (London and Boston, MA: Faber & Faber 1993), 12.

135 Michael Coren, 'And the Invisible Swarms Will Have to Die', *Independent*, 2 January 1993 Also idem., *The Invisible Man: The Life and Liberties of H. G. Wells* (London: Bloomsbury, 1993), for fuller development.

136 Notes Stone, *Breeding Superman*, 107, 'It is clear that the class-prejudices of the mainstream eugenicists were invariably accompanied by racial prejudices; indeed one could go so far as to say that the two forms of prejudice were inseparable, and fed one another'.

137 Stocking, *Victorian Anthropology*, 229–30, 234–5.

138 Ibid., 234.

139 Annegret Ehmann, 'From Colonial Racism to Nazi Racial Policy: The Role of the So-Called Mischlinge', in Berenbaum and Peck, *Holocaust*, 118.

140 Ibid., 118–19. For more on Fischer see also Paul Weindling *Health, Race and German Politics between National Unification and Nazism, 1870–1945* (Cambridge: Cambridge University Press, 1989), 436–9; Benno Müller-Hill, *Murderous Science, Elimination by Scientific Selection of Jews, Gypsies and Others, Germany 1933–1945*, trans. George R. Fraser (New York: Cold Spring Harbor Laboratory Press, 1998), 'On the Role and Self-Image of Some Anthropologists'.

141 Ehmann, 'Colonial Racism', 118–19.

142 See especially Sander L. Gilman, *Franz Kafka, The Jewish Patient* (New York and London: Routledge, 1995), 14–18; idem., *The Jew's Body* (New York and London: Routledge, 1991).

143 See Weindling, *Health*, 70–2; Bernard Harris, 'Pro-Alienism, Anti-Alienism and the Medical Profession in Late-Victorian and Edwardian Britain', in Ernst and Harris, *Race*, 194–202, for British medical opinions of Jewish ailments and failings, which, though still essentially negative, are somewhat at variance from their German counterparts.

144 Quoted in Alex Bein, 'Jewish Parasite, Notes on the Semantics of the Jewish Problem with Special Reference to Germany' *Leo Baeck Year Book*, 9 (1964), 32. Also David Bodanis, *Web of Words, the Ideas behind Politics* (Macmillan: Basingstoke, 1988), chapter 2, 'Pasteur II: Hitler's Bacteria'; Mosse, *Crisis*, 31–9, and Stern, *Politics*, chapter 1, 'Paul de Lagarde and a Germanic Religion' for more on Lagarde.

145 George du Maurier, *Trilby* (London: Penguin, 1994 [first published 1893]). See also Daniel Pick, *Svengali's Web, the Alien Encounter in Modern Culture* (New Haven, CT, and London: Yale University Press, 2000).

146 Quotes, and commentary, from Leon Poliakov, *History of Anti-Semitism*, vol. 4, *Suicidal Europe 1870–1933*, trans. George Klin (Oxford: Littman Library and Oxford University Press, 1985), 11–12.

147 Ibid., 10, quoting from Nietzsche, *Beyond Good and Evil* (1886).

148 Quoted in Mendes-Flohr and Reinharz, *The Jew*, 291. Mosse, *Crisis*, 93–8; Martin Woodroffe, 'Racial Theories of History and Politics: The Example of Houston Stewart Chamberlain', in Paul Kennedy and Anthony Nicholls, eds, *Nationalist*

and Racialist Movements in Britain and Germany before 1914 (Macmillan: London and Basingstoke, 1981), 143–52, for more on Chamberlain.

149 Arendt, *Origins*, 164–5; Greenfield, *Nationalism*, 172, for more on this 'Germanic nobility' versus 'Celtic bourgeoisie' theme.

150 Balibar, 'Racism', 62–3. Balibar aside, there has been strikingly little written on the connections between race and class thinking. It is implicit, rather than explicit, in Ronald Aronson *Dialectics of Disaster, a Preface to Hope* (London: Verso, 1983), much praised in Volume I of this work. Nor, despite the all-embracing label of totalitarianism are these particular connections properly developed in Arendt's *Origins*. One important 'veteran' exception, however, is F. A. Voigt, *Unto Caesar* (London: Constable, 1938). Notes Voigt (174): 'The Marxist myth is of a universal Golden Age in which class, nation and state will vanish … the National Socialist myth is of a Heroic age in which men of masterful personality will lead hierarchically organised but racially homogenised communities'. I am indebted to Dan Stone for bringing Voigt's extraordinarily compelling and prescient study to my attention.

151 Again Voigt, *Unto Caesar*, 22, 'The "inevitably" catastrophic nature of the "final decision" leaves the Marxist quite unperturbed. He is indifferent to human suffering and does not care in the least whether a hundred or a hundred million perish. On the contrary, he grows expansive in the contemplation of the wars and upheavals that are needed to engender the Millennium.' Voigt, indeed, later asserts (45), 'Marxism is eschatology without God'. See also Arnold Künzli, *Karl Marx. Eine Psychographie* (Vienna: Europa Verlag, 1966), for Marx as a latter-day Hebrew prophet, though also Julius Carlebach, *Marx and the Radical Critique of Judaism* (London: Routledge and Kegan Paul, 1978); Robert S. Wistrich, *Revolutionary Jews from Marx to Trotsky* (London: Harrap, 1976), 4, for repudiations of this line of argument.

152 A. J. P. Taylor, ed., Karl Marx and Friedrich Engels, *The Communist Manifesto* (London: Penguin, 1967), for the classic 1848 Marxist text.

153 Voigt, *Unto Caesar*, chapters 2 and 3. Also Arendt, *Origins*, 67–84, though with the proviso that her focus is specifically on Nazi and Stalinist comparisons.

154 Quoted in Biddiss, *Age*, 123. Leszek Kolakowski, *Main Currents of Marxism: Its Rise, Growth and Dissolution*, vol. 2: *The Golden Age*, trans. P. S. Falla (Oxford: Clarendon Press, 1978), chapter 4, 'Bernstein and Revisionism', for more on the thesis and its reception amongst Marxists.

155 Marx and Engels, *Communist Manifesto*, 84.

156 Ibid., 92. See also Tom Bottomore, ed., *Dictionary of Marxist Thought* (Oxford: Blackwell, 2nd edn, 1991), 327, for Marx's 'Eighteenth Brumaire of Louis Bonaparte' (1851–2), description of the 'lumpenproletariat' as '"the refuse of all classes", a "disintegrated mass" comprising "ruined and adventurous offshoots of the bourgeoisie, vagabonds, discharged soldiers, discharged jailbirds … pickpockets, brothel keepers, rag-pickers, beggars" etc.'.

157 Marx, 'Notes on Feuerbach' (1845), quoted in Pollard, *Idea*, 128.

158 See Kolakowski, *Main Currents*, vol. 2, 408–11, for the emergence of the idea of 'permanent revolution', as developed by Parvus and Trotsky.

159 Notes Misha Glenny, *The Balkans 1804–1999, Nationalism, War and the Great Powers* (London: Granta Books, 1999), 303. 'In the final fourteen years of the nineteenth century, assassins around the world claimed the lives of major public figures at an average rate of one a year … however … from 1900 to 1913 forty heads of state, politicians and diplomats fell victim to the terrorists' bullet or bomb.' See James Joll, *The Anarchists* (London: Methuen, 1969), chapter 5, 'Terrorism and Propaganda by the Deed', for more on anarchist violence in this period.

160 Zeev Sternhell, with Mario Sznajder and Maia Asheri, *The Birth of Fascist Ideology, from Cultural Rebellion to Political Revolution*, trans. David Maisel (Princeton, NJ: Princeton University Press, 1994), 50. Also J. J. Roth, *The Cult of Violence, Sorel and the Sorelians* (Berkeley and Los Angeles: University of California Press, 1980).

161 Sternhell, *Birth*, chapter 1, 'Georges Sorel and the Antimaterialist Revision of Marxism'; Kolakowski, *Main Currents*, 2, chapter 7, 'Georges Sorel: A Jansenist Marxism', for the debate around Sorel's relationship to Marxism.

162 Sternhell, *Birth,* 'Introduction', and chapter 5, 'The Mussolini Crossroads: From the Critique of Marxism to National Socialism and Fascism', for the alleged Sorelian roots of the fascist movement but also David D. Roberts, 'How Not to Think About Fascism and Ideology, Intellectual Antecedents and Historical Meaning', *Journal of Contemporary History,* 35:2 (2000), 185–211, for doubts on the Sorelian relationship to Italian fascism.

163 See Cummins, *Marx*, chapter 6, 'The Problem of Russia'.

164 See Robert Conquest, ed., Tibor Szamuely, *The Russian Tradition* (London: Fontana, 1974), part 2, 'The Russian Revolutionary Tradition', for the background.

165 Amongst the vast literature on the subject see Robert Conquest, *Lenin* (London: Fontana, 1972), chapter 3, 'What is to be Done?', Robert Service, *Lenin; A Political Life*, vol. 1: *The Strengths of Contradiction* (Basingstoke and London: Macmillan, 1985), 88–93.

166 Biddiss, *Age*, 126; George L. Mosse, *The Culture of Western Europe, the Nineteenth and Twentieth Centuries* (Boulder, CO, and London: Westview Press, 3rd edn, 1988), 172–5, on Blanqui and Blanquism. Neil Harding, *Lenin's Political Thought*, vol. 1: *Theory and Practice in the Democratic Revolution* (London and Basingstoke: Macmillan, 1977), esp. 226–37; Kolakowski, *Main Currents*, vol. 2, 381–98, for critical discussions of Lenin's views on insurrection and the degree to which they represented a Marxist deviation.

167 Theodore Dan, *Origins of Bolshevism*, trans. Joel Carmichael (London: Secker and Warburg, 1964), chapter 9, 'Bolshevism and Menshevism'. The cause célèbre was whether the Jewish Bund, in fact the very first Marxist party founded in the Russian empire, would be allowed an autonomy within the RSDLP, thereby presupposing a federal party framework.

168 M. Şükrü Hanioğlu, *The Young Turks in Opposition* (New York and Oxford: Oxford University Press, 1995), chapter 8, 'The First Congress of Ottoman Opposition in Paris and its Consequences'.

169 However, see Alan Bullock, *Hitler and Stalin, Parallel Lives* (London: Fontana Press, 1993), 19–26, for some largely speculative thoughts on the shaping of the young Hitler's worldview.

170 Carey, *Intellectuals*, chapter 1, 'The Revolt of the Masses'; Stone, *Breeding Superman*, esp. chapters 2–4. For *the* contemporary attempt at analysis of *fin-de-siècle* angst see Max Nordau, *Degeneration* (Lincoln, NB, and London: University of Nebraska Press, 1993 [first published 1892]).

171 See George L. Mosse, *Nationalism and Sexuality, Middle-Class Morality and Sexual Norms in Modern Europe* (London and Madison: University of Wisconsin Press, 1985), for the classic wide-ranging analysis; also restated in idem., *The Image of Man, the Creation of Modern Masculinity* (New York and Oxford: Oxford University Press, 1996). Also Sander L. Gilman, *Difference and Pathology, Stereotypes of Sexuality, Race and Madness* (Ithaca, NY, and London, Cornell University Press, 1985), and, more generally, Klaus Theweleit, *Male Fantasies*, 2 vols (Cambridge: Polity Press, 1987/9).

172 See Sander L. Gilman, *Jewish Self-Hatred: Anti-Semitism and the Hidden Language of the Jews* (Baltimore: Johns Hopkins University Press, 1986); Leon Poliakov, *The History of Anti-Semitism*, vol. 3: *From Voltaire to Wagner*, trans. Miriam Kochan (London: Routledge and Kegan Paul, 1975), 409–29; Carlebach, *Marx*; Wistrich, *Revolutionary Jews*, esp. chapter 1, 'Jews and Socialism'; Edmund Silberner, 'Was Marx an Anti-Semite?', *Historia Judaica*, 11 (1949), 3–52, for further exploration of this theme, from somewhat different perspectives.

173 See Zeev Sternhell, *Ni Droite, ni gauche: l'ideologie fasciste en France* (Paris: Éditions du Seuil, 1983), chapter 1, 'D'un avant-guerre à l'autre'.

174 Arendt, *Origins*, 107.

175 Ibid., 44. See also John Boyer, *Political Radicalism in Late Imperial Vienna, Origins of the Christian Social Movement, 1848–1897* (Chicago: Chicago University Press, 1987), for the background.

176 Jack London, *The Iron Heel* (Edinburgh: Rebel Inc., 1999 [first published 1908]).

177 Alon Confino, *The Nation as a Local Metaphor: Wurttemberg, Imperial Germany and National Memory, 1871–1918* (Chapel Hill: University of North Carolina Press, 1997), 214.

178 Hewitson, *National Identity*, 255.

179 Hans-Ulrich Wehler, *The German Empire 1871–1918*, trans. Kim Traynor (Leamington Spa: Berg Publishers, 1985), for the classic attempt to link these two factors, the argument being that the Wihelmine state sought to head off social discontent by mobilising public opinion around a programme of 'social imperialism'.

180 Mayer, *Persistence*, esp. 88–102, for a necessary corrective to the German singularity argument.

5 Ascendant Imperialisms

1 Anthony Pagden, *Peoples and Empires* (London: Weidenfeld and Nicolson, 2001), 8.

2 See idem., *Ideologies of Empire in Spain, Britain and France c.1500–c.1800* (New Haven, CT, and London: Yale University Press, 1995); especially chapters 1 and 2. Also Dominic Lieven, *Empire, the Russian Empire and its Rivals* (London: John Murray, 2000), 8–17.

3 Pagden, *Peoples*, 8.

4 See Lieven, *Empire*, 17–24, for further discussion.

5 See Immanuel Wallerstein, 'World System or World Systems?', in André Gunder Frank and Barry K. Gillis, eds, *The World System, Five Hundred Years or Five Thousand?* (London and New York: Routledge, 1993), 292–6, for one of his more recent restatements on the concept of 'world empire'.

6 Kappeler, *Russian Empire*, 114, for instance on Russia.

7 Ibid., chapters 7 and 8; Lieven, *Empire*, 190–3. More generally on imperial Habsburg ethnic policy in this period, see Robert A. Kann, *The Multinational Empire, Nationalism and National Reform in the Habsburg Monarchy 1848–1918*, vol. 2: *Empire Reform* (New York: Octagon Books, 1970).

8 McNeill, *Pursuit*, 143.

9 Mann, *Sources*, vol. 2, 261.

10 Geoffrey Barraclough, *An Introduction to Contemporary History* (London: C.A. Watts and Co., 1964).

11 See Sebastian Balfour, *The End of the Spanish Empire, 1898–1923* (Oxford: Clarendon Press, 1997).

12 See António José Telo, *Economia e imperio no Portugal contemporaneo* (Lisbon: Edicoes Cosmos, 1994); Maarten Kuitenbrouwer, *The Netherlands and the Rise of Modern Imperialism: Colonies and Foreign Policy, 1870–1902*, trans. Hugo Beyer (Oxford: Berg, 1991), for further background.

13 See, W. O. Henderson, *The German Colonial Empire* (London: Frank Cass, 1993); L. H. Gann and Peter Duigan, *The Rulers of German Africa 1884–1914* (Stanford, CA: Stanford University Press, 1977).

14 See W. G. Beasley, *Japanese Imperialism 1894–1945* (Oxford: Clarendon Press, 1997).

15 Ronald Hyam, *Britain's Imperial Century, a Study of Empire and Expansion, 1815–1914* (Basingstoke: Macmillan, 1993), for an excellent overview.

16 Quoted in Giddens, *Nation-State*, 223. See also Connor, *Frontier Wars*, 9–10, for a long list of some of these conflicts between 1788 and 1838.

17 See Robert Aldrich, *Greater France, a History of French Overseas Expansion* (Basingstoke: Macmillan, 1996), 97–100 on the French, post-1884 'New Imperialism'.

18 Lieven, *Empire*, 46.

19 See Philip S. Foner, *The Spanish–Cuban–American War and the Birth of American Imperialism, 1895–1902*, 2 vols (New York: Monthly Review Press, 1972);

Joseph Smith, *The Spanish–American War, Conflict in the Caribbean and the Pacific 1895–1902* (London and New York: Longman, 1994).

20 Arendt, *Origins*, esp. 131–2.

21 This still would beg the question whether the primary motor to the new phase of imperialism was capitalism itself, as for instance, Lenin, in his 1916 study, 'Imperialism the Highest Stage of Capitalism' proposed, or, rather, motivated by 'irrational' and essentially atavistic impulses on the part of European ruling elites, as famously developed in Joseph Schumpeter's 1951 critique, *Imperialism and Social Classes*. These big questions, however, must remain outside the scope of this analysis, which is primarily concerned with the *impact* of the new imperialism.

22 See, for instance, Arendt, *Origins*, 127–31.

23 See Jeremy Black, *Maps and History, Constructing Images of the Past* (New Haven, CT, and London: Yale University Press, 1997), especially chapter 3, 'Nationalism and Eurocentrism in Nineteenth-Century Historical Atlases'.

24 Limerick, *Legacy*, 55. More generally, see Scott, *Seeing*, 33–52.

25 See Peter Hopkirk, *The Great Game: The Struggle for Empire in Central Asia* (London: John Murray, 2nd edn, 1992); Michael Edwardes, *Playing the Great Game, a Victorian Cold War* (London: Hamish Hamilton, 1975). See also more recently, Karl E. Mayer and Shareen Blair Brysac, *Tournament of Shadows, the Great Game and the Race for Empire in Asia* (London: Little, Brown, 2001). Interestingly, all these accounts tend to foreground the key military and diplomatic actors in the 'Game' but with much less attention paid – except in passing – to the consequences for the populations who happened to be in the way.

26 Michael Geyer and Charles Bright, 'Global Violence and Nationalizing Wars in Eurasia and America: The Geopolitics of War in the Mid-Nineteenth Century', *Comparative Studies in Society and History*, 38:4 (1996), esp. 626–34, independently of the thesis herein, speak in very similar terms of a 'Eurasian seam' of conflict. The critical difference between their provocative argument and mine is that they see the transmission of imperial conflicts into Europe emanating from autonomous', decentred', Eurasian factors, rather than being themselves a by-product of Western impact.

27 See Glenny, *Balkans*, 143–51.

28 See Willis Brooks, 'Russia's Conquest and Pacification of the Caucasus: Relocation becomes a Pogrom in the Post-Crimean War Period', *Nationalities Papers*, 23 (1995), 675–86 for more on this theme.

29 See Justin McCarthy, *Death and Exile: The Ethnic Cleansing of Ottoman Muslims, 1821–1922* (Princeton, NJ: Darwin Press, 1995), 39–60.

30 Noam Chomsky, arguing with regard to the US liberal media presentation of news in the context of the Cold War, has proposed that atrocities are effectively packaged in three basic forms: a) 'constructive', i.e. those which serve US interests; b) 'benign', which are irrelevant to its concerns; and c) 'nefarious', which

can be blamed on official enemies. See Milan Rai, *Chomsky's Politics* (London and New York: Verso, 1995), 27–8.

31 Mark Mazower, *The Balkans* (London: Weidenfeld and Nicolson, 2000), 11, quotes Edith Durham, the perceptive British traveller and commentator on the Balkans, for her summary of Western values thus: 'When a Muslim kills a Muslim it does not count. When a Christian kills a Muslim it is a righteous act; when a Christian kills a Christian it is an error of judgement better not talked about; it is only when a Muslim kills a Christian that we arrive at full-blown atrocity'. For the Western shift towards 'discovery' and empathy with oppressed Christians in the Ottoman empire see Maria Todorova, *Imagining the Balkans* (New York and Oxford: Oxford University Press, 1997), 97–102. More generally McCarthy, *Ethnic Cleansing*, on the impact of the *anti-Muslim* atrocities.

32 Samuel P. Huntington, *The Clash of Civilisations and the Remaking of World Order* (London: Touchstone Books, 1998), esp. 125–30, 207–18. It might be noted that Huntington, too, is also very focused on geo-strategic and cultural fault-lines but with rather different assumptions and agendas to those herein.

33 See Donald Bloxham, 'Three Imperialisms and a Turkish Nationalism: International Stresses, Imperial Disintegration and the Armenian Genocide', *Patterns of Prejudice*, 36:4 (2002), 37–58, for a cogent analysis of this theme.

34 See H. L. Wesseling, *Divide and Rule, the Partition of Africa 1880–1914,* trans. Arnold J. Pomerans (Westport, CT, and London: Praeger, 1996), esp. 113–19, for the 1884 conference. See Kader Asmal, 'Juridical Aspects of the Berlin Conference, 1884–5: Contribution to the New Colonial Order', in Brian Wood, ed., *Namibia, 1884–1994, Readings in Namibian History and Society* (London and Lusaka: Namibia Support Committee and United Nations Institute for Namibia, 1988), 152–70, for the *realpolitik* behind the rhetoric.

35 Quoted in Felix Gross, *Rhodes of Africa* (London: Cassell and Co., 1956), 90.

36 See V. Y. Mudimbe, *The Idea of Africa* (Bloomington and Indianapolis: Indiana University Press, 1994), esp. 1–15 and chapter 3, 'The Power of the Greek Paradigm', for the savage and exotic in European discourses on Africa.

37 See, for example, Roland Oliver, *The African Experience* (London: Weidenfeld and Nicolson, 1991), 118, for the explorer Heinrich Barth's 1851 graphic record of the atrocity he witnessed when accompanying a Borno raiding party in west Africa.

38 See Jules Marchal, *L'État Libre du Congo, paradis perdu, l'histoire du Congo, 1876–1900*, 2 vols (Borgloon: Éditions Paula Bellings, 1996), vol. 1, 132–3; Neal Ascherson, *The King Incorporated, Leopold II in the Age of Trusts* (London: George Allen and Unwin, 1963), chapter, 20, 'Leopold and the Anti-Slavery Conference of 1889'. For more general background on Arab slaving, see John Laffin, 'The Arabs as Slavers', in Willem A. Veenhoven, ed., *Case Studies on Human Rights and Fundamental Freedoms, a World Survey* (The Hague: Martinus Nijhoft, 1976), vol. 4, 433–59.

39 See James O. Gump, *The Formation of the Zulu Kingdom in South Africa, 1750–1840* (San Francisco: Mellen Research University Press, 1990), for historical background. That said, see Carolyn Hamilton, ed., *The Mfecane Aftermath, Reconstructive Debates in Southern African History* (Johannesburg and Pietermaritzburg: Witwatersrand University Press and University of Natal Press, 1995), for the emerging historiography which disputes the *Mfecane* impact on local African societies compared with that of late eighteenth- early nineteenth-century white settlement at Cape Colony and Delgoa Bay slave trading.

40 In addition to Marchal, *L'État*, see also idem., *E.D. Morel contre Leopold*, 2 vols (Paris: Éditions L'Harmattan, 1996); Adam Hochschild, *King Leopold's Ghost: A Story of Greed, Terror and Heroism in Colonial Africa* (London: Macmillan, 1998); Ascherson, *The King Incorporated*, for more on the scope, scale and viciousness of Leopold's programme. At the time of writing, a Belgian historical commission, at the instigation of the state-funded Royal Museum for Central Africa, is investigating claims, implicit or explicit in Hochschild and Marchal's work, that genocide was the outcome of Leopold's rule in the Congo. See Andrew Osborn, 'Belgium Exhumes its Colonial Demons', *Guardian*, 13 July 2002.

41 See Pomeranz, *Great Divergence*, 265–9, for a particularly cogent exposition on this theme.

42 See Herbert S. Klein, *The Atlantic Slave Trade* (Cambridge: Cambridge University Press, 1999), chapter 6, 'The Middle Passage', for a detailed breakdown of figures. Klein notably downgrades previous estimates of Africans transhipped to the Americas ranging between nearly 12 and over 14 million. See Philip D. Curtin, *The Atlantic Slave Trade, a Census* (Madison and Milwaukee: University of Wisconsin Press, 1969), chapter 1, 'The Slave Trade and the Numbers Game: A Review of the Literature'.

43 I am indebted to my Southampton colleague, Dr John Oldfield, for current research estimates on this score. Other estimates, however, do propose figures as high as 15 per cent mortality either in the 'Middle Passage', or in the first year of 'seasoning'. See Seymour Drescher, 'The Atlantic Slave Trade and the Holocaust: A Comparative Analysis', in Alan S, Rosenbaum, ed., *Is the Holocaust Unique? Perspectives on Comparative Genocide* (Boulder, CO: Westview Press, 1996), 67.

44 Drescher, 'Atlantic Slave Trade', 67.

45 Jean-Paul Sartre, 'On Genocide', *Ramparts* (Feb. 1968), 37–42. For comments for and against Sartre's position see Churchill, *Little Matter*, 416–17; Kuper, *Genocide*, 14, 44–5.

46 These figures refer to the Belgian Congo only. See Hochschild, *King Leopold's Ghost*, chapter 15, 'A Reckoning', especially 230–3 for assessment. The figure of 5 million doubles if one also takes account of the overall demographic downturn. See note below.

47 See Lindqvist, *Exterminate*, 'Preface'; Joseph Conrad, *Heart of Darkness* (London: Penguin, 1973 [first published 1902]).

48 Peter Warwick, *Black People and the South African War 1899–1902* (Cambridge: Cambridge University Press, 1983), 4, notes that in the area of conflict in southern Africa, in 1899, there were 1 million whites compared with 4 million blacks, and another almost 0.5 million coloureds, mostly in Cape Colony. There was also by this time an Asian community of 100,000, mostly in Natal.

49 See V. Y. Mudimbe, *The Invention of Africa, Gnosis, Philosophy and the Order of Knowledge* (Bloomington and Indianapolis: Indiana University Press, 1988), esp. chapter 1, 'Discourse of Power and Knowledge of Otherness', for European cultural conceptions of Africa and tendencies towards an ethnocentric reductionism. On changing attitudes to Africans and African history, see also Basil Davidson, *Africa in History* (London: Granada, 1974), 15–19.

50 The statement of von Trotha (November 1904) which Cocker, *Rivers*, 328, uses as the title of his comparative study.

51 See Jan-Bart Gewald, *Herero Heroes, a Socio-Political History of the Herero of Namibia 1890–1923* (Oxford: James Currey, 1999), for more on the Herero, their culture, environment and neighbours.

52 Cocker, *Rivers*, 327.

53 Horst Drechsler, *Let Us Die Fighting, the Struggle of the Herero and Nama against German Imperialism 1884–1915* (London: Zed Press, 1980), 153–4.

54 See Henrik Lundtofte, '"Ich glaube, dass die Nation als solche vernichtet werden muss ..." radikaliseringen af den tyske nedkaempelse af hereroopstanden 1904', *Den Jyske Historiker*, 90 (Dec. 2000), 74–105 (I am indebted to Steven Jensen for provision of an English version of this article); Isabel V. Hull, 'Military Culture and the Production of "Final Solutions" in the Colonies: The Example of Wilhelminian Germany', in Ben Kiernan and Robert Gellately, eds, *The Spectre of Genocide: Mass Murder in Historical Perspective* (New York and Cambridge: Cambridge University Press, 2003), 141–62: A more radical case of disputing actual genocide comes from Karla Poewe, *The Namibian Herero, a History of their Psychosocial Disintegration and Survival* (Lewiston, NY, and Queenston, ON: Edwin Mellen Press 1985), 64–5, who argues for instance, that von Trotha's extermination order (see n. 59 below) was a case of psychological warfare intended to frighten the Herero away from German troops, rather than to kill them.

55 See Jehuda L. Wallach, *The Dogma of the Battle of Annihilation: The Theories of Clausewitz and Schlieffen and their Impact on the German Conduct of Two World Wars* (Westport, CT: Greenwood Press, 1986).

56 Cocker, *Rivers*, 331. See also Gewald, *Herero Heroes*, 171–5.

57 Lundtofte, 'Ich glaube', 84–7.

58 Ibid., 87.

59 Quoted in Helmut Bley, *South-West Africa under German Rule, 1894–1914* (London: Heinemann, 1971), 163–4.

60 Drechsler, *Let Us Die*, 160–1. See also Tilman Dedering, '"A Certain Rigorous Treatment of all Parts of the Nation": The Annihilation of the Herero in German South West Africa, 1904', in Levene and Roberts, *Massacre*, 211–12.

61 See Trutz von Trotha, "'The Fellows Can Just Starve': On Wars of "Pacification" in the African Colonies of Imperial Germany and the Concept of "Total War,'" in Boemeke, *Anticipating Total War*, 431, n. 55, for a comment on the Prussian code of honour which disallowed *direct* extermination of women and children. Also Lundtofte, 'Ich glaube', 92.

62 Cocker, *Rivers*, 332.

63 Quoted in John Bridgman, *The Revolt of the Hereros* (Berkeley and Los Angeles: UCLA Press, 1968), 145.

64 Drechsler, *Let Us Die*, 212–14, for the casualty figures.

65 Röhl, *Kaiser*, 14, significantly notes that in the wake of the battle of Tannenberg, in 1914, the kaiser proposed to kill 90,000 Russian prisoners of war by driving them onto a barren spit in the Baltic Sea, where they would starve and thirst to death.

66 See Dedering, 'Certain Rigorous Treatment', 222, n. 81, who raises the issue more as question than a confirmation. See also discussion in Hull, 'Military Culture', 141–3. However, for a much more thoroughgoing case for the connections between Herero genocide and Holocaust, see Jürgen Zimmerer, *Deutsche Herrschaft über Afrikaner. Staatlicher Machtanspruch und Wirklichkeit im Kolonialen Namibia* (Hamburg: LIT, 2001).

67 See amongst others, Christopher R. Browning, *The Path to Genocide: Essays on Launching the Final Solution* (Cambridge and New York: Cambridge University Press, 1992), 106–8; Richard Breitman, *Official Secrets, What the Nazis Planned, What the British and Americans Knew* (New York: Hill and Wang, 1999), 60: Christian Gerlach, 'German Economic Interests, Occupation Policy, and the Murder of the Jews in Belorussia, 1941–43', in Ulrich Herbert, ed., *National Socialist Extermination Policies, Contemporary German Perspectives and Controversies* (New York and Oxford: Berghahn Books, 2000), 220, for differing views on the Himmler order and its significance.

68 Cocker, *Rivers*, 298.

69 Arendt, *Origins*, 136–8.

70 See Stocking, *Victorian Anthropology*, 236–7.

71 Quoted in Bodley, *Victims*, 2.

72 Quoted in Lindqvist, *Exterminate*, 130–1. On Knox and Ratzel more generally, see 122–46.

73 Quoted in Martin Gilbert, *The Holocaust, the Jewish Tragedy* (London: Collins, 1986), 282.

74 Hochshild, *King Leopold's Ghost*, 233.

75 See Marchal, *Morel*, esp. chapter 1, 'Edmund D. Morel'; Hochshild, *King Leopold's Ghost*, 177–228; William Roger Louis and Jean Stengers, *E.D. Morel's History of the Congo Reform Movement* (Oxford: Clarendon Press, 1968). See also Morel's own account: E. D Morel, *Red Rubber, the Story of the Rubber Slave Trade Flourishing on the Congo in the Year of Grace 1906* (London: T. Fisher Unwin, 1906).

76 Hochshild, *King Leopold's Ghost*, 188.

77 Thomas Pakenham, *The Scramble for Africa: The White Man's Conquest of the Dark Continent from 1876 to 1912* (New York: Random House, 1991), 607–8.

78 Bley, *South-West Africa*, 97.

79 Drechsler, *Let Us Die*, 16.

80 Bley, *South-West Africa*, 112–13.

81 John H. Wellington, *South West Africa and its Human Issues* (Oxford: Oxford University Press, 1967), 196.

82 See above, Chapter 4, 197–8.

83 Quoted in Dedering, Certain Rigorous Treatment', 215. See also Zimmerman, *Anthropology*, 244–5 for Felix von Luschan's coveting of such skulls and the rumours in the German press that thousands of them had been shipped to Germany.

84 Bley, *South West Africa*, 151.

85 Wellington, *South West Africa*, 213.

86 See Gay, *Cultivation*, 86–7.

87 Quoted in Hochschild, *King Leopold's Ghost*, 188.

88 See William Worger, *South Africa's City of Diamonds: Mine Workers and Monopoly Capitalism in Kimberley 1867–1895* (New Haven, CT, and London: Yale University Press, 1985).

89 Drechsler, *Let Us Die*, 93, 81.

90 M. A. P. Meilink-Roelofsz, *Asian Trade and European Influence in the Indonesian Archipelago between 1500 and about 1630* (The Hague: Martinus Nijhoff, 1962), 219; Boxer, *Dutch Seaborne Empire*, 99. Both Meilink-Roelofsz and Boxer refer to the Banda island extermination essentially only in passing, an issue for comment in itself. Meilink-Roelofsz, however, does give some indication of the collapse of the indigenous population, prior to 1621, under the impact of external destabilisation and war.

91 The previous year –1650 – the Herren XII, the VOC Board Directors, had issued instructions confirming that where the monopoly was enforced, the inhabitants were to be 'well treated'. See C. R. Boxer, *John Compagnie in War and Peace, a Short History of the Dutch East Indian Company 1602–1799* (Hong Kong: Heinemann Asia, 1979), 21–2.

92 Boxer, *Dutch Seaborne Empire*, 99.

93 See for instance, Pakenham, *Scramble*, 464, on the extirpation of the January 1895 Brass rebellion.

94 See Marchal, *L'État*, vol. 1, chapter 11, 'Esclavage sous l'appellation libération'; Hochschild, *King Leopold's Ghost*, 123–4.

95 Hochschild, *King Leopold's Ghost*, 231.

96 Ibid., 228–9.

97 Marchal, *L'État*, vol. 1, 354–7. See more generally, part 3, 'La regne de la terreur', for a much fuller catalogue of atrocities and killings.

98 See Hochschild, *King Leopold's Ghost*, 280; W. E. Hardenburg, *The Putumayo: The Devil's Paradise* (London: T. Fisher Unwin, 1912).

99   Hochschild, *King Leopold's Ghost*, 300.

100   See Terence Ranger, *Peasant Consciousness and Guerrilla War in Zimbabwe, a Comparative Study* (London: James Currey, 1985), 26–34, for what has been dubbed 'self-peasantisation': the widespread efforts of African societies to reform themselves, in order to avoid becoming labourers for the settler market. See also Ran Greenstein, *Genealogies of Conflict, Class, Identity and State in Palestine/ Israel and South Africa* (Hanover, NH, and London: Wesleyan University Press, 1995), 168–73, for an interesting discussion of the potentialities of native economic self-development in the context of white hegemony.

101   Pakenham, *Scramble*, 48; Gump, *Dust*, 35–7, for the *Mfecane* background to the specifically Hlubi tragedy.

102   Wellington, *South West Africa*, 218.

103   See Drechsler, *Let Us Die*, esp. 4–6, 33; Richard A. Voeltz, *German Colonialism and the South West Africa Company 1894–1914* (Ohio: Ohio University Press, 1988), 4–10. See also Lundtofte, 'Ich glaube', 75–6, for his dismissal of Chalk and Jonassohn's extrapolation of Drechsler's argument that the Hereros were 'victims of a perpetrator who killed those who blocked his access to wealth'. Chalk and Jonassohn, *History*, 231.

104   Cocker, *Rivers*, 306–8; Palmer, *Colonial Genocide*, 180–1.

105   Dan Stone, 'White Men with Low Moral Standards? German Anthropology and the Herero Genocide', *Patterns of Prejudice*, 35:2 (2001), 39, 41, quoting a German colonial journal of 1896 and the official German military history of the Herero war (1906).

106   Mike Davis, *Late Victorian Holocausts, El Niño Famines and the Making of the Third World* (London and New York: Verso, 2001), 200. One might note, however, that rinderpest was itself a probable by-product of ecological imperialism through the importation of infected Russian cattle, intended as the meat ration for the Italian invasion of Eritrea. See John Lonsdale, 'The Conquest State of Kenya', in Moor and Wesseling, *Imperialism*, 101; Richard Pankhurst and Douglas H. Johnson, 'The Great Drought and Famine of 1888–2 in Northeast Africa', in Johnson and David M. Anderson, eds, *The Ecology of Survival, Case Studies from Northeast African History* (London and Boulder, CO: Lester Crook Academic Publishing and Westview Press, 1988), 48–52.

107   Davis, *Late Victorian Holocausts*, 201.

108   Drechsler, *Let Us Die,* 98.

109   Wellington, *South West Africa*, 197; Voeltz, *German Colonialism*, 54.

110   Cocker, *Rivers*, 310–11.

111   Drechsler, *Let Us Die*, 118–19.

112   Voeltz, *German Colonialism*, 66–8.

113   See Neville Alexander, 'The Namibian War of Anti-Colonial Resistance 1904–7', in Wood, *Namibia*, 195. The abuse of the Herero by German traders which Bridgman, *Hereros*, 59, takes to be the key catalyst to revolt, of its own, seems to me to be questionable. It was the build-up of many factors leading to an absolute

loss of autonomy – albeit with the underlying issue of land seizure, as noted particularly by Drechsler, *Let Us Die*, 132, which led to insurrection.

114 Drechsler, *Let Us Die*, 143.

115 Cocker, *Rivers*, 316.

116 See Charles-Robert Ageron, *Histoire de l'Algérie contemporaine* (Paris: Universitaires de France, 1964); 10–16, 38–42; M. Emerit, 'La question algérienne en 1871', *Revue d'Histoire Moderne et Contemporaine*, 19 (1972), 256–64. See also Bruce Vandervort, *Wars of Imperial Conquest 1830–1914* (London: UCL Press, 1998), 56–70, for a good overview of the military struggle. J. L. Miège, 'French Action and Indigenous Reaction in the Maghrib, 1880–1914', in H. L. Wesseling, ed., *Expansion and Reaction, Essays in European Expansion and Reaction in Africa and Asia* (Leiden: Leiden University Press, 1978), 103–15, for the longer-term destabilisation.

117 V. G. Kiernan, *European Empires from Conquest to Collapse, 1815–1960* (London: Fontana and Leicester University Press, 1982), 29, notes that from the name of a Kabyle tribe that regiments of 'Zouaves' were formed. See also Douglas Porch, 'Bugeaud, Gallieni, Lyautey: The Development of French Colonial Warfare', in Peter Paret, ed., *Makers of Modern Strategy, from Machiavelli to the Nuclear Age* (Oxford: Clarendon Press, 1986), 384–5.

118 Davis, *Late Victorian Holocausts*, 98–9; Aldrich, *Greater France*, 205–8. Michel's reference to 'lessons in cannibalism' harks back to the sixteenth-century essay by Michel de Montaigne, 'On Cannibalism', where he proposed that the atrocities committed by 'civilised' Frenchmen during the religious wars proved that they were more savage than Brazilian cannibals. See Rawson, *God*, 4–9. See also Porch, 'Bugeaud', 386, 393–8; C. Fourniau, 'Colonial Wars before 1914: The Case of France in Indochina', in J. A. de Moor and H. L. Wesseling, eds, *Imperialism and War, Essays in Colonial Wars in Asia and Africa* (Leiden: E.J. Brill and University of Leiden Press, 1989), 84–6, for comparable examples of French punitive expedition rampage.

119 Kiernan, *European Empires*, 47.

120 See Andrew Ward, *Our Bones are Scattered, the Cawnpore Massacres* (London: Henry Holt and Co., 1996).

121 Quoted in Bernard Porter, *The Lion's Share, a Short History of British Imperialism 1850–1983* (Harlow: Longman, 1984), 31; Christopher Hibbert, *The Great Mutiny, India 1857* (London: Penguin, 1978), chapter 2, 'Soldiers and Sepoys', for an overview of grievances.

122 See Hibbert, *Great Mutiny*; esp. 331, 340–2, and chapter 19, 'The Fall of Lucknow'. Also Ward, *Our Bones*, part 4; Victor Kiernan, *The Lords of all Humankind, European Attitudes to Other Cultures in the Age of Empire* (London: Serif, 1995, [first published 1969]), 'The Mutiny and its Effects', 47–53.

123 Michael Lieven, '"Butchering the Brutes all over the Place", Total War and Massacre in Zululand, 1879', *History*, 84:276 (Oct. 1999), 620. More generally see

Donald R. Morris, *The Washing of the Spears: A History of the Rise of the Zulu Nation under Shaka and its Fall in the Zulu War of 1879* (London: Jonathan Cape, 1966).

124 See Rodney Davenport and Christopher Saunders, *South Africa, a Modern History* (Basingstoke and London: Macmillan, 5th edn, 2000); Noel Mostert, *Frontiers: The Epic of South Africa's Creation and the Tragedy of the Xhosa People* (New York: Alfred A. Knopf, 1992), 1249–54. The strongly millenarian backdrop linked to European land seizure, environmental degradation and famine is a feature here which strongly links these events to other last-ditch cases of native resistance throughout this volume.

125 Lieven, 'Butchering the Brutes', 631.

126 See Terence O. Ranger, *Revolt in Southern Rhodesia 1896–97, a Study in African Resistance* (London: Heinemann, 1967), esp. chapter 10, 'The Risings in African Political History'.

127 Arthur Kepple-Jones, *Rhodes and Rhodesia. The White Conquest of Zimbabwe 1884–1902* (Kingston and Montreal: McGill-Queen's University Press, 1983), chapters 11 and 12. Ranger, *Revolt*, chapters 4 and 6–8, for the contours and chronology of the insurrections.

128 Kepple-Jones, *Rhodes*, chapter 4, 'The Pioneers and their Rivals'.

129 Ibid., chapter 8, 'Bricks without Straw'.

130 Gewald, *Herero Heroes*, 8.

131 Speaking of East Africa, G. C. K. Gwassa, 'The German Intervention and African Resistance in Tanzania', in I. N. Kimambo and A. J. Temu, eds, *A History of Tanzania* (Nairobi: Heinemann, 1969), 94, notes 'In such conditions some Africans had the sense to use the Germans in the existing political game. In other words, they sought to enlist the Germans in a way that would ensure both the extermination of rivals and the friendships of the Germans.'

132 Ranger, *Revolt*, 32–7. See also Peter Becker, *Path of Blood, the Rise and Conquests of Mzilikazi, Founder of the Matabele Tribe of Southern Africa* (London: Penguin, 1972), for a more colourful narrative.

133 Kepple-Jones, *Rhodes*, chapters 6 and 7, 'Jameson's War i: The Incidents and the Intrigue' and 'ii: The Victory of the Maxim Gun'; Ranger, *Revolt*, 92–101.

134 Pakenham, *Scramble*, 500.

135 Kepple-Jones, *Rhodes,* 563.

136 See Lawrence Vambe, *An Ill-Fated People, Zimbabwe Before and After Rhodes* (London: Heinemann, 1972), 154.

137 See Ranger, *Revolt,* 2–4, for the repeated and almost unanimously negative settler and administrator verdict on the craven and febrile nature of Shona society. Also Robin H. Palmer, 'War and Land in Rhodesia in the 1890s', in Bethwell A. Ogot, ed., *War and Society in Africa, Ten Studies* (London: Frank Cass, 1972), 93.

138 Vambe, *Ill-Fated People*, 124, 134. For Vambe's own VaShawasha people, the uprising is known as the Chindunduma.

139 Gewald, *Herero Heroes,* chapter 7, 'This Land is Not Yours, It is the Property of America and the Herero, 1915–23', for the changes in Hereroland wrought by

the First World War. See also Poewe, *Namibian Herero*, for longer-term processes of psychic as well as physical dislocation, survival and revitalisation.

140 Lundtofte, 'Ich glaube', 103. See also the various discussions pervading Boemeke, *Anticipating Total War*, part 4, 'The Experience of War'.

141 Though essentially contemporary, and hence post-colonial in its terms of reference, see James C. Scott, *Weapons of the Weak, Everyday Forms of Peasant Resistance* (New Haven, CT, and London: Yale University Press, 1985); especially chapter 2, 'Normal Exploitation, Normal Resistance', for the classic study of grass-roots peasant struggle without recourse to 'collective outright defiance'. See also Terence O. Ranger, 'African Initiatives and Resistance in the Face of Partition and Conquest', in A. Adu Boahen, ed., *General History of Africa*, vol. 7: *Africa under Colonial Domination 1880–1935* (London and Nairobi: Heinemann and UNESCO, 1985), 67–85, for forms of resistance to colonial rule.

142 See Alfred Draper, *The Amritsar Massacre, Twilight of the Raj* (Leatherhead and Ashford: Buchan and Enright, 1985), 14. See also the concluding remarks of Sengoopta, *Imprint*, 204, on the degree to which despotic imperial rule in India combined with 'intense insecurity'.

143 Davis, *Late Victorian Holocausts*, 173 estimates that in Gujarat up to 1 in 6 of its population died in the famine.

144 See Christine Kinealy, *The Great Catastrophe: The Irish Famine, 1845–52* (Dublin: Gill and Macmillan, 1994); Peter Gray, *Famine, Land and Politics: British Government and Irish Society, 1843–1850* (Dublin: Irish Academic Press, 1999).

145 Davis, *Late Victorian Holocausts*, esp. part 1, 'The Great Drought, 1876–1878', and part 2, 'El Niño and the New Imperialism, 1888–1902'.

146 See Stuart Creighton Miller, *'Benevolent Assimilation', the American Conquest of the Philippines, 1899–1903* (New Haven, CT, and London: Yale University Press, 1982), for a suitably acerbic dismantling of American self-deception.

147 Vambe, *Ill-Fated People*, 124. See also Ranger, *Revolt*, 17–24, 212–19, for the significance of the Mwari cult in the Shona revolt and European misperceptions of it.

148 Cocker, *Rivers*, 316.

149 See G. C .K. Gwassa, 'African Methods of Warfare during the Maji-Maji War, 1905–1907', in Ogot, *War*, 123–48. See particularly, 123, where Gwassa refers to a German officer, Eduard Haber, who, acknowledging the skilled and systematic African campaign assumed it was either a discharged askari or Arab who was leading it – in other words, doubting an African ability to undertake an anti-colonial insurrection of their own volition.

150 Ibid., 139, quoting Captain Wagenheim operating in the Monogoro region: 'In my view only hunger and want can bring about a formal submission. Military action alone will remain more or less a drop in the ocean'.

151 See J. Iliffe, *Tanganikya under German Rule, 1905–1912* (Cambridge: Cambridge University Press, 1979), 201–2. More generally chapter 6, 'The Maji-Maji Rebellion, 1905–7'.

152 See Davis, *Late Victorian Holocausts*, 133–8; Pankhurst and Johnson, 'The Great Drought', 57–65, for the already vastly destabilised conditions in the Sudan as a result of El Niño-related drought and subsequent famine. Also Vandervort, *Wars*, 170–7, for a militarily standard, and Lindqvist, *Exterminate*, 63–9, for a more charged reading of the battle and post-battle killings at Omdurman.

153 P. M. Holt, *A Modern History of the Sudan: From the Funj Sultanate to the Present Day* (London: Weidenfeld and Nicolson, 1961), 78–9. See part 11, 'The Mahdist State', for a fuller background.

154 Miège, 'French Action', 106, for the *Le Temps* editorial, of 1885, demanding constant vigilance against the potential anti-colonial alliance of Mahdism, the Sanusi and the Turks.

155 Pakenham, *Scramble*, 652.

156 See *Perang Kolonial Belanda di Aceh/The Dutch Colonial War in Aceh* (Banda, Aceh: Documentation and Information Centre of Aceh, 2nd edn, 1990), esp. 187–94; Dutch sources referred to in Kuitenbrouwer, *Netherlands*, 321, put the death toll from the 1904 operation at 3,000 villagers, including 1,200 women and children.

157 Robert M. Levine, *Vale of Tears: Revisiting the Canudos Massacre in Northeastern Brazil, 1893–1897* (Berkeley and Los Angeles: UCLA Press, 1992), 190.

158 Ibid. See also Levine's shorter article, 'The Canudos Massacre: A Hundred Years On', in Levene and Roberts, *Massacre*, 185–204.

159 Han Woo-keun, *The History of Korea* (Seoul: Eul-Yoo Publishing Co., 1970), 354–7, and chapter 28, 'The Tonghak Revolt'; Stewart Lone, *Japan's First Modern War, Army and Society in the Conflict with China, 1894–95* (London: St Martin's Press, 1994), 25–7.

160 Davis, *Late Victorian Holocausts*, 125. See also Han, *History*, 413.

161 Davis, *Late Victorian Holocausts*, 178–86; Diana Preston, *A Brief History of the Boxer Rebellion, China's War on Foreigners, 1900* (London: Constable and Robinson, 2002), 26–30.

162 See Immanuel C. Y. Hsu, *The Rise of Modern China* (Oxford and New York: Oxford University Press, 1970), 462–3.

163 Ibid., 466. More generally, Preston, *Brief History*, chapter 2, 'Boxers and Devils'.

164 Preston, *Brief History*, 289–90, notes that not less than 30,000 Catholic Christians alone were killed. Some 200 missionaries and their families were amongst others also massacred. For further (though in terms of atrocity more diluted) details on the course of the siege, see Peter Fleming, *The Siege at Peking* (London: Readers Union, 1959).

165 Röhl, *Kaiser*, 13–14, quotes a section of the speech thus: '... you must avenge the death not only of the envoy but of many other Germans and Europeans ... pardon will not be given, prisoners will not be taken. Whoever falls into your hands will fall to your sword. Just as a thousand years ago the Huns under King Attila made a name for themselves for ferocity ... so may the name of Germany

become known in China in such a way that no Chinaman will ever dare to look a German in the eye with a squint.'

166 Preston, *Brief History*, chapter 18, 'The Spoils of Peking'. Also F. Laritier, 'La guerre des Boxers: une expédition internationale, 1900', *Revue historique des armées*, 1(1992), 115–23.

167 See Preston, *Brief History*, 298–300.

168 Sabrine Dabrinhaus, 'An Army on Vacation? The German War in China, 1900–1901', in Boemeke, *Anticipating Total War*, 466.

169 Drechsler, *Let Us Die*, 164–5.

170 Pakenham, *Scramble*, 652.

171 Dabrinhaus, 'Army', 468–9.

172 Ibid., 469.

173 Dedering, 'Certain Rigorous Treatment', 212, 214.

174 Gay, *Cultivation*, 89–90.

175 See Romain H. Rainero, 'The Battle of Adowa on 1st March 1896: A Reappraisal', in Moor and Wesseling, *Imperialism*, 189–200, for a perspicacious reading of Adowa's broad significance. Also Vandervort, *Wars*, 156–64, for the battle itself and its specific impact on Italian politics and society; Pankhurst and Johnson, 'The Great Drought', 48–57, for the backdrop of invasion, drought, rinderpest and famine.

176 Best, *Humanity*, 139–41. Just as a reminder that native resisters to European encroachment were also perfectly capable of ignoring the laws of war, Vandervort, *Wars*, 64, notes that *after* the battle of Adowa the thousand surviving captured Eritrean and Tigrayan askaris who had fought on the side of the Italians had their right hands and left feet cut off by Menelik's victorious, Christian army.

177 Best, *Humanity*, 162.

178 See for instance, Kristin L. Hoganson, *Fighting for American Manhood, How Gender Politics Provoked the Spanish–American and Philippine–American Wars* (New Haven, CT, and London: Yale University Press, 1998), esp. chapter 2, 'Cuba and the Restoration of American Chivalry'.

179 Ibid., chapter 6, 'The Problem of Male Degeneracy and the Allure of the Philippines'; Richard E. Welch, Jr., *The United States and the Philippine–American War, 1899–1902* (Chapel Hill: University of North Carolina Press, 1979), 101–6.

180 An historic memory of such potent significance, argues Michel-Rolph Trouillot, that it literally had to be airbrushed out of it. See idem., *Silencing the Past, Power and the Production of History* (Boston: Beacon Press, 1995), chapter 3, 'An Unthinkable History, the Haitian Revolution as a Non-Event'. James, *Black Jacobins*, for the actual history.

181 See Ada Ferrer, *Race, Nation and Revolution, Cuba 1868–1898* (Chapel Hill and London: University of North Carolina Press, 1999).

182 Brian McAllister Linn, *The US Army and Counter-Insurgency in the Philippine War 1899–1902* (Chapel Hill and London: University of North Carolina Press, 1989), 23, 53.

183 Ferrer, *Race*, 152.

184 see Miller, *Benevolent Assimilation,* 9; Balfour, *End*, 21–2. Also Hoganson, *Fighting*, 49–51, for suitably lurid and sado-erotic US 'yellow press' accounts of Weyler's atrocities.

185 Miller, *'Benevolent Assimilation'*, 237–38; Welch, *United States*, 40–1; also chapter 9, 'The Press, Atrocities and Patriotic Pride'.

186 Glenn Anthony May, 'Was the Philippine–American War a "Total War"?', in Boemeke, *Anticipating Total War*, 446–7.

187 Welch, *United States*, 41, 38.

188 May, 'Philippine–American War', 453.

189 Linn, *US Army*, 155.

190 Reynaldo Clemena Ileto, *Pasyon and Revolution: Popular Movements in the Philippines 1840–1910* (Manila: Atanco de Manila University Press, 1979), 208–9. Ileto in using the term 'genocide' infers here a population collapse through starvation and illness rather than direct physical extermination.

191 Quoted in Linn, *US Army*, 54.

192 Quoted in Davis, *Late Victorian Holocausts*, 199. However, the much more sanguine figure of 200,000 fatalities through 'famine, disease and other war-related calamities', as offered by Welch, *The United States*, 42, is catastrophic enough.

193 S. B. Spies, *Methods of Barbarism: Roberts and Kitchener and Civilians in the Boer Republics, January 1900–May 1902* (Cape Town: Human and Rousseau, 1977), esp. chapter 6, 'Kitchener's Initial Measures: December 1900 to March 1901'.

194 A. C. Martin, *The Concentration Camps 1900–1902* (Cape Town: Timmins, 1957), 6–7.

195 Pakenham, *Scramble*, 578–79; Martin, *The Concentration Camps*, 6–7. Warwick, *Black People*, 145, notes that a figure of 29,927 Boer fatalities in the camps amounted to some 10 per cent of the Boer republics' populations. Warwick also notes, however, that the proportionate mortality in the black *refugee* camps – in which at least 14,000 died – actually exceeded that of the concentration camps.

196 See notably Emily Hobhouse, *Report of a Visit to the Camps of Women and Children in the Cape and Orange River Colonies* (London: Friars Printing Association, 1901).

197 The words of the Liberal leader, Sir Henry Campbell-Bannerman, interestingly seem to portend Lemkin's original efforts at a definition of genocide as presented to the 1933 Madrid conference. Quoted in Warwick, *Black People*, 145.

198 Ibid., 164; Pakenham, *Scramble*, 579.

199 Pakenham, *Scramble*, 648–9. Warwick, *Black People*, 95, puts the Zulu casualties at between 3,500 and 4,000.

200 G. H. Mungeam, *British Rule in Kenya 1895–1912* (Oxford: Clarendon Press, 1966), 171–80. In addition to Churchill's venom, the issue was also pursued by a R. Popham Lobb, a conscientious Colonial Office official who compiled a report showing that, as well as the hundred massacred in the 1908 Kisii raid, which had precipitated Churchill's ire, 2,426 tribespeople had been killed in six other separate 'minor expeditions' between 1902 and 1906. Nearly 100,000 animals, in

other words, these peoples' livelihoods, had also been slaughtered, or taken away. For Lobb's efforts, he was removed to another posting. Lonsdale, 'Conquest State', 87–120, provides an immaculate analysis of the structural state-building underpinnings to the escalation in British military violence in Kenya. Also Ranger, *Revolt*, 350–1, for further parallels between the nature of grass-roots, religiously inspired supra-tribal Nandi resistance to the British, and other revolts in east and southern Africa.

201 Dedering, 'Certain Rigorous Treatment', 214.

202 Cocker, *Rivers*, 355; Wellington, *South West Africa*, 231.

203 See Gewald, *Herero Heroes*, chapter 7, 'This Land is not Yours', for the Hereros' partially successful post-1918 efforts to regain some of their land.

204 Quoted in Cocker, *Rivers*, 356. More generally, see Wellington, *South West Africa*, chapter 16, 'Apartheid'.

205 Cocker, *Rivers*, 357.

206 Quoted in Gewald, *Herero Heroes*, 274.

207 Iliffe, *Tanganikya*, 200–2 where evidence of the demographic collapse, in the wake of the famine, is made manifest through the return of forest, the tsetse fly and elephants to previously well-cultivated regions.

208 See Philip Knightley, *The First Casualty, from the Crimea to Vietnam, the War Correspondent as Hero, Propagandist and Mythmaker* (London and Melbourne: Quartet Books, 1978). Though lacking in reference to the sort of colonial campaigns described here, Knightley's coverage of mostly War Type One campaigns provides a penetrating insight into the ongoing way in which military commanders and political establishments massage, repackage and airbrush out news to suit state as well as their own personal interests.

209 See E. E. Evans-Pritchard, *The Sanusi of Cyrenaica* (London: Oxford University Press, 1949), esp. chapter 3, 'The First Italo-Sanusi War (1911–17)'.

210 Kiernan, *European Empires*, 156.

211 Ibid., 166.

212 J. Gooch, *Army, State and Society in Italy 1870–1915*, quoted in Vandervort, *Wars*, 206. See also Angelo del Boca, *Gli italiani in Libia*, vol. 1: *Tripoli bel suol d'amore 1860–1922* (Rome and Bari: Laterza, 1986), for a comprehensive survey of the Italian invasion and aftermath.

213 Giorgio Rochat, 'La repressione della resistenza Arabe in Cirenaica nel 1930–31: Nei Documenti dell'Archivo Graziani', *Il Movimento di Liberazione in Italia*, 25:110 (1973), 3–39; Evans-Pritchard, *The Sanusi*, 191, puts the number of Bedouin in these concentration camps at 80,000, and the total population loss between 1911 and 1932 at something between one-third and one-half.

214 Quoted in Evans-Pritchard, *The Sanusi*, 198. Following the exterminatory phase, the fascist state did attempt to encapsulate Bedouin survivors and returning refugees into the Italian system. However, both the attempt at the detribalisation and at the sedentarisation failed.

6 Declining Powers

1 See Hedley Bull, *The Anarchical Society, a Study of Order in World Politics* (Basingstoke: Macmillan, 1977), for more on this theme.

2 Kennedy, *Rise*, chapter 6, 'The Coming of the Bipolar World', for Austrian and Russian relative positions compared with the other powers.

3 See Kann, *Multinational Empire*, vol. 2, chapter 19, 'Nationalism Reconsidered'; Robin Okey, *The Habsburg Empire, c. 1765–1918. From Enlightement to Eclipse* (Basingstoke: Macmillan, 2001), chapter 7, 'Liberalism'.

4 See Glenny, *Balkans*, 225–6.

5 See George F. Kennan, *The Other Balkan Wars, a 1913 Carnegie Endowment Inquiry in Retrospect with a New Introduction and Reflections on the Present Conflict* (Washington, DC: Carnegie Endowment for International Peace, 1993 [first published 1914]), notably chapter 4, 'The War of the Nationalities'; McCarthy, *Death and Exile*, 164, for a (possibly inflated) estimate of nearly 1.5 million Muslims displaced from the Macedonian region in the period 1911–14. The impact and legacy of Balkan wars, ethnic cleansing and atrocities will be further considered in the next volume of this work.

6 See Louise Nalbandian, *The Armenian Revolutionary Movement: The Development of Armenian Political Parties through the Nineteenth Century* (Berkeley and Los Angeles: University of California Press, 1963), 118–26, 176–8, for the thinking and strategy of both Hunchak and Dashnak revolutionary parties on this score.

7 This is hardly to diminish the scale, or ugliness of the atrocities. See Januarius A. MacGahan, *The Turkish Atrocities in Bulgaria* (Geneva: n.p., 1966), for a contemporary news reporter's first-hand account of the *bashi-bazouk* killings. See also James J. Reid, 'Batak 1876: A Massacre and its Significance', *Journal of Genocide Research*, 2:3 (2000), 375–409, for the killing of some 8,000 Bulgarian villagers by Ottoman regulars and irregulars – as first reported by MacGahan – at the epicentre of the insurrection.

8 Glenny, *Balkans*, 138–51, for the terms of the Berlin settlement.

9 See for example H. N. Brailsford, *Macedonia, its Races and their Future* (London: Methuen, 1906), 135–6, for a brazen personal account of a failed attempt by a radical Bulgarian splinter group to blow up a mosque at Friday evening prayers in order to precipitate the 'inevitable' Turkish counter-massacre.

10 See Tessa Hoffman and Gerayer Koutcharian, 'The History of Armenian–Kurdish Relations in the Ottoman Empire', *Armenian Review*, 39:4 (1986), 30, n. 71, 33–4, with regard, for instance, to the Balikli and Zaza, two not insignificant Islamicised and Kurdified groupings with notable Armenian linguistic and ethnic traits.

11 Christopher J. Walker, *Armenia: The Survival of a Nation* (London: Croom Helm, 1980), 156–64, for details.

12 See Robin Okey, 'State, Church, and Nation in the Serbo-Croat speaking Lands of the Habsburg monarchy 1850–1914', in Donal A. Kerr et al., eds, *Compara-*

tive Studies on Governments and non-Dominant Ethnic Groups in Europe 1850–1940, Religion, State and Ethnic Groups (Dartmouth: New York University Press and European Science Foundation, 1992), vol. 2, 51–78.

13 See Geoffrey Hosking, *Russia, People and Empire, 1552–1917* (London: Harper-Collins, 1997), xix, for the distinction.

14 See Hans Kohn, *Pan-Slavism, its History and Ideology* (Notre Dame, IL: University of Notre Dame Press, 1953), for the full treatment; Michael Boro Petrovich, *The Emergence of Russian Pan-Slavism, 1856–1870* (New York: Columbia University Press, 1956), for the more specifically Russian understanding of it.

15 Peter Holquist, '"To Count, to Extract and to Exterminate," Population Politics in Late Imperial and Soviet Russia', in Ronald Grigor Suny and Terry Martin, eds, *A State of Nations, Empire and Nation-Making in the Age of Lenin and Stalin* (Oxford: Oxford University Press, 2001), 114. See also Robert E. Dickinson, *The German Lebensraum* (London: Penguin, 1943), for a detailed examination of specifically German imaginings of this nature.

16 See Andrew Gladding Whiteside, *Socialism of Fools, Georg Ritter von Schönerer and Austrian Pan-Germanism* (Berkeley and Los Angeles: University of California Press 1975) and idem. *Austrian National Socialism before 1918* (The Hague: Martinus Nijhoff, 1962), for more on these feelings of grievance and of the central role of the pan-Germanist, von Schönerer, in attempting to politically mobilise them.

17 David Saunders, *Russia in the Age of Reaction and Reform 1801–1881* (Longman: Harlow, 1992), 283.

18 See Jacob M. Landau, *Pan-Turkism: From Irredentism to Cooperation* (London: Hurst and Co., 1983), esp. chapter 2, 'Pan-Turkism in the Ottoman Empire, Genesis and Flowering'; George Georgiades Arnakis, 'Turanism, an Aspect of Turkish Nationalism', *Balkan Studies*, 1 (1960), 19–32.

19 Jacob M. Landau, *Pan-Turkism in Turkey* (London: Hurst and Co., 1995), 52.

20 See both W. G. Beasley, 'Japan and Pan-Asianism: Problems of Definition', and J. Y. Wong, 'Sun Yat-sen and Pan-Asianism', in Janet Hunter, ed., *Aspects of Pan-Asianism* (London: Suntory Toyota International Centre, 1987), for rather sceptical views on the strength or significance of pan-Asianism in Chinese nationalist circles.

21 Lieven, *Empire*, 137. More broadly see Jacob M. Landau, *The Politics of Pan-Islam, Ideology and Organisation* (Oxford: Clarendon Press, 1994), chapter 1, 'The Hamidian Era, an Imperial Ideology'.

22 Lieven, *Empire*, 130.

23 Karpat, 'Millets and Nationality', 107–34; Roderic Davison, 'Nationalism as an Ottoman Problem and the Ottoman Response', in William H. Haddad and William Ochsenwald, eds, *Nationalism in a Non-National State, the Dissolution of the Ottoman Empire* (Columbus: Ohio State University Press, 1977), 25–56, for more on the complexities of Ottoman state–communal relations.

24 See Richard G. Hovannisian, *Armenia, on the Road to Independence, 1918* (Berkeley and Los Angeles: University of California Press, 1967), 37, and by way of comparison, McCarthy, *Muslims*, 50–9.

25 John King Fairbank, *The Great Chinese Revolution 1800–1985* (New York: Harper and Row, 1986), 81. Ternon, *État criminel*, 287, quotes the figure of 40 million dead, mostly indirect deaths from famine, as a result of Taiping. Perhaps this highlights the degree to which nobody really knows the death toll from all these events. See Jack Gray, *Rebellions and Revolutions, China from the 1800s to 2000* (Oxford: Oxford University Press, 2nd edn, 2002), chapter 3, 'The Taiping Rebellions, 1850–1864', for a broad analysis.

26 See Jonathan D. Spence, *God's Chinese Son, the Taiping Heavenly Kingdom of Hong Xinquan* (New York and London: W.W. Norton and Co., 1996). Also E. Zürchner, 'Western Expansion and Chinese Reaction: A Theme Reconsidered', in Wesseling, *Expansion*, 70–2, for a succinct but valuable analysis of Western influence in the making of Taiping.

27 See Sechin Jagchid, 'Discrimination against Minorities in China', Veenhoven, *Case Studies*, vol. 2, 391–2; François Thierry, 'Empire and Minority in China', in Gérard Chaliand, ed., *Minority Peoples in the Age of Nation-States*, trans. Tony Berrett (London: Pluto Press, 1989), 76–7.

28 June Teufel Dreyer, *China's Forty Millions, Minority Nationalities and National Integration in the People's Republic of China* (Cambridge, MA, and London: Harvard University Press, 1976), 3.

29 Thierry, 'Empire', 85; S. C. M. Paine, *Imperial Rivals. China, Russia and their Disputed Frontier* (Armonk, NY, and London: M.E. Sharpe, 1996), for the longer-term consequences.

30 Thierry, 'Empire', 85.

31 Ibid., 88.

32 The figure quoted by Wen-Djang Chu, *The Moslem Rebellion in North-West China 1862–1878, a Study of Government Minority Policy* (The Hague and Paris: Mouton and Co., 1966), 1. The vast death toll appears not to have been entirely the result of direct physical extermination. According to Owen Lattimore, *Pivot of Asia, Sinkiang, the Inner Asian Frontiers of China and Russia* (Boston: Little, Brown, 1950), 126, some 30 per cent of the tribe were directly exterminated while something in the region of 40 per cent died of possibly smallpox epidemic either before, or in the wake of the Qing onslaught. Twenty per cent possibly fled to Russia. Others were reduced to slavery. That said there is little extant information in western European scholarship on this dramatic event.

33 See Morris Rossabi, 'Muslim and Central Asian Revolts', in Jonathan D. Spence and John E. Wills, Jr., eds, *From Ming to Ch'ing, Conquest, Region, and Contnuity in Seventeenth-Century China* (New Haven, CT, and London: Yale University Press, 1979), 169–99.

34 Kappeler, *Russian Empire*, 43–4. Few of the 100,000–150,000 Kalmyks who responded to the Chinese invitation made it to Dzangaria, succumbing instead to the intervening desert and attacks from rival Kazakh and Kirghiz tribes.

35 Chu, *Moslem Rebellion*, 190.

36 While Chu presents no figures on the overall Sinkiang population of the period, one might extrapolate backwards from the Chinese 1982 census statistics, (tabulated in Burger, *Report*, 228–9) – putting the Uighur population of the region, at 5.95 million, with other ethnic groups numbering tens of thousands, or hundreds of thousands – to assume a significant eighteenth- and ninteenth-century indigenous population, even after the Dzangar catastrophe. According to Paine, *Imperial Rivals*, 129, n. 4, for instance, the Illi valley alone had a population of 350.000 before the uprising, that had been reduced to 130,000, by 1876.

37 See Dru C. Gladney, *Muslim Chinese, Ethnic Nationalism in the People's Republic* (Cambridge, MA: Harvard University Press, 1991) for more on the Muslim Hui.

38 Rossabi, 'Muslim and Central Asian Revolts', 180–1.

39 Ibid., 193. The role of the Naqshbandi in state–communal dynamics will appear again more centrally in Volume III's discussion of Turkey's inter-war conflicts with its Kurdish minority.

40 Again, while he does not offer figures for Sinkiang itself, Chu, *Moslem Rebellion*, vii, quotes sources which claim that the overall population of Kansu, both Muslim and non-Muslim, was reduced from 15 million to only 1 million, as a result of the fighting, mostly through starvation.

41 Hsu, *Rise*, 382; Rossabi, 'Muslim and Central Asian Revolts', 172–3, for more on the politico-religious role of the *khojas* in Central Asia.

42 David Gillard, *The Struggle for Asia 1828–1914, a Study in British and Russian Imperialism* (London: Methuen and Co., 1977), 129.

43 Chu, *Moslem Rebellion*, 166–7.

44 Ibid., 118–25.

45 Ibid., 177.

46 Ibid., 171–6.

47 Thierry, 'Empire', 85; Owen Lattimore, *Inner Asian Frontiers of China* (Oxford and New York: Oxford University Press, 1988 [first published 1940]), 183–7. Unfortunately, this author is aware of no specific assessment of the mortality as a result of Tso Tsung-t'ang's campaign. A figure of 1 million Sinkiang casualties for the period 1862–77 comes from Linda K. Benson, 'The Turkic Peoples of China', in Margaret Bainbridge, ed., *The Turkic Peoples of the World* (London and New York: Kegan Paul International, 1993), 55, but is itself clearly derived from another (unspecified) source.

48 Fairbank, *Great Chinese Revolution*, 117. Paine, *Imperial Rivals*, chapter 4, 'Ethnic Tensions: The Muslim Uprising and Russian Invasion', for the contours of the Sino-Russian stand-off.

49 Hsu, *Rise*, 388.

50 Lieven, *Empire*, 210.

51 See Kappeler, *Russian Empire*, chapter 5, 'Colonial Expansion in Asia in the Nineteenth Century', for the broad contours of these developments. See also Mark Bassin, 'Inventing Siberia–Visions of the Russian East in the Early Nineteenth Century', *American Historical Review*, 96:3 (1991), 763–94, for US frontier comparisons.

52 Stephen Shenfield, 'The Circassians, a Forgotten Genocide?', in Levene and Roberts, *Massacre*, 154–5; Kappeler, *Russian Empire*, 153–7, for these and other examples of Russian extirpatory violence. Also Yuri Slezkine, *Arctic Mirrors: Russia and the Small Peoples of the North* (Ithaca, NY: Cornell University Press, 1994).

53 Hosking, *Russia*, 22, agrees, as does Firuz Kazemzadeh, 'Russian Penetration of the Caucasus', in Taras Hunczak, ed., *Russian Imperialism from Ivan the Great to the Revolution* (New Brunswick, NJ: Rutgers University Press, 1974), 261.

54 See Lionel Kochan, *Russia in Revolution, 1890–1918* (London: Weidenfeld and Nicolson, 1966), 10–13, for Witte's famous 1898 memorandum to the tsar, setting out his fears of ultimate neo-colonial status for Russia.

55 Robert Seely, *Russo-Chechen Conflict, 1800–2000, a Deadly Embrace* (London and Portland, OR: Frank Cass, 2001), 19.

56 Moshe Gammer, *Muslim Resistance to the Czar: Shamil and the Conquest of Chechnia and Daghestan* (London: Frank Cass, 1994), 24.

57 Porch, 'Bugeaud', 380–1, on the increasing French resort to a form of genocidal warfare in Algeria in the 1840s. For Russian comparisons see Paul B. Henze, 'Fire and Sword in the Caucasus: the 19th Century Resistance of the North Caucasian Mountaineers', *Central Asian Survey*, 2:1 (1983), 5–44. Also see Anna Zelkina, *In Quest for God and Freedom: The Sufi Response to the Russian Advance in the North Caucasus* (London, Hurst and Co., 2000) for the role of the Naqshbandi in the evolution and bolstering of Caucasian anti-imperial resistance, 5–44; Kiernan, *European Empires*, 58–9, 74–6.

58 Shenfield, 'Circassians', 150; Paul B. Henze, 'Circassian Resistance to Russia', in Marie Benningsen Broxup, ed., *The North Caucasus Barrier: The Russian Advance towards the Muslim World* (London: Hurst and Co., 1992), 66–70.

59 Gammer, *Muslim Resistance*, 25.

60 Henze, 'Fire', 6.

61 Lieven, *Empire*, 213. See also Hosking, *Russia*, 21.

62 See Hosking, *Russia*, 315–20, for a succinct commentary on the war-reform connection.

63 Saunders, *Russia*, 208, 278–89; Gillard, *Struggle*, 96.

64 See Willis Brooks, 'Russia's Conquest and Pacification of the Caucasus: Relocation becomes a Pogrom in the Post-Crimean War Period', *Nationalities Papers*, 23:4 (1995), 675–86, for an exposition on this theme. Also Gillard, *Struggle*, 96; Lieven, *Empire*, 210–11.

65 See Max Beloff, *The Foreign Policy of Soviet Russia, 1929–1941*, vol. 2: *1936–1941* (London and New York: Royal Institute of International Affairs and Oxford University Press, 1949), 301–2, 309, n. 5. Also Anthony Read and David Fisher, *The*

Deadly Embrace, Hitler, Stalin and the Nazi-Soviet Pact 1939–1941 (New York and London, W.W. Norton and Co., 1988), 529, for Soviet foreign minister, Molotov's direct reference to the Black Sea 'as England's historic gateway for attack on the Soviet Union', during the Crimean war, in his ill-fated November 1940 meeting with Hitler.

66 Henze, 'Circassian Resistance', 80–7.

67 Seely, *Russo-Chechen Conflict*, 57.

68 Gillard, *Struggle*, 104. See also Henze, 'Circassian Resistance', 76.

69 See Hosking, *Russia*, 319–20; Hans Rogger, *Jewish Policies and Right-Wing Politics in Imperial Russia* (Basingstoke: Macmillan, 1986), 12.

70 Rogger, *Jewish Policies*, 13. More generally see John Doyle Klier, *Imperial Russia's Jewish Question, 1855–1881* (Cambridge: Cambridge University Press, 1995).

71 Hosking, *Russia*, part 4, chapter 3, 'Russification'.

72 Shenfield, 'Circassians', 151.

73 Ibid., 154. See also Austin Lee Jersild, 'Imperial Russification, Dagestani Mountain Dwellers in Russian Exile', in John Morison, ed., *Ethnic and National Issues in Russian and East European History, Selected Papers from the Fifth World Congress of Central and East European Studies, Warsaw 1995* (Basingstoke: Macmillan, 2000), 29–45, for one comparable, small-scale but disastrous example of forcible relocation and attempted sedentarisation, in the 1870s, in which 400 of the most vulnerable of a 1,600-strong mountain-people group died during, or immediately after, migration to Saratov province.

74 Kappeler, *Russian Empire*, 183.

75 See Moshe Gammer, 'Russian Strategies in the Conquest of Chechnia and Daghestan, 1825–1859', in Broxup, *North Caucasus Barrier*, 45–61.

76 Holquist, 'To Count', 117.

77 Ibid., 118.

78 Shenfield, 'Circassians', 152.

79 Quoted in ibid., 153.

80 Henze, 'Circassian Resistance', 111, 103–4; also Kazemzadeh, 'Russian Penetration', 262.

81 As reported in Seely, *Russo-Chechen Conflict*, 60.

82 Shenfield, 'Circassians', 154. It is difficult to gauge how accurate these figures are in the absence of fuller demographic data. Holquist, 'To Count', 119, for instance puts the combined mortality from the Russian campaigns and their aftermath at half a million. Putting aside the issue of direct mass murder versus more generalised population collapse, the reality of mass expulsion, however, is self-evident. Kappeler, *Russian Empire*, 184, cites the figure of only 44,746 Circassians domiciled in the Russian empire in 1897.

83 See Kiernan, *European Empires*, 20–1, 27–9.

84 Holquist, 'To Count', 118.

85 Ibid., 116.

86 Notes Henze, 'Circassian Resistance', 111, of the mass dislocation and destruction of so many eastern Anatolian peoples, beginning with the Circassian events of the 1860s: 'None of these ethnic disasters is entirely unrelated to the others'.

87 See Jelle Verheij, 'Die armenischen Massaker von 1894–1896. Anatomie und Hintergrunde einer Krise', in Hans-Lukas Kieser, ed., *Die armenische Frage und die Schweiz (1896–1923)* (Zurich: Chronos, 1999), 69–133, for the first full critical study, in many decades.

88 See for example, Erich Feigl, *A Myth of Error: Turkey, Europe and Public Opinion* (Vienna and Munich: Amalthea, 1999), Vahakn N. Dadrian, compiled, *The Ottoman Empire: A Troubled Legacy, Views, Comments and Judgements by Noted Experts Worldwide* (Williamsburg, VA: Association of Genocide Scholars 1997), for the opposite ends of the spectrum.

89 Bedr Khan, an avant-gardist nineteenth-century exponent of the Kurdish nation astutely noted that, 'it was primarily the Kurd who was denounced before civilisation as a marauder and murderer'. Quoted in John Joseph, *The Nestorians and their Muslim Neighbours: A Study of Western Influences on their Relations* (Princeton, NJ: Princeton University Press, 1961), 119, See also Charles Glass, 'How the Kurds were Betrayed', *Times Literary Supplement*, 6 September 1996, 14–15, for more on the Kurdish bad press.

90 See Walker, *Armenia*, 145–6; Philip Mansel, *Constantinople, City of the World's Desire 1453–1924* (London: Penguin, 1995), 330.

91 See Jeremy Salt, *Imperialism, Evangelism and the Ottoman Armenians, 1878–1896* (London: Frank Cass, 1993), chapter 10, 'The Armenian Agitation'; Roy Douglas, 'Britain and the Armenian Question, 1894–7', *Historical Journal*, 19:1 (1976), 113–33; Manoug Joseph Somakian, *Empires in Conflict, Armenia and the Great Powers, 1895–1920* (London and New York: I.B. Tauris, 1995), 25–6. See also E. J. Dillon, 'The Condition of Armenia', *Contemporary Review*, 68 (Aug. 1895), 153–89, for a notable example of the British atrocity genre of this period, republished as *Prelude to Genocide, Conditions of Life among the Armenians in Anatolia, 1890–1895* (Armenian Genocide Resource Centre, 2001).

92 Vahakn N. Dadrian, *The History of the Armenian Genocide, Ethnic Conflict from the Balkans to Anatolia to the Caucasus* (Oxford: Berghahn Books, 1996), 115–17. See also Walker, *Armenia*, 136–44.

93 Robert F. Melson, *Revolution and Genocide: On the Origins of the Armenian Genocide and the Holocaust* (Chicago: Chicago University Press, 1992), 45, quoting the British Constantinople report and the Mus-based Commission of Inquiry. Verheij, 'armenischen Massaker', 83, for larger, British-based estimates.

94 Vahakn N. Dadrian, 'The Role of the Turkish Military in the Destruction of Ottoman Armenians: A Study in Historical Continuities', *Journal of Political and Military Sociology*, 20:2 (1992), 262–3.

95 Quoted in Melson, *Revolution*, 51.

96 Verheij, 'armenischen Massaker'; 83–4; Salt, *Imperialism*, chapter 7, 'The Ambassadors Propose'.

97 Dadrian, *History*, 120.

98 See Nalbandian, *Armenian Revolutionary Movement*, 109–14, 122–6; Verheij, 'armenischen Massaker', 84, for a more charitable interpretation of its intentions.

99 Walker, *Armenia*, 152–6; Mansel, *Constantinople*, 330–1; Verheij, 'armenischen Massaker', 84–5, for details.

100 See J. Lepsius, *Armenia and Europe, An Indictment* (London: Hodder and Stoughton, 1897), 4–18 and 154–78, for the Urfa massacre; Walker, *Armenia*, 156–64; Verheij, 'armenischen Massaker', 85–8, for the more general massacre sequence.

101 Dadrian, *History*, 148.

102 Bat Ye'or, *The Dhimmi, Jews and Christians under Islam*, trans. David Maisel et al. (Rutherford, NJ, and London: Fairleigh Dickinson University Press and Associated University Presses, 1985), for further discussion. See also Lepsius, *Armenia*, 21–30, for the nature of the atrocities committed.

103 I am grateful to Hans-Lukas Kieser, for clarification on this score. See also his *Der verpasste Friede. Mission, Ethnie und Staat in den Ostprovinzen der Türkei 1839–1938* (Zurich: Chronos, 2000), esp. 198–203, 540–3. Also Walker, *Armenia*, 155, for a further if possibly exceptional example of an attack on Armenian Catholics, near Dolmabahche.

104 See Dadrian, *History*, 147.

105 Nalbandian, *Armenian Revolutionary Movement*, 176–8; Walker, *Armenia*, 167; Mansel, *Constantinople*, 332–3.

106 Melson *Revolution*, 69, 247.

107 See Lepsius, *Armenia*, 58–61. Lepsius' evaluation of military–civil coordination derived, in part, from consular reports, is today considered largely accurate and authoritative. Few historians would agree with Stanford J. Shaw and Ezel Kural Shaw, *History of the Ottoman Empire and Modern Turkey*, vol. 2: *Reform, Revolution and the Republic: The Rise of Modern Turkey 1808–1975* (Cambridge: Cambridge University Press, 1977), 204, in their argument that the massacres were the result of a general security breakdown and that little could be done until the following spring, when the army could be brought in to restore law and order.

108 Lepsius, *Armenia*, 330–1, in his overall statistical analysis offers the figure of 88,243 Armenian deaths but considers this ultimately an underestimate, given the mortality from 'unregistered villages' and remote locations. See also the careful evaluation of the widely different estimates by Melson, *Revolution*, 46–7.

109 Melson, *Revolution*, 47.

110 Lepsius, *Armenia*, 330, chapter 4, 'A List of Crimes', for specific atrocities directed against churches, pastors and their congregations.

111 Joseph, *Nestorians*, 62–4, estimates that as many as one-fifth of the specifically 50,000-strong Hakkari community were slaughtered.

112 See Ussama Makdisi, *The Culture of Sectarianism, Community, History and Violence in Nineteenth-Century Ottoman Lebanon* (Berkeley, Los Angeles and London: University of California Press, 2000).

113 Ibid., esp. 10, and chapter 5, 'Reinventing Mount Lebanon'.

114 See Kamal Madhar Ahmad, *Kurdistan during the First World War* (London: Saqi Books, 1994), 156, for the example of a Major Mason's speech to the Royal Geographical Society in London, 1919, recalling that traditional Christian–Muslim relations in eastern Anatolia were the best between any two peoples in the Middle East. See more generally Donald Quataert, *The Ottoman Empire, 1700–1922* (Cambridge: Cambridge University Press, 1995), 172–83, for a more general endorsement of good, historically grounded inter-ethnic relations in the empire.

115 Hoffman and Koutcharian, 'History', 3, 5.

116 Ahmad, *Kurdistan*, 55–6; McDowall, *Modern History*, 89.

117 Ernest E. Ramsaur, Jr., *The Young Turks* (Princeton, NJ: Princeton University Press, 1957), 65–76, 124–9. Hanioğlu, *Young Turks*, 197–9, however, notes the fractiousness of the conference when it came to matters of ethnic cooperation.

118 See Mesrob K. Krikorian, *Armenians in the Service of the Ottoman Empire, 1860–1908* (London: Routledge and Kegan Paul, 1977), 107–8.

119 Ibid., throughout for the scope and depth of this participation.

120 Hoffman and Koutcharian, 'History', 12. See also Ronald Grigor Suny, 'Religion, Ethnicity, and Nationalism, Armenians, Turks, and the End of the Ottoman Empire', in Omer Bartov and Phyllis Mack, eds, *In God's Name, Genocide and Religion in the Twentieth Century* (New York and Oxford: Berghahn Books, 2001), 33–9, on the degree to which 'nationalisation' of the Armenian community took place against the backdrop of increasing social and economic, metropolitan versus country tensions *within* the community, not say the degree to which Armenian leaders looked to the Porte to resolve them.

121 Libaridian, 'Ultimate Repression', 216.

122 Lieven, *Empire*, 153.

123 Justin McCarthy, *Muslims and Minorities, the Population of Ottoman Anatolia at the End of Empire* (New York and London: New York University Press, 1983), 2.

124 Nalbandian, *Armenian Revolutionary Movement*, 69; Walker, *Armenia*, 95.

125 See McCarthy, *Death and Exile*, 29–32.

126 Richard G. Hovannisian, 'Historical Dimensions of the Armenian Question, 1878–1923', in idem., ed., *The Armenian Genocide in Perspective* (New Brunswick, NJ, and London: Transaction Books, 1986), 22.

127 McCarthy, *Death and Exile*, 89–91, 112–14. The figures may come from a notably polemical and partisan account. Even, however, if McCarthy's statistical extrapolations are inaccurate, the general point is correct. Ethnic cleasing was a critical element of this campaign.

128 Hoffman and Koutcharian, 'History', 33.

129 Ibid., 29–36 where the quite bitter contemporary controversy surrounding the different ethnic demographic weights is analysed at some length. The most that can be said, however, for Armenian national claims to predominance on the pla-

teau, is that 'they were the largest minority in an area where all races formed a minority'. Walker, *Armenia*, 96.

130 Salt, *Imperialism*, 86.

131 Ibid., 82–90.

132 Nalbandian, *Armenian Revolutionary Movement*, 175; J. K. Hassiotis, 'The Greeks and the Armenian Massacres (1890–1896)', *Neo-Hellenika*, 4 (1981), 73–4, for the close collaboration between the two parties. Other Armenians were also taken with the Bulgarian cause. For instance, Mkrtich Portukalian, the founder of the Armenakan, the very first Armenian revolutionary party later put in the shade by its upstart rivals, was enthusiastic about the creation of a Bulgarian state on the grounds that he considered it 'a postive precedent for the promotion of the Armenian cause'.

133 Nalbandian, *Armenian Revolutionary Movement*, 108–9, 166–9: Hratch Dasnebadian, *History of the Armenian Revolutionary Federation Dashnaktsutiun 1890/1924* (Milan: OEMME Edizione, 1989), chapter 1, 'Formation, Purpose, Expansion, 1890–1895'.

134 Unsympathetic commentators include Ramsaur, *Young Turks*, 9, who argues that the 1894 uprisings show that the revolutionaries 'were prepared to sacrifice their own people in order to attract the attention of the European powers to their desires'. Similarly, Mansel, *Constantinople*, 333, argues that both Abdulhamid and the revolutionary parties treated the Armenians of the capital as if they were pawns. Equally, however, those writing from an armenophile standpoint including Walker, *Armenia*, 135, and Nalbandian, *Armenian Revolutionary Movement*, 160, portray the uprisings as an essentially opportunistic response to an apparently disintegrating empire, while Hovannisian, *Armenia, On the Road*, 23, highlights the parties' lack of political comprehension, naiveté and weakness.

135 Mansel, *Constantinople*, 330; Walker, *Armenia*, 145–6.

136 Hoffman and Koutcharian, 'History', 15.

137 Anaide Ter Minassian, *Nationalism and Socialism in the Armenian Revolutionary Movement* (Cambridge, MA: Zoryan Institute, 1983), 4.

138 Shaw and Shaw, *History*, vol. 2, 202–3, 302.

139 Hoffman and Koutcharian, 'History', 16.

140 Nalbandian, *Armenian Revolutionary Movement*, 122, Walker, *Armenia,* 156.

141 Nalbandian, *Armenian Revolutionary Movement*, 144–5.

142 See Melson, *Revolution*, 59–60.

143 Halil İnalcik and Donald Quataert, eds, *An Economic and Social History of the Ottoman Empire 1300–1914* (Cambridge: Cambridge University Press, 1994), 761–62.

144 Roderic Davison, *Reform in the Ottoman Empire 1856–76* (Princeton, NJ: Princeton University Press, 1963), for the classic study of Tanzimat. Also see Shaw and Shaw, *Reform*, chapter 2, 'The Era of Modern Reform, the Tanzimat, 1839–1876'; Erik J. Zürcher, *Turkey, a Modern History* (London and New York: I.B. Tauris, 1993), chapter 5, 'The Era of Tanzimat 1839–71'.

145 Simon Bromley, *Rethinking Middle East Politics, State Formation and Development* (Cambridge: Polity Press, 1994), 54, notes that, by 1875, one-third to one-half of all Ottoman public revenues went on servicing the debt, effectively forcing a bankrupt government to accept the post-1881 Western control on its finances. For more on these developments see Roger Owen, *The Middle East in the World Economy 1800–1914* (London: Methuen, 1981), chapter 4, 'The Ottoman Road to Bankruptcy and the Anatolian Economy 1850–1881'; Christopher Clay, *Gold for the Sultan, Western Bankers and Ottoman Finance 1856–1881* (London: I.B. Tauris, 2000); Immanuel Wallerstein, Hale Decdeli and Resat Kasaba, 'The Incorporation of the Ottoman Empire into the World Economy', in Huri İslamoğlu-İnan, ed., *The Ottoman Empire and the World-Economy*, (Cambridge: Cambridge University Press, 1987), 88–97.

146 Hilmar Kaiser, *Imperialism, Racism, and Development Theories, the Construction of a Dominant Paradigm on Ottoman Armenians* (Ann Arbor, MI: Gomidas Institute, 1997), for a notably coruscating attack on some of these interpretations and assumptions.

147 Bromley, *Rethinking Middle East Politics*, 52–4; Charles Issawi, 'Transformation of the Economic Position of the Millets in the 19th century', in Braude and Lewis, *Christians and Jews*, vol. 1, 261–84.

148 Selim Deringil, *The Well-Protected Domains, Ideology and the Legitimation of Power in the Ottoman Empire 1876–1909* (London and New York: I.B. Tauris, 1999), chapter 5, '"They Confuse and Excite the Mind": The Missionary Problem'; Salt, *Imperialism*, chapter 3, 'The Missionary Impact'; Kieser, *Der verpasste Friede*.

149 Gladney, *Muslim Chinese*, 22.

150 See, for instance, Aron Rodrigue, *French Jews, Turkish Jews, the Alliance Israélite Universelle and the Politics of Jewish Schooling in Turkey, 1860–1925* (Bloomington and Indianapolis: Indiana University Press, 1990).

151 See Glenny, *Balkans*, 114–17, for the Greek Orthodox ferocity in the face of the Bulgarian religious breakaway to create their own Exarchate.

152 Deringil, *Well-Protected Domains*, 120.

153 Joseph, *Nestorians*, 21, 8, 13, 44.

154 See Suny 'Religion', 34–5; Melson, *Revolution*, 55.

155 See Balakian, *Black Dog*, 226–35, for an interesting family-based account of this process.

156 See Harry Jewel Sarkiss, 'The Armenian Renaissance 1500–1863', *Journal of Modern History*, 9: 4 (1937), 433–48; Walker, *Armenia*, 49–56, 97–8.

157 Kaiser, *Imperialism*, chapter 3, 'German Stereotypes of Armenians and World War 1', paradoxically, is the best introduction to these widely held Western attitudes.

158 See Stephen Astourian, 'Genocidal Process: Reflections on the Armeno-Turkish Polarization', in Richard G. Hovannisian, ed., *The Armenian Genocide, History, Politics, Ethics* (New York: St Martin's Press, 1992), 60. Astourian also notes how Armenians were vilified by Turkish defenders of the Hamidian regime on the

very grounds that the Armenians were 'allies of the much-hated West', not to say a 'cipher for modernity'.

159 Quoted in Nalbandian, *Armenian Revolutionary Movement*, 84.

160 Quoted in McDowall, *Modern History*, 56–7.

161 Joseph, *Nestorians*, 62–4.

162 Ibid., 64.

163 Martin van Bruinessen, *Aghas, Shaiks and State, the Social and Political Structure of Kurdistan* (London and Atlantic Highlands, NJ: Zed Books, 1990), 25, 180. The further irony is that the Mar Shamun – not unlike the Maronite patriarch – was in this period a declared enemy of the Protestant missionaries and threatened anathema against any member of the congregation who associated with them. See Salt, *Imperialism*, 33. This, doubly ironically, did not prevent the American missionaries' Hakkari outpost being locally dubbed 'the fortress'.

164 See Leila Tarazi Fawaz, *Occasion for War: Civil Conflict in Lebanon and Damascus in 1860* (London and New York: I.B. Tauris, 1994), chapter 5, 'International Response'.

165 See Astourian, 'Genocidal Process', 60; Suny 'Religion', 43.

166 See Walker, *Armenia*, 145–6, with reference to Abdulhamid's 1889 conversation with his confidante, Arminius Vambery, that he would sooner allow his head to be severed from his body 'than to permit the formation of a separate Armenia'. Also Verheij, 'armenischen Massaker', 99–105, for corroboration of Abdulhamid's central role as the driving force behind the massacres.

167 Lepsius, *Armenia*, 76.

168 Suny, 'Religion', 31, quoting from an article by Aron Rodrigue.

169 See Deringil, *Well-Protected Domains*, 69–75. See also ibid., 171–2, and Stephen Duguid, 'The Politics of Unity: Hamidian Policy in Eastern Anatolia', *Middle Eastern Studies*, 9:2 (1973), 139–56, for the growing congruence between loyalty and Muslim identity.

170 Figures from Tim Judah, *The Serbs, History, Myth and the Destruction of Yugoslavia* (New Haven, CT, and London: Yale University Press, 1997), 101.

171 Kann, *Multinational Empire*, vol. 2, 302, 304, for imperial demographic statistics by ethnicity.

172 Noel Malcolm, *Bosnia, a Short History* (London and Basingstoke: Papermac, 1994), 158; Janko Pleterski, 'The Southern Slav Question, 1908–1914', in Mark Cornwall, ed., *The Last Years of Austria-Hungary* (Exeter: University of Exeter Press, 1990), 88.

173 John Reed, *War in Eastern Europe, Travels through the Balkans in 1915* (London: Phoenix, 1994 [first published Scribners, 1916]), 41–7; Mark Mazower, 'Two Wars: Serbia 1914–1918 and 1941–1944', unpublished paper, 'Cultures of Killing' conference, Birkbeck College, July 2000, 6. I am indebted to Prof. Mazower for a copy of the paper.

174 See Peter Caddick-Adams, 'The Western Balkans', in John Bourne, Peter Liddle and Ian Whitehead, eds, *The Great World War 1914–1945*, vol. 2: *Who Won? Who Lost?* (London: HarperCollins, 2001), 123.

175 See Edward Crankshaw, *The Fall of the House of Habsburg* (London: Longmans, 1963), 'Prologue, The House of Austria', for more of this sense of Habsburg self.

176 Lieven, *Empire*, 181, 130.

177 Caddick-Adams, 'Western Balkans', 123.

178 Quoted in Mann, *Sources*, vol. 2, 346.

179 Okey, *Habsburg Monarchy*, 312–14, for discussion.

180 Ibid., 304–9.

181 Robert Musil, *The Man Without Qualities*, trans. Sophie Wilkins (London: Picador, 1995 [first published 1930]). vol. 1, 26–31. See David S. Luft, *Robert Musil and the Crisis of European Culture 1880–1942* (Berkeley and Los Angeles: University of California Press, 1980), esp. chapter 5, 'The Man Without Qualities', for discussion.

182 See Kann, *Multinational Empire*, 2, chapter 20, 'The Social Democrats'; Theodor Hanf, 'Reducing Conflict through Cultural Autonomy: Karl Renner's Contribution', in Uri Ra'anan et al., eds, *State and Nation in Multi-Ethnic Societies, the Breakup of Multinational States* (Manchester: Manchester University Press, 1991), 33–52; Ephraim Nimni, 'Nationalist Multiculturalism in Late Imperial Austria as a Critique of Contemporary Liberalism: The Case of Bauer and Renner', *Journal of Political Ideologies*, 4: 3 (1999), 289–314.

183 Crankshaw, *Fall*, 67–70.

184 Okey, *Habsburg Monarchy*, 337.

185 Quoted in ibid., 362.

186 See Z. A. B. Zeman, *The Making and Breaking of Communist Europe* (Oxford: Blackwell, 1991), 43–5.

187 Nevertheless, John R. Lampe and Marvin R. Jackson, *Balkan Economic History, 1550–1950: From Imperial Borderlands to Developing Nations* (Bloomington: Indiana University Press, 1982), 225–36, note the general weakness of Great Power financial support and penetration of the new Balkan states.

188 Quoted in Mazower, *Balkans*, 91–2.

189 Glenny, *Balkans*, 280–2.

190 See Charles Jelavich, 'Serbian Textbooks: Toward Greater Serbia or Yugoslavia?', *Slavic Review*, 42:4 (1983), 601–19.

191 Pleterski, 'Southern Slav Question', 88.

192 Ibid., 84–7. For a detailed contemporary analysis, see R. W. Seton-Watson, *The Southern Slav Question and the Habsburg Monarchy* (New York: Howard Fertig, 1969 [first published 1911]).

193 Glenny, *Balkans*, 253,

194 Malcolm, *Bosnia*, 136–7, for discussion of these anxieties.

195 Glenny, *Balkans*, 251.

196 Ibid., 200–5; Douglas Dakin, *The Greek Struggle in Macedonia, 1897–1913* (Thessaloniki: Institute for Balkan Studies, 1993), 198–209; Voin Bozhinov, L. Panayotov, eds, *Macedonia, Documents and Materials* (Sofia: Bulgarian Academy of Sciences 1978), part 3, 'National-Liberations Struggles 1878–1918'.

197 See Lieven, *Empire*, 130–1.

198 For more generally on these developments see George W. Gawrych, 'The Culture and Politics of Violence in Turkish Society 1903–13', *Middle Eastern Studies*, 22:3 (1985), 307–30; James J. Reid, 'Total War, the Annihilation Ethic and the Armenian Genocide 1870–1918', in Hovannisian, *Armenian Genocide, History, Politics, Ethics*, 35, 43.

199 See Zürcher, *Turkey*, 94. The Reval meeting between the two monarchs was intended to seal the new Anglo-Russian entente, bringing to an end the rivalry between the two empires, dating back over the previous century.

200 Malcolm, *Bosnia*, 150.

201 See F. R. Bridge, 'The Foreign Policy of the Monarchy, 1908–1918', in Cornwall, *Last Years*, 10–13; Samuel R. Williamson, Jr., *Austria-Hungary and the Origins of the First World War* (Basingstoke: Macmillan, 1991), 68–70.

202 See Ernst Christian Helmreich, *The Diplomacy of the Balkan Wars, 1912–1913* (Cambridge, MA: Harvard University Press, 1938), chapter 4, 'Russia and the Balkan States'.

203 See Kennan, *Other Balkan Wars*, for full details.

204 Quoted in Judah, *Serbs*, 95.

205 Williamson, *Austria-Hungary*, 67–8; Glenny, *Balkans*, 289.

206 Quoted in Mazower, *Balkans*, 97.

207 See Malcolm, *Bosnia*, 138 and idem., *Kosovo, a Short History* (London and Basingstoke: Macmillan, 1998), 253.

208 See Crankshaw, *Fall*, 397–9, for an assessment of von Hotzendorf's role.

209 The symbolic significance of the battle has been repeated, of course, more recently at the half-millennium anniversary of the event, in 1989, at which the Yugloslav president, Slobodan Milosevic, used the occasion to rekindle the flames of Serbian nationalism. For discussion of Serbian nationalist myth-making associated with the battle see Malcolm, *Kosovo*, 75–80; Anzulovic, *Heavenly Serbia*, especially chapter 5, 'A Vicious Circle of Lies and Fears'.

210 Glenny, *Balkans*, 304–5.

211 Ibid., 303, Glenny notes that, between 1900 and 1913, forty heads of state, politicians and diplomats fell victim to terrorist bullets or bombs.

212 Bridge, 'Foreign Policy', 19.

213 See Williamson, *Austria-Hungary*, 205–7, 212–16.

214 Reed, *War*, 42.

215 See Glenny, *Balkans*, 315–16.

216 Reed, *War*, 41–50. See R. G. D. Laffin, *The Serbs, the Guardians of the Gate* (New York: Dorset Press, 1989 [first published 1917]), 194–7, despite its polemical style for further corroborating evidence.

217 Caddick-Adams, 'Western Balkans', 126.

218 Ibid. Also Laffin, *Serbs*, 221–8.

219 Mazower, 'Two Wars', 2, refers to the comprehensive post-war study by R. A. Reiss, *Les Infractions aux règles et Lois de la Guerre* (Lausanne: Payot, 1918), 60–2. See also Judah, *Serbs*, 99.

220 Karl Kraus, *In These Great Times*, scene 24, quoted in Zeman, *Making*, 50.

221 James Joll, '1914: The Unspoken Assumptions', in H. W. Koch, ed., *The Origins of the First World War* (Basingstoke: Macmillan, 1972), 318.

Select Bibliography

This bibliography lists the principal works that supported this study.
Fuller references are to be gleaned from the endnotes.

Ageron, Charles-Robert, *Histoire de l'Algérie contemporaine* (Paris: Universitaires de France, 1964).

Ahmad, Kamal Madhar, *Kurdistan during the First World War* (London: Saqi Books, 1994).

Aldrich, Robert, *Greater France, a History of French Overseas Expansion* (Basingstoke: Macmillan, 1996).

Anderson, Benedict, *Imagined Communities: Reflections on the Origins and Spread of Nationalism* (London: Verso, 2nd edn, 1991).

Anderson, Fred, *Crucible of War, The Seven Years' War and the Fate of Empire in British North America* (New York: Alfred A. Knopf, 2000).

Anderson, Margaret Lavinia, 'The Kulturkampf and the Course of German History', *Central European History*, 19:1 (1986), 82–115.

Anderson, Perry, *Passages from Antiquity to Feudalism* (London: New Left Books, 1974).

Anzulovic, Branimir, *Heavenly Serbia, from Myth to Genocide* (New York: New York University Press, 1999).

Arendt, Hannah, *The Origins of Totalitarianism* (New York: Meridian, 1958).

Aronson, Ronald, *Dialectics of Disaster, a Preface to Hope* (London: Verso, 1983).

Ascherson, Neal, *The King Incorporated, Leopold II in the Age of Trusts* (London: George Allen and Unwin, 1963).

Aschheim, Steven E., 'The Jew Within: The Myth of the Judaization in Germany', in Jehuda Reinharz and Walter Schatzberg, eds, *The Jewish Response to German Culture* (Hanover, NH: University Press of New England, 1985), 212–41.

Attwood, Bain, and Foster, S. G., eds, *Frontier Conflict, the Australian Experience* (Canberra: National Museum of Australia, 2004).

Axtell, James, and Sturtevant, W. C., 'The Unkindest Cut, or who Invented Scalping?', *William and Mary Quarterly*, 3rd Series, 37:3 (1980), 451–72.

Baer, Yitzhak F., *Galut* (New York: Schocken Books, 1947).

Balakian, Peter, *Black Dog of Fate: A Memoir* (New York: Basic Books, 1997).

Balfour, Sebastian, *The End of the Spanish Empire, 1898–1923* (Oxford: Clarendon Press, 1997).

Balesi, Charles J., *The Time of the French at the Heart of North America, 1673–1818* (Chicago: Alliance Française Chicago, 1992).

Balibar, Étienne, and Wallerstein, Immanuel, *Race, Nation, Class, Ambiguous Identities* (London: Verso, 1991).

Barber, Malcolm, *The Cathars, Dualist Heretics in Languedoc in the High Middle Ages* (Harlow: Longman, 2000).

Baron, Salo, 'Ghetto and Emancipation, Shall we Revise the Traditional View?', *The Menorah Journal*, 14:6 (1928), 513–26.

Barraclough, Geoffrey, *An Introduction to Contemporary History* (London: C.A. Watts and Co., 1964).

Bartlett, Robert, *The Making of Europe, Conquest, Civilisation and Cultural Change 950–1350* (London: Penguin, 1994).

Barzun, Jacques, *Darwin, Marx, Wagner, Critique of a Heritage* (New York: Doubleday Anchor Books, 2nd edn, 1958).

Bayertz, Kurt, 'Science and Aesthetics in *Fin-de-Siècle* Germany', in Mikuláš Teich and Roy Porter, eds, *Fin de Siècle and its Legacy* (Cambridge: Cambridge University Press, 1990).

Beasley, W. G., *Japanese Imperialism, 1894–1945* (Oxford: Clarendon Press, 1997).

Becker, Peter, *Path of Blood, the Rise and Conquests of Mzilikazi, Founder of the Matabele Tribe of Southern Africa* (London: Penguin, 1972).

Bein, Alex, 'Jewish Parasite, Notes on the Semantics of the Jewish Problem with Special Reference to Germany', *Leo Baeck Year Book*, 9 (1964), 3–40.

Belich, James, *The New Zealand Wars and the Victorian Interpretation of Racial Conflict* (Auckland: Auckland University Press, 1986).

Beloff, Max, *The Foreign Policy of Soviet Russia, 1929–1941*, vol. 2: *1936–1941* (London and New York: Royal Institute of International Affairs and Oxford University Press, 1949).

Benedict, Philip, et al., eds, *Reformation, Revolt and Civil War in France and the Netherlands 1555–1585* (Amsterdam: Royal Netherlands Academy of Arts and Science, 1999).

Berenbaum, Michael, and Peck, Abraham J., eds, *The Holocaust and History, the Known, the Unknown, the Disputed and the Reexamined* (Bloomington and Indianapolis: Indiana University Press, 1998).

Berndt, Catherine H., and Berndt, Ronald M., *The Barbarians, an Anthropological View* (London: Pelican Books, 1973).

Bernheimer, Richard, *Wild Men in the Middle Ages: A Study in Art, Sentiment and Demonology* (Cambridge, MA: Harvard University Press, 1978).

Best, Geoffrey, *Humanity in Warfare* (New York: Columbia University Press, 1980).

——, ed., *Permanent Revolution, the French Revolution and its Legacy, 1789–1989* (London: Fontana, 1988).

Biddiss, Michael A., *The Age of the Masses, Ideas and Society in Europe since 1870* (London: Penguin, 1977).

Birnbaum, Pierre, and Katznelson, Ira, eds, *Paths of Emancipation, Jews, States and Citizenship* (Princeton, NJ: Princeton University Press, 1995).

Black, Jeremy, *Culloden and the '45* (London: St Martin's Press, 1997).

——, *Maps and History, Constructing Images of the Past* (New Haven, CT, and London: Yale University Press, 1997).

Blackbourn, David, *Populists and Patricians, Essays in Modern German History* (London: Allen and Unwin, 1987).

——, *Marpingen Apparitions of the Virgin Mary in Bismarkian Germany* (Oxford: Clarendon Press, 1993).

——, *The Fontana History of Germany 1780–1918, the Long Nineteenth Century* (London: Fontana, 1997).

——, and Eley, Geoff, *The Peculiarities of German History, Bourgeois Society and Politics in Nineteenth-Century Germany 1780–1918, the Long Nineteenth Century* (Oxford and New York: Oxford University Press, 1984).

Bley, Helmut, *South-West Africa under German Rule, 1894–1914* (London: Heinemann, 1971).

Blick, Jeffrey P., 'The Iroquois Practice of Genocidal Warfare', *Journal of Genocide Research*, 3:3 (2001), 405–29.

Bloxham, Donald, 'Three Imperialisms and a Turkish Nationalism, International Stresses, Imperial Disintegration and the Armenian Genocide', *Patterns of Prejudice*, 36:4 (2002), 37–58.

Boahen, A. Adu, ed., *General History of Africa*, vol. 7: *Africa under Colonial Domination 1880–1935* (London and Nairobi: Heinemann and UNESCO, 1985).

Del Boca, Angelo, *Gli italiani in Libia*, vol. 1: *Tripoli bel suol d'amore 1860–1922* (Rome and Bari: Laterza, 1986).

Bodanis, David, *Web of Words, the Ideas behind Politics* (Basingstoke: Macmillan, 1988).

Bodley, John H., *Victims of Progress* (Palo Alto, CA: Maybury, 2nd edn, 1982).

Boemeke, Manfred F., Chickering, Roger, and Forster, Stig, *Anticipating Total War, the German and American Experiences, 1871–1914* (Cambridge and Washington, DC: German Historical Institute and Cambridge University Press, 1999).

Borah, Woodrow, and Cook, Sherburne F., *The Aboriginal Population of Central Mexico on the Eve of the Spanish Conquest* (Berkeley: University of California , 1963).

——, *Essays in Population History: Mexico and the Caribbean*, Ibero-Americana no 45 (Berkeley: University of California Press, 1971).

Borchardt, Knut, *The Industrial Revolution in Germany 1700–1914* (London: Fontana, 1972).

Bottigheimer, Karl S., *English Money and Irish Land: the 'Adventurers' in the Cromwellian Settlement of Ireland* (Oxford: Oxford University Press, 1971).

Bottomore, Tom, ed., *Dictionary of Marxist Thought* (Oxford: Blackwell, 2nd edn, 1991).

Bourne, Russell, *The Red King's Rebellion, Racial Politics in New England 1675–76* (New York: Oxford University Press, 1990).

Boxer, C. R., *The Christian Century in Japan, 1549–1650* (Berkeley and Los Angeles: University of California Press, 1951).

——, *John Compagnie in War and Peace, a Short History of the Dutch East Indian Company 1602–1799* (Hong Kong: Heinemann Asia, 1979).

Boyer, John, *Political Radicalism in Late Imperial Vienna, Origins of the Christian Socialist Movement, 1848–1897* (Chicago: Chicago University Press, 1987).

Bozhinov, Voin, and Panayotov, L., eds, *Macedonia, Documents and Materials* (Sofia: Bulgarian Academy of Sciences, 1978).

Brailsford, H. N., *Macedonia, its Races and their Future* (London: Methuen, 1906).

Braude, Benjamin, and Lewis, Bernard, eds, *Christians and Jews in the Ottoman Empire, the Functioning of a Plural Society*, vol. 1: (New York and London: Holmes and Meier, 1982).

Braudel, Fernand, *The Mediterranean World in the Age of Philip II*, trans. Sian Reynolds (London: Fontana/Collins, 1972).

Brégeon, Jean-Joël, *Carrier et la terreur nantaise* (Paris: Perrin, 1987).

Breitman, Richard, *Official Secrets, What the Nazis Planned, What the British and Americans Knew* (New York: Hill and Wang, 1999).

Brewer, John, *The Sinews of Power, War, Money and the English State 1688–1783* (London: Unwin Hyman, 1989).

Bridgman, John, *The Revolt of the Hereros* (Berkeley and Los Angeles: University of California Press, 1968).

Briggs, Robin, *Witches and Neighbours, the Social and Cultural Context of European Witchcraft* (London: Fontana Press, 1997).

Brooks, Willis, 'Russia's Conquest and Pacification of the Caucasus: Relocation becomes a Pogrom in the Post-Crimean War Period', *Nationalities Papers*, 23:4 (1995), 675–86.

Brown, Dee, *Bury My Heart at Wounded Knee, an Indian History of the American West* (London: Vintage, 1991).

Brown, Peter, *The Rise of Western Christendom, Triumph and Diversity AD 200–1000* (Oxford and Malden, MA: Blackwell, 1996).

Browning, Christopher R., *The Path to Genocide: Essays on Launching the Final Solution* (Cambridge and New York: Cambridge University Press, 1992).

Broxup, Marie Beningsen, ed., *The North Caucasus Barrier: The Russian Advance towards the Muslim World* (London: Hurst and Co., 1992).

Brubaker, Rogers, *Citizenship and Nationhood in France and Germany* (Cambridge, MA, and London: Harvard University Press, 1992).

Bruinessen, Martin van, *Aghas, Shaiks and State, the Social and Political Structure of Kurdistan* (London and Atlantic Highlands, NJ: Zed Books, 1990).

Bull, Hedley, *The Anarchical Society, a Study of Order in World Politics* (Basingstoke: Macmillan, 1977).

Bullock, Alan, *Hitler and Stalin, Parallel Lives* (London: Fontana Press, 1993).

Burger, Julian, *Report from the Frontier: The State of the World's Indigenous Peoples* (London: Zed Books, 1987).

Burleigh, Michael, 'The Knights, Nationalists and the Historians: Images of Medieval Prussia from the Enlightenment to 1945', *European History Quarterly*, 17 (1987), 35–55.

——, *Germany Turns Eastwards, a Study of Ostforschung in the Third Reich* (Cambridge: Cambridge University Press, 1988).

——, *Death and Deliverance, 'Euthanasia' in Germany, 1900–1945* (Cambridge: Cambridge University Press, 1994).

Butler, Jon, *The Huguenots in America: A Refugee People in New World Society* (Cambridge, MA: Harvard University Press, 1983).

Caddick-Adams, Peter, 'The Western Balkans', in John Bourne, Peter Liddle and Ian Whitehead, eds, *The Great World War 1914–1945*, vol. 2: *Who Won? Who Lost?* (London: HarperCollins, 2001), 121–39.

Cahm, Eric, *The Dreyfus Affair in French Society and Politics* (London: Longman, 1996).

Calloway, Colin G., *The American Revolution in Indian Country, Crisis and Diversity in Native American Communities* (Cambridge: Cambridge University Press, 1995).

Cameron, Euan, *Waldensees, Rejections of Holy Church in Medieval Europe* (Oxford: Blackwell, 2000).

Canny, Nicholas, 'The Ideology of English Colonization: From Ireland to America', *William and Mary Quarterly*, 30 (1973), 575–98.

——, *Making Ireland British, 1580–1650* (Oxford: Oxford University Press, 2001).

Carey, John, *The Intellectuals and the Masses, Pride and Prejudice among the Literary Intelligentsia, 1880–1939* (London and Boston: Faber and Faber, 1993).

Carlebach, Julius, *Marx and the Radical Critique of Judaism* (London: Routledge and Kegan Paul, 1978).

Carlton, Charles, *Going to the Wars: The Experience of the British Civil Wars 1638–51* (London: Routledge, 1952).

Carranco, Lynwood, and Beard, Estle, *Genocide and Vendetta, the Round Valley Wars of North California* (Norman: University of Oklahoma Press, 1981).

Cesarani, David, ed., *Port Jews, Jewish Communities in Cosmopolitan Maritime Trading Centres, 1550–1950* (London: Frank Cass, 2002).

Chaliand, Gérard, ed., *Minority Peoples in the Age of Nation-States*, trans. Tony Berrett (London: Zed Press, 1980).

Chalk, Frank, and Jonassohn, Kurt, *The History and Sociology of Genocide* (New Haven, CT, and London: Yale University Press, 1990)

Challener, Richard D., *The French Theory of the Nation in Arms 1866–1939* (New York: Russell and Russell, 1965).

Charny, Israel W., ed., *Encyclopaedia of Genocide*, 2 vols (Santa Barbara, CA, and Denver, CO: ABC-CLIO, 1999).

Chazan, Robert, *European Jewry and the Third Crusade* (Berkeley and Los Angeles: University of California Press, 1987).

Chejne, Anwar G., *Islam and the West: The Moriscos, a Cultural and Social History* (Albany: State University of New York Press, 1983).

Christiansen, Eric, *The Northern Crusades, the Baltic and the Catholic Frontier 1100–1525* (London and Basingstoke: Macmillan, 1980).

Chu, Wen-Djang, *The Moslem Rebellion in North-West China 1862–1878, a Study of Government Minority Policy* (The Hague and Paris: Mouton and Co., 1966).

Churchill, Ward, *A Little Matter of Genocide, Holocaust and Denial in the Americas: 1492 to the Present* (San Francisco: City Light Books, 1997).

Clark, Stuart, *Thinking with Demons, the Idea of Witchcraft in Early Modern Europe* (Oxford: Oxford University Press, 1997).

Clasen, C.-P., *The Anabaptists. A Social History, Switzerland, Austria, Moravia, South and Central Germany* (Ithaca, NY, and London: Cornell University Press, 1972).

Clay, Christopher, *Gold for the Sultan, Western Bankers and Ottoman Finance 1856–1881* (London: I.B. Tauris, 2000).

Cobb, Richard, *The People's Army* (New Haven, CT, and London: Yale University Press, 1987).

Cocker, Mark, *Rivers of Blood, Rivers of Gold, Europe's Conflict with Tribal Peoples* (London: Jonathan Cape, 1998).

Cohen, Mark R., *Under Crescent and Cross, the Jews in the Middle Ages* (Princeton, NJ: Princeton University Press, 1994).

Cohn, Norman, *The Pursuit of the Millennium: Revolutionary Millenarians and Mystical Anarchists of the Middle Ages* (London: Paladin, 1967).

Colley, Linda, *Britons, Forging the Nation 1707–1837* (London: Pimlico, 1994).

Confino, Alon, *The Nation as a Local Metaphor: Wurttemberg, Imperial Germany and National Memory, 1871–1918* (Chapel Hill: University of North Carolina Press, 1997).

Connor, John, *The Australian Frontier Wars, 1788–1838* (Sydney: University of New South Wales Press, 2002).

Conquest, Robert, *Lenin* (London: Fontana, 1972).

Cook, Noble David, *Born to Die, Disease and New World Conquest, 1492–1650* (Cambridge: Cambridge University Press, 1998).

Cook, Sherburne F., *The Conflict between the California Indians and White Civilisation* (Berkeley and Los Angeles: University of California Press, 1976).

——, *The Indian Population of New England in the Seventeenth Century* (Berkeley and Los Angeles: University of California Press, 1976).

Coren, Michael, *The Invisible Man: The Life and Liberties of H.G. Wells* (London: Bloomsbury, 1993).

Cornwall, Mark, ed., *The Last Years of Austria-Hungary* (Exeter: University of Exeter Press, 1990).

Costen, Michael, *The Cathars and the Albigensian Crusade* (Manchester: Manchester University Press, 1997).

Cottret, Bernard, *Terre d'exil; L'Angleterre et ses refugiés français et wallons de la réforme à la révocation de l'Édit de Nantes 1550–1700* (Paris: Aubier, 1985).

Crankshaw, Edward, *The Fall of the House of Habsburg* (London: Longmans, 1963).

Creed, Barbara, and Hoorn, Jeanette, eds, *Body Trade, Captivity, Cannibalism and Colonialism in the Pacific* (New York and Annandale, NSW: Routledge and Pluto Press, 2001).

Cronon, William, *Changes in the Land: Indians, Colonists and the Ecology of New England* (New York: Hill and Wang, 1983).

Crook, Paul, *Darwinism, War and History, the Debate over the Biology of War from the Origins of Species to the First World War* (Cambridge: Cambridge University Press, 1994).

Crosby, Alfred W., *Ecological Imperialism: The Biological Expansion of Europe, 900–1900* (Cambridge: Cambridge University Press, 1986).

Cummins, Ian, *Marx, Engels and National Movements* (London: Croom Helm, 1980).

Curthoys, Ann, and Docker, John, 'Introduction, Genocide: Definitions, Questions, Settler Colonies', *Aboriginal History*, 25 (2001), 1–15.

Curtin, Philip D., *The Atlantic Slave Trade, a Census* (Madison and Milwaukee: University of Wisconsin Press, 1969).

Cutler, Allan Harris, and Cutler, Helen Elmquist, *The Jew as Ally of the Muslim; Medieval Roots of Anti-Semitism* (Notre Dame, IN: University of Notre Dame Press, 1986).

Dadrian, Vahakn N., 'The Role of the Turkish Military in the Destruction of Ottoman Armenians: A Study in Historical Continuities', *Journal of Political and Military Sociology*, 20:2 (1992), 257–8.

——, *The History of the Armenian Genocide, Ethnic Conflict from the Balkans to Anatolia to the Caucasus* (Oxford: Berghahn Books, 1996).

——, ed., *The Ottoman Empire: A Troubled Legacy, Views, Comments and Judgements by Noted Experts Worldwide* (Williamsburg, VA: Association of Genocide Scholars, 1997).

Dakin, Douglas, *The Greek Struggle in Macedonia, 1897–1913* (Thessaloniki: Institute for Balkan Studies, 1993).

Daly, Mary, *Gyn Ecology: The Meta-Ethics of Radical Feminism* (London: Women's Press, 1979).

Darwin, Charles, *On the Origin of Species by Means of Natural Selection: Or the Preservation of Favoured Races in the Struggle for Life*, ed. J. W. Burrow (London: Penguin, 1968 {first published John Murray, 1859}).

Dan, Theodore, *Origins of Bolshevism*, trans. Joel Carmichael (London: Secker and Warburg, 1964).

Dasnebadian, Hratch, *History of the Armenian Revolutionary Federation Dashnaksutiun 1890/1924* (Milan: OEMME Edizione, 1989).

Daunton, Mark, and Halpern, Rick, eds, *Empire and Others: British Encounters with Indigenous Peoples, 1600–1850* (London: UCL Press, 1999).

Davidson, Basil, *Africa in History* (London: Granada, 1974).

Davies, Norman, *God's Playground: A History of Poland*, vol. 1: *The Origins to 1795* (Oxford: Clarendon Press, 1981).

——, *Europe, a History* (London: Pimlico, 1997).

Davies, R. W., 'Forced Labour under Stalin, the Archive Revelations', *New Left Review*, 214 (Nov./Dec. 1995), 62–80.

Davis, Mike, *Late Victorian Holocausts, El Niño Famines and the Making of the Third World* (London and New York: Verso, 2001).

Davis, Natalie Zemon, *Society and Culture in Early Modern France* (Stanford, CA: Stanford University Press, 1975).

Davison, Roderic, 'Nationalism as an Ottoman Problem and the Ottoman Response', in William H. Haddad and William Ochsenwald, eds, *Nationalism in a Non-National State, the Dissolution of the Ottoman Empire* (Columbus: Ohio State University Press, 1977), 25–56.

Deringil, Selim, *The Well-Protected Domains, Ideology and the Legitimation of Power in the Ottoman Empire 1876–1909* (London and New York: I.B. Tauris, 1999).

Dillon, E. J., *Prelude to Genocide, Conditions of Life among the Armenians in Anatolia 1890–1895* (Armenian Genocide Research Centre, 2001).

Dikotter, Frank, *The Discourse of Race in Modern China* (Stanford, CA: Stanford University Press, 1992).

Dobyns, Henry F., 'Estimating Aboriginal Populations: An Appraisal of Techniques with a New Hemispheric Estimate', *Current Anthropology*, 7 (1966), 395–416.

Douglas, Roy, 'Britain and the Armenian Question, 1894–7', *Historical Journal*, 19:1 (1976), 113–33.

Dowd, Gregory Evans, *A Spirited Resistance, the North American Indian Struggle for Unity, 1745–1815* (Baltimore and London: Johns Hopkins University Press, 1992).

Doyle, William, and Haydon, Colin, eds, *Robespierre* (Cambridge: Cambridge University Press, 1999).

Drake, James D., *King Philip's War: Civil War in New England 1675–76* (Amherst: University of Massachusetts Press, 1999).

Draper, Alfred, *The Amritsar Massacre, Twilight of the Raj* (Leatherhead and Ashford: Buchan and Enright, 1985).

Dreschler, Horst, *Let Us Die Fighting, the Struggle of the Herero and Nama against German Imperialism 1884–1915* (London: Zed Press, 1980).

Dreyer, June Teufel, *China's Forty Millions, Minority Nationalities and National Integration in the People's Republic of China* (Cambridge, MA, and London: Harvard University Press, 1976).

Duguid, Stephen, 'The Politics of Unity: Hamidian Policy in Eastern Anatolia', *Middle Eastern Studies*, 9:2 (1973), 139–56.

Dumont, Louis, *Homo Hierarchicus, The Caste System and its Implications* (London: Paladin, 1972).

Earle, Rebecca, '"Two Pairs of Pink Satin Shoes!!": Clothing, Race and Identity in the Americas, 17th–19th Centuries', *History Workshop Journal*, 52 (2001), 175–95.

Edwards, John, *The Jews in Christian Europe, 1400–1700* (London and New York: Routledge, 1988).

Eley, Geoff, *From Unification to Nazism: Reinterpreting the German Past* (Boston: Allen and Unwin, 1986).

——, and Suny, Ronald Grigor, *Becoming National, a Reader* (New York and Oxford: Oxford University Press, 1996).

Ellis, Peter Berresford, *Hell or Connaught! The Cromwellian Colonisation of Ireland 1652–1660* (London: Hamish Hamilton, 1975).

Emerit, M., 'La question algérienne en 1871', *Revue d'histoire moderne et contemporaine*, 19 (1972), 256–64.

Ernst, Waltraud, and Harris, Bernard, eds, *Race, Science and Medicine 1700–1960* (London: Routledge, 1999).

Evans, Raymond, with Saunders, Kay, and Cronin, Kathryn, *Exclusion, Exploitation and Extermination: Race Relations in Colonial Queensland* (Sydney: Australia and New Zealand Book Company, 1975).

Evans, Richard J., *Rereading German History 1800–1996, from Unification to Reunification* (London and New York: Routledge, 1997).

Evans-Pritchard, E. E., *The Sanusi of Cyrenaica* (London: Oxford University Press, 1949).

Fabre-Vassas, Claudine, *The Singular Beast, Jews, Christians and the Pig,* trans. Carol Volk (New York: Columbia University Press, 1997).

Fairbank, John King, *The Great Chinese Revolution 1800–1985* (New York: Harper and Row, 1986).

Fawaz, Leila Tarazi, *Occasion for War: Civil Conflict in Lebanon and Damascus in 1860* (London and New York: I.B. Tauris, 1994).

Feher, Ferenc, ed., *The French Revolution and the Birth of Modernity* (Berkeley and Los Angeles: University of California Press, 1990),

Fein, Helen, 'Genocide:A Sociological Perspective', *Current Sociology,* 38:1 (1990), 1–126.

Felsenstein, Frank, *Anti-Semitic Stereotypes: A Paradigm of Otherness in English Popular Culture, 1660–1830* (Baltimore and London: Johns Hopkins University Press, 1995).

Fenn, Elizabeth A., 'Biological Warfare in Eighteenth Century America', *Journal of American History,* 86:4 (2000), 1554–8.

Ferrer, Ada, *Race, Nation and Revolution, Cuba 1868–1898* (Chapel Hill and London: University of North Carolina, 1999).

Finzsch, Norbert, and Jutte, Robert, eds, *Institutions of Confinement: Hospitals, Asylums and Prisons in Western Europe and North America, 1500–1950* (Cambridge: Cambridge University Press, 1996).

Fischer, Fritz, *War of Illusions, German Policies from 1911 to 1914,* trans. Marian Jackson (London: Chatto and Windus, 1975).

Fleming, Peter, *The Siege at Peking* (London: Readers Union, 1959).

Fletcher, Richard, *The Conversion of Europe, from Paganism to Christianity 371–1386 AD* (London: HarperCollins, 1997).

——, *Moorish Spain* (London: Phoenix Press, 2001).

Flora, Peter, et al., eds, *State Formation, Nation-Building and Mass Politics in Europe, the Theory of Stein Rokkan* (Oxford: Oxford University Press, 1999).

Foner, Philip S., *The Spanish-Cuban-American War and the Birth of American Imperialism, 1895–1902,* 2 vols (New York: Monthly Review Press, 1972).

Foucault, Michel, *Discipline and Punish, the Birth of the Prison,* trans. Alan Sheridan (London: Penguin, 1979).

Frankel, Jonathan, and Zipperstein, Steven J., eds, *Assimilation and Community: The Jews in Nineteenth-Century Europe* (Cambridge: Cambridge University Press, 1992).

Freeden, Michael, 'Eugenics and Progressive Thought: A Study in Ideological Affinity', *Historical Journal,* 22:3 (1979), 645–71.

Frend, W. H. C., *The Rise of Christianity* (Philadelphia: Fortress Press, 1984).

Furet, François, *The French Revolution, 1770–1814* (Oxford: Blackwell, 1992).

——, and Ozouf, Mona, eds, *A Critical Dictionary of the French Revolution* (Cambridge, MA: Harvard University, 1978).

Gammer, Moshe, *Muslim Resistance to the Czar: Shamil and the Conquest of Chechnia and Daghestan* (London: Frank Cass, 1994).

Gann, L. H., and Duigan, Peter, *The Rulers of German Africa 1884–1914* (Stanford, CA: Stanford University Press, 1977).

Garrisson, Janine, *l'Édit de Nantes et sa révocation, histoire d'une intolerance* (Paris: Éditions du Seuil, 1985).

Gawrych, George W., 'The Culture and Politics of Violence in Turkish Society 1903–13', *Middle Eastern Studies*, 22:3 (1985), 307–30.

Gay, Peter, *The Cultivation of Hatred*, vol. 3: *The Bourgeois Experience, Victoria to Freud* (London: HarperCollins, 1994).

Gellner, Ernest, *Nations and Nationalism* (Oxford: Blackwell, 1983).

Gentles, Ian, *The New Model Army in England, Ireland and Scotland 1645–1653* (Oxford: Oxford University Press, 1992).

Gewald, Jan-Bart, *Herero Heroes, a Socio-Political History of the Herero of Namibia 1890–1923* (Oxford: James Currey, 1999).

Geyer, Michael, and Bright, Charles, 'Global Violence and Nationalizing Wars in Eurasia and America: The Geopolitics of War in the Mid-Nineteenth Century', *Comparative Studies in Society and History*, 38:4 (1996), 619–57.

Geyl, Pieter, *The Revolt of the Netherlands 1555–1609* (London: Benn, 1980 [first published 1958]).

Gibson, Charles, *The Aztecs under Spanish Rule* (Stanford, CA: Stanford University Press, 1964).

Giddens, Anthony, *Capitalism and Modern Social Theory* (Cambridge: Cambridge University Press, 1971).

——, *The Nation-State and Violence* (Cambridge: Polity Press, 1985).

Gilbert, Martin, *The Holocaust, the Jewish Tragedy* (London: Collins, 1986).

Gillard, David, *The Struggle for Asia 1828–1914, a Study in British and Russian Imperialism* (London: Methuen and Co., 1977).

Gilman, Sander L., *Jewish Self-Hatred: Anti-Semitism and the Hidden Language of the Jews* (Baltimore: Johns Hopkins University Press, 1986).

——, *The Jew's Body* (New York and London: Routledge, 1991).

——, *Franz Kafka, the Jewish Patient* (New York and London: Routledge, 1995).

Gladney, Dru C., *Muslim Chinese, Ethnic Nationalism in the People's Republic* (Cambridge, MA: Harvard University Press, 1991).

Glenny, Misha, *The Balkans 1804–1999, Nationalism, War and the Great Powers* (London: Granta Books, 1999).

Goertz, Hans-Jürgen, *The Anabaptists* (London and New York: Routledge, 1996).

Goldstein, Robert A., *French-Iroquois Diplomatic and Military Relations 1609–1701* (The Hague: Mouton, 1969).

Goltz, Colmar von der, *The Nation in Arms: A Treatise on Modern Military Systems and the Conduct of War*, trans. Philip A. Ashworth (London: Hugh Rees, 2nd edn, 1906).

Goodall, Heather, *Invasion to Embassy, Land in Aboriginal Politics in New South Wales, 1770–1972* (Sydney: Allen and Unwin, 1996).

Gould, Stephen Jay, *Ever Since Darwin, Reflections on Natural History* (London: Pelican, 1980).

Gray, Jack, *Rebellions and Revolutions, China from the 1800s to 2000* (Oxford: Oxford University Press, 2nd edn, 2002).

Gray, Peter, *Famine, Land and Politics: British Government and Irish Society, 1843–1850* (Dublin: Irish Academic Press, 1999).

Green, Abigail, *Fatherlands, State-Building and Nationhood in Nineteenth Century Germany* (Cambridge: Cambridge University Press, 1987).

Greenfield, Liah, *Nationalism, Five Roads to Modernity* (Cambridge, MA: Harvard University Press, 1992).

Greer, Donald, *The Incidence of the Terror during the French Revolution* (Cambridge, MA: Harvard University Press, 1935).

Gross, Felix, *Rhodes of Africa* (London: Cassell and Co., 1956).

Güiraldes, Alfredo M. Serres, *La estrategia del general Roca* (Buenos Aires: Editorial Pleamar, 1979).

Guiraudon, Virginie, 'Cosmopolitanism and National Priority: Attitudes towards Foreigners in France between 1789 and 1794', *History of European Ideas*, 13:5 (1991), 591–604.

Gump, James O., *The Formation of the Zulu Kingdom in South Africa, 1750–1840* (San Francisco: Mellen Research University Press, 1990).

——, *The Dust Rose Like Smoke: The Subjugation of the Zulu and the Sioux* (Lincoln, NB, and London: University of Nebraska Press, 1994).

Hadfield, Andrew, 'Briton and Scythian: Tudor Representations of Irish Origins', *Irish Historical Studies*, 28 (1993), 390–408.

Hagen, William W., *Germans, Poles and Jews, the Nationality Conflict in the Prussian East, 1772–1914* (Chicago: Chicago University Press, 1980).

Hall, Edith, *Inventing the Barbarian, Greek Self-Definition through Tragedy* (Oxford: Oxford University Press, 1989).

Hall, John A., *Powers and Liberties, the Causes and Consequences of the Rise of the West* (Oxford: Blackwell, 1985).

Hamilton, Carolyn, ed., *The Mfecane Aftermath, Reconstructive Debates in Southern African History* (Johannesburg and Pietermaritzburg: Witwatersrand University Press and University of Natal Press, 1995).

Hanf, Theodor, 'Reducing Conflict Through Cultural Autonomy: Karl Renner's Contribution', in Uri Ra'anan et al., eds, *State and Nation in Multi-Ethnic Societies, the Break up of Multinational States* (Manchester: Manchester University Press, 1991), 33–52.

Hanioğlu, M. Şükrü, *The Young Turks in Opposition* (New York and Oxford: Oxford University Press, 1995).

Hanke, J. Lewis, *All Mankind is One: A Study of the Disputation between Bartholomé de las Casa and Juan Ginés de Sepúlveda in 1550 on the Intellectual and Religious Capacity of American Indians* (Dekalb: Illinois University Press, 1974).

Hardenburg, W. E., *The Putumayo: The Devil's Paradise* (London: T. Fisher Unwin, 1912).

Harding, Neil, *Lenin's Political Thought*, vol. 1: *Theory and Practice in the Democratic Revolution* (London and Basingstoke: Macmillan, 1977).

Hartog, François, *The Mirror of Herodotus, the Representation of the Other in the Writing of History*, trans. Janet Lloyd (Berkeley and Los Angeles: University of California Press, 1988).

Hassiotis, J. K., 'The Greeks and the Armenian Massacres (1890–1896)', *Neo-Hellenika*, 4 (1981), 73–4.

Haude, Sigrun, *In the Shadow of 'Savage Wolves'. Anabaptist Munster and the German Reformation During the 1530s* (Boston: Humanities Press, 2000).

Heather, Peter, 'The Huns and the End of the Roman Empire in Western Europe', *English Historical Review*, 110:435 (1995), 4–41.

Helmreich, Ernst Christian, *The Diplomacy of the Balkan Wars, 1912–1913* (Cambridge, MA: Harvard University Press, 1938).

Hemming, John, *Red Gold, the Conquest of the Brazilian Indians, 1500–1760* (Cambridge, MA: Harvard University Press, 1978).

Henderson, W. O., *The German Colonial Empire* (London: Frank Cass, 1993).

Henze Paul B., 'Fire and Sword in the Caucasus: The 19th Century Resistance of the North Caucasian Mountaineers', *Central Asian Survey*, 2:1 (1983), 5–44.

Hess, Andrew, 'The Moriscos: An Ottoman Fifth Column in Sixteenth Century Spain', *American Historical Review*, 74 (1968), 1–25.

Hewitson, Mark, *National Identity and Political Thought in Germany, Wilhelmine Depictions of the French Third Republic 1890–1914* (Oxford: Clarendon Press, 2000).

Heymann, Frederick G., *John Žižka and the Hussite Revolution* (Princeton, NJ: Princeton University Press, 1955).

Hibbert, Christopher, *The Great Mutiny, India 1857* (London: Penguin, 1978).

Higonnet, Patrice, *Goodness Beyond Virtue* (Cambridge, MA, and London: Harvard University Press, 1998).

Hobhouse, Emily, *Report of a Visit to the Camps of Women and Children in the Cape and Orange River Colonies* (London: Friars Printing Association, 1901).

Hobsbawm, Eric, *Nations and Nationalism since 1780: Programme, Myth, Reality* (Cambridge: Cambridge University Press, 1990).

——, and Ranger, Terence, eds, *The Invention of Tradition* (Cambridge: Cambridge University Press, 1983).

Hochschild, Adam, *King Leopold's Ghost: A Story of Greed, Terror and Heroism in Colonial Africa* (London: Macmillan, 1998).

Hoffman, Tessa, and Koutcharian, Gerayer, 'The History of Armenian–Kurdish Relations in the Ottoman Empire', *Armenian Review*, 39:4 (1986), 1–45.

Hoganson, Kristin L., *Fighting for American Manhood, How Gender Politics Provoked the Spanish–American and Philippine–American Wars* (New Haven, CT, and London: Yale University Press, 1998).

Holquist, Peter, '"To Count, to Extract and to Exterminate," Population Politics in Late Imperial and Soviet Russia', in Ronald Grigor Suny and Terry Martin, eds, *A State of Nations, Empire and Nation-Making in the Age of Lenin and Stalin* (Oxford: Oxford University Press, 2001), 111–44.

Holt, P. M., *A Modern History of the Sudan: From the Funj Sultanate to the Present Day* (London: Weidenfeld and Nicolson, 1961).

Hood, John Y. B., *Aquinas and the Jews* (Philadelphia: University of Pennsylvania Press, 1995).

Horsman, Reginald, *Expansion and American Indian Policy 1783–1812* (East Lansing: Michigan State University Press, 1967).

Hosking, Geoffrey, *Russia, People and Empire, 1552–1917* (London: HarperCollins, 1997).

Hovannisian, Richard G., *Armenia, on the Road to Independence, 1918* (Berkeley and Los Angeles: University of California Press, 1967).

——, ed., *The Armenian Genocide in Perspective* (New Brunswick, NJ, and London: Transaction Books, 1986).

——, ed., *The Armenian Genocide, History, Politics, Ethics* (New York: St Martin's Press, 1992).

Hsia, R. Pochia, *The Myth of Ritual Murder, Jews and Magic in Reformation Germany* (New Haven, CT, and London: Yale University Press, 1988).

Hsu, Immanuel C. Y., *The Rise of Modern China* (Oxford and New York: Oxford University Press, 1970).

Hughes, Robert, *The Fatal Shore: A History of the Transportation of Convicts to Australia 1787–1868* (London: Collins Harvill, 1987).

Hunt, Lynn, *Politics, Culture and Class in the French Revolution* (Berkeley and Los Angeles: University of California Press, 1984).

Hunter, Janet, ed., *Aspects of Pan-Asianism* (London: Suntory Toyota International Centre, 1987).

Huntington, Samuel P., *The Clash of Civilisations and the Remaking of World Order* (London: Touchstone Books, 1998).

Hyam, Ronald, *Britain's Imperial Century, a Study of Empire and Expansion, 1815–1914* (Basingstoke: Macmillan, 1993).

Hyman, Paula E., *The Jews of Modern France* (Berkeley and Los Angeles: University of California Press, 1998).

Ileto, Reynaldo Clemena, *Pasyon and Revolution: Popular Movements in the Philippines 1840–1910* (Manila: Atanco de Manila University Press, 1979).

Illiffe, J., *Tanganikya under German Rule, 1905–1912* (Cambridge: Cambridge University Press, 1979).

İnalcik, Halil, and Quataert, Donald, eds, *An Economic and Social History of the Ottoman Empire 1300–1914* (Cambridge: Cambridge University Press, 1994).

İslamoğlu-İnan, Huri, ed., *The Ottoman Empire and the World-Economy* (Cambridge: Cambridge University Press, 1987).

Jacobs, Wilbur R., 'The Fatal Confrontation: Early Native–White Relations on the Frontiers of Australia, New Guinea and America – A Comparative Study', *Pacific Historical Review*, 40 (1971), 283–309.

——, *Dispossessing the American Indian, Indians and Whites on the Colonial Frontier* (Norman and London: University of Oklahoma, 1985).

Jaher, Frederic Cople, *The Jews and the Nation: Revolution, Emancipation, State Formation, and the Liberal Paradigm in America and France* (Princeton, NJ, and Oxford: Princeton University Press, 2002).

Jahoda, Gloria, *The Trail of Tears: The Story of the American Indian Removals, 1813–1855* (New York: Holt, Rinehart and Winson, 1975).

James, C. L. R., *Black Jacobins, Toussaint L'Ouverture and the San Domingo Revolution* (London: Allison and Busby, 1989 [first published 1938]).

Jelavich, Charles, 'Serbian Textbooks: Toward Greater Serbia or Yugoslavia?', *Slavic Review*, 42:4 (1983), 601–19.

Jennings, Francis, *The Invasion of America, Indians, Colonialism and the Cant of Conquest* (New York and London: W.W. Norton and Co., 1976).

——, *The Ambiguous Iroquois Empire: The Covenant Chain Confederation of Indian Tribes with the New England Colonies* (New York: W.W. Norton, 1984).

——, *The Creation of America, Through Revolution to Empire* (Cambridge: Cambridge University Press, 2000).

Joll, James, *The Anarchists* (London: Methuen, 1969).

——, '1914: The Unspoken Assumptions', in H. W. Koch, ed., *The Origins of the First World War* (Basingstoke: Macmillan, 1972), 307–28.

Jones, A. H. M., *Constantine and the Conversion of Europe* (Harmondsworth: Penguin, revised edn, 1972).

Jones, E. L., *The European Miracle, Environments, Economies and Geopolitics in the History of Europe and Asia* (Cambridge: Cambridge University Press, 1981).

Jones, Peter, ed., *The French Revolution in Social and Political Perspective* (London: Arnold, 1996).

Joseph, John, *The Nestorians and their Muslim Neighbours: A Study of Western Influences on their Relations* (Princeton, NJ: Princeton University Press, 1961).

Judah, Tim, *The Serbs, History, Myth and the Destruction of Yugoslavia* (New Haven, CT, and London: Yale University Press, 1997).

Kaiser, Hilmar, *Imperialism, Racism, And Development Theories, the Construction of a Dominant Paradigm on Ottoman Armenians* (Ann Arbor, MI: Gomidas Institute, 1997).

Kamen, Henry, *The Spanish Inquisition, an Historical Revision* (London: Phoenix Giant, 1998).

Kaminsky, H., *A History of the Hussite Revolution* (Berkeley and Los Angeles: University of California Press, 1967).

Kann, Robert A., *The Multinational Empire, Nationalism and National Reform in the Habsburg Monarchy 1848–1918*, vol. 2: *Empire Reform* (New York: Octagon Books, 1970).

Kaplan, Steve Laurence, *Disputed Legacies, the Historians' Feud 1789/1989* (Ithaca, NY, and London: Cornell University Press, 1995).

——, *Farewell Revolution, The Historians' Feud 1789/1989* (Ithaca, NY, and London: Cornell University Press, 1995).

Kappeler, Andreas, *The Russian Empire: A Multiethnic History*, trans. Alfred Clayton (Harlow: Longman, 2001).

Katz, Steven T., *Historicism, the Holocaust and Zionism* (New York and London: New York University Press, 1992).

——, *The Holocaust in Historical Context*, vol. 1: *The Holocaust and Mass Death before the Modern Age* (New York and Oxford: Oxford University Press, 1994).

Kedourie, Elie, *Nationalism* (Oxford and Cambridge, MA: Blackwell, 4th edn, 1994).

Keeley, Lawrence, *War before Civilisation* (New York and Oxford: Oxford University Press, 1996).

Kelly, Alfred, *The Descent of Darwin: The Popularisation of Darwinism in Germany, 1860–1914* (Chapel Hill: University of North Carolina Press, 1981).

Kennan, George F., *The Other Balkan Wars, a 1913 Carnegie Endowment Inquiry in Retrospect with a New Introduction and Reflections on the Present Conflict* (Washington, DC: Carnegie Endowment for International Peace, 1993 [first published 1914]).

Kennedy, J. H., *Jesuit and Savage in New France* (Hamden, CT: Archon Books, 1970).

Kennedy, Paul, *The Rise and Fall of the Great Powers* (London: Fontana Press, 1989).

——, and Nicholls, Anthony, eds, *Nationalist and Racialist Movements in Britain and Germany before 1914* (Basingstoke and London: Macmillan, 1981).

Kenny, Kevin, *The American Irish, a History* (Harlow: Longman, 2000)

Kepple-Jones, Arthur, *Rhodes and Rhodesia. The White Conquest of Zimbabwe 1884–1902* (Kingston and Montreal: McGill-Queen's University Press, 1983).

Khalidi, Rashid, et al., eds, *The Origins of Arab Nationalism* (New York and London: Columbia University Press, 1991).

Kiernan, Ben, and Gellately, Robert, eds, *The Spectre of Genocide: Mass Murder in Historical Perspective* (Cambridge and New York: Cambridge University Press, 2003).

Kiernan, V. G., *European Empires from Conquest to Collapse, 1815–1960* (London: Fontana and Leicester University Press, 1982).

——, *The Lords of all Humankind, European Attitudes to Other Cultures in the Age of Empire* (London: Serif, 1995 [first published 1969]).

Kieser, Hans-Lukas, *Der verpasste Friede. Mission, Ethnie und staat in den Ostprovinzen der Türkei 1839–1938* (Zurich: Chronos, 2000).

Kimambo, I. N., and Temu, A. J., eds, *A History of Tanzania* (Nairobi: Heinemann, 1969).

Kinealy, Christine, *The Great Catastrophe: The Irish Famine, 1845–52* (Dublin: Gill and Macmillan, 1994).

King, Desmond, *In the Name of Liberalism, Illiberal Social Policy in the United States and Britain* (Oxford: Oxford University Press, 2000).

Klassen, John Martin, *The Nobility and the Making of the Hussite Revolution* (New York and Boulder, CO: East European Quarterly, 1978).

Klein, Herbert S., *The Atlantic Slave Trade* (Cambridge: Cambridge University Press, 1999).

Klier, John Doyle, *Imperial Russia's Jewish Question, 1855–1881* (Cambridge: Cambridge University Press, 1995).

Knecht, Robert J., *The French Civil Wars, 1562–1598* (Harlow: Longman, 2000).

Knightly, Philip, *The First Casualty, from the Crimea to Vietnam, the War Correspondent as Hero, Propagandist and Mythmaker* (London and Melbourne: Quartet Books, 1978).

Kochan, Lionel, *Russia in Revolution, 1890–1918* (London: Weidenfeld and Nicolson, 1966).

Kohn, Hans, *Pan-Slavism, Its History and Ideology* (Notre Dame, IN: University of Notre Dame Press, 1953).

——, *The Idea of Nationalism* (New York: Collier-Macmillan, 2nd edn, 1967).

Kolakowski, Leszek, *Main Currents of Marxism: Its Rise, Growth and Dissolution*, vol. 2: *The Golden Age,* trans. P.S. Falla (Oxford: Clarendon Press, 1978)

Krikorian, Mesrob K., *Armenians in the Service of the Ottoman Empire* (London: Routledge and Kegan Paul, 1977).

Kuitenbrouwer, Maarten, *The Netherlands and the Rise of Modern Imperialism: Colonies and Foreign Policy, 1870–1902*, trans. Hugo Beyer (Oxford: Berg, 1991).

Kuper, Leo, *Genocide: Its Political Use in the Twentieth Century* (New Haven, CT, and London: Yale University Press, 1981).

Kupperman, Karen Ordahl, *Indians and English, Facing Off in Early America* (Ithaca, NY, and London: Cornell University Press, 2000).

Labrousse, Elisabeth, *Une foi, une loi, un roi, essai sur la révocation de l'Édit de Nantes* (Geneva and Paris: Payot, 1985).

Ladurie, Emmanuel Le Roy, *Montaillou, Cathars and Catholics in a French Village 1294–1324*, trans. Barbara Bray (London: Penguin, 1978).

Laffin, R. G. D., *The Serbs, the Guardians of the Gate* (New York: Dorset Press, 1989 [first published 1917]).

Lambert, Malcolm, *The Cathars* (Oxford: Blackwell, 1998).

Lampe, John R., and Jackson, Marvin R., *Balkans Economic History, 1550–1950: From Imperial Borderlands to Developing Nations* (Bloomington: Indiana University Press, 1982).

Lancaster, Jane F., *Removal Aftershock, the Seminoles' Struggle for Survival in the West, 1836–1866* (Knoxville: University of Tennessee Press, 1994).

Landau, Jacob M., *Pan-Turkism: From Irredentism to Cooperation* (London: Hurst and Co., 1983)

Langmuir, Gavin, *Towards a Definition of Antisemitism* (Berkeley and Los Angeles: University of California Press, 1990).

Laritier, F., 'La guerre des Boxers: une expédition internationale, 1900', *Revue historique des armées*, 1 (1992), 115–23.

Larner, Christina, *Witchcraft and Religion, the Politics of Popular Belief* (Oxford: Blackwell, 1984).

Lattimore, Owen, *Pivot of Asia, Sinkiang, the Inner Asian Frontiers of China and Russia* (Boston: Little, Brown, 1950).

Lavender, David, *The Penguin Book of the American West* (London: Penguin, 1965).

Lenman, Bruce, *The Jacobite Risings in Britain 1689–1746* (London: Eyre Methuen, 1980).

——, *England's Colonial Wars, 1550–1688* (London: Pearson, 2001).

Leon, Abram, *The Jewish Question, a Marxist Interpretation* (New York: Pathfinder Press, 1970).

Lepsius, J., *Armenia and Europe, an Indictment* (London: Hodder and Stoughton, 1897).

Lestringant, Frank, *Cannibals, the Discovery and Representation of the Cannibal from Columbus to Jules Verne*, trans. Rosemary Morris (Cambridge: Cambridge University Press, 1997).

Levack, Brian P., *The Witchhunt in Early Modern Europe* (London: Longman, 2nd edn, 1995).

Levene, Mark, and Roberts, Penny, eds, *The Massacre in History* (New York and Oxford: Berghahn Books, 1999).

Lévi-Strauss, Claude, *The Elementary Structures of Kinship*, trans. James Harle Bell, et al. (London: Eyre and Spottiswoode, 1969).

Levine, Robert M., *Vale of Tears: Revisiting the Canudos Massacre in Northeastern Brazil, 1893–1897* (Berkeley and Los Angeles: University of California Press, 1992).

Levy, Richard S., *The Downfall of the Anti-Semitic Parties in Imperial Germany* (New Haven, CT, and London: Yale University Press, 1975).

Lewis, Gwynne, *The French Revolution, Rethinking the Debate* (London: Routledge, 1993).

Lewy, Guenter, *The Nazi Persecution of the Gypsies* (Oxford and New York: Oxford University Press, 2000).

Lieven, Dominic, *Empire, the Russian Empire and its Rivals* (London: John Murray, 2000).

Lieven, Michael, "'Butchering the Brutes all over the Place", Total War and Massacre in Zululand, 1879', *History*, 84:276 (1999), 624–32.

Limerick, Patricia M., *The Legacy of Conquest, the Unbroken Past of the American West* (New York and London: W.W. Norton and Co., 1981).

Lindqvist, Sven, *'Exterminate all the Brutes'*, trans. Joan Tate (London: Grant Books, 1998).

Linn, Brian McAllister, *The US Army and Counter-Insurgency in the Philippine War 1899–1902* (Chapel Hill and London: University of North Carolina, 1989).

London, Jack, *The Iron Heel* (Edinburgh: Rebel Inc., 1999 [first published 1908]).

Lone, Stewart, *Japan's First Modern War, Army and Society in the Conflict with China, 1894–95* (London: St Martin's Press, 1994).

Loos, Noel, *Invasion and Resistance: Aboriginal-European Relations on the North Queensland Frontier 1861–1897* (Canberra: Australian National University Press, 1982).

Lopez, Barry Holstun, *Of Wolves and Men* (New York: Dent, 1978).

Lundtofte, Henrik, "'Ich glaube, dass die Nation als solche vernichtet werden muss …'" radikaliseringen af den tyske nedkaempelse af hereroopstanden 1904', *Den Jyske Historiker*, 90 (Dec. 2000), 74–105.

Macartney, C. A., *National States and National Minorities* (London: Royal Institute of International Affairs, 1934).

McCarthy, Justin, *Death and Exile: The Ethnic Cleansing of Ottoman Muslims, 1821–1922* (Princeton, NJ: Darwin Press, 1995).

——, *Muslims and Minorities, the Population of Ottoman Anatolia at the End of Empire* (New York and London: New York University Press, 1983).

Maccoby, Hyam, *Revolution in Judaea, Jesus and the Jewish Resistance* (New York: Taplinger Publishing Co., 1980).

McFarlane, Anthony, *The British in the Americas, 1480–1815* (London and New York: Longman, 1994).

McGregor, Russell, *Imagined Destinies: Aboriginal Australians and the Doomed Race Theory, 1880–1939* (Melbourne: Melbourne University Press, 1997).

McLoughlin, William G., *Cherokee Renaissance in the New Republic* (Princeton, NJ: Princeton University Press, 1986).

MacMullen, Ramsey, *Christianising the Roman Empire* (New Haven, CT, and London: Yale University Press, 1984).

McNeill, William H., *Plagues and Peoples* (London: Penguin, 1979).

——, *The Pursuit of Power, Technology, Armed Force and Society since AD.1000* (Oxford: Basil Blackwell, 1983).

Mahoney, Michael R., 'The Zulu Kingdom as a Genocidal and Post-Genocidal Society *c.*1810 to the Present', *Journal of Genocide Research*, 5:2 (2003), 251–68.

Makdisi, Ussama, *The Culture of Sectarianism, Community, History and Violence in Nineteenth-Century Ottoman Lebanon* (Berkeley and Los Angeles: University of California Press, 2000).

Malcolm, Noel, *Kosovo, a Short History* (London and Basingstoke: Macmillan, 1998).

——, *Bosnia, a Short History* (London and Basingstoke: Macmillan, 1994).

Mann, Michael, *Sources of Social Power,* 2 vols (Cambridge: Cambridge University Press, 1986/1993).

Mann, Vivien B., Glick, Thomas F., and Dodds, Jerrilyn D., eds, *Convivienca: Jews, Muslims and Christians in Medieval Spain* (New York: Braziller, 1992).

Mansel, Philip, *Constantinople, City of the World's Desire 1453–1924* (London: Penguin, 1995).

Marchal, Jules, *L'État Libre du Congo, paradis perdu, l'histoire du Congo, 1876–1900,* 2 vols (Borgloon: Éditions Paula Bellings, 1996).

——, *E.D. Morel contre Leopold,* 2 vols (Paris: Éditions L'Harmattan, 1966).

Marcus, Jacob R., *The Jew in the Medieval World: A Source Book 315–1791* (Cincinnati: Sinai Press, 1938).

Marrus, Michael Robert, *The Politics of Assimilation: a Study of the French-Jewish Community at the Time of the Dreyfus Affair* (Oxford: Clarendon, 1971).

Martin, A. C., *The Concentration Camps 1900–1902* (Cape Town: Timmins, 1957).

Martin, Jean-Clément, *La Vendée de la mémoire, 1800–1980* (Paris: Éditions du Seuil, 1989).

——, and Lardière, Xavier, *Le Massacre des Lucs, Vendée 1794* (Vouille: Geste, 1992).

Martin, Joel W., *Sacred Revolt, the Muskogee's Struggle for a New World* (Boston: Beacon Press, 1991).

Marx, Karl, and Engels, Friedrich, *The Communist Manifesto* Taylor, ed. A. J. P. Taylor, (London: Penguin, 1967).

Mathiez, Albert, *Robespierre, Terroriste* (Paris: La renaissance du livre, 1921).

Mauzi, Robert, *Idée du bonheur au XVIIIe siècle* (Paris: Colin, 1960).

Mayer, Arno J., *The Persistence of the Old Regime, Europe to the Great War* (London: Croom Helm, 1981).

——, *The Furies, Violence and Terror in the French and Russian Revolutions* (Princeton, NJ: Princeton University Press, 2000).

Mazower, Mark, *The Balkans* (London: Weidenfeld and Nicolson, 2000).

——, 'Two Wars: Serbia 1914–1918 and 1941–1944', unpublished paper, 'Cultures of Killing' Conference, Birkbeck College, July 2000.

Mechoulan, Henry, *El Honor de Dios, Indios, judios y moriscos en el Siglo de Oro* (Barcelona: Editorial Argos Vergara, S.A., 1981).

Meilink-Roelofsz, M. A. P., *Asian Trade and European Influence in the Indonesian Archipelago between 1500 and about 1630* (The Hague: Martinus Nijhoff, 1962).

Melson, Robert F., *Revolution and Genocide: On the Origins of the Armenian Genocide and the Holocaust* (Chicago: Chicago University Press, 1992).

Mendes-Flohr, Paul R., and Reinharz, Jehuda, *The Jew in the Modern World, Documentary History* (New York: Oxford University Press, 1980).

Mill, John Stuart, *Utilitarianism, Liberty and Representative Government* (London: Everyman edn, 1910).

Miller, Stuart Creighton, *'Benevolent Assimilation', the American Conquest of the Philippines, 1899–1903* (New Haven, CT, and London: Yale University Press, 1982).

Minassian, Anaide Ter, *Nationalism and Socialism in the Armenian Revolutionary Movement* (Cambridge, MA: Zoryan Institute, 1983).

Moe, Nelson, *The View from Vesuvius: Italian Culture and the Southern Question* (Berkeley and Los Angeles: University of California Press, 2002).

Moor, J. A. de, and Wesselling, H. L., eds, *Imperialism and War, Essays in Colonial Wars in Asia and Africa* (Leiden: E.J. Brill and University of Leiden Press, 1989).

Moore, Barrington, Jr., *Social Origins of Dictatorship and Democracy* (London: Penguin, 1967).

Moore, R. I., *The Formation of a Persecuting Society: Power and Deviance in Western Europe, 950–1250* (Oxford: Blackwell, 1987).

Moorhead, Alan, *The Fatal Impact, an Account of the Invasion of the South Pacific, 1767–1840* (London: Penguin, 1968).

Morel, E. D., *Red Rubber, the Story of the Rubber Trade Flourishing on the Congo in the Year of Grace 1906* (London: T. Fisher Unwin, 1906).

Morris, Donald R., *The Washing of the Spears: A History of the Rise of the Zulu Nation under Shaka and its Fall in the Zulu War of 1879* (London: Jonathan Cape, 1966).

Moses, A. Dirk, 'An Antipodean Genocide? The Origins of the Genocidal Moment in the Colonisation of Australia', *Journal of Genocide Research*, 2:1 (2000), 89–106.

Mosse, George L., *The Crisis of German Ideology: Intellectual Origins of the Third Reich* (London: Weidenfeld and Nicolson, 1964).

——, *Nationalism and Sexuality, Middle-Class Morality and Sexual Norms in Modern Europe* (London and Madison: University of Wisconsin, 1985).

——, *Toward the Final Solution, a History of European Racism* (New York: Howard Fetig, 2nd edn, 1985).

——, *The Culture of Western Europe, the Nineteenth and Twentieth Centuries* (Boulder, CO, and London: Westview Press, 3rd edn, 1988).

——, *The Image of Man, The Creation of Modern Masculinity* (New York and Oxford: Oxford University Press, 1996).

Mostert, Noel, *Frontiers; The Epic of South Africa's Creation and the Tragedy of the Xhosa People* (New York: Alfred A. Knopf, 1992).

Mudimbe, V. Y., *The Invention of Africa, Gnosis, Philosophy and the Order of Knowledge* (Bloomington and Indianapolis: Indiana University Press, 1988).

——, *The Idea of Africa* (Bloomington and Indianapolis: Indiana University Press, 1994).

Müller-Hill, Benno, *Murderous Science, Elimination by Scientific Selection of Jews, Gypsies and Others, Germany 1933–1945,* trans. George R. Fraser (New York: Cold Spring Harbor Laboratory Press, 1998).

Mungeam, G. H., *British Rule in Kenya 1895–1912* (Oxford: Clarendon Press, 1966).

Naimark, Norman M., *Fires of Hatred, Ethnic Cleansing in Twentieth Century Europe* (Cambridge, MA, and London: Harvard University Press, 2001).

Nalbandian, Louise, *The Armenian Revolutionary Movement: The Development of Armenian Political Parties through the Nineteenth Century* (Berkeley and Los Angeles: University of California Press, 1963).

Nimni, Ephraim, 'Nationalist Multiculturalism in Late Imperial Austria as a Critique of Contemporary Liberalism: The Case of Bauer and Renner', *Journal of Political Ideologies*, 4:3 (1999), 289–314.

Nirenberg, David, *Communities of Violence, Persecution of Minorities in the Middle Ages* (Princeton, NJ: Princeton University Press, 1996).

Nobles, Gregory H., *American Frontiers, Cultural Encounters and Continental Conquest* (New York: Hill and Wang, 1997).

Nordau, Max, *Degeneration* (Lincoln, NB, and London: University of Nebraska Press, 1993 [first published 1892]).

Oberman, Heiko A., *The Roots of Anti-Semitism in the Age of Renaissance and Reformation* (Philadelphia: Fortress, 1984).

Ogot, Bethwell A., ed., *War and Society in Africa, Ten Studies* (London: Frank Cass, 1972).

Okey, Robin, 'State, Church, and Nation in the Serbo-Croat Speaking Lands of the Habsburg Monarchy 1850–1914', in Donal A. Kerr, et al., eds, *Comparative Studies on Governments and Non-Dominant Ethnic Groups in Europe 1850–1940*, vol. 2: *Religion, State and Ethnic Groups* (Dartmouth: New York University Press and European Science Foundation, 1992), 51–78.

——, *The Habsburg Empire c. 1765–1918. From Enlightenment to Eclipse* (Basingstoke: Macmillan, 2001).

Oliphant, John, *Peace and War on the Anglo-Cherokee Frontier, 1756–63* (Basingstoke: Palgrave, 2001).

Oliver, Roland, *The African Experience* (London: Weidenfeld and Nicolson, 1991).

Ortiz, Antonio Dominguez, and Vincent, Bernard, *Historia de los moriscos, Vida tragedia de una minoria* (Madrid: Biblioteca de la Revista de Occidente, 1978).

Outram, Dorinda, *The Enlightenment* (Cambridge: Cambridge University Press, 1995).

Owen, Roger, *The Middle East in the World Economy 1800–1914* (London: Methuen, 1981).

Pagden, Anthony, *The Fall of Natural Man; The American Indian and the Origins of Comparative Ethnology* (Cambridge: Cambridge University Press, 1982).

——, *Ideologies of Empire in Spain, Britain and France c. 1500–1800* (New Haven, CT, and London: Yale University Press, 1995).

——, *Peoples and Empires* (London: Weidenfeld and Nicolson, 2001).

Paine, S. C. M., *Imperial Rivals, China, Russia and their Disputed Frontier* (Armonk, NY, and London: M.E. Sharpe, 1996).

Pakenham, Thomas, *The Scramble for Africa: The White Man's Conquest of the Dark Continent from 1876 to 1912* (New York: Random House, 1991).

Palmer, Alison, *Colonial Genocide* (Adelaide: Crawford House Publishing, 2000).

Pankhurst, Richard, and Johnson, Douglas H., 'The Great Drought and Famine of 1888–92 in Northeast Africa', in Douglas H. Johnson and David M. Anderson, eds, *The Ecology of Survival, Case studies from Northeast African History* (London and Boulder, CO: Lester Crook Academic Publishing and Westview Press, 1988), 47–70.

Paret, Peter, *Internal War and Pacification: The Vendée 1789–1796* (Princeton, NJ: Monograph, no. 12, 1961).

——, ed., *Makers of Modern Strategy, from Machiavelli to the Nuclear Age* (Oxford: Clarendon Press, 1986).

Parker, Geoffrey, *The Dutch Revolt* (Ithaca, NY, and New York: Cornell University Press, 1977).

——, *The Grand Strategy of Philip II* (New Haven, CT, and London: Yale University Press, 1998).

——, *Empire, War and Faith in Early Modern Europe* (London: Allen Lane, 2002).

Parkman, Francis, *History of the Conspiracy of Pontiac* (New York: Book League of America, 1929).

Parry, J. H., *The Spanish Seaborne Empire* (London: Penguin, 1973).

Paul, Diane B., 'Eugenics and the Left', *Journal of the History of Ideas*, 45:4 (1984), 567–90.

Pearce, Roy Harvey, *Savagism and Civilisation: A Study of the Indian and the American Mind* (Baltimore: Johns Hopkins University Press, 1965).

Pelt, Robert Jan van, and Dwork, Deborah, *Auschwitz, 1270 to the Present* (New Haven, CT, and London: Yale University Press, 1996).

Perang Kolonial Belanda di Aceh/The Dutch Colonial War in Aceh (Banda, Aceh: Documentation and Information Centre of Aceh, 2nd edn, 1990).

Petitfrère, Claude, *La Vendée et les Vendéens* (Paris: Éditions Gallimard/Juillard, 1981).

Pick, Daniel, *Faces of Degeneration, a European Disorder c.1848–1918* (Cambridge: Cambridge University Press, 1989).

——, *War Machine, the Rationalisation of Slaughter in the Modern Age* (New Haven, CT, and London: Yale University Press, 1993).

——, *Svengali's Web, the Alien Encounter in Modern Culture* (New Haven, CT, and London: Yale University Press, 2000).

Pipes, Daniel, *Conspiracy, How the Paranoid Style Flourishes and Where it Comes From* (New York and London: Free Press, 1997).

Plank, Geoffrey, *An Unsettled Conquest, The British Campaign against the Peoples of Arcadia* (Philadelphia: University of Pennsylvania Press, 2001).

Poewe, Karla, *The Namibian Herero, a History of their Psychosocial Disintegration and Survival* (Lewiston, NY, and Queenston, ON: Edwin Mellen Press, 1985).

Poliakov, Leon, *History of Anti-Semitism*, vol. 3: *From Voltaire to Wagner,* trans. Miriam Kochan (London: Routledge and Kegan Paul, 1975) and vol. 4: *Suicidal Europe 1870–1933*, trans. George Klin (Oxford: Littman Library and Oxford University Press, 1985).

Pollard, Sidney, *The Idea of Progress, History and Society* (London: Pelican, 1971).

Pomeranz, Kenneth, *The Great Divergence: Europe, China and the Making of the Modern World Economy* (Princeton, NJ: Princeton University Press, 2000).

Porter, Bernard, *The Lion's Share, a Short History of British Imperialism 1850–1983* (Harlow: Longman, 1984).

Porter, Roy, *The Enlightenment* (Basingstoke: Palgrave, 2nd edn, 2001).

Prebble, John, *Culloden* (London: Penguin, 1967).

Preston, Diana, *A Brief History of the Boxer Rebellion, China's War on Foreigners, 1900* (London: Constable and Robinson, 2002).

Prucha, Francis Paul, *Americanising the American Indians, Writings by the Friends of the Indian, 1880–1900* (Lincoln, NB, and London: University of Nebraska Press, 1978).

Pulzer, Peter, *The Rise of Political Antisemitism in Germany and Austria* (London: Halban, 1988).

Quataert, Donald, *The Ottoman Empire, 1700–1922* (Cambridge: Cambridge University Press, 1995).

Rai, Milan, *Chomsky's Politics* (London and New York: Verso, 1995).

Ramsaur, Ernest E., Jr., *The Young Turks* (Princeton, NJ: Princeton University Press, 1957).

Ranger, Terence O., *Peasant Consciousness and Guerilla War in Zimbabwe, a Comparative Study* (London: James Currey, 1985).

——, *Revolt in Southern Rhodesia 1896–97, a Study in African Resistance* (London: Heinemann, 1967).

Rawson, Claude, *God, Gulliver and Genocide, Barbarism and the European Imagination, 1492–1945* (Oxford University Press, 2001).

Reece, R. H. W., *Aborigines and Colonists, Aborigines and Colonial Society in New South Wales in the 1830s and 1840s* (Sydney: Sydney University Press, 1974).

Reed, John, *War in Eastern Europe, Travels through the Balkans in 1915* (London: Phoenix, 1994 [first published Scribners, 1916]).

Reid, James J., 'Batak 1876: a Massacre and its Significance', *Journal of Genocide Research*, 2:3 (2000), 375–409.

Remini, Robert V., *Andrew Jackson and his Indian Wars* (London: Penguin, 2001).

Reynolds, Henry, *The Other Side of the Frontier, Aboriginal Resistance to the European Invasion of Australia* (London: Penguin Books, 1968).

——, *An Indelible Stain? The Question of Genocide in Australian History* (Ringwood: Viking, 2001).

Richards, Eric, *The Highland Clearances, People, Landlords and Rural Turmoil* (Edinburgh: Birlinn, 2000).

Rochat, Giorgio, 'La repressione della resistenza Arabe in Cirenaica nel 1930–31: Nei Documenti dell'Archivo Graziani', *Il Movimento di Liberazione in Italia*, 25:110 (1973), 3–39.

Rodrigue, Aron, *French Jews, Turkish Jews, The Alliance Israélite Universelle and the Politics of Jewish Schooling in Turkey, 1860–1925* (Bloomington and Indianapolis: Indiana University Press, 1990).

Rogger, Hans, *Jewish Policies and Right-Wing Politics in Imperial Russia* (Basingstoke: Macmillan, 1986)

Röhl, John C. G., *The Kaiser and his Court: Wilhem II and the Government of Germany*, trans. Terence F. Cole (Cambridge: Cambridge University Press, 1987).

Roper, Lyndal, *Oedipus and the Devil: Witchcraft, Sexuality and Religion in Early Modern Europe* (London: Routledge, 1994).

Rose, Paul Lawrence, *Wagner, Race and Revolution* (London: Faber, 1992).

Rosenbaum, Alan S., ed., *Is the Holocaust Unique? Perspectives on Comparative Genocide* (Boulder: Westview Press, 1996).

Rossabi, Morris, 'Muslim and Central Asian Revolt', in Jonathan D. Spence and John E. Wills, Jr., eds, *From Ming to Ch'ing, Conquest, Region, and Continuity in Seventeenth-Century China* (New Haven, CT, and London: Yale University Press, 1979), 169–99.

Roth, J. J., *The Cult of Violence, Sorel and the Sorelians* (Berkeley and Los Angeles: University of California Press, 1980).

Rothschild, Joseph, *East Central Europe between Two World Wars* (Seattle: University of Washington Press, 1977).

Rousseau, Jean-Jacques, *Discourse of Political Economy and The Social Contract*, trans. Christopher Betts (Oxford: Oxford University Press, 1994).

Rubenstein, Richard L., *The Age of Triage: Fear and Hope in an Overcrowded World* (Boston: Beacon Press, 1983).

Rubin, Miri, *Gentile Tales, the Narrative Assault on Late Medieval Jewry* (New Haven, CT, and London: Yale University Press, 1999).

Rudé, George, *The Crowd in the French Revolution* (London and Oxford: Oxford University Press, 1967).

——, *Robespierre, Portrait of a Revolutionary Democrat* (London: Collins, 1975).

Russell, Lynette, ed., *Colonial Frontiers: Indigenous-European Encounters in Settler Societies* (Manchester and New York: Manchester University Press, 2001).

Ryan, Lyndall, *The Aboriginal Tasmanians* (Sydney: Allen and Unwin, 2nd edn, 1996).

Salt, Jeremy, *Imperialism, Evangelism and the Ottoman Amenians, 1878–1896* (London: Frank Cass, 1993).

Sarkiss, Harry Jewel, 'The Armenian Renaissance 1500–1863', *Journal of Modern History*, 9:4 (1937), 433–48.

Sartre, Jean-Paul, 'On Genocide', *Ramparts* (Feb. 1968), 37–42.

Saunders, David, *Russia in the Age of Reaction and Reform 1801–1881* (Harlow: Longman, 1992).

Schama, Simon, *Citizens: A Chronicle of the French Revolution* (London: Viking Press, 1989).

Schwarzfuchs, Simon, *Napoleon, the Jews and the Sanhedrin* (Boston: Routledge and Kegan Paul, 1979).

Scott, James C., *Weapons of the Weak, Everyday Forms of Peasant Resistance* (New Haven, CT, and London: Yale University Press, 1985).

Searle, G. R., *The Quest for National Efficiency, a Study in British Politics and Political Thought, 1899–1914* (London and Atlantic Highlands, NJ: Ashfield Press, 1990).

Secher, Reynauld, *Le Génocide franco-français, La Vendée-Vengé* (Paris: Presses Universitaires de France, 4th edn, 1992).

Seely, Robert, *Russo-Chechen Conflict, 1800–2000, a Deadly Embrace* (London and Portland, OR: Frank Cass, 2001).

Service, Robert, *Lenin, a Political Life*, vol. 1: *The Strengths of Contradiction* (Basingstoke and London: Macmillan, 1985).

Seton-Watson, R. W., *The Southern Slav Question and the Habsburg Monarchy* (New York: Howard Fertig, 1969 [first published 1911]).

Sharma, Ursula, *Caste* (Buckingham and Philadelphia: Open University Press, 1999).

Shaw, Stanford, and Shaw, Ezel Kural, *History of the Ottoman Empire and Modern Turkey*, vol. 2: *Reform, Revolution and the Republic: The Rise of Modern Turkey 1808–1975* (Cambridge: Cambridge University Press, 1977).

Sheehan, Bernard W., *Seeds of Extinction, Jeffersonian Philanthropy and the American Indian* (Chapel Hill: University of North Carolina Press, 1973).

Sheehan, J. J., 'What is German History? Reflections on the Role of the *Nation* in German History and Historiography', *Journal of Modern History*, 53:1 (1981), 1–23.

Sheils, W. J., ed., *Persecution and Toleration, Studies in Church History*, 21 (Oxford: Blackwell, 1984).

Shils, Edward A., *The Torment of Secrecy: The Background and Consequences of American Security Policies* (London: William Heinemann, 1956).

Showalter, Dennis E., *Little Man, What Now? Der Stuermer in the Weimar Republic* (Hamden, CT: Archon Books, 1982).

Silberner, Edmund, 'Was Marx an Anti-Semite?', *Historia Judaica*, 11 (1949), 3–52.

Simpson, L. B., *The Encomienda in New Spain* (Berkeley: University of California Press, 1966).

Slezkine, Yuri, *Arctic Mirrors: Russia and the Small Peoples of the North* (Ithaca, NY: Cornell University Press, 1994).

Slotkin, Richard, *Regeneration through Violence, the Myth of the American Frontier, 1600–186,* (Middletown, CT: Wesleyan University Press, 1973).

Smith, Anthony D., *The Ethnic Origins of Nations* (Oxford: Blackwell, 1986).

——, *Myths and Memories of the Nation* (Oxford: Oxford University Press, 1999).

Smith, Dennis Mack, *Modern Italy, A Political History* (New Haven, CT, and London: Yale University Press, 1997 [first published 1969]).

Smith, Joseph, *The Spanish-American War, Conflict in the Caribbean and the Pacific 1895–1902* (London and New York: Longman, 1994).

Smith, Woodruff D., *The Ideological Origins of Nazi Imperialism* (New York and Oxford: Oxford University Press, 1986).

Somakian, Manoug Joseph, *Empires in Conflict, Armenia and the Great Powers, 1895–1920* (London and New York: I.B. Tauris, 1995).

Sorkin, David, 'The Port Jew: Notes toward a Social Type', *Journal of Jewish Studies*, 50:1 (Spring, 1999), 87–97.

Spence, Jonathan D., *God's Chinese Son, the Taiping Heavenly Kingdom of Hong Xinquan* (New York and London: W.W. Norton and Co., 1996).

Spies, S. B., *Methods of Barbarism: Roberts and Kitchener and Civilians in the Boer Republics, January 1900–May 1902* (Cape Town: Human and Rousseau, 1977).

Stannard, David, *American Holocaust, the Conquest of the New World* (New York and Oxford: Oxford University Press, 1992).

——, *Before the Horror, the Population of Hawai'i on the Eve of Western Contact* (Honolulu: Social Science Research Institute and University of Hawai'i Press, 1989).

Starkey, Armstrong, *European and Native American Warfare, 1675–1815* (Norman: University of Oklahoma Press, 1998).

Stern, Fritz, *The Politics of Cultural Despair: A Study in the Rise of the Germanic Ideology* (Berkeley and Los Angeles: University of California Press, 1974).

Sternhell, Zeev, *Ni droite, ni gauche: ideologie fasciste en France* (Paris: Éditions du Seuil, 1983).

——, with Sznajder, Mario, and Asheri, Maia, *The Birth of Fascist Ideology, from Cultural Rebellion to Political Revolution*, trans. David Maisel (Princeton, NJ: Princeton University Press, 1994).

Stocking, George W., Jr., *Victorian Anthropology* (New York: Free Press, 1987).

Stone, Dan, *Breeding Superman, Nietzsche, Race and Eugenics in Edwardian and Interwar Britain* (Liverpool: Liverpool University Press, 2002).

——, 'White Men with Low Moral Standards? German Anthropology and the Herero Genocide', *Patterns of Prejudice*, 35:2 (2001), 33–45.

Stone, Gerald, *The Smallest Slavonic Nation: The Sorbs of Lusatia* (London: Athlone Press, 1972).

Stone, Norman, *Europe Transformed 1878–1919* (London: Fontana, 1983).

Stow, Kenneth R., *Alienated Minority, the Jews of Medieval Latin Europe* (Cambridge, MA, and London: Harvard University Press, 1992).

Suny, Ronald Grigor, 'Religion, Ethnicity, and Nationalism, Armenians, Turks, and the End of the Ottoman Empire', in Omer Bartov and Phyllis Mack, eds, *In God's Name, Genocide and Religion in the Twentieth Century* (New York and Oxford: Berghahn Books, 2001), 23–61.

Sutherland, D. M. G., *France 1789–1815, Revolution and Counter-Revolution* (London: Fontana Press, 1985).

Svaldi, David, *Sand Creek and the Rhetoric of Extermination, a Case Study in Indian–White Relations* (Lanham, MD: University Press of America, 1989).

Szporluk, Roman, *Communism and Nationalism, Karl Marx versus Friedrich List* (New York and London: Oxford University Press, 1988).

Tackett, Timothy, 'The West in France in 1789: The Religious Factors in the Origins of the Counter-Revolution', *Journal of Modern History*, 4 (1982), 715–45.

Talmon, J. L., *The Origins of Totalitarian Democracy* (London: Sphere, 1970).

Tatz, Colin, *Aboriginals and Uranium and Other Essays* (Melbourne: Heinemann, 1982).

Tawney, R. H., *Religion and the Rise of Capitalism: An Historical Study* (London: John Murray, 1926).

Taylor, Bruce, 'The Enemy Within and Without: An Anatomy of Fear on the Spanish Mediterranean Littoral', in William G. Naphy and Penny Roberts, eds, *Fear in Early Modern Society* (Manchester: Manchester University Press, 1997), 78–99.

Telo, António José, *Economia e imperio no Portugal comtemporaneo* (Lisbon: Edicoes Cosmos, 1994).

Ternon, Yves, *L'État criminel: Les Génocides au XXe siècle* (Paris: Éditions du Seuil, 1995).

Thomas, Keith, *Religion and the Decline of Magic: Studies in Popular Belief in Sixteenth and Seventeenth Century England* (London: Penguin, 1971).

————, *Man and the Natural World, Changing Attitudes in England, 1500–1800* (London: Penguin, 1984).

Thornton, Russell, *American Indian Holocaust and Survival: A Population History since 1492* (Norman: University of Oklahoma, 1987).

Tilly, Charles, *The Vendée* (Cambridge, MA: Harvard University Press, 1964).

————, *Coercion, Capital and European States AD. 990–1990* (Oxford: Blackwell, 1990).

Todorov, Tzvetan, *The Conquest of America, the Question of the Other*, trans. Richard Howard (New York: HarperPerennial, 1984).

Toynbee, Arnold, *Mankind and Mother Earth, a Narrative History of the World* (Oxford: Oxford University Press, 1976).

Trachtenberg, Joshua, *The Devil and the Jews, the Medieval Conception of the Jew and its Relationship to Modern Anti-Semitism* (New York: Harper and Row, 1966).

Trevor-Roper, Hugh, *The European Witch Craze of the Sixteenth and Seventeenth Centuries and Other Essays* (London: Penguin, 1969).

Trouillot, Michel-Rolph *Silencing the Past, Power and the Production of History* (Boston: Beacon Press, 1995).

Tsuzuki, Chushichi, *The Pursuit of Power in Modern Japan, 1825–1995* (Oxford: Oxford University Press, 2000).

Tuck, Richard, *The Rights of War and Peace, Political Thought and the International Order from Grotius to Kant* (Oxford and New York: Oxford University Press, 1999).

Turnbull, Clive, *Black War, the Extermination of the Tasmanian Aborigines* (Melbourne: Lansdowne Press, 1948).

Utley, Robert M., *The Indian Frontier of the American West 1846–1890* (Albuquerque: University of New Mexico Press, 1984).

Vambe, Lawrence, *An Ill-Fated People, Zimbabwe before and after Rhodes* (London: Heinemann, 1972).

Vandervort, Bruce, *Wars of Imperial Conquest 1830–1914* (London: UCL Press, 1998).

Veenhoven, Willem A., ed., *Case Studies on Human Rights and Fundamental Freedoms, a World Survey*, 5 vols (The Hague: Martinus Nijhoft, 1976).

Verheij, Jelle, 'Die armenischen Massaker von 1894–1896. Anatomie und Hintergrunde einer Krise', in Hans-Lukas Kieser, ed., *Die Armenische Frage und die Schweiz (1896–1923)* (Zurich: Chronos, 1999), 69–133.

Voeltz, Richard A., *German Colonialism and the South West Africa Company 1894–1914* (Ohio: Ohio University Press, 1988).

Voigt, F. A., *Unto Caesar* (London: Constable, 1938).

Volkov, Shulamit, 'Antisemitism as a Cultural Code. Reflections on the History and Historiography of Antisemitism in Imperial Germany', *Leo Baeck Year Book*, 23 (1976), 25–46.

Waldinger, Renée et al., eds, *The French Revolution and the Meaning of Citizenship* (Westport, CT, and London: Greenwood Press, 1992).

Walker, Christopher J., *Armenia: The Survival of a Nation* (London: Croom Helm, 1980).

Wallace, Anthony F. C., *The Long Bitter Trail, Andrew Jackson and the Indians* (New York: Hill and Wang, 1993).

——, *Jefferson and the Indians, The Tragic Fate of the First Americans* (Cambridge, MA: Harvard University Press, 1999).

Wallerstein, Immanuel, 'World System or World Systems?', in André Gunder Frank and Barry K. Gillis, eds, *The World System, Five Hundred Years or Five Thousand?* (London and New York: Routledge, 1993), 292–6.

Wallimann, Isidor and Dobkowski, Michael, eds, *Genocide and the Modern Age* (Westport, CT: Greenwood Press, 1987).

Ward, Andrew, *Our Bones are Scattered, the Cawnpore Massacres* (London: Henry Holt and Co., 1996).

Warwick, Peter, *Black People and the South African War 1899–1902* (Cambridge: Cambridge University Press, 1983).

Watson, Don, *Caledonia Australis: Scottish Highlanders on the Frontier of Australia* (Sydney: Collins, 1984).

Weber, Eugen, *Peasants into Frenchmen: The Modernisation of Rural France 1870–1914* (Stanford, CA: Stanford University Press, 1976).

Weber, Max, *The Protestant Ethic and the Spirit of Capitalism*, trans. Talcott Parsons (London: Routledge, 1992 [first published 1930]).

Wehler, Hans-Ulrich, *The German Empire 1871–1918*, trans. Kim Traynor (Leamington Spa: Berg Publishers, 1985).

Weiner, Marc A., *Richard Wagner and the Anti-Semitic imagination* (Lincoln, NB: University of Nebraska Press, 1995).

Weindling, Paul, *Epidemics and Genocide in Eastern Europe, 1890–1945* (Oxford: Oxford University Press, 2000).

——, *Health, Race and German Politics between National Unification and Nazism, 1870–1945* (Cambridge: Cambridge University Press, 1989).

Weiss, Yfaat, 'Homeland as Shelter or as Refuge? Repatriation in the Jewish Context', *Tel Aviver Jahrbuch für deutsche Geschichte*, 27 (1990), 195–219.

Welch, Richard E., Jr., *The United States and the Philippine–American War, 1899–1902* (Chapel Hill: University of North Carolina Press, 1979).

Wellington, John H., *South West Africa and its Human Issues* (Oxford: Oxford University Press, 1967).

Wesselling, H. L., *Divide and Rule, The Partition of Africa 1880–1914*, trans. Arnold J. Pomerans (Westport, CT, and London: Praeger, 1996).

——, ed., *Expansion and Reaction, Essays in European Expansion and Reaction in Africa and Asia* (Leiden: Leiden University Press, 1978).

Wheeler, James Scott, *Cromwell in Ireland* (Dublin: Gill and Macmillan, 1999).

White, Richard, *The Middle Ground, Indians, Empires and Republics in the Great Lakes Region, 1650–1815* (Cambridge, Cambridge University Press, 1991).

Whiteside, Andrew Gladding, *Socialism of Fools, Georg Ritter von Schönerer and Austrian Pan-Germanism* (Berkeley and Los Angeles: University of California Press, 1975).

——, *Austrian National Socialism before 1918* (The Hague: Martinus Nijhoft, 1962).

Wilken, Robert L., *John Chrysostom and the Jews: Rhetoric and Reality in the late 4th Century* (Berkeley and Los Angeles: University of California Press, 1983).

Willems, Wim, *In Search of the True Gypsy, From Enlightenment to Final Solution* (London: Frank Cass, 1997).

Williams, E. N., *The Ancien Régime in Europe, Government and Society in the Major States, 1648–1789* (London: Penguin, 1970).

Williams, Stephen, *Diocletian and the Roman Recovery* (London: B.T. Batsford Ltd, 1981).

Williamson, Samuel R., Jr., *Austria-Hungary and the Origins of the First World War* (Basingstoke: Macmillan, 1991).

Wilson, James, *The Earth Shall Weep: A History of Native America* (London: Picador, 1998).

Wilson, Stephen, *Ideology and Experience, Antisemitism in France at the Time of the Dreyfus Affair* (Rutherford and London: Farleigh Dickinson and Associated Universities Press, 1982).

Winock, Michel, *Nationalism, Antisemitism and Fascism in France* (Stanford, CA: Stanford University Press, 1998).

Winter, J. M., *The Great War and the British People* (Basingstoke: Macmillan, 1986).

Wishart, David J., *An Unspeakable Sadness, the Dispossession of the Nebraska Indians* (Lincoln, NB, and London: University of Nebraska Press, 1994).

Wistrich, Robert, *Revolutionary Jews from Marx to Trotsky* (London: Harrap, 1976).

———, ed., *Terms of Survival, The Jewish World Since 1945* (London and New York: Routledge, 1995).

Wolf, Phillippe, 'The 1391 Pogrom in Spain: Social Crisis or Not?', *Past and Present*, 50 (1971), 4–18.

Wood, Brian, ed., *Namibia, 1884–1994, Readings in Namibian History and Society* (London and Lusaka: Namibia Support Committee and United Nations Institute for Namibia, 1988).

Woo-Keun, Han, *The History of Korea* (Seoul: Eul-Yoo Publishing Company, 1970).

Wright, J. Leitch, Jr., *Creeks and Seminoles, the Destruction and Regeneration of the Muscogulge People* (Lincoln, NB, and London: University of Nebraska Press, 1986).

Ye'or, Bat, *The Dhimmi, Jews and Christians under Islam*, trans. David Maisel, et al. (Rutherford, NJ, and London: Fairleigh Dickinson University Press and Associated University Presses, 1985).

Zamoyski, Adam, *The Polish Way, a Thousand Year History of the Poles and their Culture* (London: John Murray, 1987).

Zelinka, Anna, *In quest for God and Freedom: The Sufi Response to the Russian Advance in the North Caucasus* (London: Hurst and Co., 2000).

Zeman, Z. A. B., *The Making and Breaking of Communist Europe* (Oxford: Blackwell, 1991).

Zimmerer, Jürgen, *Deutsche Herrschaft über Afrikaner. Staatlicher Machtanspruch und Wirklichkeit im Kolonialen Namibia* (Hamburg: LIT, 2001).

Zimmerman, Andrew, *Anthropology and Antihumanism in Wilhelmine Germany* (Chicago: Chicago University Press, 2002).

Zürcher, E. J., *Turkey, a Modern History* (London and New York: I.B. Tauris, 1993).

Index